CICS/VS ONLINE SYSTEM DESIGN AND IMPLEMENTATION TECHNIQUES

DAVID LEE

CCD ONLINE SYSTEMS DATA PROCESSING SERIES

Copyright © 1986 by CCD Online Systems, Inc.

Library of Congress Catalog Card number 86-071263
ISBN: 0-9611810-7-9

Published by CCD Online Systems, Inc.
P. O. Box 795759
Dallas, Texas 75379

Library of Congress Cataloging in Publication Data

Lee, Shyh-Yuan David

    CICS/VS Online System Design And Implementation Techniques

    Includes index.

    1. CICS/VS   2. COBOL

InterTest is a registered trademark of On-line Software International, Inc.

IBM is a registered trademark of International Business Machines Corporation.

To my parents, Mr. & Mrs. Ching-Chieh Lee

CCD ONLINE SYSTEMS DATA PROCESSING SERIES

CICS/VS Command Level Programming With COBOL Examples
By David Lee $29.95 ISBN 0-9611810-1-X

A complete & practical guide to CICS/VS Command Level Programming. 273 practical COBOL examples and 15 sample programs address all CICS major applications. 295 big 8.5x11 technique-packed pages. Contents are printed in two colors. Contents include: BMS control statements, BMS mapset coding, CICS command usage, CICS program structure, coding, testing, and implementation, Pseudo Conversational programming, CICS internal table setup, CEDF debugging, Dynamic table handling, Online report printing, VSAM file processing, Alternate Index design, setup, and processing, Dump reading, Abend handling, and more. Sample programs include: Menu, Add, Update, Delete, Browse, Browse/Update, four Online printing techniques, Dynamic Table processing, VSAM file setup and processing, Screen Refreshing, Independent CICS program coding, and Automatic Transaction Initiation (ATI).

IMS/VS DB/DC Online Programming Using MFS And DL/I
By David Lee $29.95 ISBN 0-9611810-2-8

A complete & practical guide to IMS/VS Online programming using MFS and DL/I. 245 practical COBOL examples and 9 sample MPP programs with 8 MFS formats address all IMS/VS online major applications. 310 big 8.5x11 technique-packed pages. Contents are printed in two colors. Contents include: MFS Formatting, MFS language utility control statements, MFS format structure and coding, MPP program structure, coding, testing, and implementation, BTS II JCL setup and testing, BMP programming, Data Communication DL/I calls and much more. Sample programs include: Menu, Add, Update/Delete, Browse/Update, Online report printing, Update using two MFS formats, and independent MPP program.

IMS/VS DL/I Programming With COBOL Examples By David Lee $29.95
ISBN 0-9611810-4-4

A complete & practical guide to IMS/VS batch programming using DL/I with introduction to IMS/VS Online programming. 212 practical COBOL examples and 10 sample IMS/VS programs. 305 big 8.5x11 pages. Contents are printed in two colors. Contents include: IMS/VS system environment, Data Base concept and terminology, Data Base DL/I calls, DL/I batch program structure, coding, testing and implementation, BTS II testing, Data Base access methods, DBD & PSB generation, batch program JCL setup, Data Base load, Logical Data Base and Secondary Index design, allocation and manipulation, and introduction to IMS/VS Online programming: MFS format coding, Data Communication DL/I calls, MPP and BMP program structure, coding and testing.

VSAM Coding In COBOL And VSAM AMS
By David Lee $19.95 ISBN 0-9611810-6-0

Become a VSAM expert in just one month! A complete and practical guide to COBOL coding on VSAM files and VSAM Access Method Services (AMS). 53 practical AMS examples with complete JCL to satisfy all your needs for VSAM AMS commands. 14

COBOL batch sample programs that process all three types of VSAM files (KSDS, ESDS, and RRDS) in all three access modes. Many practical COBOL examples. Book contents are printed in two colors. It is in big 8.5x11 size, 201 technique-packed pages. COBOL batch program structure, and coding on all three types of VSAM files in sequential, random, or skip sequential modes. VSAM file DELETE, DEFINE, REPRO, LISTCAT, PRINT, VERIFY, and load using AMS commands. VSAM file backup, restore, and reorganization, VSAM alternate index design, define, load, and processing, and VSAM files setup for CICS/VS.

CICS/VS Online System Design And Implementation Techniques
By David Lee $29.95 ISBN 0-9611810-7-9

This book is a must for all CICS programmers and analysts who want to gain three years of heavy CICS experience within several months. It contains four parts. Part one covers the CICS/VS advanced features, Part two covers CICS/VS online system design and implementation techniques, Part three lists 100 most common CICS application problems that application programmers must face on a daily basis and their solutions, and Part four presents 15 most important CICS applications, each is demonstrated by a sample CICS program.

CICS/VS advanced features include VSAM Alternate Indexing, DL/I Interface, Online report printing, Message Routing, Temporary Storage, Transient Data, and Program error handling, backout, and recovery. CICS/VS design techniques include Menu-driven, Pseudo Conversational, Modular Programming, Screen Layout design, Security, Priority, Time-out, Re-insert, efficient input data transmition and editing, and design of six major CICS applications. The testing and implementation techniques include storage dump reading, CICS internal tables setup, VSAM test files creation, INTERTEST usage, and CECI, CMSG, CEMT, CSMT, ALLO and FREE transactions.

The list of 100 most common CICS problems with their solutions is the result of author's 10-year CICS experience with over 280 CICS screen installation. It will show you the causes of daily CICS problems and their solutions. It should take care most of your CICS problems for the next five years. Part four presents 15 most important CICS applications, each is carefully chosen and is demonstrated by a CICS sample program.

Contract Programming For DP Professionals
By David Lee $29.95 ISBN 0-9611810-8-7

An average contract programmer makes between $6500 and $9500 per month. The demand for experienced DP professionals is greater than ever and contracts normally last longer than one year. How long can you afford not to go contracting? If you have at least two years of experience in Data Processing, this book could be the best investment you'll ever make. David Lee, the author, has completed CICS/IMS contracts that worth over $400,000.00. This book covers everything you need to know about contract programming: the most demanded DP skills today, the locations of IBM mainframes & PCMs, How to purchase the contacts of IBM mainframe sites from research firms, Client data base setup, Future projects lead, Marketing your services using IBM PC, Price your services to beat consulting firms, Draw a service brochure, What should a proposal consist of, Fixed price or hourly rate? How to quote a fixed-price contract, How to make a presentation, Time table set up, Paymeny schedule, and Draw a contract agreement without a lawyer. The hourly-rate contract agreement, the fixed-price contract agreement, and sample proposal are included. David Lee has built up an impressive record of success as a CICS/IMS consultant for both large and small firms. He has installed over twenty CICS/IMS online systems for fourteen companies.

Send the purchase order in the back of this book with check or money order to:

CCD Online Systems, Inc.
P. O. Box 795759
Dallas, Texas 75379

To order by credit card (VISA or M/C):

Call Toll Free 1-800-851-5072 (Outside Texas)
                1-214-248-7642 (In Texas)
                9AM - 5PM Central Time

Allow 1 to 2 weeks for delivery.

PREFACE

This book is intended for CICS programmers, programmer/analysts, project leaders and CICS system designers who are interested in the CICS advanced features, CICS online system design and implementation techniques, and resolving the CICS application problems that they must face on a daily basis. CICS/VS and IMS/VS DB/DC systems are the two major Teleprocessing systems for IBM mainframes and their compatibles. This book contains the following four parts:

Part 1. CICS/VS advanced features
Part 2. CICS/VS online system design and implementation techniques
Part 3. 100 CICS/VS application problems that an application programmer must face on a daily basis and their solutions
Part 4. 15 CICS major applications and sample programs.

Part 1 of this book addresses the CICS/VS advanced features which include VSAM alternate Index design, setup and processing, DL/I data base concept and terminology, DL/I call interface, CICS/DL/I program coding, BMS commands, Message Routing, Terminal Paging, On-line report printing, Terminal Control, Temporary Storage Control, Transient Data Control, Interval Control, Storage Control, Program Control, other control operations and error handling and recovery.

Part 2 of this book addresses CICS/VS online system design and implementation techniques which include CICS screen design, CICS program design, molular program design, pseudo conversational programming, menu-driven design, four ways to pass data amoung CICS programs, security design, task priority consideration, Re-insert technique, the design of the nine CICS major applications, CICS internal tables setup, VSAM file creation, CEDF testing, the usage of INTERTEST debugging tool, CECI, Tracing, Dump reading, CMSG, CEMT, CSMT and dynamic file allocation and de-allocation.

Part 3 of this book lists 100 CICS application problems that a CICS application programmer must face on a daily basis and their solutions. Many un-experienced CICS programmers can be easily defeated by daily CICS production problems. This list will ensure that you are aware of the causes of these common CICS application problems and their solutions.

Part 4 of this book contains 15 CICS major applications, each one is demonstrated by a CICS program. Each application in Part 4 is carefully chosen and represents one CICS major application that you must know. These CICS major applications include: Menu, Add, Inquire/Update/Delete, Browse/Update, Print a 24x80 report, Print a 24x80 report with OVERFLOW, Print a 66x132 report, Print any-size report, Create data in TS queue, Review/Update/Create data in TS queue, Automatic Task Initiation (ATI), CICS Dynamic Table setup and processing, Screen Refreshing, Independent CICS program design, Submit batch job JCL from CICS, Abend-handling CICS program design, and Print utility transaction coding.

I hope this book along with my first CICS book, CICS/VS Command Level Programming With COBOL Examples, will satisfy all your needs for CICS/VS Command Level programming and CICS Online system design, testing, Implementation. Good luck on your adventures in CICS/VS.

David Lee
CCD Online Systems, Inc.
Dallas, Texas, USA

ABOUT THE AUTHOR

David Lee is a CICS/IMS consultant for CCD Online Systems, Inc., a Dallas-based computer consulting, education and publishing firm delicated to increasing understanding of advanced IBM mainframe software.

David Lee has built up an impressive record of success as a computer consultant for both large and small firms. His clients include manufacturing, services, wholesale, retailing, chemicals, marketing, insurance, commercial metals, banking, electronics, medical, health, and many more.

His newly published book from CCD Online Systems, Inc., CICS/VS Online System Design And Implementation Techniques, distills his many years of practical CICS/VS experience into a comprehensive step-by-step CICS/VS system design and implementation guide. His four other CICS/IMS/VSAM books have been used by more than 25,000 Data Processing professionals. As an CICS/IMS consultant, David Lee has designed, programmed, and implemented more than twenty online CICS/VS or IMS/VS DB/DC systems for fourteen companies, many of which are Fortune 500 companies.

In addition to holding a B.S. in Computer Science from National Chiao-Tung University in Taiwan, Mr. Lee also holds a M.S. in Computer Science from The University of Texas at Arlington.

CONTENTS   PAGE

PART 1.   CICS/VS ADVANCED FEATURES

PART 1. CICS/VS ADVANCED FEATURES

CHAPTER 1. FILE CONTROL AND VSAM FILES

CICS/VS supports VSAM, ISAM, BDAM, and DL/I data bases. If you want to process VSAM, ISAM, or BDAM files, then File Control commands (i.e. READ) must be used. If you want to process DL/I data bases, then DL/I call interface (i.e. GU) must be used. Since ISAM and BDAM files have been obsolete for over ten years, most of the CICS/VS shops today use either VSAM files or DL/I data bases. At least 90% of CICS/VS shops use VSAM files, the rest use DL/I data bases.

Every Teleprocessing system always contains two major components: data base and data communication components. The data base component handles the data base or file processing and the data communication component handles the data transfer and formatting between the application programs and the terminal devices. For CICS/VS, its data base component consists of two features: File Control and DL/I Interface. The File Control commands are used to process VSAM, ISAM, or BDAM files. The DL/I Interface calls are used to process the DL/I data bases. In this chapter, we'll cover the File Control feature of CICS/VS. In Chapter 2, we'll cover the DL/I Interface.

For CICS/VS, the data communication component consists of two features: Basic Mapping Support (BMS) and Terminal Control. The BMS commands allow the CICS programs to send a format screen with the output data to the terminal and receive the input data entered from the terminal into the CICS program. It can also be used to build and transmit a report to terminals or printers (Message Routing). BMS of CICS/VS will format the input and output data and handle the special characteristics of the terminal devices to achieve the data and device independence. The Terminal Control of CICS/VS will send or receive a stream of data to and from the terminal. It is not as useful as BMS since it has no data formatting capability. It only handles a stream of data to and from the terminal. We'll cover BMS in Chapter 3 and Terminal Control in Chapter 4.

In this chapter, we'll concentrate our efforts on the File Control. The File Control feature of CICS/VS supports VSAM, ISAM, and BDAM files. ISAM and BDAM files are obsolete for over ten years. Not too many CICS/VS shops are still using ISAM or BDAM files. The majority of CICS/VS shops use VSAM files. Therefore, we'll cover VSAM primary file, VSAM Alternate Index and File Control commands in this chapter.

The File Control commands allow you to create, update, delete, read, or browse VSAM records. The READ command is used to read a VSAM record. The READ command with the UPDATE option and the REWRITE command are used to update a VSAM record. The DELETE command is used to delete a VSAM record. The STARTBR, READNEXT, and ENDBR commands are used to browse a group of VSAM records sequentially. The WRITE command is used to create a new VSAM record. The RESETBR command is used to reset the starting point during a browse operation. The READPREV command is used to retrieve the previous record during a browse operation.

In the following sections, we'll cover:

  1.1. VSAM Primary File Setup
       We will shows you how to delete, define, load, and initialize a VSAM KSDS file
       and then set up its entry in the FCT table and the CICS startup JCL.

1.2. VSAM Alternate Index

We'll show you how to design, define, build a VSAM alternate index and then set up its entry in the FCT and the CICS startup JCL. We will cover both unique and non-unique alternate index key.

1.3. VSAM files in CICS/VS environment

We will cover the life cycle of VSAM primary and alternate index files. VSAM file delete, define, initialization, load, FCT entry setup, the CICS startup JCL setup, File Control commands, and VSAM file rebuild, backup, restore and reorganization.

1.1. VSAM Primary File Setup

There are three types of VSAM files: KSDS, RRDS and ESDS. The majority of VSAM files used in CICS/VS are KSDS files. KSDS files allows random access by key (i.e. customer number), sequential access and skip sequential access. RRDS files also allow random access but this is performed through the use of the Relative Record Number instead of a key field in the record. ESDS files do not allow the random access. Therefore, RRDS and ESDS files are not very popular in CICS/VS. If ESDS files are used, they are used as output files for off-line batch processing.

Before you can process a VSAM file in CICS/VS or batch region, the VSAM file must have been defined through the use of the DEFINE CLUSTER command of VSAM Access Method Services (AMS). After the VSAM file has been defined, you can then write a COBOL batch program or use the REPRO command of AMS to load the VSAM file with records. After the VSAM file has been defined and loaded, you can then set up its entry in the File Control Table (FCT). Each VSAM file to be processed in CICS/VS must have one entry in the FCT. After the FCT entry has been set up, your system programmer must set up one DD card (OS/VS) or DLBL card (DOS/VS) in the CICS startup JCL for each VSAM file to be used in CICS/VS. When CICS/VS is brought up, the VSAM files will be allocated and ready to be processed through the use of the File Control commands. In the CICS startup JCL, your system programmer also needs to include one VERIFY command for each VSAM file (including alternate index) to ensure the consistant end of file information in both the VSAM file and the VSAM catalog.

We'll show you how to allocate a VSAM file using AMS (Access Method Services) commands. After the VSAM file has been allocated, you must load the VSAM file with records or create at least one dummy record on the file before it can be opened to CICS/VS for processing. CICS/VS prohibits a null (empty) VSAM file to be processed. Therefore, if the VSAM file is to be created exclusively from CICS/VS region, then you need to create a dummy record in the file and then delete it right away before it can be processed in CICS/VS. If the records can be loaded from other VSAM or non-VSAM file, then you need to use the REPRO command of AMS to load this VSAM file with records. After the VSAM file has been defined (DEFINE CLUSTER), loaded (REPRO) or initilized (COBOL batch program), you need to set up its entry in the File Control Table (FCT). All VSAM files to be processed under CICS/VS must have one entry in the FCT. Otherwise, invalid dataset name condition (DSIDERR) will occur when you try to process this VSAM file through the use of the File Control commands.

1.1.1. Define A VSAM File

There are two types of VSAM files you can define: suballocated or unique VSAM file. A suballocated VSAM file occupies a VSAM space with other suballocated VSAM files and the VSAM space upon which it occupies must have been defined through the use of the DEFINE SPACE command prior to the define of the suballocated VSAM file. A unique VSAM file occupies a VSAM space by itself and the VSAM space is allocated dynamically when the VSAM file is defined. Therefore, there is no need to issue a DEFINE SPACE command to allocate the VSAM spaces for the unique VSAM files. You only need to issue the DEFINE CLUSTER command to define the unique VSAM files.

There are three types of VSAM files: KSDS, ESDS and RRDS. At least 95% of VSAM files used in CICS/VS are KSDS files. Thus we'll only show you how to define VSAM KSDS files. For more information on how to define VSAM ESDS and RRDS files, please refer to author's another book entitled VSAM Coding In COBOL And VSAM AMS. It covers everything you need to know about VSAM AMS and COBOL coding on VSAM files.

You can define a VSAM file in the master catalog or in one of the user catalogs. There is only one master catalog in the entire VSAM environment and optionly one or more VSAM user catalogs may be defined. Each user catalog has one entry in the master catalog. If your shop uses suballocated VSAM files, then your system programmer will define the VSAM spaces for you. He will normally define the entire disk volume as a single VSAM space. Thus you only need to find out which volume (disk) is to be used for your VSAM test or production files. Then you can issue the DEFINE CLUSTER command to define the VSAM files upon the VSAM space on that volume.

The following example shows how to define a suballocated VSAM file in the user catalog USERCAT:

```
    OS/VS:

//EXMP      JOB  (1500,CUST0001),'LEE',CLASS=6,
//               NOTIFY=LEE,MSGCLASS=X
//JOBCAT     DD   DSN=MASTCAT,DISP=OLD
//STEP      EXEC PGM=IDCAMS,REGION=512K
//STEPCAT    DD   DSN=USERCAT,DISP=OLD
//SYSPRINT   DD   SYSOUT=*
//SYSIN      DD   *
  DEFINE CLUSTER(NAME(CUSTOMER.MASTER) -
              VOL(VOL1) -
              RECORDS(10000 1000) -
              RECORDSIZE(200 200) -
              KEYS(5 0) -
              SHR(2 3) -
              FREESPACE(20 10) -
              INDEXED -
              IMBED -
              REPLICATE) -
        DATA(NAME(CUSTOMER.MASTER.DATA) -
```

```
                        CISZ(6144)) -
            INDEX(NAME(CUSTOMER.MASTER.INDEX) -
                        CISZ(512)) -
            CATALOG(USERCAT)
  /*
  //


  DOS/VS:


  // JOB   EXMP DEFINE A SUBALL KSDS IN USER CAT
  // EXEC IDCAMS,SIZE=64K
     (Same as above DEFINE CLUSTER)
  /*
  /&
```

In the above examples, the VSAM file cluster name is CUSTOMER.MASTER and it resides on the disk volume VOL1. The primary allocation is 10000 records and the second allocation is 1000 records. It is a fixed-length VSAM file whose record length is 200 bytes long. The key is 5 bytes long and starts with the first byte. The CI free space percentage is 20% and CA free space percentage is 10%. This is a KSDS file (INDEXED). It will be cataloged in the user catalog named USERCAT since we specify the CATALOG parameter.

The following example shows how to define a unique VSAM KSDS file in the user catalog:

```
  OS/VS:

  //EXMP      JOB (1500,CUST0001),'LEE',CLASS=6,
  //              NOTIFY=LEE,MSGCLASS=X
  //JOBCAT    DD DSN=USERCAT2,DISP=OLD
  //STEP      EXEC PGM=IDCAMS,REGION=512K
  //STEPCAT   DD DSN=USERCAT1,DISP=OLD
  //DD1       DD UNIT=3350,VOL=SER=VOL1,DISP=OLD
  //SYSPRINT  DD SYSOUT=*
  //SYSIN     DD *
   DEFINE CLUSTER(NAME(CUSTOMER.MASTER) -
                  FILE(DD1) -
                  VOL(VOL1) -
                  CYL(10 3) -
                  RECORDSIZE(200 200) -
                  KEY(5 0) -
                  IMBED -
                  UNIQUE -
                  REPLICATE) -
            DATA(NAME(CUSTOMER.MASTER.DATA) -
                  CISZ(6144)) -
            INDEX(NAME(CUSTOMER.MASTER.INDEX) -
                  CISZ(512))
  /*
  //
```

```
DOS/VS:

// JOB     EXMP DEFINE A UNQ KSDS IN USER CAT
// DLBL    DD2,'USERCAT1',,VSAM
// EXTENT  SYS001,111111
// ASSGN   SYS002,X'151'
// DLBL    DD1,'CUSTOMER.MASTER',,VSAM
// EXTENT  SYS002,VOL1,1,0,20,300
// EXEC    IDCAMS,SIZE=AUTO
   (Same as above DEFINE CLUSTER)
/*
/&
```

In the above examples, the primary allocation for this VSAM file is 10 cylinders and the secondary allocation is 3 cylinders. This is a unique KSDS file (UNIQUE). When the VSAM file type is not specified, the default is INDEXED (KSDS). We did not specify the CATALOG operand since the //STEPCAT DD statement will make sure the VSAM file will be created in the user catalog USERCAT1.

After the above JCL has been executed, the VSAM KSDS file will be defined in the VSAM user catalog. Now you can load the data into it using the AMS REPRO command or a COBOL batch program.

1.1.2.   VSAM File Initialization or Loading

After a VSAM file has been defined through the use of the DEFINE CLUSTER command, you must create a dummy record on it or load it with records. CICS/VS does not allow a null (empty) VSAM file to be processed through its File Control commands. If you want to create this new VSAM file exclusively from CICS/VS, then you have to create a dummy record in the VSAM file before it can be opened for process under CICS/VS. If you want to load the new VSAM file with records from other file, you can use the REPRO command or write a COBOL batch program to do it.

When a VSAM file is to be created completely from CICS/VS region, you need to create a dummy record into it after the VSAM file has been defined. The dummy record can be anything you like. After the dummy record is created, you can go ahead delete it in the same COBOL batch program that creates it or leave it in the file. If you delete this dummy record after it has been created, CICS/VS will not consider this VSAM file as an empty file and you'll be able to open and process it in CICS/VS. Therefore, it is better for you to delete the dummy record right after it is created.

The following example shows how to create a dummy record into the VSAM file and then delete it:

```
ID DIVISION.
PROGRAM-ID. CUST001.
REMARKS. INITIALIZE A VSAM KSDS FILE.
ENVIRONMENT DIVISION.
CONFIGURATION SECTION.
```

```
       INPUT-OUTPUT SECTION.
       FILE-CONTROL.
           SELECT CUSTMAST ASSIGN TO SYS040-CUSTMST
                   ORGANIZATION IS INDEXED
                   ACCESS IS DYNAMIC
                   RECORD KEY IS CUST-KEY
                   FILE STATUS IS CUST-STATUS.
       DATA DIVISION.
       FILE SECTION.
       FD  CUSTMAST
           LABEL RECORD IS STANDARD.
       01  CUST-REC.
           02  CUST-KEY    PIC X(5).
           02  FILLER      PIC X(195).
       WORKING-STORAGE SECTION.
       01  CUST-STATUS    PIC X(2).
       PROCEDURE DIVISION.
           OPEN OUTPUT CUSTMAST.
           IF CUST-STATUS NOT = '00'
               DISPLAY 'CUSTOMER FILE OPEN ERROR' CUST-STATUS
               STOP RUN.
           MOVE LOW-VALUES TO CUST-REC.
           WRITE CUST-REC.
           IF CUST-STATUS NOT = '00'
               DISPLAY 'CUSTOMER FILE WRITE ERROR' CUST-STATUS
               STOP RUN.
           CLOSE CUSTMAST.
           IF CUST-STATUS NOT = '00'
               DISPLAY 'CUSTOMER FILE CLOSE ERROR' CUST-STATUS
               STOP RUN.
           OPEN I-O CUSTMAST.
           MOVE LOW-VALUES TO CUST-KEY.
           DELETE CUSTMAST.
           IF CUST-STATUS NOT = '00'
               DISPLAY 'CUSTOMER FILE DELETE ERROR' CUST-STATUS
               STOP RUN.
           CLOSE CUSTMAST.
           IF CUST-STATUS NOT = '00'
               DISPLAY 'CUSTOMER FILE CLOSE ERROR' CUST-STATUS
               STOP RUN.
           DISPLAY 'CUSTOMER FILE INITIALIZED SUCCESSFULLY'.
           STOP RUN.
```

After you have successfully compiled the above COBOL batch program, you can use the following JCL to run this program:

```
OS/VS:

//CUST001   JOB  (1500,CUST0001),'LEE',CLASS=6,
//               NOTIFY=LEE,MSGCLASS=X
//CUST001   EXEC PGM=CUST001,REGION=512K
//SYSOUT    DD   SYSOUT=*
//SYSPRINT  DD   SYSOUT=*
```

6

```
//SYSUDUMP DD    SYSOUT=*
//CUSTMST  DD    DSN=CUSTOMER.MASTER,DISP=OLD
/*
//
```

DOS/VS:

```
// JOB     CUST001 INITIALIZE CUSTOMER FILE
// ASSGN   SYS040,X'231'
// DLBL    CUSTMST,'CUSTOMER.MASTER',,VSAM
// EXTENT  SYS040,VOL1
// EXEC    CUST001,SIZE=AUTO
/*
/&
```

If the VSAM file you have just defined can be loaded from other file, you can use the REPRO command or a COBOL batch program to load the records. The following example shows how to copy a portion of the production customer file into the test customer file using the REPRO command after the test file has been defined:

OS/VS:

```
//CUST001    JOB  (1500,CUST0001),'LEE',CLASS=6,
//                NOTIFY=LEE,MSGCLASS=X
//STEP       EXEC PGM=IDCAMS,REGION=512K
//DD1        DD DSN=CUSTOMER.MASTER.PROD,DISP=OLD
//DD2        DD DSN=CUSTOMER.MASTER.TEST,DISP=OLD
//SYSPRINT   DD SYSOUT=*
//SYSIN      DD *
 REPRO INFILE(DD1) OUTFILE(DD2) COUNT(100)
/*
//
```

DOS/VS:

```
// JOB     CUST001 REPRO VSAM FILE
// ASSGN   SYS004,X'151'
// DLBL    DD1,'CUSTOMER.MASTER.PROD',,VSAM
// EXTENT  SYS004,VOL1
// ASSGN   SYS005,X'152'
// DLBL    DD2,'CUSTOMER.MASTER.TEST',,VSAM
// EXTENT  SYS005,VOL2
// EXEC    IDCAMS,SIZE=64K
 REPRO INFILE(DD1) OUTFILE(DD2) COUNT(100)
/*
/&
```

The above examples will copy the customer test file from the production file. Only 100 records will be copied since we specify COUNT(100).

1.1.3. VSAM File Setup For CICS/VS

After the VSAM file has been defined and initialized (low-value record) or loaded (REPRO or batch program), you can then set up the FCT entry for it. Each VSAM file to be processed in CICS/VS must have one entry created in the FCT. If the VSAM file contains one or more alternate indexes, each alternate index must also have one FCT entry. After the FCT entry has been set up in the FCT, your system programmer must include one DD or DLBL card for each VSAM file in the CICS/VS startup JCL. One VERIFY command for each VSAM file should also be included in the CICS startup JCL to verify each VSAM file when CICS/VS is brought up in the morning. This VERIFY command will ensure that the end of file information in the VSAM catalog is consistant with that in the VSAM file itself.

The FCT entry describes the VSAM file type (KSDS), service requests (i.e. DELETE or READ), record format (fixed- or variable-length), and other control information. The following example shows how to create the FCT entry for a VSAM KSDS file (customer file):

```
DFHFCT TYPE=DATASET,DATASET=CUSTMST,ACCMETH=(VSAM,KSDS),      X
       SERVREQ=(GET,PUT,NEWREC,UPDATE,DELETE,BROWSE,SHARE),   X
       STRNO=1,BUFND=2,BUFSP=09216,BUFNI=1,                   X
       RECFORM=FIXED,FILSTAT=OPENED,LOG=YES
```

In the above example, we specify the FCT entry for the customer master VSAM KSDS file (CUSTMST). The VSAM file type is KSDS (ACCMETH=(VSAM,KSDS)). All file operations will be allowed. You can issue READ (GET), REWRITE (PUT and UPDATE), WRITE (PUT and NEWREC), DELETE (DELETE), STARTBR, READNEXT, ENDBR, READPREV, and RESETBR (BROWSE). This VSAM file is shareable so it can be read from the batch region while CICS/VS is up. The string number is 1. That means CICS/VS allows at most one request to process this VSAM file at the any time. When you issue a READ with UPDATE option, CICS/VS will increase the string count for this file by one. When you issue a REWRITE, DELETE or UNLOCK, CICS/VS will decrease the string count for this file by one. The record format for this VSAM file is fixed-length. You must specify this RECFORM=FIXED for all fixed-length VSAM files since the default is variable-length. For a variable-length VSAM file, you must specify the LENGTH option in the File Control commands. Otherwise, LENGERR condition will occur. FILSTAT=OPENED specifies that you want CICS/VS to open this file for you when CICS/VS is brought up. A VSAM file must be opened before you can issue File Control commands on it. Otherwise, NOTOPEN exceptional condition occurs. You should specify FILSTAT=OPENED for most of your VSAM files. The VSAM files that you do not want to open when CICS is brought up are those that should not be processed until the time has come. For example, you do not want to open the order file until 3 PM since the order entry clerks come in at 3 PM each day to enter the orders. In this case, the order file should be closed when CICS is brought up and should be opened at 3 PM using CSMT or CEMT transaction.

LOG=YES in the above FCT entry specifies that this VSAM file is to be backed out when the CICS task that processes this file is terminated abnormally. You should define all your VSAM files with LOG=YES to back out the updates when a CICS task is abended in order to re-enter that transaction. If the VSAM file is not backed out when the CICS task abends, then your VSAM files may be out of sync and you may have trouble to re-enter that transaction. When a CICS task is abended, CICS will call in dynamic transaction backout program to restore all VSAM files that are defined with LOG = YES and updated by this task back to the status when the task is started or to the last syncpoint if SYNCPOINT command has been issued. Your system programmer must have installed the dynamic transaction backout program which is an option to CICS/VS before if you want that to happen when a CICS task abends.

After the VSAM file has been set up in the FCT, your system programmer must include one DD (OS/VS) or DLBL (DOS/VS) card for each VSAM file to be processed in CICS/VS. A VERIFY card is also included in the CICS startup JCL to verify each VSAM file while it is brought up. The DD card for the VSAM primary file is as follow:

```
//CICSJCL   JOB CICS STARTUP JCL
//CUSTMST   DD DSN=CUSTOMER.MASTER,DISP=SHR
//CUSTNAM   DD DSN=CUSTOMER.MASTER.NAME,DISP=SHR
//VERIFY    EXEC PGM=IDCAMS,COND=EVEN
 VERIFY FILE(CUSTMST)
 VERIFY FILE(CUSTNAM)
/*
//
```

In the above example, we specify the data set name as the label and use the VSAM file cluster name in the DSN= operand. We also verify each VSAM file before it is opened to CICS for processing. If a VSAM file contains one or more alternate indexes, each alternate index must have a DD or DLBL card and one VERIFY command in the CICS startup JCL. The DSN name (OS/VS) or File ID (DOS/VS) must be the alternate index path name instead of the alternate index entry name. If you specify the alternate index entry name as the DSN or the File ID, the record you retrieve will be the alternate index record itself rather than the primary file record. The label specified in the DD or DLBL statement and in the FILE option of the VERIFY command should be the name that you specify in the FCT. You should also use this name in the DATASET option in the File Control commands.

The CICS startup JCL is a set of JCL cards stored in the partitioned data set (PDS) just like any other batch job JCL. If you want to bring up CICS/VS region, you only need to submit this set of JCL and wait for several minutes. After the CICS is up and running, you can then use CSSN transaction to sign on to CICS region. After you have signed on to CICS, the VSAM files that are opened by the CICS startup JCL are ready to be processed by CICS transactions.

1.1.4.   VSAM File Processing and File Control Commands

After the VSAM file has been defined, initialized or loaded, its FCT entry has been set up, its DD or DLBL card and VERIFY command have been included in the CICS startup JCL, you can then submit the CICS startup JCL to bring up CICS. When CICS/VS is brought up, the VSAM files will be enabled and opened and they are now ready to be processed in the CICS/VS region. You can then issue the following File Control commands to process these VSAM files:

1. READ - to read a VSAM record for inquiry or update
2. WRITE - to create a new VSAM record
3. DELETE - to delete a VSAM record
4. REWRITE - to update a VSAM record that has just been retrieved through the use of the READ command with UPDATE option.
5. UNLOCK - to release the exclusive control of a VSAM record.
6. STARTBR - to set up the starting point for a browse operation.
7. READNEXT - to read the next VSAM record during a browse.
8. ENDBR - to end a browse operation.
9. RESETBR - to reset the starting point during a browse.
10. READPREV - to read the previous VSAM record during a browse.

We'll discuss some techniques and problems that may occur while using these File Control commands in the following sections.

1.1.4.1. READ Command

The READ command can be used to read a VSAM record for inquiry (without UPDATE), read a VSAM record for update (with UPDATE), and read the next available VSAM record (with GTEQ). When you issue a READ command without UPDATE option, you only want to retrieve the VSAM record for inquiry. If you issue a READ command with the UPDATE option, you want to retrieve that record for update. In this case, the key must be moved to the RIDFLD field before you can issue this READ command. After the record to be updated has been retrieved, you need to move the new data into the record layout and then issue a REWRITE command. You should not try to update the key field. After examining the record you have just retrieved for update and you have determined that there is no need to update this record, you should issue an UNLOCK command to release the exclusive control over the VSAM control interval that contains that record.

If no UNLOCK command is issued, the string number for this VSAM file will not be decreased. If total number of CICS tasks that use this CICS program is more than the string number specified in its FCT entry, the additional CICS tasks will be hung.

The GTEQ option in the READ command can be used to update VSAM records sequentially. This is the only way to update a group of VSAM records sequentially. You cannot use STARTBR, READNEXT, and ENDBR to update a group of VSAM records sequentially since no update is allowed during a browse operation. For example, we want to update the status field of all sales order details of any given sales order number. The key of the sales order detail file is the sales order number plus the detail sequence number, a 3-byte numeric field. The following example shows how to update the status of each detail to 'C' (cancel) for the sales order 5000 using a READ command with the GTEQ option:

```
WORKING-STORAGE SECTION.
01   ORDDET-REC.
     02   ORDDET-KEY.
          03   ORDDET-ORDRNO     PIC 9(5).
```

```
      03  ORDDET-SEQNO      PIC 9(3).
      02  ORDDET-STATUS          PIC X(1).
      02  FILLER                 PIC X(191).
  PROCEDURE DIVISION.
      EXEC CICS HANDLE CONDITION
              NOTFND(A200-UPD-COMPLETE)
              END-EXEC.
      MOVE 5000 TO ORDDET-ORDRNO.
      MOVE 1    TO ORDDET-SEQNO.
  A100-READ-NEXT-DETAIL.
      EXEC CICS READ DATASET('ORDDET') INTO(ORDDET-REC)
              RIDFLD(ORDDET-KEY) GTEQ END-EXEC.
      IF ORDDET-ORDRNO NOT = 5000
         GO TO A200-UPD-COMPLETE.
      EXEC CICS READ UPDATE DATASET('ORDDET') INTO(ORDDET-REC)
              RIDFLD(ORDDET-KEY) END-EXEC.
      MOVE 'C' TO ORDDET-STATUS.
      EXEC CICS REWRITE DATASET('ORDDET') FROM(ORDDET-REC)
              END-EXEC.
      ADD 1 TO ORDDET-SEQNO.
      GO TO A100-READ-NEXT-DETAIL.
  A200-UPD-COMPLETE.
```

In the above example, we retrieve the first detail record using a READ command with the GTEQ option. After the record has been retrieved, we then check to see if this detail belongs to order 5000. If not, the update is completed. If this is a detail record for the order 5000, we then read this record again for update. After the record has been read for update, we move the new status ('C') into the status field and then issue a REWRITE command to update the record. Now we need to increase the key by 1 and then go back to read the next detail.

1.1.4.2.   WRITE Command

The WRITE command is used to create a new VSAM record. Before you can issue a WRITE command, you must move the key and the data of the new record to the record I/O area. For CICS/VS Version 1, Release 6 or later release, you must move the key to both the key field in the record I/O area and key field specified in the RIDFLD option if they are not the same field. Many CICS users encounter this problem during the conversion from Release 1.5 to 1.6.

The following example shows how to create a new customer to the customer file:

```
  01  CUST-REC.
      02  CUST-KEY   PIC 9(5).
      02  CUST-NAME  PIC X(20).

      MOVE 1000      TO CUST-KEY.
      MOVE 'LEE'     TO CUST-NAME.
      EXEC CICS WRITE DATASET('CUSTMST')
                  FROM(CUST-REC)
                  RIDFLD(CUST-KEY)
                  END-EXEC.
```

If you want to use a data field other than the key field in the record I/O area in the RIDFLD option, then you need to move the key value to both fields:

```
01  CUST-REC.
    02  CUST-KEY     PIC 9(5).
    02  CUST-NAME    PIC X(20).
01  CUSTOMER-KEY     PIC 9(5).

    MOVE 1000        TO CUST-KEY CUSTOMER-KEY.
    MOVE 'LEE'       TO CUST-NAME.
    EXEC CICS WRITE  DATASET('CUSTMST')
                     FROM(CUST-REC)
                     RIDFLD(CUSTOMER-KEY)
                     END-EXEC.
```

If the record I/O area is defined in LINKAGE SECTION, then you need to issue a GETMAIN command to acquire the record I/O area before you can move the key and data into it:

```
WORKING-STORAGE SECTION.
01  WS-SPACE          PIC X(1) VALUE ' '.
LINKAGE SECTION.
01  DFHCOMMAREA       PIC X(100).
01  BLLCELLS.
    02  FILLER        PIC S9(8) COMP.
    02  CUST-PTR      PIC S9(8) COMP.
01  CUST-REC.
    02  CUST-KEY      PIC 9(5).
    02  CUST-NAME     PIC X(20).
PROCEDURE DIVISION.
    EXEC CICS GETMAIN SET(CUST-PTR) LENGTH(25)
              INITIMG(WS-SPACE) END-EXEC.
    MOVE 1000    TO CUST-KEY.
    MOVE 'LEE'   TO CUST-NAME.
    EXEC CICS WRITE DATASET('CUSTMST')
                    FROM(CUST-REC)
                    RIDFLD(CUST-KEY)
                    END-EXEC.
```

The only two exceptional conditions you need to watch out for the WRITE commands are NOSPACE and DUPREC. The NOSPACE condition occurs when there is no more space in this VSAM file to add this new record. In this case, you need to disable the transaction of this CICS program to prevent the users from using it. Then you need to close this VSAM file using CSMT or CEMT transaction. After the VSAM file is closed, you can then go to the batch region to do a re-organization on this file. The only difference between this re-organization and the normal re-organization is you need to use a bigger space (RECORDS or CYL or TRK) in the DEFINE CLUSTER command. So you still issue a REPRO command, DELETE CLUSTER command, DEFINE CLUSTER command and then REPRO the VSAM file from its backup tape.

The DUPREC condition occurs when the key of the new record has already existed. If this is a fixed-length VSAM file, then the LENGTH option needs not be specified in the WRITE command. If this is a variable-length VSAM file, then you need to move the actual length of this new record to the data field specified in the LENGTH option before you issue the WRITE command. If no LENGTH option is specified for a variable-length VSAM file, LENGERR condition occurs.

If you try to create a new record for a VSAM file with one or more alternate indexes and there is no more space in the alternate index file, no exceptional condition will occur for the WRITE command. VSAM just creates the new record in the primary file and no alternate index record will be created. But when you try to access this VSAM file through this alternate index key, you will get ILLOGIC condition. In this case, CICS notifies you that your VSAM file and its alternate index file are not in sync. You should close both files and rebuild only the alternate index by specifying a bigger space for it.

1.1.4.3.   REWRITE Command

This command is used to update a VSAM record that has been retrieved through the use of the READ command with the UPDATE option. Before you issue the REWRITE command, you should move the updates to the record I/O area. But you should not try to modify the key, you can only modify the data fields within the record I/O area. You do not need to specify the RIDFLD option in the REWRITE command since VSAM knows the record you are going to update is the one that has been retrieved.

In a CICS online update application, you should issue the READ with UPDATE option only after the input fields have been edited successfully. You should not issue a READ with UPDATE option before the editing since CICS will maintain an exclusive control over the control interval that contains that record and in result, no other CICS tasks can process that control interval.

The following example shows how to issue a REWRITE command to update the customer name:

```
01   CUST-REC.
     02   CUST-KEY     PIC 9(5).
     02   CUST-NAME    PIC X(20).

     MOVE 1000 TO CUST-KEY.
     EXEC CICS READ DATASET('CUSTMST')
                    INTO(CUST-REC)
                    RIDFLD(CUST-KEY)
                    END-EXEC.
     MOVE 'LEE' TO CUST-NAME.
     EXEC CICS REWRITE DATASET('CUSTMST')
                    FROM(CUST-REC)
                    END-EXEC.
```

There is no exceptional condition you need to watch out for the REWRITE command.

1.1.4.4. DELETE Command

This DELETE command is used to delete a VSAM record or a group VSAM records with the same generic key. The generic delete can only be performed on a VSAM file that is not specified with LOG=YES in its FCT entry. When a VSAM file is specified with LOG=YES in its FCT entry, CICS will try to back out the updates made on this VSAM file when the CICS task is terminated abnormally. This will allow you to fix the problem and enter the same transaction again later. If a VSAM file is not specified with LOG=YES, it will not be backed out when the CICS task that processes that file abends.

Most of VSAM files are specified with LOG=YES, therefore, you cannot perform the generic delete.

You can delete a VSAM record directly or indirectly. If the VSAM record has been retrieved for update through the use of the READ command with UPDATE option, you can issue a DELETE command without RIDFLD option to delete the retrieved record. You can also move the key of the record to be deleted to the record ID field (RIDFLD), and then issue a DELETE command with RIDFLD option to delete the VSAM record directly.

The following example shows we want to delete customer 1000 that has been retrieved for update:

```
MOVE 1000 TO CUST-KEY.
EXEC CICS READ DATASET('CUSTMST')
               INTO(CUST-REC)
               RIDFLD(CUST-KEY)
               END-EXEC.
EXEC CICS DELETE DATASET('CUSTMST') END-EXEC.
```

The following example shows we want to delete customer 1000 directly:

```
MOVE 1000 TO CUST-KEY.
EXEC CICS DELETE DATASET('CUSTMST')
          RIDFLD(CUST-KEY)
          END-EXEC.
```

In the above example, we move the customer number 1000 to a key field and then issue a DELETE command with RIDFLD option to delete customer 1000. NOTFND condition occurs when the record you try to delete does not exist.

The following example shows how to perform a generic delete to delete all sales order details for the sales order 1000. Assume that the key of the sales order detail file is the order number plus the detail sequence number. We'll use the sales order number as the generic key to delete all sales order details with sales order number equal to 1000:

```
WORKING-STORAGE SECTION.
01   ORDRDET-REC.
     02   ORDRDET-KEY.
          03   ORDRDET-ORDRNO   PIC 9(5).
          03   ORDRDET-SEQNO    PIC 9(3).
```

```
      02  ORDRDET-PRODUCT         PIC X(15).
PROCEDURE DIVISION.
      ....
      MOVE 1000 TO ORDRDET-ORDRNO.
      EXEC CICS DELETE DATASET('ORDRDET')
                       RIDFLD(ORDRDET-KEY)
                       KEYLENGTH(5)
                       GENERIC
                       END-EXEC.
```

In the above example, we specify the key of the sales order detail file (ORDRDET-KEY) in the RIDFLD field and then specify the length of the order number (5 bytes) in KEYLENGTH option. CICS will then use this order number to perform the generic delete to delete all detail records with the same generic key (order number).

1.1.4.5.   UNLOCK Command

This UNLOCK command is used to release the exclusive control of the record that has been retrieved for update through the READ command with UPDATE option. After a record has been retrieved for update, CICS will maintain an exclusive control over the control interval that contains this record. You should issue a REWRITE (update), DELETE (delete) or UNLOCK command to release the exclusive control so other CICS tasks can access this control interval. If you don't, the string count for this VSAM file will be increased by 1 for each CICS task that uses this CICS program. When the total number of CICS tasks that use this program exceeds the string number you specify for this VSAM file in its FCT entry, the additional CICS tasks will be hung waiting for this VSAM file to be released. In this case, the entire CICS system will be hung eventually.

The default string number is 1, that means at most one request can access this VSAM file at the any time. Therefore, if you do not want to update or delete the retrieved record, then you should issue an UNLOCK command to release the VSAM file for other CICS tasks.

There are no exceptional conditions you need to watch out for this UNLOCK command.

1.1.4.6.   Browse Operations

The browse operation is a unique feature of VSAM file. You can retrieve a group of records sequentially. This feature is also called skip sequential processing. When a VSAM record is retrieved, VSAM will remember the location of the record you have just retrieved. When you issue another retrieval request during a browse operation, VSAM will use the location of the last record retrieved to get the next record. This way VSAM saves some time in retrieving the next record. So the browse operation is different from the READ command with GTEQ (greater than or equal to) option which is a random retrieval.

You can use the browse operation to retrieve all sales order details for any given order number or to retrieve customers starting with any given key. In order to perform a browse operation, you need to issue a STARTBR command to set up the starting key, a

READNEXT command for each record to be retrieved, and an ENDBR command to end the browse operation. Before you can issue a STARTBR command, you need to move the starting key to the data field specified in the RIDFLD option. You should use the same data field specified in the STARTBR command in the READNEXT command. When there are no more records on the file (ENDFILE condition) or you have determined that the browse should be terminated, you should issue an ENDBR command to inform CICS that the browse operation is to be terminated.

The following example shows how to browse the sales order detail file and display up to fifteen details for the order number 1000. Assume that the key to the sales order detail file is the sales order number plus the detail sequence number, a 3-byte numeric field.

```
WORKING-STORAGE SECTION.
01  ORDRDET-REC.
    02  ORDRDET-KEY.
        03  ORDRDET-ORDRNO     PIC 9(5).
        03  ORDRDET-SEQNO      PIC 9(3).
    02  ORDRDET-ORDRQTY        PIC 9(3).
01  LINE-CTR                   PIC 9(2).
PROCEDURE DIVISION.
    EXEC CICS HANDLE CONDITION
              NOTFND(A140-ENDBR-ORDRDET)
              ENDFILE(A140-ENDBR-ORDRDET)
              ERROR(A900-ERROR)
              END-EXEC.
    MOVE 0     TO LINE-CTR.
    MOVE 1000  TO ORDRDET-ORDRNO.
    MOVE 1     TO ORDRDET-SEQNO.
    EXEC CICS STARTBR DATASET('ORDRDET')
                      RIDFLD(ORDRDET-KEY)
                      END-EXEC.
A120-READNEXT-ORDRDET.
    EXEC CICS READNEXT DATASET('ORDRDET')
                       INTO(ORDRDET-REC)
                       RIDFLD(ORDRDET-KEY)
                       END-EXEC.
    IF ORDRDET-ORDRNO NOT = 1000
       GO TO A140-ENDBR-ORDRDET.
    ADD 1 TO LINE-CTR.
    .... MOVE DETAIL TO MAP I/O AREA ...
    IF LINE-CTR < 15
       GO TO A120-READNEXT-ORDRDET.
A140-ENDBR-RDRDET.
    EXEC CICS ENDBR DATASET('ORDRDET') END-EXEC.
    .... SEND MAP ....
A900-ERROR.
```

During the browse operation, you can only issue the browse commands, you cannot issue the File Control commands like READ or DELETE. If you do, INVREQ condition occurs. During the browse, you cannot update the record you have just retrieved. However, you can browse the VSAM file through the alternate index key and after the record has been retrieved, you can issue a READ command with UPDATE option to retrieve this record for update using the primary key and update this record. This type of applications is used so often that you need to know how to do it. Assume that we want to cancel all invoices for a given customer. The customer number plus the invoice number is set up as the unique alternate index key and the invoice number is the primary key to the invoice file.

```
WORKING-STORAGE SECTION.
01  INVOICE-REC.
    02  INV-ALT-KEY.
        03  INV-CUSTNO    PIC 9(5).
        03  INV-PRIMARY-KEY.
            04  INV-INVOICE-NO PIC 9(8).
    02  INV-STATUS PIC X(1).
01  LINE-CTR        PIC 9(2).
PROCEDURE DIVISION.
    EXEC CICS HANDLE CONDITION
              NOTFND(A140-ENDBR-INVCUST)
              ENDFILE(A140-ENDBR-INVCUST)
              ERROR(A999-ABEND)
              END-EXEC.
    MOVE 0    TO LINE-CTR.
    MOVE 1000 TO INV-CUSTNO.
    MOVE 1    TO INV-INVOICE-NO.
    EXEC CICS STARTBR DATASET('INVCUST')
                      RIDFLD(INV-ALT-KEY)
                      END-EXEC.
A120-READNEXT-INVCUST.
    EXEC CICS READNEXT DATASET('INVCUST')
                       INTO(INVOICE-REC)
                       RIDFLD(INV-ALT-KEY)
                       END-EXEC.
    IF INV-CUSTNO NOT = 1000
       GO TO A140-ENDBR-INVCUST.
    ADD 1 TO LINE-CTR.
*   UPDATE THIS INVOICE
    EXEC CICS READ DATASET('INVOICE')
                   INTO(INVOICE-REC)
                   RIDFLD(INV-PRIMARY-KEY)
                   END-EXEC.
    MOVE 'C' TO INV-STATUS.
    EXEC CICS REWRITE DATASET('INVOICE')
                      FROM(INVOICE-REC)
                      END-EXEC.
    GO TO A120-READNEXT-INVCUST.
A140-ENDBR-INVCUST.
    EXEC CICS ENDBR DATASET('INVCUST') END-EXEC.
    ...
A999-ABEND.
```

In the above example, we start the browse operation with customer number 1000 using the alternate index key. Then we issue the READNEXT command to retrieve the first invoice record for customer number 1000. After the record has been retrieved, we need to make sure it belongs to customer 1000. If it is, we can then issue a READ command with UPDATE option using the primary key. Then we move the cancel status 'C' to the status field and issue a REWRITE command to update the primary record. We then go back to issue a READNEXT command to retrieve the next invoice record under customer 1000. The primary file data set name is 'INVOICE' and the alternate index file data set name is 'INVCUST'. The primary key is the invoice number and alternate index key is the customer number plus the invoice number. Since we have included the primary key as the last part of the alternate index key, we can define the alternate index key as unique. Therefore, we do not specify DUPKEY condition for the READNEXT command.

You need to set up the NOTFND condition when you issue a STARTBR command. This condition occurs when there is no record on the file with key equal or greater than the key you specify in the RIDFLD option. When NOTFND condition occurs, you should go to issue an ENDBR command to end the browse. If you don't, the browse will be ended when the CICS task is terminated.

You need to set up the ENDFILE condition when you issue a READNEXT command. This condition occurs when there are no more records in the file. That means you have just retrieved the last record on the file and then you issue another READNEXT command.

VSAM also allows you to read the previous record from the current record using the READPREV command. However, to retrieve the previous record, you must have a base record as the current one. For example, we want to know the sequence number of the last sales order detail record for sales order 1000 in the file. We need to know that when we try to create a new detail for that sales order. The key to the sales order detail file is the sales order number plus the sequence number. The sequence number is assigned sequentially when a new detail record is created. We can use the READPREV command to get the last detail record of this sales order number as follows:

```
WORKING-STORAGE SECTION.
01  ORDRDET-REC.
    02  ORDRDET-KEY.
        03  ORDRDET-ORDRNO    PIC 9(5).
        03  ORDRDET-SEQNO     PIC 9(3).
    02  ORDRDET-ORDRQTY       PIC S9(5)V99 COMP-3.
PROCEDURE DIVISION.
    EXEC CICS HANDLE CONDITION
              NOTFND(A900-NOTFND)
              END-EXEC.
    COMPUTE ORDRDET-ORDRNO = 1000 + 1.
    MOVE 1 TO ORDRDET-SEQNO.
    EXEC CICS STARTBR DATASET('ORDRDET')
                      RIDFLD(ORDRDET-KEY)
                      END-EXEC.
    EXEC CICS READPREV DATASET('ORDRDET')
                       INTO(ORDRDET-REC)
                       RIDFLD(ORDRDET-KEY)
                       END-EXEC.
```

```
      EXEC CICS ENDBR DATASET('ORDRDET') END-EXEC.
      ADD 1 TO ORDRDET-SEQNO.
      .... NOW YOU GET THE SEQNO FOR NEW RECORD ....
A900-NOTFND.
```

In the above example, we start the browse operation with the first detail record of the sales order number 1001. Then we issue a READPREV command to retrieve the previous record of the first detail of sales order 1001. After this record has been retrieved, we can add 1 to its sequence number to get the new sequence number for the new record. The trouble about using the READPREV command is that the STARTBR command may get a NOTFND condition when there is no record on the file with key equal to or greater than the one we specified in the RIDFLD option. In this case, you cannot issue a READPREV command. In the above example, we will get NOTFND condition when 1000 is the highest order in that file. For this reason, you need to create a dummy record with HIGH-VALUES as the key in the file if a READPREV command is to be used in the CICS programs to process this file. This dummy record will ensure the STARTBR command will not get NOTFND condition and subsequent READPREV command can be issued.

1.2.   VSAM Alternate Index

Alternate Index is a unique feature of VSAM. It allows your CICS programs to access the VSAM files through the alternate index keys in addition to the primary key. Since the COBOL SORT verb is not allowed in the online CICS programs and you may try to access a VSAM file using a sequence that is different from the primary key. For example, the key to the customer master file, a VSAM KSDS file, is the customer number. If the customer calls to order products from us, he may not remember the customer number we have assigned to him. In this case, we can set up the customer name as the alternate index key to this customer master file. Then we can read the customer master record using the customer name as the key to retrieve the same customer record. After the customer record has been read, we can then use the customer number on the record to place the order.

VSAM alternate index is an important feature for CICS applications, the majority of important VSAM KSDS files used in CICS/VS contain one or more alternate indexes. At least 15% of VSAM files carry one or more alternate indexes. Many CICS applications may not be possible if VSAM alternate Index feature is not allowed.

For example, we normally set up the name as the alternate index key to the customer or vendor file so they can be accessed by name in addition to the customer or vendor number. We normally set up the customer number as the alternate index key to the invoice file so we can browse all invoices in the invoice file for any given customer. The invoice number is the primary key of the invoice file. We can also set up the store number as the alternate index key to the inventory file so we can browse all products for any given store number. We can also set up the purchase order number as the alternate index key to the sales order file so we can answer the customer's questions on a sales order using the customer's purchase order as the key.

When you need an additional key to a VSAM file, you can define an alternate index upon this VSAM file. Then VSAM will maintain the alternate index for you automatically. That means the CICS application programs do not need to maintain the records in the alternate index file. VSAM will do that for you automatically. When you create a new customer on the customer file, VSAM will create its alternate index record in the index file for you. When a customer is deleted from the customer file, its alternate index record will be deleted by VSAM automatically. When you update a customer and the customer name (alternate index key) has been changed, its alternate index record will be deleted and a new alternate index record will be created to reflect this change.

A majority of VSAM files are KSDS files and most of them are updated through CICS/VS on-line applications. However, the COBOL SORT verb cannot be used in the CICS programs. Therefore, alternate indexes are set up mostly to satisfy the on-line CICS/VS application needs. It is very important that you know how to design, define, load, process and reorganize a VSAM file with alternate indexes.

An alternate index consists of an alternate index file and a path. The alternate index file is a VSAM KSDS file that contains the index records. Each index record contains an alternate index key as the key, and the primary key and a 5-byte control area as the data. The path defines the relationship between the VSAM primary file and its alternate index file so when the VSAM primary file is updated, VSAM will use this relationship defined by the path to maintain the alternate index file.

If you want to define a VSAM file with one alternate index from scratch, here is what you need to do:

1. Define the primary file using the DEFINE CLUSTER command.
2. Create a dummy record or load the VSAM file with one or more records using the REPRO command or a COBOL batch program.
3. Define the alternate index file using the DEFINE AIX command.
4. Define the alternate index path using the DEFINE PATH command.
5. Build the alternate index file from the primary file using the BLDINDEX command.
6. Set up FCT entries for both the VSAM primary file and the alternate index paths.
7. Add a DD or DLBL card for both the primary and alternate index path in the CICS/VS startup JCL.
8. Add a VERIFY command for both the primary and alternate index path in the CICS startup JCL.

If you want to create an alternate index upon an existing VSAM KSDS file, here is what you need to do:

1. Close the VSAM file to CICS/VS.
2. Perform step 3, 4, 5 in the above procedure.
3. Set up FCT entry for the alternate index path.
4. Add DD or DLBL card and VERIFY command for the alternate index path in the CICS startup JCL.

The alternate index file can be completely rebuilt using the VSAM primary file as the input in the BLDINDEX command. That is the reason why you only need to back up the primary file during the VSAM reorganization. There is no need to back up the alternate index file during the re-organization process.

1.2.1. VSAM Alternate Index Design

VSAM allows you to define an alternate index key as unique or nonunique. If an alternate index key is defined as nonunique, more than one records in the primary file can have the same alternate index key. If an alternate index key is defined as unique, then each record in the primary file contains an unique alternate index key. You should define all your alternate indexes as unique. Here is the reason. If you want to define an alternate index key as nonunique, then you need to specify the average and maximum lengths of the alternate index record when you define the alternate index file itself. The maximum record length is determined by how many duplicates allowed for that alternate index key. Therefore, during the alternate index file define, you have already specified the maximum number of duplicates allowed. VSAM will only maintain up to the maximum number of primary records with duplicated alternate index key in its index record. The maximum length of this alternate index file is defined in the DEFINE AIX command. Those duplicates that exceed the limit will not be maintained due to no spaces in the variable-length index record. That means you will lose the alternate indexing capability for those primary records that exceed the total number of duplicates. How many VSAM files can you put a limit on the number of duplicates allowed on its alternate index? The answer is very few. That is the reason why you should define all your alternate indexes as unique.

Many CICS shops use non-unique alternate index keys because they do not want to re-arrange the VSAM record layout in order to make the key unique. Since re-arrange of the record layout will result in VSAM file convertion and changing all batch and online CICS programs that use these VSAM files.

When a VSAM alternate index is defined as unique, you can access the primary file through the alternate index key just like you access it through the primary key. The only differences are the key and the data set name used in the File Control commands. The key should be the alternate index key instead of the primary key. The dataset name should be the name for the alternate index path instead of that of the primary file. However, you should only issue read-only and browse commands on the alternate index key. For example, you should not try to update a customer using the customer name sequence. You should update the customer using the customer number. You should specify GET and BROWSE in the service request (SERVREQ=) in its FCT entry.

VSAM only allows you to specify a consecutive area within the record as the alternate index key. In order to make the alternate index key unique, you need to put the primary key immediately following the desired alternate index field and make the entire area as the alternate index key. For example, you should define the customer number right behind the customer name in the customer record layout and make the entire area (customer name and customer number) as the alternate index key. Since the customer number is unique to this record, this alternate index key that includes the customer number will also be unique. Since we do not know the customer number when we try to retrieve the customer record through the alternate index key, you will use a partial or full customer name as the starting point to browse the customer records and display all customers with the same generic key (customer name) on the terminal for the user to select the right customer. After the right customer has been selected, you can then retrieve that customer using the primary key to display that customer for detail information. Therefore, when you attach the primary key as last part of the alternate index key, you will normally use browse operation rather than the READ command to get to the desired customer record using the alternate index key.

From the above discussion, we know the design of the alternate index starts when you design the VSAM primary file record layout. If this VSAM file is an existing file, you may need to convert the file in order to accommadate the alternate index key. Many compaines have rejected the idea of converting the VSAM files in order to make them unique so they do not need to change batch programs that process these VSAM files. So the only way to do that is to define the alternate index key nonunique and risk the loss of index data for those additional primary records that exceed the maximum number of duplicates allowed.

The following example shows we want to define the customer name as the alternate index key to the customer master file. The primary key to this file is the customer number. In order to make the alternate index key unique, we need to include the customer number as the last part of the alternate index key in the record layout:

```
01   CUST-RECORD.
     02   CUST-ALT-KEY.
          03   CUST-NAME      PIC X(20).
          03   CUST-PRM-KEY.
               04   CUST-NO   PIC X(5).
     02   FILLER              PIC X(175).
```

Then we can specify the CUST-ALT-KEY as the alternate index key when we define the index file using the DEFINE AIX command. We can still define the customer number as the primary key in the DEFINE CLUSTER command when we define this VSAM file.

1.2.2.   VSAM Alternate Index Define

After the VSAM file has been defined, you can then define the alternate index file using the DEFINE AIX command. This DEFINE AIX command simply defines a VSAM KSDS file to store the alternate index records. The alternate index record contains the alternate index key (customer name and customer number) as the key, primary key (customer number) and a 5-byte control area as the data. After the alternate index file has been defined, you need to define the path. After the path has been defined, you can then load the alternate index file using its primary file as input. The primary file must contain at least one record before you can execute the BLDINDEX command. The following example shows how to define a VSAM file with one alternate index:

```
OS/VS:

//EXMPL      JOB (1500,CUST0001),'LEE',CLASS=6,
//               NOTIFY=LEE,MSGCLASS=X
//STEP       EXEC PGM=IDCAMS,REGION=512K
//SYSPRINT   DD SYSOUT=*
```

```
//SYSIN     DD *
  DELETE  CUSTOMER.MASTER CLUSTER
  DEFINE  CLUSTER(NAME(CUSTOMER.MASTER) -
                  VOL(VOL1) -
                  RECORDS(10000 1000) -
                  RECORDSIZE(200 200) -
                  SHR(2 3) -
                  KEYS(5 20) -
                  FREESPACE(20 10) -
                  INDEXED -
                  IMBED -
                  REPLICATE) -
          DATA(NAME(CUSTOMER.MASTER.DATA) CISZ(6144)) -
          INDEX(NAME(CUSTOMER.MASTER.INDEX) CISZ(512))
  DEFINE  AIX(NAME(CUSTOMER.MASTER.ALT) -
                  VOL(VOL1) -
                  RECORDSIZE(35 35) -
                  SHR(2 3) -
                  KEYS(25 0) -
                  CYL(3 1) -
                  FREESPACE(10 10) -
                  IMBED -
                  REPLICATE -
                  RELATE(CUSTOMER.MASTER) -
                  UNIQUEKEY -
                  UPGRADE) -
          DATA(NAME(CUSTOMER.MASTER.ALT.D)) -
          INDEX(NAME(CUSTOMER.MASTER.ALT.I))
  DEFINE  PATH(NAME(CUSTOMER.MASTER.PATH) -
          PATHENTRY(CUSTOMER.MASTER.ALT) -
          UPDATE)
/*
//
```

Where:

The DELETE CLUSTER command will delete the VSAM file along with all its alternate indexes and paths, if exist. We put the DELETE CLUSTER command in front of the DEFINE CLUSTER command so this set of JCL can also be used in the reorganization. The DEFINE CLUSTER command will define the VSAM primary file itself. The DEFINE AIX command defines the alternate index file itself. An alternate index file is a VSAM KSDS file that contains one data component and one index component. The DEFINE PATH command defines the relationship between the VSAM primary file and its alternate index file. The path name must be used in the CICS/VS startup JCL when you try to set up the alternate index path in CICS/VS for that VSAM file. The BLDINDEX command can be used to load the alternate index file from the primary file if the primary file contains at least one record. This will make the primary file and its alternate index file in sync. After the BLDINDEX command has been executed, you can open both files to CICS/VS. After that, CICS/VS will then keep both files in sync for you automatically.

In the above example, after we've defined the customer master file using the DEFINE

CLUSTER command, we can then define the alternate index file using the DEFINE AIX command. After the alternate index file has been defined, we can then define the path using the DEFINE PATH command.

When a new record is added into this customer master file, an index record will also be added into the index file by VSAM automatically. If a customer record is deleted from the customer file, its index record will also be deleted. If the alternate key in the customer record has been changed, its index record will be deleted and a new index record will be created to reflect this change. Thus VSAM maintains the alternate index records for you automatically. Thus you do not need to get involved with the maintenance of the alternate index file in your CICS programs.

In the above example, we specify KEYS(5 20) as the key for the customer primary file since the customer number starts on the 21st byte of the record and is 5 bytes long. The record size for this customer master is 200 bytes long (RECORDSIZE(200 200)). We specify KEYS(25 0) as the alternate index key for the index file since the alternate key starts at the first byte of the record and is 25 bytes long (customer name plus customer number). The index record size is 35 bytes long since the alternate index key is 25 bytes long, the primary key (customer number) is 5 bytes long and the control area is also 5 bytes long. We specify UNIQUEKEY to indicate the alternate index key is unique.

You can also set up an alternate index upon an existing VSAM KSDS file. In this case, you need to issue the DEFINE AIX command to define the alternate index file and the the DEFINE PATH command to define the relationship between the primary VSAM file and its alternate index file. After the alternate index file and the path have been defined, you can then issue the BLDINDEX command to build the index file from the existing primary VSAM file. After that, the primary and alternate index files are in sync. You can then open both files to CICS/VS for processing, VSAM will then maintain the alternate index file for you automatically.

The following example shows how to define the alternate index file and the path for the same customer master file under DOS/VS:

```
DOS/VS:

// JOB     EXMPL DEFINE AIX AND PATH
// DLBL    CUSTNAM,'CUSTOMER.MASTER.ALT',,VSAM
// EXTENT  SYS040,VOL1
// EXEC    IDCAMS,SIZE=AUTO
  DELETE CUSTOMER.MASTER.ALT FILE(CUSTNAM) PURGE
  DEFINE AIX(NAME(CUSTOMER.MASTER.ALT) -
         RELATE(CUSTOMER.MASTER) -
         FILE(CUSTNAM) -
         RECSZ(35 35) -
         CYL(3 1) -
         FREESPACE(10 10) -
         IMBED -
         REPLICATE -
         UPGRADE -
         KEY(25 0) -
         VOL(VOL1) -
```

```
            UNQK -
            SHR( 2  3)) -
            DATA(NAME(CUSTOMER.MASTER.ALT.D)) -
            INDEX(NAME(CUSTOMER.MASTER.ALT.I)) -
            CATALOG(USERCAT)
     DEFINE PATH(NAME(CUSTOMER.MASTER.PATH) -
            FILE(CUSTNAM) -
            PATHENTRY(CUSTOMER.MASTER.ALT) -
            CATALOG(USERCAT)
   /*
   /&
```

1.2.3.   VSAM Alternate Index Build

If you try to set up an alternate index upon an existing VSAM file and the alternate index file and its path have been defined, you can then build the index file using the primary file as the input to the BLDINDEX command. Since the index record contains the alternate index key as the key and the primary key and a 5-byte control area as data, the index file can be built or re-built completely from the primary file. The primary file must contain at least one record before you issue the BLDINDEX command. This BLDINDEX command is also used in reorganization to re-build the index file from the primary file after the primary file has been reorganized. Therefore, there is no need to back up the index file to tape during the reorganization. You only need to backup the primary file.

The following example shows how to build an alternate index file from an existing VSAM KSDS file with records:

```
OS/VS:

//EXMP      JOB (1500,CUST0001),'LEE',CLASS=6,
//             NOTIFY=LEE,MSGCLASS=X
//STEP      EXEC PGM=IDCAMS,REGION=512K
//DD1       DD DSN=CUSTOMER.MASTER,DISP=OLD
//DD2       DD DSN=CUSTOMER.MASTER.ALT,DISP=OLD
//SYSPRINT DD SYSOUT=*
//SYSIN     DD *
 BLDINDEX INFILE(DD1) -
          OUTFILE(DD2)
/*
//
```

In the above example, we must specify the alternate index entry name (NAME) specified in the DEFINE AIX command as the DSN name (not the path name). The INFILE parameter identifies the VSAM primary file as the input file, and the OUTFILE parameter identifies the alternate index file, a VSAM KSDS file, to be built. The VSAM primary file contains all the necessary information to completely rebuild its alternate index file. After the BLDINDEX command has been executed successfully, both the primary and alternate index files are in sync. You can open both files to CICS/VS for processing after the BLDINDEX command is executed successfully. CICS/VS will then take it from there to maintain the alternate index file for you automatically.

25

The following example shows how to build the same alternate index file from the VSAM primary file in DOS/VS:

```
DOS/VS:

// JOB      EXMPL BUILD ALTERNATE INDEX FILE
// ASSGN    SYS007,X'233'
// DLBL     DD1,'CUSTOMER.MASTER',,VSAM
// EXTENT   SYS007,VOL1
// DLBL     DD2,'CUSTOMER.MASTER.ALT',,VSAM
// EXTENT   SYS007,VOL1
// EXEC     IDCAMS,SIZE=AUTO
 BLDINDEX INFILE(DD1) -
          OUTFILE(DD2)
/*
/&
```

1.2.4.   VSAM Alternate Index Processing

After the alternate index file and its path have been defined and the index file has been loaded from the primary file, the next step you need to take is to set up the VSAM primary file and its alternate index in the FCT. We have shown you how to set up the VSAM primary file entry in the FCT. Here, we will only show you how to set up the FCT entry for the alternate index. Each alternate index must have one FCT entry before you can process the primary file using the alternate index key sequence in CICS/VS. However, you should perform read-only or browse operations through the alternate index key. For example, you should only read the customer records using the READ command or browse commands in the customer name sequence. You should not try to update, delete, or create the customer records using the customer name sequence. In order to prevent CICS programs from updating VSAM primary file through the alternate index path, you can specify GET and BROWSE in the SERVREQ= parameter in its FCT entry. The following example shows the alternate index entry for the customer name alternate index path:

```
DFHFCT TYPE=DATASET,DATASET=CUSTNAM,ACCMETH=(VSAM,KSDS),   X
       SERVREQ=(GET,BROWSE),BASE=CUSTMST,                  X
       STRNO=1,BUFND=2,BUFSP=09216,BUFNI=1,                X
       RECFORM=FIXED,FILSTAT=OPENED
```

For an alternate index file, you should allow only read or browse operations for CICS programs and let VSAM maintain the index file for you. The BASE= parameter specifies the data set name of its base cluster (primary file).

After the FCT entries have been set up for both the VSAM primary file and its alternate index, you should then ask your system programmer to include these two files in the CICS startup JCL. We have shown you how to include the DD or DLBL card and VERIFY command for the VSAM primary file. Here we'll show you how to include these for an alternate index. You should use the path name (NAME) specified in the DEFINE PATH command as the DSN name (OS/VS) or the File ID (DOS/VS) rather than the alternate index entry name (NAME) specified in the DEFINE AIX command. If you use the later, CICS will return the alternate index record to you instead of the primary record when you retrieve the file through the alternate index key. The following example shows how to set up the DD card or DLBL card for both the primary file and its alternate index path in the CICS startup JCL:

```
//CICSJCL   JOB CICS STARTUP JCL
//CUSTMST   DD DSN=CUSTOMER.MASTER,DISP=SHR
//CUSTNAM   DD DSN=CUSTOMER.MASTER.PATH,DISP=SHR
//VERIFY    EXEC PGM=IDCAMS,SIZE=512K
 VERIFY FILE(CUSTMST)
 VERIFY FILE(CUSTNAM)
/*
//
```

After you have included these VSAM files in the CICS startup JCL, you can then submit this set of JCL to bring up the CICS/VS region. After the CICS/VS region has been brought up, you are now ready to process the VSAM files with alternate indexes.

The following example shows we want to browse all customers starting with name 'ABC'. Assume that the primary key to this customer file is the customer number and the customer name plus the customer number has been set up as the alternate index key (unique). We can browse the customer records as following:

```
WORKING-STORAGE SECTION.
01   CUSTOMER-REC.
     02   CUST-ALT-KEY.
          03   CUST-NAME.
               04   CUST-NAME-13   PIC X(3).
               04   FILLER         PIC X(17).
          03   CUST-PRIMARY-KEY.
               04   CUST-NO     PIC X(5).
     02   FILLER                 PIC X(175).
01   LINE-CTR                    PIC 9(2).
PROCEDURE DIVISION.
     EXEC CICS HANDLE CONDITION
               NOTFND(A140-ENDBR-CUSTNAM)
               ENDFILE(A140-ENDBR-CUSTNAM)
               END-EXEC.
     MOVE 0          TO LINE-CTR.
     MOVE 'ABC'      TO CUST-NAME.
     MOVE LOW-VALUES TO CUST-NO.
     EXEC CICS STARTBR DATASET('CUSTNAM')
                    RIDFLD(CUST-ALT-KEY)
                    END-EXEC.
 A100-READ-NEXT-CUST.
     EXEC CICS READNEXT DATASET('CUSTNAM')
                    RIDFLD(CUST-ALT-KEY)
                    INTO(CUSTOMER-REC)
                    END-EXEC.
     IF CUST-NAME-13 NOT = 'ABC'
        GO TO A140-ENDBR-CUSTNAM.
     .... MOVE CUSTOMER TO MAP I/O AREA ...
     ADD 1 TO LINE-CTR.
```

```
         IF LINE-CTR < 16
            GO TO A100-READ-NEXT-CUST.
     A140-ENDBR-CUSTNAM.
            EXEC CICS ENDBR DATASET('CUSTNAM') END-EXEC.
            .... SEND MAP ....
```

In the above example, we set up the starting point at 'ABC' by issuing a STARTBR
command on the alternate index path. Then we issue a READNEXT command to
retrieve the customer record. The record you retrieve is the customer primary record not
the alternate index record. After the record has been retrieved, you can then move it to
the map I/O area. Then you should go back to get the next customer until there are no
more records on the file (ENDFILE), the map is full or no more customer with the first
three bytes of name equal to 'ABC'. From this example, we know that accessing a VSAM
file through its alternate index key is similar to accessing that through the primary key
if the alternate index key is defined as unique.

Even you can retrieve a VSAM record using its alternate index key, but most of the time,
you would use alternate index key for browse only since we do not know the primary
key of the record which is part of the alternate index key. For example, we want to display
up to 20 invoices for any given customer number on the terminal. Therefore, we use the
the customer number as the generic key to browse the invoice file through the alternate
index sequence (the alternate index key is the customer number plus invoice number).
When the customer number in the retrieved invoice record has changed, we know that
there are no more invoices for this customer. In order to make the alternate index unique,
we include the primary key (invoice number) as the last part of the alternate index key.
This makes the random retrieval through the alternate index key impossible since, most
of the time, we do not know the primary key. Thus we can only use the first part (customer
number) of the alternate index key to perform generic browse and display all records
for the that customer and then let the user choose the desired invoice if detail information
is desired.

If you define an alternate index key as nonunique, then the DUPKEY condition occurs
when the first record in the file that contains a nonunique alternate index key. To retrieve
the rest of records with the same key, you should start a browse operation if the command
you issue that caused DUPKEY is the READ command. If you are already in a browse
operation when DUPKEY condition occurs, then the READNEXT command will
retrieve the records with duplicated alternate index key in the sequence in which they
are added to the file. The DUPKEY condition will occur for each of all records with the
duplicate key except for the last record. When the last record is retrieved, you will get
a NORMAL condition. This will let you know all records with that key have been
retrieved. The following example shows we want to retrieve all customers with customer
name equal to 'ABC COMPANY'.

```
     EXEC CICS HANDLE CONDITION
             DUPKEY(A100-STARTBR-CUSTNAM)
             END-EXEC.
     MOVE 'ABC COMPANY' TO CUST-NAME.
     EXEC CICS READ DATASET('CUSTNAM')
                INTO(CUSTOMER-REC)
                RIDFLD(CUST-NAME)
                END-EXEC.
```

```
      .... NO DUPLICATE ....
A100-STARTBR-CUSTNAM.
    EXEC CICS STARTBR DATASET('CUSTNAM')
                      RIDFLD(CUST-NAME)
                      END-EXEC.
    EXEC CICS HANDLE CONDITION
              DUPKEY(A130-PROCESS-RECORD)
              END-EXEC.
A120-READ-NEXT-CUSTNAM.
    EXEC CICS READNEXT DATASET('CUSTNAM')
                       RIDFLD(CUST-NAME)
                       INTO(CUSTOMER-REC)
                       END-EXEC.
    .... LAST RECORD WITH SAME KEY ...
A125-ENDBR-CUSTNAM.
    EXEC CICS ENDBR DATASET('CUSTNAM') END-EXEC.
A130-PROCESS-RECORD.
    .... PROCESS THE RECORD WITH KEY 'ABC COMPANY' ...
    GO TO A120-READ-NEXT-CUSTNAM.
A140-ENDBR-CUSTNAM.
    EXEC CICS ENDBR DATASET('CUSTNAM') END-EXEC.
```

In the above example, we read the customer file using the customer name (non-unique alternate index key). If DUPKEY condition occurs, we know that there are more than one customer with the same customer name ('ABC COMPANY'). In this case, we should issue a STARTBR command to browse all these customers with the same name. The first READNEXT command will retrieve the same customer record (first customer with name equal to 'ABC COMPANY'). We need to issue as many READNEXT commands as it takes to get to the last customer with the same name. The DUPKEY condition will occur for each customer with the same customer name except for the last one. When the last customer is retrieved, no DUPKEY condition will occur. In this case, we know we have just retrieved the last customers with the same customer name and we should issue an ENDBR command to end this browse operation.

1.3.   VSAM File Maintenance

In this section we'll discuss the life cycle of a VSAM file. A VSAM file must be defined through the use of the DEFINE CLUSTER command. Then it can be loaded with records through the use of the REPRO command or a COBOL batch program. After the VSAM file has been defined and loaded, you can then set up its FCT entry and your system programmer can include this VSAM file in the CICS startup JCL. The CICS startup JCL will verify (VERIFY) and allocate (DD or DLBL statement) this VSAM file when CICS/VS is brought up in the morning.

After the CICS/VS region is up, the VSAM file will normally be opened and enabled. A VSAM file must be opened and enabled before CICS tasks can process it. If a VSAM file is specified with FILSTAT=OPENED in its FCT entry, it will be opened when the CICS/VS region is brought up. If a VSAM file cannot be opened and enabled that normally means something wrong with that file.

At 5 PM, your computer operator will shut down the CICS/VS region. When a CICS/VS region is shut down, all VSAM files will be closed for batch jobs. Before any batch job can process these VSAM files, your computer operator will normally back up these VSAM files to tapes, delete them, define them, and then restore them from the back up tapes. The process of back up and restore is called reorganization which is used to improve the VSAM performance. When the VSAM files have been backed up and restored, the freespace within the VSAM files will be re-distributed to gain better performance. The back up tapes will be kept for recovery purposes in case the batch update jobs fail later that night or VSAM files were damaged the next day in the CICS/VS region.

In this section, we'll cover how to rebuild a VSAM file when it is damaged in the CICS/VS region, and how to back up, restore or reorganize a VSAM file with or without alternate indexes.

1.3.1.   VSAM File Rebuild

If a VSAM file is damaged in the CICS/VS region, you need to close it to CICS/VS using CSMT or CEMT transaction and then go to the batch region to rebuild it. If this VSAM file also contains one or more alternate indexes, you not only need to close the VSAM file itself but also all its alternate index files to CICS/VS in order to rebuild the VSAM file. If a VSAM primary file is damaged, then the rebuild must also include all its alternate indexes. The alternate index file can be rebuilt completely from its primary file after the primary file has been rebuilt. The reason that we want to close its alternate indexe files when a VSAM file is damaged is to prevent the CICS tasks from accessing the primary file through its alternate indexes.

To close a VSAM primary file or alternate index file to CICS/VS, you need to use CSMT or CEMT transaction. After the File has been closed, you can then sign off from CICS/VS region and go to batch region to rebuild the files. The following example shows how to close a VSAM file to CICS/VS:

```
CSMT CLO,DAT,FILEID=CUSTMST
```

If the alternate index file has been damaged and the primary file is still in normal status, you still need to close both the primary file and alternate index file to CICS/VS in order to rebuild the alternate index file. This will prevent CICS tasks from updating the primary file. When a VSAM primary file is updated, its alternate index file may need to be updated to reflect this update.

While you are in the batch region, you need to perform the following steps in order to rebuild a VSAM primary file:

1. Use the REPRO command to back up the VSAM file to tape. If the REPRO command does not work because the VSAM file has been damaged, then you need to skip this step and use the latest backup tape to restore the VSAM file in the step 4.

2. Use the DELETE command to delete the VSAM primary file. It will also delete all its alternate index files and paths (if exist).

3. Use the DEFINE CLUSTER command to define the VSAM file. When you issue a DELETE CLUSTER command, the VSAM file is deleted. Therefore, you need to define it before you can restore it from the backup tape.

4. Use the REPRO command to restore the VSAM file from its backup tape created in step 1. If no backup tape can be created from the step 1, you should then use the latest backup tape.

   After the VSAM file has been restored, you can then go to CICS/VS region and use the CSMT or CEMT transaction to open it. After the VSAM file has been opened, it is ready to be used.

   If the VSAM file contains one or more alternate indexes, then you need to rebuild these alternate indexes as well after the VSAM primary file has been restored in the step 4 above:

5. Use the DEFINE AIX command to define alternate index file. When you issue a DELETE command to delete the VSAM primary file in the step 2 above, its alternate index files and paths will also be deleted. Therefore, you must define the alternate index file and path before you can rebuild the alternate index file.

6. Use the DEFINE PATH command to define the relationship between the alternate index file and its primary file.

7. Use the BLDINDEX command to rebuild the alternate index file completely from its primary file.

   There is no need to back up the alternate index file since it can be rebuilt completely from its primary file.

After the alternate index has been defined, and rebuilt, you can then go to CICS/VS region and use CSMT or CEMT transaction to open these alternate index files as well. When you issue a DELETE CLUSTER command in the step 1, VSAM will delete the primary file along with all its alternate indexes. Therefore, you do not need to delete the alternate index again before you define it in the step 5.

If you only want to rebuild the alternate index file itself, then after you have closed both the primary file and the alternate index file to CICS/VS, you need to issue a DELETE command to delete the alternate index entry name (NAME) specified in the DEFINE AIX command before you can perform step 5, 6 and 7. This is because no DELETE command were issued for the primary file. Therefore, the alternate index file is still existing.

1.3.2. VSAM File Back Up

After the CICS/VS region has been shut down and before any batch jobs are to be executed, you need to back up all your VSAM files to tapes for recovery purposes. You may need them when the subsequent batch update jobs fail or when the VSAM files are damaged the next day in the CICS/VS region. The loss of one or more important VSAM files without back up tapes may disable one or more CICS application systems and may cause the job of your DP director. That is why most of the CICS shops spend several hours each night to back up all or some of their VSAM files.

The REPRO command is used to back up a VSAM file to tape. The input file (INFILE) in the REPRO command is your VSAM file and the output file (OUTFILE) is the back up tape. If this VSAM file contains one or more alternate indexes, you do not need to back up these alternate index files because the alternate index files can be completely rebuilt from its primary file. We'll show you a complete JCL that can be used to back up, delete, define, restore or reorganize a VSAM file with or without alternate indexes.

1.3.3.   VSAM File Reorganization

After VSAM files have been backed up to tapes, you may want to reorganize some of your VSAM files in order to gain better performance. The frequency of the reorganization on each VSAM file depends on how often this VSAM file is updated. You can use the LISTCAT command to list the information on this VSAM file to determine if this VSAM file needs to be reorganized.

When the LISTCAT report shows too many CI or CA splits, or when there are no more spaces for that VSAM file, it is time for you to reorganize that VSAM file. Heavy-traffic VSAM files are normally reorganized every night.

In order to reorganize a VSAM file, you need to back up the VSAM file to tape using the REPRO command, delete the file using the DELETE CLUSTER command, define the VSAM file using the DEFINE CLUSTER command, and then restore the VSAM file from its backup tape using the REPRO command:

1. Use the REPRO command to back up the VSAM file to tape.

2. Use the DELETE command to delete the VSAM file.

3. Use the DEFINE CLUSTER command to define the VSAM file.

4. Use the REPRO command to restore the VSAM file from its backup tape.

After the VSAM file has been restored, the freespace within the VSAM file will be re-distributed to gain better performance.

The following example shows how to reorganize a VSAM KSDS file with one alternate index:

```
OS/VS:

//EXMPL      JOB (1500,CUST0001),'LEE',CLASS=6,
//               NOTIFY=LEE,MSGCLASS=X
//*    BACKUP VSAM KSDS FILE TO TAPE
//STEP1       EXEC PGM=IDCAMS,REGION=512K
//DD1         DD DSN=CUSTOMER.MASTER,DISP=OLD
//DD2         DD DSN=CUSTOMER.MASTER.BACKUP,
//               DISP=(NEW,PASS,DELETE),
```

```
//                UNIT=(TAPE,,DEFER),LABEL=RETPD=30,
//                DCB=(RECFM=FB,LRECL=200,BLKSIZE=2000)
//SYSPRINT   DD SYSOUT=*
//SYSIN      DD *
 REPRO INFILE(DD1) -
       OUTFILE(DD2)
//* DELETE AND DEFINE VSAM KSDS FILE
//STEP2      EXEC PGM=IDCAMS,REGION=512K,COND=(0,NE,STEP1)
//SYSPRINT   DD SYSOUT=*
//SYSIN      DD *
 DELETE CUSTOMER.MASTER CLUSTER
 DEFINE CLUSTER(NAME(CUSTOMER.MASTER) -
                VOL(VOL1) -
                RECORDSIZE(200 200) -
                SHR(2 3) -
                KEYS(5 20) -
                CYL(10 1) -
                FREESPACE(20 10) -
                IMBED -
                REPLICATE) -
        DATA(NAME(CUSTOMER.MASTER.DATA) CISZ(6144)) -
        INDEX(NAME(CUSTOMER.MASTER.INDEX) CISZ(512))
//*    RESTORE VSAM KSDS FILE FROM BACKUP TAPE
//STEP3      EXEC PGM=IDCAMS,REGION=512K,COND=(0,NE,STEP2)
//DD1        DD DSN=CUSTOMER.MASTER.BACKUP,DISP=(OLD,KEEP,KEEP),
//               UNIT=(TAPE,,DEFER)
//DD2        DD DSN=CUSTOMER.MASTER,DISP=OLD
//SYSPRINT   DD SYSOUT=*
//SYSIN      DD *
 REPRO INFILE(DD1) -
       OUTFILE(DD2)
//* DEFINE ALTERNATE INDEX FILE AND PATH
//STEP4      EXEC PGM=IDCAMS,REGION=512K,COND=(0,NE,STEP2)
//SYSPRINT   DD SYSOUT=*
//SYSIN      DD *
 DEFINE AIX(NAME(CUSTOMER.MASTER.ALT) -
            VOL(VOL1) -
            RECORDSIZE(35 35) -
            SHR(2 3) -
            KEYS(25 0) -
            CYL(2 1) -
            FREESPACE(10 10) -
            IMBED -
            REPLICATE -
            RELATE(CUSTOMER.MASTER) -
            UNIQUEKEY -
            UPGRADE) -
        DATA(NAME(CUSTOMER.MASTER.ALT.D)) -
        INDEX(NAME(CUSTOMER.MASTER.ALT.I))
 DEFINE PATH(NAME(CUSTOMER.MASTER.PATH) -
            PATHENTRY(CUSTOMER.MASTER.ALT) -
            UPDATE)
//*    REBUILD ALTERNATE INDEX FILE FROM PRIMARY VSAM KSDS
//STEP5      EXEC PGM=IDCAMS,REGION=512K,COND=(0,NE,STEP4)
//DD1        DD DSN=CUSTOMER.MASTER,DISP=OLD
//DD2        DD DSN=CUSTOMER.MASTER.ALT,DISP=OLD
//SYSPRINT   DD SYSOUT=*
//SYSIN      DD *
 BLDINDEX INFILE(DD1) -
          OUTFILE(DD2)
/*
//
```

```
DOS/VS:

// JOB    EXMPL REORGANIZE A KSDS WITH ALT INDEX
// ASSGN  SYS006,X'150'
// DLBL   DD1,'CUSTOMER.MASTER',,VSAM
// EXTENT SYS006,VOL1
// ASSGN  SYS007,SYS030
// TLBL   DD2,'CUSTOMER.MASTER.BACKUP',30
// EXEC   IDCAMS,SIZE=AUTO
 REPRO INFILE(DD1) -
       OUTFILE(DD2 ENV(BLKSZ(2000) PDEV(2400) RECFM(FB) -
                  RECSZ(200) SLBL))
/*
* DELETE AND DEFINE VSAM KSDS FILE
// EXEC IDCAMS,SIZE=AUTO
 DELETE CUSTOMER.MASTER CLUSTER
 DEFINE CLUSTER(NAME(CUSTOMER.MASTER) -
                VOL(VOL1) -
                RECORDSIZE(200 200) -
                SHR(2 3) -
                KEYS(5 20) -
                CYL(10 2) -
                FREESPACE(20 10) -
                IMBED -
                REPLICATE) -
        DATA(NAME(CUSTOMER.MASTER.DATA) CISZ(6144)) -
        INDEX(NAME(CUSTOMER.MASTER.INDEX) CISZ(512))
/*
* RESTORE VSAM KSDS PRIMARY FILE
// ASSGN  SYS006,SYS030
// TLBL   DD1,'CUSTOMER.MASTER.BACKUP',30
// ASSGN  SYS007,X'150'
// DLBL   DD2,'CUSTOMER.MASTER',,VSAM
// EXTENT SYS007,VOL1
// EXEC IDCAMS,SIZE=AUTO
 REPRO INFILE(DD1 ENV(RECFM(FB) PDEV(2400) -
                  BLKSZ(2000) RECSZ(200) SLBL)) -
        OUTFILE(DD2)
/*
* DEFINE ALTERNATE INDEX FILE AND PATH
// EXEC IDCAMS,SIZE=AUTO
 DELETE CUSTOMER.MASTER.ALT
 DEFINE AIX(NAME(CUSTOMER.MASTER.ALT) -
            VOL(VOL1) -
            RECORDSIZE(35 35) -
            SHR(2 3) -
            KEYS(25 0) -
            CYL(2 1) -
            FREESPACE(10 10) -
            IMBED -
            REPLICATE -
            RELATE(CUSTOMER.MASTER) -
            UNIQUEKEY -
            UPGRADE) -
        DATA(NAME(CUSTOMER.MASTER.ALT.D)) -
        INDEX(NAME(CUSTOMER.MASTER.ALT.I))
 DEFINE PATH(NAME(CUSTOMER.MASTER.PATH) -
        PATHENTRY(CUSTOMER.MASTER.ALT) -
        UPDATE)
/*
*   BUILD ALTERNATE INDEX FROM PRIMARY FILE
// ASSGN  SYS006,X'150'
// DLBL   DD1,'CUSTOMER.MASTER',,VSAM
// EXTENT SYS006,VOL1
```

```
// DLBL     DD2,'CUSTOMER.MASTER.ALT',,VSAM
// EXTENT   SYS006,VOL1
// EXEC     IDCAMS,SIZE=AUTO
 BLDINDEX INFILE(DD1) -
          OUTFILE(DD2)
/*
/&
```

In the above examples, if you just want to back up the VSAM file, you can just execute the REPRO command. If you just want to rebuild the alternate index file, you only need to perform the DELETE command on the alternate index entry name, and then execute the DEFINE AIX command, the DEFINE PATH command, and the BLDINDEX command as shown in the above examples.

1.3.4. CSMT And CEMT Transactions

You can use CSMT or CEMT transaction to inquire about or set VSAM files in CICS/VS. You can inquire about the VSAM file status by issuing:

```
ENTER:    CSMT INQ,SIN,DAT,FILEID=CUSTMST

RECEIVE:  FILE ID --------- STATUS --------
          CUSTMST  OPEN,READ,UPDATE,ADD,EXCL,
          BROWSE, ENABLED
          **END**

          TIME=09:29:07  DATE=09/06/86
```

To open a VSAM file:

```
ENTER:    CSMT OPE,DAT,FILEID=CUSTMST
```

To close a VSAM file:

```
ENTER:    CSMT CLO,DAT,FILEID=CUSTMST
```

You can also use CEMT to inquire about, open or close a VSAM file.

You can also use ALLO and FREE transactions to dynamically open and close a VSAM file:

To open and allocate a file dynamically:

```
ENTER:    ALLO CUSTMAT CUSTOMER.MASTER
```

To close and deallocate a VSAM file dynamically:

```
ENTER:    FREE CUSTMST
```

The ALLO transaction will dynamically allocate and open a VSAM file. The FREE transaction will dynamically close and deallocate a VSAM file to CICS/VS.

CHAPTER 2.   DL/I INTERFACE AND DL/I DATA BASES

CICS/VS supports VSAM, ISAM, BDAM and DL/I data bases. ISAM and BDAM files have been obsolete for over ten years and very few CICS shops are still using these two types of files. Today, most of companies use either VSAM files or DL/I data bases. At least 90% of CICS/VS shops use VSAM files and the rest use DL/I data bases. The File Control commands are used to process VSAM, ISAM and BDAM files and DL/I calls are used to process DL/I data bases.

2.1.   DL/I Data Base Concept And Terminology

A DL/I data base is a collection of interrelated data items organized in a hierarchic structure. Each data item within a data base represents the smallest piece of data application programs can process through the use of DL/I calls. Each data item normally consists of a sequence field (key) and many data fields. The sequence field is used to retrieve and store this data item. The data fields describe the contents of this data item. The data item at each level of the hierarchy depends upon the preceeding level of the hierarchy.

Figure 2.1 shows a sales order data base. This sales order data base consists of three data items: Sales Order Header (SOH), Sales Order Detail (SOI), and Shipment Detail (SHP). The Sales Order Header contains the sales order header information like sales order number (key), customer number, purchase order number and total order amount. Each sales order must have one sales order header. Each sales order detail represents one product the customer ordered and contains sales order detail information like detail sequence number (key), product code, order quantity, unit price, and product description. Each sales order may have one or more sales order details in this detail data item. The Shipment Detail represents the shipment made against each sales order detail and contains shipment detail information like shipment release number (key) and ship quantity. One sales order detail may be shipped one or more times before it is completely shipped. Therefore, each sales order detail may have zero to n shipment details.

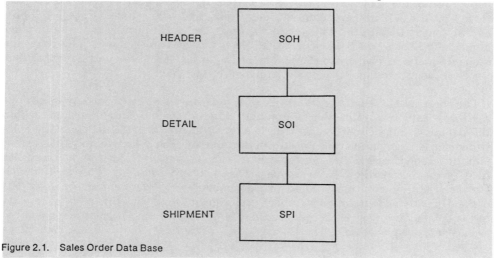

Figure 2.1.   Sales Order Data Base

37

A DL/I data base must be defined by your Data Base Administrator (DBA) through the use of IMS/VS utility called DBDGEN. The result of this DBDGEN is the DBD (Data Base Description Block) of the DL/I data base. After the DBD has been generated for a data base, you can then write COBOL batch program that issues the DL/I calls to load the data into the DL/I data base. After the DL/I data base has been defined and loaded. You can then write DL/I batch or CICS/DL/I programs to process this DL/I data base. However, before you can test and implement your DL/I batch or CICS/DL/I program, you need to generate a PSB (Program Specification Block) for this application program through the use of IMS/VS utility called PSBGEN. Within the CICS/DL/I program, you need to issue DL/I calls to process the DL/I data bases and you still use BMS commands to send the map to the terminal and receive the map to the program. So the CICS/DL/I programs still have the same structure as CICS/VSAM programs. The only difference is that you need to issue DL/I calls instead of File Control commands.

Each application program (DL/I batch or CICS/DL/I program) can request information from the DL/I data base and sees only that information defined for that application program. The rest of the information within the data base is secured from unauthorized access of this program. This is accomplished through the Program Specification Block (PSB) generated for each application program. Each application program (DL/I batch or CICS/DL/I program) must have a PSB generated for it before it can be tested and implemented. The PSB is generated through an IMS/VS utility named PSBGEN by the application programmer or DBA. Within the PSB, you specify all the data bases to be processed by this application program and all the data items (segments) within each data base to be processed. This way, your CICS/DL/I program or DL/I batch program can only process the data bases specified in the PSB and only those segments that are specified within each data base in the PSB. The use of PSBs for application programs allows certain degree of data independency of the physical structure of the data base and the sequence of the data items within the data base. So even if the structure of a DL/I data base has changed, you may not need to change the application programs that use it.

Let us compare the difference between using VSAM KSDS files and using DL/I data bases to store the above sales order information. If VSAM KSDS files are to be used, three VSAM KSDS files are required: Sales Order Header File, Sales Order Detail File, and Shipment Detail File. The key to the Sales Order Header file is the sales order number. The key to the Sales order Detail file is the sales order number plus the detail sequence number. The key to the Shipment Detail file is the sales order number plus the detail sequence number plus the shipment release number.

If DL/I data bases are to be used for this sales order information, then there is only one sales order data base to store this information. However, there are three data items within this data base: Sales Order Header, Sales Order Detail, and Shipment Detail. The Sales Order Header segment is at the top level of the hirarchy. The Sales Order Detail segment is at the second level and the Shipment Detail segment is at the third level. The sequence field for the Sales Order Header segment is the sales order number. That for the Sales Order Detail segment is the detail sequence number. The sales order number is not part of the sequence field for this Sales Order Detail segment since DL/I uses pointers to point to the details for any given header. So there is no need to use the sales order number as part of the sequence field. The sequence field for the Shipment Detail segment is the shipment release number. There is no need to include the sales order number and the detail sequence number as part of the sequence field for the Shipment Detail segment for the same reason.

2.1.1.   Data Base Organization

Hierarchical Structure

All data items within a DL/I data base are organized in hierarchical structure. The data items are called "segment types". Each segment type may have zero to n segment occurrences. For example, the Sales Order Header is a segment type and it may contain 1000, 1001, and 1005 as the segment occurrences.

The segment is the smallest piece of data an application program can process through the use of DL/I calls. When you issue a DL/I call to retrieve a piece of data within the data base, the smallest piece of data you can get is a segment. In the above sales order data base, there are three segment types: header, detail, and shipment detail segments.

A parent segment is a segment with a dependent segment beneath it in the hierarchy. A child segment is any segment depending on another segment above it in the hierarchy. In the above example, the detail segment is the parent segment of the shipment detail segment and the child segment of the header segment. Each segment type may consist of many data fields, one of which may be defined as the sequence field (key) for that segment. For example, the header segment may consist of the following data fields: order number (sequence field), customer number, purchase order number and total order amount. The order number can be defined as the sequence field to this header segment during the data base definition (DBDGEN). The sequence field is used by DL/I to store and retrieve segment occurrences within the data base.

Levels

The successive dependencies of a hierachical structure are called "levels". In Figure 2.1 there are three levels: the header is the top level, the detail is the second level and the shipment detail is the third level. A DL/I data base may have a maximum of fifteen levels. Most of the DL/I data bases are between one and four levels.

Traversal

DL/I allows the application program to access the DL/I data base sequentially or randomly. With sequential access, DL/I traverse a hierarchical structure from top to bottom, front to back, left to right. At every position, it seeks the first segment occurrence of the first child segment of this segment type. If there is no child segment for this segment type, it seeks the next segment occurrence of the current segment type. If the current segment occurrence is the last one within the current segment type, it seeks the first segment occurrence of the segment type at the same level under the same parent segment occurrence. If not exists, it seeks the level immediately above. The data base in Figure 2.2 would be traversed through in the following sequence: A1, B1, C1, D1, D2, E1, F1, G1, H1.

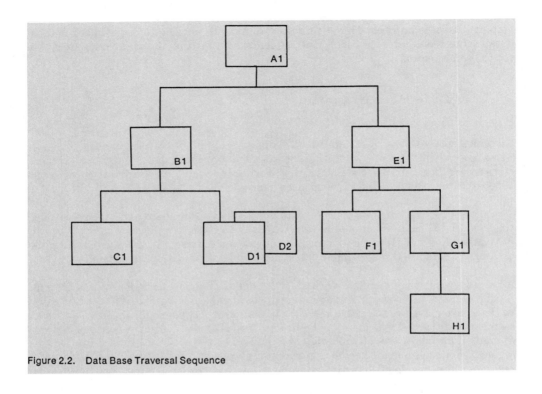

Figure 2.2. Data Base Traversal Sequence

Root Segments

The segment at the top of the hierarchy is called the root segment. In the sales order data base, the sales order header segment is the root segment. The simplest form of a DL/I data base contains only the root segment.

Twin Segments

Twin segments are multiple segment occurrences of the same segment type under a single parent. In Figure 2.2, D1 and D2 are twins. Another example, all the sales order detail segment occurrences under the sales order header 1000 are twins.

Hierarchical Path

A hierarchical path is the sequence of segment occurrences, one per level, leading directly from a segment at one level to a particular segment at a lower level. In Figure 2.2, A1-E1-G1-H1 and B1-D1 are both paths. DL/I allows the application program to retrieve or update a path in one single DL/I call. This type of DL/I calls are called path calls. For example, you can retrieve A1-B1-C1 segment occurrences in a single DL/I path call instead of using three separate DL/I calls to retrieve A1, B1 and C1 seperately. A1-B1-

C1 is also a path. Another example, you can retrieve the sales order detail segment occurrence 001 of the sales order header 1000 and the sales order header segment occurrence 1000 into the I/O area in one single DL/I call.

Data Base Record

A single root segment occurrence and all its dependents are defined as a data base record. In Figure 2.2, Both A1-E1-F1 and A1-E1-G1-H1 are data base records.

Limit On the Design Of Data Bases

The maximum number of levels a data base can have is 15. The maximum number of segment types a data base can have is 255. There is no limit on the maximum number of segment occurrences as long as the storage allows.

There are four data structures you need to know about: physical Data Base, Logical Data Base, Application Data Structure, and Logical Data Structure.

Physical Data Base

Most of DL/I data bases are physical data bases. A physical data base consists of one or more segment types in the physical storage. The Sales Order Data Base is a physical data base. You can define a physical data base through the use of IMS/VS utility named DBDGEN.

Logical Data Base

A logical data base can be defined upon existing physical data bases to meet the application requirements. For example, when a shipment is made against a sales order in our Sales Order data base, a shipment header will be created in the shipment header physical data base and a shipment detail will be created in the shipment detail segment of the sales order data base for each sales order detail shipped. If we want to display all shipment details for a given shipment release header, there is no data structure that will meet this application requirement. In this case, we can define a logical relationship between the shipment header segment in the shipment header data base and the shipment detail segment of the sales order data base. This logical data base will use the shipment header as the parent and the shipment detail as the child. The application can then access this logical data base and display all shipment details for any given shipment header.

The logical data base is also defined through the use of IMS/VS DBDGEN utility after the physical data bases upon which the logical relationship is to be defined have been defined. Figure 2.3 shows this logical data base built upon the two physical data bases. A majority of data bases are physical data bases. You only need to define logical data bases when the logical structure exists upon physical data bases to meet the application requirement.

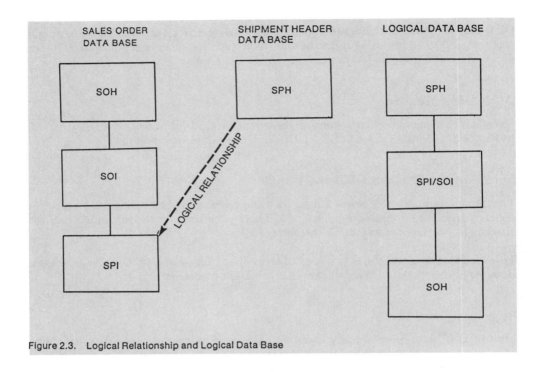

Figure 2.3. Logical Relationship and Logical Data Base

Application Data Structure

Before you can test and implement a DL/I batch or CICS/DL/I program, a Program Specification Block (PSB) must be generated through the PSBGEN utility. The result of this PSBGEN utility is the PSB control block in the PSB load library. The PSB specifies the data bases and segments within each data base to be processed by this application program. Each data base to be processed by this program must have been specified in the PSB. Only the segments that are specified in the PSB for each data base can be processed in this program. These segments are called sensitive segments since the program is only sensitive to these segments. The PSB represents the application data struture toward these data bases from the application program's viewpoint and it enhances the data independency and security.

Logical Data Structure

Each data base to be processed by the application program must be specified in the PSB of that program. For each data base specified in the PSB, you need to specify the segments you want to process. The control block specified within the PSB for each data base is called Program Communication Block (PCB). One PSB may have one or more PCBs depending on how many data bases this program is to process. Thus each PCB in the PSB represents a logical data structure toward a data base from the application program viewpoint.

42

Data Base Load

After a data base has been defined through the DBDGEN utility, it can then be loaded with data through an user-written DL/I batch program. After the data base has been defined and loaded, you need to generate the PSB for each program that is to process DL/I data bases using the PSBGEN utility. After the PSB has been generated, you still need to put the CICS/DL/I program name, CICS mapset, and dynamic table (i.e. store table if any) into PPT, put the transaction ID and its associated CICS/DL/I program name into PCT. Each DL/I data base must have one entry created in the FCT. Your system programmer still need to include the DD or DLBL statements in the CICS startup JCL for the DL/I data bases to be used in CICS/VS region. No VERIFY command needs to be issued for a DL/I data base.

Data Base Processing

After the DL/I data base has been defined, loaded, and set up and the PSBs of CICS/DL/I programs have been generated, it can then be processed in the CICS region. Instead of using the File Control commands, DL/I calls must be used to process DL/I data bases within your CICS/DL/I programs. Each DL/I call is a call subroutine that specifies the call function (i.e. GU call), PCB mask (which data base to process), segment I/O area (where to store the segment occurrence) and SSAs (sequence field value at each level).

2.1.2.   DL/I Calls

In order to process DL/I data bases in the CICS application programs, you must issue DL/I calls instead of the File Control commands. The File Control commands can only be used with VSAM, BDAM, or ISAM files. The DL/I calls has the following format:

```
CALL 'CBLTDLI' USING DL/I-call-function
                     PCB-mask
                     segment-I/O-area
                     SSAs.
```

DL/I-call-function

specifies the DL/I function you want to perform on this data base. The DL/I function can be read (GU, GN, GNP), read with update intent (GHU, GHN, GHNP), update (REPL), delete (DLET), or add (ISRT).

PCB-mask

specifies the PCB mask of the data base to be processed by this DL/I call. The PCB masks of all data bases to be processed in this CICS/DL/I program must be specified in LINKAGE SECTION. Each PCB mask specified in LINKAGE SECTION represents one PCB in the PSB. Therefore, the PCB mask you specify in the DL/I call indicates which data base in the PSB to be processed. The sequence of the PCB masks specified in LINKAGE SECTION must be exact the same as that of PCBs in the PSB. So when a PCB mask is specified in a DL/I call, DL/I knows which PCB in the PSB to use to process this call. For example, if you specify the customer data base as the second PCB in the PSB, then you should specify its PCB mask in LINKAGE SECTION as the second PCB mask. When this PCB mask is used in a DL/I call, DL/I will use the second PCB in the PSB to process the call. Therefore, you must use the PSB source code to code their corresponding PCB masks in LINKAGE SECTION.

The PCB mask has the following standard format:

```
01   PCB-MASK.
     02   PCB-DBD-NAME          PIC X(8).
     02   PCB-SEG-LEVEL         PIC X(2).
     02   PCB-STATUS            PIC X(2).
     02   PCB-PROCOPTS          PIC X(4).
     02   PCB-DLI-RSVD          PIC X(4).
     02   PCB-SEGMENT-NAME-FB   PIC X(8).
     02   PCB-FB-KEY-LENGTH     PIC S9(5) COMP.
     02   PCB-NO-SENSEGS        PIC S9(5) COMP.
     02   PCB-FB-KEY-AREA       PIC X(n).
```

The status code (PCB-STATUS) and the DBD name (PCB-DBD-NAME) are the only two fields within a PCB mask you need to be concerned with. Only the length of the last field (key feed back area) can be different from one PCB mask to another. The rest of the fields within a PCB mask have standard length. After each DL/I call has been executed, DL/I will place the execution status into the status field in the PCB mask. It is your responsibility to check the returned status in the PCB mask and in the User Interface Block (UIB). If the DL/I call is successful, spaces will be returned in the status field of its PCB mask and low-values will be returned in the UIBRCODE of the UIB. The data base name will also be returned in the DBD name field in the PCB mask. You can also get the DBD name in the EIBRSRCE field. When you code the PCB mask in LINKAGE SECTION, you can just code the following:

```
01   ORDR-PCB-MASK.
     02   FILLER            PIC X(10).
     02   ORDR-PCB-STATUS   PIC X(2).
01   CUST-PCB-MASK.
     02   FILLER            PIC X(10).
     02   CUST-PCB-STATUS   PIC X(2).
```

After each DL/I call, you must check the returned status in the PCB mask to see if the call is successful. If it is an unrecoverable error, you should terminate the CICS program using the ABEND command.

segment-I/O-area

specifies the segment I/O area where the segment occurrence is to be loaded, updated, or created. For example, you specify this area in a GU call to store the retrieved segment occurrence. The I/O area for each segment within a DL/I data base is normally set up as a copy book member. Thus the application programmer only needs to copy the desired segments into WORKING-STORAGE SECTION. After a successful retrieval, the segment I/O area will contain the retrieved segment. Before you issue an ISRT (add) or a REPL (update) call, you need to put the new segment or updated segment into its segment I/O area.

The following example shows we want to retrieve the sales order header 5000:

```
       WORKING-STORAGE SECTION.
       *   ORDER HEADER SEGMENT I/O AREA
       COPY ORDRHDR.
       *   ORDRHDR COPY BOOK
       *   01   ORDR-HDR-SEGMENT.
       *        02   ORDR-HDR-ORDR-NO     PIC 9(5).
       *        02   ORDR-HDR-PONO        PIC X(15).
       *        02   ORDR-HDR-CUSTNO      PIC X(5).
       *        02   ORDR-HDR-TOTAMT      PIC S9(7)V99 COMP-3.
       01   GU-CALL       PIC X(4) VALUE 'GU '.
       LINKAGE SECTION.
       01   DFHCOMMAREA      PIC X(100).
       01   BLLCELLS.
            02   FILLER        PIC S9(8) COMP.
            ....
       01   ORDR-PCB.
            02   FILLER            PIC X(10).
            02   ORDR-PCB-STATUS PIC X(2).
       PROCEDURE DIVISION.
            ....
            MOVE 1000 TO SOH-SSA-ORDER-NO.
            CALL 'CBLTDLI' USING GU-CALL
                            ORDR-PCB
                            ORDR-HDR-SEGMENT
                            SOH-SSA.
```

In the above example, we specify ORDRHDR as the copy book of the order header segment I/O area. Then we copy it into WORKING-STORAGE SECTION and specify ORDR-HDR-SEGMENT as the segment I/O area in the DL/I call (GU).

SSA-1 to SSA-n

These areas contain segment search arguments (SSAs) which are used by DL/I to narrow the field of search to a particular segment type or to a particular segment occurrence to be manipulated at each level of the data base. There can be a maximum of one SSA per level. If the SSA is not specified at one level, DL/I will follow the rules to calculate the default SSA.

The following example shows how to retrieve the sales order detail with sequence number 003 of the sales order header 1000. We need two SSAs: one for the sales order header segment and the other for the sales order detail segment. The first part of SSA specifies the segment type to be processed. The second part of SSA specifies the search field value(s) to be used for comparison in order to find a qualified segment occurrence at that level. The segment type specified in the SSA for the sales order header segment must

45

be 'ORDRHDR ' and that for the sales order detail must be 'ORDRDET '. The segment type names and search field names in the SSAs are specified in the DBD for this data base.

```
      *     SALES ORDER HEADER SEGMENT SSA
      01    SOH-SSA.
            02    SOH-SSA-SEGMENT-NAME    PIC X(8) VALUE 'ORDRHDR '.
            02    FILLER                  PIC X(1) VALUE '('.
            02    SOH-SSA-FIELD-NAME      PIC X(8) VALUE 'SOHKEY  '.
            02    SOH-SSA-REL-OP          PIC X(2) VALUE ' ='.
            02    SOH-SSA-ORDER-NO        PIC 9(5).
            02    FILLER                  PIC X(1) VALUE ')'.
      *     SALES ORDER DETAIL SEGMENT SSA
      01    SOI-SSA.
            02    SOI-SSA-SEGMENT-NAME    PIC X(8) VALUE 'ORDRDET '.
            02    FILLER                  PIC X(1) VALUE '('.
            02    SOI-SSA-FIELD-NAME      PIC X(8) VALUE 'SOIKEY  '.
            02    SOI-SSA-REL-OP          PIC X(2) VALUE ' ='.
            02    SOI-SSA-DETAIL-SEQ      PIC 9(3).
            02    FILLER                  PIC X(1) VALUE ')'.
      PROCEDURE DIVISION.
            MOVE 1000     TO SOH-SSA-ORDER-NO.
            MOVE 3        TO SOI-SSA-DETAIL-SEQ.
            CALL 'CBLTDLI' USING GU
                          ORDR-PCB
                          SOI-SEG
                          SOH-SSA SOI-SSA.
```

In the above example, we specify the sales order header segment name in the header SSA and the sales order detail segment name in the detail SSA. We also specify 1000 as the sales order number in the header SSA and 003 as the detail sequence number in the detail SSA. DL/I will search the header segment to find the sales order 1000 and then search the detail segment under this header 1000 to find the detail with sequence number equal to 003. Thus SSAs are used to narrow the search of fields to a particular segment type and/or to a particular segment occurrence.

The SSA may consist of from one to three elements: the segment name, command codes, and qualification statements. The segment name is required and must be specified. It identifies the segment type at each level and narrows the search of field to a particular segment type. The command codes are optional and specified only as required. The command codes specifies advanced DL/I functions (like setting up parentage for subsequent GNP calls) to be performed. One or more command codes may be specified. An asterisk (*) following the segment name in the SSA indicates the existing of command codes and a blank or left parenthesis ends the command codes. The qualification statements are optional and one or more qualification statements may be specified. The qualification statement identifies a particular segment occurrence to be manipulated.

segment name

This 8-byte field must contain the segment type to be processed. The application program must be sensitive to this segment type. Otherwise, the DL/I call will fail. That means when you generate the PSB for this application program, you should specify this segment type as the sensitive segment in the PCB of this data base. The segment name must be identical to that in the DBD. You should use DBD source codes as the source to code the SSA copy book members for this data base. The SSA for each segment in the data base is normally set up as a copy book, thus the application programmer only needs to copy the required SSA copy book members into WORKING-STORAGE SECTION. The following example shows a PSB with SOHSEG and SOISEG segments specified as the sensitive segments:

```
PCB     TYPE=DB,DBDNAME=SLSORD,PROCOPT=AP,KEYLEN=11
SENSEG  NAME=SOHSEG,PARENT=0
SENSEG  NAME=SOISEG,PARENT=SOHSEG
PCB     TYPE=DB,DBDNAME=CUSMST,PROCOPT=GO,KEYLEN=5
SENSEG  NAME=CUSSEG,PARENT=0
PSBGEN  LANG=COBOL,PSBNAME=ORDR100,CMPAT=YES
FINISH
END
```

In the above example, SOHSEG and SOISEG are defined as sensitive segments (SENSEG) in the PCB of the sales order data base (SLSORD) in the PSB of the DL/I application program ORDR100. The second PCB in this PSB is for the customer data base.

Commands Codes

One or more command codes may be specified following the segment name to request the advanced functions to be performed by DL/I. For example, F command code can be specified in the SSA to request DL/I to start the search of the field from the first segment occurrence of the specified segment name instead of from the current data base position. The command codes are optional and normally will not be specified. The following example shows three types of SSAs: the SSA without command codes and qualification statements, the SSA with only command codes, and the fully qualified SSA with command codes and qualification statements. b in the following examples represents blank.

```
SOHSEGbbb                        (unqualified SSA)

SOHSEGbb*Fb                      (unqualified SSA with command code)

SOHSEGbb*P(SOHKEYbbb=01000) (qualified SSA with command code)
```

Most of DL/I calls are specified without command codes and have at most one qualification statement.

Qualification Statements

One or more qualification statements may be specified to narrow the search of field to a particular segment occurrence. If more than one qualification statement are to be specified within a SSA, then the boolean operator * (AND) or + (OR) must be used to connect these qualification sytatements. Most of SSAs have no qualification statement or have only one qualification statement. In this case, no boolean operators are needed.

Each qualification statement consists of a search field name, a relational operator, and a comparative value. The search field name specifies a key field or data field within the specified segment type to be tested with the specified comparative value. The search field must be defined in the FIELD statement in the DBD before it can be used in the SSA. Most of the time, the search field is the key field. The relational operator specifies the test condition to be performed. The comparative value specifies the value to be used to test the condition. For example, we want to retrieve the sales order header 1000. Then the segment name in the SSA must be SOHSEG (header segment), the search field name must be SOHKEY (sales order number), the relational operator must be '=', and the comparative value must be 01000. The SSA for this header segment is as follows:

```
SOHSEG    (SOHKEY    =01000)
```

Begin Qualification Character

A left parenthesis, (, starts one or more qualification statements.

Field Name

This 8-byte field contains the key field or data field name within the segment whose contents are to be compared with the following specified comparative value. For example, the sales order number (key) and sales order status are both specified in the DBD of the sales order data base. Then you can search the header segment occurrences for either a particular order number or status. This is one of the unique features of DL/I. The following example shows a data field SOISTS (detail status) is specified along with the sequence field SOIKEY (detail sequence number) in the DBD of the sales order data base:

```
              DBD      NAME=SLSORD,ACCESS=(HDAM,OSAM),             X
                       RMNAME=(RMN020,1,600,3600)
      DSG1    DATASET  DD1=SLSORDD,DEVICE=3350,BLOCK=(3656),SCAN=3
              SEGM     NAME=SOHSEG,PARENT=0,BYTES=400,PTR=(T)
              FIELD    NAME=(SOHKEY,SEQ,U),BYTES=5,START=1
              SEGM     NAME=SOISEG,PARENT=((SOHSEG,DBLE)),         X
                       BYTES=300,PTR=(TB)
              FIELD    NAME=(SOIKEY,SEQ,U),BYTES=3,START=1
              FIELD    NAME=SOISTS,BYTES=2,START=4,TYPE=C
              DBDGEN
              FINISH
              END
```

In the above example, we specify SOHKEY as the sequence field of the header segment SOHSEG, SOIKEY as the sequence field of the detail segment SOISEG and SOISTS as the data field in the detail segment SOISEG. Thus we can search the detail segment for the sequence field SOIKEY or for the data field SOISTS.

Relational Operator

This two-byte relational operator specifies how the contents of the field name specified are to be compared with the following comparative value specified. The contents of the field name specified must be equal to (b= or EQ), greater than (b or GT), less than (b< or LT), greater than or equal to (= or GE), less than or equal to (<= or LE), or not equal to (¬= or NE) the comparative value specified. The following example shows the SSA of the sales order header segment to retrieve the sales order 1000:

```
SOHSEG   (SOHKEY    =01000)
```

The relational operator in the above example is ' =' (EQ).

Comparative Value

This field specifies the value to be used to compare with the contents of the specified field. The length of this comparative value must be equal to its length specified in the DBD. If the length of the comparative value specified is less than the length of the field specified in the DBD, numeric zeros will be used to pad the numberic value in front and spaces will be used to pad the alphameric field in the back. The following example shows how to specify the comparative values for numeric and alphameric field names:

```
SOHSEG   (SOHKEY    =01000)
SOISEG   (SOISTS    =A )
```

In the above examples, the length of SOHKEY is defined as 5 bytes long in the DBD, so we need to specify 01000 rather than 1000 as the comparative value. The length of SOISTS is defined as two bytes long and it is an aplameric field. Therefore, we specify 'A ' as its comparative value with space padded in the back.

If more than one SSA are to be specified in a DL/I call, they must be specified in the sequence of the hierarchical path. That means the SSA at the higher level must be specified in front of those at the lower levels. The SSA for each segment type is normally set up as a copy book, so the application programmer only needs to copy the required SSAs into WORKING-STORAGE SECTION. In order to be able to use the same SSA copy book to build SSA with or without command codes, a SSA copy book is normally set up as follows:

```
 01   SOH-SSA.
      02   SOH-SSA-SEGMENT-NAME      PIC X(8) VALUE 'SOHSEG  '.
      02   FILLER                    PIC X(1) VALUE '*'.
      02   SOH-SSA-COMMAND-CODES.
           03   SOH-SSA-CMD-CD-1     PIC X(1) VALUE '-'.
           03   SOH-SSA-CMD-CD-2     PIC X(1) VALUE '-'.
      02   SOH-SSA-QUALIFIER         PIC X(1) VALUE '('.
      02   SOH-SSA-FIELD-NAME        PIC X(8) VALUE 'SOHKEY  '.
      02   SOH-SSA-REL-OP            PIC X(2) VALUE ' ='.
      02   SOH-SSA-ORDER-NO          PIC 9(5).
      02   FILLER                    PIC X(1) VALUE ')'.
```

In the above SSA copy book, we specify null command code '-' in the two-byte field reserved for the command codes. Since null command codes will be ignored by DL/I, no operation will take place. Using the above SSA copy book member, we can issue DL/I calls with or without commands as follows:

```
*    QUALIFIED SSA WITHOUT COMMAND CODES
     MOVE 1000 TO SOH-SSA-ORDER-NO.
     CALL 'CBLTDLI' USING GU ORDR-PCB SOH-SEG SOH-SSA.

*    QUALIFIED SSA WITH COMMAND CODE
     MOVE 'P'   TO SOH-SSA-CMD-CD-1.
     MOVE 1000  TO SOH-SSA-ORDER-NO.
     CALL 'CBLTDLI' USING GU ORDR-PCB SOH-SEG SOH-SSA.
     MOVE '-'   TO SOH-SSA-CMD-CD-1.

*    UNQUALIFIED SSA
     MOVE ' '   TO SOH-SSA-QUALIFIER.
     CALL 'CBLTDLI' USING GN ORDR-PCB SOH-SEG SOH-SSA.
     MOVE '('   TO SOH-SSA-QUALIFIER.
```

In the above examples, we can build a SSA without command codes by specifying the correct relational operator and comparative value. In the second example above, we move the command code 'P' (set up parentage) to the first command code field. Since '*' following the segment name indicates the existence of the command codes and 'P' is a valid command code, thus the request of setting up the parentage at header 1000 will be performed by DL/I. The last example above shows how to construct an unqualified SSA by moving a blank to the left parenthsis field. A blank in this field indicates no qualification statement.

The SSA at each level should be specified in the DL/I call whenever you can to reduce the search time. By using qualified SSAs, the application program may not be effected by the change of the data base and in results higher degree of data independency can be achieved.

2.2.   DL/I Call Functions

The DL/I call function specified as the first parameter in a DL/I call tells DL/I which function is to be performed upon the data base. You can retrieve, update, delete, browse or add DL/I data base information by specifying the correct function. There are five types of data base DL/I calls:

1. Get calls (GU, GN, and GNP)
   This group of DL/I calls are used to retrieve the segment occurrence for review only from the data base randomly (GU) or sequentially (GN and GNP). No update is to be performed after the retrieval.

2. Get Hold calls (GHU, GHN, and GHNP)
   This group of DL/I calls are used to retrieve the segment occurrence from the data base randomly or sequentially with update intent. After the segment occurrence has been retrieved by one of these DL/I calls, a REPL or DLET call is to be issued to update (REPL) or delete (DLET) the retrieved segment occurrence.

3. Insert call (ISRT)
   The ISRT call is used to add a new segment occurrence into an existing data base or a new data base during the initial load.

50

4. Delete call (DLET)

The DLET call is used to delete a segment occurrence along with all its dependents from the data base. Before you can issue a DLET call, one of the get hold calls must be issued to retrieve the segment occurrence to be deleted.

5. Replace call (REPL)

The REPL call is used to update a segment occurrence which has been retrieved through the use of one of the get hold calls (GHU, GHN, and GHNP).

2.2.1.   Get Calls (GU, GN, GNP)

There are three data base DL/I calls in this group: GU (Get Unique), GN (Get Next), and GNP (Get Next Within Parent). The GU call is used to retrieve a segment occurrence randomly. Normally you issue a GU call with a fully qualified SSA at each level to retrieve a particular segment occurrence. For example, if we want to retrieve the sales order detail 001 of the sales order header 1000, we can issue a GU call with qualified SSAs at both header and detail segments.

The GN call is used to retrieve the next segment occurrence that satisfies the search critiria specified in the SSAs from the current data base position. The data base position can be established through the GU or GN call. After the data base position has been established, a subsequent GN call will start the search from the current data base position to try to find a segment occurrence that satisfies this call. We can use unqualified GN calls to traverse through the entire data base.

A GNP call will perform the same function as a GN call except that the search will be conducted only on the children for the established parent segment occurrence. For example, we want to display all the detail segment occurrences for the sales order header 1000. First, we need to issue a GU call to retrieve header 1000 in order to establish the parentage at header 1000, then we issue GNP calls to retrieve only the details for the header 1000. You should specify an unqualified SSA at the sales order detail seqment level.

GU (Get Unique)

The GU call is used to retrieve a segment occurrence for review randomly. For example, we want to retrieve the sales order detail 001 of the sales order header 1000:

```
MOVE 1000 TO SOH-SSA-ORDER-NO.
MOVE 1    TO SOI-SSA-DETAIL-SEQ.
CALL 'CBLTDLI' USING GU ORDR-PCB SOI-SEG SOH-SSA SOI-SSA.
```

In addition to retrieve a segment occurrence randomly, the GU call can also be used to set up the parentage at the retrieved segment occurrence for the subsequent GNP or GHNP calls. After the parentage has been established through the use of a GU call, you can then issue GNP or GHNP calls to retrieve the children of the established parent sequentially. The following example shows we want to retrieve all detail segment occurrences of the sales order header 1000:

```
01   SOI-SSA    PIC X(9) VALUE 'SOISEG    '.

*    SET UP PARENTAGE AT HEADER 1000
     MOVE 1000 TO SOH-SSA-ORDER-NO
     CALL 'CBLTDLI' USING GU ORDR-PCB SOH-SEG SOH-SSA.
*    RETRIEVE NEXT DETAIL OF HEADER 1000
A100-READ-NEXT-DETAIL.
     CALL  'CBLTDLI' USING GNP ORDR-PCB SOI-SEG
                                SOH-SSA  SOI-SSA.
     IF (UIBRCODE NOT = LOW-VALUES) OR
        (ORDR-PCB-STATUS NOT = SPACES AND 'GE')
        EXEC CICS ABEND ABCODE('ABCD') END-EXEC.
     IF ORDR-PCB-STATUS = 'GE'
        GO TO B100-NO-MORE-DETAILS.
     .... PROCESS RETRIEVED DETAIL ....
     GO TO A100-READ-NEXT-DETAIL.
```

GN Call (Get Next)

The GN call is used to retrieve the next segment occurrence that satisfies the search critiria from the current data base position. The GN call is normally used in the following two situations:

1. To traverse through the entire data base sequentially. You may need to do this when you try to convert an old data base to a new one. In this case, you need to traverse through the entire old data base, retrieve each segment occurrence, and then use the retrieved segment occurrence to load the new data base. This can be accomplished by repeatedly issuing the GN call without SSAs. Following each GN call, you should examine the level number, segment name, and status code in the PCB mask to determine which segment you have just retrieved in order to process it.

2. To browse the HIDAM root segment occurrences in the sequence of the root key. This can be accomplished by specifying an unqualified SSA using the root segment name in the GN call. HIDAM and HDAM data bases are the two most used DL/I access methods.

The following example shows how to traverse through the entire sales order data base:

```
A100-GET-NEXT-SEGMENT.
     CALL 'CBLTDLI' USING GN ORDR-PCB IO-AREA.
     .... CHECK SEGMENT TYPE AND END OF DATA BASE STATUS
     GO TO A100-GET-NEXT-SEGMENT.
```

Where IO-AREA must be big enough to contain even the biggest segment in the data base. After you have retrieved each segment occurrence, you can use the information returned by DL/I in the PCB mask to determine the segment type and then move the IO-AREA to the correct segment layout area before you try to process the retrieved segment.

The following example shows how to browse HIDAM root segments:

```
01   SOH-SSA      PIC X(9) VALUE 'SOHSEG   '.

A100-READ-NEXT-ROOT.
     CALL 'CBLTDLI' USING GN ORDR-PCB SOH-SEG SOH-SSA.
     .... CHECK RETURNED STATUS ....
     GO TO A100-READ-NEXT-ROOT.
```

In the above example, we specify the SSA at the SOHSEG level without the command codes and qualification statements, thus all the root segment occurrences (SOHSEG) will be qualified and retrieved sequentially.

GNP Call (Get Next Within Parent)

A GNP call is used to retrieve the next segment occurrence under the present parent that satisfies the call. This GNP call is normally used to sequentially browse the details for a given header. For example, we want to retrieve all detail segment occurrences for the sales order header 1000. Before you can issue a GNP call, the parentage must have been established. Therefore, you can issue a GU call to retrieve the header 1000 and establish the parentage at header 1000. Then we can repeatly issue GNP call to retrieve all details under header 1000:

```
01   SOH-SSA.
     02   SOH-SSA-SEG-NAME      PIC X(8) VALUE 'SOHSEG   '.
     02   FILLER                PIC X(1) VALUE '('.
     02   SOH-SSA-FIELD-NAME    PIC X(8) VALUE 'SOHKEY   '.
     02   FILLER                PIC X(2) VALUE ' ='.
     02   SOH-SSA-ORDER-NO      PIC 9(5).
     02   FILLER                PIC X(1) VALUE ')'.
01   SOI-SSA.
     02   SOI-SSA-SEG-NAME      PIC X(8) VALUE 'SOISEG   '.
     02   FILLER                PIC X(1) VALUE ' '.

*    SET UP PARENTAGE AT HEADER 1000
     MOVE 1000 TO SOH-SSA-ORDER-NO.
     CALL 'CBLTDLI' USING GU ORDR-PCB SOH-SEG SOH-SSA.
     IF (UIBRCODE NOT = LOW-VALUES) OR
        (ORDR-PCB-STATUS NOT = SPACES)
        EXEC CICS ABEND ABCODE('ABCD') END-EXEC.
     ... HEADER 1000 RETRIEVED SUCCESSFULLY ...
A100-READ-NEXT-DETAIL.
     CALL 'CBLTDLI' USING GNP ORDR-PCB SOI-SEG SOH-SSA SOI-SSA.
     IF (UIBRCODE NOT = LOW-VALUES) OR
        (ORDR-PCB-STATUS NOT = SPACES AND 'GE')
        EXEC CICS ABEND ABCODE('ABCD') END-EXEC.
     IF ORDR-PCB-STATUS = 'GE'
        GO TO A120-NO-MORE-DETAIL.
     .... PROCESS RETRIEVED DETAIL ....
     GO TO A100-READ-NEXT-DETAIL.
```

In the above example, we issue a GU call to establish the parentage at header 1000. Then we issue GNP calls to retrieve the details under header 1000. We use an unqualified SSA at the detail segment level, so all details under header 1000 will be qualified. When 'GE' status is returned, we know there are no more details under header 1000.

2.2.2.   Get Hold Calls (GHU, GHN, GHNP)

There are three DL/I calls within this group: GHU (Get Hold Unique), GHN (Get Hold Next), and GHNP (Get Hold Next Within Parent). The functions of these get hold calls are identical to that of GU, GN, and GNP respectively except that get hold calls have update intent. That means the DL/I call immediately following the get hold call will be a REPL or DLET call to update (REPL) or delete (DLET) the retrieved segment.

GHU (Get Hold Unique)

The GHU call is used to retrieve a segment randomly with the update intent. The following example shows we want to change the status of header 1000 to 'A':

```
WORKING-STORAGE SECTION.
01  SOH-SSA.
    02  FILLER          PIC X(19) VALUE
        'SOHSEG  (SOHKEY   ='.
    02  SOH-SSA-ORDER-NO PIC 9(5).
    02  FILLER          PIC X(1) VALUE ')'.

    MOVE 1000 TO SOH-SSA-ORDER-NO.
    CALL 'CBLTDLI' USING GHU ORDR-PCB SOH-SEG SOH-SSA.
    IF (UIBRCODE NOT = LOW-VALUES) OR
        (ORDR-PCB-STATUS NOT = SPACES)
        EXEC CICS ABEND ABCODE('ABCD') END-EXEC.
    MOVE 'A' TO ORDR-HDR-STATUS.
    CALL 'CBLTDLI' USING REPL ORDR-PCB SOH-SEG.
    .... CHECK STATUS ....
```

GHN (Get Hold Next)

The GHN call is used to retrieve the next segment occurrence from the current data base position that satisfies this call with the update intent. The following example shows we want to change the status of all sales order header segment occurrences to 'A'. Assume that the sales order data base is a HIDAM data base.

```
01  SOH-SSA     PIC X(9) VALUE 'SOHSEG    '.

A100-GET-NEXT-HDR.
    CALL 'CBLTDLI' USING GHN ORDR-PCB SOH-SEG SOH-SSA.
    IF (UIBRCODE NOT = LOW-VALUES) OR
        (ORDR-PCB-STATUS NOT = SPACES AND 'GE')
        EXEC CICS ABEND ABCODE('ABCD') END-EXEC.
    MOVE 'A' TO ORDR-HDR-STATUS.
    CALL 'CBLTDLI' USING REPL ORDR-PCB SOH-SEG.
    .... CHECK RETURNED STATUS ....
    GO TO A100-GET-NEXT-HDR.
```

In the above example, we use an unqualified SSA at the SOHSEG header segment. Therefore, all headers will be qualified and retrieved for update. After the header has been retrieved, we can then update the status and then issue a REPL call.

GHNP (Get Hold Next Within Parent)

A GHNP call is used to retrieve the next segment occurrence under the present parent that satisfies the call with the update intent. The parentage must be set up before you issue the GHNP call. This call is normally used to update all details for any given header. The header must have been established as the parent before the GHNP call can be issued. The following example shows we want to change the status of all detail segment occurrences for the sales order header 1000:

```
    WORKING-STORAGE SECTION.
    01  SOH-SSA.
        02  FILLER              PIC X(19) VALUE 'SOHSEG  (SOHKEY   ='.
        02  SOH-SSA-ORDER-NO PIC 9(5).
        02  FILLER              PIC X(1) VALUE ')'.
    01  SOI-SSA             PIC X(9) VALUE 'SOISEG   '.

    *   SET UP PARENTAGE AT HEADER 1000
        MOVE 1000 TO SOH-SSA-ORDER-NO.
        CALL 'CBLTDLI' USING GU ORDR-PCB SOH-SEG SOH-SSA.
        .... CHECK RETURNED STATUS ....
    A100-READ-NEXT-DETAIL.
        CALL 'CBLTDLI' USING GHNP ORDR-PCB SOI-SEG SOH-SSA SOI-SSA.
        IF (UIBRCODE NOT = LOW-VALUES) OR
           (ORDR-PCB-STATUS NOT = SPACES AND 'GE')
           EXEC CICS ABEND ABCODE('ABCD') END-EXEC.
        IF ORDR-PCB-STATUS = 'GE'
           GO TO A120-NO-MORE-DETAIL.
        MOVE 'A' TO SOI-STATUS.
        CALL 'CBLTDLI' USING REPL ORDR-PCB SOI-SEG.
        GO TO A100-READ-NEXT-DETAIL.
    A120-NO-MORE-DETAIL.
```

2.2.3 ISRT Call

An ISRT call is used to add a new segment occurrence into an existing data base or a new data base during the initial load. All segment occurrences at the higher levels from the top of the hierarchy along the hierarchical path to the segment to be added must exist before you can issue this ISRT call. For example, in order to add the sales order detail 003 under the sales order header 1000, the header 1000 must have existed or this ISRT call must be a path call which will also insert the header 1000. To issue an ISRT call, you should specify qualified SSAs at all parent levels and an unqualified SSA at the segment level to be added. The following example shows how to insert the sales order detail 003 under the sales order header 1000:

```
    01  SOH-SSA.
        02  SOH-SSA-SEG-NAME    PIC X(8) VALUE 'SOHSEG  '.
        02  FILLER              PIC X(1) VALUE '('.
        02  SOH-SSA-FIELD-NAME  PIC X(8) VALUE 'SOHKEY  '.
        02  FILLER              PIC X(2) VALUE ' ='.
        02  SOH-SSA-ORDER-NO    PIC 9(5).
        02  FILLER              PIC X(1) VALUE ')'.
    01  SOI-SSA.
        02  SOI-SSA-SEG-NAME    PIC X(8) VALUE 'SOISEG  '.
        02  FILLER              PIC X(1) VALUE ' '.
```

```
.... MOVE DATA AND KEY TO SOI-SEG ....
MOVE 1000 TO SOH-SSA-ORDER-NO.
CALL 'CBLTDLI' USING ISRT ORDR-PCB SOI-SEG SOH-SSA SOI-SSA.
IF (UIBRCODE NOT = LOW-VALUES) OR
   (ORDR-PCB-STATUS NOT = SPACES AND 'II')
   EXEC CICS ABEND ABCODE('ABCD') END-EXEC.
IF ORDR-PCB-STATUS = 'II'
   GO TO A100-DETAIL-ALREADY-EXISTS.
.... ADD SUCCESSFULLY ....
```

In the above example, we specify a fully qualified SSA for the sales order header segment (SOHSEG) and an unqualified SSA for the sales order detail segment (SOISEG). When the detail is to be added, DL/I will use the sequence field contents to determine the location of this detail within the data base.

When trying to add a new segment occurrence, you should not issue a GU call first to check to see if this segment occurrence exists. Since the ISRT call also performs the same checking as a GU call. If the sequence field of the segment occurrence to be inserted exists, an 'II' status will be returned in the PCB mask of the data base you try to process. If you want to load a HIDAM, HSAM, or HISAM data base, all root segments must be loaded in their ascending sequence of the root segment sequence field and all dependents of a root segment must be inserted immediately following the root insertion in their hierarchical sequence.

If you try to initially load a data base, then you need to specify L as the processing option in its PSB. If you try to add a new segment occurrence to an existing data base, you only need to specify A as the processing option in its PSB.

2.2.4.   DLET Call

A DLET call is used to delete the segment occurrence along with all its dependents from the data base. Before you can issue a DLET call, the segment occurrence to be deleted must have been retrieved through the use of one of the get hold calls (GHU, GHN, or GHNP). The following example shows how to delete the sales order detail 003 of the sales order header 1000:

```
01  SOH-SSA.
    02  SOH-SSA-SEG-NAME      PIC X(8)  VALUE 'SOHSEG  '.
    02  FILLER                PIC X(1)  VALUE '('.
    02  SOH-SSA-FIELD-NAME    PIC X(8)  VALUE 'SOHKEY  '.
    02  FILLER                PIC X(2)  VALUE ' ='.
    02  SOH-SSA-ORDER-NO      PIC 9(5).
    02  FILLER                PIC X(1)  VALUE ')'.
01  SOI-SSA.
    02  SOI-SSA-SEG-NAME      PIC X(8)  VALUE 'SOISEG  '.
    02  FILLER                PIC X(1)  VALUE '('.
    02  SOI-SSA-FIELD-NAME    PIC X(8)  VALUE 'SOIKEY  '.
    02  FILLER                PIC X(2)  VALUE ' ='.
    02  SOI-SSA-DETAIL-SEQ    PIC 9(3).
    02  FILLER                PIC X(1)  VALUE ')'.

*   RETRIEVE THE DETAIL 003 OF HEADER 1000
    MOVE 1000 TO SOH-SSA-ORDER-NO.
    MOVE 3    TO SOI-SSA-DETAIL-SEQ.
```

```
CALL 'CBLTDLI' USING GHU ORDR-PCB SOI-SEG SOH-SSA SOI-SSA.
IF (UIBRCODE NOT = LOW-VALUES) OR
   (ORDR-PCB-STATUS NOT = SPACES)
     EXEC CICS ABEND ABCODE('ABCD') END-EXEC.
CALL 'CBLTDLI' USING DLET ORDR-PCB SOI-SEG.
.... CHECK STATUS ....
```

In the above example, we specify fully qualified SSAs in the GHU call for both SOHSEG and SOISEG segment types in order to retrieve the detail 003 of the header 1000. After the detail 003 has been retrieved, we then issue a DLET call to delete it. After the delete call has been executed, the detail 003 along with all its dependents (shipment details for the detail 003 if any) will be deleted.

2.2.5.   REPL Call

A REPL call is used to update the segment occurrence which was previously retrieved through the use of one of the get hold calls (GHU, GHN, or GHNP). You can only change the data fields not the sequence field. The following example shows we want to change the status of the sales order detail 3 of the sales order header 1000:

```
WORKING-STORAGE SECTION.
01   SOH-SSA.
     02   FILLER           PIC X(19) VALUE 'SOHSEG   (SOHKEY   ='.
     02   SOH-SSA-ORDER-NO PIC 9(5).
     02   FILLER           PIC X(1) VALUE ')'.
01   SOI-SSA.
     02   FILLER           PIC X(19) VALUE 'SOISEG   (SOIKEY   ='.
     02   SOI-SSA-SEQNO    PIC 9(3).
     02   FILLER           PIC X(1) VALUE ')'.

*    RETRIEVE DETAIL 003 OF HEADER 1000
     MOVE 1000 TO SOH-SSA-ORDER-NO.
     MOVE 3    TO SOI-SSA-SEQNO.
     CALL 'CBLTDLI' USING GHU ORDR-PCB SOI-SEG SOH-SSA SOI-SSA.
     IF (UIBRCODE NOT = LOW-VALUES) OR
        (ORDR-PCB-STATUS NOT = SPACES)
          EXEC CICS ABEND ABCODE('ABCD') END-EXEC.
     MOVE 'A' TO SOI-SEG-STATUS.
     CALL 'CBLTDLI' USING REPL ORDR-PCB SOI-SEG.
```

In the above example, we issue a GHU call to retrieve the detail 3 of the header 1000 for update using two fully qualified SSAs. After the detail 003 has been retrieved, we move the update to the SOI-SEG segment layout and then issue a REPL call to rewrite the segment. Note that there are no SSAs specified in the REPL call since DL/I assumes that the segment occurrence to be updated is the one that was retrieved by the previous get hold call. You should issue a REPL or DLET call right after the get hold call. There should not have any other DL/I call issued using the same PCB between the get hold call and the REPL or DLET call.

2.3.   Status Codes

After the execution of each DL/I call, DL/I will load the PCB mask you specify in the DL/I call and UIB with the execution results. One of the fields in the PCB mask is the status code. After a successful completion of a DL/I call, DL/I will load this status field with blanks. If a non-blank status code is returned, that does not mean the execution of the DL/I call fails. For example, a 'GE' status code will be returned if there are no more sales order detail segment occurrence for a given sales order number in a GNP call. In this case, we know we have retrieved and processed all sales order details for the given order header. In addition to the status code in the PCB mask, you must also check the return status code in the User Interface Block (UIBRCODE). This two-byte area will contain LOW-VALUES (binary zeros) when a DL/I call is successful. If a DL/I call fails, this area contains a value other than LOW-VALUES.

It is the responsibility of the application programmer to check the returned status in both the PCB mask and the UIB after each DL/I call to make sure the call is successful before he continues to execute the next statement. The following example shows how to define the PCB masks and UIB in LINKAGE SECTION and check the returned status following a DL/I call in CICS/VS:

```
      WORKING-STORAGE SECTION.
      01   SOH-SSA.
           02   FILLER                PIC X(19) VALUE 'SOHSEG   (SOHKEY   ='.
           02   SOH-SSA-ORDER-NO PIC 9(5).
           02   FILLER                PIC X(1) VALUE ')'.
      LINKAGE SECTION.
      01   DFHCOMMAREA               PIC X(100).
      01   BLL-CELLS.
           02   FILLER                PIC S9(8) COMP.
           02   UIB-PTR               PIC S9(8) COMP.
           02   PCB-ADDR-LIST-PTR     PIC S9(8) COMP.
           02   ORDR-PCB-PTR          PIC S9(8) COMP.
           02   CUST-PCB-PTR          PIC S9(8) COMP.
      01   DLIUIB COPY DLIUIB.
      01   PCB-ADDR-LIST.
           02   ORDR-PCB-ADDR         PIC S9(8) COMP.
           02   CUST-PCB-ADDR         PIC S9(8) COMP.
      01   ORDR-PCB.
           02   FILLER                PIC X(10).
           02   ORDR-PCB-STATUS       PIC X(2).
      01   CUST-PCB.
           02   FILLER                PIC X(10).
           02   CUST-PCB-STATUS       PIC X(2).
      PROCEDURE DIVISION.
      ....
           MOVE 1000 TO SOH-SSA-ORDER-NO.
           MOVE 3    TO SOI-SSA-DETAIL-SEQ.
           CALL 'CBLTDLI' USING GU ORDR-PCB SOI-SEG SOH-SSA SOI-SSA.
           IF (UIBRCODE NOT = LOW-VALUES) OR
              (ORDR-PCB-STATUS NOT = SPACES AND 'GE')
                EXEC CICS ABEND ABCODE('ABCD') END-EXEC.
           IF ORDR-PCB-STATUS = 'GE'
                GO TO A120-DETAIL-NOTFND.
           .... DETAIL 3 RETRIEVED SUCCESSFULLY ....
```

In the above example, after the GU call has been executed, we need to check the returned status in the PCB mask and the UIB. If 'GE' status code was returned in the PCB mask, that means the detail 003 does not exist. If a blank status code was returned in the status code of the PCB mask, that means the GU call is completed successfully and the detail 003 has been retrieved. If a status code in the PCB mask is not equal to 'GE' or spaces or UIB return code is not equal to LOW-VALUES, we need to abend the CICS task.

The error information you can collect and print before the CICS task is abended is as follows:

1. DBD name returned in the PCB mask.
   You can get this from EIBRSRCE.

2. Returned status code in the PCB mask.
   It is in the status code of the PCB mask.

3. Location where the abend occurred.
   You should move the paragraph location to a data area when the paragraph changes.

4. Other useful information like DL/I call function and SSAs.

2.4. CICS/DL/I Program Structure And Coding

If DL/I data bases are to be used in the CICS/VS region, you need to issue DL/I calls instead of the File Control commands to process DL/I data bases. The DL/I data bases are defined by your DBA through the use of IMS/VS utility named DBDGEN. After the DL/I data base has been defined, you can write a COBOL/DL/I batch program to load the data base with data. Then you can write CICS/DL/I programs to process the data bases. Before you can test and implement your CICS/DL/I program, you need to generate a PSB for each CICS/DL/I program. This PSB will specify the DL/I data bases and the segments within each data base to be processed by this CICS/DL/I program. You still need to put the CICS/DL/I programs, CICS mapsets, and dynamic tables (i.e. store table) into the PPT, CICS transaction code and its associated CICS/DL/I program into the PCT, and each DL/I data base must have one entry in the FCT.

In this section, we'll show you how to code a CICS/DL/I program to process DL/I data bases. Instead of using File Control commands, you should use DL/I calls to process DL/I data bases. You will still use the SEND MAP and the RECEIVE MAP commands to communicate with the terminals for your input and output needs. The editing of input data and preparation of output data for the CICS map is still the same. The CICS control operations can still be used to control the operations of a CICS task. You still need to pass data through the communication area (DFHCOMMAREA) or Temporary Storage Queue.

2.4.1. ID DIVISION.

There is no difference between coding ID DIVISION for a COBOL batch program and coding a CICS/DL/I program. You can still need to specify PROGRAM-ID. The AUTHOR, REMARKS, DATE-WRITTEN, and DATE-COMPILED are optional. Only PROGRAM-ID is required. The following example shows an ID DIVISION for a CICS/DL/I program:

```
ID DIVISION.
PROGRAM-ID. CUST001.
REMARKS.    INQUIRE/UPDATE A CUSTOMER.
```

2.4.2. ENVIRONMENT DIVISION.

There is no need to code ENVIRONMENT DIVISION for a CICS program no matter if VSAM files or DL/I data bases are used. Since CICS File Control and DL/I Interface will handle the File I/O operations between the CICS program and the data sets, you can just specify ENVIRONMENT DIVISION without specifying any SECTIONs. Following ENVIRONMENT DIVISION, you should specify DATA DIVISION:

```
ID DIVISION.
PROGRAM-ID. CUST001.
REMARKS.    INQUIRE/UPDATE A CUSTOMER.
ENVIRONMENT DIVISION.
DATA DIVISION.
```

2.4.3. DATA DIVISION.

There are only two SECTIONs needed to be specified in the DATA DIVISION: WORKING-STORAGE SECTION and LINKAGE SECTION. There is no need to code the FILE SECTION, since DL/I will get the data base information from DBDs generated for DL/I data bases.

2.4.3.1. WORKING-STORAGE SECTION.

In WORKING-STORAGE SECTION, you should specify the following work areas to be used in the PROCEDURE DIVISION:

1. DL/I call function table.
   This table contains a list of symbolic names with values of DL/I call functions to be used in the DL/I calls in PROCEDURE DIVISION.

2. SSAs for data base segments to be processed.
   Each sensitive segment in the PCB specified in the PSB for this CICS/DL/I program normally has a corresponding SSA specified in WORKING-STORAGE SECTION. The SSA is normally defined as a copy book member, you only need to copy the desired SSAs into WORKING-STORAGE SECTION and then use them in DL/I calls. The SSAs are used in DL/I calls to narrow the search of field to a particular segment type and/or to a particular segment occurrence.

3. Segment I/O areas.
   Segment I/O areas are used in DL/I calls to receive the retrieved segment or to store the updated or new segment before it is written to the DL/I data base. The segment I/O area is normally defined as a copy book member. Therefore, you only need to copy the desired segments into WORKING-STORAGE SECTION. Each sensitive segment normally should be copied into WORKING-STORAGE SECTION.

4. Other work areas to be used in PROCEDURE DIVISION.
   Just like in a COBOL batch program, you should define any intermediate work areas to be used in PROCEDURE DIVISION in WORKING-STORAGE SECTION.

DL/I Call Function Table

Since you cannot specify DL/I call function as a literal in a DL/I call, one DL/I call function table is normally set up as a copy book member in a partitioned data set for the entire installation. This table contains a list of symbolic names with the DL/I call functions as value. Thus the application programmer only needs to copy it into WORKING-STORAGE SECTION and then use the desired symbolic names in the DL/I calls. The following example shows a DL/I function table:

```
01   DLICALLS.
     02   GU                PIC  X(4)  VALUE  'GU  '.
     02   GN                PIC  X(4)  VALUE  'GN  '.
     02   GNP               PIC  X(4)  VALUE  'GNP '.
     02   GHU               PIC  X(4)  VALUE  'GHU '.
     02   GHN               PIC  X(4)  VALUE  'GHN '.
     02   GHNP              PIC  X(4)  VALUE  'GHNP'.
     02   REPL              PIC  X(4)  VALUE  'REPL'.
     02   ISRT              PIC  X(4)  VALUE  'ISRT'.
     02   DLET              PIC  X(4)  VALUE  'DLET'.
     02   PSB-SCHEDL        PIC  X(4)  VALUE  'PCB '.
     02   PSB-TERM          PIC  X(4)  VALUE  'TERM'.

WORKING-STORAGE SECTION.
01 DLICALLS COPY DLICALLS.
LINKAGE SECTION.
PROCEDURE DIVISION.
     . . . .
     CALL 'CBLTDLI' USING GU ORDR-PCB SOH-SEG SOH-SSA.
```

In the above example, we set up a DL/I call function table which contains a list of DL/I functions. Then we copy this table into WORKING-STORAGE SECTION and use the symbolic name GU which contains DL/I call function 'GU ' (Get Unique) in the table to retrieve the sales order header segment.

SSAs

SSAs are specified in DL/I calls to narrow the search of field to a particular segment type and/or a particular segment occurrence. You should specify the SSA at each level of the hierarchical structure in the get or get hold calls whenever possible to achieve the data independence and reduce the processing time in some cases. Normally, there is a SSA copy book member set up for each segment type. Thus the application programmer only needs to copy the desired SSAs into WORKING-STORAGE SECTION and then use them in the DL/I calls. Since a SSA may consist of three elements: segment name, command codes and qualification statements, the SSA copy book has to be able to handle different combinations of the above three. The following SSA copy book for the sales order header segment can be used to build unqualified SSA, SSA with or without command codes and SSA with and without qualification statements:

```
Copy book member name: SOHSSA

    01  SOH-SSA.
        02  SOH-SSA-SEG-NAME        PIC X(8) VALUE 'SOHSEG  '.
        02  SOH-SSA-CMD-STARTS      PIC X(1) VALYE '*'.
        02  SOH-SSA-CMD-CDS.
            03  SOH-SSA-CMD-CD-1    PIC X(1) VALUE '-'.
            03  SOH-SSA-CMD-CD-2    PIC X(1) VALUE '-'.
        02  SOH-SSA-QUALIFIER       PIC X(1) VALUE '('.
        02  SOH-SSA-FIELD-NAME      PIC X(8) VALUE 'SOHSEG  '.
        02  SOH-SSA-REL-OP          PIC X(2) VALUE ' ='.
        02  SOH-SSA-ORDER-NO        PIC 9(5).
        02  FILLER                  PIC X(1) VALUE ')'.
```

Using the above SSA copy book, we can build the following SSAs for desired applications:

```
    WORKING-STORAGE SECTION.
    COPY SOHSSA.
    PROCEDURE DIVISION.
*       FULLY QUALIFIED SSA TO RETRIEVE HEADER 1000
        MOVE 1000 TO SOH-SSA-ORDER-NO.
        CALL 'CBLTDLI' USING GU ORDR-PCB SOH-SEG SOH-SSA.

*       UNQUALIFIED SSA TO BROWSE ROOTS
        MOVE ' ' TO SOH-SSA-QUALIFIER.
        CALL 'CBLTDLI' USING GN ORDR-PCB SOH-SEG SOH-SSA.
        MOVE '(' TO SOH-SSA-QUALIFIER.

*       FULLY QUALIFIED SSA WITH COMMAND CODE P
        MOVE 'P'  TO SOH-SSA-CMD-CD-1.
        MOVE 1000 TO SOH-SSA-ORDER-NO.
        CALL 'CBLTDLI' USING GU ORDR-PCB SOH-SEG SOH-SSA.
        MOVE '-'  TO SOH-SSA-CMD-CD-1.
```

Segment I/O Areas

The segment I/O area is used in a DL/I call to store the segment to be retrieved, updated or added. A copy book member is normally set up for each segment within a data base. Thus the application programmer only needs to copy those segments specified in the PSB as the sensitive segments into WORKING-STORAGE SECTION and use them in the DL/I calls in PROCEDURE DIVISION. The following example shows the segment I/O area for the sales order header segment:

```
Copy book member name: SOHSEG

    01  SOH-SEG.
        02  SOH-KEY.
            03  SOH-ORDER-NO        PIC 9(5).
        02  SOH-CUSTOMER-NO         PIC 9(5).
        02  SOH-PO-NO               PIC X(15).
        02  SOH-TOT-AMT             PIC S9(7)V99 COMP-3.
```

```
WORKING-STORAGE SECTION.
COPY SOHSEG.
LINKAGE SECTION.
PROCEDURE DIVISION.
    ....
     MOVE 1000 TO SOH-SSA-ORDER-NO.
     CALL 'CBLTDLI' USING GU ORDR-PCB SOH-SEG SOH-SSA.
```

In the above example, we copy the copy book member SOHSEG of the sales order header segment into WORKING-RAGE SECTION, then we use SOH-SEG as the segment I/O area in the GU call. After the successful completion of this GU call, the retrieved segment, header 1000, will be stored in SOH-SEG.

2.4.3.2.   LINKAGE SECTION.

In LINKAGE SECTION, you should specify the following data areas:

1. DFHCOMMAREA (communication area)
   The communication area will contain data passed from the previous program or data you saved from the last send map session. Since the pseudo conversational programming is to be used in all CICS programs, DFHCOMMAREA is needed for almost every CICS program.

2. BLL Cells
   In order to address work areas outside your CICS program, a list of pointers must be defined following DFHCOMMAREA. Each pointer in this list will be used to address one of the subsequent 01-level work area. The work areas to be addressed by these pointers include: User Interface Block (UIB), PCB mask address list, all PCB masks and other work areas (i.e. map I/O areas).

3. UIB (User Interface Block)
   The UIB will contain the address of the PCB mask address list and the UIB return code after the PSB has been scheduled. The address of PCB mask address list must be moved to the corresponding pointer to address the PCB mask address list. The PCB mask address list contains the addresses of all PCB masks. The UIBRCODE must be checked for each DL/I call to make sure the call is successful.

4. PCB Mask Address List
   The PCB mask address list contains a list of addresses of all PCB masks. After you have scheduled the PSB, the UIBPCBAL field in the User Interface Block (UIB) contains the address of this list. You should move UIBPCBAL to the pointer set up for the PCB mask address list. After the move, you can then access the addresses of all PCB masks in this list. You should then move these PCB mask addresses in the list to their corresponding pointers so you can use all PCB masks in the DL/I calls.

5. PCB masks
   The PCB masks must be specified for each PCB in the PSB. You should use the PSB source codes to code the PCB masks in LINKAGE SECTION. The sequence

of PCB masks must be identical to that of PCBs in the PSB. You only need to specify the status code field within a PCB mask. The rest of the fields are not used.

In the following sections, we'll discuss these five areas in LINKAGE SECTION in greater details.

DFHCOMMAREA

The DFHCOMMAREA (communication area) is used to pass the data saved in the previous program to the current program or to pass data between the SEND MAP session and the RECEIVE MAP session within the same CICS program. After the current program has been invoked, the data passed or saved will be in DFHCOMMAREA. Since the pseudo conversational programming technique must be used in every CICS program, DFHCOMMAREA is needed in almost every CICS program.

BLL Cells

The base locator for linkage (BLL) mechanism is used to address work areas outside the CICS program. All work areas defined in WORKING-STORAGE SECTION are static storages and allocated when the CICS program is invoked. But the work areas you define in LINKAGE SECTION are dynamic storages and are allocated during the execution of the CICS commands like the READ command with SET option or when the PSB is scheduled. You need to define a list of pointers, one for each subsequent 01-level work area, to address these work areas. The first pointer in this list is reserved for CICS. Each subsequent pointer will point to one subsequent 01- level work area. The following example shows a typical LINKAGE SECTION of a CICS/DL/I program:

```
LINKAGE SECTION.
01   DFHCOMMAREA              PIC X(100).
01   BLL-CELLS.
     02   FILLER              PIC S9(8) COMP.
     02   DLIUIB-PTR          PIC S9(8) COMP.
     02   PCB-MASK-ADDR-LIST-PTR   PIC S9(8) COMP.
     02   CUST-PCB-PTR        PIC S9(8) COMP.
     02   ORDR-PCB-PTR        PIC S9(8) COMP.
01   DLIUIB                   COPY DLIUIB.
01   PCB-MASK-ADDR-LIST.
     02   CUST-PCB-ADDR       PIC S9(8) COMP.
     02   ORDR-PCB-ADDR       PIC S9(8) COMP.
01   CUST-PCB
     02   FILLER              PIC X(10).
     02   CUST-PCB-STATUS     PIC X(2).
01   ORDR-PCB.
     02   FILLER              PIC X(10).
     02   ORDR-PCB-STATUS     PIC X(2).
```

In the above example, we set up DFHCOMMAREA for the communication area. Then we set up a list of pointers. The first pointer is reserved for CICS/VS. The second pointer points to the first 01-level work area which is the User Interface Block (UIB). The third pointer in this list (PCB-MASK-ADDR-LIST-PTR) points to the second 01-level work area (PCB-MASK-ADDR-LIST). The fourth pointer (CUST-PCB-PTR) points to the third 01-level work area (CUST-PCB) and so on. Each pointer in the list must be defined as a full-word binary (PIC S9(8) COMP).

DLIUIB (User Interface Block)

The User Interface Block (UIB) is an interface area used by CICS-DL/I routine to load the results of the DL/I calls. You should copy it (DLIUIB) into LINKAGE SECTION for every CICS/DL/I program. There are only two fields in the UIB: UIBPCBAL and UIBRCODE. Before you can issue any DL/I call, you should schedule the PSB. After the PSB has been scheduled, UIBPCBAL contains the address of the PCB mask address list. By moving UIBPCBAL to PCB-MASK-ADDR-LIST-PTR in the above example, you can access PCB-MASK-ADDR-LIST. The PCB-MASK-ADDR-LIST contains the addresses or all subsequent PCB masks (CUST-PCB and ORDR-PCB). After the PCB-MASK-ADDR-LIST can be accessed, you can then move the addresses of the PCB masks within this list to their corresponding pointers in the BLL cells. After that, you can use PCB masks in the DL/I calls. Therefore, before you can issue any DL/I calls within your CICS/DL/I program, you need to schedule the PSB. After the PSB has been scheduled, you can access the UIB, PCB mask address list, and all PCB masks. You only need to schedule the PSB once for the CICS task. When you issue a RETURN command with TRANSID option, the PSB is released. When the program is invoked the next time, you need to schedule the PSB again.

The second field in the UIB is UIBRCODE which is a 2-byte field. It contains the DL/I return code after the execution of the DL/I call. You should check this field and the status code in the PCB mask for every DL/I call issued to ensure that the call is successful. CICS-DL/I routine will return LOW-VALUES (binary zeros) to this field following a successful execution of a DL/I call. If this UIBRCODE contains any value other than LOW-VALUES, you should issue an ABEND command to abend the CICS task.

You can copy a copy book member named DLIUIB in order to copy this UIB into LINKAGE SECTION.

PCB Mask Address List

This list contains addresses of all subsequent PCB masks. After the PSB has been scheduled, the address of this list will be stored in UIBPCBAL. So you can just move UIBPCBAL to the pointer of this list set up in the BLL pointer list to establish the addressibility of this list. After this list can be accessed, it contains addresses of all subsequent PCB masks. You can then move these addresses to their corresponding pointers in the BLL pointer list in order to address the PCB masks. After the PCB masks can be accessed, you can use them in the DL/I calls. The following example shows how to address the PCB masks using the LINKAGE SECTION we specified in the above example:

```
WORKING-STORAGE SECTION.
01  PSB-SCHEDULE     PIC X(4) VALUE 'PCB '.
01  PSB-NAME         PIC X(8) VALUE 'CUST001 '.
```

```
LINKAGE SECTION.
PROCEDURE DIVISION.
    CALL 'CBLTDLI' USING PSB-SCHEDULE PSB-NAME DLIUIB-PTR.
    IF UIBRCODE NOT = LOW-VALUES
        EXEC CICS ABEND ABCODE('ABCD') END-EXEC.
    MOVE UIBPCBAL        TO PCB-MASK-ADDR-LIST-PTR.
    MOVE CUST-PCB-ADDR   TO CUST-PCB-PTR.
    MOVE ORDR-PCB-ADDR   TO ORDR-PCB-PTR.
    ... YOU CAN ISSUE ANY DL/I CALL NOW ...
```

In the above example, after we have scheduled the PSB, we check to see if the schedule call is successful. If not, we will abend the transaction. If the PSB is scheduled successfully, we can then move the the address of the PCB mask address list in UIBPCBAL to its pointer in the BLL pointer list (PCB-MASK-ADDR-LIST-PTR). After we have addressed the PCB mask address list, it will contain the addresses of all subsequent PCB masks. We can then move the addresses of the PCB masks in this list to their corresponding pointers to address PCB masks. After the PCB masks have been addressed, you can use them in any DL/I call.

In order to schedule the PSB, you need to specify 'PCB ' as the DL/I call function, the PSB name as the second parameter in the schedule call and the pointer of the UIB as the third and last paramter. The PSB name is specified when you generate the PSB using the IMS/VS utility PSBGEN. The PSB name is a 8-byte alphameric field. After the PSB schedule call is executed, you can access the UIB since CICS-DL/I routine will put the address of the UIB into the pointer we specify in this call.

Before you can issue any DL/I call for a CICS task, you need to schedule the PSB and address the work areas defined in the LINKAGE SECTION. This procedure is very standard in every CICS/DL/I program so you only need to set up your LINKAGE SECTION the way we did in the above example and then schedule the PSB and address these work areas. When you issue a RETURN command with TRANSID option, the CICS task is terminated and the PSB is released. Therefore, when this CICS program is invoked the next time, you need to schedule the PSB and address these areas again.

If the initial map output session does not require any DL/I call, then you do not need to schedule the PSB and address these areas. For example, you try to send a blank order entry map to the terminal for the user to enter a new order and then you issue a RETURN command with TRANSID option. In this case, there is no DL/I call needed to be issued. Therefore, you do not need to schedule the PSB and address these areas defined in LINKAGE SECTION.

PCB Masks

The PCB masks are used in DL/I calls to identify the data base to be processed by this call. You should use the PSB as the source to code PCB masks in LINKAGE SECTION. Each PCB in the PSB must have a corresponding PCB mask in LINKAGE SECTION. The sequence of PCB masks in LINKAGE SECTION must be identical to that of their corresponding PCBs in the PSB. This way when you specify a PCB mask in a DL/I call, CICS-DL/I routine will use the sequence of this PCB mask in LINKAGE SECTION to get the corresponding PCB in the PSB. After the execution of a DL/I call, DL/I will return the status code into the PCB mask specified in the DL/I call. You should examine the returned status code in the PCB mask and in UIBRCODE following each DL/I call to see if the call is successful. If a DL/I call is successful, blanks will be returned in the status code field in the PCB mask. If a non-blank status code is returned, you should then determine if you need to terminate this CICS task.

We have memtioned how to established the addressibility of PCB masks in the preceeding section.

The following example shows the complete listing of this sample customer update program up to LINKAGE SECTION.

```
ID DIVISION.
PROGRAM-ID. CUST001.
REMARKS.       INQUIRE/UPDATE A CUSTOMER.
ENVIRONMENT DIVISION.
DATA DIVISION.
WORKING-STORAGE SECTION.
01  COMM-AREA.
    02  CA-CUSTNO             PIC 9(5).
    02  CA-CUSTNAME           PIC X(20).
    02  CA-CRTLMT             PIC 9(9).
    02  EDIT-TAB.
        03  EDIT              OCCURS 2 PIC X(1).
01  XCTL-MENU-AREA           PIC X(30).
01  AXCU01I                  COPY XXCU01.
01  CUST-SEG.
    02  CUST-KEY.
        03  CUST-CUSTNO       PIC 9(5).
    02  CUST-NAME            PIC X(20).
    02  CUST-CREDIT-LMT      PIC S9(7) COMP-3.
01  CUST-SSA.
    02  CUST-SSA-SEG-NAME    PIC X(8) VALUE 'CUSTSEG '.
    02  FILLER              PIC X(1) VALUE '('.
    02  CUST-SSA-FIELD-NAME  PIC X(8) VALUE 'CUSTKEY '.
    02  FILLER              PIC X(2) VALUE ' ='.
    02  CUST-SSA-CUST-NO    PIC 9(5).
    02  FILLER              PIC X(1) VALUE ')'.
01  DLICALLS.
    02  GU                  PIC X(4) VALUE 'GU  '.
    02  GN                  PIC X(4) VALUE 'GN  '.
    02  GNP                 PIC X(4) VALUE 'GNP '.
    02  GHU                 PIC X(4) VALUE 'GHU '.
    02  GHN                 PIC X(4) VALUE 'GHN '.
    02  GHNP                PIC X(4) VALUE 'GHNP'.
    02  ISRT                PIC X(4) VALUE 'ISRT'.
    02  REPL                PIC X(4) VALUE 'REPL'.
    02  DLET                PIC X(4) VALUE 'DLET'.
    02  PSB-SCHEDULE        PIC X(4) VALUE 'PCB '.
    02  PSB-TERM            PIC X(4) VALUE 'TERM'.
01  PSB-NAME                PIC X(8) VALUE 'CUST001 '.
LINKAGE SECTION.
01  DFHCOMMAREA             PIC X(100).
01  BLLCELLS.
    02  FILLER              PIC S9(8) COMP.
```

```cobol
        02   DLIUIB-PTR              PIC S9(8) COMP.
        02   PCB-MASK-ADDR-LIST-PTR  PIC S9(8) COMP.
        02   CUST-PCB-PTR            PIC S9(8) COMP.
        02   ORDR-PCB-PTR            PIC S9(8) COMP.
    COPY DLIUIB.
    01  PCB-MASK-ADDR-LIST.
        02   CUST-PCB-ADDR           PIC S9(8) COMP.
        02   ORDR-PCB-ADDR           PIC S9(8) COMP.
    01  CUST-PCB.
        02   FILLER                  PIC X(10).
        02   CUST-PCB-STATUS         PIC X(2).
    01  ORDR-PCB.
        02   FILLER                  PIC X(10).
        02   ORDR-PCB-STATUS         PIC X(2).
    PROCEDURE DIVISION.
    *    SCHEDULE PSB AND ADDRESS UIB & PCB MASKS
         CALL 'CBLTDLI' USING PSB-SCHEDULE PSB-NAME DLIUIB-PTR.
         MOVE UIBPCBAL          TO PCB-MASK-ADDR-LIST-PTR.
         MOVE CUST-PCB-ADDR     TO CUST-PCB-PTR.
         MOVE ORDR-PCB-ADDR     TO ORDR-PCB-PTR.
         EXEC CICS HANDLE CONDITION
                 MAPFAIL(A900-MAPFAIL)
                 ERROR(A910-ERROR)
                 END-EXEC.
         EXEC CICS HANDLE AID
                 CLEAR(A899-XCTL-MENU)
                 ANYKEY(A900-MAPFAIL)
                 END-EXEC.
         MOVE DFHCOMMAREA      TO COMM-AREA.
         IF EIBTRNID = 'CU01' AND EIBCALEN = 100
            GO TO A200-RECEIVE-MAP.
    *    CONTROL IS JUST TRANSFERRED FROM MENU PROGRAM
    *    READ CUSTOMER FOR DISPLAY
         MOVE 1000             TO CUST-SSA-CUST-NO.
         CALL 'CBLTDLI' USING GU CUST-PCB CUST-SEG CUST-SSA.
         IF UIBRCODE = LOW-VALUES AND CUST-PCB-STATUS = SPACES
            NEXT SENTENCE
         ELSE
            EXEC CICS ABEND ABCODE('ABCD') END-EXEC.
         .... HEADER 1000 RETRIEVED SUCCESSFULLY ...
         .... MOVE HEADER 1000 TO MAP I/O AREA
         EXEC CICS SEND MAP('AXCU01')
                 MAPSET('XXCU01')
                 ERASE
                 CURSOR
                 END-EXEC.
         EXEC CICS RETURN TRANSID('CU01')
                 COMMAREA(COMM-AREA)
                 LENGTH(100)
                 END-EXEC.
    A200-RECEIVE-MAP.
         EXEC CICS RECEIVE MAP('AXCU01')
                 MAPSET('XXCU01')
                 END-EXEC.
```

2.4.4.   PROCEDURE DIVISION.

In PROCEDURE DIVISION, you issue DL/I calls to process DL/I data bases. But before you can process any DL/I data base, you must schedule the PSB. After the PSB has been scheduled, you can then use the returned address in UIBPCBAL to address PCB masks. You only need to schedule the PSB when you need to process DL/I data bases. If a CICS task does not process DL/I data bases, you do not need to schedule the PSB. For example, an order entry CICS program is first invoked by the menu program to display the order entry screen for the user to enter a new order, then return the control to CICS. In this case, there is no DL/I call needs to be issued at this time, thus there is no need to schedule the PSB. But after the user has entered the new order information and hits the ENTER key, you need to verify the input data with DL/I data base or to add the new order to the data base, then you need to schedule the PSB before you can issue the DL/I calls.

After the PSB has been scheduled and PCB masks have been addressed, you can then issue DL/I calls to process DL/I data bases. After the execution of each DL/I call has been completed, you need to check the UIBRCODE in the User Interface Block (UIB) and the status code in the PCB mask to ensure the call is successful. The following example shows after the input data has been received and edited, we want to update the customer in the customer data base:

```
PROCEDURE DIVISION.
    EXEC CICS HANDLE CONDITION
              MAPFAIL(A900-MAPFAIL)
              ERROR(A910-ERROR)
              END-EXEC.
    EXEC CICS HANDLE AID
              CLEAR(A899-XCTL-TO-MENU)
              ANYKEY(A900-MAPFAIL)
              END-EXEC.
    MOVE DFHCOMMAREA TO COMM-AREA.
*   SCHEDULE PSB THEN RETRIEVE CUSTOMER FOR DISPLAY
    CALL 'CBLTDLI' USING PSB-SCHEDLUE PSB-NAME DLIUIB-PTR.
*   PSB HAS BEEN SCHEDULED, NOW ADDRESS PCB MASKS
    MOVE UIBPCBAL        TO PCB-MASK-ADDR-LIST-PTR.
    MOVE CUST-PCB-ADDR   TO CUST-PCB-PTR.
    MOVE ORDR-PCB-ADDR   TO ORDR-PCB-PTR.
    IF EIBTRNID = 'CU01' AND EIBCALEN = 100
        GO TO A200-RECEIVE-MAP.
*   USE CUSTOMER# PASSED FROM MENU TO RETRIEVE CUSTOMER FOR
*   DISPLAY
    MOVE CA-CUSTNO       TO CUST-SSA-CUST-NO.
    CALL 'CBLTDLI' USING GU CUST-PCB CUST-SEG CUST-SSA.
*   CHECK TO SEE IF GU CALL FAILS
    IF UIBRCODE = LOW-VALUE AND CUST-PCB-STATUS = SPACES
        NEXT SENTENCE
    ELSE
        EXEC CICS ABEND ABCODE('CU01') END-EXEC.
*   CUSTOMER HAS BEEN RETRIEVED, MOVE IT TO MAP I/O AREA
    .... MOVE CUSTOMER INFORMATION TO MAP ....
*   SEND MAP TO THE TERMINAL
    EXEC CICS SEND MAP('AXCU01') MAPSET('XXCU01')
              ERASE CURSOR END-EXEC.
```

```
*      POST TRANSID ON THIS TERMINAL FOR NEXT SESSION
       EXEC CICS RETURN TRANSID('CU01')
                        COMMAREA(COMM-AREA)
                        LENGTH(100)
                        END-EXEC.
*      IF SECOND TIME AROUND, RECEIVE THE UPDATES FROM MAP
A200-RECEIVE-MAP.
       EXEC CICS RECEIVE MAP('AXCU01') MAPSET('XXCU01')
                        END-EXEC.
*      EDIT UPDATES IN MAP I/O AREA
*      CHECK IF ALL UPDATES ARE OK. IF SO, UPDATE CUSTOMER
       IF ALL-INPUT-OK
           GO TO A160-UPDATE-CUSTOMER.
*      INPUT DATA INVALID, SEND BACK FOR CORRECTION
       MOVE 'INPUT INVALID, CORRECT INTENSED' TO MSGO.
A250-SEND-MAP-DATAONLY.
       EXEC CICS SEND MAP('AXCU01') MAPSET('XXCU01')
                        CURSOR DATAONLY END-EXEC.
       EXEC CICS RETURN TRANSID('CU01')
                        COMMAREA(COMM-AREA)
                        LENGTH(100)
                        END-EXEC.
*      ALL UPDATES ARE OK, NOW GHU CUSTOMER THEN REPL CUSTOMER
A160-UPDATE-CUSTOMER.
       MOVE CA-CUSTNO        TO CUST-SSA-CUST-NO.
       CALL 'CBLTDLI' USING GHU CUST-PCB CUST-SEG CUST-SSA.
*      CHECK STATUS TO SEE IF GHU CALL IS SUCCESSFUL
       IF UIBRCODE = LOW-VALUE AND CUST-PCB-STATUS = SPACES
           NEXT SENTENCE
       ELSE
           EXEC CICS ABEND ABCODE('CU01') END-EXEC.
*      THE CUSTOMER HAS BEEN RETRIEVED FOR UPDATE
       IF EDIT(1) = 'G'
           MOVE CA-CUSTNAME TO CUST-NAME.
       IF EDIT(2) = 'G'
           MOVE CA-CRTLMT    TO CUST-CREDIT-LMT.
*      NOW REWRITE THE CUSTOMER
       CALL 'CBLTDLI' USING REPL CUST-PCB CUST-SEG.
*      CHECK TO SEE IF REPL CALL OK
       IF UIBRCODE = LOW-VALUE AND CUST-PCB-STATUS = SPACES
           NEXT SENTENCE
       ELSE
           EXEC CICS ABEND ABCODE('CU01') END-EXEC.
*      REPL IS SUCCESSFUL, NOW SEND MAP WITH SUCCESSFUL MSG
       MOVE 'UPDATE COMPLETE SUCCESSFULLY' TO MSGO.
       MOVE -1 TO CUSTNAML.
       GO TO A250-SEND-MAP-DATAONLY.
A899-XCTL-TO-MENU.
       MOVE SPACES TO XCTL-MENU-AREA.
       EXEC CICS XCTL PROGRAM('XCU00')
                        COMMAREA(XCTL-MENU-AREA)
                        LENGTH(30)
                        END-EXEC.
A900-MAPFAIL.
       MOVE -1 TO CUSTNAML.
       GO TO A250-SEND-MAP-DATAONLY.
A910-ERROR.
       EXEC CICS ABEND ABCODE('CU01') END-EXEC.
```

From the above example, we know that there is no difference in coding a CICS program using VSAM files or coding a CICS program using DL/I data bases except for the following:

1. Before you can issue DL/I calls, you need to schedule the PSB. The PSB needs to be scheduled only once for each CICS task. When the CICS task is terminated, the PSB is released. When this program is invoked again, you need to schedule the PSB again if DL/I calls are to be issued.

2. After the execution of each DL/I call, you need to check two status codes: one in UIBRCODE and the other in the status code of the PCB mask specified in this call.

3. You need to issue DL/I calls rather than File Control commands.

4. DL/I data bases are defined through the use of IMS/VS utility named DBDGEN. VSAM files are defined through the DEFINE CLUSTER command of Access Method Services (AMS).

5. One PSB must be generated for each DL/I batch or online CICS/DL/I program through the use of IMS/VS utility PSBGEN. You can only test and implement a DL/I program after its PSB has been generated.

6. You need to set up one entry in the FCT for each DL/I data base to be used in CICS/VS. The DL/I data base includes physical data base, logical data base and secondary index data base.

2.5. Sample CICS/DL/I Program

The following is a complete listing of this customer update CICS/DL/I program. It will be invoked by the menu program after the function number 2 and a valid customer number are entered on the menu screen. After it is invoked, it will use the customer number passed in DFHCOMMAREA to read (GU) the customer from the customer data base and display the customer on the terminal for update. After the SEND MAP command is issued to display the customer, it will issue a RETURN command with TRANSID to terminate the program. When the user enters the updates on the terminal and then hits the ENTER key, this inquiry/update program will be invoked. It will then issue a RECEIVE MAP command to receive the updates. After all updates are valid, it will issue a GHU call to retrieve the customer for update, move the updates to the customer segment I/O area and then issue a REPL call to rewrite the customer.

Source Program Listing:

```
ID DIVISION.
PROGRAM-ID. XCU01.
REMARKS. INQUIRE/UPDATE A CUSTOMER.
ENVIRONMENT DIVISION.
DATA DIVISION.
WORKING-STORAGE SECTION.
01  COMM-AREA.
    02  CA-CUSTNO    PIC 9(5).
```

```
          02  CA-CUSTNAM    PIC X(20).
          02  CA-CRDLMT     PIC 9(7).
          02  EDIT-TAB.
              03  EDIT OCCURS 2 PIC X(1).
          02  FILLER        PIC X(64).
      01  XCTL-MENU-AREA    PIC X(30).
      01  AXCU01I           COPY XXCU01.
      01  CUST-SEG.
          02  CUST-KEY.
              03  CUST-CUSTNO  PIC 9(5).
          02  CUST-NAME       PIC X(20).
          02  CUST-CREDIT-LMT  PIC S9(7) COMP-3.
      01  CUST-SSA.
          02  CUST-SSA-SEG-NAME    PIC X(8) VALUE 'CUSTSEG '.
          02  FILLER              PIC X(1) VALUE '*'.
          02  CUST-SSA-CMD-CD1    PIC X(1) VALUE '-'.
          02  CUST-SSA-CMD-CD2    PIC X(1) VALUE '-'.
          02  CUST-SSA-QUALIFIER  PIC X(1) VALUE '('.
          02  CUST-SSA-FIELD-NAME PIC X(8) VALUE 'CUSTKEY '.
          02  CUST-SSA-REL-OPR    PIC X(2) VALUE ' ='.
          02  CUST-SSA-CUST-NO    PIC 9(5).
          02  FILLER              PIC X(1) VALUE ')'.
      01  DLICALLS.
          02  GU                  PIC X(4) VALUE 'GU  '.
          02  GN                  PIC X(4) VALUE 'GN  '.
          02  GNP                 PIC X(4) VALUE 'GNP '.
          02  GHU                 PIC X(4) VALUE 'GHU '.
          02  GHN                 PIC X(4) VALUE 'GHN '.
          02  GHNP                PIC X(4) VALUE 'GHNP'.
          02  ISRT                PIC X(4) VALUE 'ISRT'.
          02  REPL                PIC X(4) VALUE 'REPL'.
          02  DLET                PIC X(4) VALUE 'DLET'.
          02  PSB-SCHEDULE        PIC X(4) VALUE 'PCB '.
          02  PSB-TERM            PIC X(4) VALUE 'TERM'.
      01  PSB-NAME                PIC X(8) VALUE 'XCU01   '.
      01  WS-CRDLMT               PIC 9(7).
      01  DFHAID                  COPY DFHAID.
      LINKAGE SECTION.
      01  DFHCOMMAREA             PIC X(100).
      01  BLL-CELLS.
          02  FILLER              PIC S9(8) COMP.
          02  DLIUIB-PTR          PIC S9(8) COMP.
          02  PCB-MASK-ADDR-LIST-PTR PIC S9(8) COMP.
          02  CUST-PCB-PTR        PIC S9(8) COMP.
          02  ORDR-PCB-PTR        PIC S9(8) COMP.
      01  DLIUIB COPY DLIUIB.
      01  PCB-MASK-ADDR-LIST.
          02  CUST-PCB-ADDR       PIC S9(8) COMP.
          02  ORDR-PCB-ADDR       PIC S9(8) COMP.
      01  CUST-PCB.
          02  FILLER              PIC X(10).
          02  CUST-PCB-STATUS     PIC X(2).
      01  ORDR-PCB.
          02  FILLER              PIC X(10).
          02  ORDR-PCB-STATUS     PIC X(2).
      PROCEDURE DIVISION.
      *   SCHEDULE PSB AND ADDRESS UIB & PCB MASKS
```

```
              CALL 'CBLTDLI' USING PSB-SCHEDULE PSB-NAME DLIUIB-PTR.
              MOVE UIBPCBAL        TO PCB-MASK-ADDR-LIST-PTR.
              MOVE CUST-PCB-ADDR TO CUST-PCB-PTR.
              MOVE ORDR-PCB-ADDR TO ORDR-PCB-PTR.
              EXEC CICS HANDLE CONDITION
                      MAPFAIL(A900-MAPFAIL)
                      ERROR(A910-ERROR)
                      END-EXEC.
              EXEC CICS HANDLE AID
                      CLEAR(A899-XCTL-MENU)
                      ANYKEY(A900-MAPFAIL)
                      END-EXEC.
              MOVE DFHCOMMAREA TO COMM-AREA.
              IF EIBTRNID = 'CU01' AND EIBCALEN = 100
                 GO TO A200-RECEIVE-MAP.
              MOVE CA-CUSTNO TO CUST-SSA-CUST-NO.
              CALL 'CBLTDLI' USING GU CUST-PCB CUST-SEG CUST-SSA.
              IF (UIBRCODE NOT = LOW-VALUES) OR
                 (CUST-PCB-STATUS NOT = SPACES)
                 EXEC CICS ABEND ABCODE('CU01') END-EXEC.
              MOVE LOW-VALUES          TO AXCU010.
              MOVE CUST-CUSTNO          TO CUSTNOO.
              MOVE CUST-NAME            TO CUSTNAMO.
              MOVE CUST-CREDIT-LMT      TO WS-CRTLMT.
              MOVE WS-CRTLMT            TO CRDLMTO.
              MOVE -1                   TO CUSTNAML.
              MOVE SPACES               TO EDIT-TAB.
              MOVE 'UPDATE NAME AND CREDIT LIMIT' TO MSGO.
              EXEC CICS SEND MAP('AXCU01') MAPSET('XXCU01')
                      ERASE CURSOR END-EXEC.
              EXEC CICS RETURN TRANSID('CU01') COMMAREA(COMM-AREA)
                      LENGTH(100) END-EXEC.
          A200-RECEIVE-MAP.
              EXEC CICS RECEIVE MAP('AXCU01') MAPSET('XXCU01')
                      END-EXEC.
      *     EDIT NAME AND CREDIT LIMIT
              IF CUSTNAML > 0
                 MOVE CUSTNAMI TO CA-CUSTNAM
                 MOVE 'G'        TO EDIT(1)
                 MOVE ' '        TO CUSTNAMA.
              IF CRDLMTL > 0
                 IF CRDLMTI NUMERIC
                    MOVE CRDLMTI     TO WS-CRDLMT
                    MOVE WS-CRDLMT TO CA-CRDLMT
                    MOVE 'G'         TO EDIT(2)
                    MOVE '&'         TO CRDLMTA
                 ELSE
                    MOVE 'R'         TO CRDLMTA
                    MOVE 'B'         TO EDIT(2)
                    MOVE -1          TO CRDLMTL
                    MOVE 'INVALID CREDIT LIMIT' TO MSGO.
      *     CHECK ANY BAD INPUT FIELD ('B')
              IF EDIT(1) NOT = 'B' AND EDIT(2) NOT = 'B'
                 GO TO A300-UPDATE-CUSTOMER.
          A250-SEND-MAP-DATAONLY.
              EXEC CICS SEND MAP('AXCU01') MAPSET('XXCU01')
                      DATAONLY CURSOR END-EXEC.
```

```
              EXEC CICS RETURN TRANSID('CU01') COMMAREA(COMM-AREA)
                    LENGTH(100) END-EXEC.
       A300-UPDATE-CUSTOMER.
           MOVE CA-CUSTNO  TO CUST-SSA-CUST-NO.
           CALL 'CBLTDLI' USING GHU CUST-PCB CUST-SEG CUST-SSA.
           IF (UIBRCODE NOT = LOW-VALUES) OR
              (CUST-PCB-STATUS NOT = SPACES)
               EXEC CICS ABEND ABCODE('CU01') END-EXEC.
           IF EDIT(1) = 'G'
               MOVE CA-CUSTNAM  TO CUST-NAME.
           IF EDIT(2) = 'G'
               MOVE CA-CRDLMT   TO CUST-CREDIT-LMT.
           CALL 'CBLTDLI' USING REPL CUST-PCB CUST-SEG.
           IF (UIBRCODE NOT = LOW-VALUES) OR
              (CUST-PCB-STATUS NOT = SPACES)
               EXEC CICS ABEND ABCODE('CU01') END-EXEC.
           MOVE 'UPDATE COMPLETED SUCCESSFULLY' TO MSGO.
           MOVE -1 TO CUSTNAML.
           GO TO A250-SEND-MAP-DATAONLY.
       A899-XCTL-MENU.
           MOVE SPACES TO XCTL-MENU-AREA.
           EXEC CICS XCTL PROGRAM('XCU00')
                          COMMAREA(XCTL-MENU-AREA)
                          LENGTH(30)
                          END-EXEC.
       A900-MAPFAIL.
           IF EIBAID = DFHENTER
               MOVE 'NO DATA WAS ENTERED' TO MSGO
           ELSE
               MOVE 'YOU HIT THE WRONG KEY' TO MSGO.
           MOVE -1 TO CUSTNAML.
           GO TO A250-SEND-MAP-DATAONLY.
       A910-ERROR.
           EXEC CICS ABEND ABCODE('CU01') END-EXEC.
```

Screen Layout:

```
                    INQUIRY/UPDATE A CUSTOMER

    CUSTOMER NUMBER: 99999

    CUSTOMER NAME  : XXXXXXXXXXXXXXXXXXX

    CREDIT LIMIT   : 999999999


    CLEAR=MENU
    XXXXXXXXXXXXXXXXXXXXXXXXXXXXXXXXXXXXXXXXXXXXXXXXXXXXXXXXX
```

CICS Mapset XXCU01:

```
XXCU01    DFHMSD TYPE=&SYSPARM,LANG=COBOL,TIOAPFX=YES,MODE=INOUT,       X
              STORAGE=AUTO,CTRL=(FREEKB,FRSET),TERM=3270,DATA=FIELD
AXCU01    DFHMDI SIZE=(24,80)
          DFHMDF POS=(01,28),LENGTH=25,INITIAL='INQUIRY/UPDATE A CUSTOMEX
              R'
          DFHMDF POS=(03,03),LENGTH=16,INITIAL='CUSTOMER NUMBER:'
```

74

```
CUSTNO     DFHMDF  POS=(03,20),LENGTH=05
           DFHMDF  POS=(05,03),LENGTH=16,INITIAL='CUSTOMER NAME   :'
CUSTNAM    DFHMDF  POS=(05,20),LENGTH=20,ATTRB=UNPROT
           DFHMDF  POS=(05,41),LENGTH=01
           DFHMDF  POS=(07,03),LENGTH=16,INITIAL='CREDIT LIMIT    :'
CRDLMT     DFHMDF  POS=(07,20),LENGTH=09,ATTRB=NUM
           DFHMDF  POS=(07,30),LENGTH=01
           DFHMDF  POS=(10,03),LENGTH=10,INITIAL='CLEAR=MENU',      X
               ATTRB=(ASKIP,BRT)
MSG        DFHMDF  POS=(11,03),LENGTH=60,ATTRB=(ASKIP,BRT)
           DFHMSD  TYPE=FINAL
           END
```

The PPT must contain XCU01 (CICS/DL/I program) and XXCU01 (CICS mapset). The PCT must contain CU01 (Transaction code) and XCU01 (CICS/DL/I program). The FCT table must have entries for the DL/I data bases: SLSORD and CUSTMST.

The PSB source listing for this CICS/DL/I program is as follows:

```
PCB      TYPE=DB,DBDNAME=CUSTMST,PROCOPT=AP,KEYLEN=5
SENSEG   NAME=CUSTSEG,PARENT=0
PCB      TYPE=DB,DBDNAME=SLDORD,PROCOPT=GO,KEYLEN=11
SENSEG   NAME=SOHSEG,PARENT=0
PSBGEN   LANG=COBOL,PSBNAME=XCU01,CMPAT=YES
FINISH
END
```

CHAPTER 3. BASIC MAPPING SUPPORT (BMS)

There are two ways you can communicate with CICS terminals or printers: Terminal Control and BMS. The Terminal Control commands can only be used to send a small stream of data to the terminal or receive a small stream of data into the CICS program from the terminal. They do not have the data formatting capabilty like BMS commands. Therefore, the Terminal Control commands are not that useful as the BMS commands.

There are two important Terminal Control commands that you will use most frequently: the SEND FROM and the RECEIVE INTO commands. You can use the SEND FROM command of the Terminal Control to send a small message to the terminal to inform the user. For example, when the NOTOPEN (file not open) condition occurs, you can use the SEND FROM command to inform the user this situation and then issue a RETURN command to terminate the task. In this case, there is no need to use the SEND MAP command since we just want to send a small message to inform the user that the file he tries to use is not open. The SEND FROM command can also be used to print an online report which we'll cover in Chapter 4. The RECEIVE INTO command can be used to develop an independent CICS program that can be invoked by entering its transaction code with the input data. For example, we can develop a customer update program which is to be invoked by entering its transaction code and the customer number on a clear screen. We'll cover how to use the Terminal Control feature for your CICS application needs in Chapter 4.

The BMS commands can be divided into two major groups: Message Routing commands and non Message Routing commands. There are two CICS commands that belong to the non Message Routing BMS commands: the SEND MAP and the RECEIVE MAP commands. You will use these two commands in almost every CICS programs to send the output map and to receive the input map. There are five Message Routing commands: ROUTE, SEND MAP ACCUM, SEND PAGE, SEND TEXT ACCUM, and PURGE MESSAGE commands. The Message Routing BMS commands are only used in Message Routing CICS programs. A Message Routing program builds and transmits the message (report) to display terminals or printers. It is an output-only operation. There is no input data to be received into a Message Routing program. Only a small portion of your CICS programs will employ this Message Routing technique. However, Message Routing represents one of the two methods to print an online report. At least 10% of your CICS programs will be report-printing programs. Therefore, you need to know how to write a Message Routing program to print an online report.

The Message Routing commands are used to build and route a message to display terminals or printers. The message normally contains one or more pages, and each page has a standard format. For example, we want to display or print all the sales order details for any given sales order number. Assume that each page contains seventeen details. This sales order may have more than one page of details. If the message is to be sent to a printer, then the entire message will be printed. If the message is to be transmitted to a display terminal, then only the first page of details will be displayed after the message has been routed to the terminal. In this case, the user must hit the CLEAR key and then enter the Terminal Paging commands to retrieve the remaining pages within the message. After the user has finished with this message, he needs to issue a Message Purging command to delete the message.

When Message Routing commands are used, they are used mostly to print on-line reports. The other method to print an online report is to use the SEND FROM command of the Terminal Control operation.

In this chapter, we'll concentrate our efforts on the Basic Mapping Support: BMS non Message Routing commands, Message Routing commands, Terminal Paging commands and Message Routing Applications.

3.1. Non-Message-Routing BMS Commands

A majority of CICS programs use non Message Routing commands to communicate with the display terminals. There are two BMS commands within this catagory: the SEND MAP and the RECEIVE MAP commands. The SEND MAP command is used to send a CICS map with program-prepared output data to the terminal. The RECEIVE MAP command is used to receive the input data entered on a CICS map from the terminal into the CICS program. You'll use these two BMS commands in almost every CICS program that requires terminal I/O operations. A CICS mapset must be created before you can use these two commands. The following example shows we want to read the customer and display it on the terminal:

```
WORKING-STORAGE SECTION.
01  AXCU03I  COPY XXCU03.
LINKAGE SECTION.
01  DFHCOMMAREA     PIC X(100).
PROCEDURE DIVISION.
    EXEC CICS HANDLE CONDITION
            NOTFND(A900-NOTFND)
            MAPFAIL(A910-MAPFAIL)
            ERROR(A920-ERROR)
            END-EXEC.
    EXEC CICS HANDLE AID
            CLEAR(A899-XCTL-TO-MENU)
            ANYKEY(A910-MAPFAIL)
            END-EXEC.
    MOVE DFHCOMMAREA TO COMM-AREA.
    IF EIBTRNID = 'CU03'AND EIBCALEN = 100
        GO TO A200-RECEIVE-MAP.
    EXEC CICS READ DATASET('CUSTMST')
                INTO(CUST-REC)
                RIDFLD(CA-CUSTNO)
                END-EXEC.
    MOVE LOW-VALUES    TO AXCU030.
    MOVE CUST-NO       TO CUSTNOO.
    MOVE CUST-NAME     TO CUSTNAMO.
    MOVE CUST-CRDLMT   TO CRDLMTO.
    MOVE -1            TO CUSTNAML.
    MOVE 'UPDATE NAME AND CREDIT LIMIT' TO MSGO.
    MOVE SPACES        TO EDIT-TAB.
    EXEC CICS SEND MAP('AXCU03') MAPSET('XXCU03')
                ERASE CURSOR END-EXEC.
    EXEC CICS RETURN TRANSID('CU03')
```

```
                          COMMAREA(COMM-AREA)
                          LENGTH(100)
                          END-EXEC.
     A200-RECEIVE-MAP.
         EXEC CICS RECEIVE MAP('AXCU03') MAPSET('XXCU03')
                   END-EXEC.
         .... EDIT INPUT FIELDS ...
         IF ALL-INPUT-FIELDS-OK
            GO TO A300-UPDATE-CUSTOMER.
         MOVE 'INPUT INVALID' TO MSGO.
         EXEC CICS SEND MAP('AXCU03') MAPSET('XXCU03')
                   DATAONLY CURSOR END-EXEC.
         EXEC CICS RETURN TRANSID('CU03')
                          COMMAREA(COMM-AREA)
                          LENGTH(100)
                          END-EXEC.
```

3.1.1.   SEND MAP Command

The first time you send a CICS map, you should specify the ERASE option in the SEND MAP command. This will erase whatever displayed on the terminal before the map is sent. The second through the last time you try to send this map, you should specify the DATAONLY option in the SEND MAP command. This will send only the data you move to the output map I/O area without erasing the current display. This will save you data transmition time to transmit the output data from the CICS program to the terminal. There is no need to specify the FROM option in a SEND MAP command since CICS will use the map I/O area of the map you specified.

After each SEND MAP command is issued, you should issue a RETURN command with TRANSID option. This technique is called pseudo conversational programming. The RETURN command will return the control to CICS and terminate the current task. However, the transation code you specify in the TRANSID option will be post on this terminal. Any response to this terminal will initiate this transaction code and its associated CICS program specified in the PCT will be invoked. After the CICS program is invoked again, you should get the data you save from DFHCOMMAREA and then issue a RECEIVE MAP command to receive the input data entered on the terminal into the CICS program.

If you issue a SEND MAP command and then a RECEIVE MAP command, this technique is called conversational programming. In this case, after the SEND MAP command is executed, the CICS program along with all its resources will not be released. It is waiting for the user to response to the terminal. When the response is made on this terminal, the RECEIVE MAP command will then be executed. So the CICS task is waiting for the response from the user. If the user goes out to lunch and never come back, the CICS task will still be waiting until it is timed out or the CICS/VS region is shut down. The CICS program along with its resources will be wasted if conversational programming technique is used. This is not acceptable for all data centers. So you must issue a RETURN command with TRANSID option following each SEND MAP command. When the CICS program is invoked again, you should then issue the RECEIVE MAP command and get the data saved in the communication area.

If you define your map I/O area in LINKAGE SECTION instead of WORKING STORAGE SECTION, then you need to issue a GETMAIN command to acquire the map I/O area before you can move the output data into it and then issue a SEND MAP command. When you try to issue a RECEIVE MAP command you should specify the SET option to acquire the map I/O area and store the input map.

```
LINKAGE SECTION.
01  DFHCOMMAREA      PIC X(100).
01  BLL-CELLS.
    02  FILLER       PIC S9(8) COMP.
    02  MAP-PTR      PIC S9(8) COMP.
01  AXCU03I          COPY XXCU03.
PROCEDURE DIVISION.
    ....
    EXEC CICS GETMAIN SET(MAP-PTR)
                LENGTH(1920)
                END-EXEC.
    MOVE LOW-VALUES TO AXCU03O.
    ... MOVE OUTPUT DATA TO AXCU03O ...
    EXEC CICS SEND MAP('AXCU03') MAPSET('XXCU03')
            ERASE CURSOR END-EXEC.
    EXEC CICS RETURN TRANSID('CU03')
                COMMAREA(COMM-AREA)
                LENGTH(100)
                END-EXEC.
A200-RECEIVE-MAP.
    EXEC CICS RECEIVE MAP('AXCU03') MAPSET('XXCU03')
            SET(MAP-PTR) END-EXEC.
    IF CUSTNAML > 0
    ....
```

LOW-VALUES And SPACES

When you issue a SEND MAP command and the input/output field in the map I/O area contains LOW-VALUES (binary zeros), no data will be transmitted to the terminal. If the ERASE option is specified, the INITIAL values you specify in the mapset definition will be displayed. If there is no INITIAL= parameter specified for this field, no data will be displayed. If the DATAONLY option is specified in this SEND MAP command, whatever displayed on the terminal will not be changed since LOW-VALUES means no data is to be sent to this field.

However, if an input/output field in the map I/O area contains SPACES, then spaces will be treated as any non-LOW-VALUES data and will be sent to the terminal to erase whatever displayed on the terminal. If the MDT of this field has been turned on before this SEND MAP command is issued and the user does not enter anything on this field after this map have been sent, the spaces will be received into the input area of this field if the user hits ENTER key.

If the MDT of a map field is turned off and no data is entered on this field, the input area of this data field will contain LOW-VALUES after the map has been received.

If the terminal is hung when you try to send a map to the terminal using the SEND MAP command, you should check to see if any alphameric output map field in the map I/O area contains packed-decimal (COMP-3) data. For example, you define the amount as ATTRB=NUM in the mapset definition and you move the amount in the record that is defined as COMP-3 to its output field.

```
AMT DFHMDF POS=(03,03),LENGTH=7,ATTRB=NUM

01  CUST-REC.
    ......
    02  CUST-AMT    PIC S9(7) COMP-3.

    MOVE CUST-AMT TO AMTO.
    ... SEND MAP ...
```

AMTI and AMTO will be generated by BMS as PIC X(7). So when you try to move a S9(7) COMP-3 data to X(7) area, we'll hang your own terminal.

You can also specify the ALARM option when issuing a SEND MAP command to produce a sound to catch the user's attention. For example, you can issue a SEND MAP command with the ALARM option when the input data is invalid. But most of the time, the users do not like to be told that they are making a mistake so the ALARM option is normally not used.

Before you issue a SEND MAP command, you can set the MDT of each field the way you want it. This is the best time to set the MDT for the output fields. If you do not set the attribute byte of an output field before you issue a SEND MAP command and its MDT is off during the last input operation, then BMS will set the MDT of this field using its attribute value define in the CICS mapset or the last input operation. If the user enters input data on that field during the last input operation and FRSET is not specified in the CTRL= of the mapset definition or the following SEND MAP command, then the MDT will still be on for the next input operation. If FRSET is specified, the MDT will be turned off for the next input operation. FRSET will turn off the MDT for the last input operation.

You can also position the cursor where you want it in the SEND MAP command. You just need to move -1 to the length field of the output field where you want to put the cursor and then issue a SEND MAP with CURSOR option. If there are more than one map field that contain -1 in their length field, the cursor will sit on the first one in the map. You can also use IC in the mapset definition to position the cursor, but this method is not flexible since the cursor will be positioned on that field for any output operation. The following example shows how to position the cursor on the order number:

```
MOVE -1 TO ORDRNOL.
EXEC CICS SEND MAP('AXCU03') MAPSET('XXCU03')
        ERASE CURSOR END-EXEC.
```

Before you issue a SEND MAP command, you should save all data that is to be used in the RECEIVE MAP session in the communication area. After the SEND MAP command is issued, you should issue a RETURN command with TRANSID and COMMAREA options. This will terminate this program, post the next transaction code on this terminal and save the data in the communication area. Any response to this terminal will initiate the transaction code. This transaction code is normally set up in the PCT to invoke the same CICS program. After this CICS program is invoked, you can get the data you save in DFHCOMMAREA and issue a RECEIVE MAP command to receive the input data. The following example shows how to issue a SEND MAP command:

```
MOVE 'UPDATE DESIRED FIELDS' TO MSGO.
MOVE -1    TO ORDERL.
MOVE SPACES TO EDIT-TAB.
EXEC CICS SEND MAP('AXCU03') MAPSET('XXCU03')
          ERASE CURSOR END-EXEC.
EXEC CICS RETURN TRANSID('CU03')
                 COMMAREA(COMM-AREA)
                 LENGTH(100)
                 END-EXEC.
```

3.1.2.   RECEIVE MAP Command

When the user enters updates and then hits ENTER key, the CICS program will be invoked again. This time, you should get the data you save in the communication area (DFHCOMMAREA) and then issue a RECEIVE MAP command. The RECEIVE MAP command will receive the input data entered on the terminal into the map I/O area. You only need to use one RECEIVE MAP format:

```
EXEC CICS RECEIVE MAP('AXCU03') MAPSET('XXCU03')
          END-EXEC.
```

The input data will be received into AXCU03I that is defined in WORKING-STORAGE SECTION. If you define the map I/O area in LINKAGE SECTION, then you need to issue:

```
LINKAGE SECTION.
01  DFHCOMMAREA    PIC X(100).
01  BLL-CELLS.
    02  FILLER     PIC S9(8) COMP.
    02  MAP-PTR    PIC S9(8) COMP.
01  AXCU03I        COPY XXCU03.
PROCEDURE DIVISION.
    EXEC CICS RECEIVE MAP('AXCU03') MAPSET('XXCU03')
              SET(MAP-PTR) END-EXEC.
    IF ORDRNOL > 0
       IF ORDRNOI NUMERIC
          . . . .
```

In the above example, after you have issued a RECEIVE MAP command, CICS will acquire the map I/O area for you and put the received input data into it. Now you can edit the input data in the map I/O area.

However, the RECEIVE MAP command has the capability to branch the control to the label within the CICS program. If the user enters the input data and then hits the ENTER key, the control will go to the next statement following the RECEIVE MAP command. If no input data was entered and no FSET (MDT on) is defined for any field in the mapset definition, the MAPFAIL condition will occur if the user hits the ENTER key. The MAPFAIL condition occurs when there is no input data to be transmitted. When the user hits any key other than the key defined in the HANDLE AID command, the control will go to the label specified for ANYKEY in the HANDLE AID command. If ANYKEY is not specified and no input fields with MDT turned on, MAPFAIL condition will occur. The ANYKEY in the HANDLE AID command will prevail over the MAPFAIL in the HANDLE CONDITION command.

If the user hits a key that has been defined in the HANDLE AID command, the control will go to the label specified for it after the RECEIVE MAP command is issued. Therefore, you need to issue the HANDLE AID command before you issue a RECEIVE MAP command.

If the MDT of an input field is off, its input field will contain LOW-VALUES after the RECEIVE MAP command is issued. If the user enters input data on a field, the input field will contain the input data after the RECEIVE MAP command is issued. In this case, the MDT is turned on when the input data is entered. When the MDT of an input field is turned on and the user does not enter or change the data currently displayed on that field, the data displayed will be received into the program.

The following example explains how the control will go after the RECEIVE MAP command is issued:

```
        EXEC CICS HANDLE CONDITION
                  MAPFAIL(A900-MAPFAIL)
                  ERROR(A910-ERROR)
                  END-EXEC.
        EXEC CICS HANDLE AID
                  CLEAR(A899-XCTL-TO-MENU)
                  ANYKEY(910-MAPFAIL)
                  END-EXEC.
        IF EIBTRNID = 'CU03' AND EIBCALEN = 100
           GO TO A200-RECEIVE-MAP.
        .... MOVE OUTPUT DATA TO MAP I/O AREA
        EXEC CICS SEND MAP('AXCU03') MAPSET('XXCU03')
                  ERASE CURSOR END-EXEC.
        EXEC CICS RETURN TRANSID('CU03')
                          COMMAREA(COMM-AREA)
                          LENGTH(100)
                          END-EXEC.
    A200-RECEIVE-MAP.
        EXEC CICS RECEIVE MAP('AXCU03') MAPSET('XXCU03')
                  END-EXEC.
        IF CUSTNAML > 0
```

```
            MOVE CUSTNAMI TO CA-CUSTNAM.
        ....
    A899-XCTL-TO-MENU.
        EXEC CICS XCTL PROGRAM('XCU01')
                       COMMAREA(WS-CU01)
                       LENGTH(30)
                       END-EXEC.

    A900-MAPFAIL.
        MOVE 'NO DATA WAS ENTERED' TO MSGO.
        MOVE -1  TO CUSTNAML.
        EXEC CICS SEND MAP('AXCU03') MAPSET('XXCU03')
                  AONLY CURSOR END-EXEC.
        EXEC CICS RETURN TRANSID('CU03')
                         COMMAREA(COMM-AREA)
                         LENGTH(100)
                         D-EXEC.
    A910-ERROR.
        EXEC CICS ABEND ABCODE('CU03') END-EXEC.
```

In the above example, if the user enters the customer name and credit limit and hits ENTER key, the control will go to the next statement following the RECEIVE MAP command. If the user did not enter input data but hit ENTER key, the MAPFAIL condition will occur and the control will go to A900-MAPFAIL. If the user hits CLEAR key, the control will go to A899-XCTL-TO-MENU after the RECEIVE MAP command is issued. If the user hits any key other than CLEAR or ENTER key, the control will go to the label (A900-MAPFAIL) set up for ANYKEY. You need to issue the HANDLE AID command before you issue the RECEIVE MAP command.

How can you determine you need to issue a RECEIVE MAP command rather than the SEND MAP command when the CICS program is invoked? You can use the EIBTRNID and EIBCALEN in the EIB table. When you issue a SEND MAP command, you will then issue a RETURN command with TRANSID and COMMAREA options. In the above example, when the CICS program is invoked the second time, EIBTRNID will contain CU03 and EIBCALEN will contain 100. In this case, you know this is not the first time the program is invoked and you need to issue a RECEIVE MAP command.

When the program is first invoked by the menu program, EIBTRNID will still contain CUST which is the transaction code for the menu program. In this case, you need to read the customer and display it for update.

3.2.   Message Routing Commands

The Message Routing commands of BMS are used only in Message Routing programs. A Message Routing program will build and transmit a message (report) to one or more terminals. The terminal can be a display terminal or a printer. Most of the time, you will use Message Routing technique to print an online report. If the message is to be transmitted to a display terminal, then the users must be trained to use Terminal Paging commands to retrieve the remaining pages within the message and to delete the message when it is no longer needed. The concept behind the Terminal Paging commands is too complicated for most of the users. That is why the Message Routing technique is only used to print an online report instead of displaying a report on the terminal. It is one of the two techniques that can be used to print an online report. At least 10% of your CICS programs will be report printing programs.

The message routing program performs an output-only operation. After the message is built and transmitted, the program itself is normally terminated by a RETURN command. At this time, the message is no longer within the control of the issuing CICS program. The user must delete it when he has finished with this message.

There are five Message Routing commands:

1. ROUTE
   It is used to set up the list of terminals or printers that are to receive the message. If you want to print this report on the printer, then you should set up the printer ID in the route list.

2. SEND MAP ACCUM
   It is used to send a CICS map to build the message. This command is normally issued repeatly to build a message. The map can be the entire page or only a portion of the page. A report normally contains more than one page. Therefore, more than one SEND MAP ACCUM command must be issued to build the entire message (report).

3. SEND TEXT ACCUM
   It is used to send a stream of data to build the message. If the data will not be defined in a CICS map, then this command should be used instead of the SEND MAP ACCUM command. It is normally used to build one detail line at a time. Therefore, many SEND TEXT ACCUM commands must be issued in order to build the entire message.

4. SEND PAGE
   It is used to signal the completion of the message building and possibly transmit the message to its destination. When the entire message is built, you should issue this command to print or display the report.

5. PURGE MESSAGE
   It is used to delete the uncompleted message when errors have been encountered during the message building process. This command is normally used in the error-handling routine to purge the uncompleted message.

You can send the same message to more than one terminal or printer. For example, if you want to print the sales order in the headquarter and the plant, then you need to set up the printers in the ROUTE command for both the headquarter and the plant.

If the message is to be delivered to two different device types, then you may need to divide the page into three maps: header map, detail map and trailer map. If the message is to be routed to the terminals with the same device type, then you can define the entire page as a header map.

After the message has been built using the SEND MAP ACCUM or the SEND TEXT ACCUM command, you can then issue a SEND PAGE command to route the message to its destinations (terminals or printers). If the message is routed to a display terminal, then only the first page of the message will be displayed. The user should then hit the CLEAR key and enter the Terminal Paging commands to retrieve the remaining pages within the message. After the message is no longer needed, the user can enter the Message Purging command to purge the message.

If the message is routed to a printer, the printing will start as soon as the SEND PAGE command is executed. The entire message will be printed and there are no Terminal Paging commands needed to be used.

CICS uses the Temporary Storage to store the message before you send it to the terminals. The most important thing you need to do when you try to use the Message Routing technique is to put a limit on the size of the message. If you don't, when there is no more temporary storage to store your message, your CICS task will wait for the resource to become available and in the meantime still use the temporary storage for the uncompleted message. When more and more CICS tasks request the temporary storage, all CICS tasks will be hung and eventually the entire CICS system will be hung. So you should always specify the maximum number of records to be processd to build the message within the Message Routing program to prevent it from hanging the entire CICS system. Normally, a report should not exceed 15 regular pages (24x80 = 1920 bytes/page) or 30K bytes.

When the report exceeds the limit you specify in your CICS print program, you should issue a SEND PAGE command to send the message and release the temporary storage for other CICS tasks.

When you try to design a CICS print program, you should always consider the re-print capability. That means if the printer is jammed or out of service while you send the message, you should be able to re-print this report. This can be done by setting up this CICS program as a transaction to be started (by the START command) from the menu program or any other CICS program. The data can be passed from the issuing CICS program to the print program through the use of the FROM option in the START command. After the START command is issued, the print transaction will be initiated. This will invoke the print program itself. When the print program is invoked, it should issue a RETRIEVE command to retrieve the data passed to it and print the report. After the report is printed, it should then issue a RETURN command without any option to terminate itself. If the printer is jammed when it tries to print the report, you can re-print the report from the menu screen.

We'll use one example to show how you can use the Message Routing commands to satisfy your application programming needs. Assume that we want to print all sales order details for any given sales order number. This print program will be started by the START command issued within the menu program. The sales order number is passed in the FROM option of the START command. After this print program is invoked, it will issue a RETRIEVE command to retrieve the sales order number passed from the menu program. The key to the sales order detail file is the sales order number plus a 3-byte sequence number. The sequene number is assigned sequentially when the sales order detail record is created.

We'll issue a ROUTE command to set up the route list for the printers where we want to print this report. Then we use the sales order number as the generic key to browse the sales order detail file. For each sales order detail record retrieved, we'll print it on one print line. Therefore, we can set up only one header map in the mapset. Each print page will contain one header map. We use the SEND MAP ACCUM command to send the header map to create one page in the message. Each page contains 17 sales order details. When there are no more details on the file for this sales order number, you should issue an ENDBR command to end the browse operation and then issue the SEND PAGE command to print the report. After the report has been transmitted and printed, you should issue a RETURN command to terminate the program.

The entire program listing for this CICS print program is listed in Chapter 13.6.

3.3. Terminal Paging Commands

If a message is routed to a display terminal, only the first page of the message will be displayed. The user should hit CLEAR key to erase the first page and then enter the Terminal Paging commands to retrieve the remaining pages within the message. After the current message has been reviewed, the user should issue the Message Purging commands to purge the current message.

In the preceeding print program, if you specify a display terminal instead of a printer in the route list, then the report will be displayed on the terminal instead of being printed in the printer. No changes need to be made to this print program in order to display the report on the terminal.

The Terminal Paging commands that are used to retrieve the pages within a message all start with the same characters which are defined by your system programmer. For example, all Terminal Paging commands start with 'P/' and all Message Purging commands start with 'T/'.

To retrieve a page within the current message, you need to hit CLEAR key to erase the first page of the message and then enter:

```
P/n     ... to go to page n
P/+n    ... to go to next n pages forward
P/-n    ... to go to previous n pages backward
P/N     ... to go to the next page
P/L     ... to go to the last page
P/C     ... to re-display the current page
```

To purge message:

```
T/A     ... to purge all messages destinated for or being displayed
            on that terminal
T/B     ... to purge the message being displayed on that terminal
            and all messages chained to it
T/C     ... to purge the current message and any message chained to
            it
T/H     ... to purge all messages chained to the base message being
            displayed on that terminal
T/R     ... to purge all messages queued for immediate delivery to
            the terminal
```

To copy pages:

```
C/tttt
```

This allows you to print the page being displayed on the terminal to the printer. Where tttt is the printer ID.

'P/', 'T/' and 'C/' are defined by your system programmer. Therefore, you need to consult your system programmer before you issue those commands.

3.4. Message Routing Applications

In Section 3.2, we introduce the Message Routing technique using the SEND MAP ACCUM command. Each page within the message consists of one header map. The header map contains the sales order header information, 17 sales order details and 2 space lines. We only need to define the entire page within the message as one header map when we try to send the message to the same device type.

3.4.1. SEND MAP ACCUME Using OVERFLOW

If you know that the device types of all terminals specified in the ROUTE commands are different, you should define the entire page of the report as one header map, one detail map and one trailer map. For example, we want to print the sales order on two different printer types, each with different line numbers in a page. The header map will contain the sales order header information. The detail map contains only one detail record and occupies one line. The trailer map occupies two lines and contains the footing. Using three maps for a page, you need to set up the OVERFLOW condition for the detail map. When there are no more spaces to create the detail map in the page, OVERFLOW condition occurs. In this case, you need to send the trailer map for the current page, send the header map for the next page and then send the detail map the caused the OVERFLOW condition again. OVERFLOW condition will occur.

You still need to issue a ROUTE command to set up the printer list. For each page, you need to send a header map, 17 detail maps, and one trailer map. When you try to send the 18th detail map, OVERFLOW condition occurs. When there are no more sales order details for that sales order number, you should then issue a SEND PAGE command to print the message.

The entire print program using SEND MAP ACCUM with OVERFLOW is listed in Chapter 13.7.

3.4.2. SEND TEXT ACCUM Command

If you want to print an online report that uses up to 132 columns on each line. You can either use the SEND FROM command or use the SEND TEXT ACCUM command. In this section, we'll show you how to print an online report using the SEND TEXT ACCUM command. You can also use this technique to print any report that print less than 132 columns on each line. In this case, you only need to pad spaces at the end of each line to make it up to 132 bytes per line.

Before you can test your print program using the SEND TEXT ACCUM command, you should ask your CICS system programmer to change the page size of the printer that is to print this report to PGESIZE=(11,132) on its TCT entry. The reason we choose 11 lines and 132 columns is that we want to be able to print up to 132 columns on one line and the regular computer paper normally can print 66 lines. The complete source program listing and the program description are in Chapter 13.8.

CHAPTER 4. TERMINAL CONTROL

There are two ways you can communicate with the CICS terminals or printers: Terminal Control and BMS. The Terminal Control commands are not that useful as BMS commands since they do not have the data formatting capability. You can only send a stream of data to the terminal or receive a stream of data into the CICS program.

Two Terminal Control commands are used most frequently: the SEND FROM and the RECEIVE INTO commands. The SEND FROM command is used for the following two purposes:

1. Send a message to the terminal:
   For example, you can send a small message to the terminal to inform the user that the file is not open. In this case, there is no need to send a CICS map to the terminal since we just want to send a small message. After the message has been sent, you should then issue a RETURN command to terminate the CICS program.

2. Print a stream of data on the printer:
   This is one of the two methods to print an online report in CICS/VS. Before you can issue a SEND FROM command to print the report from an output data stream, you should insert the new line (DFHBMPNL), the end of message (DFHBMPEM) and the form feed (X'0C' and X'0D') characters into the output data stream to control the report format. You can print up to 1920 bytes of output data stream at a time. We'll show you how to code the print utility program in Chapter 13.13 that can be started by any CICS program that needs to print an online report.

The RECEIVE INTO command can be used in an independent CICS program or when you perform the unit test. An independent CICS program is designed to be invoked by entering its transaction code and input data on a clear screen. For example, we can design a customer update program to be invoked by entering its transaction code and the customer number on a clear screen. After this customer update program is invoked, it should issue a RECEIVE INTO command to receive the transaction code and the customer number into the program. Then it will use the customer number to retrieve the customer and display it on the terminal. So instead of passing the customer number from the menu program in a menu-driven system, an independent customer update program gets tthe customer number from the terminal. This technique can also be used to perform unit test on your CICS program within a menu-driven system without going through the menu program. You just need to modify your CICS program so it will be invoked by entering its transaction code with the input data on the terminal. After you have finished the unit testing for this CICS program, you can then change the program back to hook up with the menu program so it can be invoked by the menu program.

4.1. SEND FROM Command

When you encounter problems in a CICS program, you can issue the SEND FROM command to inform the user the situation and then issue a RETURN command to terminate the program. You should only do this when the situation you have encountered is recoverable. If an unrecoverable error is encountered, you should issue an ABEND command to abend the task and produce the storage dump. The file not open (NOTOPEN) condition can be a recoverable situation so we can issue a SEND FROM command to inform the user and terminate the task normally. The following example shows how to issue the SEND FROM command:

```
WORKING-STORAGE SECTION.
01  WS-MSG          PIC X(60).
01  WS-MSG-LENG     PIC S9(4) COMP VALUE +60.

    EXEC CICS HANDLE CONDITION
              NOTOPEN(900-NOT-OPEN)
              END-EXEC.
    MOVE 1000 TO ORDER-NO.
    EXEC CICS READ DATASET('ORDER')
              INTO(ORDER-REC)
              RIDFLD(ORDER-NO)
              END-EXEC.
    .... ORDER HAS BEEN RETRIEVED ....

900-NOT-OPEN.
    MOVE 'ORDER FILE NOT OPEN - HIT CLEAR' TO WS-MSG.
    EXEC CICS SEND FROM(WS-MSG) LENGTH(WS-MSG-LENG)
              ERASE END-EXEC.
    EXEC CICS RETURN END-EXEC.
```

In the above example, we issue a SEND FROM command to notify the user that the order file is not open. The current screen will be erased before the message is sent. After the message is sent to the terminal, we issue a RETURN command to terminate the CICS program. The user should hit the CLEAR key to erase the message and then enter the next CICS transaction or call the computer room to open the file.

The SEND FROM command can also be used to print an online report. However, it has the following two disadvantages:

1. Up to 1920 bytes of data can be printed. If the report is greater than 1920 bytes, more than one SEND FROM command must be issued.

2. If more than one SEND FROM command need to be issued, you need to enqueue the printer using the ENQ command to prevent other CICS print tasks from printing reports between two SEND FROM commands.

From the above discussion, we know the SEND FROM command is easy to use but you need to aware of its disadvantages. Many CICS shops develop a print utility program that is to be initiated by any CICS program that needs to print the report. These issuing CICS programs do not need to issue the SEND FROM command themself. They only need to pass the data to be printed and specify which printer to print this report. Normally, the Message Routing technique is considered complicated by many CICS programmers. Therefore, this print utility program can solve the problems for many CICS programmers.

The SEND FROM command can only print up to 1920 bytes of data. However, the output can be compressed before you print it. That means you can truncate all the trailing spaces of each print line and then insert a new line control character (DFHBMPNL) after that. For example, if a print line contains only 30 bytes of data and 102 bytes of spaces, it only needs to occupy 30 bytes for the data and one byte for the new line control character in the output data stream. That means more lines can be printed for each SEND FROM command if the print CICS program will compress the data before the SEND FROM command is issued. If that CICS program does not want to compress the data, less lines will be printed. You can also choose to compress only the blank lines. For example, your report contains many blank lines, you can use only one byte of the new line character to represent one space line in the output data stream.

The following example shows how to issue a START command to initiate this print utility program to print a report:

The first CICS program will use this print utility program to print a report that prints 132 columns on each line and performs the form feed before the report is printed. The printer ID is 'K01P':

Issuing CICS program:

```
WORKING-STORAGE SECTION.
01  PRINT-DATA-LENGTH        PIC S9(4) COMP.
01  PRINT-DATA.
    02  PRINT-LINE-LENGTH    PIC S9(4) COMP VALUE +132.
    02  PRINT-FORM-FEED      PIC X(1).
    02  PRINT-LINES.
        03  PRINT-LINE       OCCURS 14 TIMES PIC X(132).

    MOVE 'Y'   TO PRINT-FORM-FEED.
    MOVE +1851 TO PRINT-DATA-LENGTH.
    EXEC CICS START TRANSID('CU11')
             FROM(PRINT-DATA)
             LENGTH(PRINT-DATA-LENGTH)
             TERMID('K01P')
             END-EXEC.
    MOVE 'PRINT REQUEST COMPLETED' TO MSGO.
    EXEC CICS SEND MAP('AXCU03') MAPSET('XXCU03')
             DATAONLY CURSOR END-EXEC.
```

The following CICS program will use the same print utility program to print a report that prints 85 columns on each line. No form feed is to be performed before the report is to be printed. The printer ID is 'K02P'. Since the maximum length of data to be printed by a SEND FROM command is 1920 bytes, we can only pass 22 lines (22 x 85 = 1870) of data.

Issuing CICS program 2:

```
WORKING-STORAGE SECTION.
01  PRINT-DATA-LENGTH        PIC S9(4) COMP.
01  PRINT-DATA.
```

```
02   PRINT-LINE-LENGTH     PIC S9(4) COMP VALUE +85.
02   PRINT-FORM-FEED       PIC X(1).
02   PRINT-LINES.
     03   PRINT-LINE       OCCURS 22 TIMES PIC X(85).

MOVE 'N'  TO PRINT-FORM-FEED.
MOVE +1873 TO PRINT-DATA-LENGTH.
EXEC CICS START TRANSID('CU11')
                FROM(PRINT-DATA)
                LENGTH(PRINT-DATA-LENGTH)
                TERMID('K02P')
                END-EXEC.
MOVE 'P/O PRINTED SUCCESSFULLY' TO MSGO.
EXEC CICS SEND MAP('AXP003') MAPSET('XXP003')
          DATAONLY CURSOR END-EXEC.
```

We'll cover the coding of this print utility program in Chapter 13.9 and 13.11.

4.2.   RECEIVE INTO Command

The RECEIVE INTO command can be used in an independent CICS program to receive the transaction code and the input data after the CICS program is invoked by entering the transaction code with the input data on a clear screen. This technique can also be used to perform the unit test for a CICS program within a menu-driven system.

If the customer update program is to be invoked by the menu program after the user has entered the function number 2 and a valid customer number and the coding of the menu program has not finished, then you can test your update program independently by changing the program as follows:

```
WORKING-STORAGE SECTION.
01   RECE-AREA.
     02   RECE-TRAN-ID  PIC X(4).
     02   RECE-COMMA    PIC X(1).
     02   RECE-CUST-NO  PIC 9(5).
01   RECE-LENGTH        PIC S9(4) COMP VALUE +10.
01   CUSTOMER-REC       COPY CUSTMAST.
01   WS-MSG             PIC X(60).
01   WS-MSG-LENG        PIC S9(4) COMP VALUE +60.
LINKAGE SECTION.
01   DFHCOMMAREA        PIC X(100).
PROCEDURE DIVISION.
     EXEC CICS HANDLE CONDITION
               LENGERR(A900-LENGTH-ERROR)
               END-EXEC.
     EXEC CICS HANDLE AID
               ....
               END-EXEC.
     MOVE DFHCOMMAREA TO COMM-AREA.
     IF EIBTRNID = 'CU02' AND EIBCALEN = 100
        GO TO A200-RECEIVE-MAP.
     EXEC CICS RECEIVE INTO(RECE-AREA) LENGTH(RECE-LENGTH)
          END-EXEC.
     EXEC CICS READ DATASET('CUSTMAST')
```

```
                         RIDFLD(RECE-CUST-NO)
                         INTO(CUSTOMER-REC)
                         END-EXEC.
                .... DISPLAY CUSTOMER ....
        A900-LENGTH-ERROR.
              MOVE 'INPUT FORMAT IS INVALID, CU02,12345' TO WS-MSG.
              EXEC CICS SEND FROM(WS-MSG) LENGTH(WS-MSG-LENG)
                              ERASE END-EXEC.
              EXEC CICS RETURN END-EXEC.
```

After the user has entered 'CU02.12345' on the terminal, this CICS program will be invoked since the transaction code CU02 points to this program in the PCT. After this program is invoked, it should issue a RECEIVE INTO command to receive the transaction code (CU02) and the customer number into the CICS program. If the length of the data entered is greater then 10 bytes, the LENGERR condition occurs. In this case, the control will go to the paragraph named A900-LENGTH-ERROR to issue a SEND FROM command to inform the user the correct input format. After the user has seen the message, he should hit the CLEAR key to erase the message and enter the transaction code with the correct input data format again.

4.3. SEND FROM Command For Printing

You can also use the SEND FROM command to print an on-line report. In this section, we'll show you how to write a print utility program which will be invoked by a START command issued in any CICS program that wants to print a report. The report can be any size in line length. The CICS program that issues the START command should pass the following information to this print utility program:

1. The print line length.

2. Form feed or not before printing the report

3. data to be printed in line format.

The CICS program that issues the START command is as follows:

```
        WORKING-STORAGE SECTION.
        01   PRINT-DATA-LENGTH        PIC S9(4) COMP.
        01   PRINT-DATA.
             02   PRINT-LINE-LENGTH    PIC S9(4) COMP VALUE +132.
             02   PRINT-FORM-FEED      PIC X(1).
             02   PRINT-LINES.
                  03   PRINT-LINE      OCCURS 14 PIC X(132).
        LINKAGE SECTION.
        01   DFHCOMMAREA              PIC X(100).
        PROCEDURE DIVISION.
             .... MOVE EACH PRINT LINE TO PRINT-LINE(I) ...
             .... UP TO 14 LINES CAN BE MOVED INTO PRINT-LINES ...
             .... IF FORM FEED IS REQUIRED, MOVE 'Y' ....
             MOVE 'Y' TO  PRINT-FORM-FEED.
             .... SPECIFY TOTAL NUMBER OF BYTES TO BE PRINTED ....
             MOVE +1851 TO PRINT-DATA-LENGTH.
```

```
     .... START THE PRINT TRANSACTION PRNT ....
     EXEC CICS START TRANSID('CU11')
                     FROM(PRINT-DATA)
                     LENGTH(PRINT-DATA-LENGTH)
                     TERMID('K01P')
                     END-EXEC.
```

In the print program XCU11 that is to be invoked by the transaction code CU11, you should perform the following functions:

1. Truncate all the trailing spaces in each line.
   This step is optional. If you do not want to truncate the trailing spaces within each print line, then less lines will be printed for each SEND FROM command issued.

2. Insert a new line character (DFHBMPNL) following the last character of the compressed line.
   When this new line character in the output data stream is encountered, the printer will advance to the first column of the next line.

3. Insert X'0C' and X'0D' as the first two bytes of output data if the form feed is requested by the issuing CICS program.
   If the form feed has been requested by the issuing CICS program ('Y' in PRINT-FORM-FEED), then you should insert these two characters as the first two bytes of the output data stream. When the printer encounters these two characters, it will return the carriage to the column 1 of the same line and then perform the form feed. The reason we need X'0C' (carriage return) is because the last report printing may leave the carriage of the printer in the middle of the print line. If you do not insert this character, the printer will print your first print line starting with the column where the carriage is.

4. Insert the end of the message printer control character (DFHBMPEM) as the last byte of output data.
   The end of message character must be the last character in the output data stream to singal the completion of the data to be printed. If you do not insert this character in the output data stream, CICS will print the data in the buffer between the last print line and the end of the buffer (1920 bytes) as output data. For example, your output data stream is 1876 bytes long and no end of message character has been inserted as the 1877th character, then 44 spaces (1920 - 1876 = 44) will be printed after you have printed the last line.

5. Issue a SEND FROM command to send the output data to the printer.
   You should specify the output data stream that you have constructed in the FROM option of the SEND FROM command. This output data stream contains carriage return, form feed, new line, end of message printer control characters and output print lines.

The issuing CICS program can supply the data to be printed in any desired line length. The line length must be specified in the data to be passed. If the form feed is required before the report is printed, it must indicate that in the PRINT-FORM-FEED field. The line length will be used by this print utility program to interpret the data passed and construct the output data stream for the SEND FROM command.

Each printer control character will occupy one byte in the output data stream, but it will not occupy any space in the report. These printer control characters are only used to control the printing operations and not part of the report to be printed. The complete listing of this print utility program is in Chapter 13.13. Chapter 13.8 shows a CICS program that starts this print transaction.

CHAPTER 5. TEMPORARY STORAGE CONTROL

The Temporary Storage queues can be used to pass data amoung CICS programs. For example, we want to create the entire sales order in the temporary storage queue instead of the sales order file so we can review or update it later before we create it in the VSAM file. After we has reviewed or updated the sales order stored in the temporary storage queue, the sales order will then be created in the sales order file. In this case, the temporary storage queue that contains the sales order is created in one CICS program and then reviewed or updated in the other CICS program. These two CICS programs are not related by the XCTL or LINK command so we cannot use the communication area to pass the data. The other reason we use the temporary storage to store the sales order is that we do not know how many sales order details for any given sales order. The temporary storage queue is better suited to store the detail records than the communication area since the temporary storage queue may contain one or more records. After the sales order has been created in the file, we can then delete the temporary storage queue.

In the above example, we save the sales order in the temporary storage queue for later use. The temporary storage queue is identified by a 1- to 8-charater queue name. A temporary storage queue can contain one or more records. You can retrieve these temporary storage queue records sequentially or randomly. You can also update the queue records. There is no limit on how many times you can read or update the temporary storage queue records. You can only delete the entire TS queue and you cannot delete TS queue records individually.

You can pass the data from the current CICS program to the next program to be invoked through the use of the XCTL or LINK command in the communication area. If the current program will not invoke the CICS program that is to receive the data from this program, then you should create the data to be passed in the temporary storage queue and retrieve it later in the other CICS program. The temporary storage queue you create will exist until you delete it or CICS/VS is shut down.

Therefore, the temporary storage queue works like a VSAM RRDS file that is created in one CICS program and reviewed or updated in another CICS program. You can create the TS queue in the main storage or auxiliary storage (disk). If the temporary storage queue is to be used only for a short period time (less than one second), then you should use the main storage. Otherwise, the auxiliary storage should be used. Most of the time, you should use the auxiliary storage since the time interval normally exceeds one second. There is no CICS internal table needed to be set up by your system programmer before you can use the temporary storage queue. However, you need to make sure the temporary storage queue you are going to create is unique to your terminal or transaction by attaching the terminal ID as part of the queue name. When the same CICS program that creates the temporary storage queue is used concurrently by many terminal users, the temporary storage queue created by each user will be unique if you use the terminal ID as part of the queue name.

Temporary storage is also used by CICS internally for the following purposes:

1. BMS paging request

2. Message routing
3. START command with FROM option
4. CEDF displays

If auxiliary storage is used for a temporary storage queue, then a VSAM ESDS file must be defined. Your system programmer must use VSAM AMS DEFINE CLUSTER command to define this ESDS file. The DD or DLBL statement for this ESDS file must be included in the CICS startup JCL. The label for this DD or DLBL statement should be DFHTEMP. The following example shows a DD card included in the CICS startup JCL:

```
//DFHTEMP DD DSN=CICS.TEMP.STORAGE,DISP=SHR
```

When a temporary storage queue record is created, an item number will be assigned sequentially by CICS. This item number should be used if you want to retrieve or update this record later. The item number can be obtained by specifying the ITEM option in the WRITEQ TS command. After the temporary storage queue record is created, the item number assigned for this record is in the data field you specify in the ITEM option. If you want to retrieve a queue record randomly, then the queue name and the item number of that record must be supplied in the READQ TS command.

You should always issue a DELETEQ TS command before you try to create the first record in the temporary storage queue that uses main storage (MAIN). This will ensure that there is no left-over temporary storage queue from the last CICS task that created this TS queue. The TS queue that uses main storage is not a recoverable when a CICS task abends. When the temporary storage queue is no longer needed, you should issue a DELETEQ TS command to delete the queue. After the queue is deleted, the temporary storage will be released.

If you know the TS queue name, you can use a CICS transaction named CEBR to browse the queue records on 3270 terminal. By entering CEBR transaction with the QUEUE subcommand, you can browse, copy, or purge the TS queues. But you cannot read an output transient data queue.

Using the temporary storage queues has the following advantages:

1. There are no CICS internal tables needed to be set up in order to create a TS queue. After your system programmer has set up the ESDS file for the temporary storage, you can use it at any time you want to without asking any other system information.

2. The record length can be fixed- or variabl-length. So you can create different types of records in the same queue. But most of the time, you would create records with the same length.

3. More than one records can be created in the queue. So the TS queue works like a small RRDS file and you can create as many records as you like. When you try to retrieve the records, you only need to supply the queue name and their item number (if random access).

4. No key needs to be set up for the queue record, all you need to do is to move the data you want to store into a data area and then specify this data area in the FROM option of the WRITEQ TS command. CICS will assign an item number to each record you create.

5. You can retrieve or update the queue records as many times as you like. Unlike transient data queues that can be read only once, you can process a TS queue record as many times as you wish.

6. You can retrieve the queue records randomly or sequentially. If you try to retrieve a queue record randomly, the queue name and the item number of the record to be retrieved must be specified in the READQ TS command.

7. You can delete the TS queue in any CICS program at any time. There are no rules set for the queue deletion, you can delete it as soon as it is no longer needed. You just need to specify the queue name in order to delete it.

8. You can create the TS queue in the main storage or in the auxiliary storage.

Temporary Storage commands are as follows:

1. WRITEQ TS
   It is used to create a TS queue record.

2. READQ TS
   It is used to read a TS queue record.

3. WRITEQ TS REWRITE
   It is used to update a TS queue record.

4. DELETEQ TS
   It is used to delete the entire TS queue.

5.1.   WRITEQ TS Command

This command is used to create a queue record in a temporary storage queue. You need to specify that the main storage or auxiliary storage is to be used to store this queue. You also need to give the queue a name that will be unique to each user in case this CICS program is to be used by many users concurrently. When a queue record is created, it will be added to the end of the queue. CICS will assign sequentially an item number to the record. This item number should be used later if you want to randomly retrieve this record. The item number assigned by CICS starts with 1. There is no key in the queue record itself, you can store data starting with the first byte. The WRITEQ TS command has the following format:

```
EXEC CICS WRITEQ TS QUEUE(data-area)
                    FROM(data-area)
                    LENGTH(data-value)
```

```
               [ITEM(data-area)]
               [MAIN|AUXILIARY]
               END-EXEC.
```

Exceptional condition: NOSPACE

QUEUE(data-area) specifies the name of the queue you want to create. The queue name must be up to eight characters long. You should always use the terminal ID (EIBTRMID) as part of the queue name in order to make it unique to each terminal when this CICS program is used concurrently by many users.

FROM(data-area) specifies the queue record area that contains the data to be created in the queue.

LENGTH(data-value) specifies the length of the record layout area. You should move the actual length of the record to be added to the data field specified in the LENGTH option before you issue this WRITEQ TS command.

ITEM(data-area) specifies a data area that is to contain the item number that CICS has assigned to the record. This is optional. If you want to know the item number assigned to this record for later use, then you can specify this option. Most of the time, you do not need to know. In this case, you do not need to specify ITEM. After the record is created, it will contain the item number assigned to it. The data area to store the item number must be defined as a half-word binary (PIC S9(4) COMP).

MAIN|AUXILIARY specifies whether you want to store the queue in the main storage (MAIN) or auxiliary storage (disk). If the use of the TS queue will last less than one second, then you should specify MAIN. If the queue will be used to pass the data between two CICS programs that belong to the same task (through the use of XCTL or LINK command), then MAIN should be used. If the use of the queue will last longer than one second, the auxiliary storage should be used. The first TS queue record created will determine which type of storage is to be used for the subsequent records in the same TS queue. You cannot create the same TS queue in both main storage and auxiliary storage.

The following example shows that we want to create a sales order detail in the TS queue:

```
       WORKING-STORAGE SECTION.
       01  QUEUE-RECORD.
           02  Q-ORDER-NO      PIC 9(5).
           02  Q-DETAIL-NO     PIC 9(3).
           02  Q-PRODUCT-CODE  PIC X(15).
           02  Q-ORDERQTY      PIC S9(5) COMP-3.
           02  Q-UNIT-PRICE    PIC S9(7)V99 COMP-3.
       01  QUEUE-LENGTH        PIC S9(4) COMP VALUE +31.
       01  QUEUE-NAME.
           02  QUEUE-TRMID     PIC X(4).
           02  QUEUE-TRNID     PIC X(4) VALUE 'CU03'.
       01  QUEUE-ITEM          PIC S9(4) COMP.
       PROCEDURE DIVISION.
```

```
        ....
        EXEC CICS HANDLE CONDITION
                QIDERR(A000-BUILD-Q-RECORD)
                END-EXEC.
*       DELETE THE QUEUE (IF ANY) BEFORE YOU CREATE IT
        MOVE EIBTRMID     TO QUEUE-TRMID.
        EXEC CICS DELETEQ TS QUEUE(QUEUE-NAME) END-EXEC.
A000-BUILD-Q-RECORD.
        .... MOVE SALES ORDER DETAIL TO QUEUE-RECORD ...
        EXEC CICS WRITEQ TS QUEUE(QUEUE-NAME)
                        FROM(QUEUE-RECORD)
                        LENGTH(QUEUE-LENGTH)
                        MAIN
                        END-EXEC.
        GO TO A000-BUILD-Q-RECORD.
```

In the above example, we use the terminal ID from EIBTRMID and the transaction ID (CU03) as the queue name. We move the sales order detail into the queue record layout area before we issue a WRITEQ TS command. We specify MAIN (main storage) is to be used to store this TS queue. Before you create the first record in a TS queue that uses MAIN storage, it is a good practice to delete the queue first. The TS queue that uses MAIN storage is not recoverable. Therefore, when a CICS task abends after it has created a TS queue in the main storage, the TS queue will not be backed out. So when you re-enter the same transaction later, that TS queue is still there. If there is no left-over queue from the last CICS task that use this program, QIDERR condition occurs.

5.2.   READQ TS Command

This command is used to retrieve a TS queue record. You can read a TS queue record randomly or sequentially. If you want to retrieve it randomly, then you need to specify the ITEM option in the READQ TS command and move the item number of the record to be retrieved into the data area specified in the ITEM option before you issue this READQ TS command. CICS assigns an item number to each TS queue record when it is created. The item number is assigned sequentially and starts with 1. If no ITEM option is specified in the READQ TS command, the next record within the queue will be retrieved. CICS remembers which queue record was the last one retrieved by any CICS task. The READQ TS command has the following format:

```
        EXEC CICS READQ TS QUEUE(data-area)
                        [SET(pointer-ref)|INTO(data-area)]
                        LENGTH(data-area)
                        [NEXT|ITEM(data-value)]
                        END-EXEC.

        Exceptional conditions: QIDERR, ITEMERR, LENGERR
```

QUEUE(data-area) specifies the TS queue name that you want to access. The queue name is assigned when you create the queue. It is one to eight bytes long. If the queue name specified cannot be found, the QIDERR condition occurs.

SET(pointer-ref) specifies the pointer that addresses the queue record area defined in LINKAGE SECTION. If you define the queue record area in LINKAGE SECTION, then you need to use the SET option. After the queue record is retrieved, CICS will set the address of the record in the pointer.

INTO(data-area) specifies the TS queue record layout area that is to be used to store the retrieved TS queue record. The data area must be defined in WORKING-STORAGE SECTION.

LENGTH(data-area) specifies the maximum length of the TS record that is to be retrieved. After the record is retrieved, the actual record length will be stored in this data area. If the length of the record retrieved is greater that that specified, the LENGERR condition occurs. You should move the maximum record length into the data area before you issue the READQ TS command. If all the records within this queue have the same length, then you should specify this length.

NEXT specifies that the next record is to be retrieved. This implies the sequential retrieval. CICS remembers the last record you retrieved. Therefore, when you specify the NEXT option in the READQ TS command, CICS will retrieve the next record. This is the default if both NEXT and ITEM are not specified.

ITEM(data-value) specifies the item number of the TS queue record to be retrieved. When a TS queue record is created through the use of the WRITEQ TS command, CICS will sequentially assign an item number to this record. The item number of the record must be specified if you want to retrieve this record randomly. This item number data area must be defined a half-word binary field (PIC S9(4) COMP).

Expectional Condtions

QIDERR

This condition occurs when the TS queue name you specify in the QUEUE option does not exist.

ITEMERR

This condition occurs when the item number you specify in the ITEM option for the record your try to retrieve does not exist. It can also occur when there are no more records in the queue to be retrieved when you issue a sequential read (NEXT option).

LENGERR

This condition occurs when the length of the TS queue record retrieved is greater than that specified in the LENGTH option.

Unlike TD queue records which can only be read once, you can retrieve or update TS queue records as many times as you like.

The following example shows how to retrieve all TS queue records sequentially starting from the top of the queue:

```
WORKING-STORAGE SECTION.
01  QUEUE-RECORD     PIC X(100).
01  QUEUE-LENGTH     PIC S9(4) COMP VALUE +100.
01  QUEUE-NAME.
    02  QUEUE-TRMID PIC X(4).
    02  QUEUE-TRNID PIC X(4) VALUE 'CU03'.
01  QUEUE-ITEM       PIC S9(4) COMP.
PROCEDURE DIVISION.
    EXEC CICS HANDLE CONDITION
              QIDERR(A910-ERROR)
              ITEMERR(A900-EOJ)
              ERROR(A910-ERROR)
              END-EXEC.
    MOVE EIBTRMID TO QUEUE-TRMID.
A100-READ-NEXT-Q-RECORD.
    EXEC CICS READQ TS QUEUE(QUEUE-NAME)
                    INTO(QUEUE-RECORD)
                    LENGTH(QUEUE-LENGTH)
                    NEXT
                    END-EXEC.
    .... PROCESS TS QUEUE RECORD JUST RETRIEVED ...
    GO TO A100-READ-NEXT-Q-RECORD.
A900-EOJ.
    EXEC CICS DELETEQ TS QUEUE(QUEUE-NAME) END-EXEC.
    EXEC CICS RETURN END-EXEC.
A910-ERROR.
    EXEC CICS ABEND ABCODE('CU03') END-EXEC.
```

In the above example, we issue the READQ TS command with the NEXT option to retrieve the TS queue records sequentially. Since this is the first time we retrieve the queue records, CICS will start with item number 1. After the record has been retrieved, we'll process it and then go back to read the next one. If there are no more records in the TS queue, the ITEMERR condition occurs. In this case, we'll go to delete the queue and terminate the CICS program.

If this TS queue can be accessed by other CICS programs, you cannot be so sure about what was the last record retrieved. In this case, you should use the random retrieval to read the records from item number 1.

The following example shows how to retrieve all records in the TS queue randomly. In order to retrieve the TS records randomly, you need to specify the ITEM option and move the item number of the record to be retrieved into the data area specified for the ITEM option:

```
WORKING-STORAGE SECTION.
01  QUEUE-RECORD     PIC X(100).
01  QUEUE-LENGTH     PIC S9(4) COMP VALUE +100.
01  ITEM-NUMBER      PIC S9(4) COMP.
```

```
01  QUEUE-NAME.
    02  QUEUE-TRMID PIC X(4).
    02  QUEUE-TRNID PIC X(4) VALUE 'CU03'.
PROCEDURE DIVISION.
    EXEC CICS HANDLE CONDITION
              ITEMERR(A900-NO-MORE-ITEM)
              ERROR(A910-ERROR)
              END-EXEC.
    MOVE EIBTRMID TO QUEUE-TRMID.
    MOVE +0       TO ITEM-NUMBER.
A100-READ-NEXT-Q-RECORD.
    ADD 1 TO ITEM-NUMBER.
    EXEC CICS READQ TS QUEUE(QUEUE-NAME)
                       INTO(QUEUE-RECORD)
                       LENGTH(QUEUE-LENGTH)
                       ITEM(ITEM-NUMBER)
                       END-EXEC.
    .... PROCESS THE RETRIEVED RECORD ....
    GO TO A100-READ-NEXT-Q-RECORD.
A900-NO-MORE-ITEM.
    .... NO MORE RECORDS ....

*   READ ITEM NUMBER 2 RECORD RANDOMLY
    MOVE +2 TO ITEM-NUMBER.
    EXEC CICS READQ TS QUEUE(QUEUE-NAME)
                       INTO(QUEUE-RECORD)
                       LENGTH(QUEUE-LENGTH)
                       ITEM(ITEM-NUMBER)
                       END-EXEC.

A910-ERROR.
```

In the above example, we use random retrieval to retrieve the records starting with item number 1 until there are no more records in the queue (ITEMERR). You need to specify ITEM option in order to retrieve the record randomly. You can retrieve or update a TS queue as many times as you like.

The READQ TS command is also used when you try to update a queue record. You should issue a READQ TS command to retrieve the record you try to update, move updates to the record layout and then issue a WRITEQ TS REWRITE command to update the queue record.

5.3.   WRITEQ TS REWRITE Command

This command is used to update a queue record. To update a queue record, you should issue a READQ TS command to retrieve the record you try to update, move updates to its record layout, and then issue this WRITEQ TS REWRITE command to update the record. The WRITEQ TS REWRITE command has the following format:

```
EXEC CICS WRITEQ TS QUEUE(name)
                    FROM(data-area)
                    LENGTH(data-value)
```

106

```
                  ITEM(data-area) REWRITE
                  [MAIN|AUXILIARY]
                  END-EXEC.
```

Exceptional condition: none

The ITEM option must be specified to indicate the item number of the record to be
updated. The REWRITE option must be specified to indicate that an update is to be
performed instead of a creation. You should also specify the storage type in which this
queue was created. The default is AUXILIARY. So if you specify MAIN in the WRITEQ
TS command when you create this TS queue, you should specify MAIN when you try
to update the queue records.

The following example shows how to update the order quantity of the queue record with
the item number equal to 2:

```
      WORKING-STORAGE SECTION.
      01  ITEM-NUMBER      PIC S9(4) COMP.
      01  QUEUE-RECORD.
          02  Q-ORDERNO  PIC 9(5).
          02  Q-DETAILNO PIC 9(3).
          02  Q-PRODUCT  PIC X(15).
          02  Q-ORDERQTY PIC 9(5).
      01  QUEUE-LENGTH     PIC S9(4) COMP VALUE +28.
      01  QUEUE-NAME.
          02  QUEUE-TRMID PIC X(4).
          02  QUEUE-TRNID PIC X(4) VALUE 'CU03'.
      PROCEDURE DIVISION.
          MOVE +2        TO ITEM-NUMBER.
          MOVE EIBTRMID TO QUEUE-TRMID.
          EXEC CICS READQ TS QUEUE(QUEUE-NAME)
                          INTO(QUEUE-RECORD)
                          LENGTH(QUEUE-LENGTH)
                          ITEM(ITEM-NUMBER)
                          END-EXEC.
          MOVE 100       TO Q-ORDERQTY.
          EXEC CICS WRITEQ TS QUEUE(QUEUE-NAME)
                           FROM(QUEUE-RECORD)
                           LENGTH(QUEUE-LENGTH)
                           ITEM(ITEM-NUMBER)
                           REWRITE
                           AUXILIARY
                           END-EXEC.
```

In the above example, we move +2 to the item number before we issue a READQ TS
command to retrieve the second record in the queue. After the record has been retrieved
randomly, we can move the update to its record layout and then issue a WRITEQ TS
REWRITE command. We need to specify ITEM in this command in order to identify
the record we want to update.

5.4.   DELETEQ TS Command

This command is used to delete the entire TS queue when it is no longer needed. You cannot delete the individual TS queue records, you can only delete the entire queue. It is also a good pratice to issue this command when you try to create the first record in a TS queue that uses the main storage. This will ensure there is no left-over TS queue from the last task that executed this CICS program and failed. When a CICS task abends, no back out will be performed on the TS queues that use MAIN storage. So the TS queue that is created by the last CICS task associated with this terminal that uses this program may exist. If you do not issue a DELETEQ TS command, the queue records will be added to the end of the queue. When you try to process them, you may not know you are processing queue records created by the last CICS task.

The DELETEQ TS command has the following format:

```
EXEC CICS DELETEQ TS QUEUE(name) END-EXEC.

Exceptional condition: QIDERR
```

QUEUE(name) specifies the name of the TS queue that is to be deleted. If the name specified cannot be found, QIDERR condition occurs.

QIDERR

This condition occurs when the TS queue to be deleted does not exist.

After the TS queue is deleted, all storage associated with the queue will be released. You should delete the TS queue when it is no longer needed.

The following example shows how to delete a TS queue:

```
MOVE EIBTRMID TO QUEUE-TRMID.
EXEC CICS DELETEQ TS QUEUE(QUEUE-NAME) END-EXEC.
```

CHAPTER 6. TRANSIENT DATA CONTROL

The Transient Data Control of CICS/VS provides an excellent way to pass data amoung CICS tasks or between CICS/VS region and batch regions.

There are two types of transient data queues: Intrapartition and Extrapartition transient data queues. The intrapartition transient data queue is used to queue data within the CICS region or partition. The data in this type of queue is used amoung CICS tasks. For example, you can store the sales order numbers in an intrapartition TD queue within one CICS program and then print all sales orders from the queue in the other CICS program. The extrapartition transient data queue is used to collect output data in the CICS region for off-line batch processing. The data in this type of queue is used to transfer information between the CICS region/partition and batch region/partition. For example, you can log the terminal ID, and operator ID for all CICS tasks into an extrapartition TD queue and then print the queue (a sequential data set) by the operator sequence at night after the CICS/VS region is shut down. All TD queues must be specified in the DCT, each for each TD queue.

6.1.   Intrapartition Transient Data Sets

The intrapartition transient data queue can be a VSAM ESDS file or a direct access data set. If VSAM ESDS is to be used, your system programmer must use the DEFINE CLUSTER command of AMS to define the intrapartition transient data set before it can be used in CICS. A DD or DLBL statement must be provided in the CICS startup JCL to identify this intrapartition transient data queue. An intrapartition TD queue can only be defined as variable-length. It can be specified as reusable or non-reusable. If an intrapartition transient data queue is defined as reuseable (REUSE=YES in the DCT entry), the storage is released when all records stored in the control interval have been read by the READQ TD commands. If an intrapartition transient data queue is defined as nonreusable, the storage can only be freed when you issue a DELETEQ TD command after all records in the queue have been read.

An intrapartition TD queue can be used for the following purposes:

1. Batch queues
2. Automatic Task Initiation (ATI)
3. Audit
4. Terminal output

6.1.1.   Batch Queues

This type of TD queue is a good way to collect output data from many CICS tasks that execute the same CICS program. After the data has been collected in the queue, you can then enter another CICS transaction to process this TD queue. The CICS program that is invoked by this transaction must issue the READQ TD command to retrieve one queue record at a time and then process it. After the retrieved record has been processed, it should go back to retrieve the next one until QZERO condition occurs. QZERO condition occurs when there are no more records in the queue.

For example, you want to print a sales order after it has been created. You can do it through the use of an intrapartition TD queue. You can create a queue record that contains only the sales order number in the sales order create CICS program. Twice a day, you can invoke a CICS transaction to process all sales orders in the queue. For each record, you want to print the sales order. The reasons that you only want to queue the sales orders are:

1. You want to change the pre-print form in the printer before you print the sales orders. So this printer can also be used to print other reports that use different pre-print forms.

2. You want to invoke the sales order print program only once to print all sales orders currently in the queue. So instead of invoking the print program for each sales order created, you want to print them all together at the same time. This will save some loading time for this print program since we only load this program twice a day.

6.1.2. Automatic Task Initiation (ATI)

You can also use Automatic Task Initiation (ATI) technique to invoke a CICS transaction when the total number of records in an intrapartition TD queue has reached the trigger level specified in its DCT entry. For example, we want to invoke the above sales order print transaction automatically when the total number of sales orders in the above TD queue has reached 30. In this case, we need to set up the print transaction (PRNT) and the trigger level (30) for that TD queue in the DCT. The DCT entry for this intrapartition transient data set used in the ATI application is as follows:

```
L860    DFHDCT    TYPE=INTRA,DESTFAC=TERMINAL,DESTID=L860,        X
                  DESTRCV=NO,REUSE=YES,RSL=1,TRANSID=PRNT,        X
                  TRIGLEV=30
```

In the above example, we specify this is an intrapartition transient data set (TYPE=INTRA). The destination (queue name) is L860 (DESTID=L860). The TD queue is reusable (REUSE=YES) so when the TD queue record is read, its storage occupied by that record will be released. The resource security level is 1. The transaction to be invoked when the trigger level (30) is reached is PRNT. The trigger level is set at 30. You can dynamically alter the trigger level through the use of the CSMT transaction:

```
CSMT TRIGGER,n,DESTID=L860
```

Where n is the new trigger level. You can also inquire about the current trigger level for the destination L860 as follows:

```
CSMT TRI,INQ,DESTID=L860
```

After the print program is invoked, it will issue a READQ TD command to retrieve the queue record and use the sales order number in the record to retrieve and print the sales order. After the retrieved sales order has been printed, it should go back to read the next record in the queue until there are no more records in the queue (QZERO). When QZERO condition occurs, you should issue a RETURN command to terminate the program. The storage occupied by this TD queue will be released since we define REUSE=YES in its DCT entry.

If an intrapartition TD queue is defined as non-reusable in the DCT entry, then the storage that is occupied by this queue will not be released by the READQ TD command, you need to issue a DELETQ TD command to release the queue storage after you have processed all the records in the queue. However, an intrpartition transient data queue used in the ATI application is normally defined as reusable.

6.1.3. Audit

Both extrapartition and intrapartition TD queues may also be used to collect output data from CICS tasks for auditing purposes. For example, you can define an extrapartition TD queue to collect all updates to the inventory file. All CICS programs that update the inventory record must create both before and after image of the record in this TD queue. After CICS/VS has been shut down at 5 PM, you can then use a COBOL batch program to sort this extrapartition TD queue by the part number and list the records. This report will show how the inventory of any given part number was updated from CICS online order entry, shipping, inventory control and purchasing systems. If you use an intrpartition transient data queue, you can issue the READQ TD command to display all updates on the CICS terminal for auditing.

6.1.4. Terminal Output

You can also use intrapartition queues to accumulate the on-line report you are going to print from CICS tasks. Therefore, you need to store the lines you want to print in the intrapartition TD queue and specify a trigger level of 1 and the printer ID as the destionation in the DCT. When you write a record to the TD queue, the print program can be invoked and it will read the queue record (print line) and print it on the printer. This is not the best way to print an on-line report since you need to enqueue the printer to prevent other CICS tasks from mixing their reports with yours.

Indirect Destinations

For the above terminal output operations, you can specify a logical destination as the indirect destination in the DCT. Then you need to specify another DCT entry that will identifies the physical device as the destination to be used to receive that output. This way, if the printer is broken, you only need to replace the printer ID in the DCT with a working printer and then recompile the DCT. You do not need to recompile the CICS programs that use this TD queue since the CICS programs only specify the indirect destination. Therefore, you need to specify the indirect destination as the queue name in the WRITEQ TD command. This queue record will be created in the queue whose name is the physical device. The following DCT entries show this relationship:

```
DFHDCT TYPE=INDIRECT,DESTID=L778,INDDEST=L860
DFHDCT TYPE=INTRA,DESTFAC=TERMINAL,DESTID=L860,    X
       DESTRCV=NO,REUSE=YES,RSL=1,TRANSID=PRNT,         X
       TRIGLEV=30
```

In the above example, we specify an indirect destination L778 which will point to an intrapartition TD queue named L860 (INDDEST=L860). Then we set up another DCT entry to describe this L860 destination as we normally do. In the CICS programs that create the TD queue records, you should specify the indirect destination L778 as the TD queue name in the WRITEQ TD command.

```
EXEC CICS WRITEQ TD QUEUE('L778')
                    FROM(QUEUE-RECORD)
                    LENGTH(QUEUE-LENGTH)
                    END-EXEC.
```

If the output is to be directed to another physical device, the CICS programs that create the TD queue do not need to be changed since they can still use the same indirect destination. You only need to change the physical device name (L860) in the DCT to another working printer ID and re-assemble this DCT table.

6.2.   Extrapartition Transient Data Sets

The extrapartition transient data sets are sequential files. They can be on disks or tapes. The TD queue name must be defined in the DCT. Your system programmer must include a DD or DLBL statement in the CICS startup JCL for each DCT entry of the extrapartition TD queue and the ddname must match that specified in the DSCNAME operand of the DCT entry. The DCT entry for an extrapartition transient data set is as follows:

```
LOGA      DFHDCT TYPE=EXTRA,DESTID=LOGA,DSCNAME=LOGUSR,RSL=1
```

Where TYPE=EXTRA specifies this is an extrapartition transient data set. The destination is LOGA (DESTID=LOGA) and ddname specified in the DD or DLBL statement in the CICS startup JCL must be LOGUSR (DSCNAME=LOGUSR). The resource security level is equal to 1.

The extrapartition transient data queue can only be defined for input or output but not for both. If input is defined, the information is to be passed from the batch region/partition to CICS/VS. In this case, you should issue the READQ TD command to retrieve the TD queue records and no WRITEQ TD command should be issued. If output is defined for the extrapartition transient data set, the information is to be collected from CICS tasks in the CICS/VS region and then passed to the batch region/partition for off-line batch processing. In this case, you can only issue the WRITEQ TD command to create the TD queue records and no READQ TD command should be issued. After the output data is collected in the extrapartition TD queue, it will be processed by batch programs at night after CICS/VS has been shut down. These extrapartition transient data queues are sequential data sets using QSAM (OS/VS) or SAM (DOS/VSE). The record length can be fixed or varable, blocked or unblocked. No recovery will be performed for an extrapartition TD queue.

The extrapartition transient data queues can be used for the following purposes:

1. Batch data transfer
2. Sequential Devices
3. Audit

6.2.1. Batch Data Transfer

The extrapartition TD queues are excellent tool to collect output data from CICS tasks. For example, you can define an extrapartition TD queue to collect the data for CICS transactions. Each record in this queue contains the transaction code, the operator ID, and the terminal ID. You can create one record in this queue for each CICS task. Then after 5 PM, you can shut down CICS/VS and then sort this TD queue which is a sequential file by the operator ID and list the CICS tasks by the operator sequence. From this report, you can see how many transactions executed for each CICS operator. If you sort this queue by the transaction code, you can see how many users use this transaction a day.

You can also set up an extrapartition TD queue to collect all updates to the inventory files. All CICS programs that update the inventory file must create both before and after image of the inventory record in this TD queue. After the CICS/VS region has been shut down, you can then sort this TD queue, a sequential file, by the product code and then list this sorted file. From this report, you can see how an inventory record was updated by the online order entry, shipping, inventory control, manufacturing, and purchasing systems.

6.2.2. Sequential Devices

You can specify a card reader, line printer, disk or tape as an extrapartition TD queue to CICS/VS. Then you can create the TD queue records into these sequential devices. In the above Batch Data Transfer, we would specify disk or tape as the output devices. However, you can specify the card reader as the output device. In this case, you will create TD queue records into the reader queue. This allows you to develop CICS applications that will submit the batch JCL statements (TD queue records) to the reader queue. We'll show you how to develop CICS applications to submit batch JCL to reader queue for execution in Chapter 13.12.

6.2.3. Audit

Since we can collect output data from all CICS users into an extrapartition TD queue, we can use this TD queue to collect the data for auditing purposes. In this case, the TD queue will be defined for output only and a VSAM ESDS file will be defined for this TD queue. The CICS tasks from which the auditing data is to be collected will issue the WRITEQ TD command to create TD queue records. After the CICS/VS region is shut down, we can then sort this ESDS file and list it.

6.3. Transient Data Control Commands

There are three Transient Data Control commands. The WRITEQ TD command is used to create a record in the queue. The READQ TD command is used to read a queue record. Each queue record can only be read once. If the queue is defined as reusable in the DCT, the storage will be released after the READQ TD command is executed. If it is defined as non-reusable, the storage will not be released after the READQ TD command is executed and you need to issue a DELETEQ TD command after all queue records have been read in order to release the storage. In the following sections, we'll discuss how to issue these three TD queue commands. There are no differences in coding these TD commands between using an extrapartition TD and an intrapartition TD queue.

6.3.1. WRITEQ TD Command

This command is used to create a queue record in a transient data queue. It has the following format:

```
EXEC CICS WRITEQ TD QUEUE(name)
                    FROM(data-area)
                    [LENGTH(data-value)]
                    END-EXEC.

Exceptional conditions: LENGERR, NOSPACE, NOTOPEN, QIDERR
```

QUEUE(name) specifies the TD queue name. The name must be one to four characters and must be specified on the DCT.

FROM(data-area) specifies the queue record I/O area that contains the record to be created.

LENGTH(data-value) specifies the length of the queue record to be created. You must move the actual length of the record to be created to this area before you can issue this WRITEQ TD command. The LENGTH is required if the TD queue is defined as a variable-length data set or the data set is not on disk for CICS/VS/DOS. A TD queue is a sequential file and can be defined as fixed- or variable-length file.

Exceptional Condition

LENGERR

This condition occurs in any of the following situations:

1. The LENGTH option is not coded for a variable-length TD data set.

2. The length specified in the LENGTH option is greater than the maximum record size specified for the queue in the DCT.

3. The length specified is not equal to the record length for a fixed-length data set.

4. The LENGTH option is not coded for a queue other than disk involving fixed-length records.

NOSPACE

This condition occurs when there is no more space in the intrapartition TD queue.

114

NOTOPEN

This condition occurs if the queue is closed. The queue must be opened to CICS/VS before you can issue any TD commands.

QIDERR

This condition occurs when the destination (TD queue name) specified is not on the DCT. All TD queue names must be specified in the DCT.

The following example shows how to create a queue record into a TD queue:

```
WORKING-STORAGE SECTION.
01  QUEUE-RECORD      PIC X(100).
01  QUEUE-LENGTH      PIC S9(4) COMP VALUE +100.
PROCEDURE DIVISION.
    .... MOVE DATA TO QUEUE-RECORD ....
    EXEC CICS WRITEQ TD QUEUE('L300')
                        FROM(QUEUE-RECORD)
                        LENGTH(QUEUE-LENGTH)
                        END-EXEC.
```

You do not need to specify any exceptional condition for the WRITEQ TD command.

6.3.2.   READQ TD Command

This command is used to read a queue record from a TD queue. You can read each queue record only once. If the queue is defined as reusable, the storage of the queue record will be released after the READQ TD command is executed. If the queue is defined as non-reusable, then the storage of the queue record will not be released after the READQ TD command is issued. In this case, you should issue a DELETEQ TD command to release the storage after all records in the queue (QZERO) have been retrieved. CICS remembers which record in the queue is the last record you retrieved, so when you issue a READQ TD command, it will retrieve the next record in the queue. If there are no more records in the queue, QZERO condition occurs.

The READQ TD command has the following format:

```
EXEC CICS READQ TD QUEUE(name)
                   {SET(pointer-ref)|INTO(data-area)}
                   [LENGTH(data-area)]
                   END-EXEC.
```

Exceptional conditions: QIDERR, QZERO, LENGERR, NOTOPEN

QUEUE(name) specifies the TD queue name to be read. The queue name is one to four characters long and must be in the DCT.

SET(pointer-ref) specifies the pointer that addresses the queue record I/O area defined in LINKAGE SECTION.

INTO(data-area) specifies the queue record I/O area defined in WORKING-STORAGE SECTION where you want to store the retrieved queue record.

LENGTH(data-area) specifies the maximum record length of this queue. If this option is specified, it must contain the maximum length of the record before you issue this READQ TD command. After this command is executed, CICS will put the actual record length of the retrieved record in this area. This LENGTH option must be specified if the queue is defined as variable-length or your installation is under CICS/VS/DOS. If the queue is defined as fixed-length, then this option can be omitted. In this case, if you specify it, it must contain the record length specified in the DCT.

Exceptional Conditions

QIDERR

This condition occurs when the queue name specified is not on the DCT.

QZERO

This condition occurs when there are no more records in the queue. You should always specify this condition in the HANDLE CONDITION command when you need to issue the READQ TD command.

LENGERR

This condition occurs in any of the following situations:

1. The LENGTH option is not coded for a variable-length TD queue.

2. The length of the record retrieved is longer than the length specified in the LENGTH option.

3. The length specified in the LENGTH option is not equal to the record length of a fixed-length queue.

4. The LENGTH option is not specified for the queue other than disk, involving fixed-length records.

The following example shows how to retrieve a queue record from the TD queue we've just created in the preceeding example using the WRITEQ TD command:

```
WORKING-STORAGE SECTION.
01   QUEUE-RECORD      PIC X(100).
01   QUEUE-LENGTH      PIC S9(4) COMP VALUE +100.
PROCEDURE DIVISION.
     EXEC CICS READQ TD QUEUE('L300')
                        INTO(QUEUE-RECORD)
                        LENGTH(QUEUE-LENGTH)
                        END-EXEC.
```

You cannot indicate which queue record to be read since CICS will always retrieve the next record in the queue. Each queue record can be read only once. Since we do not know if this TD queue is defined as variable- or fixed-length, we specify the LENGTH option to avoid possible LENGERR condition.

You should also use the READQ TD command to read an intrapartition TD queue when the trigger level is reached and the transaction code specified in its DCT entry is initiated. In the associated CICS program of this transaction code, you should issue the READQ TD command to retrieve the queue record until there are no more records in the queue (QZERO condition). The following example shows how this CICS program should do after it is invoked. Assume that we create one TD queue record in the L300 queue for each sales order created in the order creation CICS program. When the total number of records in this queue has reached 30, CICS will initiate a transaction named PRNT which will invoke the sales order print program XPRNT to print all sales orders in the queue. The queue record contains only the sales order number.

The DCT entry for this Intrapartition TD queue is as follows:

```
L300        DFHDCT TYPE=INTRA,DESTFAC=TERMINAL,DESTID=L300,     X
                   DESTRCV=NO,REUSE=YES,TRANID=PRNT,TRIGLEV=30
```

The PCT entry for this transaction PRNT:

```
            DFHPCT TYPE=ENTRY,TRANSID=PRNT,PROGRAM=XPRNT,       X
                   TRANSEC=02,TRANPRTY=001,TWASIZE=0,           X
                   DVSUPRT=NONV,TCLASS=2
```

In the Sales Order Creation CICS Program:

```
WORKING-STORAGE SECTION.
01   QUEUE-RECORD.
     02   QUEUE-ORDER-NO     PIC 9(5).
01   QUEUE-LENGTH            PIC S9(4) COMP VALUE +5.
LINKAGE SECTION.
01   DFHCOMMAREA             PIC X(100).
PROCEDURE DIVISION.
     .... A SALES ORDER CREATED IN VSAM KSDS FILE ...
     MOVE ORDR-ORDER-NO TO QUEUE-ORDER-NO.
     EXEC CICS WRITEQ TD QUEUE('L300')
                      FROM(QUEUE-RECORD)
                      LENGTH(QUEUE-LENGTH)
                      END-EXEC.
```

In the Sales Order Print CICS Program XPRNT:

```
WORKING-STORAGE SECTION.
01   QUEUE-RECORD.
     02   QUEUE-ORDR-NO  PIC 9(5).
01   QUEUE-LENGTH        PIC S9(4) COMP VALUE +5.
PROCEDURE DIVISION.
     EXEC CICS HANDLE CONDITION
               QZERO(A900-EOJ)
               ERROR(A910-ERROR)
               END-EXEC.
```

```
A100-READ-NEXT-Q-RECORD.
     EXEC CICS READQ TD QUEUE('L300')
                         INTO(QUEUE-RECORD)
                         LENGTH(QUEUE-LENGTH)
                         END-EXEC.
     .... PRINT SALES ORDER RETRIEVED ....
     GO TO A100-READ-NEXT-Q-RECORD.
A900-EOJ.
     EXEC CICS RETURN END-EXEC.
A910-ERROR.
     EXEC CICS ABEND ABCODE('PRNT') END-EXEC.
```

In the above example, after the CICS print program is invoked, we'll issue the READQ TD command to retrieve the queue record and process it. When there are no more records in the queue, QZERO condition occurs. In this case, we'll issue a RETURN command to terminate this CICS program. Since this CICS program is invoked by the transaction code (PRNT) specified in the DCT when the trigger level (30) has been reached, you only need to issue a RETURN command to terminate it.

6.3.3.   DELETEQ TD Command

This command is used to delete an intrapartition transient data set that is defined as non-reusable in the DCT. After this command is executed, the storage associated with this TD queue will be released. If the TD queue is defined as reusable, the storage of the record will be released after a READQ TD command is issued. However, if the TD queue is defined as non-reusable, the READQ TD command will not release the storage occupied by that record. Therefore, the size of the queue will continue to grow until you issue a DELETEQ TD command. You should issue this DELETQ TD command only after all records in the queue have been read. This command has the following format:

```
EXEC CICS DELETEQ TD QUEUE(name) END-EXEC.

Exceptional condition: QIDERR
```

QUEUE(name) specifies the TD queue to be deleted. It must be on the DCT and defined as non-reusable intrapartition TD queue.

QIDERR occurs when the queue name specified is not on the DCT.

The following example shows how to delete the intrapartition TD queue named L330:

```
EXEC CICS DELETEQ TD QUEUE('L330') END-EXEC.
```

6.4.   Transient Data Applications

In this section, we'll shows you three most used TD queue applications. The first one is the Automatic Task Initiation (ATI) application. The second one is an extrapartition TD queue created for off-line batch processing. The third one is to submit the JCL from a CICS program to the reader queue using the sequential device (card reader) as the extrapartition TD queue.

6.4.1. Automatic Task Initiation (ATI)

A sales order print transaction (PRNT) will be initiated when the total number of records in the intrapartition TD queue is equal to the trigger level specified in its DCT entry. A TD queue record will be created when a sales order is created in the order file. We want to print the sales order after it has been created. Instead of starting (START command) the sales order print transaction (PRNT) for each sales order created, we want to write the sales order to a TD queue and initiate this print transaction only when there are 30 (trigger level) sales orders in the queue. This way, the print transaction only needs to be loaded once in order to print all 30 sales orders. We have shown you how to code the sales order create program that creates the TD queue and the DCT entry for this intrapartition TD queue in Section 6.3.2. Here we'll show you how to write this sales order print program that is to be invoked by the print transaction PRNT. This CICS program must perform the following functions:

1. Issue the READQ TD command to retrieve the next record in the queue.

2. Use the sales order number in the retrieved record to read the sales order information from the order file.

3. Print the sales order information.

4. Go back to step 1 until QZERO condition occurs.

5. When there are no more records in the TD queue, QZERO condition occurs. In this case, you should issue a RETURN command to terminate this print transaction.

The complete listing of this CICS print program is in Chapter 13.14.

6.4.2. Extrapartition TD queue For Off-line Batch Processing

We'll set up an extrapartition TD queue to collect output data from all CICS programs that update the inventory file. For each update to the inventory record, two TD queue records will be created. One is the old image of the record and the other is the new image of the record. This TD queue must be specified in the DCT, and the DD statement for this VSAM ESDS file must be included in the CICS startup JCL. Your system programmer must define this VSAM file through the use of the DEFINE CLUSTER command. All the CICS programs that are to update the inventory file must issue the WRITEQ TD command to create two records in the queue:

```
WORKING-STORAGE SECTION.
01  INVENTORY-REC      PIC X(200).
01  INVENTORY-LENG     PIC S9(4) COMP VALUE +200.
LINKAGE SECTION.
01  DFHCOMMAREA        PIC X(100).
PROCEDURE DIVISION.
*      READ INVENTORY RECORD FOR UPDATE
       EXEC CICS READ DATASET('INVENT')
                      INTO(INVENTORY-REC)
                      RIDFLD(PRODUCT-CODE)
```

```
                    UPDATE
                    END-EXEC.
    *     CREATE BEFORE IMAGE OF INVENTORY RECORD
          EXEC CICS WRITEQ TD QUEUE('INVT')
                            FROM(INVENTORY-REC)
                            LENGTH(INVENTORY-LENG)
                            END-EXEC.
          .... MOVE UPDATES TO INVENTORY-REC ...
    *     CREATE AFTER IMAGE IN TD QUEUE
          EXEC CICS WRITEQ TD QUEUE('INVT')
                            FROM(INVENTORY-REC)
                            LENGTH(INVENTORY-LENG)
                            END-EXEC.
    *     REWRITE INVENTORY RECORD
          EXEC CICS REWRITE DATASET('INVENT')
                            FROM(INVENTORY-REC)
                            END-EXEC.
```

In the above example, we retrieve the inventory record for update. Then we create the current inventory record in the TD queue. Then we move the updates to the inventory record I/O area. Now the record contains the new information. So we create the after-image of the record into the TD queue and then issue a REWRITE to update the record.

After the CICS region has been shut down, you can then sort this VSAM ESDS file by the product code sequence. Since this TD queue records were created in the entry sequence by many CICS programs, the records are not in the product code sequence. After the ESDS file has been sorted, we can then use a COBOL batch program to print it. The report will show all the updates for any given product code from all CICS online systems like order entry, shipping, production, shipping, inventory control and purchasing.

6.4.3.   Submit JCL to Reader Queue From CICS

Most of CICS online systems can not be complete without batch programs. These batch programs perform report printing and batch update functions that are too expensive to be done in the CICS/VS region. However, the CICS users like to be able to request the execution of these batch jobs from the CICS online menu. Otherwise, you need to do it for them by submitting the batch JCL from the batch region.

You can accomplish this type of application requirement by defining the card reader (reader queue) as an extrapartition transient data queue. Then you can create CICS programs that issue the WRITEQ TD command to write the JCL statements as the queue records into this reader queue. When the JCL has been submitted to this reader queue from CICS/VS, it will be executed in the batch region just like it is submitted from the batch region. The reader TD queue should be defined as fixed-length (80 bytes per record) data set. Each queue record represents a JCL card. In order to submit a batch job, you need to issue more than one WRITEQ TD command, one for each JCL statement in the batch job.

Normally, you would display an online menu that contains all the batch jobs to be requested and ask the user to select one or more on the menu. When the user has made the selections, you would issue many WRITEQ TD commands for each job he selected. After all the JCL statements have been created in the reader queue, you can then send a message saying the jobs have been requested.

Since you can only execute the read-only batch jobs while CICS/VS is up, you must make sure the JCL for the batch update jobs will only be executed after the CICS/VS region has been shut down. This can be accomplished by specifying proper CLASS= in the JOB card.

The complete listing of this CICS program that submits the batch job JCL to the reader queue is in Chapter 13.12.

CHAPTER 7. OTHER CONTROL OPERATIONS

In this chapter, we'll discuss other CICS control operations from a designer viewpoint. These control operations are as follows:

7.1. Program Control
The Program Control operation allows you to transfer the control from the present program to the next one (XCTL), link to a subroutine program (LINK), load and release a CICS constant table dynamically (LOAD and RELEASE), return the control to the next higher level (RETURN), abend the CICS task (ABEND), and transfer control to a label within the CICS program or to an abend-handling program (HANDLE ABEND).

7.2. Task Control
The Task Control operation allows you to suspend the execution of a CICS task (SUSPEND), enqueue a CICS resource (ENQ) or dequeue a resource (DEQ).

7.3. Interval Control
The Interval Control operation allows you to start a CICS transaction (START), retrieve the data passed from the starting CICS program (RETRIEVE), cancel a future task (CANCEL), synchronize the time and date of CICS to OS/VS (ASKTIME), request the posting when the time has expired (POST), delay the processing of a task (DELAY), suspend a task until the time has expired (WAIT EVENT).

7.4. Storage Control
The Storage Control operation allows you to acquire and release a data area defined in LINKAGE SECTION (GETMAIN and FREEMAIN).

Before we start to discuss how to use the above CICS control operations, we need to know how a CICS task is initiated. There are four ways you can initiate a CICS task:

1. Entering a transaction code on a clear screen.
   For example, you can enter the transaction code of a menu program to invoke the menu program. This method is normally used to initiate the menu screen.

2. A transaction can be initiated when the trigger level specified in the DCT has been reached.
   For example, we will create a record in an intrapartition transient data queue. When this record is created, CICS will check to see if the total number of records in the queue has reached the trigger level specified in the DCT entry for the queue. If it has, the transaction code specified in that DCT entry will be initiated. This will invoke its associated CICS program of that transaction code. This technique is called Automatic Task Initiation (ATI).

3. Interval Control
   You can issue a START command with TRANSID option to initiate a CICS transaction. After the transaction in the TRANSID option is initiated, the CICS program associated with that transaction is invoked. For example, you can issue

a START command to initiate a CICS print transaction to print the sales order.

4. RETURN command with TRANSID option.

This is normally used after the SEND MAP command is issued and you want to return the control to CICS and post the transaction of this CICS program to this terminal. Any response to this terminal will initiate that transaction. In result, the associated CICS program of that transaction will be invoked and it should issue a RECEIVE MAP command to receive the input data entered on the terminal into the CICS program. This technique is called pseudo conversational programming which is required by all CICS shops to code CICS programs that perform terminal I/O operations.

In the following sections, we'll discuss all these CICS control operations.

7.1   Program Control

The Program Control operation allows you to control the execution of a CICS program. There are seven CICS commands in this Program Control operation:

1. XCTL

It allows you to pass the control from the present CICS program to the next one at the same level without expecting the control to return. For example, after the function number and a valid customer number have been entered on the menu screen, we want to pass the control from the customer menu program to the customer update program to display that customer for update. In this case, the XCTL command should be used.

2. LINK

It allows you to link to a CICS subroutine program. After the execution of that subroutine program has finished, the control is expected to return to the very next statement following the LINK command. For example, the customer editing CICS program can be used in both the customer create program and customer update program. Then you can create this editing program as a subroutine program which will be linked by these two CICS main programs. The data you need to pass to this subroutine program is the map I/O area that contains the new or update fields. Following the LINK command in the main program, you should then check to see if any invalid input field exists.

3. LOAD

This command allows you to load a CICS constant table into LINKAGE SECTION of the CICS program. After the table has been loaded, you can then access the table contents. If a table (i.e. store table) will be changed very frequently, then you should consider to set it up as a CICS constant table. When the table is changed, you only need to reassemble the table and you do not need to recompile all CICS programs that use this table since the table is loaded into the program dynamically.

4. RELEASE

After the table that was loaded through the use of the LOAD command is no longer needed, it should be deleted through the use of this RELEASE command. After the command is issued, the table is no longer available to this CICS program. If no RELEASE command is issued, the table will be released at the termination of the CICS task.

5. RETURN

This command is used to return the control from a CICS main program to CICS, or from a subroutine CICS program to the linking main program. A transaction can be specified if you expect the response from the terminal user to complete a transaction. When the RETURN command is executed, the task is terminated.

6. ABEND

This command terminates a CICS task abnormally. It is normally used in the error-handling routine within the CICS program to terminate the task. When a CICS task is terminated this way, a storage dump will be created in the dump dataset and the transaction backout program will be called in to back out protected resources (CICS files with LOG=YES).

7. HANDLE ABEND

This command allows the CICS program to continue the execution when an abend is to occur. You should try to back out the CICS resources or collect the error information for debugging in the abend-handling program or routine specified in this HANDLE ABEND command and then issue an ABEND command to terminate the task.

7.1.1. XCTL Command

This command passes the control from the current CICS program to the next one at the same level. Data can also be passed to the next program in the communication area. After this command has been executed, the current CICS program will be terminated and the next one will be invoked. However, the CICS task is not terminated. So a CICS task can execute more than one CICS program. The EIBTRNID still contains the same transaction code after the XCTL command is executed. Since a majority of CICS on-line systems are menu-driven systems, this command is used in the menu program to pass the control from the menu program to the other CICS program in the same system (i.e. customer update program). It can also be used in the other CICS program (i.e. customer update program) to pass the control back to the menu program when the desired function (customer update) is completed. This command has the following format:

```
EXEC CICS XCTL PROGRAM(name)
               [COMMAREA(data-area) LENGTH(data-value)]
               END-EXEC.

Exceptional condition: PGMIDERR
```

PROGRAM(name) sppecifies the next program to be invoked. The program name must be specified in the PPT. Otherwise, PGMIDERR condition occurs. The program name must be one to eight characters long.

COMMAREA(data-area) specifies the communication area that contains the data to be passed to the next program. After the next program is invoked, the passed data is in DFHCOMMAREA of LINKAGE SECTION of that program. CICS will address DFHCOMMAREA for you so you can access DFHCOMMAREA as soon as the program is invoked.

LENGTH(data-value) specifies the length of the communication area that is to be passed to the next program. If COMMAREA option is specified, the LENGTH option is required. You should check the length of DFHCOMMAREA used in the next program to define your communication area in the current program. If the next program uses 100 bytes for its DFHCOMMAREA in LINKAGE SECTION, then you should define the communication area as 100 bytes no matter how small the data is to be passed. The communication area used in the next program normally contains the data passed from the current program and the data needed to be saved between the SEND MAP and the RECEIVE MAP commands.

The following example shows we want to pass the control from the menu program to the customer update program. The customer number entered on the menu screen will be passed to the customer update program. Assume that the length of DFHCOMMAREA of the Customer Update program is defined as 100 bytes long.

In the Menu program:

```
WORKING-STORAGE SECTION.
01   COMM-AREA.
     02   CA-CUST-NO     PIC X(5).
     02   FILLER         PIC X(95).
PROCEDURE DIVISION.
     .... PASS CONTROL TO UPDATE PROGRAM ....
     MOVE SPACES       TO COMM-AREA.
     MOVE WS-CUST-NO TO CA-CUST-NO.
     EXEC CICS XCTL PROGRAM('UPDPGM')
                    COMMAREA(COMM-AREA)
                    LENGTH(100)
                    END-EXEC.
```

In the Update program UPDPGM:

```
LINKAGE SECTION.
01   DFHCOMMAREA.
     02   CUST-NO     PIC X(5).
     02   OTHER-DATA PIC X(95).
PROCEDURE DIVISION.
     IF EIBTRNID = 'UPDT' AND EIBCALEN = 100
        GO TO 200-RECEIVE-MAP.
     EXEC CICS READ DATASET('CUSTMAST')
                    INTO(CUST-RECORD)
                    RIDFLD(CUST-NO)
                    END-EXEC.
```

In the above example, we allocate a 100-byte communication area in the menu program because the length of DFHCOMMAREA for the customer update program is 100 bytes long. After the customer update program is invoked, the customer number is in DFHCOMMAREA. CICS will address DFHCOMMAREA for you so you can use the customer number passed (CUST-NO) as soon as the update program is invoked. We use this customer number to read the customer master file.

7.1.2. LINK Command

This command is used to link from a CICS main program to a subroutine CICS program and after the execution of this subroutine program is completed, the control is to return to the next statement following the LINK command in the main program. You should issue a RETURN command without any other option as the last statement in the subroutine program to return to the main program. When a group of codes is to be used in more than one CICS programs, you can create a subroutine program to contain only this group of codes. Then the CICS programs that need to perform this group of codes can issue a LINK command to invoke the subroutine program. The data can be passed from the CICS main program that issues the LINK command to the subroutine program through the communication area (COMMAREA option in the LINK command).

The subroutine CICS program should not issue any SEND MAP or RECEIVE MAP command to perform any terminal I/O operations. If you try to issue a RETURN command with TRANSID option in a subroutine program, an INVREQ (invalid request) condition will occur. This is because you can only issue a RETURN command with TRANSID option when you are at the highest level. The subroutine program is one level lower than the issuing CICS main program.

There is no difference between setting up a subroutine program and a normal CICS main program. You still need to set up its PPT entry. No PCT entry is needed for this subroutine program since no transaction code is to be used to invoke this program. It can only be invoked through the LINK command. No HANDLE AID command should be issued since no terminal I/O operatios are to be performed. However, you can still set up HANDLE CONDITION command since other CICS operations can be used.

How do you determine when you need a subroutine CICS program? For example, the customer editing program can be used by the customer create program and customer update program. We can then set up this customer editing program as a subroutine CICS program which will be linked (LINK) by both the customer create and the customer update programs. The data needs to be passed to this subroutine program is the map I/O area (the symbolic map) which contains the input data to be edited.

However, the LINK command will generate many CALL subroutines. Therefore, you should try to avoid using LINK command whenever you can. If the subroutine program is very small, you should repeat it in the main programs instead of using the LINK command.

When the LINK command is issued, the subroutine program still belongs to the same CICS task and no change will be made on the EIBTRNID. The subroutine CICS program is one level lower than the issuing CICS main program. You can not only pass the data from the main program to the subroutine CICS program, but also pass the data updated by the subroutine program to the main program after the control has returned to the main program. The communication area updated by the subroutine program can be accessed by the main program after the control has returned to the main program.

The LINK command has the following format:

```
EXEC CICS LINK PROGRAM(name)
               [COMMAREA(data-area) LENGTH(data-value)]
               END-EXEC.

Exceptional condition: PGMIDERR
```

PROGRAM(name) specifies the name of the subroutine program that is to be linked to. The program name must be in the PPT. Otherwise, PGMIDERR condition occurs.

COMMAREA(data-area) specifies the communication area that contains the data to be passed to the subroutine program. This area can also be used to pass the data back to the linking main program. After the subroutine program is invoked, the data passed will be in DFHCOMMAREA of LINKAGE SECTION within the subroutine program. CICS will address DFHCOMMAREA for you when the subroutine program is invoked so you can access the data passed after the linked program is invoked.

LENGTH(data-value) specifies the length of the communication area that contains the data to be passed to the subroutine program. If COMMAREA option is specified, LENGTH option must also be specified. You should use the length of DFHCOMMAREA in the subroutine program in this LENGTH option.

The following example shows we want to link to a subroutine program named EDITPGM to perform the editing:

Linking CICS main program:

```
WORKING-STORAGE SECTION.
01  AXCU03I COPY XXCU03.
PROCEDURE DIVISION.
    EXEC CICS LINK PROGRAM('EDITPGM')
                   COMMAREA(AXCU03I)
                   LENGTH(1920)
                   END-EXEC.
```

Linked Subroutine program EDITPGM:

```
WORKING-STORAGE SECTION.
01  AXCU03I COPY XXCU03.
LINKAGE SECTION.
01  DFHCOMMAREA     PIC X(1920).
PROCEDURE DIVISION.
    MOVE DFHCOMMAREA TO AXCU03I.
    .... EDIT INPUT FIELDS IN AXCU03I ...
    EXEC CICS RETURN END-EXEC.
```

After the subroutine program is completed, a RETURN command should be issued to return the control to the next statement following the LINK command in the linking program. The length of the communication area specified in the LINK command should be equal to that of DFHCOMMAREA in the subroutine program.

7.1.3.   RETURN Command

This command is used to return the control from the current CICS program to the other CICS program at the next higher level or to CICS/VS. After this command is issued at the highest level, the CICS task is terminated. A CICS task can only be terminated by the RETURN command or by CICS/VS itself (i.e. abend). If this RETURN command is issued in a linked subroutine program, the control is returned to the next statement following the LINK command of the main program. After the control returns to the main program, it will execute the next statement following the LINK command. If the RETURN command is issued in a CICS program at the highest level, the control is returned to CICS/VS. After the control returns to CICS, the terminal user should enter the next transaction. For example, you enter a CICS transaction code to invoke the menu program. Then this menu program is at the highest level. If you issue a RETURN command without any other option, the control is returned to CICS/VS. Following that, CICS will try to interpret the first four characters of the next input data as the transaction code. If the user does not enter a valid transaction, CICS will send a message saying this is not a valid transaction.

This RETURN command also allows you to post the next transaction to be initiated when the response is made to the terminal. You will issue a RETURN command with TRANSID option after the SEND MAP command has been issued. This will terminate the CICS program, and post the transaction of this CICS program on the terminal. Any response (enter updates or hit any control key) will initiate the transaction code we have post on that terminal.

The RETURN command has the following format:

```
EXEC CICS RETURN [TRANSID(name)
                 [COMMAREA(data-area) LENGTH(data-value)]]
                 END-EXEC.
```

```
Exceptional condition: INVREQ
```

TRANSID(name) specifies the transaction code to be initiated if the terminal user enters the input data or hits any control key on this terminal. You should issue a RETURN with TRANSID option following each SEND MAP command. This technique is called pseudo conversational programming.

COMMAREA(data-area) specifies the data area that contains the data to be passed to the program that is to be invoked by the transaction code specified in the TRANSID option. After the CICS program is invoked, the data passed to it is in DFHCOMMAREA of LINKAGE SECTION of this CICS program.

LENGTH(data-value) specifies the length of the communication area specified in the COMMAREA option. You should specify the length of DFHCOMMAREA for the next program to be invoked.

INVREQ condition occurs when you try to issue a RETURN command with TRANSID option in a CICS program that is not at the highest level. For example, you will get INVREQ condition if you try to issue a RETURN command with TRANSID option in a subroutine program (LINK command).

The following example shows how to return to CICS/VS from the customer menu program after the user has determined that he wants to get out of this system. The menu program is invoked by entering the menu transaction code on a clear screen. Therefore, the menu program is at the highest level (so does the customer update program since XCTL is used).

```
EXEC CICS RETURN END-EXEC.
```

The following example shows how to return the control from the linked subroutine program to the linking main program. You should issue a RETURN command without any other option as the last statement in a subroutine program:

```
EXEC CICS RETURN END-EXEC.
```

The following example shows how to issue a SEND MAP command to send the menu screen and then return to CICS/VS with the transaction code of the menu program post on this terminal:

```
        LINKAGE SECTION.
        01  DFHCOMMAREA     PIC X(100).
        PROCEDURE DIVISION.
            IF EIBTRNID = 'MENU' AND EIBCALEN = 100
                GO TO A200-RECEIVE-MAP.
            .... PREPARE FOR INITIAL SEND MAP ....
            EXEC CICS SEND MAP('AXMENU') MAPSET('XXMENU')
                    ERASE CURSOR END-EXEC.
            EXEC CICS RETURN TRANSID('MENU')
                            COMMAREA(DFHCOMMAREA)
                            LENGTH(100)
                            END-EXEC.
        A200-RECEIVE-MAP.
            EXEC CICS RECEIVE MAP('AXMENU') MAPSET('XXMENU')
                            END-EXEC.
```

In the above example, we issue a RETURN command with TRANSID option after we have sent the map to the terminal. This will terminate this CICS program and post the transaction code of this CICS program on this terminal. The data to be passed to the next session is saved in the communication area. When the user enters the input data or presses any control key, the transaction MENU will be initiated. This will invoke this CICS program once again since we specify MENU to point this menu program in the PCT. This time, you should go to issue a RECEIVE MAP command to receive the input data into the CICS program for editing. This type of processing is called pseudo conversational programming and is required by all data centers to code the CICS programs.

After you have issue a SEND MAP command, you should always issue a RETURN command with TRANSID option to terminate the CICS program and post the transaction of this program on that terminal. Any response to that terminal will initiate that transaction specified in the TRANSID option and that CICS program will be invoked. After that CICS program is invoked again, you should go to issue a RECEIVE MAP command to receive the input data or the control key.

The reason we want to issue the RETURN command with TRANSID option between the SEND MAP and RECEIVE map command is we do not want to tie up the CICS resources allocated to this task. If we do not issue this RETURN command between the SEND MAP and RECEIVE MAP command, that CICS program will be waiting for the user to response to that terminal. If the user goes out to lunch and never come back to enter the response, the RECEIVE MAP command will never be executed. All resources allocated for this CICS task will be wasted. But if you issue a RETURN with TRANSID option, the CICS task will be terminated and all its resources will be released. The control will be returned only after the response has been made on the terminal.

7.1.4. LOAD Command

This command is used to load a constant table (i.e. store table) into LINKAGE SECTION of a CICS program. Before you can load a constant table, the following steps must have been taken:

1. Write an assembler batch program to catalog the constant table in the CICS load module library. This program contains many DC statements to define and load the table contents.

2. Put the table name (load module program ID) into the PPT. There is no need to set up the PCT entry. The table name will then be used in the LOAD command.

3. Define the table in LINKAGE SECTION of the CICS program. Since the table is to be loaded dynamically, you need to set up an address pointer in the pointer list and a 01-level data area to define this table.

After the table has been set up in the CICS system and in the CICS program, you can then use the LOAD command load this table into LINKAGE SECTION. After it has been loaded, you can use it. When the table is no longer needed, you should delete this table by issuing a RELEASE command.

Why and when do you need to set up a table this way? If a table is very small, the contents of the table are changed very frequently, or the fast access time is needed, then you should set up the table this way. When you issue a LOAD command to load a table, the main storage will be used. The main storage is a precious CICS resource so you should not try to load a big table. The access time in the main storage is many times faster than in auxiliary storage (disk). When a table is to be used by many CICS programs and requires very fast access time, you can set up the table this way. For example, you set up a security table that is to be used by all CICS programs to check to user's authority of using the system.

The LOAD command has the following format:

```
       EXEC CICS LOAD PROGRAM(name)
                     [SET(pointer-ref)]
                     [LENGTH(data-area)]
                     [HOLD]
                     END-EXEC.
```

Exceptional condition: PGMIDERR

PROGRAM(name) specifies the constant table name. It must be one to eight characters long and must be specified in the PPT. This is also the load module name you specify for this table when you try to catalog it in the CICS load libaray.

SET(pointer-ref) specifies the pointer that addresses this constant table defined in LINKAGE SECTION. After the LOAD command is issued, the data area addressed by this pointer contains the table.

LENGTH(data-area) specifies the length of this constant table. If the table is to be changed frequently, you should not specify the length. So when the table is changed, you do not need to change the length and recompile this CICS program.

HOLD specifies the table is to be held until the RELEASE command is issued. If HOLD is not specified, the table will be deleted after the CICS task is terminated normally or abnormally. So if a table should exist until the CICS region is shut down, then you should specify HOLD option.

PGMIDERR condition occurs when the table name specified in the PROGRAM option is not in the PPT. You should create a PPT entry for each constant table set up. No PCT entry is needed for a constant table.

The following example shows how to load a store table into a CICS program. Each entry in the store table contains the store number and location. We want to get the location for any given store number:

```
    LINKAGE SECTION.
    01  DFHCOMMAREA        PIC X(100).
    01  BLL-CELLS.
        02  FILLER         PIC S9(8) COMP.
        02  STOR-TBL-PTR   PIC S9(8) COMP.
    01  STORE-TABLE.
        02  STORE-TOT-NUMBER   PIC 9(4).
        02  STORE-ENTRY OCCURS STORE-TOTAL TIMES.
            03  STORE-NO        PIC 9(3).
            03  STORE-LOCATION PIC X(20).
    PROCEDURE DIVISION.
        EXEC CICS LOAD PROGRAM('STORTBL')
                       SET(STOR-TBL-PTR)
                       END-EXEC.
        MOVE STORE-TOT-NUMBER TO STORE-TOTAL.
        SEARCH STORE-ENTRY
              WHEN STORE-NO = WS-STORE
                  MOVE STORE-LOCATION TO WS-LOCATION
                  GO TO STORE-FOUND.
```

In the above example, we define the store table in LINKAGE SECTION. We set up a pointer (STOR-TBL-PTR) to address the store table (STORE-TABLE). The table contains the total number of entries and store entries. Since the total number of entries in the store table will be increased everyday. You should define the OCCURS using a variable (STORE-TOTAL) and the value of this variable will be determined only when the table is loaded. The total number of stores is the first data field in this table. When the total number of table entries is increased, the user will increase this number while adding the new entries. After the LOAD command is issued, you should move the total number of entries in the table to the variable specified in the OCCURS. Then you can use the data in the table.

If you do not want to increase the number of entries in the table, then you can define the table without the total number of entries as follows:

```
LINKAGE SECTION.
01  DFHCOMMAREA         PIC X(100).
01  BLL-CELLS.
    02  FILLER          PIC S9(8) COMP.
    02  STOR-TBL-PTR    PIC S9(8) COMP.
01  STORE-TABLE.
    02  STORE-ENTRY         OCCURS 40 TIMES.
        03  STORE-NO    PIC 9(3).
        03  STORE-LOCATION PIC X(20).
PROCEDURE DIVISION.
    EXEC CICS LOAD PROGRAM('STORETBL')
                   SET(STOR-TBL-PTR)
                   END-EXEC.
    MOVE STORE-NO(1) TO STORENOO.
    MOVE STORE-LOCATION(1) TO LOCATO.
```

If the table is greater than 4096 bytes, then you need to set up one additional pointer for every 4096 bytes of storage. After the LOAD command is issued, you'll get the address for the first pointer. You need to add 4096 to the first pointer in order to get the address of the second pointer and so on:

```
01  BLL-CELLS.
    02  FILLER      PIC S9(8) COMP.
    02  PTR-1       PIC S9(8) COMP.
    02  PTR-2       PIC S9(8) COMP.
01  STORE-TABLE.
    02  STORE-ENTRY         OCCURS 300 TIMES.
        03  STORE-NO        PIC 9(3).
        03  STORE-LOCATION PIC X(20).
PROCEDURE DIVISION.
    EXEC CICS LOAD PROGRAM('STORETBL')
                   SET(PTR-1)
                   END-EXEC.
    COMPUTE PTR-2 = PTR-1 + 4096.
*   NOW YOU CAN ACCESS ANY ENTRY IN THE TABLE
    MOVE STORE-LOCATION(300) TO LOCATO.
```

7.1.5. RELEASE Command

This command is used to delete the table that was loaded into the main storage by the LOAD command. When the table is no longer needed, you should issue a RELEASE command to delete the table and release the main storage it occupies. A table will be deleted by CICS when the CICS task is terminated normally or abnormally if HOLD option was not specified in the LOAD command. If HOLD is specified in the LOAD command, you can only delete this table through the use of the RELEASE command. In this case, CICS will not delete the table when the task is terminated.

The RELEASE command has the following format:

```
EXEC CICS RELEASE PROGRAM(name) END-EXEC.

Exceptional condition: PGMIDERR
```

PROGRAM(name) specifies the table to be deleted. If the name is not on the PPT, PGMIDERR condition occurs.

The following example shows how to delete the store table:

```
EXEC CICS RELEASE PROGRAM('STORTBL') END-EXEC.
```

7.1.6. ABEND Command

This command is used to terminate the CICS program abnormally. When a data exception occurs, CICS will abend the task with ASRA abend code. When an exceptional condition occurs and that exceptional condition and ERROR are not specified in the HANDLE CONDITION command, CICS will take the default action for that exceptional condition which is normally to abend the task. If that exceptional condition is not specified but ERROR is specified in the HANDLE CONDITION command, control will go to the label set up for the ERROR. In the ERROR routine, you should issue the ABEND command to abend the task.

When an abend occurs, CICS will produce a storage dump in the current dump dataset and call in Dynamic Transaction Backout program to restore you VSAM files and other protected CICS resources back to the status when the task was started.

However, if you use HANDLE CONDITION or HANDLE ABEND command to set up labels or CICS program to handle these error conditions. In this case, the abend will not be performed by CICS and you are responsible to abend the task yourself. The control will go to the label or program you specify in these two commands. In the routing that handles the error condition, you should perform house-keeping, error message printing and the issue an ABEND command to terminate the task abnormally. If you issue a RETURN command instead of an ABEND command, the task will be terminated normally. In this case, the storage dump and dynamic transaction backout will not be performed by CICS since CICS assumes the task is completed normally. If the ABEND command is issued, the task will be terminated abnormally. In results, CICS will create the storage dump and perform the backout for that task.

In the production CICS system, the storage dump producted by the CICS task abend is the only way to notify the CICS programmer about the problems within the CICS programs. If you issue a RETURN command to terminate the CICS task when an exceptional condition occurs, you will never know the problem.

If the transaction backout is not performed, your VSAM files may be out of sync. The ABEND command will make sure the task is terminated abnormally. In results, the VSAM files updated by this task will be backed out so you can re-enter the same CICS transaction after you have fixed the problem.

The ABEND command has the following format:

```
EXEC CICS ABEND [ABCODE(name)] [CANCEL] END-EXEC.
```

ABCODE(name) specifies that the task-related storage is to be dumped and the name of this dump. The dump code is used to identify the dump for this task and it may consist of up to four characters. The dump data set consists of many storage dumps. You can use the task number, the transaction code, and the dump code to identify your own dump.

CANCEL specifies that you want to cancel all exits at any level in the task set up by the HANDLE ABEND command. If you have issued any HANDLE ABEND command prior to this ABEND command, then you should specify this CANCEL option to terminate the task right here. If the HANDLE ABEND command has been set up and the CANCEL option is not specified in the ABEND command, the control will go to the label or program set up in the HANDLE ABEND command.

The following example shows we want to abend the task when the VSAM file is not in normal condition:

```
EXEC CICS HANDLE CONDITION
          ERROR(900-ERROR)
          NOTFND(500-NOT-FND)
          END-EXEC.
EXEC CICS READ DATASET('CUSTMAST')
               INTO(CUSTOMER-REC)
               RIDFLD(CUST-NO)
               END-EXEC.
.... PROCESS THE RETRIEVED CUSTOMER ....
500-NOT-FND.
    .... CUSTOMER NOT FOUND ....
900-ERROR.
    EXEC CICS ABEND ABCODE('CU03') END-EXEC.
```

If the error condition is a recoverable condition, you may not want to abend the task. For example, the NOTOPEN condition occurs in a read-only CICS task, you do not need to issue an ABEND command to abend the task since this is a recoverable condition and there is no need to product a storage dump for CICS programmers. You only need to notify the user and terminate the task normally using a RETURN command. The user can then call the computer operator to open the file and try again. The following example shows we want to notify the terminal user and terminate the task normally when the customer file is not open:

```
        EXEC CICS HANDLE CONDITION
              NOTOPEN(900-NOT-OPEN)
              NOTFND(910-NOT-FND)
              ERROR(920-ERROR)
              END-EXEC.
        EXEC CICS READ DATASET('CUSTMAST')
                INTO(CUSTOMER-REC)
                RIDFLD(CUST-NO)
                END-EXEC.
        .... PROCESS THE RETRIEVED CUSTOMER ....
  900-NOT-OPEN.
        MOVE 'CUSTOMER FILE NOT OPEN' TO WS-MSG.
        EXEC CICS SEND FROM(WS-MSG) LENGTH(WS-MSG-LENG)
                ERASE END-EXEC.
        EXEC CICS RETURN END-EXEC.
```

In short, the ABEND command is normally issued in the error-handling routine or program to abend the task in order to get the storage dump and dynamic transaction backout.

7.1.7.   HANDLE ABEND Command

You can set up exit routine or program to which the control is to branch when CICS is to abend the task. For example, we can set up a common routine that will print the error message and then terminate the task when CICS is about to terminate the task abnormally. So when the CICS programmer tries to debug the abend, he can look at the error message printed in addition to the storage dump. Normally, the error message printed is all you need to determine the problem of a CICS abend. Only if you cannot determine the problem this way, you read the storage dump.

For example, you try to add 1 to a numeric field that contains alphabetic data, CICS will try to abend this task with ASRA abend code. Since you have set up the HANDLE ABEND command, the abend will not be performed and the control will go to the label or program you set up in the HANDLE ABEND command. In this label or program, you can print the abend location and then abend the task using the ABEND command.

If you do not issue a HANDLE ABEND command, then the CICS task will be abended with a storage dump. The CICS programmer can only look at the storage dump to debug the abend. The error message that is to be printed can contain the abend location within the CICS program, VSAM file name, CICS command, exceptional condition, return code, terminal ID, transaction code, CICS program ID, date, time, operator ID and more. From the error message printed, you may not need to read the dump in order to debug this abend.

However, when the control is transferred to the label specified in the HANDLE ABEND command, you should issue an ABEND command to terminate the CICS task after the error message has been printed. This way, CICS will product the storage dump and perform the backout for this task. If the program is specified instead, then CICS will abend the task for you after the program has been executed.

The HANDLE ABEND command has the following format:

```
EXEC CICS HANDLE ABEND {PROGRAM(name)|LABEL(label)|
                        CANCEL|RESET}
                        END-EXEC.
```

Exceptional condition: PGMIDERR

PROGRAM(name) specifies the CICS program to be given control when a CICS abend is to occur. That CICS program name must be in the PPT. Normally, there is one such abend-handling program in the entire CICS shop so every CICS program can use it to handle the abend. This abend-handling program will be linked by the issuing CICS program and it should use EIB fields for that task to print the error message and then issue a RETURN command to return to the program that caused the abend. After the control has been returned, CICS will then abend the task for you. Therefore, unlike using the label, CICS will abend the task if program is specified in the HANDLE ABEND command.

LABEL(label) specifies the label within this CICS program to which the control is to be branched when a CICS abend is to occur. The difference between using the label and the program in the HANDLE ABEND command are:

1. It is more difficut to pass the abend location to the abend-handling program if you specify a program instead of a label. But you can set up a label within the CICS program and then issue an XCTL command within that label to invoke the abend-handling program and pass the abend location to it. The abend location is normally identified by the paragraph number.

2. CICS will abend the task for you if PROGRAM is specified in the HANDLE ABEND command. However, you need to issue an ABEND command yourself if you use the LABEL.

3. CICS will use the LINK command to link to the program you specify and use GO TO to branch the control to the label if a label is specified.

CANCEL specifies the exit set up by the previous HANDLE ABEND command within this CICS program is to be ignored. If more than one HANDLE ABEND command have been issued, you should specify this option to de-activate the exits set up by previous HANDLE ABEND commands.

RESET specifies that an exit cancelled by a previous HANDLE ABEND CANCEL command is to be reactivated.

PGMIDERR

This condition occurs when the program specified in the PROGRAM option is not in the PPT.

The following example shows we want to start a transaction that will print the error message when the CICS abend is to occur:

```
        EXEC CICS HANDLE ABEND
                LABEL(900-ABEND-ROUTINE)
                END-EXEC.
        .... WS-CTR CONTAINS LOW-VALUE ....
        ADD 1 TO WS-CTR.
        ....
   900-ABEND-ROUTINE.
        .... MOVE EIB FIELDS INTO ERROR-MSG ...
        EXEC CICS START TRANSID('PRNT')
                     FROM(ERROR-MSG)
                     LENGTH(100)
                     TERMID('K01P')
                     END-EXEC.
     EXEC CICS ABEND ABCODE('CU03') END-EXEC.
```

In the above example, we add 1 to WS-CTR which contains LOW-VALUES. Therefore, CICS will abend this task. However, we have set up a label (900-ABEND-ROUTINE) within this program to handle the abend. So the control will go to the label named 900-ABEND-ROUTINE. This routine will start a CICS print transaction PRNT which will print the error information we've stored in ERROR-MSG and then issue an ABEND command to abend the task. You have to issue an ABEND command in order to product a storage dump and perform the dynamic transaction backout for this task. However, you only need to issue a RETURN command if an abend-handling program is specified in the PROGRAM option. In this case, after the control is returned from this abend-handling program, CICS will abend the task for you.

The following example shows how to set up a common abend-handling CICS program that can be used in all CICS programs:

```
    EXEC CICS HANDLE ABEND
                    PROGRAM('ABPGM')
                    END-EXEC.
    ... WS-CTR CONTAINS LOW-VALUES ...
    ADD 1 TO WS-CTR.
```

When we try to add 1 to WS-CTR, abend is to occur and the abend-handling program named ABPGM will be linked (LINK command) to by this CICS program. In this abend-handling CICS program ABPGM, you should use EIB fields of this task to collect and print the error message and then issue a RETURN command to return the control to the CICS program that causes the abend. If this CICS program is at the highest level, CICS will abend the task for you. Therefore, you do not need to issue an ABEND command in this ABPGM program. When the abend-handling program is invoked, it is still in the control of the same CICS task as the CICS program that caused the abend. Therefore, you can get information from EIB fields. However, it is more difficult to pass information (like abend location) from the abended CICS program to this abend-handling program. That is the reason you should try to use the following technique:

```
      EXEC CICS HANDLE ABEND
                     LABEL(900-ABEND)
                     END-EXEC.
      ADD 1 TO WS-CTR.
      ....
  900-ABEND.
      .... MOVE ERROR INFOMATION TO ERROR-MSG ...
      EXEC CICS XCTL PROGRAM('ABPGM')
                     COMMAREA(ERROR-MSG)
                     LENGTH(100)
                     END-EXEC.
```

In the abend-handling program ABPGM you should print the error information from
EIB fields and data in DFHCOMMAREA passed from the abended CICS program. Then
you need to issue an ABEND command in the program ABPGM to terminate the task.
This way all CICS programs can XCTL to this abend-handling program and pass the
error information to it. The error information needs to be printed by the abend-handling
program is:

1. abend location within the CICS program.
    You should define a data field that is to contain the current paragraph identifier
    (i.e. 'A100') and pass it to that abend-handling program.

2. the last resource name used (EIBRSRCE).
    If the resource is a file, it contains the data set name (as in EIBDS). For TD or TS
    queues, it contains the queue name. For Terminal Control commands, it contains
    the terminal ID. From the contents of this field, we know the last CICS command
    we issued.

3. the record key (passed from the abended CICS program).
    Sometimes, a particular record may cause the abend. The key can identify that
    record.

4. the CICS command that caused the abend (EIBFN).
    This EIBFN field identifies the last CICS command issued. It is a 2-byte data field.
    In this abend-handling program, you should use the EIBFN value table in the IBM
    manual to translate this field into the CICS command issued.

5. the return code (EIBRCODE).
    This is a 6-byte field that contains the return status of the last CICS command
    issued. You can use this field to determine what exceptional condition caused the
    abend. You should use the return code table in the IBM manual to translate this
    field into the exceptional condition raised by the last CICS command.

6. the terminal ID (EIBTRMID).
    This field contains the terminal ID associated with the abended task.

7. the date and time-of-day (EIBDATE and EIBTIME).

8. the operator ID (ASSIGN OPID).

   You can use ASSIGN command to get the operator ID signed on to this terminal. So you can call him and ask any question you may have regarding the abended task.

9. Transaction ID (EIBTRNID).

10. CICS program ID.

    The program ID can be passed from the abended program through the communication area.

11. CICS task number (EIBTASKN).

    You can use this task number to identify its storage dump in the dump dataset in case you need to read the storage dump.

If you can start a print transaction in this abend-handling CICS program to print the above error information and then issue an ABEND command to terminate the task, the CICS programmer can determine the cause of the abend from this error message right away. If there is no printer delicated to the CICS abend messages, you can define an extrapartition TD queue and write the error message to this queue in the abend-handling program instead of printing it in the printer. After the CICS/VS region is shut down at 5 PM, you can then sort and print this queue (sequential data set) by the program ID or transaction code.

7.2.   Task Control

There are three commands in this group:

1. SUSPEND

   This command is used to suspend the execution of the current task and transfer the control to the CICS tasks with higher priority. Upon the completion of all CICS tasks with higher priority, the execution of the current task will resume at the statement following the SUSPEND command. This command is used in a processor-intensive CICS program to prevent the program from monopolizing the CPU.

2. ENQ

   This command is us+ed to enqueue a CICS resource (like printer) for exclusive use by this CICS task. If the resource is being used by another task while the ENQ command is issued, ENQBUSY condition occurs.

3. DEQ

   This command is used to release the exculsive control of a CICS resource that is enqueued through the ENQ command. As soon as the resource is no longer needed by this task, you should issue a DEQ command to release the exculsive control of the resource, so other CICS tasks waiting for this resource can use it.

7.2.1.   SUSPEND Command

CICS/VS executes CICS tasks concurrently according to priority assigned to each CICS task. The priority of a CICS task is the combination of the transaction priority (specified in the PCT), the terminal priority (specified in the TCT) and the operator priority (specified in the SNT). 1 is the lowest priority and 255 is the highest. If the combination of all these three priorities is greater than 255, 255 is assumed. A CICS task with highest priority is executed when it is ready to be processed. The control is returned to CICS/VS when there are no more tasks to be executed.

The SUSPEND command is used to give up the control of the processor for the current task to allow tasks with higher priority to proceed. When there are no more tasks with higher priority to execute, the control returns to this task. When a CICS task is given control, it will execute until a CICS command is issued. When a CICS command is issued, the control return to CICS for other CICS tasks waiting to be executed. If a CICS program does not issue any CICS command for a long period of time, it will monopolize the CPU unless you issue a SUSPEND command.

The SUSPEND command has the following format:

```
EXEC CICS SUSPEND END-EXEC.
```

If there is no task with higher priority waiting to be excuted when you issue this SUSPEND command, control will return to this task for execution.

7.2.2.   ENQ Command

CICS/VS is running under multiple-tasking environment, many CICS tasks can be processed concurrently. Therefore, sometimes it is necessary to schedule the use of a CICS resource to prevent more than one CICS task from using the same resource at the same time. For example, when a terminal user enters a valid customer number for update, you may want to allow only one user to update the same customer at any time. Then you can issue an ENQ command to enqueue the customer number for the exclusive use of this task. When the second user tries to issue the ENQ command to enqueue the same customer number for update, the ENQBUSY exceptional condition occurs. We can then send a message to inform the second user that the customer is being updated and he should try it later. In this case, the customer number (5 bytes) is the resource that you should enqueue.

When you issue a READ command with UPDATE option, CICS will use this ENQ facility to enqueue the record you are going to update. When you issue a REWRITE, DELETE or UNLOCK command, CICS will use the DEQ facility to dequeue the record. But you only issue a READ command to display the record for update and you issue a READ command with UPDATE option only after the valid updates have been entered on the terminal. This create a gap for the second user to come in to display the same record for update. The second user may display the old record for update before the record is updated by the first user. So the second user can display the old customer and update the customer based on the old information. When he tries to issue a REWRITE command, the new record will not contain the updates made by the first user.

To resolve this problem, you can issue an ENQ command to enqueue the customer number before you display it on the terminal for update. If the customer number has been enqueued by the other user, ENQBUSY condition occurs. In this case, you can get out and inform the second user that the customer is being updated. However, the best way is to save the customer record you try to display and then pass it to the RECEIVE MAP session. When you are ready to update the customer, compare the old record with the one you have just retrieved through the READ command with UPDATE option. If both are the same, you should proceed to issue the REWRITE command. Otherwise, you should send a message saying that the customer is being updated. The customer update program logic is as follows:

```
LINKAGE SECTION.
01  DFHCOMMAREA  PIC X(200).
PROCEDURE DIVISION.
    IF EIBTRNID = 'CU02' AND EIBCALEN = 200
       GO TO A200-RECEIVE-MAP.
    .... READ THE CUSTOMER ...
    EXEC CICS SEND MAP('AXCU02') MAPSET('XXCU02')
           ERASE CURSOR END-EXEC.
*   SAVE CUSTOMER RECORD IN COMM AREA FOR LATER COMPARE
    EXEC CICS RETURN TRANSID('CU02')
                     COMMAREA(CUSTOMER-REC)
                     LENGTH(200)
                     END-EXEC.
A200-RECEIVE-MAP.
    EXEC CICS RECEIVE MAP('AXCU02') MAPSET('XXCU02')
              END-EXEC.
    .... EDIT UPDATES ...
    IF ANY-INVALID-INPUT-EXISTS
       GO TO A300-BAD-INPUT-DATA.
*   UPDATE CUSTOMER
    EXEC CICS READ DATASET('CUSTMAST')
                   INTO(CUSTOMER-REC)
                   RIDFLD(CUST-NO)
                   UPDATE
                   END-EXEC.
*   COMPARE CUSTOMER RECORD CONTENTS
    IF CUSTOMER-REC NOT = DFHCOMMAREA
       GO TO A400-DOUBLE-UPDATE.
    ... MOVE UPDATES TO CUSTOMER-REC ...
    EXEC CICS REWRITE DATASET('CUSTMAST')
                      FROM(CUSTOMER-REC)
                      END-EXEC.
A400-DOUBLE-UPDATE.
    EXEC CICS UNLOCK DATASET('CUSTMAST') END-EXEC.
    MOVE 'THIS CUSTOMER IS BEING UPDATED, TRY IT LATER'
         TO WS-MSG.
    EXEC CICS SEND FROM(WS-MSG) LENGTH(WS-MSG-LENG)
              ERASE END-EXEC.
    EXEC CICS RETURN END-EXEC.
```

When you try to use the SEND FROM command to print an on-line report, you may want to enqueue the printer upon which the report is to be printed until the entire report has been printed to prevent other users from using the same printer. This way, the report of the other user will not mix with yours. Since the SEND FROM command can only print up to 1920 bytes of data to the printer. If your report is bigger than 1920 bytes, more than one SEND FROM command must be issued. The ENQ command should be used before you issue the first SEND FROM command to enqueue the printer. If ENQBUSY condition occurs, you should send a message saying that the printer is in use and the user should try it later. In this case, the printer ID is the resource that you should enqueue. If you use the START command to initiate a print transaction and more than one START command is needed to print the entire report, you should try to ENQ the printer before you issue the first START command.

If you use message routing technique to print an on-line report, you do not need to enqueue the printer since the report will be printed in its entirety before the second report will be printed.

You can also issue an ENQ command to enqueue a CICS program, so only one user can use it at any time. This may become necessary when the CICS program is a processor-intensive program. If the second task tries to enqueue the same CICS program, the ENQBUSY exceptional condition occurs. In this case, you can send a message to the terminal to inform the second user that this CICS program is being used and he should try it later. In this case, the program ID (8 bytes) is the resource you should enqueue.

The ENQ command has the following format:

```
EXEC CICS ENQ RESOURCE(data-area) [LENGTH(data-value)]
              END-EXEC.
```

Exceptional condition: ENQBUSY

RESOURCE(data-area) specifies the resource that is to be enqueued. This resource may be a customer number, a printer ID, a program ID or any thing that can uniquely identify this resource.

LENGTH(data-value) specifies the length of the data area that is specified in the RESOURCE option.

ENQBUSY

This condition occurs when the resource that is to be enqueued is in use. That means the resource has been enqueued by other task. When this condition occurs, you should issue a SEND FROM command to inform the user that the resource is not available and then issue a RETURN command to terminate the CICS program. After the user has seen the message, he should hit the CLEAR key to erase the message and he is ready to enter the next CICS transaction. If you do not set up this ENQBUSY condition when you issue an ENQ command and the resource has been enqueued by other CICS task, this CICS task will be suspended until the resource is dequeued by the task that enqueued it. That means the user's terminal will be hung waiting for the resource to become available. If the resource is available while you issue an ENQ command, the control will return to the next statement following the ENQ command.

The following example shows we want to enqueue the customer number to be updated so only one user can update the same customer number at any time. This ENQ command should be issued before you try to read and display the customer for subsequent update. If the customer number is being used, we will notify the user the situation:

```
WORKING-STORAGE SECTION.
01   CUST-NO        PIC X(5).
01   WS-MSG         PIC X(40).
01   WS-MSG-LENG    PIC S9(4) COMP VALUE +40.
PROCEDURE DIVISION.
     EXEC CICS HANDLE CONDITION
               ENQBUSY(900-CUST-IN-USE)
               END-EXEC.
     EXEC CICS ENQ RESOURCE(CUST-NO) LENGTH(5) END-EXEC.
     .... CUSTOMER IS OK FOR READ, DISPLAY AND UPDATE ....
     .... AFTER UPDATE IS COMPLETED ....
     EXEC CICS DEQ RESOURCE(CUST-NO) LENGTH(5) END-EXEC.

900-CUST-IN-USE.
     MOVE 'CUSTOMER IS IN USE, TRY IT LATER' TO WS-MSG.
     EXEC CICS SEND FROM(WS-MSG) LENGTH(WS-MSG-LENG) ERASE
               END-EXEC.
     EXEC CICS RETURN END-EXEC.
```

In the above example, we set up the ENQBUSY condition in the HANDLE CONDITION command. We then try to enqueue the customer number to be updated. If this customer number has been enqueued by the other CICS task that uses this CICS program, the ENQBUSY condition occurs. In this case, we should notify the user that the customer number is being updated by other user and issue a RETURN command to terminate the program.

7.2.3.   DEQ Command

The DEQ command is used to release the exclusive control of the resource that has been enqueued through the use of the ENQ command. After the resource is no longer needed, you should issue a DEQ command to release the exclusive control of the resource, so other CICS tasks waiting for this resource can use it. If a CICS task was suspended because the resource was not available, it will become dispatchable when the resource is dequeued. The DEQ command has the following format:

```
EXEC CICS DEQ RESOURCE(data-area) [LENGTH(data-value)]
          END-EXEC.
```

If the resource you try to dequeue does not exist, this command will be ignored. No exceptional condition will occur for this DEQ command. After the resource is no longer needed, you should issue a DEQ command to release the resource. If a CICS task enqueues a resource but does not issue a DEQ command, the resource is released when the task is terminated. The following example shows how to dequeue the customer we have just enqueued in the preceeding example:

```
EXEC CICS DEQ RESOURCE(CUST-NO) LENGTH(5) END-EXEC.
```

7.3. Interval Control

CICS/VS Interval Control operations perform time-controlled functions. These functions will be executed at the exact time specified. When the time specified expires, the function will be performed. There are total of seven Interval Control commands, but only two are used most often: the START and RETRIEVE commands.

The START command is normally used to start a transaction to print a report. For example, you want to print the sales order after the sales order is created. You can then issue a START command in the sales order create program to initiate a CICS transaction code which will invoke the sales order print program. The sales order number can be passed in the START command to the transaction to be started.

You can also use the START command in a screen refreshing application to initiate the same transaction at a specified time interval after you have displayed the latest information on the screen. For example, the airline company wants to display the latest information about the departure and arrival time of the flights. After this CICS program is invoked, it will go get the information and display it on the terminal, issue a START command to initiate itself within 30 seconds and then terminate itself. When the 30-seconds time interval has expired, this program will be initiated. It will display the latest information again, issue a START command to initiate itself within 30 seconds, and terminate itself. This way, the CICS program only needs to be initiated once and it will start itself every 30 seconds to display the latest information.

The RETRIEVE command is used in the started program to retrieve the data passed to it from the CICS program that issues the START command. For example, after the sales order print program is invoked, it should issue a RETRIEVE command to retrieve the sales order number passed to it by the sales order create program. Then it should use this sales order number to retrieve and print the order.

In addition to the START and RETRIEVE commands, there are five Interval Control commands: CANCEL, DELAY, POST, WAIT EVENT, and ASKTIME commands. These five commands are rarely used by CICS application programmers.

The CANCEL command is used to cancel the previous interval control command. If you have started a transaction at a future time, you can issue a CANCEL command to cancel that task before it is executed. For example, you can issue a CANCEL command in the screen-refreshing program to cancel the future transaction if the user decides to cancel the screen-refreshing session for any reason.

The DELAY command suspends the execution of the issuing task for a period of time or until a special time has expired. After the excution of this DELAY command, the task will be suspended. When the time has expired, it will become dispatchable.

The POST command requests notification when a specified time has expired. CICS/VS will reset a data area with special values to indicate that the time specified in the POST command has expired. It is the responsibility of the issuing CICS program to check the contents of this data area to see if the time has expired or to issue a WAIT EVENT command to suspend the processing of the task until the time has expired.

The WAIT EVENT command is used to suspend the processing of a task until the time specified in the previous POST command has expired. The combination of issuing the POST command and the WAIT EVENT command has the same effect as the DELAY command. However, using the POST command allows you to perform other jobs while checking if the time has expired.

The ASKTIME command will update the CICS/VS time-of-day and EIBTIME and EIBDATE of the issuing task. CICS will copy the date and time-of-day from OS/VS or DOS/VSE.

In the following sections, we'll discuss these seven Interval Control commands in greater details.

7.3.1.   START Command

This command is used to initiate a transaction at a specified time. When the time expires, the transaction specified will be initiated. When a CICS transaction is initiated, its associate CICS program specified in the PCT will be invoked. Data can be passed from the issuing CICS program to the associated program of the initiated transaction in the START command. If data is to be passed, the RETRIEVE command should be issued in the invoked CICS program to retrieve the data passed. The START command is normally used to start a CICS print transaction. If the Message Routing technique is to be used in the print program, no TERMID option should be specified in the START command since the ROUTE command should set up the printer list. If the SEND FROM command is to be used to print the report, then you should specify the printer in the TERMID option in the START command.

The START command can also be used in the screen-refreshing applications to initiate itself at a specified interval. After the START command is executed, a new CICS task will be initiated when the specified time expired. However, the execution of the issuing task will continue at the next statement following the START command.

The START command has the following format:

```
EXEC CICS START  [INTERVAL(hhmmss) |INTERVAL(0) |TIME(hhmmss)]
                 TRANSID(name)
                 [REQID(name)]
                 [FROM(data-area)  LENGTH(data-value)]
                 [TERMID(name)]
                 END-EXEC.

Exceptional conditions: TERMIDERR, TRANSIDERR
```

INTERVAL(hhmmss) specifies the interval to be elapsed before this transaction is to be initiated. hh means hour, mm means minute, and ss means second. For example, INTERVAL(013010) specifies that this transaction is to be initiated in one hour, 30 minitues and 10 seconds.

INTERVAL(0) specifies that the transaction is to be initiated immediately. This is the default. Normally, you will not specify INTERVAL and take the default (INTERVAL(0)) when you try to start a print transaction. The report will be printed immediately.

TIME(hhmmss) specifies the time of day the transaction is to be initiated. For example, TIME(153000) specifies this transaction is to be initiated at 3:30 PM.

TRANSID(name) specifies the transaction to be initiated when the time expires. This transaction code must be in the PCT. Otherwise, TRANSIDERR occurs. This is a required option.

REQID(name) specifies the request identification for this START command. You only need to specify this option when you may need to issue a CANCEL command to cancel this future task later. This name field should be defined as a 8-byte alphameric field (PIC X(8)). You can get the request ID from EIBREQID field after the START command is executed. For example, you can issue a START command with this option using the terminal ID (EIBTRMID) as the request name in the screen-refreshing program. When the user decides to cancel the session, you can issue a CANCEL command with the terminal ID in the REQID option to cancel the future task.

FROM(data-area) specifies a data area that contains the data to be passed to the started transaction. For example, you can pass the sales order number to the sales order print program using this FROM option. If no data is to be passed, FROM option can be omitted. In the started program, you should issue a RETRIEVE command to retrieve the data passed.

LENGTH(data-value) specifies the length of the data area specified in the FROM option. This option is required if the FROM option is specified.

TERMID(name) specifies the terminal or printer to be associated with this task. A CICS task can be initiated with or without a terminal associated with it. If a CICS task is initiated without a terminal, then you cannot monitor its execution through CEDF. For example, you can start a print transaction without specifying the TERMID option, then this print program should use Message Routing technique to set up the printer in the route list as the destination of the message. If you start a transaction using the printer in the TERMID option, then you can issue the SEND FROM command to print the report. The terminal ID is a 4-byte field and must be defined in the TCT.

TERMIDERR condition occurs when the terminal specified in the TERMID option is not in the TCT.

TRANSIDERR condition occurs when the transaction code spacified in the TRANSID option is not in the PCT.

When the FROM option is specified in a START command, CICS will use the temporary storage to store the data to be passed to the started program.

The following example shows how to start a print transaction to print an on-line report on the printer K01P:

```
EXEC CICS START TRANSID('PRNT')
                FROM(SALES-ORDER-NO)
                LENGTH(5)
                TERMID('K01P')
                END-EXEC.
```

In the above example, we specify the transaction PRNT is to be initiated immediately. The data to be passed to the started print program is the sales order number. The length of this sales order number is 5 bytes long. The printer associated with this print transaction is K01P. So in the print program, you only need to issue the SEND FROM command to send the output data. CICS/VS will then use its associated terminal (printer K01P) to print the report. In order to monitor the excution of this print program using CEDF transaction, you should enter 'CEDF K01P' on the second terminal before the START command is issued by the first terminal. This way, the CEDF displays for this print program will be displayed on the second terminal.

If you do not want to specify the TERMID option in the START command, then no terminal is associated with this task. In this case, there is no way you can monitor the execution of this started task under CEDF. In order to test this type of CICS tasks under CEDF, you should change the CICS program to use the RECEIVE INTO command to receive the input data to this program for your testing. After you have completely tested this started program, you can then change it back so it can be started by the START command. If no TERMID option is specified in the START command, you need to use the Message Routing technique to set up the destination for the output message in order to print the report.

In the screen refreshing application, you need to start the same transaction at a specified time interval after you have issued the SEND MAP command. You need to specify the present terminal in the TERMID option, so the SEND MAP command will send the CICS map to this display terminal. You can also use the EIBTRMID as the request ID in the REQID option of the START command so you can cancel the future task using the request ID when the terminal user decides to stop the screen refreshing displays.

In the started program, you should perform read-only operations. No update operations should be performed since the started task will be a new task. If this started task is abended, backout will only be performed for this started task and no backout will be performed for the task that issues the START command. Therefore, your files may be out of sync. This is the reason why you should not start a transaction that will update VSAM files.

If the started transaction is a print transaction, you should consider the re-print capability for this report. That means, you should always allow the user to be able to start this transaction from the menu screen. In case the printer jammed during the report printing, you can start this task again from the menu screen.

7.3.2.   RETRIEVE Command

This command is used within the started CICS program to retrieve the data passed from the CICS program that issued the START command. For example, we start a print transaction within the sales order create program to print the sales order. The sales order number is the data specified in the FROM option of the START command. After the started program is invoked, it should issue a RETRIEVE command to retrieve the sales order. The data area specified in the FROM option of the START command should have the same format as that specified in the INTO option of the RETRIEVE command.

When the started program is invoked, you should issue the RETRIEVE command to retrieve the data and then process the retrieved data. After the retrieved data has been processed, you should go back to issue another RETRIEVE command to retrieve the next data for the next task. For example, two users have started the sales order print transaction from two different terminals and both want to print the sales order in the same printer named K01P. The data stored in the temporary storage will contain two sales orders. One RETRIEVE command can only retrieve data for one task. So more than one RETRIEVE command should be issued to process all data in the temporary storage. When there are no more data in the temporary storage, ENDDATA condition occurs. In this case, you should issue a RETURN command to end this started program. This type of design will save some loading time for this started program since it process data stored by more than one task.

The RETRIEVE command has the following format:

```
EXEC CICS RETRIEVE {SET(pointer-ref)|INTO(data-area)}
                    LENGTH(data-area)
                    END-EXEC.
```

Exceptional conditions: ENDDATA, LENGERR, NOTFND

INTO(data-area) specifies the data area that is to store the data to be retrieved. The data area must be defined in WORKING-STORAGE SECTION.

SET(pointer-ref) specifies an address pointer that is used to address the data area defined in LINKAGE SECTION. The data area will be used to store the data to be retrieved.

LENGTH(data-area) specifies the length of the data area to be used to store the data to be retrieved. You should move the actual length of the data you try to retrieve into this data area before you issue this RETRIEVE command. If the length you specified in this LENGTH option is less than the actual length of the data retrieved, LENGERR condition occurs.

ENDDATA

This condition occurs when there is no more data to be retrieved. When this condition occurs, you should issue a RETURN command to terminate this task. It is a good practice to go back to issue a RETRIEVE command after the current task has been processed. Since many users may request the same CICS transaction at the same time. Therefore the temporary storage may contain more than one record. Each record represents a new task. When you try to retrieve the record for the next task and there are no more records, ENDDATA condition occurs.

LENGERR

This condition occurs when the length of data you specified in the LENGTH option is less than the actual length of the data retrieved.

NOTFND

This condition occurs when no data was passed from the CICS program that issued the START command. That means no FROM option was specified in the START command.

The following example shows how to retrieve the sales order number passed from the sales order create program discussed in the preceeding section:

```
WORKING-STORAGE SECTION.
01  ORDER-NO    PIC X(5).
01  ORDER-LENG  PIC S9(4) COMP VALUE +5.
PROCEDURE DIVISION.
    EXEC CICS HANDLE CONDITION
            ENDDATA(900-EOJ)
            END-EXEC.
100-READ-NEXT-RECORD.
    EXEC CICS RETRIEVE INTO(ORDER-NO)
                    LENGTH(ORDER-LENG)
                    END-EXEC.
    .... PRINT THE SALES ORDER ....
    GO TO 100-READ-NEXT-RECORD.
900-EOJ.
    EXEC CICS RETURN END-EXEC.
```

The above example is a typical started CICS program. We set up ENDDATA condition in the HANDLE CONDITION command to handle no-more-record condition. We then issue a RETRIEVE command to retrieve the sales order number passed to this program. Then we print the sales order we've just retrieved and then go back to get the next one. If many users request the same transaction (PRNT) at the same time, this print program can be used to print all sales orders stored for it. This will save CICS/VS some valuable time to load and unload the print program. When there are no more records to be retrieved, ENDDATA condition occurs. In this case, you should issue a RETURN command to terminate this program.

7.3.3.   CANCEL Command

This command can be used to cancel the request made through the use of the POST, DELAY or START command. For example, in the screen refreshing application, if the terminal user decides to terminate the screen refreshing sessions, then the CANCEL command can be issued to cancel the future task that is to be initiated on this terminal when the specified time interval has expired. Before you can issue a CANCEL command, your START, POST, or DELAY command must be issued with REQID option. The request identifier in the REQID option should then be used in the CANCEL command to cancel that request.

The CANCEL command has the following format:

```
EXEC CICS CANCEL [REQ(name) [TRANSID(name)]] END-EXEC.

Exceptional conditions: NOTFND, INVREQ
```

REQID(name) specifies the identification of the request that is to be cancelled. This option must be specified if you want to cancel the request made by the START, DELAY or POST command. No REQID option is required when you try to cancel a POST command issued by the same task.

TRANSID(name) specifies the transaction identification that is to be cancelled. This transaction ID must be on the PCT. When you try to cancel a START command, you should specify both REQID and TRANSID options.

INVREQ

This condition occurs when CICS/VS has determined this CANCEL command is invalid.

NOTFND

This condition occurs when the request identifier specified in the REQID option cannot be found.

The following example shows how to start a screen refreshing program and then cancel the future task when the user decides to terminate the sessions:

```
.... GET LATEST INFOMATION FROM VSAM FILE ....
.... DISPLAY INFOMATION ON TERMINAL ...
EXEC CICS SEND MAP('TIMEINF') MAPSET('TIMEINA')
          ERASE CURSOR END-EXEC.
.... START ITSELF IN 30 SECONDS ....
EXEC CICS START TRANSID('REFH')
                INTERVAL(000030)
                REQID(EIBTRMID)
                TERMID(EIBTRMID)
                END-EXEC.
.... TERMINATE THE CURRENT TASK ....
EXEC CICS RETURN END-EXEC.
```

When the user hits CLEAR key to cancel the screen refreshing session, you should issue the following to cancel the future task:

```
EXEC CICS CANCEL REQID(EIBTRMID) TRANSID('REFH') END-EXEC.
```

In the above examples, we get the latest information from the VSAM files and then display it on the associated terminal. Then we start this transaction (REFH) in 30 seconds and then terminate the current task. The user can see the latest information on the terminal now. When 30 seconds has elapsed, this program will be initiated again to display the latest information and start itself in 30 seconds. We use the terminal ID as the request ID so we can cancel the future task if we have to. When the user hits the CLEAR key on the terminal, we will issue a CANCEL command to cancel this future task. In this CANCEL command, we specify the terminal ID as the request identification and the transaction ID of the task to be cancelled.

7.3.4. ASKTIME Command

This command is used to update the CICS/VS time-of-day clock and the EIBDATE and EIBTIME fields. Each CICS task has its own EIB table. This EIB table consists of many EIB fields. EIBDATE contains the task starting date and EIBTIME contains starting time-of-day of the task. Normally, you'll issue this command before you issue any Interval Control command so the date and time-of-day of CICS/VS will be consistant with that of OS/VS or DOS/VSE.

```
EXEC CICS ASKTIME END-EXEC.

No exceptional condition.
```

7.3.5. DELAY Command

This command is used to suspend the processing of the issuing task for a time interval or until a specified time has expired. You'll not use this command very often. After the DELAY command is executed, the current task will be suspended until the specified time has expired. After the time has expired, the task becomes dispatchable. The DELAY command has the following format:

```
EXEC CICS DELAY [INTERVAL(hhmmss) |INTERVAL(0) |TIME(hhmmss)]
                [REQID(name)]
                END-EXEC.
```

```
Exceptional conditions: EXPIRED, INVREQ
```

INTERVAL(hhmmss) specifies the time interval for which the issuing task is to be suspended. For example, INTERVAL(003000) specifies that the task is to be suspended for 30 minutes.

INTERVAL(0) specifies this DELAY function is to supersede the previous POST command.

TIME(hhmmss) specifies that the issuing task is to be suspened until the specified time.

REQID(name) specifies the identifier of the request of this DELAY command. You should specify this option if you may need to cancel the DELAY command later. This request identifier must be specified in the CANCEL command in order to cancel this DELAY request.

EXPIRED

This condition occurs when the time specified in the DELAY command has already expired when this command is issued.

INVREQ

This condition occurs when CICS/VS has determined that this DELAY command is an invalid type of request.

The following example shows how to suspend the execution of the issuing task for 30 minutes:

```
EXEC CICS DELAY INTERVAL(003000) END-EXEC.
```

The following example shows how to suspend the processing of the task until 3:30 PM:

```
EXEC CICS DELAY TIME(153000) REQID(EIBTRMID) END-EXEC.
```

We specify the terminal ID as the request ID in the above example so we can cancel this DELAY command if we have to.

7.3.6.   POST Command

This command is used to request CICS/VS to update a data area when the time specified in the POST command has expired. The CICS program that issues this command should check this data area to see if it has been posted by CICS. If it has, the time has expired. You can also issue the WAIT EVENT command following the POST command to suspend the processing of the issuing task until the time has expired.

The POST command has the following format:

```
EXEC CICS POST [INTERVAL(hhmmss)|INTERVAL(0)|TIME(hhmmss)]
               SET(pointer-ref)
               [REQID(name)]
               END-EXEC.

Exceptional conditions: INVREQ, EXPIRED
```

INTERVAL(hhmmss) specifies the interval to be elapsed before the timer event control area is to be posted by CICS.

TIME(hhmmss) specifies the time the timer event control area is to be posted.

SET(pointer-ref) specifies the pointer that address the timer event control area. This area must be 4 bytes long. It contains low-values initially. When the specified time has expired, CICS/VS will set the first byte of this area to X'40' (space) and the third byte to X'80'. The issuing CICS program should check this area at intervals in order to find out if the time has expired.

REQID(name) specifies the identifier of the request for this POST command. This name must be up to 8 bytes long. You only need to specify this option when you need to issue a CANCEL command from other CICS task to cancel this POST command.

INVREQ

This condition occurs when CICS/VS has determined that this command type is invalid.

EXPIRED

This condition occurs when the time specified in the DELAY command has expired when this command is executed.

The following example shows how to issue a POST command:

```
WORKING-STORAGE SECTION.
01  WS-X80-BYTE-2  PIC S9(4) COMP.
01  F REDEFINES WS-X80-BYTE-2.
    02  FILLER     PIC X(1).
    02  WS-X80     PIC X(1).
LINKAGE SECTION.
01  DFHCOMMAREA    PIC X(100).
01  BLLCELLS.
    02  FILLER     PIC S9(8) COMP.
    02  PTR-1      PIC S9(8) COMP.
01  TIMER-EVENT-AREA.
    02  TIMER-BYTE-1 PIC X(1).
    02  FILLER       PIC X(1).
    02  TIMER-BYTE-3 PIC X(1).
    02  FILLER       PIC X(1).
PROCEDURE DIVISION.
    MOVE +80  TO WS-X80-BYTE-2.
    EXEC CICS POST INTERVAL(003000)
                SET(PTR-1)
                REQID(EIBTRMID)
                END-EXEC.
    ....
100-CHECK-EVENT.
    IF TIMER-BYTE-1 = ' ' AND TIMER-BYTE-3 = WS-X80
       GO TO 200-TIME-IS-UP.
    .....
    GO TO 100-CHECK-EVENT.
```

In the above example, we define a timer event control area in LINKAGE SECTION for CICS/VS to post when the time specified (within 30 minutes) has expired. We then issue the POST command to address this area. Then we check this area at intervals to see if CICS/VS has posted the new data in this area. If this area has been posted, we know the 30-minute interval has expired.

7.3.7.   WAIT EVENT Command

This command is used to suspend the processing of a task until the specified time has expired. This command is normally issued following the POST command to suspend the processing of a task for the time interval or until the time has expired. The POST command specifies the expiration time and the WAIT EVENT suspends the processing of the task. The combination of these two commands has the same effect as the DELAY command. However, the WAIT EVENT command can be issued other than the task that issued the POST command.

154

The WAIT EVENT command has the following format:

```
EXEC CICS WAIT EVENT ECADDR(pointer-ref) END-EXEC.
```

ECADDR(pointer-value) specifies the pointer value that addresses the timer event control area. When the time has expired, CICS/VS will update this area. The WAIT EVENT command will suspend the processing of this task until CICS/VS has post this area when the time specified in the POST command has expired.

The following example shows how to issue the POST and WAIT EVENT commands to suspend the processing of a task until the time has expired:

```
EXEC CICS POST INTERVAL(003000) SET(PTR-1) REQID(EIBTRMID)
          END-EXEC.
EXEC CICS WAIT EVENT ECADDR(PTR-1) END-EXEC.
```

This will suspend the processing of the task for 30 minutes.

7.4.   Storage Control

When you define the map I/O areas, record layout areas, or work areas in the LINKAGE SECTION, the storage they occupy will not be allocated until you issue a CICS command (i.e. READ command) with SET ootion or a Storage Control command named GETMAIN command. The data areas you define in WORKING-STORAGE SECTION will be allocated by CICS automatically when the CICS program is loaded. But the storage for a data area defined in LINKAGE SECTION will only be available after you have explicitly acquired it.

For example, you can issue a READ command with SET option to retrieve a VSAM record and place the retrieved record in a data area defined in the LINKAGE SECTION. The SET option in the READ command will load the address of the retrieved record in the pointer reference specified in the SET option. After the address has been set, you can access this data area in the LINKAGE SECTION. But you cannot access this data area before you issue the READ command with SET option. However, you may not want to issue the CICS command with SET option in order to acquire the area. For example, you try to move output data to a map I/O area defined in LINKAGE SECTION. In this case, you cannot move data into it before you acquire this area. So you need to issue the GETMAIN command to acquire this map I/O area before you move output data into it. When the storage area acquired by the GETMAIN command is no longer needed, you should issue a FREEMAIN command to release this storage area. If no FREEMAIN command is issued, the storage area will be released when the task is terminated normally or abnormally.

7.4.1.   GETMAIN Command

This command acquires a data area defined in LINKAGE SECTION. After the storage area has been acquired, you can then move data into it. For example, you define the symbolic description map in the LINKAGE SECTION, you need to issue a GETMAIN command to acquire this area before you can move the output data to this map I/O area. When yo try to create a new record to a VSAM file, you need to issue a GETMAIN command to acquire the record I/O area defined in LINKAGE SECTION before you can move the key and data into the record. If you define the intermediate data areas to be used in PROCEDURE DIVISION in LINKAGE SECTION, then you need to issue this GETMAIN command to acquire these work areas before you use them in PROCEDURE DIVISION. You should define all your intermediate work areas under one or more 01-level data areas, then issue a GETMAIN commad to acquire storage for each 01-level data area. You should always use a group name at 01-level for many small data fields.

When a GETMAIN command is issued, CICS will dynamically allocate the main storage for the area specified.

The GETMAIN command has the following format:

```
EXEC CICS GETMAIN SET(pointer-ref)
                  LENGTH(data-value)
                  [INITIMG(data-value)]
                  END-EXEC.
```

    Exceptional condition: NOSTG

SET(pointer-ref) specifies the pointer that addresses the data area to be acquired. The pointer-reference must be defined as a full-word binary (PIC S9(8) COMP).

LENGTH(data-value) specifies the length of the data area to be acquired. The length must be defined as a half-word binary field. The maximum length that can be specified is 32767 bytes (32K).

INITIMG(data-value) specifies an one-byte initial value in hexadecimal form to initilize the data area to be acquired.

NOSTG

This condition occurs when there are no main storages available for this request.

The following example shows we want to acquire three data areas defined in LINKAGE SECTION:

```
WORKING-STORAGE SECTION.
01  WS-SPACE            PIC X(1) VALUE SPACES.
LINKAGE SECTION.
01  DFHCOMMAREA         PIC X(200).
01  BLLCELLS.
    02  FILLER          PIC S9(8) COMP.
    02  MAP-PTR         PIC S9(8) COMP.
    02  CUST-REC-PTR    PIC S9(8) COMP.
    02  USER-AREA-PTR   PIC S9(8) COMP.
01  AXCU01I             COPY XXCU01.
```

```
01  CUSTMAST              COPY CUSTMAST.
01  USER-AREA.
    02  WS-CTR            PIC 9(3).
    02  WS-NAME           PIC X(20).
PROCEDURE DIVISION.
    EXEC CICS GETMAIN SET(MAP-PTR)
                      LENGTH(1920)
                      END-EXEC.
    MOVE LOW-VALUES   TO AXCU010.
    .... MOVE DATA TO MAP I/O AREA ...
    EXEC CICS GETMAIN SET(CUST-REC-PTR)
                      LENGTH(200)
                      INITIMG(WS-SPACE)
                      END-EXEC.
    .... MOVE KEY AND DATA TO CUSTMAST ...
    .... WRITE THE CUSTOMER RECORD ....
    EXEC CICS GETMAIN SET(USER-AREA-PTR)
                      LENGTH(23)
                      INITIMG(WS-SPACE)
                      END-EXEC.
    EXEC CICS SEND MAP('AXCU01') MAPSET('XXCU01')
              ERASE CURSOR END-EXEC.
    EXEC CICS RETURN TRANSID('CU01')
                     COMMAREA(COMM-AREA)
                     LENGTH(200)
                     END-EXEC.
100-RECEIVE-MAP.
    EXEC CICS RECEIVE MAP('AXCU01') MAPSET('XXCU01')
              SET(MAP-PTR) END-EXEC.
    .... EDIT MAP INPUT FIELDS IN MAP I/O AREA ...
```

In the above example, we define three areas in LINKAGE SECTION. Each area is addressed by a pointer reference in BLLCELLS. In order to access the area defined in LINKAGE SECTION, its pointer reference must contains the address of its data area acquired. When a CICS command with SET option is executed, the pointer reference specified in the SET option will be loaded with the address of the data area acquired. Before we can move output data to this map I/O area, we must issue a GETMAIN command. When you try to receive the input map into this map I/O area, you do not need to issue a GETMAIN command, you can just issue the RECEIVE MAP command with SET option. In this case, CICS will acquire this map I/O area for you automatically.

You do not need to count how big is your map I/O area, you only need to specify 1920 in the LENGTH option (24 x 80) since a 3270 model 2 map I/O area can contain up to 1920 bytes.

Using the same LINKAGE SECTION as in the above example, we can acquire a record area to be used for a new record:

```
EXEC CICS GETMAIN SET(CUST-REC-PRT)
                  LENGTH(200)
                  INITIMG(WS-SPACE)
                  END-EXEC.
```

```
... MOVE KEY AND DATA TO CUSTMAST ....
EXEC CICS WRITE DATASET('CUSTMAST')
               FROM(CUSTMAST)
               RIDFLD(CUST-NO)
               END-EXEC.
```

In the above example, we need to acquire the customer record area defined in LINKAGE SECTION before we can move key and data into it. You do not need to acquire this record area first when you want to retrieve a customer record into this area:

```
EXEC CICS READ DATASET('CUSTMAST')
               SET(CUST-REC-PTR)
               RIDFLD(WS-CUST-NO)
               END-EXEC.
.... DATA FIELDS IN CUSTMAST CAN NOW BE ACCESSED ...
```

In the above example, we issue a READ command with SET option. CICS will acquire this record area for you and put the retrieved customer into this area. However, you cannot use the key field within CUSTMAST in the RIDFLD option since the record area is not available when you try to issue the READ command. Therefore WS-CUST-NO must be defined in WORKING-STORAGE SECTION or must have been acquired through the GETMAIN command.

Using the same LINKAGE SECTION above, we can acquire the user area that contains intermediate fields to be used in PROCEDURE DIVISION:

```
EXEC CICS GETMAIN SET(USER-AREA-PTR)
                  INITIMG(WS-SPACE)
                  LENGTH(23)
                  END-EXEC.
MOVE 0 TO WS-CTR.
```

You should group all your intermediate fields under one or more 01-level group names. You should not try to acquire many small areas separately.

7.4.2.   FREEMAIN Command

When the main storage acquired through the GETMAIN command is no longer needed, you should release it as soon as possible through the FREEMAIN command. If a main storage area is not freeed through the FREEMAIN command, it will be freed when the task is terminated normally or abnormally.

The FREEMAIN command has the following format:

```
EXEC CICS FREEMAIN DATA(data-area) END-EXEC.

No exceptional condition.
```

DATA(data-area) specifies the data area to be released.

The following examples show how to release all three areas we have acquired in the preceeding examples:

```
EXEC CICS FREEMAIN DATA(AXCU01I) END-EXEC.
EXEC CICS FREEMAIN DATA(CUSTMAST) END-EXEC.
EXEC CICS FREEMAIN DATA(USER-AREA) END-EXEC.
```

If you define the file record area in LINKAGE SECTION, the storage acquired through
File Control command with SET option will be released when you issue a REWRITE,
DELETE, WRITE or UNLOCK command. For example, you issue a READ with
UPDATE and SET options to retrieve a customer for update and then issue a REWRITE
command with FROM option. After the REWRITE command is issued, the storage you
acquired through the READ command with UPDATE and SET options will be released
and all data in the record area will be lost.

CHAPTER 8.   ERROR HANDLING, BACKOUT AND RECOVERY

In this chapter, we'll show you how to handle the program error and how CICS will try to recover the protected resources when the task is abended.

8.1.   Error Handling

There are two major types of errors that may occur while executing a CICS program: data exception (with ASRA as abend code) and exceptional condition. The data exception normally is caused by trying to process a numeric field that contains alphabetic data or by accessing a data area defined in LINKAGE SECTION that has not been acquired (protection error). You do not need to code any routine within the CICS program to handle this type of errors (ASRA) since you only want to know the COBOL statement that caused the abend and the contents of the data fields in that COBOL statement at the time the data exception occurs (ASRA). If no HANDLE ABEND command is set up prior to the data exception, CICS will terminate this task abnormally. When a task is abended by CICS, CICS will produce a storage dump for this task and perform the dynamic transaction backout to restore the protected resources (i.e. VSAM files specified with LOG=YES in the FCT).

The storage dump will tell you which COBOL statement caused the abend and the contents of data fields within the statement at the time of the abend. So it is easier for you to read the storage dump that is produced by CICS when the transaction is abended. You should not specify the HANDLE ABEND command to handle the data exception. You just need to let CICS abend the task and read the storage dump for debugging.

The following example shows how you can handle the abend caused by data exception within your CICS program:

```
PROCEDURE DIVISION.
    EXEC CICS HANDLE CONDITION
              NOTFND(A900-NOTFND)
              ENDFILE(A910-ENDFILE)
              MAPFAIL(A920-MAPFAIL)
              ERROR(A930-ERROR)
              END-EXEC.
    EXEC CICS HANDLE AID
              CLEAR(A800-XCTL-TO-MENU)
              PF1(A820-NEXT-PAGE)
              PF2(A840-PREV-PAGE)
              ANYKEY(A920-MAPFAIL)
              END-EXEC.
    MOVE DFHCOMMAREA TO COMM-AREA.
    IF EIBTRNID = 'CU05' AND EIBCALEN = 100
        GO TO A200-RECEIVE-MAP.
A100-SEND-INIT-SCREEN.
    .... WS-CTR CONTAINS LOW-VALUES ...
    ADD 1 TO WS-CTR.
```

In the above example, we did not set up the HANDLE ABEND command. Therefore, CICS will abend the task when we try to add 1 to WS-CTR that contains LOW-VALUES. When the abend occurs, CICS will produce a storage dump and perform the backout. You can then use the storage dump with ASRA as the abend code to determine which COBOL statement caused the abend and the contents of WS-CTR at the time of the abend. So you should let CICS handle the data exception rather than using the HANDLE ABEND command to handle it yourself.

The second type of errors is the exceptional condition which may occur while executing a CICS command. If that exceptional condition (i.e. NOTFND) is specified in the HANDLE CONDITION command, the control will go to the label specified for that exceptional condition. If that exceptional condition (NOTFND) is not specified in the HANDLE CONDITION command and the general error condition ERROR is specified, the control will go to the label specified for ERROR. In the label specified for ERROR, you should XCTL to an abend-handling program (ABPGM) with the abend location. If both the exceptional condition (NOTFND) and ERROR are not specified in the HANDLE CONDITION command and no HANDLE ABEND command is issued, CICS will take the default action of that exceptional condition (abend the task for NOTFND). Normally the default action is to terminate the task abnormally which will produce a storage dump and cause dynamic transaction backout to be performed. The following example shows how to handle errors caused by the exceptional condition within your CICS program:

```
LINKAGE SECTION.
01  DFHCOMMAREA     PIC X(100).
PROCEDURE DIVISION.
    EXEC CICS HANDLE CONDITION
            NOTFND(A900-NOTFND)
            ENDFILE(A910-ENDFILE)
            MAPFAIL(A920-MAPFAIL)
            ERROR(A930-ERROR)
            END-EXEC.
    EXEC CICS HANDLE AID
            CLEAR(A800-XCTL-TO-MENU)
            PF1(A820-NEXT-PAGE)
            PF2(A840-PREV-PAGE)
            ANYKEY(A920-MAPFAIL)
            END-EXEC.
    MOVE DFHCOMMAREA TO COMM-AREA.
    IF EIBTRNID = 'CU04' AND EIBCALEN = 100
        GO TO A200-RECEIVE-MAP.
A100-SEND-INIT-SCREEN.
    MOVE LOW-VALUES  TO AXCU050.
    MOVE 0           TO WS-LINE-CTR.
    MOVE CA-CUSTNO   TO CUST-NO.
    MOVE 'A100'      TO CA-LOCATION.
    EXEC CICS STARTBR DATASET('CUSTMAST')
                    RIDFLD(CUST-NO)
                    END-EXEC.
A120-READNEXT-CUSTMAST.
    MOVE 'A120'      TO CA-LOCATION.
    EXEC CICS READNEXT DATASET('CUSTMAST')
                    INTO(CUSTOMER-REC)
                    RIDFLD(CUST-NO)
                    END-EXEC.
    ADD 1 TO WS-LINE-CTR.
```

```
     .... MOVE RETRIEVED CUSTOMER TO MAP ...
     IF WS-LINE-CTR < 15
         GO TO A120-READNEXT-CUSTMAST.
 A140-ENDBR-CUSTMAST.
     MOVE 'A140' TO CA-LOCATION.
     EXEC CICS ENDBR DATASET('CUSTMAST') END-EXEC.
 A160-SEND-MAP-ERASE.
     MOVE 'A160' TO CA-LOCATION.
     EXEC CICS SEND MAP('AXCU05') MAPSET('XXCU05')
             ERASE CURSOR END-EXEC.
     EXEC CICS RETURN TRANSID('CU05')
                     COMMAREA(COMM-AREA)
                     LENGTH(100)
                     END-EXEC.
 A200-RECEIVE-MAP.
     MOVE 'A200' TO CA-LOCATION.
     EXEC CICS RECEIVE MAP('AXCU05') MAPSET('XXCU05') END-EXEC.
     ....
 A900-NOTFND.
     IF CA-LOCATION = 'A100'
         MOVE 'NO MORE CUSTOMERS TO DISPLAY' TO MSGO
         GO TO A140-ENDBR-CUSTMAST.
     GO TO A930-ERROR.
 A910-ENDFILE.
     IF CA-LOCATION = 'A120'
         GO TO A140-ENDBR-CUSTMAST.
     GO TO A930-ERROR.
 A920-MAPFAIL.
     IF EIBAID = DFHENTER
         MOVE 'NO DATA WAS ENTERED' TO MSGO
     ELSE
         MOVE 'WRONG KEY WAS HIT'   TO MSGO.
     PERFORM B100-SEND-MAP-DATAONLY THRU
             B109-SEND-MAP-DATAONLY-EXIT.
 A930-ERROR.
     EXEC CICS XCTL PROGRAM('ABPGM')
                     COMMAREA(CA-LOCATION)
                     LENGTH(4)
                     END-EXEC.
```

In the above example, we set up NOTFND condition for the STARTBR command, ENDFILE condition for the READNEXT command, MAPFAIL condition for the RECEIVE MAP, and ERROR condition for general error condition. The setup of the ERROR condition in the HANDLE CONDITION command will enable us to be in control for any type of exceptional condition that may occur during the execution of a CICS command. However, it is your responsibility to abend the task in the label specified for ERROR since the control will go to the label specified for ERROR when the exceptional condition occurs. So after the control goes to A930-ERROR, you need to issue an ABEND command in the abend-handling program ABPGM. The ABEND command will abend the task and in results the storage dump of this task will be created and backout will be performed by CICS. Note that we move a unique location to CA-LOCATION in each paragraph and pass this location to the abend-handling program ABPGM. Therefore, the error message printed by ABPGM will contain the abend location.

After the abend-handling program ABPGM is invoked, it should print the error message and then issue an ABEND command to abend the task. If there is no CICS printer set up for error messages, you can use an extrapartition transient dataset to store these error messages produced by CICS transactions. After the CICS/VS has been shut down, you can then sort and print this extrapartition transient dataset (a sequential data set) by the transaction code. Then this report can be distributed to CICS programmers the next morning for debugging.

It is not recommand to use the HANDLE ABEND command to handle a CICS abend since the abends caused by data exception do not need any special handling. You only need to let CICS terminate the task abnormally and read the dump. For exceptional condition errors, you should use ERROR condition to take care of other exceptional conditions not specified in the HANDLE CONDITION command. If you want to use an abend-handling program to handle all CICS abends, then you can issue an XCTL command from the label specified for ERROR to transfer the control to this abend-handling program.

When you issue an XCTL command to go to an abend-handling program, both the issuing program and this abend-handling program belong to the same task. Therefore, you can still use the EIB fields to print the error message.

If there is no abend-handling program set up in your shop, then you should start a print transaction to print the error message and then issue an ABEND command yourself. The A930-ERROR routine in the above example can be replaced as follows:

```
A930-ERROR.
        .... MOVE ERROR INFORMATION TO ERROR-MSG ...
        EXEC CICS START TRANSID('PRNT')
                        FROM(ERROR-MSG)
                        LENGTH(ERROR-MSG-LENG)
                        TERMID('K01P')
                        END-EXEC.
        EXEC CICS ABEND ABEND('CU05') END-EXEC.
```

In the above example, we want to print the error information on the printer K01P by starting the print transaction PRNT. After the error message has been printed, we need to issue an ABEND command to abend the task. If you issue a RETURN command instead of an ABEND command, the task will be terminated normally and no storage dumping and backout will be performed. In this case, your VSAM files may be out of sync.

When a CICS task abends, CICS will call in dynamic transaction backout program to restore the VSAM files back to the status when the task is initiated or at the last syncpoint. A syncpoint is established when a task is started or when a SYNCPOINT command is issued. The backout process will enable you to re-enter the same transaction like nothing ever happened after you have fixed the problem. The dynamic transaction backout program is an option of CICS/VS. Most of the CICS shops enable this feature to protect the intergrity of the CICS resources. Your system programmer must specify LOG=YES for the VSAM files in the FCT. Otherwise, no backout will be performed on these VSAM files.

When a CICS task is abended, CICS will display the system abend message on the top portion of the screen. It would be better if you can print the error information in the local printer. If the error message is displayed on the terminal, the application programmer must rely on the user to report the problems. The abend message printed in the local printer can then be distributed to CICS programmers for debugging.

The error message to be printed should contain the following information:

1. The abend location within the CICS program.
   Before you issue any CICS command, you should move an unique number to a data field which will be used in the printed information to indicate where the abend occurred.

2. The last resource name used (EIBRSRCE).
   If the resource is a file, EIBRSRCE contains the file name. For TD and TS queues, it contains the queue name. For Terminal Control commands, it contains the terminal ID. From the contents of this field, we know the last CICS resource we used.

3. The key of the record in process (passed from the program that caused the abend).
   If it is the VSAM record that caused the abend, you should try to print the key of the record. Many times, the abend is caused by bad data within a particular record. Therefore, you should print the record key.

4. The last CICS command issued (EIBFN):
   If it is the exceptional condition that caused the abend, you can use EIBFN to determine the CICS command that caused this exceptional condition.

5. The return code of CICS command (EIBRCODE).
   When exceptional condition occurs during the execution of a CICS command, EIBRCODE indicates that exceptional condition.

6. The terminal ID associated with the task (EIBTRMID).

7. Starting date and time-of-day of the task (EIBDATE and EIBTIME).

8. The operator ID.
   The operator ID can be obtained as follows:

   ```
   WORKING-STORAGE SECTION.
   01  WS-OPERID     PIC X(3).

   EXEC CICS ASSIGN OPID(WS-OPERID) END-EXEC.
   ```

9. Transaction ID (EIBTRNID).

10. CICS Program ID.
    The program ID can be passed from the CICS program that caused the abend to the abend-handling program.

11. CICS task number (EIBTASKN).
   You can use the task number to identify the storage dump for this task.

You do not need to copy anything into WORKING-STORAGE SECTION in order to use EIB fields. They are available to you when the CICS task is initiated. EIB fields are unique for each CICS task. So when you issue an XCTL command to go to the abend-handling program, you are still in the same task. Therefore, you can still get the EIB fields for the abended program.

The error information is very important to CICS programmers since it indicates most of the abend causes on one or two print lines. In many cases, CICS programmers do not need to read the storage dump in order to debug the abend. The abend location in the error message tells you where the abend occurs within the program and it is the most important piece of information within the error messge. The EIBFN shows you the last CICS command issued. The EIBRCODE indicates the exceptional condition for the excution of the last CICS command. The EIBDS or EIBRSRCE indicates which VSAM file caused the abend. The record key can pin-point the record that contains the bad data.

If the error message still cannot tell you the problem of a CICS task abend, you may want to re-run the same transaction under CEDF or INTERTEST monitoring. When CEDF or INTERTEST is allowed in the production CICS system, normally no update on main storage is allowed. However, you do not need to modify the main storage in order to resolve the CICS abend. If CEDF and INTERTEST are not allowed in the production system, then you need to get the storage dump and start your debugging from the dump. The dump reading technique is very simple, we'll show you how to read a storage dump in Chapter 11.7.

If you specify PROGRAM option in the HANDLE ABEND command, no data can be passed through the communication area to the abend-handling program. Therefore, the most important piece of information (the abend location) cannot be passed to the program specified in the PROGRAM option. If you specify the LABEL option in the HANDLE ABEND command, you need to issue the ABEND command yourself after the control has been passed to the label specified in the LABEL option. CICS will not abend the task for you. However, if the PROGRAM option is specified, no ABEND command is needed in the abend-handling program since CICS will abend the task for your after the control is returned from this abend-handling program to the issuing program.

8.2.   SYNCPOINT

When a CICS task performs many file update operations for a long period of time, you may not want to expose the CICS task to the possibility of being backed out by CICS when an error is encountered. In this case, you can issue a SYNCPOINT command at the end of each Logical Unit of Work (LUW) to indicate that a syncpoint has been reached. If the dynamic transaction backout occurs when a task is abended, it only backs out the protected resources up to the last syncpoint and no backout will be performed beyong the last syncpoint. If no SYNCPOINT command is issued, the backout program will restore the protected resources to the status when the task is initiated. CICS considers the beginning of the task as a syncpoint. The SYNCPOINT command has the following format:

```
EXEC CICS SYNCPOINT END-EXEC.
```

However, before you can issue a SYNCPOINT command, you need to organize the updates to protected resources so a SYNCPOINT command can be issued at the end of an LUW. For example, you want to create a sales order detail for each sales order detail entered on the terminal. For each sales order detail, you need to add a detail record to the sales order detail file and update the total order amount of the sales order header in the sales order header file. In order to prevent CICS from backing out the detail record after it has been added to the detail file, you need to design your CICS program to add the detail record, update the total amount and then issue a SYNCPOINT command. Assume that the user can enter 15 details on the terminal. After we have received and edited the input map, we need to add those 15 details. If the CICS program abends while it tries to add the 15th record, CICS will only back out the updates to the detail and header files for the 15th detail. No backout will be performed for the 14 details we have added. Both the detail and header files are in sync when we issue a SYNCPOINT command. The total order amount is always equal to the total amount of the details added. So the section that adds a detail and updates the order total is considered a Logical Unit of Work.

If you do not update the total order amount after the creation of each detail record and you only update the total order amount when all 15 details have been created successfully, you should not issue a SYNCPOINT command after each detail has been created. The total order amount in the header file and detail file are not in sync after each detail record is created.

When a CICS task is started by a transaction code, the syncpoint is at the beginning of this task. If no SYNCPOINT command is issued, then the backout will restore the VSAM files back to the status when the task is started. If one or more SYNCPOINT commands are issued, the backout will restore the VSAM files back to the status when the last SYNCPOINT command was issued.

8.3.   Backout And Recovery

In addition to VSAM files, the following resources can also be backed out if they are defined as protected:

1. DL/I data bases
2. Intrapartitioned transient data sets
3. Auxiliary temporary storage
4. VTAM Terminal messages
5. TCT user area (TCTUA)
6. Communication area (COMMAREA).
7. TIOA (Terminal I/O Area).

CICS uses a dynamic log in main storage for each CICS transaction to store the before-image of the deleted or updated records. If the dynamic log is to small to hold these image records, temporary storage will be used. When dynamic transaction backout occurs, this dynamic log will be used to restore the VSAM files or DL/I data bases.

The temporary storage queues using the main storage (MAIN) will not be backed out when a CICS task abends. No recovery will be tried by Dynamic Transaction Backout program. So if your CICS program creates a temporary storage queue in main storage and then it abends. The temporary storage queue will still be existing (no backout) when you try to re-enter the same transaction. That is why it is a good practice to issue a DELETEQ TS command to purge any outstanding temporary storage queue using the main storage (MAIN) before you create the first record in it. For a protected auxiliary temporary storage queue, the queue will be backed out when the task abends to allow the re-enter of the same transaction.

When a CICS task is terminated by CICS abnormally, a task-related storage dump will be created in the current dump data set. Normally, there are two dump data sets (DFHDUMPA and DFHDUMPB) in the entire CICS/VS system and only one is active at any time. The task-related storage dump contains terminal I/O areas, file I/O areas, file work areas, program working storage used by that task and a trace table. The trace table is normally defined to contain 1000 entries.

Before you can print the storage dumps in the current dump dataset, you need to issue CSMT SWI to close the current dump dataset and switch the active one to the other one. Then you use the dump print utility program in the batch region to print the entire dump dataset. You can then use the transaction code, the abend code, or the task number to identify your own dump.

PART 2. **CICS/VS ONLINE SYSTEM DESIGN AND IMPLEMENTATION TECHNIQUES**

CHAPTER 9. APPLICATION DESIGN TECHNIQUES

In this chapter, we'll discuss the following topics regarding the CICS application design:

1. CICS screen design
2. CICS program design
3. Passing data amoung CICS programs
4. Security design
5. Transmit and Edit Input Data Only Once
6. Re-insert Technique

9.1.   CICS Screen Design

9.1.1.   Screen Layout

A CICS screen format normally consists of the following information:

1. Header Lines
2. Detail Lines
3. Control key Line
4. Message Line

The header lines may consist of the following information:

1. Transaction ID
   This is used by the terminal user or CICS programmer for communication purposes. You can get it from EIBTRNID. It is used to identify the screen. For example, CU02 is displayed on the customer update screen. So you can refer this screen as CU02 when you discuss the problems of this screen with your users. Some CICS shops define this field as the first named field in the mapset definition with ATTRB=(ASKIP,FSET). This way, MAPFAIL condition will never occur since the transaction ID will be received into the CICS program for every input operation.

2. Header title
   The title specifies the function to be performed for this screen. For example, you can specify 'CUSTOMER UPDATE' as the title in the header lines for the customer update screen.

3. Terminal ID:
   The terminal ID can be obtained from EIBTRMID. It can be used to identify the problem terminal for a CICS task. You can display this field on the terminal in case you need to monitor the execution of the CICS task running on this terminal.

4. Date and Time
   It is a good practice to display the date (CURRENT-DATE or EIBDATE) and time-of-day (TIME-OF-DAY or EIBTIME) on the screen so when the user presses the hard-copy key to print the screen contents, it always contains the starting date and time-of-day of the problem task.

The detail lines contain the detail information of the screen. For example, all the customer detail information will be displayed in the middle of the customer update screen.

The control key line contains the control keys to be used for this screen. For example, in the customer update screen, CLEAR=MENU specifies that the control is to return to the MENU screen when the CLEAR key is pressed. The control keys are used in almost every CICS on-line application. They are used for two major functions. One is to transfer the control from the current program to the next one. For example, CLEAR=MENU specifies the control should be transferred from the current customer update program to the menu program. The other function is to perform a pre-defined function. For example, PF1=NEXT PAGE in the control key line of the customer browse screen specifies that the next page of customers is to be displayed if PF1 is pressed.

The control key line is normally defined as ATTRB=(ASKIP,BRT) to catch user's attention. The control keys that can be specified are PA keys, PF keys, CLEAR key, and ENTER key.

The message line contains the instruction to tell the user what to do next or to inform him a situation. For example, if the input customer credit limit is not numeric, you can send a message to this message line to inform the user about that situation. The message line is normally defined as ATTRB=(ASKIP,BRT) to catch the user's attention.

Figure 9.1 shows the screen format for the customer inquire/update/delete program:

```
CU02  XX/XX/XX HH:MM     INQUIRE/UPDATE/DELETE A CUSTOMER        XXXX

CUSTOMER NO  : 99999

CUSTOMER NAME: XXXXXXXXXXXXXXXXXXXX

CREDIT LIMIT : 9999999

INVOICE AMT  : 9999999


                              NEXT CUSTOMER NO: 99999

CLEAR=MENU, PF1=DELETE
XXXXXXXXXXXXXXXXXXXXXXXXXXXXXXXXXXXXXXXXXXXXXXXXXXXXXXXXXXXXXXXXXXXXXXXXXXXXX
```

Figure 9.1. Inquire/Update/Delete A Customer

9.1.2. Map Field Define

An attribute byte will be assigned to each CICS map field. Therefore, you need to allow one byte of space in the screen layout for each map field. You should not define a map field that starts with the first column of the first line on the screen, since there is no space to put its attribute byte. If you define the transaction code in POS=(01,01), the first byte of line 1 will be used by its attribute byte.

However, you can use 80th byte of line 24 as the last byte of a map field. For example, we normally define the message line with POS=(24,01),LENGTH=79. The message line will start with column 2 and its last byte will be at column 80.

We normally define a stopper to stop the user from entering more data on an unprotected field than it is defined. For example, we define the customer number with LENGTH=5 and ATTRB=NUM. This customer number is defined as five bytes long and is an unprotected numeric field. However, the user can enter more than five bytes of data on this field if there is no other field defined within one-byte range. So we will define a stopper following an unprotected field. You should not define a named map field which is two bytes apart from an unprotected map field. Since you need to define a stopper for the unprotected field to prevent the user from entering more data than it is defined. In order to define a stopper, you need to have at least three bytes apart between the unprotected field and the next map field. If you have only two bytes, it will be too small for a stopper, since the second byte is occupied by the attribute byte of the next map field and two actual bytes are needed to define this stopper field (one for the attribute byte and the other for +he stopper itself). If there is only one byte apart between an unprotected field and the map field that immediately follows, then no stopper is needed since the attribute byte of the map field that follows will occupy this byte and serve as a stopper.

The following example shows why two bytes apart between the unprotected customer number and the credit limit should be avoided:

```
CUSTOMER NO/CREDIT LMT: XXXXX   999999999
```

It is recommended that you specify FRSET in the CTRL= parameter in the DFHMSD macro when you define a mapset. This will turn off the MDT of an unprotected map field after its input data has been received. The input data should only be received and edited once. If you do not specify FRSET and input data has been entered on an unprotected field, its MDT will be left on for the next input operation after the input data has been received. If the MDT of a map field stays on like that, the data on the map field will be received into the program and edited as a map field with new input data for every input operation. This is very time-consuming and an inefficient way to process an online transaction. Each input field should only be transmitted and edited only once. After the input field has been edited and it is a valid data, you should save it in the communication area and turn off its MDT. After the MDT of this field is turned off, LOW-VALUES will be received into the program for the next input operation. This way the input data will only be transmitted and edited once.

It is recommended that ATTRB=FSET should not be specified for an unprotected map field. When the user enters input data on this field, the MDT of this field will be turned on and the input data entered will be received into the program. In this case, you only need to edit the input data when its length is greater than 0. If you specify FSET for an unprotected field in a CICS mapset, the length of the input field will be greater than 0 even when there is no input data entered. You lose the ability to tell if any input data is entered by the user if FSET is specified for an unprotected field. The second disadvantage of using FSET on an unprotected field is that the data on this field will be transmitted into the CICS program from the terminal for each input operation unless you turn off its MDT in the CICS program.

9.1.3.   One CICS Map Per CICS Program

CICS is running under multiple tasking environment. Each day, millions of CICS tasks are executed in an average CICS shop. The way you write your CICS programs and mapsets will effect the response time of your CICS transactions. The easiest way to cut down the response time for a CICS transaction is to use less resources as possible. The CICS resources include main storages, auxiliary storages, files, programs, and mapsets. The rule number one is that you should not try to process two CICS screens within one CICS program. The reason is very simple. Your CICS program can only process one screen at any given time. The codes used to process the second map will be loaded into the virtual storage when the CICS program is invoked to process the first screen. You waste the storages that are occupied by the codes of the second screen. So always use one CICS map within one CICS program and then use XCTL command to transfer the control to the second program when the second screen is to be processed. Message Routing technique requires all CICS maps (header, detail and trailer maps) within the CICS mapset be presented within the program. So this rule does not apply to the Message Routing technique.

9.2.   CICS Program Design

9.2.1.   Menu-Driven Design

A majority of CICS online systems are menu-driven. That means the user only needs to enter the transaction code of the menu program to invoke the menu screen and then selects the desired function and enters the required and/or optional fields on the menu screen. After the selection has been made on the menu screen, the desired screen will appear on the terminal. For example, the user can enter 'CUST' on a clear terminal to invoke the menu screen of the customer maintenance system. After the menu screen has been displayed, he can enter the function number 2 and a valid customer number to display that customer for update. You can list all the functions to be performed in this system on the menu screen. The menu-driven design provides the following advantages:

1. The user only needs to remember the transaction code of the menu program in order to perform all functions within this system. He does not need to remember the transaction codes of the rest of CICS programs within the system. If you design a CICS transaction to be invoked by entering its transaction code with input data, then the user need to remember the transaction code of each CICS program within the system and its input format.

2. The required and/or optional fields can be prompted on the menu screen so the user does not need to remember the input format of each function.

3. The security only needs to be imposed in the menu program. After the menu program has been invoked by the transaction code entered, you can check to see if this user is authorized to use this system. After the user has selected the desired function on the menu screen, you can check to see if he is authorized to use that function in the menu program. If you use independent transaction design, then you need to perform the security checking in each CICS program.

4. You can transfer the control from one function to the other within the same system by simply pressing a control key. For example, you can press PF1 to go to the delete customer screen from the update customer screen.

5. You can audit user's activity of using this system since all users must go through the menu program in order to perform the desired functions within this system.

9.2.2.   Modular Program Design

Each CICS program should be designed to accept a minimum amount of data and perform a pre-defined function. This way it can be invoked by any CICS program that needs to transfer the control to it. This approach is called the modular program design. For example, we can design the sales order print program so it can be invoked by any CICS program that needs to print the sales order. The sales order number is the only input data needs to be passed to this print program. This print program should get the sales order information and print it on the printer. You can also design the customer update program so it can be invoked by any CICS program that needs to come to this program to perform the customer update function. The only input data needs to be passed to this customer update program is the customer number to be updated. For example, you can select one of the customers displayed by the customer browse program to go to this customer update program.

A CICS online system normally consist of 10 to 20 CICS programs. If you approach each program using the modular program design, you can transfer the control from one CICS program to the next one by simply pressing a control key. For example, you can press PF1 to go to the customer print program to print the current customer from the customer update program since the customer number used by the customer update program is the only data needs to be passed to the customer print program. You can also hit the CLEAR key to go to the menu program from the customer update program since no data needs to be passed in order to invoke the menu program.

However, there are two ways you can write CICS programs to perform a function in CICS. One is to write only one CICS program to perform the function and the other is to write two CICS programs to perform the function. For example, we want to write a CICS transaction to update a customer. This CICS transaction will be invoked by the menu program when the function number 2 and a valid customer number are entered. The customer number to be updated will be passed from the menu program. You can write a single CICS program to perform the customer update function or write two CICS programs to perform the same update function.

9.2.3.   One CICS Program Per Function

Most of CICS programs today use this technique. For example, we can write a CICS program to perform the customer update fnction as follows after the control is transferred from the menu program to this update program:

1. Get the customer number passed from the menu program in DFHCOMMAREA.

2. Read the customer from the customer file using the passed customer number.

3. Display the customer on the terminal using the SEND MAP command.

4. Issue a RETURN command with TRANSID option to terminate the task and post the transaction code of this update program on the terminal.

When the user has updated the customer and hit the ENTER key, this update program will be invoked. You should continue the process as follows:

5. Issue a RECEIVE MAP command to receive the updates.

6. Edit and process the updates.

From the above discussion, we know this customer update program not only displays the customer to be updated but also receives, edits, and processes the updates.

From the above example, we know any CICS program that performs terminal I/O operations can be designed to consist of two parts. The first part of the program is to send the initial map to the terminal, terminate itself and post the transaction ID of this program on the terminal. When any response to this terminal is made, this program will be invoked to perform the second part. The second part of the program should receive, edit, and process the input data. In addition to these two parts, this CICS program also has to handle the control keys and exceptional conditions and send the error map if the input data is invalid.

9.2.4. Two CICS Programs Per Function

In addition to the above technique that uses only one CICS program, you can see another type of CICS program design technique that was used in the old CICS macro level programs developed before 1975 when CICS/VS command level language was not available. This type of design divides the above two parts into two separate CICS programs. The first CICS program will send the initial map to the terminal and then issue a RETURN command with TRANSID option to terminate itself and post the transaction ID of the second CICS program on this terminal. Any response to this terminal will invoke the second CICS program which should receive, edit, and process the input data. Therefore, two CICS programs must be specified in the PPT and only the transaction ID of the second program should be specified in the PCT. There is no PCT entry for the first program. Any CICS program that needs to invoke this function must issue an XCTL command to invoke the first program.

This type of design will cut down the size of both CICS programs but the total resources used by two CICS programs are normally greater than the single CICS program that performs both functions. It is easier for CICS programmers to maintain one function (i.e. customer update function) in one single CICS program. The codes that perform the initial send map is normally relatively small comparing to the rest of the codes. So it is not that much of saving in storage and response time if you use two CICS programs instead of one to perform the desired function. For easier maintenance, it is recommanded that one single CICS program instead of two be used to perform the desired function.

9.2.5. Pseudo Conversational Programming

You must use pseudo conversational programming technique to code all your CICS programs that need to perform terminal I/O operations. You should issue a RETURN command with TRANSID option between the SEND MAP and the RECEIVE MAP commands. This RETURN command will terminate the task, post the transaction code of this CICS program on the terminal and store the necessary data in communication area (COMMAREA). Any response to this terminal will invoke the same CICS program. After the program is invoked again, you should check EIBTRNID and EIBCALEN to determine if this is the second time the program is invoked. If it is, you should go to issue a RECEIVE MAP command to receive the input data and continue the transaction. The data you saved in the communication area before you issue the RETURN command will be in DFHCOMMAREA when this program is invoked again.

If you do not issue a RETURN command with TRANSID option between the SEND MAP and the RECEIVE MAP commands, the CICS task will not be terminated. It will wait for the response of the user after the SEND MAP command has been executed. Only when the user responses to the terminal, the RECEIVE MAP command will be executed. If the user goes out to lunch and never comes back to response to the terminal, all the resources allocated to this task will still be waiting until the CICS/VS is shut down. This is not acceptable for all CICS shops.

9.3.   Passing Data Among CICS Programs

There are several ways to pass the data between or amoung CICS programs:

1. Using communication area in the XCTL, LINK or RETURN commands.
   It is the most used method to pass data between two CICS programs (XCTL or LINK) or to itself (RETURN).

2. Using TWA to pass data between two CICS programs that belong to the same task. TWA is initiated when a CICS task is initiated and released when the task is terminated. Therefore, you should not use TWA to pass data between the SEND MAP and the RECEIVE MAP sessions in a pseudo conversational program. It can only be used to pass data between two CICS programs that are related by the XCTL or LINK command. In this case, both programs belong to the same task. However, the communication area can be used not only in this case but also can be used to pass data to itself. Therefore, TWA is obsolete and replaced by the communication area.

3. Temporary storage queue.
   It is the most used method to pass data to another CICS program that is not to be invoked by the present program or data to be passed is a small file contains many records.

4. Intrapartition transient data queue.
   It is used to create data in one CICS program and then process the stored data in the other CICS program. The extrapartition transient data queue cannot be used to pass data amoung CICS programs since you can only define it as input or output but not both.

9.3.1.   Communication Area

The communication area is the best way to pass data between two CICS programs or to itself. It can be specified in the COMMAREA option in the XCTL or LINK command to pass the data from the current program to the next one specified in the PROGRAM option. You can also save the necessary data in the communication area before you issue a RETURN command with TRANSID and COMMAREA options. When the program is invoked again, the data saved is in the DFHCOMMAREA in LINKAGE SECTION of this program. If a CICS program is invoked by the XCTL or LINK command, the data passed from the issuing program is in DFHCOMMAREA of LINKAGE SECTION of the program invoked. DFHCOMMAREA is addressed by CICS, so there is no need to perform any dynamic allocation before you use it. It is available for you as soon as the program is invoked. For example, we want to pass the customer number entered on the menu screen to the customer update program, we can issue an XCTL command with COMMAREA option:

In the menu program:

```
EXEC CICS XCTL PROGRAM('UPDTCUST')
               COMMAREA(WS-CUST-NO)
               LENGTH(5)
               END-EXEC.
```

In the customer update program:

```
LINKAGE SECTION.
01   DFHCOMMAREA.
     02   CUST-NO    PIC X(5).
PROCEDURE DIVISION.
     EXEC CICS READ DATASET('CUSTMAST')
                    RIDFLD(CUST-NO)
                    INTO(CUST-REC)
                    END-EXEC.
```

In the above examples, we pass the customer number in the communication area of the XCTL command to the customer update program. After the customer update program has been invoked, CICS will address DFHCOMMAREA for you. The customer number passed from the menu program is in DFHCOMMAREA of LINKAGE SECTION. We can use the customer number right away to read the customer master file after the customer update program is invoked.

You can also pass the data to a subroutine CICS program in the LINK command. The subroutine CICS program can pass the data back to the main program. The following example shows we want to pass the customer number to a subroutine program and the invoice number for that customer number will be returned from the subroutine program to the main program:

In the main program:

```
WORKING-STORAGE SECTION.
01   COMM-AREA.
     02   CA-CUST-NO    PIC 9(5).
     02   CA-INVOICE-NO PIC X(7).
PROCEDURE DIVISION.
     . . . .
```

```
       MOVE 5000    TO CA-CUST-NO.
       MOVE SPACES TO CA-INVOICE-NO.
       EXEC CICS LINK PROGRAM('CUSTINV')
                      COMMAREA(COMM-AREA)
                      LENGTH(12)
                      END-EXEC.
  *    NOW YOU CAN USE INVOICE NUMBER PASSED FROM SUBROUTINE
       MOVE CA-INVOICE-NO TO PRINT-INVOICE-NO.
```

In the subroutine program:

```
       LINKAGE SECTION.
       01  DFHCOMMAREA.
           02  CUST-NO    PIC 9(5).
           02  INVC-NO    PIC X(7).
       PROCEDURE DIVISION.
           EXEC CICS READ DATASET('CUSTMAST')
                          RIDFLD(CUST-NO)
                          INTO(CUSTOMER-REC)
                          END-EXEC.
           ...
           MOVE WS-INVOICE-NO TO INVC-NO.
           EXEC CICS RETURN END-EXEC.
```

In the above examples, we pass the customer number to the subroutine program and reserve a space for the invoice number in the communication area so the subroutine program can pass the invoice number for this customer to the main program. Following the LINK command in the main program, we can access the invoice number passed from the subroutine program. If no data is to be passed from the subroutine program to the main program, then you do not need to reserve the space for it.

You can also pass data to the current program itself while you use pseudo conversational programming:

```
       LINKAGE SECTION.
       01  DFHCOMMAREA.
           02  CUST-NO     PIC 9(5).
       PROCEDURE DIVISION.
           IF EIBTRNID = 'CU03' AND EIBCALEN = 5
              GO TO A200-RECEIVE-MAP.
           EXEC CICS READ DATASET('CUSTMAST')
                          RIDFLD(CUST-NO)
                          INTO(CUSTOMER-REC)
                          END-EXEC.
           .... MOVE CUSTOMER TO MAP I/O AREA ....
           EXEC CICS SEND MAP('AXCU03') MAPSET('XXCU03')
                          ERASE CURSOR END-EXEC.
           EXEC CICS RETURN TRANSID('CU03')
                            COMMAREA(DFHCOMMAREA)
                            LENGTH(5)
                            END-EXEC.
       A200-RECEIVE-MAP.
           EXEC CICS MAP('AXCU03') MAPSET('XXCU03')
```

179

```
               END-EXEC.
        MOVE CUST-NO TO WS-CUST-NO.
        . . . .
```

In the above example, we get the customer number passed from the menu program in DFHCOMMAREA when this customer update program is invoked the very first time. We then use the customer number to read the customer file to get the customer for display. We issue a SEND MAP command to display the customer and then issue a RETURN command with TRANSID option to terminate this task and save the customer number in the communication area (COMMAREA). When the user enters the updates and hits the ENTER key, this customer update program will be invoked the second time. This time we need to go to issue the RECEIVE MAP command. We can also get the customer number saved in DFHCOMMAREA after this program is invoked the second time. Therefore, we use the communication area not only to pass data from the menu program to this customer update program but also to pass data from the SEND MAP session to the RECEIVE MAP session.

9.3.2.   TWA

The TWA (Transaction Work Area) is unique to each CICS task. When a CICS task is initiated, its TWA will be initiated. When the task is terminated, its TWA will be released. Before you can use TWA in a CICS program, it must have been specified in the PCT of that transaction. If no TWASIZE is specified, then no spaces will be allocated to TWA. In this case, you cannot use it. You will lose all your data after the RETURN command with TRANSID option is issued in a pseudo conversational CICS program if you use TWA to store your data for the next RECEIVE MAP session. Therefore, TWA is not suitable for a pseudo conversational program to pass data between the SEND MAP command and the RECEIVE MAP command. However, it can be used to pass data between two CICS programs that are related by the XCTL command or LINK command. In this case, both CICS programs belong to the same task. Howver, communication area is normally be used for this purpose since it can pass data not only in this situation but also between terminal I/O sessions in a pseudo conversational program.

In order to use TWA, you need to ask your system programmer to specify the TWA size for that transaction in its PCT entry:

```
DFHPCT TYPE=ENTRY,TRANSID=CUST,PROGRAM=XCU00,TRANSEC=02, X
       TRANPRTY=001,TWASIZE=512,DVSUPRT=NONV,TCLASS=2
```

In the above example, we specify TWA size as 512 bytes long for the transaction CUST that uses CICS program XCU00. Since TWA is not used any more these days, it is normally specified as TWASIZE=0 (the default).

In order to access the TWA for the current transaction, you should issue the ADDRESS command as follows:

```
WORKING-STORAGE SECTION.
01  TWA-LENG          PIC S9(4) COMP.
LINKAGE SECTION.
01  DFHCOMMAREA       PIC X(150).
01  BLLCELLS.
```

```
      02   FILLER      PIC S9(8) COMP.
      02   TWA-PTR     PIC S9(8) COMP.
 01   TWA-AREA.
      02   TWA-CUST-NO  PIC X(5).
 PROCEDURE DIVISION.
      EXEC CICS ASSIGN  TWALENG(TWA-LENG) END-EXEC.
      IF TWA-LENG > 0
          EXEC CICS ADDRESS TWA(TWA-PTR) END-EXEC
          EXEC CICS READ DATASET('CUSTMAST')
                         RIDFLD(TWA-CUST-NO)
                         END-EXEC.
```

In the above example, we use the ASSIGN command to get the length of TWA for this transaction. If no TWA is assigned in the PCT, its length will be equal to zero. If the TWA length is greater than zero, we can then use the customer number passed from the previous program in TWA to read the customer master file.

TWA is the most frequently used area to pass data between two CICS programs before 1975 when CICS command level was not available. The CICS macro level language does not have communication area feature. Therefore, you have no choice except to use TWA to pass data from the menu program to the update program. But the communication area is available for the CICS command level language, TWA is replaced by the communication area.

9.3.3.   Temporary Storage Queues

If you need to pass data amoung CICS programs, then TS queue is the best way to do it. The communication area can only be used to pass data between two CICS programs that are related by the XCTL or LINK command. If two CICS programs are not related by either of these two commands, you need to pass data to the other CICS program through the use of Temporary Storage queue. After the TS queue has been created by one CICS program, any CICS program can review, update or delete this TS queue. Therefore, data can be passed from one CICS program to another through the use of the TS queue.

You can store the data to be passed in one record or many records in the TS queue. The TS queue works like a small VSAM RRDS file that can be retrieved or updated sequentially or randomly. There is no need to define the TS queue in any CICS internal tables before you create it. You can name the TS queue anything you like and retrieve the records in the queue by the queue name and their item number. Each record in the TS queue can be retrieved or updated as many times as needed. You can only delete the entire queue and you cannot not delete the queue record individually.

For example, the CICS program A will create sales order details in the TS queue so these details can be reviewed or updated later by CICS program B. Each sales order detail will create one record in the queue. After program B has updated or reviewed the detail records in the queue, program C will read the queue records and create them in the sales order detail VSAM file. After all detail records in the queue have been created in the VSAM file, program C can then delete the queue. In this case, no record creation in the

VSAM file until all details have been reviewed or updated by the user. In this case, the TS queue serves as a small VSAM RRDS file that holds the data to be processed by other CICS programs for a while until it is no longer needed.

In order to retrieve a TS queue, the queue name and/or item number must be specified. The TS queue should include the terminal ID as part of the name in most cases so the queue will be unique to each terminal user. The item number is assigned to each record in the queue when the queue record is created. This item number should be used to identify the record if you want to retrieve that particular record.

9.3.4.   Intrapartition Transient Data Sets

There are two types of TD queues: Intrapartition and Extrapartition transient data queues. The extrapartition TD queue can be defined as input or output but not both. If it is defined as output, it is used to collect output data from CICS terminals for off-line batch processing. In this case, you can only issue the WRITEQ TD command to create the queue. If it is defined as input, it is used to transfer the data created in the batch region to CICS/VS. In this case, you can only issue the READQ TD command to retrieve the data in the queue. Therefore, you cannot use extrapartition TD queues to pass data amoung CICS programs since both input (retrieval) and output operation (creation) are normally involved in passing the data amoung CICS programs.

The most frequently used application for intrapartition TD queue is Automatic Task Initiation (ATI). In an ATI application, data to be passed is created as Intrapartition TD queue records. Each time a record is added to the TD queue, CICS will check the total number of the records in the queue to see if the trigger level specified in the DCT for this queue has been reached. If it has, the transaction specified in the DCT for that TD queue will be initiated. When the associated CICS program of the initiated transaction is invoked, it will issue the READQ TD command repeatly to retrieve the TD queue records until there are no more records in the queue (QZERO). After each retrieved record has been processed, this program will go back to issue the READQ TD command to retrieve the next one. When QZERO condition occurs, the program will issue a RETURN command to terminate itself. The spaces that are occupied by these retrieved records will be freed.

In an ATI application, data is stored in the TD queue records that will be retrieved by the invoked CICS program later. The data is passed from the CICS program that creates the TD queue records to the CICS program that processes them.

If the ATI technique is not used, you can still create the TD queue records in one CICS program and retrieve them in the second CICS program. You must request the transaction of the second CICS program from a CICS terminal instead of being invoked by CICS when the trigger level is reached in an ATI application.

Therefore, data is passed from one CICS program to the other through the use of an intrapartition TD queue.

9.4.   Security Design

There are many ways you can impose the security to allow only the authorized personnel to access CICS resources. These CICS resources include CICS/VS systems, CICS programs, CICS files, TD or TS queues, CICS terminals and CICS transactions. In the following sections, we'll address the following topics regarding the security:

1. CSSN and CSSF transactions
2. Operator security codes
3. Transaction security codes
4. Resource security level codes
5. Operator classes
6. Operator priority
7. User-designed Security

9.4.1.   CSSN and CSSF Transactions

The CSSN and CSSF transactions are CICS transactions that are used to sign on to the CICS/VS system (CSSN) or log off from a CICS/VS system (CSSF). Before a CICS user can sign on to a CICS/VS system, his system programmer must create an entry for him in the operator Sign-On Table (SNT). This SNT entry contains the following information regarding this CICS terminal operator:

1. Operator name
2. Operator Identification
3. Operator password
4. Operator security codes
5. Resource level security codes
6. Operator classes
7. Operator priority

The terminal operator must enter the operator name and password after the transaction CSSN has been entered. If the name and the password do not match with that in the SNT, the sign-on is rejected. This sign-on procedure will authorize only the CICS terminal operators that have been set up in the SNT by the system programmer to access the CICS/VS system. This step provides the initial security checking. After the operator has signed on to CICS, we can then check the security at the CICS transaction level when that CICS transaction is invoked by the operator.

When the operator signs on to CICS/VS, his SNT information will be stored in the Terminal Control Area (TCTTE) of this terminal. The SNT information in the terminal control area will be used to perform several security checking later.

The operator Identification is a three-byte field that contains the operator ID. This field can be accessed through the use of the ADDRESS command within the CICS program:

```
WORKING-STORAGE SECTION.
01  WS-OPERID    PIC X(3).
PROCEDURE DIVISION.
    EXEC CICS ASSIGN OPID(WS-OPERID) END-EXEC.
```

In the above example, after the ASSIGN command is issued, the operator ID will be stored in WS-OPERID.

The operator ID is normally used by CICS programs to perform the security checking on each individual operator that tries to use this CICS program. For example, in the salary update CICS program, you can check to see if the operator ID is equal to 'SDL' who is the only person authorized to update the employee's salary. If the operator ID is not equal to 'SDL', then you should reject the request.

9.4.2.   Operator And Transaction Security Codes

Each terminal operator can be assigned one or more operator security codes in the SNT. When the terminal operator has signed on to CICS/VS on one of the CICS terminals, the TCT entry (TCTTE) of this terminal will contain the operator's information like: operator ID, operator security codes, operator class and operator priority. The TCT entry for this terminal will be cleared when the operator logs off from this terminal. Therefore, CICS/VS or CICS programs can use the SNT information in the TCTTE to perform the security checking during the execution of a CICS task.

In order for this terminal operator to use a CICS transaction, one of his security codes assigned in the SNT must match that for this CICS transaction. The transaction security code of a CICS transaction is assigned in the PCT entry of that transaction. If the security codes do not match, the access to this CICS transaction by this terminal user is rejected.

The operator security codes can be any number ranging from 1 to 24. One or more operator security codes can be assigned to each operator in the SNT. Your system programmer can only specify any number but 1 which is given automatically to all operators specified in the SNT.

For example, your system programmer can assign a security code of 10 to a salary-update transaction and 8 to a salary-inquiry transaction in the PCT. Then only the terminal operators with the operator security code of 10 can use this salary update transaction. All payroll clerks are assigned an operator security code of 8 and only the payroll manager has security codes of 8 and 10. Therefore, the payroll manager is the only one that can initiate the salary-update transaction. However, the manager and payroll clerks can use the payroll-inquiry transaction.

9.4.3.   Resource Level Security Codes

In addition to the transaction security code, your system programmer can also specify the resource level security code for each CICS resource. The CICS resource can be TD queue (DCT), VSAM file (FCT), CICS transaction (PCT), or CICS program (PPT). If the resource level security code is specified for a CICS resource, then one of the resource level security codes of the terminal operator specified in its SNT entry must match that of this resource before the operator can access this resource. Otherwise, a security check occurs and the transaction is terminated. Most of CICS resources are not specified with resource level security codes. In this case, the operator can access these resources without any problem.

CECI and CEDF transactions are normally assigned with a resource level security code in the PCT so only the CICS programmers with that resource level security code can use them. The terminal operators in the user departments will not be able to use them since the resource level security codes assigned in the SNT for those users are not equal to that of CECI and CEDF transactions. Most of CICS resources are defined without the resource security level code and they can be accessed by any user.

9.4.4. Operator Classes

Your system programmer may assign each terminal operator with one or more operator classes in the SNT. The operator classes are used in Message Routing applications. Since you can issue a ROUTE command to route the message to specific terminals (by terminal ID), specific operators (by operator ID), or all operators in a specific operator class (by operator class). This provides another level of security to deliver the message.

9.4.5. Operator Priority

CICS/VS is running under multiple-tasking environment. At any time, many CICS tasks may be running according to their priority. A CICS task with higher priority will be run before any CICS task with lower priority. A CICS task priority is determined from the combination of the transaction, terminal and operator priorities. The transaction priority is specified in the PCT entry of that transaction. The terminal priority is specified in the TCT entry for that terminal. The operator priority is specified in the SNT entry for that operator. The highest priority is 255 and the lowest is 1. If the combination of these three priorities is greater than 255, 255 will be used.

9.4.6. User-Designed Security

The CICS system designer always wants to provide the security checking to an CICS online system in the menu program. This is normally accomplished through the set up of a terminal VSAM KSDS file. All CICS terminals specified in the TCT will have a corresponding record in this KSDS file. The key to this file is the terminal ID (EIBTRMID). The record contains the physical location, associated printer, store number, department ID, cost center and more. When an operator signs on to a CICS terminal, we'll use the terminal ID to read this terminal file and get the terminal information. We then use the terminal information to perform the security checking. For example, terminal K01A belongs to store number 003. Therefore, the operator signs on to this terminal can only process the sales orders created by the store number 003. This will ensure no operators from other stores can review or update the sales orders created by the store number 003.

You can also use the terminal record to determine if the user is authorized to use this online system. For example, we only want the personnel in the payroll department to use the online payroll system. After the user has entered the transaction to invoke the payroll menu program, we'll retrieve its terminal record to see if the department ID is equal to '002' which is the payroll department. If not, we'll reject the request even before we display the payroll menu screen. You can also use the operator ID to impose the security.

9.5. Transmit And Edit Input Data Only Once

If data is entered on an unprotected field, it should be transmitted and edited only once. It is your responsibility to make that happen to cut down the response time. CICS command level language allows you to accomplish this through the communication area, and dynamic attribute modification. You should define an unprotected field with ATTRB=NUM or ATTRB=UNPROT. You should also specify CTRL= (FRSET,FREEKB) in the DFHMSD macro. When data is entered on this unprotected field, its MDT will be turned and data will be received into the CICS program after the RECEIVE MAP command is issued:

CICS Mapset XXCU03:

```
XXCU03    DFHMSD TYPE=&SYSPARM,LANG=COBOL,TIOAPFX=YES,      X
                 MODE=INOUT,STORAGE=AUTO,CTRL=(FREEKB,FRSET),  X
                 TERM=3270,DATA=FIELD
AXCU03    DFHMDI SIZE=(24,80)
          ....
ORDRTYP   DFHMDF POS=(03,10),LENGTH=01,ATTR=UNPROT
          ....
AMT       DFHMDF POS=(06,10),LENGTH=07,ATTRB=NUM
          ....
          DFHMSD TYPE=FINAL
          END
```

CICS Program XCU03:

```
WORKING-STORAGE SECTION.
01   COMM-AREA.
     02   CA-ORDRTYP      PIC X(1).
     02   CA-AMT          PIC 9(7).
     02   EDIT-TAB.
        02   EDIT         OCCURS 2 PIC X(1).
     02   FILLER          PIC X(90).
LINKAGE SECTION.
01   DFHCOMMAREA          PIC X(100).
PROCEDURE DIVISION.
     MOVE DFHCOMMAREA TO COMM-AREA.
     IF EIBTRNID = 'CU03' AND EIBCALEN = 100
        GO TO A200-RECEIVE-MAP.
     .... SEND INITIAL MAP ....
A200-RECEIVE-MAP.
     EXEC CICS RECEIVE MAP('AXCU03') MAPSET('XXCU03') END-EXEC.
     IF ORDRTYPL > 0
        IF ORDRTYPI = 'A' OR 'B' OR 'C'
           MOVE 'G'      TO EDIT(1)
           MOVE ' '      TO ORDRTYPA
           MOVE ORDRTYPI TO CA-ORDRTYP
        ELSE
           MOVE 'BAD ORDER TYPE' TO MSGO
           MOVE 'I'              TO ORDRTYPA
           MOVE -1               TO ORDRTYPL
           MOVE 'B'              TO EDIT(1).
     IF AMTL > 0
        IF AMTI NUMERIC AND AMTI NOT = '0000000'
           MOVE 'G'   TO EDIT(2)
           MOVE '&'   TO AMTA
           MOVE AMTI  TO CA-AMT
        ELSE
```

```
MOVE 'BAD AMOUNT'    TO MSGO
MOVE 'R'             TO AMTA
MOVE -1              TO AMTL
MOVE 'B'             TO EDIT(2).
```

In the above example, we issue a RECEIVE MAP command to receive input data into the program. If the order type or the amount field is entered, its MDT will be turned on and the data entered will be received into the map I/O area (AXCU03I). We can then check the length field of the unprotected field to see if it is greater than zero. If data is entered on this field, its length will be greater than zero. We can use the length field to determine if data has been entered. If the length is greater than zero, we then edit the data to see if it is a valid data. If it is, we need to do three things:

1. indicate valid data has been entered on this field by moving 'G' (good data) to its edit switch defined in the communication area. By using this switch, we can determine if a valid data has been entered on this field.

2. Save the valid data entered in the communication area. Since we want to turn off the MDT of this field in the step 3, we need to save the valid data in the communication area. LOW-VALUES will be received into this field for the next input operation since its MDT has been turned off.

3. Turn off the MDT of the good-edited field. This will ensure no data transmission will occur during the next input operation. There is no reason to transmit the same data more than once since we have saved the good-edited data in the communication area. However, we need to unprotect this field to allow the user to enter new data if he change this mind on this field. We move ' ' for an alphameric field and '&' for a numeric field. This will unprotect that field and turn off its MDT. '&' will also turn the numeric key lock on.

Since we turn off the MDT of a good-edited field, LOW-VALUES will be received into the program and its length field will contain zero during the next input operation. Since its length will be equal to zero for the next input operation, the editing routing will not be performed. This method will ensure that the data will only be transmitted and edited once.

If the data entered is invalid after the editing, we need to do three things:

1. We need to move 'I' for an alphameric field or 'R' for a numeric field to the attribute byte of the field. This will turn on its MDT and make it unprotected. 'R' will also turn the numeric key lock on for the user to enter the numeric data. The MDT is turned on so even if the user does not correct the invalid data, the invalid data will still be received into the program and its length will still be greater than zero during the next input operation. In this case, it will go through the editing routine again and still get bad-editing. This will force the user to correct the invalid data. If the user does not correct the invalid data, the invalid field will still be high-lighted.

2. Move cursor position to the invalid field so the user does not have to move the cursor around in order to correct it.

3. Indicate that this is an invalid field in it edit switch in the communication area. This edit switch will enable us to determine later if any invalid data was entered.

   If none, then we can process the input data. Otherwise, we need to issue a SEND MAP command with the DATAONLY option to send the error map back to the terminal for correction.

If CTRL=FRSET was not specified in the DFHMSD macro, the MDT will stay on for every subsequent input operation after the data has been entered on an unprotected field. If FRSET is specified, the MDT will be turned off by BMS after we have received the entered data.

Why there are so many CICS applications that are still programmed to transmit and edit input data for each subsequent input operation after the input data has been entered? The reason is simple. This is the only technique that works when CICS macro level language is used. CICS macro level language was replaced by CICS command level in 1975. The macro level has no communication area feature. Therefore, you cannot pass data between the SEND MAP and RECEIVE MAP sessions except to transmit the data from the terminal to the program for each input operation. This technique was used by macro level CICS programmers to code the command level programms when the command level language became available. Many entry-level CICS command level programmers then learn the CICS programming techniques through the existing CICS programs which were written by those macro level programmers.

To speed up your CICS transactions, you should transmit and edit the input data only once, and process only one screen within each CICS program.

9.6. Re-Insert Technique

When a CICS program uses too much CICS resoure, you may want to terminate it and then ask the terminal operator to hit the ENTER key to resume the execution from where the program was terminated. This technique is called re-insert.

For example, you try to print a sales order with over 1000 sales order details using the message routing technique. As we know , the message routing uses the temporary storage to store the message and the message is released only after the message has been delivered. If you want to build the entire message before you print it, you may hang the entire CICS/VS system when there are no more temporary storages available for your SEND MAP ACCUM or SEND TEXT ACCUM command. Your CICS task will be waiting for the resource that is not available and in the mean time, it still occupies a big temporary storage for the uncompleted message. This will eventually hang the entire CICS system when more and more new tasks try to use the temporary storage. So it is a good practice to set a limit on the total number of records to be processed in a message routing CICS program. When that limit has been reached, you can then issue the SEND PAGE command to print the first part of the sales order, terminate the task, and then post the transaction ID of this CICS program on the terminal. When any response (ENTER key) to this terminal is made, this CICS program will be invoked and use the data saved in the communication area (the key of the last detail record) to start the message building and print the rest of the report. The limit of total number of file I/O operations is normally set at 200. Whenever your CICS programs need to perform over 200 file I/O operations, you need to consider using the re-insert technique.

The following example shows how to implement the re-insert technique in a message routing program:

```
WORKING-STORAGE SECTION.
01   COMM-AREA.
     02   ORDER-NO                PIC 9(5).
     02   RE-INSERT-AREA.
          02   RE-INSERT-SWT      PIC X(1).
          02   LAST-SEQNO         PIC 9(3).
01   WS-TOTAL-IO                  PIC 9(3).
01   END-ORDER                   PIC X(1).
01   WS-LINE-CTR                 PIC 9(2) VALUE 0.
01   WS-MSG                      PIC X(60).
01   WS-MSG-LENG                 PIC S9(4) COMP VALUE +60.
01   WS-XCTL-MENU                PIC X(30).
LINKAGE SECTION.
01   DFHCOMMAREA                 PIC X(9).
PROCEDURE DIVISION.
*    CHECK RE-INSERT OR FIRST TIME XCTL FROM MENU
     IF EIBTRNID = 'CU03' AND EIBCALEN = 9
         MOVE DFHCOMMAREA TO COMM-AREA
     ELSE
         MOVE DFHCOMMAREA TO COMM-AREA
         MOVE SPACES TO RE-INSERT-AREA.
*    SET UP ROUTE LIST
     .... SET UP PRINTERS ....
     EXEC CICS ROUTE LIST(ROUTE-LIST) END-EXEC.
     .... SEND HEADER MAP ....
*    SET UP STARTING KEY (ORDER NO PLUS SEQUENCE NO)
     MOVE ORDER-NO TO ORDRDET-ORDER-NO.
     IF RE-INSERT-SWT = 'Y'
         MOVE LAST-SEQNO TO ORDRDET-SEQNO
         ADD 1           TO ORDRDET-SEQNO
     ELSE
         MOVE 1          TO ORDRDET-SEQNO.
*    SET TOTAL I/O TO 0
     MOVE 0              TO WS-TOTAL-IO.
*    SET END OF ORDER SWITCH TO Y
     MOVE 'Y'            TO END-ORDER.
*    SET UP ENDFILE AND NOTFND
     EXEC CICS HANDLE CONDITION
               NOTFND(A140-ENDBR-ORDRDET)
               ENDFILE(A140-ENDBR-ORDRDET)
               END-EXEC.
*    START BROWSE AT STARTING KEY SET UP
     EXEC CICS START DATASET('ORDRDET')
                     RIDFLD(ORDRDET-KEY)
                     END-EXEC.
A120-READNEXT-ORDRDET.
     EXEC CICS READNEXT DATASET('ORDRDET')
```

```
                            INTO(ORDRDET-REC)
                            RIDFLD(ORDRDET-KEY)
                            END-XEC.
*       CHECK IF SAME ORDER ?
        IF ORDRDET-ORDER-NO NOT = ORDER-NO
            GO TO A140-ENDBR-ORDRDET.
        ADD 1 TO WS-TOTAL-IO WS-LINE-CTR.
        .... MOVE ORDER DETAIL TO DETAIL MAP ...
        IF WS-LINE-CTR < 17
            GO TO A120-READNEXT-ORDRDET.
*       PAGE IS FULL, SEND IT
        EXEC CICS SEND MAP('DETMAP') MAPSET('XXCU03')
                ERASE PAGING ACCUM END-EXEC.
*       CHECK IF 200 FILE I/O REACHED
        IF WS-TOTAL-IO < 200
            GO TO A120-READNEXT-ORDRDET.
        MOVE 'N' TO END-ORDER.
A140-ENDBR-ORDRDET.
        EXEC CICS ENDBR DATASET('ORDRDET') END-EXEC.
*       PRINT THE MESSAGE
        EXEC CICS SEND PAGE END-EXEC.
*       IF MORE DETAILS, ASK USER TO HIT ENTER KEY TO CONTINUE
        IF END-ORDER = 'N'
            MOVE 'HIT ENTER TO CONTINUE THE REPORT' TO WS-MSG
            EXEC CICS SEND FROM(WS-MSG) LENGTH(WS-MSG-LENG)
                        ERASE END-EXEC
            MOVE 'Y'            TO RE-INSERT-SWT
            MOVE ORDRDET-SEQNO TO LAST-SEQNO
            EXEC CICS RETURN TRANSID('CU03')
                            COMMAREA(COMM-AREA)
                            LENGTH(9)
                            END-EXEC
        ELSE
            EXEC CICS XCTL PROGRAM('MENU')
                            COMMAREA(WS-XCTL-MENU)
                            LENGTH(30)
                            END-EXEC.
```

In the above example, we set up the route list after the program is invoked. We then set up the starting key for the browse operation. If this is the first time the program is invoked (by the menu program through the XCTL command), we start the browse with sequence number 1. Otherwise, we'll use the last sequence number printed as the starting key. When there are no more details, or the end of file has reached, or 200 file I/O operations have been performed, we need to issue an ENDBR command to end the browse operation and then print the message using the SEND PAGE command. After the message has been printed, all temporary storages it occupies will be released. You should then transfer the control back to the menu program or ask the user to hit ENTER key to print the rest of the report.

When the user hits ENTER key on the terminal, this program will be invoked. After it is invoked, we can get the order number and the last sequence number from DFHCOMMAREA and continue our printing operation.

In this chapter, we'll show you how to design the following nine major CICS applications. At least of 90% of CICS applications are within these catagories:

1. Menu

    Most of CICS online systems are menu-driven. The menu program is the first CICS program to be created in the system so other CICS programmers can test their CICS programs invoked by the menu program. The user only needs to enter the transaction code of the menu program to invoke the initial menu screen. After the menu screen has been displayed, the user can then select the desired function and enter the required or optional fields. When all input data is valid, control will be transferred to the CICS program that performs the selected function. The required or optional input fields will also be passed to the desired CICS program from the menu program through the use of the communication area. At any time, the user can hit the CLEAR key on the menu screen to terminate this transaction. The security can be imposed in the menu program to allow only the authorized users to invoke the menu screen and allow authorized users to perform the selected function after the menu screen has been displayed.

2. Add

    Most of the VSAM files today are created on-line through CICS Add programs. The Add program allows the users to add one or more records to a VSAM file on-line. The editing of new records is performed on-line so the user can correct the invalid input data right away. This eliminatesthe need for the key punch operators. The users are more aware of the input data than the key punch operators. After the record has been added to the VSAM file on-line, it is available immediately for inquiry, update or delete by authorized CICS users. No required or optional fields need to be passed from the menu program. Key and data fields must be entered on the Add screen.

3. Inquire/Update/Delete

    These three functions are normally performed by a single CICS program since all three need to display the target record first. For inquiry applications, after the record has been displayed, the user can hit a pre-defined (CLEAR key) to go back to the menu screen. All fields on an inquiry screen must be protected to prevent the user from entering data. For delete applications, the user can hit a program-defined control key (PF1 key) to delete the record being displayed. All fields on a delete screen must be protected. For update applications, after the record to be updated has been displayed, the user can change the unprotected fields on the screen and then hit the ENTER key to update the record. After the record has been updated or deleted, the user can hit a pre-defined key (CLEAR key) to go back to the menu screen. The only data needs to be passed to this inquire/update/delete program from the menu program is the key of the record to be inquired, updated or deleted.

4. Browse

    Browse is an important function of on-line applications. Normally, you'll browse all details of a header or browse records through the alternate index key. Using a complete primary key to browse a VSAM KSDS file is very rare. For example, we want to browse all sales order details in the sales order detail file for any given sales order number. Assume that each screen can display up to 15 details per page. After the first page of details has been displayed, the user should be able to hit a pre-defined control key to go to display the next page or the previous page of details. At any time, the user should be able to go back to the menu screen by pressing a pre-defined key (CLEAR key). Browse operations will be performed through the use of the STARTBR, READNEXT, and ENDBR commands. The detail lines of the screen format can be defined through OCCURS= in the CICS mapset.

5. Browse/Update

   After the browse page is displayed on the terminal, the user can update the records on the screen. Since more than one records are to be updated, a special technique must be employed in order to process the records using COBOL PERFORM verb and indexing. You need to redefine the map I/O area (symbolic description map) in WORKING-STORAGE SECTION in order to use the indexing and PERFORM. To redefine the map I/O area, you need to know how CICS generates the symbolic description map (map I/O copy book).

6. Print

   At least 10% of CICS programs are print programs. You must know how to print an online report. For example, after each sales order is created, you want to print the sales order acknowledge right away so it can be sent to the customer today. However, there are four ways you can print an on-line report depending on the format of the report. We'll show you how you can choose the right technique to print your report. You can either use Message Routing (BMS) or Terminal Control. You can print 24x80, 66x132, 66x85, or any-size reports.

10.1. Menu

Most of CICS on-line applications are menu-driven systems. The user enters the transaction ID of the menu program on a clear screen to display a menu screen. After the menu scrren has been displayed, he can then select the desired function and enter its required or optional fields to invoke the desired CICS program. The data entered on the required or optional fields can be passed from the menu program to the desired program through the use of communication area.

For example, you can enter the transaction ID CUST to invoke the menu program of the customer maintenance system. After the menu program is invoked, it will issue a SEND MAP command with ERASE option to send the initial menu screen to the terminal and then issue a RETURN command with TRANSID option to terminate the menu program. After the menu screen has been displayed, the user can select function 2 (customer update function) and enter a valid customer number. After the input data has been received and edited, control will then be transferred to the customer update program. After the customer update program is invoked, it will use the customer number passed to read and display the customer for update. The user can then update the name and address of that customer and then hit the ENTER key. The customer update program can then receive, edit, and process the updates. After the customer has been updated, the custommer update program will send a small message to the terminal to notify the user that update been completed. The user can then hit CLEAR key to return to the menu screen for the next function.

Therefore, the menu program is invoked by entering its transaction ID on the terminal. After the menu program has been invoked, it should issue a SEND MAP command with ERASE option to send the menu screen to the terminal and then issue a RETURN command with TRANSID option to terminate the program and post the next transaction on the terminal. Then the user can enter the desired function number, and required/optional fields, and then hit ENTER key. Since we have post the transaction code of the menu program on this terminal, any response to this terminal will initiate this transaction which in turn will invoke the menu program again.

After the menu program is invoked the second time, it should issue a RECEIVE MAP to receive the input data. After the input data has been received, the menu program should edit the input data. The input data will be received into the map I/O area (symbolic description map) after the RECEIVE MAP command has been executed. If any input data is invalid, you should issue a SEND MAP command with DATAONLY and CURSOR options, and then issue a RETURN command with TRANSID option to terminate the program. The user can then correct the errors and hit ENTER key.

If all input fields are valid, you should move the data (i.e. customer number) to be passed to the communication area and then issue an XCTL command with the COMMAREA option to transfer the control to the desired CICS program (the customer update program). After the XCTL command has been executed, the current CICS program is terminated and the other CICS program specified in the PROGRAM option of the XCTL command will be invoked. After the second CICS program is invoked, it can get the passed data in DFHCOMMAREA of LINKAGE SECTION. CICS will address this DFHCOMMAREA for you, so you can use it as soon as the second CICS program is invoked.

When the user is on the menu screen, you should allow him to terminate this transaction by pressing a pre-defined control key (CLEAR key). You should set up a HANDLE AID command for this pre-define key so when this key is pressed at any time, the control will go to the label specified for that key. Within the routine of this label, you should issue a SEND FROM command with ERASE option to erase the menu screen and send a transaction termination message and then issue a RETURN command without TRANSID option. When the RETURN command is executed, the menu program is terminated. The user can then hit CLEAR key to erase the transaction termination message and he is ready to enter the next CICS transaction.

The menu screen for this customer maintenance system is as follows:

```
CUST   XX/XX/XX HH:SS    CUSTOMER ORDER SERVICE SYSTEM          XXXX
                                   MENU

FUNCTION: 99 CUSTOMER NO: 99999 CUSTOMER NAME: XXXXXXXXXXXXXXXXXXXX
             ORDER NO   : 99999

             01 CREATE A NEW CUSTOMER.
             02 INQUIRE/UPDATE/DELETE A CUSTOMER (CUSTOMER NO).
             03 BROWSE/UPDATE CUSTOMERS BY NAME (CUSTOMER NAME).
             04 PRINT A SALES ORDER ON 24X80 PAPER (ORDER NO).
```

```
05 PRINT A SALES ORDER ON 24X80 PAPER (ORDER NO).
06 PRINT A SALES ORDER ON 66X132 PAPER (ORDER NO).
07 PRINT A SALES ORDER ON 66X85 PAPER (ORDER NO).
08 CREATE ORDER DETAILS ON TS QUEUE (ORDER NO).
09 REVIEW/UPDATE/CREATE ORDER DETAILS (ORDER NO).
10 PRINT SALES ORDER MASTER LIST TONIGHT.

CLEAR=END, PF1=RESET
XXXXXXXXXXXXXXXXXXXXXXXXXXXXXXXXXXXXXXXXXXXXXXXXXXXXXXXXXXXXXXX
```

From this menu screen, you can see that you only need to select the desired function number and then enter the required/optional fields. We specify the required fields on the menu screen so the user does not need to remember that. The user only needs to remember the transaction ID of the menu program. All the other CICS programs within this system will be invoked by the menu program through the use of the XCTL, LINK, or START command. In many CICS shops, the menu of an online system can be invoked from the master menu. So the user only needs to remember the transaction code of the master menu in order to invoke all the menus in the CICS/VS system. In order to allow the user to invoke the menu from the master menu, you only need to modify the menu program to accept the transfer of the control from the master menu.

The system flow for this menu program is as follows:

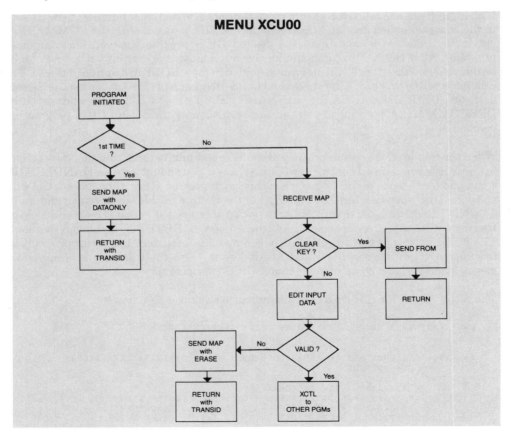

194

You can also impose the security to this on-line system in the menu program. You need to do it when this program is invoked for the very first time. This first-level security will check to see if the operator has authority to get into this on-line system. The second level of security can be imposed when the function has been selected. It will check to see if this operator has the authority to perform the selected function. For example, the update/delete function is only allowed for the manager, the clerks should only be limited to the inquiry or browse operations.

You should also program the menu program to accept the control returned from the other CICS programs in the system. For example, we want to return to the menu program when the user hits the CLEAR key on the customer update screen. After the XCTL command is issued in the customer update program, the menu program is invoked. You should program to accept this type of return and display the menu screen.

If print function is one of the functions listed on the menu screen, then you should use the START command to initiate the print transaction in the menu program. You should not try to XCTL to the print program so after the START command is issued, your terminal can be used for other functions. The print task will be initiated to print the report and then terminate itself. This gives you the re-print capability in case the printer is jammed during the printing.

The complete listing of this menu program is in Chapter 13.1.

10.2.   Add (Data Entry)

The data entry program is invoked when the user enters function number 1 and then hit ENTER key. No other fields are required to be entered on the menu screen. After the XCTL command in the menu program has been executed, the Add CICS program will be invoked. Since this is the first time it is invoked, it should clear the communication area for later use and then issue a SEND MAP command with ERASE option to send a blank screen (customer add screen) to the terminal for the user to enter a new customer. After the SEND MAP command has been issued, you should then issue a RETURN command with TRANSID option to terminate the task and post the transaction code of this Add program on this terminal. Any response to this terminal will invoke this Add program again.

The user can then enter the key (customer number) and data fields (customer name and credit limit) and then hit ENTER key. This will invoke the Add program the second time since we have post the transaction ID of this Add program on this terminal in the last RETURN command with TRANSID option. After this Add program is invoked the second time, it should issue a RECEIVE MAP command to receive the input data entered into the map I/O area (symbolic description map) and then edit the received input data. The key of the new record entered must not exist on the file. You can use the key entered to read the customer file. If NORMAL condition is returned, the key is invalid (duplicated). If NOTFND condition occurs, this is a good key.

After you have edited the input data and all input fields are valid, you can then move the input data (key and data fields) to the customer record layout and then issue a WRITE command to add the record. After a successful WRITE, you should send a message to the terminal to inform the user that the record has been added. The user can then hit the CLEAR key to go back to the menu screen or hit a pre-defined key (PF1 key) to reset the screen in order to add the next customer. You should always allow the user to reset the screen to enter the next record in a data-entry application so the user does not need to go back to the menu screen in order to add the next record.

Normally, you can see two common ways to edit the input data. We'll show you why one of these two is not recommended. We'll first introduce the right way and then compare it with the one that is not recommended.

After an input field has been received into the map I/O area, you can determine if any data has been entered on this field by checking the length of this input field (CUSTNOL). If the length of the input field is greater than zero, then input data has been entered on this field and its length field should contain the number of positions entered on this field by the user. If this customer number is defined as a 5-byte field with ATTRB=NUM, and the operator enters three bytes of data on this field, its length field (CUSTNOL) will contain 3 and its input field (CUSTNOI) will contain '00123'. If the customer number '00123' is a good customer number, you should do three things:

1. save the customer number in the communication area.

2. move '&' to CUSTNOA. '&' means unprotected, normal light, and MDT off. If the operator does not enter this field the next time, then CUSTNOL contains 0, and CUSTNOI contains LOW-VALUES. Since CUSTNOL contains zero, no editing will be performed on CUSTNOI. So you save one I/O operation (READ customer file). This will ensure the input data will be transmitted and edited only once. If the operator has to change the customer number, then CUSTNOL will be greater than zero, and CUSTNOI will contain the new customer number. In this case, the editing routine will be performed since we'll edit any input field with its length field greater than 0.

3. indicate this is good input data in the communication area.

The following example shows the right way to edit an input field:

In the CICS mapset:

```
XXCU01    DFHMSD ... CTRL=(FRSET,FREEKB) ...
CUSTNO    DFHMDF POS=(03,02),LENGTH=5,ATTBR=NUM
CUSTNAM   DFHMDF POS=(05,10),LENGTH=20,ATTRB=UNPROT
CRDLMT    DFHMDF POS=(07,10),LENGTH=7,ATTRB=NUM
```

In the CICS program:

```
WORKING-STORAGE SECTION.
01   COMM-AREA.
     02   CA-CUSTNO    PIC 9(5).
     02   CA-CUSTNAM   PIC X(20).
     02   CA-CRDLMT    PIC 9(7).
     02   EDIT-TAB.
          03   EDIT    OCCURS 3 PIC X(1).
```

```
        02  FILLER          PIC X(65).
    LINKAGE SECTION.
    01  DFHCOMMAREA         PIC X(100).
    PROCEDURE DIVISION.
        IF EIBTRNID = 'CU01' AND EIBCALEN = 100
            GO TO A200-RECEIVE-MAP.
        .... SEND INITIAL SCREEN ....
    A200-RECEIVE-MAP.
        EXEC CICS RECEIVE MAP('AXCU01') MAPSET('XXCU01')
                END-EXEC.
        IF CUSTNOL > 0
            IF CUSTNOI NUMERIC
                MOVE CUSTNOI TO CA-CUSTNO
                MOVE '&'     TO CUSTNOA
                MOVE 'G'     TO EDIT(1)
            ELSE
                MOVE 'B'     TO EDIT(1)
                MOVE 'R'     TO CUSTNOA
                MOVE -1      TO CUSTNOL
                MOVE 'CUSTOMER NO NOT NUMERIC' TO MSGO.
```

In the above example, we edit the customer number only when the input data was entered on this field (CUSTNOL 0). The input data must be numeric. Otherwise, it is a bad customer number. If the customer number is entered and numeric, then we assume this is a good customer number. When an input field is good-edited, we need to save it in the communication area, turn off its MDT and unprotect it.

If the input field is an invalid field after the editing, you should do the following four things:

1. move 'R' (numberic) or 'I' (alphameric) to the attribute field of the input field in error. This will high-light the field, turn on its MDT and unprotect this field so it can be corrected. 'R' will also turn on the numeric key lock. High-light on this field will catch the operator's attention. Turning MDT on will ensure that the data will be received into the CICS program in the next input operation no matter if the user has corrected the field or not. If the operator does not correct the error, the invalid data entered last time will be received into the program and it will still be marked as bad data after the editing has been completed. If the operator corrects the field, it will be received and re-edited again. The numberic key lock is turned on for the numeric field so the user can enter the numeric data without pressing the numeric key lock. Unprotecting the invalid field will allow the user to enter the correct data.

2. Move cursor position to the first byte of the field. So the user can correct the field without repositioning the cursor. If the cursor position has been requested by more than one field, the cursor will sit on the one with the lowest position on the screen.

3. Move error message to the message line to inform the user about the invalid fields.

4. Indicate that this is a bad field in its edit switch in the communication area.

The technique discussed above is the better way to edit the input data since any input field will be transmitted and edited only once. This will improve the response time of a CICS transaction.

The other technique to edit the input data is to turn on MDT for each field entered so it will be received into the map I/O area for each subsequent RECEIVE MAP command. This method will not use the communication area to save the input data. It will get the input data for each input operation by transmitting it from the terminal into the program. After the input data has been received, it will go through the editing routing every time. This technique will transmit and edit the input data for every input operation. Data should be transmitted and edited only once. If you use the first method, after you have edited a valid field, you will save it in the communication area and turn off its MDT. So the input data will not be transmitted for the subsequent input operatios unless it has been changed by the user. In this case, the new data will be transmitted and re-edited.

The other problem regarding the second method is that each input field will be re-edited in each input operation. Since the MDT of each input field is turned on after each input operation, the data displayed on the terminal will be transmitted into the program no matter if the user has changed it or not. The re-editing for the same data is not necessary and could be a time-consuming process if the editing involves the file I/O operation. For example, we need to read the customer file to edit the customer number to see if the key exists. If you use the second method, then READ command will be performed for each input operation no matter if the operator has changed the customer number or not. If you use the first method, the customer number will be edited only once unless it has been changed by the user.

The following example shows how two ways to use the second method:

```
XXCU01 DFHMDF ... CTRL=(FREEKB,FRSET) ...
CUSTNO DFHMDF POS=(03,02),LENGTH=5,ATTRB=(NUM,FSET)


     IF CUSTNOL > 0
         IF CUSTNOI NUMERIC
            NEXT SENTENCE
       . ELSE
            MOVE 'R' TO CUSTNOA
            MOVE -1  TO CUSTNOL
            MOVE 'BAD CUSTOMER' TO MSGO.
```

In the above example, we specify ATTRB=(NUM,FSET) to ensure the customer number will be received into the CICS program for every input operation. After the customer number has been edited as a valid field, we do not need to save it in the communication area since it will be received into the map I/O area for each subsequent input operation. We do not need to turn on the MDT since the MDT will stay on with ATTRB=(NUM,FSET).

The second way to use the second technique is not specifying FRSET in the CTRL= parameter in the DFHMSD macro:

```
XXCU01    DFHMSD ... CRTL=FREEKB ...
AXCU01    DFHMDI SIZE=(24,80)
          . . . .
CUSTNO    DFHMDF POS=(03,02),LENGTH=05,ATTRB=NUM
```

In the above example, we do not specify ATTRB=(FSET,NUM). We only specify ATTRB=NUM. However, we specify CTRL=FREEKB instead of

CTRL=(FREEKB,FRSET). When the user enters a new customer number on the screen, the MDT of this field will be turned on and the customer number will be received into the program. However, the MDT of this field will stay on for each subsequent input operation since CICS will not turn off the MDT for you (FRSET not specified) . This will transmit the customer number into the program for each input operation and in result, the customer number will be re-edit each time.

The screen format for this Customer Add program is as follows:

```
CU01  XX/XX/XX HH:SS     ADD A NEW CUSTOMER                          XXXX

CUSTOMER NO  : 99999

CUSTOMER NAME: XXXXXXXXXXXXXXXXXXX

CREDIT LIMIT : 9999999

INVOICE AMT  : 9999999


CLEAR=MENU, PF1=RESET
XXXXXXXXXXXXXXXXXXXXXXXXXXXXXXXXXXXXXXXXXXXXXXXXXXXXXXXXXXXXXXXXXXXXXXXX
```

In the preceeding screen, we define the CLEAR key to go back to menu and PF1 to reset the screen for the next new customer. This way, the user can enter the next customer without going back to the menu screen.

The flowchart for this Customer Add CICS program is as follows:

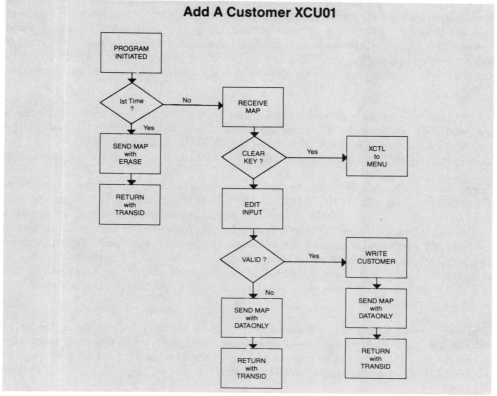

Add A Customer XCU01

199

The complete listing of this Customer Add program is in Chapter 13.2.

10.3. Inquire/Update/Delete

Normally, you can include all these three functions in one CICS program since they all need to read and display the record first. After the record has been displayed, you can then take one of the following actions:

1. Hit CLEAR key to go back to the menu screen. This is the inquiry function.

2. Enter the key of the next record to be inquired.

3. Update the record and then hit ENTER key.

4. Hit PF1 key to delete the record.

After the record has been updated or deleted, a completion message will be displayed. You can then hit CLEAR key to go back to the menu screen or enter the key of the next record to be inquired, updated or deleted to display the next record. This kind of design will enable the user to go to process the next record without going back to the menu screen.

After the user has selected function 2 and entered the customer number to be updated, inquired, or deleted on the menu screen, the menu program should edit the customer number to see if it exists. If it is not, the menu program should reject the request and ask the user to correct the customer number. Do not pass an invalid customer number to the inquire/update/delete CICS program. All CICS programs that want to go to the inquire/update/delete program must pass a valid customer number in the communication area.

After the function number 2 and a valid customer number has been entered, the menu program will issue an XCTL command with the customer number saved in the communication area (COMMAREA). After the XCTL command has been executed, the menu program will be terminated and the inquire/update/delete program will be invoked.

When the inquire/update/delete program is invoked, the customer number passed from the menu program is in DFHCOMMAREA of LINKAGE SECTION. You can use it to read its customer record from the customer file and then move the customer information to the map I/O area. After the map I/O area has been filled with data, you can issue a SEND MAP command with the ERASE option to display the customer information on the terminal and then issue a RETURN command with the TRANSID option. The transaction ID of this inquire/update/delete program should be specified in the TRANSID option so any response to this terminal will invoke this inquire/update/delete program again.

The user can then review the customer and hit CLEAR key to go back to the menu screen. He can also hit PF1 key to delete the customer. After PF1 is hit, the program will be invoked again. This time, the control will go to the label set up for PF1 key in the HANDLE AID command to delete the customer.

In this delete routine, you should use the customer number passed to this new session in DFHCOMMAREA to delete the customer. You do not need to issue a READ command with the UPDATE option to retrieve the record first. You can just specify the customer number in the RIDFLD option in the DELETE command. After the DELETE command has been issued, you should send a message saying that the customer has been deleted to the terminal. After the user has seen this message, he can then hit CLEAR key to return to the menu screen or enter the next customer number to be inquired, updated or deleted.

If the user wants to update the displayed customer, he can enters the updates and then hits ENTER key. This inquire/update/delete program will be invoked again. It should issue a RECEIVE MAP command to receive the updates into the map I/O area and then edit the updates. If any of the updates is invalid, it should perform the dynamic attribute modification and then issue a SEND MAP command with DATAONLY and CURSOR options to send the error map back to the terminal for the user to correct the invalid fields.

If all updates are valid, you should issue a READ command with the UPDATE option to retrieve the record, move the updates you saved in the communication area to the record layout and then issue a REWRITE command to update the record. You should not try to change the key of the record during the update. After the REWRITE command has been issued, you should send a message saying that the update has been completed to the terminal. After the user has seen this message, he can enter the next customer number to be inquired, updated, or deleted on the next customer field and then hit ENTER key to display the new customer. He can also hit CLEAR key to go back to the menu screen.

It is a good design to allow the user to enter the key of the next record to be processed in an inquire/update/delete application. So the user does not have to go back to the menu screen to enter the key of the next customer to be processed.

You can see we set up CLEAR key on every screen of this system to allow the user to return to the menu from any other screen at any time. You must handle CLEAR key in every CICS program since CLEAR key will erase the current screen. If you do not handle CLEAR key in the HANDLE AID command, you'll lose the current screen after the CLEAR key is hit. You may also notice that when we set up a control key to be pressed by the user to perform a pre-defined function, no data has to be entered before the control key is pressed. You should not design a screen that requires the user to enter the input data and then hit control key. This technique is used very often in the macro-level programs since CICS macro-level language does not have the feature that is performed by the HANDLE AID command of the command-level language. Therefore, many applications written in the macro-level language would require the user to enter data and hit a control key at the same time to perform a pre-defined function. In this case, the control will go to the editing routine after the input data has been received. However, if you set up the control key in the HANDLE AID command, after the RECEIVE MAP is issued, the control normally will bypass the editing routine and go to the label specified for that control key. If you need to enter input data, then ENTER key should always be used. The control key should be designed to branch to a label that does not need the input data when that key is hit.

You need to know that PA keys will not transmit data if you enter input data and hit PA key. However, PF keys will transmit data if the input data is entered and the PF key is hit.

Some compaines like to use a subroutine program that performs the editing for both Add and Update programs. Both Add and update programs will use the same CICS mapset and link to this editing program to perform the editing. The data needs to be passed to this editing program is the map I/O area.

The following is the flowchart for this Inquire/Update/Delete Customer program:

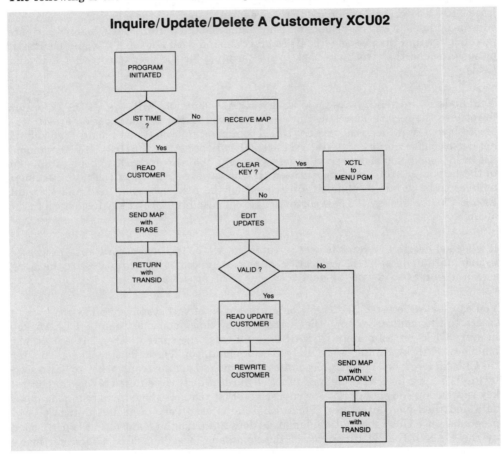

Inquire/Update/Delete A Customery XCU02

The Inquire/Update/Delete Customer program is in Chapter 13.4.

10.4. Browse

Browse is normally performed upon a segment of consecutive records. For example, we want to display all sales order details in the sales order detail file for any given sales order number. In this case, the key to this file is the sales order number plus the detail sequence number. The browse operation is performed through the use of the STARTBR, READNEXT, and ENDBR commands. The STARTBR command sets up the starting browse key. The READNEXT command will actually retrieve the next available record and is normally issued repeatedly until the screen is full or the end of the file has been reached, or the control break has occurred (sales order number has changed). The ENDBR command is issued after you have determined that browse operation should be terminated.

Since a screen can only contain so many detail lines, you should allow the user to hit a program-defined key to go to display the next page. It is also nice to allow the user to hit a pre-defined control key to display the previous page of the display from the current page. The user should also be able to hit CLEAR key to go back to the menu screen at any time on this browse screen.

In many browse applications, you need to allow the user to put an 'X' on the desired detail line and go to display the detail information of the selected record. For example, each detail line of the sales order browse screen only shows the detail sequence number, product code , product description and order quantity. If you put an 'X' on the desired sales order detail, the control will be transferred to the sales order detail program to display the detailed information about the selected sales order detail like: shipped quantity, last ship date, unit price, and discount %.

If you need to allow the user to enter data on the detail lines, then you cannot use OCCURS= in the mapset define. You can only use OCCURS= when the detail line contains display-only information and is 79 bytes long. In the next section, we will discuss how you can define detail lines for update purposes.

For the browse applications, you should also allow the user to enter the new starting key so he can browse the records starting with this new key. This is almost a required field on every browse screen. For example, the user wants to browse the details for a sales order number after the current sales order browse operation is completed. In this case, he can enter the next sales order number on this next order number field and hit ENTER key. This browse program should use this new order number as if it is passed from the menu program to display the details of this order.

The screen format for this Browse program is identical to that for Browse/Update Sales Order Detail program in the next section. The flowchart for this program is also very similar to that of the Browse/Update program. Please refer to the next section for the screen format and flowchart.

```
BRWS   XX/XX/XX HH:MM      BROWSE SALES ORDER DETAILS        XXXX PAGE: 99

NEXT ORDER NUMBER: 99999

SEL SEQ PRODUCT CODE     DESC                  ORDQTY    PRICE
 X    999 XXXXXXXXXXXXXX XXXXXXXXXXXXXXXXXXXX   99999  99999.99
 X    999 XXXXXXXXXXXXXX XXXXXXXXXXXXXXXXXXXX   99999  99999.99
 X    999 XXXXXXXXXXXXXX XXXXXXXXXXXXXXXXXXXX   99999  99999.99
 X    999 XXXXXXXXXXXXXX XXXXXXXXXXXXXXXXXXXX   99999  99999.99
 X    999 XXXXXXXXXXXXXX XXXXXXXXXXXXXXXXXXXX   99999  99999.99
 X    999 XXXXXXXXXXXXXX XXXXXXXXXXXXXXXXXXXX   99999  99999.99
 X    999 XXXXXXXXXXXXXX XXXXXXXX``XXXXXXXXXX   99999  99999.99
 X    999 XXXXXXXXXXXXXX XXXXXXXXXXXXXXXXXXXX   99999  99999.99

CLEAR=MENU, PF1=NEXT PAGE, PF2=PREV PAGE
XXXXXXXXXXXXXXXXXXXXXXXXXXXXXXXXXXXXXXXXXXXXXXXXXXXXXXXXXXXXXXXXXXXXXXXXXXXXX
```

The flowchart of this customer browse program is as follows:

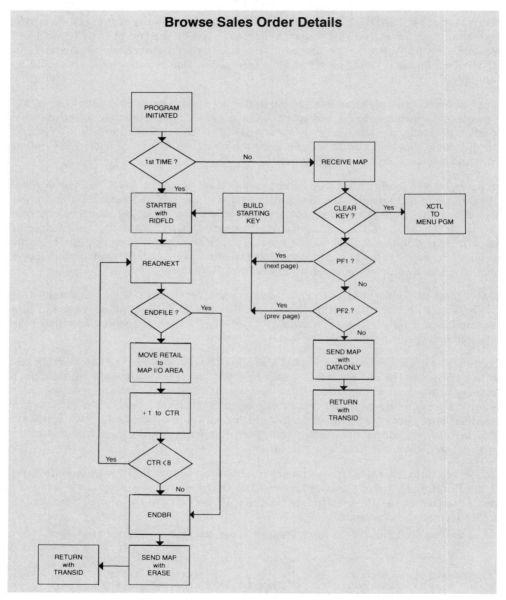

Browse Sales Order Details

10.5.   Browse/Update

In order to allow update on the detail lines in a browse operation, you need to know how
to redefine the map I/O area. The map I/O area is a copy book generated when you
assemble the CICS mapset. It contains a 12-byte control area and four generated fields

for each named field defined in the CICS mapset. Only those fields defined with a label in the mapset will be generated in the symbolic description map. The following example shows how BMS generates the map I/O area copy book:

```
XXCU03    DFHMSD ....
AXCU03    DFHMDI ZE=(24,80)
ORDER     DFHMDF POS=(03,02),LENGTH=5,ATTRB=NUM
AMT       DFHMDF POS=(05,30),LENGTH=8,ATTRB=NUM
          DFHMDF TYPE=FINAL
          END

01   AXCU03I.
     02   FILLER      PIC X(12).
     02   ORDERL      PIC S9(4) COMP.
     02   ORDERA      PIC X(1).
     02   FILLER REDEFINES ORDERA.
      03   ORDERF     PIC X(1).
     02   ORDERI      PIC X(5).
     02   AMTL        PIC S9(4) COMP.
     02   AMTA        PIC X(1).
     02   FILLER REDEFINES AMTA.
      03   AMTF       PIC X(1).
     02   AMTI        PIC X(8).
     02   FILLER      PIC X(1).
01   AXCU03O REDEFINES AXCU03I.
     02   FILLER      PIC X(12).
     02   FILLER      PIC X(3).
     02   ORDERO      PIC X(5).
     02   FILLER      PIC X(3).
     02   AMTO        PIC X(8).
     02   FILLER      PIC X(1).
```

There are three factors that will affect how BMS generates the symbolic description map:

1. Is TIOAPFX=YES specified in the DFHMSD macro? If it is, then BMS will generate a 12-byte control area in the copy book before it generates the first named map field. You should always specify TIOAPFX=YES before you can issue a SEND MAP or RECEIVE MAP without FROM or INTO option.

2. Is half-word alignment specified in the JCL used to assemble the CICS mapset. At least 50% of CICS shops set up the JCL to generate the symbolic description map using the half-word alignment. If half-word alignment is used, then you need to inclue a one-byte filler for a map field that is defined to contain even number of positions. In the above example, AMT is defined as eight (even) bytes long. Therefore, we need to include a one-byte filler following AMTI. ORDER is defined as 5 (odd) bytes long. Therefore no filler is needed following ORDERI.

3. Are extended attributes to be used for this mapset? If EXTATT=YES is secified in the DFHMSD macro for this CICS mapset, then you need to add four more bytes for each map field in the copy book to support the extended attributes. Most of the time, EXTATT=YES is not specified.

In order to use COBOL PERFORM verb to process these repeatly-generated detail lines, you need to re-define the map I/O area using OCCURS. Then you can process the data fields in each detail line in the map I/O area using the PERFORM verb and indexing. The map I/O area generated by BMS does not use OCCURS clause. Each data field in the detail line will be defined as an independent field in the CICS mapset.

The CLEAR key is used when the user wants to go back to the menu screen at any time when he is on this browse/update screen. PF1 is used to display the next page of sales order details. PF2 is used when the user wants to display the previous page of the sales order details. If the user wants to update the sales order detail lines, he can just make the updates and then hit ENTER key. After the update is completed, the user can hit CLEAR key to go to the menu screen or enter the next sales order to be processed.

In order to process PF1 key (next page), you need to save the key of the last record displayed on the current page in the communication area. Then you can use this key to build the start key for the next page. If the key is numeric, you can add 1 to the key of the last record of the current page to obtain the starting key of the next page. If the key is not numeric, you can issue a STARTBR, two READNEXT, and one ENDBR commands to get the starting key for the next page. The first READNEXT command will retrieve the last record of the current page and the next READNEXT command will retrieve the first record of the next page. You can then get the key of this record and use it for the next page operation. You should use the key of the last record on the current page to issue this STARTBR command.

You also need to save the key of the first record of each page in the communication area in order to handle the previous page request (PF2). If PF2 is pressed, you should use the key of the first record of the last page in the communication area as the starting key in the STARTBR command to display the previous page. You cannot just save the key of the first record for the last page. You need to save the key of the first record of all pages when you try to display a new page. Therefore, if the user wants to go back to page 8 from the page 10, your browse program can also handle that.

The Browse/Update screen is as follows:

```
CU03  XX/XX/XX HH:SS    BROWSE/UPDATE CUSTOMERS BY NAME   XXXX PAGE: 99

NEXT CUSTOMER NAME: XXXXXXXXXXXXXXXXXXXX

SEL CUSTOMER NAME          CUST#    CRD LMT    INV AMT
X   XXXXXXXXXXXXXXXXXXXX   99999    9999999    9999999
X   XXXXXXXXXXXXXXXXXXXX   99999    9999999    9999999
X   XXXXXXXXXXXXXXXXXXXX   99999    9999999    9999999
X   XXXXXXXXXXXXXXXXXXXX   99999    9999999    9999999
X   XXXXXXXXXXXXXXXXXXXX   99999    9999999    9999999
X   XXXXXXXXXXXXXXXXXXXX   99999    9999999    9999999
X   XXXXXXXXXXXXXXXXXXXX   99999    9999999    9999999
X   XXXXXXXXXXXXXXXXXXXX   99999    9999999    9999999
X   XXXXXXXXXXXXXXXXXXXX   99999    9999999    9999999
X   XXXXXXXXXXXXXXXXXXXX   99999    9999999    9999999
X   XXXXXXXXXXXXXXXXXXXX   99999    9999999    9999999
X   XXXXXXXXXXXXXXXXXXXX   99999    9999999    9999999
X   XXXXXXXXXXXXXXXXXXXX   99999    9999999    9999999
X   XXXXXXXXXXXXXXXXXXXX   99999    9999999    9999999
X   XXXXXXXXXXXXXXXXXXXX   99999    9999999    9999999

CLEAR=MENU, PF1=NEXT PAGE, PF2=PREV PAGE
XXXXXXXXXXXXXXXXXXXXXXXXXXXXXXXXXXXXXXXXXXXXXXXXXXXXXXXXXXXXXXXXXXXXXXXXXXXX
```

The flowchart of this Browse/Update CICS program is as follows:

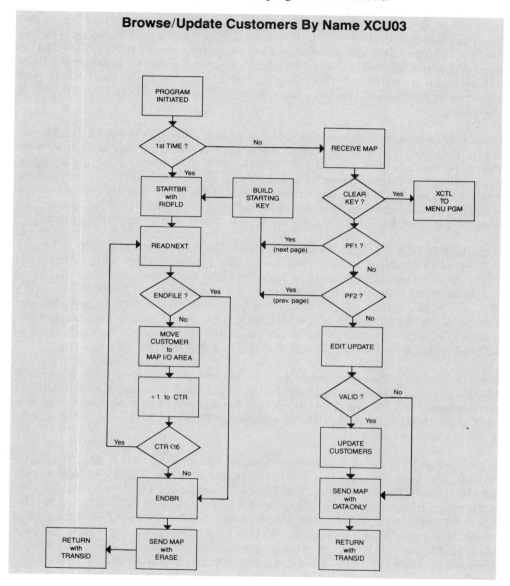

Browse/Update Customers By Name XCU03

The complete listing of the browse/update program is listed in chapter 13.5.

10.6.   Print A 24x80 Report

At least 10% of the CICS programs are on-line report print programs. Therefore, you need to know how to write a print program. However, CICS allows you to print a report in two ways: one uses Message Routing technique and the other uses Terminal Control.

If you use Message Routing technique to print a report, you have two choices. One use the SEND MAP ACCUM command and the other uses the SEND TEXT ACCUM command. If the SEND MAP ACCUM command is used, you need to set up the CICS mapset. If you use the SEND TEXT ACCUM command, then there is no CICS mapset needed to be defined and you will define the report format in WORKING-STORAGE SECTION.

A report is a message which contains one or more pages. Each page may be divided into header, detail and trailer. In most cases, you can define the entire page as a header map. Therefore, you only need to issue a SEND MAP ACCUM command to build a page in the message. This command may be issued repeatly in order to build the entire message. After the message has been built completely, you can then issue a SEND PAGE command to print the message. If an error is encountered during the message building process, you need to issue a PURGE MESSAGE command to delete the uncompleted message.

If the SEND TEXT ACCUM command is to be used, then you still need to issue a ROUTE LIST command to set up the destinations (printers), then one or more SEND TEXT ACCUM commands should be issued to build the message and then the SEND PAGE command is issued to print the message. You can print a report with line length of 40, 64, or 80 positions. If the report has a line length greater than 80 positions, you need to change the PGESIZE of the TCT entry for that printer. For example, you can specify PGESIZE = (11,132) for the printer and print up to 132 positions per line. The default line length is that specified in the TCT for that printer.

You can also insert the printer control characters into the data stream specified in the FROM option. The new line character (DFHBMPNL), end of message (DFHBMPEM), carriage return (X'0D'), and form feed (X'0C') can be inserted into the data stream. You need to specify NLEOM in the ROUTE and SEND TEXT ACCUM commands in order to use the printer control characters.

If you choose to print an on-line report using Terminal Control command (SEND FROM), you normally start this print transaction using the START command with TRANSID and TERMID options. The TRANSID option specifies the transaction code of the print program. The TERMID option specifies the printer ID that is to print this report. The data to be passed to the print transaction should be specified in the FROM option. When the START command is executed, the print task is initiated to print the report on the printer. When the print program is invoked, it will issue a RETRIEVE command to retrieve the data passed and then build the report in the output data stream. It will then issue the SEND FROM command to print the report on the printer. The data field specified in the FROM option of the SEND FROM command contains the output data stream to be printed. The output data stream will be built with printer control characters.

Using the SEND FROM command is just like using the SEND TEXT ACCUM command with NLEOM option. The advantage of using Terminal Control to print a report is that there is no limit on the length of the print line and you do not need to change PGESIZE of the TCT entry for the printer in order to print a report with line length greater than 80 positions. You can print as many characters as the printer allows (150 columns). You can print as many as 1920 bytes for each SEND FROM command. The major disadvantage is that you can only send 1920 characters of data in each SEND FROM command and if the report is longer than 1920 bytes, then you need to issue more than one SEND FROM command. Therefore, it opens up the possibility of mixing your report with others between two SEND FROM commands. In order to prevent that from happening, you need to issue an ENQ command to enqueue the printer before you print the first part of the report and then issue a DEQ command to release the printer when the report is completed.

The print utility program that is to be started by the START command and uses the SEND FROM command provides an excellent way to print any internal report. The CICS programmer does not have to know how to print an on-line report, he just supplies the output data, desired line length, and form feed request and then issue the START command to initiate the print transaction. For example, you can use this transaction in the abend-handling CICS program to print the error message on the printer that is close to the CICS programmers. You can also use this print transaction to print any report that is to be used by managers for investigation or management purposes. We'll show you how to write the print utility program and how to invoke it to print the on-line report in Chapter 13.9 and 13.13.

In the following sections, we'll show you three ways to print an on-line reports using the Message Routing technique and one way to print using Terminal Control. One uses the SEND MAP ACCUM command to print a given sales order with all its details. Each page will have 24 lines and each line has 80 positions. We'll define the entire page as one single header map. There are no detail and trailer maps needed to be defined since only one type of printer (3287 model 2) will be used. The report may have more than one page depending on how many details for that sales order. Each page contains 5 lines for the order header information, 17 sales order details, and 2 lines for the trailer (footing).

The second method will be used to print the same report as described in the first method. However, we'll define three maps for each page: header map, detail map and trailer map. The header map contains 5 lines. The detail map contains only one line. To print each sales order detail, you need to issue a SEND MAP ACCUM command using the detail map. Up to 17 details can be printed within each page. When you try to print the 18th detail, OVERFLOW condition will occur. In this case, you should send the trailer map to complete the current page, send the header map for the next page, and then go back to send the detail map that caused the OVERFLOW condition. This time, there will be no OVERFLOW condition since that condition will be reset when we send the header map. This technique can be used when you try to route the message to different type of devices. BMS will build a message for each device type. The OVERFLOW condition will occur at different time since the page size of each device may be different. This allows you to use the same program on different devices.

The third method will be used to print a sales order on 132 columns per line paper. We'll print 66 lines per page which is the most common used computer paper. Each sales order detail record will be printed on one line. We'll use the SEND TEXT ACCUM command instead of the SEND MAP ACCUM command to build the message. The page size

(PGESIZE) of the TCT entry for the printer must be defined as PGESIZE=(11,132) instead of PGESIZE=(24,80).

The fourth method will be used to print a on-line report on any-size page specified by the issuing CICS program. Each CICS shop should develop this type of print transaction so everyone who wants to print a report only needs to start the transaction. We'll show you both the invoking CICS program and the print utility program. The data to be printed and the report format must be passed to the print utility program. The printer ID must be specified in the START command. The data to be printed should not contain any printer control characters. This print utility program will insert them for you.

If the report can be printed on 24x80 pages and the page format is fixed, then you can define the page as a header map within the mapset. After the CICS mapset has been defined, you can use the Messsge Routing technique to print this report. There is no need to define the detail map and the trailer map since the header map will contain both. There is no need to set up the OVERFLOW condition since the header map will never cause this exception condition. The OVERFLOW condition will occur only if you try to send a detail map and there is no more space left within the page.

For example, we want to print a sales order with all its sales order details. The sales order header information can be obtained from the sales order header file whose key is the sales order number. Each sales order may have one or more sales order detail records in the sales order detail file whose key is the sales order number plus the sequence number.

Each page in the message contains 5 lines for the order header information, 17 detail lines and 2 lines for the trailer. More than one page may be printed for each sales order. Each page has 24 lines and each line has 80 positions. The PGESIZE for the TCT entry of this printer is (24,80). In order to print this sales order, we'll define one header map to contain all the information for a page. Therefore, one SEND MAP ACCUM command is needed for each page to be printed. Before you start to build the message, you should use the ROUTE command to set up the printer list and more than one printer can be specified in the route list. You then issue the SEND MAP command with ERASE, PAGING, and ACCUM options to send the header map for each page. You will read the sales order header file to get the order header information. Then you need to browse the sales order detail file to get all details for the sales order number. You should put a limit on total number of details to be printed to prevent this program from hanging the entire CICS system. When there are no more details to be printed, you should then issue a SEND PAGE command to transmit and print the report (message).

For Message Routing applications, you should always put a limit on the number of records to be printed to prevent the print task from using up all the avaliable temporary storage. When there are no more temporary storages, the issuing task will be suspended waiting for the resource. Since temporary storage is also used in other CICS operations like TS queue, START command, or Terminal paging, you may hang the entire CICS/VS system.

You can invoke this print program through the use of the START command. All the print programs are normally invoked through the the use of the START command. However, you do not specify the associated terminal (TERMID) for the START command. The ROUTE command within the print program will set up the printer list. There is no reason to associate a print program with a terminal unless you want to use Terminal Control command SEND FROM to print the report. So after the print transaction is initiated, the control will continue to the next statement following the START command. You can also use the XCTL or LINK command to invoke the print program. If you use the XCTL command to invoke the print program, you can use CEDF to monitor the print program on the terminal.

During the message building, you should issue a PURGE MESSAGE command if any non-recoverable error has been encountered. This command will delete the uncompleted message. When you try to send a header map in the SEND MAP ACCUM command, you always specify ERASE option to clear the printer buffer for the new page.

The flowchart for this print program to print the sales order the Message Routing technique is as follows:

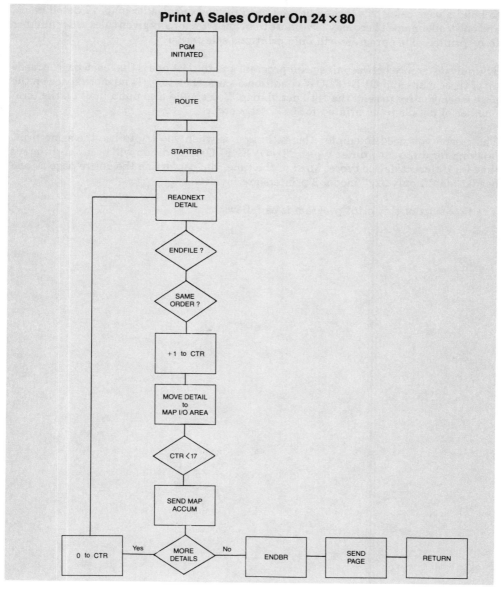

Print A Sales Order On 24 × 80

The entire CICS program, CICS mapset and report format are in Chapter 13.6.

10.7.   Print A 24x80 Paper Using OVERFLOW

This example will shows how to print a sales order with the same report format as described in the above section on 24x80 paper using the Message Routing technique. Instead of using only the header map, we'll divide each page into three maps: header, detail and trailer maps. The header map describes the order header information, the detail map occupies only one line and describes one sales order detail record and the trailer map will print 'continued on the next page' for the footing of each page. In order to build a page using this technique, you need to send one header map, 17 detail maps, and one trailer map. There may have more than one page for any given sales order number to be printed. This program will only print one sales order.

The only difference between this print program and the last one is that each page is made up of three maps and OVERFLOW condition occurs when there is no more space on the page when you try to send the 18th detail map. You should also put a limit on the total number of details to be printed for each sales order.

The reason you need to employ this technique is when you try to use the same print program for different printer types. The OVERFLOW condition will occur at different time for different device types. Most of the time, you can define the entire page as one header map if only 3287 model 2 printers are involved.

The flowchart of this print program is as follows:

Print A Sales Order on 24 × 80

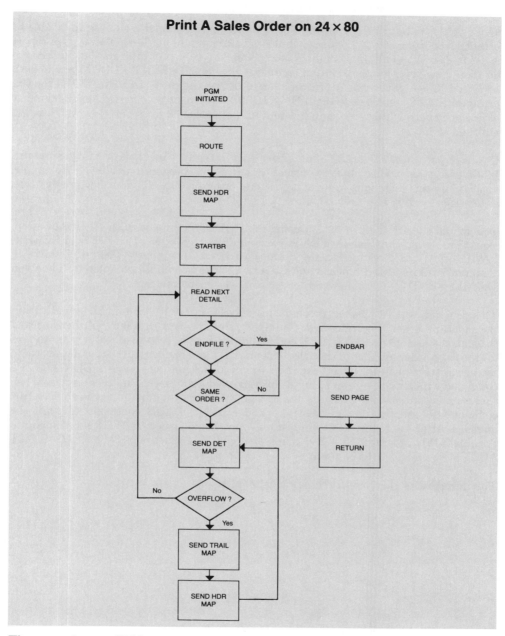

The report format, CICS program, and CICS mapset for this sales order print application is in Chapter 13.7.

10.8.   Print A 66X132 Report Using SEND TEXT ACCUM

When you need to print a report on the regular computer paper, you need to be able to print the report on 66 x 132 paper (66 lines and 132 columns per line). This type of report is used when the detail line contains more than 80 columns of information. In order to do that using the Message Routing technique (the SEND TEXT ACCUM command), you need to ask your system programmer to define the page size (PGESIZE) for the printer on its TCT entry as PGESIZE=(11,132). The reason we choose 11 as the number of lines per page is that the regular computer paper has 66 lines per page which is the multiple of 11.

If your report use less than 132 columns per line, you can still use this printing technique. In this case, you only need to move spaces to the unused columns in the line. For example, you can use this technique to print a purchase order on 66 x 85 paper (letter size). The letter-size report is also very popular.

You should specify the printer list using the ROUTE command with NLEOM option. You then issue the SEND TEXT command with FROM, LENGTH, FREEKB, PAGING, ACCUM and NLEOM options to build the report. The SEND TEXT command will be issued repeatly until the report has been built completely. Then you issue the SEND PAGE command to transmit and print the report.

This program will be invoked through the use of the START command issued within the menu program. The sales order number passed to this program will be retrieved through the use of the RETRIEVE command. We'll then browse all sales order details for the sales order number in the sales order detail file. For each sales order detail record retrieved, we will move its information to the print line and issue a SEND TEXT command with FROM option to build this retrieved detail record in the message. When there are no more detail records for this sales order, you should issue an ENDBR command to end the browse operation and a SEND PAGE command to print the message. After the report has been printed, you should issue a RETURN command to terminate this program. No CICS mapset should be defined since the SEND TEXT ACCUM command is to be used.

The flowchart of this print program is as follows:

Print 66 × 132 Report

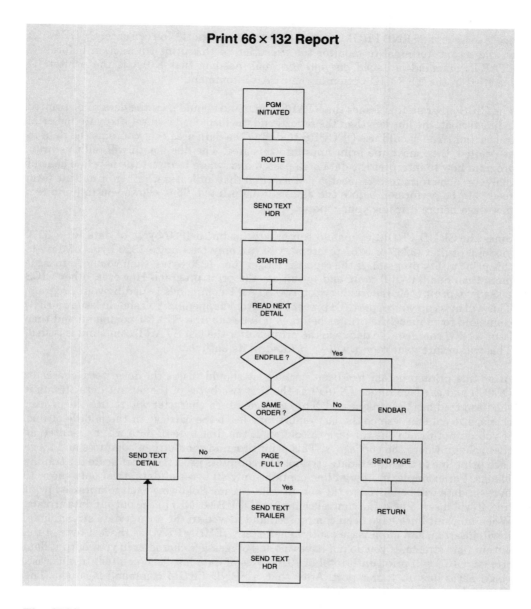

The CICS program and its report format are in Chapter 13.8.

10.9.   Print Any-Size Report Using SEND FROM

This example will show how to write a print utility program that can be used by any CICS program that needs to print any-size report. This print utility program will be invoked by the CICS program that issues the START command to initiate its transaction code. The printer ID should be specified in the START command so this print program only needs to issue the SEND FROM command to print the report. You can enter CEDF K01A on the second terminal to monitor the execution of this print transaction before the START command is issued on your terminal. Assume that K01A is the printer ID specified in the TERMID option of the START command.

The CICS program that issues the START command should pass the data to be printed in line format, the line length of the report, and the form feed request if any to this print transaction. You should use OCCURS to define the data area that contains the data to be printed, then move the print lines into this area. The line length will tell this print program how to interpret the data area passed and where to insert the new line control character. The form feed request is just a switch that indicates whether or not the form feed is to be performed before the data is to be printed. This allows you to jump to a new page before printing your report.

Since the SEND FROM command can only print up to 1920 bytes of data for a 3270 model 2 printer (3286 or 3287 printers), you can only pass up to 1920 bytes of data to this print utility program. If the report is longer than 1920 bytes, then you need to issue more than one START command to initiate the print program. However, other CICS tasks may print their reports between two START commands issued by your program. This will mess up your report. To prevent that from happening, you should issue an ENQ command to enqueue the printer before you issue the first START command and then issue a DEQ command to dequeue the printer after the last START command is issued. This will ensure your report will be printed in its entirety.

After this print program has been invoked, it should insert the form feed character (X'0C') and carriage return (X'0D') as the first two bytes of the output data stream if the form feed has been requested. The carriage return character will return the printer carriage to column 1 since the last report may leave the carriage in the middle of line. If you do not return the carriage to column 1, the first byte of data will be printed at that column where the carriage is. This print program should then compress and move each print line to the output data stream. The compress process will truncate the trailing blanks. For example, if a detail line contains only 40 bytes of data, then only those 40 bytes of data will be moved to the output data stream. Following each compressed print line, it will insert a new line control character (DFHBMPNL) in the output data stream. When all print lines have been compressed and moved to the output data stream area, it will insert an end of message control character (DFHBMPEM) as the last byte of the output data stream. If you do not have this end of message character in your output data stream, CICS will print until total of 1920 bytes of data has been printed. In this case, you'll never line up your report. After that, a SEND FROM command is issued. The output data stream you have built should be specified in the FROM option. Following the SEND FROM command, a RETURN command will be issued to end this print program.

The flowchart of this print utility program is as follows:

Print Any-Size Report

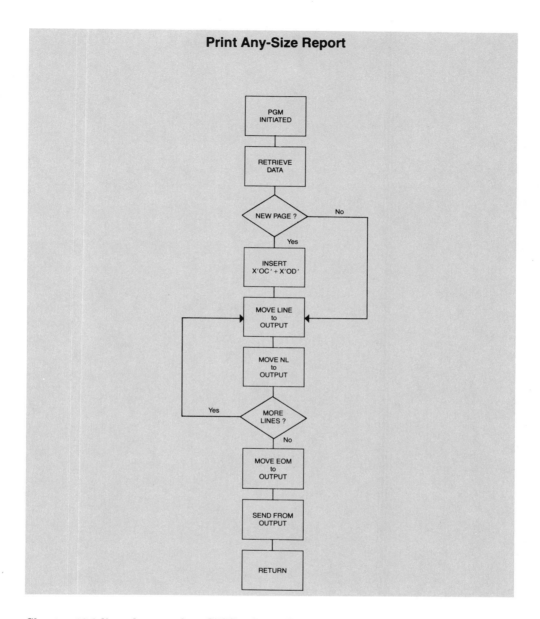

Chapter 13.9 lists the complete CICS print utility program, the report format and the invoking CICS program that issues the START command to initiate the print transaction.

CHAPTER 11. TESTING AND IMPLEMENTATION TECHNIQUES

This chapter will cover CICS testing and implementation techniques. After you have successfully compiled your CICS programs, CICS mapsets, and CICS constant tables (i.e. store table), you are ready to test the CICS transactions to see if they work. The following steps must be taken before you can actually start testing your CICS transactions in the CICS test system:

1. All CICS programs, CICS mapsets, and CICS constant tables have been successfully compiled.
   The CICS constant tables are only used in the LOAD and RELEASE commands. They are not used very frequently. If your CICS programs do not use these tables, then you do not need to worry about the constant tables.

2. Go see your system programmer to set up PPT, PCT, FCT, TCT, and DCT entries. These CICS internal tables are used during the CICS task execution time. Your system programmer should put all CICS programs, CICS mapsets, and CICS constant tables into the PPT (processing Program Table), put all CICS transaction IDs with their associated CICS program into the PCT (Program Control Table) and put all VSAM files to be processed in CICS/VS into the FCT (File Control Table). The FCT entry must also specify the service requests that CICS programs can perform upon that VSAM file. Each VSAM file must have one entry in the FCT. If alternate indexes are to be used for a VSAM file, then one entry for each alternate index path must be specified in the FCT. Each display terminal or printer to be used in a CICS/VS system must have one entry in the TCT (Terminal Control Table). If Transient Data Queues are to be used in your CICS programs, then each destination (queue) must have one entry in the DCT (Destination Control Table). Each CICS internal table (i.e. PPT) is a collection of CICS macros. Your system programmer must add new entries to each table and then use a set of JCL to assemble the table. After the table is successfully assembled, it will create a load module in the CICS system load library. When CICS/VS system is brought up each time, it will load these latest load modules (tables) for use.

3. Set up VSAM test files.
   Before you can test your CICS transactions, you need to set up VSAM test files in CICS. If this VSAM file is to be created exclusively in CICS, then you only need to define the VSAM file and then create a low-value record into it. After the low-value record has been created, you can then delete it in the same COBOL batch program. This will make CICS think that this is not a null VSAM file. You cannot just define a VSAM file and then try to process it in CICS since CICS prohibits a null file (empty file) to be processed in CICS. If this VSAM file can be copied from an existing production file, then you should define the file and then load this VSAM test file from the production file using the REPRO command. After VSAM files have been defined and loaded, you should ask your system programmer to create a FCT entry for it. After the FCT entry is created, you need to ask your system programmer to set up a DD or DLBL statement and a VERIFY statement for each VSAM file in the CICS startup JCL. Then you are ready to process this file in CICS.

After the above steps have been taken, you can sign on to CICS test system to test your CICS transactions. In each installation, there are normally two CICS systems running: CICS test system and CICS production system. The CICS test system is running in one region (OS/VS) or partition (DOS/VSE) while the CICS production system is running in another region or partition. Each CICS system has its own internal tables, files, programs, mapsets, constant tables. In addition to these two systems, some installations also have one or more training CICS systems which are used to train CICS users. The application programmers normally are able to sign on only to the CICS test system.

The CICS test system uses its own set of CICS internal tables, VSAM files, load libraries for CICS programs, mapsets, and dynamic tables. The CICS production system has its own set of resources. Therefore, you do not need to worry about screwing up the production CICS system from the CICS test system.

After the CICS transactions have been tested successfully in the CICS test system, they will be moved to CICS production system. This step is called implementation. You only need to compile your CICS programs, CICS mapsets, and CICS constant tables into the production load library instead of test system load library. Your system programmer also needs to set up your CICS programs, mapsets, and dynamic tables into the PPT, transaction IDs and associated CICS programs into the PCT, VSAM files and/or alternate indexes into the FCT, terminals and printers into the TCT, Transient Data queues into the DCT. These CICS internal tables should be the production tables which are different from their test system tables. The procedures to set up CICS transactions for CICS test system and production system are the same except for that different libraries, tables, and VSAM catalog are used.

CICS/VS provides two transactions that can be used to sign on to the CICS system. You can only test your CICS transactions after you have signed on to the CICS test system. The CICS users must also sign on to the CICS/VS production system before they can use your CICS transactions. These two CICS-supplied transactions are: CSSN and CSSF. The CSSN transaction is used to sign on to CICS and CSSF transaction is used to sign off from the CICS system. Your system programmer must create one SNT (Sign-On Table) entry for each user or programmer before he or she can sign on to the CICS system. After you have signed off from the CICS system, you cannot enter any CICS transaction.

The following example shows how to sign on to test CICS system:

1. Enter TEST then hit ENTER key.
   TEST is the system application ID assigned to the CICS test system by your system programmer. This ID can be different from one CICS shop to another.

2. Enter CSSN then hit ENTER key.
   CSSN is entered to indicate that you want to sign on to the CICS system. In response, CICS will ask you to enter the user ID and password.

3. Enter your user ID and password, then hit ENTER key.
   You should get your user ID and password from your system programmer. He must put them into your SNT entry. If both user ID and password entered match that in the SNT, CICS will inform you that sign-on has completed successfully.

4. Hit CLEAR key to erase the sign-on message.

5. You are ready to enter any CICS transaction that is defined in the PCT. For example, you can enter menu transaction.

6. When you have finished with the CICS system, you can sign off from it by entering CSSF LOGOFF on a clear screen.

CSSF transaction can be used to log off from the CICS system after you have finished with CICS. You just enter CSSF LOGOFF, you will go back to the system menu. From the system menu, you can then enter the system application ID to go to TSO/ISPF, CICS test system, or CICS production system.

After you have signed on to the CICS test system, you can enter CEDF transaction to invoke CEDF to monitor the execution of the CICS transaction that you are going to enter. CEDF will display a CICS command issued within the task both before and after the execution. You can use CEDF to check the logic flow of the task and debug the problems caused by the exceptional conditions.

You can also use CECI to issue any CICS command you like. For example, you can enter CECI SEND MAP('AXCU01') MAPSET('XXCU01') and then hit ENTER key to display the CICS map you have created to see if the map is OK.

You can also enter CMSG transaction to print a message on a printer. This allows you to test a printer to see if it works. You can also send a message to other CICS terminal using the CMSG transaction.

If you want to execute a CICS transaction without CEDF's monitoring, then you can just enter the transaction ID of its menu program on the terminal to invoke the menu screen. After the menu screen has been displayed, you can select the function you want to test your new CICS program.

Therefore, after you have signed on to CICS test system, you can test your CICS transactions using two major debugging tools: CEDF and INTERTEST. CEDF transaction comes as part of a CICS/VS system and it can be used to monitor the execution of each CICS command issued within the CICS program. INTERTEST is the most popular debugging tool for CICS/VS and is developed by On-line Software International, Inc. It has more than 2000 users. Almost everywhere you go, INTERTEST is there.

CEDF will monitor each CICS command issued within the CICS program and display the CICS command both before and after the execution. From the CICS command displayed before the execution, we know the value of the parameters that will be used for this CICS command. For example, CEDF will display the dataset name, record key, and record I/O area for the READ command. This way we know if the correct dataset, record key and record I/O areaare to be used to execute this READ command.

The CICS command displayed after the execution will tell you the results of the execution. If an exceptional condition has occurred, it will be displayed on the STATUS field. Many CICS transaction problems come from the exceptional conditions. Therefore, CEDF is an excellent tool to check out the program logic and debug the problems caused by exceptional conditions. The major disadvantages of CEDF are that it does not tell you which statement caused the abend and it has no symbolic addressing ability. When a CICS task abends due to data exception, CEDF does not tell you which statement caused the abend. You cannot examine the contents of a data field using its name under CEDF.

INTERTEST can be set on to monitor the execution of a CICS task. You can set up Unconditional Breakpoints (UBPs) within a CICS program so the execution will stop at those breakpoints so you can examine the contents of work areas. You can examine the contents of a data area by specifying its symbolic name during the breakpoint display. This symbolic addressing ability is one of the major factors that contribute the success of INTERTEST. INTERTEST will stop the execution of a CICS task at the COBOL statement that is about to cause the abend. Therefore, you know which statement within the CICS program caused the abend and you can examine any work area by name during the abend breakpoint. INTERTEST has four major transactions, each one performs a special function. The FILE transaction of INTERTEST allows you to add, update, delete, read, or browse VSAM files on-line. Therefore, you can use the FILE transaction to set up different types of test data in your VSAM files in order to test all the routines in the CICS program. The FILE transaction can work on any VSAM files in the FCT. The LIST transaction of INTERTEST allows you to review the source listing of a CICS program in the CICS/VS region. Therefore, after a CICS task abends, you do not need to log off from CICS and then go to ISPF (OS/VS) or ICCF (DOS/VSE) to review the CICS source program. You can review the compile listing of a CICS program on-line while you are in CICS.

CECI transaction of CICS/VS allows you to issue any type of CICS command on-line. Therefore, you can use this transaction to display and check out a new CICS map or you can use this transaction to process VSAM file like the FILE transaction of INTERTEST. However, CECI is not a full-screen support transaction. Therefore, no too many CICS programmers know how to use it. Most of CICS programmers prefer FILE over CECI.

CICS trace facility will produce entries for each CICS command issued within a CICS program into the trace table. When the CICS task abends, CICS will create a storage dump in the current dump dataset. The dump datasets will be printed after the CICS/VS system has been shut down. Within the storage dump for each CICS task abend, there is a trace table. Using this trace table, you can see how this task is executed. Each CICS command will produce one or more entry in the trace table. The table normally contains 1000 entries. You can also use this trace table to debug your CICS task abend.

When a CICS task abends, CICS will create a storage dump into the current dump dataset. Normally there are two dump datasets in each CICS system. When a CICS programmer needs to print his dump from the current dump dataset while CICS is up, he needs to switch (CSMT SWI) the dump dataset and close the current dump dataset. After the current dump dataset is switched and closed, he can then log off from CICS and go to batch region (TSO/ISPF or ICCF) to print the entire dump dataset using the dump print utility program. After the entire dump dataset has been printed, he can find his storage dump using the task#, abend code or transaction code. In this chapter, we'll show you how to read a CICS storage dump to debug a production CICS abend.

CEMT and CSMT transactions are used to handle CICS resources like: CICS programs, CICS transactions, CICS tasks, VSAM files, and terminals or printers. For example, you can disable a CICS transaction to prevent CICS users from using it when that CICS transaction abends. You can also use these two transactions to close a VSAM file to CICS so you can go to batch region to rebuild the file. CEMT was introduced in Version 1.5 to replace CSMT. It performs more functions than CSMT and has a better syntax.

11.1. Set Up CICS Internal Tables

There are five CICS internal tables an application programmer must know about and they are:

1. PPT (Processing Program Table)
2. PCT (Program Control Table)
3. FCT (File Control Table)
4. TCT (Terminal Control Table)
5. DCT (Destination Control Table)

Setting up CICS internal tables is the responsibility of your system programmer. However, you need to supply him with correct information in order to achieve the maximum performance. Each CICS program, CICS mapset, or CICS dynamic table (i.e. store table) must have an entry in the PPT. Each CICS transaction with its associated CICS program must have an entry in the PCT. The CICS program that will be invoked by this CICS transaction must also be specified along with its transaction ID in the PCT entry. Since we use pseudo conversational programming technique to code each CICS program that needs to perform terminal I/O operations, each CICS program that performs I/O operations must have one transaction ID specified in the PCT. You should put this transaction ID and its CICS program into the PCT. Each VSAM file to be processed in CICS/VS must have an entry in the FCT. If a VSAM file also contains one or more alternate indexes, each alternate index path must have a separate FCT entry. Each DL/I data base to be used in CICS/VS must have one entry in the FCT. Each terminal or printer to be used in CICS/VS must have a TCT entry. Each Intrapartition or extrapartition Transient Data queue to be used in CICS/VS must have one entry in the DCT.

There is one more table your system programmer must set up for each CICS user and that is Sign-On Table (SNT). Before you can use CSSN transaction to sign on to CICS/VS, your system programmer must have set up your SNT entry. Each SNT entry specifies not only the user ID and password, but also the operator security codes, operator priority, operator resource security codes, and operator classes. We have discussed these parameters of the SNT entry in Chapter 9.

In the following sections, we'll discuss these five CICS internal tables from the application programmer's viewpoint.

11.1.1. PPT

When a CICS transaction ID is entered or initiated, the CICS program specified for this transaction ID in the PCT entry will be used to search the PPT. When that CICS program entry in the PPT has been found, its load address in the PPT entry will be used by CICS to load this CICS program. After the CICS program has been loaded into the virtual storage, it will be given control. When CICS/VS is brought up each time, CICS/VS will load the load address of each CICS program specified in the PPT into PPT. If you have recompiled a CICS program, mapset, or dynamic table while CICS/VS is up, then you need to sign on to CICS/VS and issue a CSMT NEW command to reload the load address of that CICS program, mapset or dynamic table into its PPT entry. When this program is invoked the next time, the new version will be used. If you recompile a CICS program, mapset or dynamic table while CICS is not up, then you do not need to do CSMT NEW command since CICS will load the address of the new version into its PPT entry when CICS is brought up the next time.

In the production CICS system, CICS is normally brought up in the morning at 8 AM and shut down at 5 PM. Therefore, you need to do a CSMT NEW command after you have recompiled your CICS program, mapset or dynamic table while CICS is up.

There are three types of PPT entries in the PPT: CICS program, CICS mapset, and CICS dynamic table. Each CICS program, CICS mapset, and CICS dynamic table must have an entry in the PPT. You must catalog a CICS dynamic table in the CICS program load library using a batch JCL, and set up its PPT entry. Then you can issue a LOAD command to load the table into the CICS program. After the dynamic table is no longer needed, it will then be deleted through the use of the RELEASE command. If no RELEASE command is issued, the dynamic table will be deleted when the task is terminated.

If a CICS mapset contains more than one map, then only the mapset needs to be specified in the PPT. When the CICS mapset is referenced in a CICS program, all its maps will be loaded into the virtual storage.

PPT Entry For A CICS Program

Each CICS program must have one entry in the PPT and it must also be specified in the PCT along with the transaction ID if this CICS program is to be invoked by initiating a transaction code. If this CICS program performs terminal I/O operations, then it must use a transaction code. In this case, the transaction code and this CICS program must be specified in its PCT entry. If this CICS program is a subroutine program which is to be invoked by LINK command, then no PCT entry is needed.

A PPT entry for a CICS program is as follows:

```
DFHPPT TYPE=ENTRY,PROGRAM=XCU00,PGMLANG=COBOL,RES=YES
```

DFHPPT means this is a macro statement to create a PPT entry. TYPE=ENTRY specifies that an entry is to be generated in this table. PROGRAM=XCU00 specifies the CICS program name is XCU00. The CICS program name must be 1- to 8-character long and must be unique in the PPT. This program name should be used in the XCTL or LINK command. PGMLANG=COBOL specifies the programming language (COBOL) in which this CICS program is written. A CICS program can be written in COBOL, PL/I, Assembler, or RPG-II. COBOL is the most frequently used host language today for writing CICS/VS programs. RES=YES specifies that this CICS program XCU00 is a resident program. A resident program will be loaded and permanently remain in the storage when CICS/VS is brought up. A non-resident CICS program will be loaded into the virtual storage only when it is referenced. You should specify the most frequently used CICS programs as resident programs to improve the system performance.

PPT Entry for A CICS Mapset

Each CICS mapset to be used in CICS/VS must have an entry in the PPT. When the mapset name is specified in a SEND MAP or RECEIVE MAP command, the entire mapset will be loaded into the virtual storage. The mapset name will be used in the PPT instead of map names. If a CICS mapset contains more than one map, you still need to specify one PPT entry for then mapset. The following example shows a PPT entry for a CICS mapset:

```
DFHPPT ENTRY=ENTRY,PROGRAM=XXCU00,USAGE=MAP,RES=YES
```

PROGRAM=XXCU00 specifies the CICS mapset name which must be 1- to 7-character long. This mapset name must be specified as the label in the DFHMSD macro in the CICS mapset source statements. USAGE=MAP parameter specifies that this entry describes a BMS map. USAGE=MAP must be specified for CICS mapsets or programs that are infrequently referenced. If the use count for that CICS mapset or program becomes zero, the MAP storage is released if USAGE=MAP is specified for a CICS mapset or program. RES=YES specifies this mapset is a permanent resident mapset. When you specify the CICS program that uses this mapset as a resident program, it is only logical to specify its mapset as a permanent resident map.

PPT Entry for A Dynamic Table

A dynamic table is loaded into a CICS program through the LOAD command. After it is no longer needed, it can be deleted through the use of the RELEASE command. Before you can use the dynamic table in CICS/VS, you must have cataloged it in the program load library (OS/VS) or core image library (DOS/VS). The advanges of using a dynamic table is that you only need to recompile the dynamic table when it is changed and there is no need to recompile all CICS programs that use it. After the table has been re-assembled, you need to do a CSMT NEW command to load its new version into CICS. When the next LOAD command is issued, the new version of table will be used. The PPT entry for a dynamic table is as follows:

```
DFHPPT TYPE=ENTRY,PROGRAM=YTSH00,PGMLANG=COBOL
```

From the above example, you can see that there is no difference between coding a PPT entry for a CICS program and that for a dynamic table.

After your system programmer has successfully assembled the PPT table, he can then bring up CICS. When CICS/VS is brought up, it will load the load address of each CICS program specified in the PPT into PPT. When a new PPT entry is added to PPT, you can only shut down CICS and then bring it back up to get the new CICS program, mapset or dynamic table into the CICS/VS. But if this CICS program exists and is running in CICS/VS and you just change and recompile it, then you only need to sign on to CICS/VS and issue a CSMT NEW command to get the new version of the CICS program into CICS/VS. If the CICS program was in the PPT when the last time CICS is brought up and you have never compiled this program successfully, CICS will disable this CICS program. In this case, after you have compiled this CICS program successfully the first time while CICS is up, you do not need to shut down CICS. You only need to sign on to CICS and then enable the CICS program. After the CICS program has been enabled, you can then issue a CSMT NEW to get the new version of the CICS program into CICS/VS. After the CICS program has been enabled and copied into CICS, you can then enable its associated CICS transaction code.

11.1.2.   PCT

When a CICS transaction ID is entered on the terminal or initiated by other means, the CICS program specified for this transaction ID in its PCT entry will be used to search PPT. When the CICS program has been found in the PPT, its load address in the PPT entry will be used to load the CICS program into the virtual storage. After the CICS program has been loaded, it will then be given control. Since pseudo conversational programming is required for all CICS programs that perform terminal I/O operations, you need to assign a 4-character transaction code to each CICS program so you can issue a RETURN command with TRANSID option. The transaction code of this CICS program should be specified in the TRANSID option. Transaction code is also used to invoke the menu program. You can also issue a START command to initiate a CICS transaction. Whenever a transaction is used, it must be specified in the PCT with its associated CICS program.

When a CICS program is used as a subroutine program which will be linked to through the use of the LINK command, there is no transaction ID needed for this type of CICS programs. Therefore, not all CICS programs have a transaction ID associated with it in the PCT.

In a pseudo conversational CICS program, after you have sent a map to the terminal, you will issue a RETURN command with TRANSID option. This will terminate the program and post the transaction ID on this terminal. When any response to this terminal is made by the terminal operator, the transaction ID post on this terminal will be invoked. CICS will then use this transaction ID to search the PCT to find its associated CICS program. CICS will then get the load address of this program in the PPT entry to load the program and give the control to this program.

When you try to print an online report using the START command, you need to specify the transaction ID that is to be started along with the CICS print program in the PCT. The CICS print program must be specified in the PPT. Thus when the transaction ID is initiated by a CICS program, the print program specified for this transaction ID in the PCT will be loaded and given control.

When you try to use an intrapartition transient data queue in an Automatic Task Initiation (ATI) application, you must specify the transaction ID that is to be initiated in the PCT when the total number of the queue entries reach the trigger level specified in the DCT.

When you enter a transaction code to invoke the menu screen, you need to put this transaction code and the menu program into the PCT.

From the above examples, we can see that a CICS transaction can be initiated in one of the following four ways:

1. Enter the transaction ID on the terminal.
   This is how you invoke a menu screen.

2. Issue a START command to start a transaction.
   You can start a print utility transaction to print an online report.

3. Issue a RETURN command with TRANSID option.
   In a CICS program that uses pseudo conversational programming, you need to issue this type of RETURN command after each SEND MAP command is issued.

4. Create a TD queue entry to reach the trigger level specified in the DCT in order to initiate the transaction code specified in its DCT entry.

The following example shows how to define a PCT entry:

```
DFHPCT TYPE=ENTRY,TRANSID=CUST,PROGRAM=XCU00,TRANSEC=02,   X
       TRNPRTY=001,TWASIZE=0,TCLASS=2
```

DFHPCT indicates that this is a PCT macro. TYPE=ENTRY specifies that an entry is to be generated in the table. TRANSID=CUST specifies the transaction ID which must be 1- to 4-character long and must be unique within the PCT table. PROGRAM=XCU00 specifies the CICS program XCU00 that is to be invoked when this transaction (CUST) is initiated. This CICS program must be 1- to 8-character long and must be specified in the PPT. When CUST transaction is initiated, this XCU00 CICS program will be loaded and given control. TRANSEC= specifies the transaction security code for this transaction. Only the terminal operators with operator security code equal to '02' can use this transaction. Each terminal operator is assigned one or more operator security codes in the Sign-on table (SNT). When the terminal operator signs on to CICS, his security codes will be loaded into Terminal Control Table Entry (TCTTE) of that terminal. When a transaction is initiated on that terminal, the security codes of this transaction and operator will be checked to see if they match. For more information about the transaction security code and operator security codes, refer to Security Code in Chapter 9.4.2.

TRANPRTY=001 specifies the overall transaction processing priority. 1 is the lowest and the default. 255 is the higest priority. The combination of transaction priority, terminal priority, and operator priority determines the processing priority of the CICS task. For more information on the priority, refer to Priority in Chapter 9.4.5.

TWASIZE=0 specifies the TWA (Transaction Work Area) size in bytes. Since pseudo conversation programming technique is to be used in all CICS programs that perform terminal I/O operations and communication area can be used to pass data between two programs, TWA is rarely used in command-level CICS programs. TWA only lasts from the start of the task to the termination of the task. Therefore, it cannot be used in a pseudo conversational program. The default for TWASIZE is TWASIZE=0.

If you have to use TWA, you should check to see if TWA has been specified in the PCT. Its length can be obtained through the use of ASSIGN command as follows:

```
EXEC CICS ASSIGN TWALENG(WS-TWA-LENG) END-EXEC.
```

After you are sure that the length of the TWA is greater than zero, you can then address TWA of this transaction as follows:

```
LINKAGE SECTION.
01  DFHCOMMAREA      PIC X(100).
01  BLLCELLS.
    02  FILLER       PIC S9(8) COMP.
    02  TWA-PTR      PIC S9(8) COMP.
01  TWA-AREA.
    02  CUST-NO      PIC X(5).
PROCEDURE DIVISION.
    EXEC CICS ASSIGN TWALENG(WS-TWA-LENG) END-EXEC.
    IF WS-TWA-LENG > 0
        EXEC CICS ADDRESS TWA(TWA-PTR) END-EXEC
        EXEC CICS READ DATASET('CUSTMST')
                       INTO(CUSTOMER-REC)
                       RIDFLD(CUST-NO)
                       END-EXEC.
```

After you have addressed TWA, you can get the data passed from the previous program in TWA.

TCLASS=2 specifies the transaction class. The value can be decimal 1 to 10.

11.1.3.   FCT

Each VSAM file to be processed in CICS/VS must have an entry in the FCT. If this VSAM file contains one or more alternate indexes, each alternate index path must also have an entry in the FCT. The FCT entry for a VSAM primary file is different from that for an alternate index since you should not allow update request for an alternate index path. You should perform read or browse only operations through the use of an alternate index path. If you have to update a VSAM record, you should do it through the primary file.

If you use DL/I data bases instead of VSAM files, then each physical, logical and index data base must have one FCT entry. However, you only need to specify the access method (ACCMETH=DL/I) and data base DBD name (DATASET=name). A majority of your DL/I data bases will be physical data bases. The logical data bases can be built upon existing physical data bases to meet the application requirement. The index data bases are used for secondary key indexing (alternate indexing).

When CICS is brought up every time, CICS will open all the files specified with FILSTAT=OPENED. Most of VSAM files are specified with this option. Therefore, when CICS is brought up, most of VSAM files are opened and enabled and they are ready for process by CICS tasks. A VSAM file must be opened before you can enter CICS transactions to process it. Otherwise, NOTOPEN exceptional condition occurs. After you have defined this VSAM file through the use of the DEFINE CLUSTER command and you do not create at least one record for it, it will be disabled by CICS when CICS is brought up. A VSAM file must contain at least one record (even a deleted record) before it can be processed in CICS/VS. After a VSAM file has been defined and loaded, you should then set up its FCT entry. After FCT entry is set up, your system programmer must include it in the CICS startup JCL.

Your system programmer must insert one DD statement (OS/VS) or DLBL and EXTENT statements (DOS/VSE) for each VSAM file in the CICS startup JCL to allocate the VSAM file. Your system programmer must also put one VERIFY card for each VSAM file to ensure that the same end of file information has been put in the VSAM catalog and VSAM file itself. This VERIFY step is normally performed as the first step in the CICS startup JCL. If a VSAM file contains one or more alternate indexes, then your system programmer must do the same for each alternate index path in the CICS startup JCL. When you submit the CICS startup JCL in the batch region, CICS will be brought in several minimutes.

When you issue a File Control command to process a VSAM file, CICS will use the FCT to check the following:

1. Is the dataset name specified in the FCT?
    If not, DSIDERR condition occurs.

2. If the function requested is allowed for this dataset?
    If not, INVREQ condition occurs.

3. If this VSAM file is a fixed-length or variable-length file?
    If it is a variable-length file and LENGTH is not specified in the File Control command, LENGERR condition occurs.

If the VSAM file is not specified in the FCT, DSIDERR condition occurs. If the function requested (i.e. DELETE command) is not specified in the SERVREQ= parameter of the FCT entry, INVREQ (invalid request) condition occurs. If this VSAM file is specified as a variable-length file, then LENGTH option of the File Control command must be specified. If it is not specified, LENGERR condition occurs. If this is a fixed-length VSAM file, then the LENGTH option can be omitted.

The FCT entry also specifies the string count for this VSAM file. The string count specifies the total number of tasks that can access this VSAM file at the same time. When you issue a READ command with UPDATE option, the string count for this file will be increased by 1. When you issue a REWRITE, DELETE, or UNLOCK command for this file, the string count will be decreased by 1. If you forget to issue a REWRITE, DELETE or UNLOCK command following a READ command with UPDATE option, then the string count will not be decreased. If this bad program is used by many CICS users at the same time. The string count will exceed what is specified in the FCT entry, all the additional tasks accessing this this VSAM file will be hung. In this case, you should use the CORE transaction of INTERTEST to reset the DCT of TCA for the task to release the hung terminals.

The following example shows an FCT entry for a VSAM KSDS customer master file:

```
DFHFCT TYPE=DATASET,DATASET=CUSTMAST,ACCMETH=(VSAM,KSDS),   X
       SERVREQ=(GET,PUT,NEWREC,UPDATE,DELETE,BROWSE,SHARE),  X
       STRNO=1,BUFND=2,BUFSP=09216,BUFNI=1,                  X
       RECFORM=FIXED,FILSTAT=(ENABLED,OPENED),LOG=YES
```

DFHFCT specifies that this is a FCT macro. TYPE=DATASET specifies that this is a dataset entry. DATASET=CUSTMAST specifies the dataset name CUSTMAST which must be a 1- to 8-character long. This dataset name must be used in File Control commands to identify the VSAM file to be processed. ACCMETH=(VSAM,KSDS) specifies the file access method is VSAM KSDS file. VSAM has three types of access methods: KSDS, ESDS and RRDS. At least 90% of CICS VSAM files are KSDS files. SERVREQ= specifies the service requests available for this VSAM file. Most of the time, you'll specify all requests be available for this file: add, update, delete, browse and read. The following is a list of vaild requests that can be specified in this SERVREQ= parameter:

```
REQUEST     Function
GET       - data set can be read
PUT       - records can be written to this data set
NEWREC    - records can be added to this data set
            NEWREC implies PUT.
UPDATE    - records can be updated on this data set
            UPDATE implies GET and PUT were specified.
DELETE    - records can be deleted from this data set
            DELETE implies UPDATE was specified
BROWSE    - records can be browsed from this data set
SHARE     - this data set is to share resources
```

If you want all requests to be available for this VSAM file, then you should specify SERVREQ as follows:

```
SERVREQ=(NEWREC,UPDATE,DELETE,BROWSE,SHARE)
```

Since NEWREC implies PUT was specified, we do not specify PUT. Since UPDATE implies GET and PUT were specified. If this VSAM file contains one or more alternate indexes and you define the alternate index files as UPGRADE, then SHARE cannot be specified.

If you want this file to be used for review and browse operations, then you should specify:

```
SERVREQ=(GET,BROWSE,SHARE)
```

You should specify the above SERVREQ without SHARE for an VSAM alternate index path since you do not want to update a VSAM through its alternate index path. You should do it through its primary key. This will ensure the integerity of the VSAM file and its alternate indexes.

RECFORM=FIXED specifies that this is a fixed-length VSAM file. Most of the VSAM files are fixed-length. But you must specify RECFORM=FIXED in its FCT entry since the default is variable-length. If you are wondering why you got LENGERR condition for a VSAM file defined as fixed-length in the DEFINE CLUSTER command, you should check to see if its FCT entry is specified with RECFORM=FIXED.

LOG=YES specifies that you want CICS dynamic transaction backout program to restore this VSAM file back to the status when the task is initiated in case the task abends. Therefore, you can enter the same transaction again like nothing ever happened before after the problem has been fixed. Most of VSAM files are specified with LOG=YES to allow recovery. But when you specify LOG=YES, you cannot perform generic delete. That means you cannot delete a group of records using a generic key. You can detect if a VSAM file is defined with LOG=YES or not easily by entering the same transaction after it is abended. If VSAM files you try to update do not contain the same data before you entered the last transaction, you know LOG=YES was not specified for those files.

If you are under CICS/OS/VS, then you need to specify BASE=name in the FCT entry for an alternate index path. The name specified in the BASE= is the base cluster (primary file) which must have a FCT entry itself. If you don't, your alternate indexing will never work.

BUFND=number specifies the number of buffers to be used for the data component of this VSAM file. The minimum specification is the number of strings (STRNO=) plus one.

BUFNI=number specifies the number of buffers to be used for the index component of this VSAM file. The minimum specification is the number of strings (STRNO=).

BUFSP=number specifies the size in bytes of the buffer area for this VSAM file.

STRNO=number specifies the number of concurrent requests that can be processed against the data set. When the number of requests reaches this limit, CICS will queue any additional requests until one of the active requests terminates. If you issue a READ with UPDATE option and never issue a REWRITE, DELETE, or UNLOCK command, the additional requests will be queued forever. If STRNO= is not specified, STRNO=1 is assumed.

The following example shows a VSAM KSDS file (customer file) with one alternate index:

FCT entry for customer primary file:

```
      DFHFCT TYPE=DATASET,DATASET=CUSTMST,ACCMETH=(VSAM,KSDS),     X
             SERVREQ=(NEWREC,UPDATE,DELETE,BROWSE),STRNO=1,        X
             BUFND=2,BUFSP=09216,BUFNI=1,                          X
             RECFORM=FIXED,FILSTAT=OPENED,LOG=YES
```

FCT entry for customer alternate index path (by customer name):

```
      DFHFCT TYPE=DATASET,DATASET=CUSTNAM,ACCMETH=(VSAM,KSDS),     X
             SERVREQ=(GET,BROWSE),STRNO=1,BASE=CUSTMST,            X
             BUFND=2,BUFSP=09216,BUFNI=1,                          X
             RECFORM=FIXED,FILSTAT=OPENED,LOG=YES
```

Your system programmer should then specify the following in the CICS startup JCL:

```
//CUSTMST   DD DSN=CUSTOMER.MASTER,DISP=SHR
//CUSTNAM   DD DSN=CUSTOMER.MASTER.PATH,DISP=SHR

VERIFY(CUSTMST)
VERIFY(CUSTNAM)
```

11.1.4. TCT

Each terminal or printer in the CICS/VS system must have one entry in the TCT. You do not need to supply infomation to the system programmer about the new terminals and printers to be used for your new CICS applications. This is your system programmer's job. But you need to find out from him the terminal or printer IDs to be used in your applications.

When you try to print online reports using Message Routing (ROUTE LIST, SEND MAP or SEND TEXT, and SEND PAGE commands), you need to know the page size specified for your printers. If the page size specified for your printers do not satisfy your programming needs, then you need to know how to explain to your system programmer that you need a particular page size (PGESIZE). The page size of a printer will determine the page size of your report if a particular print technique is to be employed in your CICS print program. If your report does not line up with the form you try to print, it is time to look into the PGESIZE of that printer. Unless you know the PGESIZE of that printer, you may never be able to print a report on a desired form. For more information on how the page size will effect your online report format, please refer to online report printing techniques in Chapter 10.6.

If the page size is not specified in the TCT entry, the default is PGESIZE=(24,80) for 3270 model 2 terminals or printers. Four techniques have been discussed in Chapter 10 on how to print online reports on different sizes of paper. The most popular form formats are as follows:

1. 66 lines x 85 columns (letter size).
2. 66 lines x 132 columns (standard computer form).
3. 24 lines x 80 columns (standard 3270 screen size).

The following example shows a TCT entry for a 3270 model 2 display terminal:

```
DFHTCT TYPE=TERMINAL,TRMTYPE=3277,TRMIDNT=APO3,      X
       TRMPRTY=25,TRMMODL=2,TRMADDR=TRMAPO3,          X
       TRMSTAT=TRANSCEIVE,POLLPOS=1,TIOAL=512,        X
       BMSFEAT=(NOROUTEALL),                          X
       FEATURE=(AUDALARM,CTRAN),PGESIZE=(24,80)
```

The following example shows a TCT entry for a 3286 model 2 printer:

```
DFHTCT TYPE=TERMINAL,TRMTYPE=3286,TRMIDNT=APAA,       X
       TRMPRTY=25,TRMMODL=2,TRMADDR=TRMAPAA,          X
       TRMSTAT=RECEIVE,POLLPOS=1,PGESTAT=AUTOPAGE,    X
       FEATURE=PRINT,CLASS=(VIDEO,BISYNC),TIOAL=512,  X
       PGESIZE=(24,80)
```

11.1.5. DCT

Each Transient Data Queue must have one entry in the DCT. The Intrapartition transient data queue can be used in Automatic Task Initiation (ATI) applications. The Extrapartition Transient Queue is normally used to collect output data from different CICS terminals for off-line batch processing. However, it can also be used to transfer the batch data from batch region to CICS/VS region for input operations. The TD queue is normally defined as reuseable. In this case, it will be a new empty queue everytime it is opened to CICS/VS.

In an ATI application, the transaction will be initiated when a new entry is added to the queue and the total number of the entries in the queue has reached the trigger level specified in the DCT. When this transaction is initiated, it will read and process each entry in the queue until there are no more entries in the queue (QZERO). The TD queue name, trigger level, and transaction ID to be initiated when the trigger level has been reached must be specified in the DCT. For example, you want to print the sales order in both the plant and the headquarter for each sales order created. After a sales order has been created, you can create a TD queue entry with the sales order number as the only data field. When the 30th entry (trigger level) is created, a sales order print transaction will be initiated to print all the sales order in the queue. This way, all 30 sales orders can be printed at one time. If you print the sales order one at a time using the START command in the sales order create program, then you need to tear this sales order apart from other printout and the print transaction needs to be loaded for each sales order. When the print transaction is initiated in an ATI application, you should issue READQ TD command to retrieve one entry from the queue. After the queue entry has been retrieved, you can process this entry (using the sales order number to print the sales order). After the current entry has been processed, you should go back to issue another READQ TD command to retrieve the next queue entry until there are no more queue entries (QZERO) in the queue.

The following example shows how to set up an ATI application in the DCT:

```
DFHDCT TYPE=INTRA,DESTID=L770,TRIGLEV=30,TRANSID=PRNT,     X
       DESTFAC=TERMINAL
```

In the above example, we specify this is an intrapartition transient data queue (TYPE=INTRA) and the destination (queue name) is L770 (DEST=L770). The trigger level is set at 30. Therefore, when the 30th entry is added to the queue, the transaction PRNT (TRANSID=PRNT) will be initiated to process the queue entries until QZERO condition occurs. We do not specify REUSE=YES which is the default. Therefore, the storage occupied by this queue will be released when all the entries in the queue have been read (READQ TD).

The extrapartition transient data queues are used in to applications: Batch Data Transfer and Sequential Devices.

Batch Data Transfer

Data is collected in an extrapartition TD queue from CICS terminals during the day time. When CICS/VS is shut down, you can then use batch programs to process the data in

233

the extrapartition TD queue which is a sequential data set. This data transfer happens between the CICS/VS region and the batch region. The TD queues used in this type of applications must be defined as QSAM (OS/VS) or SAM for DOS/VSE.

For example, you can log all updates to an Inventory VSAM file from all CICS tasks to an extrapartition TS queue during the day time. After CICS/VS has been shut down at 5 PM, you can then sort this TD queue by the product code to produce a batch report that shows all the updates made to any product during the day.

Sequential Devices

You can also submit the batch JCL from CICS/VS using the extrapartition TD queue. Since the reader queue in the batch region or partition can be defined as an extrapartition TD queue, you can issue WRITEQ TD commands to write JCL statements to the reader queue while CICS is up. This technique will be demonstrated in Chapter 13.12.

If you specify a line printer as the TD queue name in the DCT, the the TD queue records you create will be printed in this printer. However, this is not the best way to print an online report in CICS/VS since other CICS tasks can also write TD queue records while you try to write yours. The following example shows an extrapartition TD queue entry in the DCT:

```
INVT      DFHDCT TYPE=EXTRA,DESTID=INVT,DSCNAME=INVTUSR,RSL=1
```

11.2.   Create Test And Production VSAM Files

Before you can test your CICS transactions, you must create VSAM test files that are to be used in your CICS programs. There are two sets of VSAM files in each installation: Production and Test VSAM Files. The production VSAM files are used in the production CICS and batch system and they contain the real data. The application programmers are not allowed to test their CICS programs or batch programs using the production files. Instead, VSAM test files should be used. The test VSAM files are used in the CICS test system and they contain the test data. There is no difference between creating a production VSAM file and creating a test VSAM file. You need to use VSAM AMS commands to define the VSAM spaces, define the VSAM file, and/or load the VSAM file with data.

After the VSAM file has been defined through the use of DEFINE CLUSTER command, you can load this VSAM file with data. You can use the VSAM AMS REPRO command to copy the data from other SAM or VSAM file or you can write a COBOL batch program to load the file. If this VSAM file will be created exclusively from the CICS transaction, then you only need to create (and then delete) a low-value record on it before you open it to CICS. Then you can use the CICS transaction to create the test data on this file or use FILE transaction of INTERTEST to add some test records. We'll Show you how to use FILE transaction to create, update, delete, browse, or read VSAM file later in this chapter.

For more information on how to create and maintain a VSAM file in CICS/VS, please refer to VSAM files in Chpater 1.

11.3.   CEDF Testing

CEDF and INTERTEST are the two major debugging tools available for CICS today. CEDF transaction comes with CICS/VS system. It can be implemented in both CICS test and production systems. If it is used in the CICS production system, only a few CICS programmers are authorized to use it and normally no update to main storage is allowed. Some installations even prohibit CEDF to be installed in the CICS production system. It is normally installed in the CICS test system to be used by all CICS programmers.

CEDF is very easy to use. You just enter CEDF on a clear terminal to invoke CEDF and then enter the CICS transaction that you want to monitor under CEDF. Then CEDF will monitor the task initiated by this transaction ID. CEDF will monitor each CICS command issued within the CICS task and display each CICS command both before and after the execution. From these displays, you can check the execution flow of a CICS task and debug almost all problems within your CICS programs. If the problems are caused by the exceptional conditions that occur during the execution of CICS commands, CEDF will display the exceptional condition on the terminal. If the abend is caused by data exception, CEDF will not tell you which statement within the CICS program that caused the abend. This is where INTERTEST comes in. Therefore, CEDF is an excellent tool to check out the logical flow and exceptional conditions. But it is not very helpful when it comes to pinpoint the statement that caused the data exception. INTERTEST will display the statement that caused the abend and allow you to examine the contents of data fields by their names during the abend display. In fact, many programmers use both CEDF and INTERTEST to debug their CICS programs.

You can also use CEDF to monitor the execution of a task entered from a remote terminal. For example, a user in New York City calls you about an abend caused by one of your CICS programs. You can ask him to re-enter the same transaction on his terminal and you can monitor the execution of this task on your terminal. You can do this by issuing CEDF K01A on your terminal. Where K01A is the user's terminal ID. Then you can ask him to enter the transaction on his terminal. CEDF will display the execution of that task on your terminal. This way, you do not need to enter the transaction yourself in order to monitor the execution.

You can also use CEDF to monitor a print transaction which is started by the Interval Control command START. This requires two terminals. The first terminal is used to enter the transaction which will start the print transaction and the second terminal is used to monitor the execution of this print transaction. You need to enter CEDF K01P on the second terminal before the transaction that is entered on the first terminal issues the START command. Where K01P is the printer ID you specify in the START command. Therefore, so long as a CICS task is associated with a terminal, you can monitor it under CEDF. In this case, the print task is associated with the printer K01P.

The above three CEDF monitor techniques are very important in order for you to monitor all types of CICS tasks.

CEDF will automatically display each CICS command both before and after the execution after it is invoked by the CICS programmer. No COBOL statements between two CICS commands will be displayed. After the first CICS command is executed, the second CICS command will be displayed. You can control the execution of each CICS command by pressing ENTER key. From these displays, you can determine if the logic flow is correct. You can also determine if the parameter values of each CICS command to be executed are correct from the CEDF display of the CICS command before the execution. You can also know if this CICS command is executed successfully from the CEDF after-execution display. If the execution is successful, NORMAL will be displayed on the STATUS field of the CEDF display. If an exceptional condition occurs, it will be displayed on this STATUS field.

During CEDF session, you can hit PF5 to go to review or change the work areas you define in WORKING-STORAGE SECTION or LINKAGE SECTION. By pressing PF5 key on any CEDF display, the first page of the work areas in WORKING-STORAGE SECTION will be displayed in both character and hexadecimal forms. To look at the contents of work areas defined in LINKAGE SECTION, you need the locations of these work areas when the storage is acquired. For example, in order to review the VSAM file record area that is defined in LINKAGE SECTION, you need to write down the address after the READ with SET option command is executed under CEDF. CEDF will display the contents of the pointer set by this READ command on the CEDF display. You can then hit PF5 key to review the first page of work areas defined in WORKING-STORAGE SECTION. Then you enter the address you wrote down for this file on the location field and then hit ENTER key to display this record you have just retrieved.

You can also change the parameter values before the CICS command is executed. For example, CEDF displays the READ command before its execution with value 'AA345' on RIDFLD option on the terminal. Since 'AA345' is not a valid customer number, you can move the cursor to 'AA345' and change it to '12345' (a valid customer number) then hit ENTER key to make the change. This ENTER key will not execute the READ command, it just change the parameter value. You need to hit ENTER key again in order to execute this READ command. CICS will try to read the customer record with key equal to '12345' instead of 'AA345'. This way you can test your CICS program further more before you go to correct the bugs within this CICS program.

You can also change the RESPONSE field of CEDF display after the execution of a CICS command. For example, NORMAL status has been returned by CICS for a READ command, you can change the RESPONSE field from NORMAL to NOTFND (not found) then hit ENTER key to make this change. Then you can hit ENTER key again to continue the execution, the control will go to the label you specify for the NOTFND condition in the HANDLE CONDITION command rather than go to the next statement following the READ command. This enables you to test many routines that handle the exceptional conditions.

You can also modify the contents of work areas during CEDF sessions. You can hit PF5 key at any CEDF display to go to the work areas defined in WORKING-STORAGE SECTION and then move the cursor to the location where you want to make the change and enter whatever you like on top of the data and then hit ENTER key. This enables you to change the data areas that do not contains the correct data so you can continue to test your program using the correct data. This way, you can test further more within the CICS program in one single run.

When you hit PF5, only the first page of work areas in WORKING-STORAGE SECTION will be displayed, you can hit PF8 to go to next page or PF7 to go to previous page. You can also enter the address on the location field to go to display storage contents starting with that address. When you are finished with work area content display, you should hit ENTER key to go back to the current CICS command. No other key will take you back, only the ENTER key.

At any CEDF display, you can hit PF2 to see the display in hexadecimal form. After you have finished with it, you can hit PF2 again to go back to the character form. The hexadecimal form allows you to see values of the non-character parameters (i.e. COMP-3) in the CICS command.

You can also set up CEDF to stop at a particular CICS command. You may need to do this when the CICS program abends due to a particular CICS command. You want to skip all CEDF displays prior this CICS command. You can do this by pressing PF9 on any CEDF display and enter the CICS command you want to skip to. After you have entered the CICS command, you should hit ENTER key to record this CICS command and then hit PF9 again to skip all the CEDF displays and display this particular command.

At any time, you can end the CEDF monitoring for this task by pressing PF3 key. After PF3 is pressed, CICS will execute this transaction without any interferance from CEDF. It works just like you enter the CICS transaction on the terminal without invoking CEDF. You may need to do this when you have completed your testing and you just want to execute this task without CEDF from that point.

At any time, you can abend this task by pressing PF12, entering the abend code, and then pressing PF12 key again. You may need to abend the task when you have determined that something is wrong and there is no reason to complete this task. The abend code you enter will be used to identify the storage dump produced by this task. Remember you need to hit PF12 key twice to abend the task. You have to abend the task when an un-recoverable error has occurred. This way, CICS will call in dynamic transaction backout program to restore the updates made to the VSAM files so you can re-enter the same transaction later.

At any time, you can hit PF4 to suppress CEDF displays and go to display the next map. In a pseudo conversational program, you will be asked to continue the CEDF session. After you have pressed PF4 key, you can answer 'YES' to continue CEDF or 'NO' (the default) to end the CEDF. You may need to do that when you know there is no problem from this point to the next SEND MAP command. The problem you want to test is after the RECEIVE MAP command is issued.

CEDF remembers up to ten displays for you to recall. You may need to recall the display when you forget the previous displays and you want to go back to take a look at. Since each CICS command has two CEDF displays. Therefore, up to five CICS commands will be remembered. You can hit PF10 to display the previous display. By pressing PF10 repeatly, you can recall up to ten displays.

If you just want to see the CEDF displays, you only need to hit ENTER key to see the next display during CEDF session. When the RETURN with TRANSID option is to be executed, you'll be asked to answer whether ('YES') or not ('NO') you want to continue CEDF. If you answer 'YES', then the map will be displayed for you to enter input data or press control key. This is the right place to do these two things. CEDF will also display the map when the SEND MAP command is issued. But this is not the right place to enter the input data or press the control key. If you enter the input data at this display, it will be carried over to the second map display. But if you press the control key at the first map display, the control key will be ignored. Therefore, you should enter the input data or press control key after you have answered 'YES' or 'NO' following the RETURN command with TRANSID option. If you answer 'NO' to indicate that you do not want CEDF monitoring any more, the map will be displayed and there will be no more CEDF displays from now on.

We'll use the transaction 'WCKS' to show you the CEDF displays at variable points of the execution. After you enter 'CEDF' on the terminal, the following message will be displayed:

```
THIS TERMINAL EDF MODE IS ON
```

That means the CEDF has been invoked for this terminal. Any transaction ID entered on this terminal will be under the monitoring of CEDF. You can then hit CLEAR key to erase the above message and then enter 'CUST' transaction ID on the terminal. The following CEDF display will appear on the terminal:

```
     TRANSACTION: CUST      PROGRAM: XCU00     TASK NUMBER: 0004305
     STATUS:  PROGRAM INITIATION
          EIBTIME      = +0091739
          EIBDATE      = +0086084
          EIBTRNID     = 'CUST'
          EIBTASKN     = +0004305
          EIBTRMID     = 'K01A'
          EIBCPOSN     = +00250
          EIBCALEN     = +00000
          EIBAID       = '7D'
          EIBFN        = X'0000'
          EIBRCODE     = X'000000000000'
          EIBDS        = '........'
          EIBREQID     = '........'
          EIBRSRCE     = '        '
     ENTER:  CONTINUE
     PF1 : UNDEFINED           PF2 : SWITCH HEX/CHAR     PF3 : END EDF SESSION
     PF4 : SUPRESS DISPLAYS    PF5 : WORKING STORAGE     PF6 : USER DISPLAY
     PF7 : SCROLL BACK         PF8 : SCROLL FORWARD      PF9 : STOP CONDITIONS
     PF10: UNDEFINED           PF11: UNDEFINED           PF12: UNDEFINED
```

CEDF will display the EIB fields when a transaction is initiated. You know the transaction ID, the CICS program invoked by this transaction ID, and the task number assigned by CICS. CICS assigns a unique task number for each CICS transaction. The task is terminated when a RETURN command is issued or when the transaction abends. This task number is also the key to find the storage dump of this task in the dump dataset if the task abends. PROGRAM INITIATION in the STATUS field shows that the program has just been initiated. EIB fields will be displayed with their current values. Each task has a unique EIB table. Each EIB field within this table contains certain information that can be very useful for an application programmer. For example, EIBTRNID contains the transaction ID for this task.

If you hit ENTER key, CEDF will display the first CICS command which is a SEND MAP command on the terminal:

```
 TRANSACTION: CUST     PROGRAM: XCU00      TASK NUMBER: 0004305
 STATUS:   ABOUT TO EXECUTE COMMAND
 EXEC CICS SEND
   MAP('AXCU00 ')
   FROM('.........CUST  03/25/86 09:17  CUSTOMER .....')
   CURSOR(-00001)
   TERMINAL
   ERASE
   OFFSET:X'D4508C'                          EIBFN=X'1804'
 ENTER:  CONTINUE
 PF1 : UNDEFINED
 PF4 : SUPPRESS DISPLAYS    PF2 : SWITCH HEX/CHAR     PF3 : UNDEFINED
 PF7 : SCROLL BACK          PF5 : WORKING STORAGE     PF6 : USER DISPLAY
 PF10: PREVIOUS DISPLAY     PF8 : SCROLL FORWARD      PF9 : STOP CONDITIONS
                            PF11: UNDEFINED           PF12: ABEND USER TASK
```

The STATUS field shows 'ABOUT TO EXECUTE COMMAND'. That means this is the CEDF display before the CICS command is to be executed. You can change the parameter values at this point if you see some values are incorrect. If everything is OK, you can then hit ENTER key to execute this SEND MAP command. Unlike any other CICS command, CEDF will display the map on the terminal first before executing the SEND MAP command. Therefore, a SEND MAP command will have three CEDF displays instead of two. The map will be displayed on the terminal as follows:

```
 CUST  XX/XX/XX HH:MM    CUSTOMER ORDER SERVICE SYSTEM            XXXX
                                 MENU

 FUNCTION: 99 CUSTOMER NO: 99999 CUSTOMER NAME: XXXXXXXXXXXXXXXXXXXX
             ORDER NO   : 99999

       01 CREATE A NEW CUSTOMER.
       02 INQUIRE/UPDATE/DELETE A CUSTOMER (CUSTOMER NO).
       03 BROWSE/UPDATE CUSTOMERS BY NAME (CUSTOMER NAME).
       04 PRINT A SALES ORDER ON 24X80 PAPER (ORDER NO).
       05 PRINT A SALES ORDER ON 24X80 PAPER (ORDER NO).
       06 PRINT A SALES ORDER ON 66X132 PAPER (ORDER NO).
       07 PRINT A SALES ORDER ON 66X85 PAPER (ORDER NO).
       08 CREATE ORDER DETAILS ON TS QUEUE (ORDER NO).
       09 REVIEW/UPDATE/CREATE ORDER DETAILS (ORDER NO).
       10 PRINT SALES ORDER MASTER LIST TONIGHT.

 CLEAR=END, PF1=RESET
 XXXXXXXXXXXXXXXXXXXXXXXXXXXXXXXXXXXXXXXXXXXXXXXXXXXXXXXXXXXXXXXXXXXXXXXXXXXXX
```

This is the map you are about to send. You should not enter input data or press any control key (PF, PA, CLEAR, or ENTER key) at this time. You should wait after you have answered 'YES' or 'NO' to continue CEDF session. Therefore, you should hit ENTER key to execute this SEND MAP command and display the execution results:

```
 TRANSACTION: CUST     PROGRAM: XCU00      TASK NUMBER: 004305
 STATUS:   COMMAND EXECUTION COMPLETE
 EXEC CICS SEND
   MAP('AXCU00 ')
   FROM('..........CUST  03/25/86 09:17  CUSTOMER .....')
   CURSOR(-00001)
   TERMINAL
   ERASE
   OFFSET:X'D4508C'                      EIBFN=X'1804'
   RESPONSE: NORMAL                      EIBRCODE=X'000000000000'
 ENTER:  CONTINUE
 PF1 : UNDEFINED
 PF4 : SUPRESS DISPLAYS     PF2 : SWITCH HEX/CHAR     PF3 : END EDF SESSION
 PF7 : SCROLL BACK          PF5 : WORKING STORAGE     PF6 : USER DISPLAY
 PF10: PREVIOUS DISPLAY     PF8 : SCROLL FORWARD      PF9 : STOP CONDITIONS
                            PF11: UNDEFINED           PF12: ABEND USER TASK
```

The STATUS field shows 'COMMAND EXECUTION COMPLETE'. That means this is the CEDF display after the CICS command SEND MAP has been executed. The RESPONSE field shows 'NORMAL'. That means this SEND MAP command has been executed successfully. If any exceptional condition occurs during the execution of a CICS command, it will be displayed on the RESPONSE field. For example, NOTFND condition occurs during the execution of a READ command, then NOTFND rather than NORMAL will be displayed on this RESPONSE field. You can change this RESPONSE field to any exceptional condition you like to test exceptional condition routines within the program. You can also change the RESPONSE field from an exceptional condition to NORMAL if you like.

After the execution of a CICS command (i.e. SEND MAP command) has been completed, you can continue to hit ENTER key to go to execute the next CICS command:

```
TRANSACTION: CUST     PROGRAM: XCU00      TASK NUMBER: 004305
 STATUS:  ABOUT TO EXECUTE COMMAND
EXEC CICS RETURN
  TRANSID('CUST')
  OFFSET:X'D4508C'                         EIBFN=X'0E08'
 ENTER:  CONTINUE
 PF1 : UNDEFINED          PF2 : SWITCH HEX/CHAR    PF3 : UNDEFINED
 PF4 : SUPPRESS DISPLAYS  PF5 : WORKING STORAGE    PF6 : USER DISPLAY
 PF7 : SCROLL BACK        PF8 : SCROLL FORWARD     PF9 : STOP CONDITIONS
 PF10: PREVIOUS DISPLAY   PF11: UNDEFINED          PF12: ABEND USER TASK
```

The next CICS command following the SEND MAP command is the RETURN command with TRANSID option. The RETURN command will terminate the task. If you hit ENTER key after the RETURN command with TRANSID option is first displayed, CEDF will display PROGRAM TERMINATION screen. That means the menu program is to be terminated. After you hit ENTER key on this PROGRAM TERMINATION screen, the TASK TERMINATION screen will be displayed. That means the task is to be terminated.

The PROGRAM TERMINATION and the TASK TERMINATION displays are as follows:

```
TRANSACTION: CUST     PROGRAM: XCU00      TASK NUMBER: 004305
 STATUS: PROGRAM TERMINATION
 ENTER:  CONTINUE
 PF1 : UNDEFINED          PF2 : SWITCH HEX/CHAR    PF3 : END EDF SESSION
 PF4 : SUPPRESS DISPLAYS  PF5 : WORKING STORAGE    PF6 : USER DISPLAY
 PF7 : SCROLL BACK        PF8 : SCROLL FORWARD     PF9 : STOP CONDITIONS
 PF10: PREVIOUS DISPLAY   PF11: UNDEFINED          PF12: ABEND USER TASK
```

```
TRANSACTION: CUST                     TASK NUMBER: 004305
 STATUS:  TASK TERMINATION
TO CONTINUE EDF SESSION REPLY YES
 ENTER:  CONTINUE
 PF1 : UNDEFINED          PF2 : SWITCH HEX/CHAR    PF3 : END EDF SESSION
 PF4 : SUPPRESS DISPLAYS  PF5 : WORKING STORAGE    PF6 : USER DISPLAY
 PF7 : SCROLL BACK        PF8 : SCROLL FORWARD     PF9 : STOP CONDITIONS
 PF10: PREVIOUS DISPLAY   PF11: UNDEFINED          PF12: UNDEFINED
```

On this TASK TERMINATION screen, you should answer 'YES' if you want to continue CEDF monitoring. After you have answered 'YES' or 'NO' on the TASK

TERMINATION screen, the customer maintenance system menu will be displayed again for you to enter the input data or press the control key. The menu screen is displayed as follows:

```
CUST   XX/XX/XX HH:MM      CUSTOMER ORDER SERVICE SYSTEM          XXXX
                                    MENU
FUNCTION: 99 CUSTOMER NO: 99999 CUSTOMER NAME: XXXXXXXXXXXXXXXXXXX
             ORDER NO   : 99999

          01 CREATE A NEW CUSTOMER.
          02 INQUIRE/UPDATE/DELETE A CUSTOMER (CUSTOMER NO).
          03 BROWSE/UPDATE CUSTOMERS BY NAME (CUSTOMER NAME).
          04 PRINT A SALES ORDER ON 24X80 PAPER (ORDER NO).
          05 PRINT A SALES ORDER ON 24X80 PAPER (ORDER NO).
          06 PRINT A SALES ORDER ON 66X132 PAPER (ORDER NO).
          07 PRINT A SALES ORDER ON 66X85 PAPER (ORDER NO).
          08 CREATE ORDER DETAILS ON TS QUEUE (ORDER NO).
          09 REVIEW/UPDATE/CREATE ORDER DETAILS (ORDER NO).
          10 PRINT SALES ORDER MASTER LIST TONIGHT.

CLEAR=END, PF1=RESET
XXXXXXXXXXXXXXXXXXXXXXXXXXXXXXXXXXXXXXXXXXXXXXXXXXXXXXXXXXXXXXXXXXXXXXXXXX
```

After you have entered the input data or pressed the control key on the above menu screen, the transaction 'CUST' will be initiated once again. When CUST is initiated, the customer menu program will be invoked. This is a new task. The first CEDF display will be like the one when we enter the transaction CUST on a clear terminal. The next CEDF display will be the first CICS command issued (RECEIVE MAP) within the program. The whole cycle begins.

11.4.   INTERTEST

INTERTEST is the most popular CICS testing tool today. It is developed by On-line Software International, Inc. It has more than 2000 users in the United States. There are 8000 CICS data centers in the United States today. Almost everwhere you go, INTERTEST is there. Therfore, you need to know how to use INTERTEST to debug your CICS programs in addition to CEDF.

So we have known, CEDF is an excellent testing tool to check out the logic flow of a CICS program and debug the probelms caused by the exceptional conditions which occur during the execution of CICS commands. CEDF automatically display each CICS command issued within a CICS program both before and after the execution. However, when a CICS task is abended due to data exception, CEDF will not tell you which statement within the program that caused the abend and the contents of data fields used in this statement. This is where INTERTEST comes in.

INTERTEST has the following advantages over CEDF:

1. Symbolic Addressing ability
   You can enter a data field name and INTERTEST will display its contents for you. The CORE transaction of INTERTEST is for this purposes. This is very useful when you try to examine the contents of data fields used within the abended statement during the abend screen display.

2. Abend statement display

When a CICS program abends, INTERTEST will display the statement that causes abend along with its surrounding statements on the terminal. Then you can use CORE transaction to display the contents of fields used within that abended statement that is to cause the abend. Therefore, there is no need to read the storage dump of this task in order to find out which statement caused the abend.

3. On-line source listing display

The LIST transaction of INTERTEST allows you to display the CICS program compile listing on your terminal in the CICS region. Therefore, you do not need to log off from the CICS test or production system in order to look at the latest compile listing of the CICS program.

4. On-line file manipulation

The FILE transaction of INTERTEST allows you to add, update, delete, browse, and read VSAM file on-line. This provides an excellent tool to set up the test data the way you want it. This could be the most important feature of INTERTEST since setting up desired test data is the key to the success of your CICS testing. CICS transaction CECI also allows you to issue CICS commands to perform these functions. However, it is hard to use and is not a full-screen support transaction.

5. Update main storage and system areas

The CORE transaction of INTERTEST allows you to change the contents of main storages and many system areas. For example, you can cancel a task that hangs your terminal by changing the DCT contents within TCA (Task Control Area). This way you do not need to bother your computer operator to cancel your hung terminal in the CICS test system.

The only advantage that CEDF has over INTERTEST is the automatic break points. CEDF will display each CICS command both before and after the execution and you do not need to request that. However, you need to set up Unconditional Breakpoints (UBPs) within CICS programs under INTERTEST if you want to stop at these breakpoints during the execution of the CICS program. Therefore, CEDF is an excellent tool to check out the logic flow of a CICS program and problems caused by exceptional conditions. In fact, most of the problems within a CICS program can be debugged through the use of CEDF. INTERTEST is an excellent tool when it comes down to pinpoint which statement within the CICS program causes the abend and why the program abends. INTERTEST is also good at setting up test data that way you want it through the FILE transaction.

11.4.1. Introduction To INTERTEST

Before you can use INTERTEST, you must compile your CICS programs using the JCL that is set up by your system programmer. This set of JCL contains one extra step to build the tables and information that are necessary to support INTERTEST operations in CICS.

After you have compiled your CICS programs using the new JCL, you can then sign on to CICS test system. After you get on to the test system, you can start INTERTEST by entering the following:

```
CNTL=START
```

This will start the INTERTEST. You only need to start INTERTEST once when CICS is brought up. If INTERTEST has already been started, the above command will be ignored. After INTERTEST has been started, you can issue INTERTEST transactions to set up the monitoring, process test files, and perform CICS testing. INTERTEST will be active until it is cancelled or until CICS is shut down.

After INTERTEST has been started, you can then set up your CICS programs to be monitored under INTERTEST as follows:

```
CNTL=ON,PROG=XCU00
CNTL=INCL,PROG=XCU00
```

This will include the CICS program XCU00 under the monitoring of INTERTEST. If the transaction you are going to enter involves more than one CICS program, you should include these programs as we did in the above example. If a CICS program within a CICS task is not set up for INTERTEST monitoring, then no abend screen will be displayed by INTERTEST if that CICS program causes the abend. Therefore, you would only include those CICS programs for a CICS task that may cause the abend under the monitoring of INTERTEST. After all the CICS programs you want to test have been included in INTERTEST, you can then set up the Unconditional Breakpoints (UBPs) within these CICS programs where you want the execution to stop to examine the data fields or you can just enter the transaction for execution. If no UBPs are set up, then INTERTEST only displays the abend screen when the task is about to abend. If UBPs are set up for a CICS program, INTERTEST will display the breakpoint display when the statement at the break point is to be executed. The abend screen contains the COBOL source statement that is to cause abend along with its surrounding statements.

INTERTEST has four major transactions and each one performs different functions. They are: CNTL, CORE, LIST, and FILE. CNTL transaction allows you to start INTERTEST, set up monitoring on CICS programs, CICS transactions, and CICS terminals, set up UBPs within CICS programs, and perform many other control functions. CORE transaction allows you to review or update data fields using their symbolic names or offset addresses. LIST transaction allows you to review the CICS program compile listing in the CICS region so you do not need to log off from CICS and then go to TSO/ISPF (OS/VS) or ICCF (DOS/VSE) in order to review it. FILE transaction allows you to add, update, delete, browse, or read VSAM file records on-line so you can create the test data the way you want it or repair the bad records. We will discuss all these four transactions in greater details in the following sections.

11.4.2.   CNTL Transaction

You can use CNTL transaction to start or cancel INTERTEST, set up or remove INTERTEST monitoring on CICS programs, CICS transactions, or terminals, and set up or remove Unconditional Breakpoints (UBPs).

11.4.2.1.   Start INTERTEST

When CICS is brought up in the morning, you should start INTERTEST as follows:

```
CNTL=START
```

This will start INTERTEST. You only need to do this once every time CICS is brought up. After INTERTEST has been started, you should then set up INTERTEST monitoring on the CICS programs that you try to test. When the CICS program is about to abend, INTERTEST will interrupt the execution of this task and display the abend screen that contains the statement which is about to cause the abend. You can then enter CORE transaction in the command line of this abend screen to examine or update the data fields used within the abend statement. After you have finished with these data fields, you should enter CORE=BMSG on the command line of the CORE screen to return to the abend screen. On this abend screen, you should hit ENTER key to execute this abend statement. In result, the CICS task will be abended. You should then hit PF3 to get out of INTERTEST.

11.4.2.2.   Set Up Monitoring

After INTERTEST has been started, you can then set up CICS programs, CICS transactions, or CICS terminals to be monitored by INTERTEST. If a CICS transaction is set up to be monitored by INTERTEST, then all CICS programs executed by this transaction will be monitored. A CICS transaction may execute more than one CICS program. For example, when the control is transferred from the menu program to the update program, the CICS transaction executes these two CICS programs. Therefore, if you specify the transaction code of the menu program, both menu program and the portion of the update program that issues the SEND MAP will be under the monitoring of INTERTEST.

If a CICS program is set up to be mornitored by INTERTEST, only that CICS program executed by the transaction will be monitored. If a terminal is set up to be monitored by INTERTEST, all CICS transactions or CICS programs associated with that terminal will be monitored. That means all transactions entered or executed on that terminal will be monitored.

Not all CICS programs or transactions should be monitored by INTERTEST. Only those that may cause problems should be included. You can set up or remove monitoring on CICS programs, CICS transactions, or CICS terminals, or set up or remove UBPs within CICS programs through the use of CNTL transaction. When CNTL is entered on a clear screen, CICS will display Monitoring Command Builder Screen as follows:

```
     OSI InterTest MONITORING COMMAND BUILDER - FUNCTION SELECTION

Select desired function by letter:

A Set Monitoring        E Remove Monitoring       I Status Display
B Set Breakpoints       F Remove Breakpoints      J Utility Options
C Set Replace Options   G Remove Replace Options  K System-Wide Options
D Set Protect Options   H Remove Protect Options  L Resume Task Execution
```

(Screen continued on next page)

244

```
For SET, REMOVE, or STATUS functions: Enter Program Names or Transaction Codes
                                       or Terminal Names

   Program Names      _____  _____  _____  _____  _____  _____
   Transaction Codes  ____ ____ ____ ____ ____ ____ ____ ____ ____
   Terminal Names     ____ ____ ____ ____ ____ ____ ____ ____ ____


Press ENTER KEY with data to process command or select PF key:
1 HELP        2 CNTL       3 END        4 LIST       5 CORE=Task    6 CORE=Bkpt
7 FILE        8 Prev       9            10           11 CORE=Syst   12 View
```

You can then enter A on the function field and CICS program names, CICS transaction codes or CICS terminal IDs on the blank fields and then hit ENTER key. This will set up monitoring on the programs, transactions, or terminals entered. Most of the time, you will enter either programs or transactions.

After monitoring has been set up, you can terminate this CNTL screen by pressing PF3 key. After you have get out of CNTL, you can then hit CLEAR key to erase the message and you are ready to enter the next CICS transaction.

11.4.2.3.   Set Up UBPs

You can use the Monitoring Command Builder Screen to set up UBPs within a CICS program. After this screen is invoked by entering CNTL on a clear terminal, you should enter B on the function field and enter the CICS program name in which you want to set up UBPs. You can only set up UBPs for one CICS program at a time. After you enter B and program name and then hit ENTER key, the following screen will appear:

```
   OSI InterTest MONITORING COMMAND BUILDER - COBOL BREAKPOINT LOCATIONS

    SET breakpoint locations for program XCU02    in any of the following fields:

Paragraph
   Names:  _____    _____
           _____    _____
           _____    _____

Statement
 Numbers:  _____    _____    _____    _____    _____    _____    _____    _____

 Offsets:  _____    _____    _____    _____    _____    _____    _____    _____


Terminal identification where breakpoints will take effect:        _____
Terminal identification that will receive the breakpoints:         _____


Press ENTER key with data to process command or select PF key:
1 HELP        2 CNTL       3 End        4 LIST       5 CORE=Task    6 CORE=Bkpt
7 FILE        8 Prev       9 Cond       10           11 CORE=Syst   12 View
```

You can then enter the desired UBPs in three forms: paragraph name, statement number or offset. If you do not have the latest compile listing, you may enter the paragraph name on which you want the execution to be stopped. If you have the compile listing, then you can use the statement numbers on the left margin of the program compile listing or the offsets of the statements on the right margin to set up UBPs. The easiest way is using the statement number. After you have entered UBPs on the above screen, you should then hit ENTER key to set up these UBPs. After that, you can hit PF3 key to get out of CNTL transaction and go back to CICS.

When INTERTEST stops the execution of a CICS task at one of the UBPs, you can then examine or update the contents of data fields by entering CORE transaction in the command line of this breakpoint display. You can also set up UBPs to check out the logic flow of the transaction to see if the statement at the UBP is executed. In order to check out the logic flow of a CICS program, CEDF is better than INTERTEST since CEDF will automatically display each CICS command without setting up UBPs. INTERTEST only display the breakpoint screen when the break point is set up by CICS programmers.

After the CICS programs, transactions or terminals have been set up for monitoring, they can be removed from INTERTEST monitoring. You can enter CNTL on a clear screen to display the CNTL Command Builder screen, and then enter E on the function field and the CICS programs, transactions, or terminals you want to remove from INTERTEST monitoring. You cannot mix these three types of monitoring on one screen. However, you can enter more than one entries for the each type on one screen. For example, you can remove three CICS programs from monitoring on one screen. But you cannot remove one CICS program and one CICS transaction from monitoring on the same screen. They must be done separately. After function E and entries to be removed have been entered, you should hit ENTER key to perform the monitoring removal function. After the monitoring has been removed, you should then PF3 key to terminate CNTL transaction and go back to CICS. You need to remove the monitoring on a CICS program when you have tested that program successfully.

11.4.2.4.   Remove UBPs

After UBPs are no longer needed, you can remove them using the CNTL Command Builder screen. On this screen, you can enter F (Remove Breakpoints) on the function field and the CICS program name in which the UBPs are set up. You can only remove UBPs for one CICS program at a time. Therefore, you should only enter F and one CICS program name and then hit ENTER key to display Breakpoint Location screen. On this screen, you can remove UPBs by entering them as they were entered when they were set up and then hit ENTER key to remove these UBPs entered. If you want to remove all UBPs from this program, you should enter .ALL on the paragraph name field and then hit ENTER. After UBPs have been removed, you can hit PF3 to go back to CICS.

11.4.2.5.   Breakpoint Display

When a CICS task under INTERTEST monitoring is about to abend or an UBP has been reached, INTERTEST will display a Breakpoint Display. A sample Breakpoint Display when a CICS task is about to abend is as follows:

```
     Program XCU03 stopped by InterTest in statement 1100.0 (Offset +0A13B)
   Automatic breakpoint; an attempt to change an area that does not belong
      to this task. Possible system damage has been prevented
                                                                 Back-trace
 Tran= CU03 from term K01A monitored as PROG                   1081.0 1085.1
 DFHCOMMAREA does not exist.                                   1085.1 1086.0
                                                               1096.0 1096.1
 01098         MOVE CURRENT-DATE TO DATEO.                     1096.1 1097.0
 01099         MOVE EIBTRMID     TO TERMIDO.                   1100.0 to here
 01100         MOVE 658          TO CUST-NO.
 01101         MOVE 0            TO WS-LINE-CTR.
 01102         MOVE 0            TO WS-PAGE-CTR.
 01103         MOVE SPACES       TO EDIT-TAB.
 01104         MOVE -1           TO CUSTNAML.


 Contents of relevant storage at address 000020:
 00000000                             *....*

 ==> CNTL=GO,TASK=04305,AXXXX
   Overtype the above or use a PF key or press ENTER to abend without a dump.
   1 HELP    2 CNTL menu   3 Disconnect    4 LIST     5 CORE=Task  6 CORE=Bkpt
   7 FILE    8 Backtrace   9 Exec 1 instr. 10 1 verb  11 Override  12 Resume menu
```

From the above display, we know the CICS program XCU03 is about to abend on the
statement 1100.0. The reason of the abend is this statement tries to use a data area
defined in LINKAGE SECTION that has not been acquired. The transaction ID is CU03,
the current terminal is K01A and the statement that caused abend is the statement
number 1100 which tries to move a literal to a data field named CUST-NO that has never
been acquired. The abend statement is high-lighted.

You can press PF keys to request CNTL, CORE, LIST, and FILE transactions from a
Breakpoint Display. However, you will only want to examine or update contents of data
fields during an abend Breakpoint display in most cases. You can enter CORE='CUST-
NO' on the command line at the bottom of the Breakpoint Display to display the contents
of CUST-NO. After CUST-NO has been display on CORE screen, you can enter CORE
transaction again on the command line at the bottom of the CORE screen to display or
update the next data field. You can repeat this step as many times as you need. After
you have finished with CORE transaction, you can then enter CORE=BMSG in the
command line of the current display to return to this abend Breakpoint Display. Then
you can hit ENTER key to execute this statement. In result, this CICS task will be
abended. After the task has been abended, you need to hit PF3 to get out of
INTERTEST.

11.4.3.   FILE Transaction

The FILE transaction of INTERTEST is a very powerful CICS transaction for you to
set up test data the way you want it. It can be used to add, update, delete, browse or
read VSAM file records. After a VSAM file has been defined and load with one dummy
record, you can then use FILE to add more records for your testing. You can also use
FILE to update the existing records with desired data or delete records that contain
invalid data and cause abends.

In addition to VSAM files, you can also use FILE transaction to process DL/I data bases, BDAM files, ISAM files, Temporary Storage queues, and Transient Data queues. In this section, we'll concentrate our efforts only on VSAM KSDS files.

The FILE transaction can be invoked by entering FILE on a clear screen. CICS will response with a FILE screen. You can then enter the function (read, update ..), dataset name, record ID (key) and then hit ENTER key to read, update, delete, or browse VSAM file records. In the following sections we'll show you how to add, update, delete, read, and browse VSAM records using FILE transaction.

After FILE has been entered, the following FILE screen will be display:

```
DATATYPE= FC FILEID=          MODE=      LOG=OFF TODEST=          PASSWORD=
FUNC=       SUBFUNC=     RETMETH=      ARGTYP=     SRCHTYP=
MESSAGE=
 RETNRCID=                                                      CHGELEN=
    RCID=
    DATA=                                                       SIZE=
FORMAT= D 00112233 44556677 8899AABB CCDDEEFF *              *
LOC 0000  ........ ........ ........ ........ ................
    0000                                                       DSORG=,
    0010                                                       RECFM= '
    0020                                                       LRECL= ˉ
    0030                                                       BLK    :
    0040                                                       KEY    :
    0050                                                       KEYLEN=
    0060                                                       STRNO=
    0070
    0080
    0090
    00A0
    00B0
    00C0
    00D0
    00E0
    00F0
```

In the above FILE Screen, DATATYPE=FC means you want to perform File Control command. You do not need to change this field. On FILEID= field, you should enter the dataset name you want to process. This dataset name must be specified in the FCT. On the FUNC= field, you should enter the File Control function you want to perform on this file. The following is a list of valid functions for a VSAM KSDS file:

```
GET  - read a VSAM record
GETU - read a VSAM record for update
PUT  - write a VSAM record to VSAM file
BEGB - begin a browse operation (STARTBR)
NEXT - read the next record during a browse
PREV - read the previous record during a browse
ENDB - end the browse operation
DEL  - delete a VSAM record from the VSAM file
ADDN - add a VSAM record using a new work area
ADDU - add a VSAM record using the current work area
```

If you want to read a record, you should enter the record key as C'ABC' (character form) or X'00123C' (hexadecimal form) on RCID= field. After the record has been retrieved, it will be displayed on the File Screen along with this file information. If you need to review the contents of the next page of the retrieved record, you can change the address on the LOC field and then hit ENTER key to go to the next page. At any time, you can hit CLEAR key or enter END on the function field to get out of FILE screen and go back to CICS.

For example, you can enter CUSTMAST on the FILEID, GET on the FUNC field, C'12345' on the RCID field and then hit ENTER key. The customer record with key equal to '12345' in the customer master file (CUSTMAST) will be displayed (GET).

In the following sections, we'll show you how to read, update, delete, browse, and add VSAM records using FILE screen.

11.4.3.1.   Read A VSAM Record

To read a VSAM record for inquiry, you should enter the dataset name you want to process on the FILEID field, GET on the FUNC field, and the key of the record to be read on the RCID field. You can enter the key in character or hexadecimal form. The following example shows how to read a customer record with customer number equal to '12345':

```
FILEID=CUSTMAST
FUNC=GET
RCID=C'12345'
```

The following example shows how to enter a record key in hexadecimal form:

```
RCID=X'01234C'
```

After you have entered all three fields, the record will be displayed. The information about this VSAM file will also be displayed. The following example shows a customer record with key equal to '12345' has been read:

```
DATATYPE= FC FILEID= CUSTMAST MODE=        LOG=OFF TODEST=          PASSWORD=
FUNC=        SUBFUNC=        RETMETH=      ARGTYP=    SRCHTYP=
MESSAGE= RECORD OBTAINED FOR VIEWING
  RETNRCID=                                                        CHGLEN=
        RCID=C'12345'
        DATA=                                                      SIZE= 0123
FORMAT= D 00112233 44556677 8899AABB CCDDEEFF *0123456789ABCDEF*
LOC 0000 ........ ........ ........ ........ ................
   0000   F1F2F3F4 F5C4C1E5 C9C440D3 C5C54040 *12345DAVID LEE  * DSORG=VSKS
   0010   40404040 40404040 40F0F0F5 F0F0F0F0 *       0050000* RECFM=FB
   0020   0012345C                            *...*            * LRECL=0024
   0030                                        *              * BLK    :0000
   0040                                        *              * KEY    :000
   0050                                        *              * KEYLEN=05
   0060                                        *              * STRNO=01
   0070                                        *              *
   0080                                        *              * READ
   0090                                        *              * BROWSE
   00A0                                        *              *
   00B0                                        *              *
   00C0                                        *              *
   00D0                                        *              *
   00E0                                        *              *
   00F0                                        *              *
```

On the right hand side, you can see some important information about this VSAM file. DSORG=VSKS specifies this is a VSAM KSDS file. RECFM=FB specified this VSAM file is a fixed-length file. Most of VSAM files are fixed-length files. LRECL=00C8 specifies the VSAM record length in hexadecimal form (200 bytes). BLKSIZE=0000 does not mean anything to a VSAM file since a VSAM file does not use blocks. KEYPOS=000 specifies the key starts at the first position (relative 0) within the record. KEYLEN=05 specifies the key length is 5 bytes long. STRNO=02 specifies the string number for this VSAM file is set at 2.

You can hit PF1 on this File Screen to go to the next page of the record, PF2 to go to the previous page, and PF3 to go to the beginning of the record. You can also enter the address on the LOC (location) field to display the record starting at that address. You need to do that when you want to update the contents of record at certain locations.

11.4.3.2.   Update A VSAM Record

To update a VSAM record, you need to retrieve this record through a GET, GETU, or browse operation. After the record is retrieved, you can then use CHGE function to change the record contents (except the key) one or more times and then use PUT function to rewrite this record. Assume that we want to change the status of the customer record with key equal to '12345' to '3':

1. Enter FILE on a clear screen to invoke the FILE Screen.

2. Enter CUSTMAST on the FILEID= field, GETU on the FUNC= field and C'12345' on the RCID= field to retrieve this record for update.

3. Enter CHGE on the FUNC= field, C'3' on the DATA= field and 00019 on the LOC field and then hit ENTER key to make the change. 00019 is the location of the status field in hexadecimal form. Therefore the status field is the 25th byte within the record (00019 = 25). The first byte of record is 00001 (not 00000).

4. Enter PUT on the FUNC= field and then hit ENTER key. This will rewrite the record with new status. Now you can hit CLEAR to get out of FILE screen.

You can repeat step 3 above as many times as required. If you need to update three separate fields within the record, you need to perform step 3 three times.

11.4.3.3.   Delete A VSAM Record

To delete a VSAM record, you should enter the file name on the FILEID field, DEL on the FUNC field, and the complete record key on the RCID field. The following example shows how to delete the customer record with key equal to '12345' from the customer master file CUSTMAST:

```
FILEID=CUSTMAST
FUNC=DEL
RCID=C'12345'
```

11.4.3.4. Add A VSAM Record

You can add a VSAM record from scratch or you can read an existing record and use this record as the base record to create this new record. The later method is easier. However, you need to use CHGE to change the key and data fields.

If we want to add a VSAM record using an existing record as the base record, then you need to use GET, GETU or browse (BEGB and NEXT) to retrieve the base record. After the base record has been retrieved on the FILE Screen, you can then change the FUNC field to ADDU and then hit ENTER key. This will indicate to FILE transaction that you want to use the current record as the base record for the new record to be added. You should then issue one or more CHGE functions to change the key and data fields. To see how you can use CHGE function, please refer to the update function in the preceeding section. The key of this new record must be different from the base record. After changes have been made, you can then enter PUT on the FUNC field and new key on the RCDID field to add this new record. After the record has been added, you can hit CLEAR key to get out of FILE.

If you want to add a new record from scratch, you need to enter ADDN on the FUNC field, data string on the DATA field and then hit ENTER key to obtain this work area to be used for the new record. After the work area has been obtained, you can use CHGE function to make the changes to this work area as you did for the above base record. Then you enter PUT on the FUNC field and the new key on the RCDID field to add this new record.

Let's compare the above two methods to add a new record. The first method retrieves a base record and then uses ADDU to indicate that we want to use the retrieved record as the base record to create this new record. The second method use ADDN as the function and data string on the DATA field to obtain this work area. The remaining procedures are the same.

11.4.3.5. Browse A VSAM Records

When you browse a VSAM file in a CICS program, you'll issue STARTBR, READNEXT, and ENDBR commands. When you browse a VSAM file using FILE transaction, you need to perform BEGB, NEXT, and ENDB functions. In order to browse a VSAM file on FILE Screen, you need to enter the file name on the FILEID field, BEGB on the FUNC field, the starting key (a partial or full key) on the RCID field and then hit ENTER key. This will set up the starting key for the browse operation. If no data is entered on the RCID field, the browse will start from the beginning of the file. After the starting key has been set up by BEGB function, the FUNC field will be changed to NEXT automatically. So you only need to hit ENTER key to read the first record. Each subsequent ENTER key from now on will retrieve the next record. After you have finished the browse, you can hit CLEAR key to get out of FILE screen or enter ENDB on the FUNC field to end the browse. During the browse operation, you can change NEXT on the FUNC field to PREV to read the previous record.

11.4.4. CORE Transaction

The CORE transaction of INTERTEST makes reading the CICS storage dump a history.

Its symbolic addressing capability allows you to examine or change almost any data field in the main storage. For example, you can enter CORE transaction and the data field names on a Breakpoint Display to examine or change the contents of these data fields that may cause the abend. CEDF does not have symbolic addressing capability. Therefore you need to hit PF5 key during CEDF sessions to examine or change the storage contents using offset addresses.

The storage areas of CICS main storage that can be displayed or modified include:

1. CICS program-related areas such as data fields in WORKING-STORAGE SECTION or LINKAGE SECTION.

2. CICS task-related area such as TCA (Task Control Area) or TWA (Transaction Work Area).

3. CICS system-related areas such as CSA (Common Storage Area) or CICS internal tables (PPT, PCT, FCT, DCT, TCT or SNT).

Therefore, you can use CORE transaction to display or modify the data fields within a CICS task so you know why the transaction abends or you can conduct more testing before you go back to correct the errors within a CICS program.

When a CICS task hangs your terminal for any reason, you can use CORE transaction to change DCT of TCA in order to cancel this task. In result, it will free your terminal. This is one of the most important features you need to remember for the CORE transaction. You can hang your terminal many times a day during the heavy testing. If you use CORE transaction, you do not need to ask your computer operator to free your terminal from the console. It will save you a lot of time. However, your system programmer may set up a password for the update function of the CORE transaction. In this case, you need to enter the password before you can modify the main storage contents.

You can also use CORE to display or modify the CICS internal tables. For example, your system programmer forgot to put your CICS programs, transactions, mapsets and VSAM files into the CICS internal tables and you do not want to wait until tomorrow to perform your testing. You can use CORE transaction to change some of the existing CICS programs, CICS transations, or CICS mapsets to your new programs, transactions, or mapsets so you can test them today.

11.4.4.1.   CORE Transaction At A Breakpoint Display

The most useful situation that CORE can be employed is when you are on a Breakpoint Display. Breakpoint Display is displayed when the CICS program is about to abend or at an UBP. You can enter CORE='data-name' in the command line at the bottom of this Breakpoint Display which is occupied by CNTL=GO,TASK=nnnnn. The data name must be a storage area within this CICS task. After you enter CORE='CUST-NO' and then hit ENTER key, the contents of CUST-NO will be displayed. You can then update this field using CORE transaction with CHG command or you can enter this CORE command to display as many data fields as you need. When you are finished with

CORE transaction, you can enter CORE=BMSG to return to this Breakpoint Display. If this Breakpoint Display is displayed when the CICS task is about to abend, you can hit ENTER key to abend the task. After the task has been abended, you can hit PF3 to get out of INTERTEST and return to CICS. If this is an UBP Breakpoint Display, you can hit PF9 to go to the next UBP Breakpoint Display.

Why do you want to change the contents of data fields at UBPs? If you have determined the contents of some data fields are not correct and you want to continue the testing, then you should modify these data fields to contain the valid data in order to continue the testing.

11.4.4.2.   CORE Transaction With CHG Command

After you have displayed the contents of a data field using CORE='data-name' at Breakpoint Display, you can change its contents using CORE transaction with CHG command. The following examples show how to change ORDER-QTY (PIC 9(5)) from 3 to 6:

```
CORE='ORDER-QTY'=CHGC'00006'
```

or

```
CORE='ORDER-QTY'=VERC'00003'=CHGC'00006'
```

The first one will change the order quantity to 6 no matter what is in ORDER-QTY. The second one will only change ORDER-QTY to 6 if it contains '00003'. If ORDER-QTY does not contain '00003', the change will not be made.

If you enter CORE='ORDER-QTY' first to display its contents. Then you should enter =CHGC'00006' following CORE='ORDER-QTY'. There is no need to re-enter the first part of CORE transaction that is displayed in the command line. If your system programmer has set up a password for the update function of the CORE transaction, then you'll be asked to enter the password after CHG command has been issued in the CORE transaction. After a correct password has been entered, update will be made.

When INTERTEST is implemented in the production CICS system, the CHG command of CORE transaction is normally disabled so nobody can change the contents of main storage. The FILE transaction is very useful to fix the bad data in VSAM records that caused the abends. Therefore, it is normally allowed in the production CICS system and protected by password.

CORE can also be used to fix your terminal when it is hung. When your terminal is hung for any reason, you should go to other terminal and sign on to CICS. Then you should get the task number that hangs your terminal by issuing the following CSMT command:

```
CSMT TAS
```

This CSMT command will list all active tasks with their task number and associated terminal. You can use the your terminal ID to identify the task number that hangs your terminal. After you have written down the task number, you can issue CORE transaction as follows to cancel your task:

$$CORE(000123) = TCA\ \S0+18\ \S0+18 = VERX'88' = CHGX'21'$$

This will change the first byte of DCT in TCA from X'88' to X'21'. In result, the task will be cancelled and your terminal will be released. Using CSMT or CEMT transaction to terminate a task, cancel a terminal, or put a terminal out of service may not always free your terminal when it is hung. However, using CORE transaction as described above will free the terminal every time since it alters the system area for that task.

CORE transaction also allows you to examine or update system-related areas such as CICS internal tables or CSA (Common System Area). To do that, you can enter CORE on a clear screen to display CORE Command Builder Screen as follows:

```
   OSI InterTest CORE COMMAND BUILDER - SYSTEM-RELATED AREAS   (CORE=Syst)

Specify AREA, ADDRESS, TABLE or PROGRAM to be displayed or changed:

   CICS AREA:  ____      CSA, PCT, PPT, FCT, TCT, DCT, SIT    ADDRESS: _____
                         PAM, TRT, , ATRT, ADCH, SDCH

   CICS TABLE entry:   PPT _____  FCT _____  PCT ____   TCT ____  DCT ____

   To display PROGRAM: _____    Enter  L to load or D to delete module: _

OPTIONAL OFFSET: _____

Scan value: _____           Data Formats
Scan range: _____         B to scan backwards: _    _____
                                                    | P' ' = Packed |
To VERIFY and/or CHANGE data:                       | X' ' = Hex    |
Existing data: _____       | C' ' = char   |
    New data: _____        -----------------

Press ENTER to display requested main storage or use a PF key:
1 HELP      2 CNTL     3 End       4 LIST      5 CORE=Task  6 CORE=Bkpt
7 FILE      8          9 BMSG      10          11 CORE=Syst 12
```

You can change the CICS program that will be invoked by the transaction ID CUST to XCU00 on PCT by entering CUST on PCT field, +5 on the OPTIONAL OFFSET field, and C'XCU00' on the NEW DATA field. After you press ENTER, this change will be made. Now you can use CUST to invoke your new CICS program XCU00 for testing rather than wait until your system programmer put it in the PCT and PPT. This will be a temporary change. When CICS is brought up next time, it will still use the PCT load module and your change will be gone.

You can also enter CORE=PCT (or PPT or FCT or TCT or DCT) on the terminal to display the first page of PCT, then you can search the PCT table for the transaction CUST by entering CORE=SCAN10000,C'CUST'. This will scan PCT forward for 10000 bytes to find the first character string 'CUST'. This allows you to look at the current contents of CICS internal tables.

11.4.5. LIST Transaction

The LIST transaction of INTERTEST allows you to review your CICS compile listing while you are on CICS. When you want to look at your CICS programs, you do not need to log off from CICS and then sign on to TSO/ISPF (OS/VS) or ICCF (DOS/VSE) in order to review the compile listing or CICS program source codes.

You can enter LIST on a clear screen to display LIST Source Code Viewing Screen. From this screen, you can choose to begin the display of the information with a statement number, a paragraph name, WORKING-STORAGE SECTION, LINKAGE SECTION, PROCEDURE DIVISION or other compile listing areas. The following is a LIST screen:

```
              OSI InterTest - SOURCE CODE VIEWING - (LIST)

Program= XCU03    Stmt =          Option =    (choose one option)    Margin= 01
                  Paragraph name or Search arg=
OPTIONS: 1 Procedure div  2 Working-storage  3 Linkage sect 4 D-map 5 Clist Pmap
         6 Xref      7 Procedure names    8         9 Search fwd 10 Search bwd
PFKEYS: 1 HELP     2 CNTL      3 End     4         5 FILE        6 CORE=Bkpt
         7 Page bwd 8 Page fwd 9 BMSG   10 Half    11 Half fwd   12
--------------------------------------------------------------------------------
01100        MOVE LOW-VALUES TO AXCU03O.
01101        MOVE CURRENT-DATE TO DATEO.
01102        MOVE TIME-OF-DAY TO WS-TIME-N.
01103        MOVE WS-TIME-N-HH TO WS-TIME-E-HH.
01104        MOVE WS-TIME-N-MM TO WS-TIME-E-MM.
01105        MOVE WS-TIME-E    TO TIMEO.
01106        MOVE EIBTRMID     TO TERMIDO.
01107        MOVE CUST-NO      TO CUSTNO.
01108        MOVE CUST-NAME    TO CUSTNAMO.
01109        MOVE CUST-CRDLMT  TO WS-CRDLMT.
01110        MOVE WS-CRDLMT    TO CRDLMTO.
01111        MOVE -1           TO CUSTNAML.
01112        MOVE SPACES       TO EDIT-TAB.
01113        MOVE 0            TO WS-LINE-CTR.
01114        MOVE 'ENTER INPUT DATA' TO MSGO.
```

For example, we want to look at the source program starting with PROCUDURE DIVISION, then you should enter XCU00 on the PROGRAM= field, 1 on the OPTION field, then hit ENTER. This will display the source statements starting with PROCEDURE DIVISION. You can also search a character string by entering it on 'Search arg=' field and then hit PF9 key to search forward. This character string may be anything like a data field name or a paragraph name. You can also enter the statement number on the program compile listing in order to start the display from that statement.

You can also enter the following to view a CICS program named XCU00 starting with statement 900:

```
LIST=XCU00,900
```

LIST transaction can also be invoked by pressing PF4 key from any INTERTEST Display or a Breakpoint Display. If you press PF4 on a Breakpoint Display, the program to be viewed is the one that is stopped at Breakpoint.

LIST transaction does no help you debug your CICS program that much as CORE or FILE transactions. However, it provides you with the compile listing viewing capability while your are on CICS.

11.5.   CECI And CMSG Transactions

In addition to CEDF and INTERTEST, CECI and CMSG transactions may be helpful to your testing. CECI is an IBM-supplied CICS transaction, it can interpret and execute a CICS command so you can use this transaction to perform desired CICS operations. For example, you can use CECI to send a CICS map to see if the CICS map is what you expect. You can also use CECI to read a VSAM file. CMSG transaction can be used to send a message to a terminal or printer. You can use this transaction to communicate with other CICS users or to test your printer to see if it works. In the following sections, we'll discuss these two CICS transactions in details.

11.5.1.   CECI Transaction

If your shop does not install INTERTEST, then you may need to use CECI to replace the functions performed by FILE transaction of INTERTEST. This Command-Level Interpreter will check the syntax of the CICS command you enter and execute it right away on your terminal. You can use it to maintain your VSAM files, temporary storage queues, and perform many CICS operations.

After you have successfully assembled your CICS mapset, you can use CECI to display this map on the terminal for checking. You can check the locations, lengths, attributes and initial values of CICS map fields on the screen. You can even enter the input data on the unprotected map fields. To issue a CECI transaction to send the CICS map within a CICS mapset, you enter the following on a clear screen:

```
CECI SEND MAP('AXCU00') MAPSET('XXCU00')
```

Then hit ENTER. The map AXCU00 within the mapset XXCU00 will be displayed on the terminal. This way, you do not need to wait until the CICS program that uses this map has been written in order to check out the CICS map layout. The CECI has the following general format:

```
CECI [command]
```

Where command is the CICS command. For example, you can enter the following CECI command to read the customer record with key equal to '12345' from the customer master file CUSTMAST:

```
CECI READ DATASET('CUSTMAST') RIDFLD('12345')
```

After the above line has been entered, the terminal will display the record I/O area, execution status and EIBRCODE for this command. You can enter almost every CICS command using CECI transaction. The EXEC CICS of the CICS command is optional, normally you will omit EXEC CICS and END-EXEC in the command of CECI. The output area should not be specified when you issue a CECI command. For example, the record I/O area is not specified in the preceeding example since it is an output area for the READ command. After the above CECI command is executed, the terminal will display the following screen:

```
READ DATASET('CUSTMAST') RIDFLD('12345')
STATUS:  COMMAND EXECUTION COMPLETE                    NAME=
 EXEC CICS READ
  Dataset( 'CUSTMAST' )
  SET() | Into ( '12345DAVID LEE                       ...'... )
  < Length ( +00200 ) >
  Ridfld( '12345' )
  < Keylength () <GEneric > >
  < SYsid () >
  < SEGset () | Segsetall >
  < RBa | RRn | DEBRec | DEBKey >
  < GTeg | Equal >
  < Update >


  RESPONSE: NORMAL                     EIBRCODE=X'000000000000'

 PF: 1 HELP 2 HEX 3 END 4 EIB 5 VAR 6 USER 7 SBH 8 SFH 9 MSG 10 SB 11 SF
```

You can also create an entry in the temporary Storage queue using this CECI transaction. Even CECI transaction can issue almost every CICS command, but it is not menu-driven nor full-screen support. Therefore, most of CICS programmers would use FILE transaction of INTERTEST.

11.5.2. CMSG Transaction

This transaction can be used to send a message to another terminal in the CICS system. It can also be used to print a small message on a printer to check if the printer is working. You can send a message to another CICS terminal as follows:

```
CMSG MSG='LET US GO HOME!',ROUTE=L01A,SEND
```

If L01A is a display terminal, the message will be displayed. If it is a printer, then the message will be printed. You can use this transaction to test a printer that is not printing and you want to determine if the problem comes from the CICS program or the printer. If you issue the above CMSG transaction using the printer ID in the ROUTE=. If nothing is printed on that printer after CMSG transaction is issued, then you know the problem comes from the printer itself.

11.6. Trace Control And Trace Table

When a CICS command is issued within a CICS program, CICS will create one or more entries in the trace table. The CICS program can also use Trace Control commands to create entries in the trace table. When a CICS transaction abends, this trace table will be included in the storage dump for that task. This trace table can be used as an excellent debugging tool. Normally, there are 1000 entries in the trace table. When the trace table is full, the new entries will be created at the top of the table to replace the old entries. From the trace table, you can see the execution flow of the CICS task and determine the CICS program name, the last CICS command issued before the abend and the abend code. The following is a sample of the trace table within a storage dump:

Trace Table in The Storage Dump

You can only read a storage dump to debug a CICS abend when CEDF and INTERTEST are not available. From the dump, you can determine the statement that caused the abend and the contents of data areas at the time of abend.

11.7.   Read A CICS Abend Storage Dump

You can also use the Dump Control commands within the CICS programs to dump task-related storages, or system-related areas to the current dump dataset. When a CICS task abends, CICS will automatically dump the task-related storages to the current dump dataset. There are two dump data sets in a CICS system. However, only one is active at any time. When a task abends, its storage dump will be created in the current active dump data set. When CICS is shut down, the dump data sets will be printed. However, if you do not want to wait until CICS is shut down to print your own storage dump, you need to switch the current dump data set to the other one and close the current one. This can be accomplished by entering 'CSMT SWI' on a clear screen. This will close the current dump data set and make the other one active. After this CSMT transaction is issued, CICS will display a message which will tell you which one is the new active dump data set. You can then log off from CICS and go to batch region to submit a set of JCL and specify which dump data set to be printed. After the entire dump data set has been printed, you can then use the task number, transaction code and abend code to identify your own dump.

Many times, the storage dump is all you get for a production CICS task abend. Every morning, you'll receive storage dumps that were created yesterday from the CICS abends caused by your CICS transactions. Thus you need to know how to read the storage dump to fix the CICS problems. However, reading a CICS dump is very simple. All it takes is some calculation. The following procedures can be followed to read the CICS storage dump:

Step 1:

You should get the actual address of the next statement to be executed in the last three bytes of PSW on the first page of the storage dump.

PSW 078D0007 D013DAE3

Step 2:

You should get the program entry point by adding X'18' to the PROGRAM STORAGE entry point on the first page of PROGRAM STORAGE section in the storage dump. PROGRAM STORAGE is the last part of the storage dump.

PROGRAM STORAGE ADDRESS 13C808 TO 146357 LENGTH 009B50

13C808 is the program entry point. You need to add X'18' to get the real program entry point (X'13C820'). Now you can calculate the relative address (X'12C3') of the next statement to be executed by subtracting the program entry point (X'13C820') from its actual address in the PSW (X'13DAE3').

13DAE3 - 13C820 = 12C3

Step 3:

You can use the relative address (X'12C3') of the next statement to search CONDENSED LISTING of the CICS program compile listing and find the statement number 980.

979 ADD 0012B7 980 ADD 0012C3

Therefore, statement number 980 is the next statement to be executed and statement number 979 is the statement that caused the abend.

Step 4:

Now you can use statement number 979 to find the instruction that caused the abend in the CICS program compile listing. Each statement in the CICS program will be assigned a statement number at the left margin of the statement in the compile listing.

00979 00725 ADD 1 to WS-LINE-CTR.

Step 5:

Now you want to know the contents of WS-LINE-CTR. You should use the D MAP in the CICS program compile listing to find its address. The address contains a BLL number and an offset.

WS-LINE-CTR BLL=1 02B

Now you need to know which register is used for BLL=1 from D MAP.

REGISTER ASSIGNMENT

REG 11 BL=1

From the above D MAP, we know BLL=1 uses register 11. Now you need to find out the contents of the register 11 and then add offset 02B to it to get the actual address of WS-LINE-CTR. The contents of register 0 through 15 are on the second page of the storage dump.

```
    REGS 0 THRU 15

000000 002F12D4 002F1E60 50490488 802E3928 002E94C8 0048FB0E 00001000 00002000
000020 0049476E 002F004C 002F104C 00492358 0048F3A0 002F1B94 004965F0 00000000
```

Now you can add offset 02B to the contents ('X00492358') to get its actual address in the dump.

$$00492358 + 02B = 00492383$$

You can use the actual address of WS-LINE-CTR (X'492383') to find out its contents in the storage dump. The actual address of a data field is shown at the right margin of the dump.

In many CICS shops, there are no D MAP and CONDENSED LISTING generated in their production CICS program compile listing. The D MAP and CONDENSED LISTING normally can add 40 more pages to the compile listing. Therefore, many CICS shops choose not to generate them in the CICS program compile listing. In this case, you cannot use the technique we have discussed in the above section to read the storage dump. Here, we'll introduce the other technique to read a storage dump using very little information from the CICS program compile listing. We'll use the storage dump shown in the later of this section to demonstrate how to use this second technique to read a storage dump.

Step 1:

Get the actual address of the next statement to be executed in the last three bytes of the PSW on the first page of the dump. This actual address of the next statement in this example is 490506. The PSW is a two-word (8 bytes) area. You can calculate the relative address of the next statement by subtracting the program entry point from its actual address in the PSW as discussed in the above section. Then you use this relative address to locate the next statement in the CICS program compile listing. Each COBOL statement has a relative address at the right margin of the program compile listing. After you have located the next statement in the listing, you can then locate the COBOL statement that caused the abend which is the last statement of this next statement.

Step 2:

Locate the next statement in the dump using its actual address 490506. The actual address is shown at the right margin of the dump. In this case, D705D230 is the next statement to be executed.

Step 3:

Use the first half-byte (X'D') of the second word (X'D0490506') of PSW to determine the length of the statement that caused the abend. In this case, X'D' represents B'1101'. The first two bits (B'11') represent the length in number of half-word. Therefore, the length of the statement that caused the abend is 6 bytes (3 X 2 = 6). B'11' means 3 in the length calculation. Therefore, we can get six bytes of data that is next to D705D230 (the contents of the next statement) in the storage dump. In this case, F872D230A2A6 is the contents of the COBOL statement that caused the abend.

Step 4:

Now we can calculate the actual addresses of data fields used in the abend statement. F8 in F872D230A2A6 represents a ZAP statement (Zero and Add Positive) and is an SS type of instruction. Therefore, we know the abend was caused by trying to add the second field in a ZAP instruction to the first field after the first field has been zeroed out. The first field in this statement is D230 and the second field is A2A6. D in D230 represents the register 13 and 230 in D230 represents the offset. A in A2A6 represents the register 10 and 2A6 represents the offset. In order to find the contents of the first and the second fields in this statement, we need to find out the contents of the register 10 and 13.

Step 5:

The contents of the register 10 and 13 are on the second page of the storage dump. There are two sets of contents of registers in the storage dump: one is with the PSW on the first page of the dump and the other is on the second page. You should use the one on the second page. The one on the first page with PSW is not reliable. From the second page of the storage dump, we find that register 10 contains 002F104C and register 13 contains 002F1B94. Now you can add the offset of the field to its based register in order to get the actual address of that field. In result, D230 has an actual addrsss of 2F1DC4 (002F1B94 + 230) and A2A6 has an actual address of 2F12F2 (002F104C + 2A6). Now you can search the storage dump to find the contents of these two fields using their actual address. The actual address of a data field is shown at the right margin of the dump. Therefore, the first field contains X'000000' and the second field contains '404040'. Now we know why the transaction abended. We tried to add the second field which is defined as a numeric field but contains spaces to the first field that is to be zeroed out.

From the above discussion, we know we use very little information from the CICS program compile listing to read the storage dump. We only use it to locate the COBOL statement that caused the abend.

The following figures show the PSW, register contents, abend statement, and data field contents as discussed above.

CUSTOMER INFORMATION CONTROL SYSTEM STORAGE DUMP   CCDE=ASRA   TASK=B018   DATE=06/18/84   TIME=15:06:22   PAGE   1

(handwritten: address of the next statement to be executed → see page 30 (right address is real address... left is relative...) (starting ...))

PSW   07A00007

REGS 14-4 504FCD32   *(handwritten: 00490506)*   00000000   0DC1C000   50490488   8C2E3928   002E94C8
REGS 5-11 0C49FB0E   02F1204   0CCC2C0C   0C49476E   002F1660   002F004C *(handwritten: determine how far in the program about the PSW)* CC2F104C   00492358 *(handwritten: from next statement by 6   DO = 6 bytes, so count back from next statement by 6)*

TASK CONTROL AREA (USER AREA)   ADDRESS   2E9100 TC   2E96BF   LENGTH CC05C0

(handwritten left margin: x { }   ?)

Page 1 of The Storage Dump

264

TASK CONTROL AREA (SYSTEM AREA)   ADDRESS 2E9C00 TO 2E90FF   LENGTH 0C0100

```
000000    E40406B8 002E9C00 002E9CB0 002F1EE0     8004731C 00514210 002972E0 00000000   *..........................9........*   2E9000
000020    0053F960 00000030 00C0C000 00300000     00000C00 FE50EA5C 0CC00C00 002F1894   *...9........................3.......*   2E9020
000040    002F0000 002F9368 30000300 002E97A0     00000000 00000000 00000000 00000000   *....................................*   2E9040
000060    00000000 0CC00000 00000000 C1E2D9C1     C0000000 00000000 00000000 7E2E9398   *..................ASRA..............*   2E9060
0000E0    FE2E96A8 0CC0C000 FE2E92F3 FE2E96B8     C05409C0 002E9308 00000000 0000C000   *.............3........8.............*   2E9080
0000A0    0051F37C 00000000 00000000 00000000     C2D6F1F8 00000000 00000000 002E9200   *..3...............B018..............*   2E9CA0
0000C0    C1E2D9C1 0CC00005 002E9C00 00000000     0C00C0C 00000000 00000000 0CC0C0000   *ASRA................................*   2E9CC0
0000E0    00000000 0CC00000 00000000 00000000     00000000 000000C0 00000000 0C0CC0C00   *....................................*   2E90E0
```

LIFO STACK ENTRY   ADDRESS 2E9308 TC 2E9517   LENGTH 0C0210

```
000000    42000090 00000000 FF2E9518 40C55AEA     002F015A 90C55C64 002F1E60 002F1824   *............ .E.......E*....-....*   2E9308
000020    002F1R4E 0C2F139C 00000000 002E9DA8     0C0C0C00 0053E140 00C556C0 0A509398   *...N......................E.........*   2E9328
000040    7E2E9398 002E9100 0053F0F0 FE2E9518     F0000C2C3 00EF521C 00000000 00000000   *=...........00....0.KC..............*   2E9348
000060    8B00002E 0C000000 00000000 0050ED9C     00000000 00000000 0CC00C00 00000000   *=...........................K.......*   2E9368
000080    00000000 00000000 8B000029 00300000     C0000178 C0000000 002E94C8 0CCC0C00   *.......................H............*   2E9388
0000A0    00000000 0CCC0C00 00000000 000C0000     00000000 0C51F37C 00000000 00000000   *...................3................*   2E93A8
0000C0    00000000 00000000 00000000 00000000     C0000C0C 0CC00000 0000C0000 0C0CC00    *....................................*   2E93C8
0000E0    00000000 0CC00000 00000000 08509398     C0000000 00000000 0CCC0C00 6C00C0000   *.................................E..*   2E93E8
000100    00000000 00000000 002E9460 60C E9464    002E9BB0 A0C55BB8 00000000 00000000   *.........M..E..............E........*   2E9408
000120    00000000 0CCC0C00 00000000 00000000     002E9B38 002E9B4C 0C000000 002E96C0   *..........................-...E.....*   2E9428
000140    00000000 C0000000 00000004 00000000     012C000C 00C00000 002E94C8 802E3928   *..........................H.........*   2E9448
000150   -002F1894 0C2F004C 00000000 004FDB48     002F1894 4053D9BE 00480478 004FDB48   *-...M......L........R....M..........*   2E9468
000180    002E9460 0048048 002F0010 004804C0       004FDC90 002E9000 00480478 0053D7C4   *-...M.....M........M...M...PD.*   2E9488
0001A0    0048F80E FE50EA5C FE2E9398 002E9100     A0C0C000 CC00000C 40C4C6C9 C5C9C240   *.................DFHEIB.......*   2E94A8
0001C0    0150622C 0084170F C2D6F1F8 0004731C     C2F0F8C5 000006A7 012CF206 C2C00000   *........B018..B08F....2......*   2E94C8
0001E0    000000C2 E6E2D6D3 C9D5C5C0 0C000000     000000C2 E6E2D6D3 C9D5C500 00000000   *...BWSOLINE.......BWSOLINE....*   2E94E8
000200    00C00000 00000000 00000178 00C0C0000                                                                                     2E9508
```

REGS   0 THRU 15   ADDRESS 504FE4 TO 505023   LENGTH 0C0C40

```
000000    002F12D4 002F1E60 504906EB 802E3928     002E94C3 0048EB0E 00001000 00002000   *...M...-.........H...........*   504FE4
000020    0043676E 002F004C 002F104C 00492358     0048F3A0 002F1894 CC4965F0 00000000   *.........3.....0....*   5C5004
```
R0 · R8 · R-9 · R10 · R11 · R12 · R13 · (R)

COMMON SYSTEM AREA   (A)(see p.4)   ADDRESS 53F0F0 TO 53F5EF   LENGTH 0C0500

```
000000    00000000 000C4F50 000C85A4 70504480     00000000 00000004 002E9C68 50EFD058   *....................P.......*   53F0F0
000020    00EFE058 30CF8AF0 002E9C60 002E9C00     00509418 00EFEFD6 00509398 002E9CD0   *.....0...-...-......O...........*   53F110
000040    002E9C60 002E9100 0010150C 002E9100     1506229F 00297C20 07D00100 0C000C00   *..-.......................*   53F130
000060    0052FB54 0CC01E00 40000000 0000CB16     0C04C3C 00CC5000 00544000 0084170F   *...........@....*   53F150
000080    00540108 F2FFFFFF 00000000 00541828     0000015S CCG00CG0 003B2030 D438C615   *....2...........M.F.*   53F170
0000A0    00000000 00297583 00297100 002970C0     00297200 0053FE68 0053F960 C500FF00   *...............9-E...*   53F190
0000C0    000F000B 00C00500 0053F5F0 02E02EC     00000000 00000000 0C000C00 0CC0C000    *..............*   53F1B0
0000E0    40EFF420 00EE2028 004FD51C 00D6F180     00504458 0051B048 00EFD020 004FB388   *...........50....N.01....*   53F1DC
000100    004F7880 0CC00000 00F0301C 004F4BA8     0C540940 00C74114 01ED51F8 004F8E50   *...........G....8...*   53F1F0
000120    00512338 00500218 00517FA0 00509FB8     00503B00 003B2C2C 00292C00 0C540728   *.......K........*   53F210
000140    004FD514 CC505C9B 0C000000 0050BF38     0050BBA4 004F7B7C 0C000000 00000000   *..N..........*   53F230
000160    0FC8449F 7FFFCC00 00000000 82C196A9     00EDFE9C 00000000 00000000 0CC0C0C0   *.H...........A..*   53F250
000180    00540940 00540944 0CC00000 0054095C     000C0C00 00000000 00000000 0053F0A0   *.........................0.*   53F270
0001A0    070E58F0 D19C07FF 00F8F1FC 00F8F1FD     0005DCC0 CCCC0C0C E6D6D9D2 C1D9C5C1   *.0J....81..81....WORKAREA.*   53F290
0001C0    0C00000C 001C0032 0C0C018C 04721C01     33485C01 32850C00 0C000C00 0CC00C00   *...............*   53F2B0
0001E0    1C001C00 0CC0C0C0 00CC000C 0C00000C     00000C00 0C0C0000 0CC0000C 0CC00C00   *...................*   53F2D0
```

Page 2 of The Storage Dump

TRANSACTION STORAGE -USER

ADDRESS 2F0000   TG 2F1EDF   LENGTH 0C1EE0   0C1EE0

000C20 00000000 0C000000 0CC00000 00000030 *..................M* 2F0C20
000C40 C1D2C5C3 C3C8C1D5 C7C5E240 C5096E40 *AKE CHANGES--PRESS--ENTER.* 2F0C60
000C60 40404040 4C404040 C5096E40 0C000300 *....................* 2F0C80
000C80 00000000 0000C000 00000000 00000000 *....................* 2F0CA0
         LINES TO 000CC0 SAME AS ABOVE   2F0CC0
000D00 00000000 30000000 40404040 40404040 *....................* 2F0CE0
                                                                      2F0D00
000D20 40404040 40404040 F0F0F0F0 40404040 *........OCCCO.......* 2F0D20
000D40 40404040 40404040 40404040 40404040 *....................* 2F0D40
000D60 40404040 40404040 40404040 40404040 *...........OCCCOOOOO* 2F0D60
000D80 F0F0F0F4 F0F0F0F0 F0F0F0F0 F0F0F0F0 *....................* 2F0D80
000DA0 F0F0F0F0 40404040 40404040 40404040 *....................* 2F0DA0
000DC0 40404040 40404040 40404040 40404040 *...........CCCCO....* 2F0DC0
000DE0 40404040 40404040 40404040 40404040 *....................* 2F0DE0
000E00 F0F0F0F0 40404040 40404040 40404040 *.........0..........* 2F0E00
000E20 40404040 40404040 40404040 40404040 *....................* 2F0E20
000E40 40404040 40404040 40404040 40404040 *....................* 2F0E40
000E60 C8C3C1C0 40404040 F0F0F0F0 F0F0F0F0 *........COOO..000...* 2F0E60
000E80 40404040 40404040 40404040 40404040 *..00..CCCO0000..00000* 2F0E80
000EA0 00C0C300 C0000000 F0F0F0F0 F0F0F0F0 *....................* 2F0EA0
000EC0 40404040 40404040 F0F0F0F0 03000000 *...CO0:CC0000.00000.0* 2F0EC0
000EE0 40404040 40404040 03000300 0C000000 *....................* 2F0EE0
000F00 F0F0F0F0 F5F9F0F0 F0F0F0F0 40404040 *.C00:.:CC0000..0000.0* 2F0F00
000F20 F9F6F4F0 F6F9F7F9 40404040 03000000 *.COO....0:.0000.CC...* 2F0F20
000F40 F8F4F1F5 F0F0F0F4 03CCF0F0 40404040 *HOUO2BPHTIIO 407969 1909550120* 2F0F40
000F60 F8F6F0F4 F4F1F5F0 4154C040 40404040 *O4004604846060484157007600SERVOO* 2F0F60
000F80 40404040 40404040 40404040 40404040 *06048415II 255760048157* 2F0F80
         LINES TO 000100 SAME AS ABOVE   2F0FA0
001020 F1F3F7F2 F1F3F7F2 F3F6F0F4 40404040 *   Y95000020201JIM LATCHAM 137234,* 2F1020
001060 C8C1D5C4 F1D1C9D4 40404040 D1C9D440 * LATCHAM   JIM* 2F1080
001080 40404040 40404040 D1C9D440 F1F3F6F2 * 2240   713672* 2F10A0
0010A0 F2F2F4F0 40404040 4040FFF1 F3F6F7F2 *....................* 2F10C0
0010C0 40404040 40404040 40404040 40404040 *E3901 SEGUIN RD   IRED ARROW FREIGHT LIN* 2F10E0
0010E0 E5C4C7C5 40C6D9C5 C9C7C8E3 40D9C905 *   IO TX 78219   SAN ANTON* 2F1100
001100 C9D54DE3 C7E6D8C5 D5C4D6C5 40404040 *....................* 2F1120
001120 E1C4C5C1 40404040 C9D54DE3 D9D6D6C5 *....................* 2F1140
001140 D9D6D6C5 F1F8F9F7 D9C5C44C C1D9D9C3 *LINEBOX 1897   RED ARROW FREIGHT* 2F1160
001160 40404040 40404040 E3D5E6C9 D6404040 *NTONIO TX 78297* 2F1180
         LINES TO 001200 SAME AS ABOVE   2F11A0
001220 40404040 40404040 40404040 40404040 *....................* 2F1220
001240 40404040 40404040 40404040 40404040 *........000.........* 2F1240
001260 F7404040 40404040 40404040 40404040 *   N385047* 2F1260
001280 F8F8F5F3 40404040 F0F0F0F0 40404040 *....................* 2F1280
0012A0 40404040 40404040 F0F0F0F0 40404040 * 0003 L.R..........N 0000 0* 2F12A0
0012C0 D9030401 C9D5C7D5 F0F0F0F0 40404040 *.....407969000000* 2F12C0
0012E0 C1D6404B 49C760D0 D8404B69 F0F0F0F0 *4660005194760--00 KIT, IGNITION* 2F12E0
001300 40404040 40404040 40404040 40404040 * 10 PER   .EA GO750782* 2F1320
001340 40404040 40404040 40404040 40404040 *....................* 2F1340

PROGRAM STORAGE

ADDRESS   48D460   TC   496FAF   LENGTH   0C9B50

PSW

Page 1 of the PROGRAM STORAGE

CUSTOMER INFORMATION CONTROL SYSTEM STORAGE DUMP   CODE=ASRA   TASK=BC1A   DATE=06/18/84   TIME=15:06:22   PAGE   25

TRANSACTION STORAGE -USER   ADDRESS 2F0C00 TC 2F1EDF   LENGTH 0C1EE0

001350   4000000C D340D000 0D7D9C00 2D00729C   40C00039 40C0C400 0D39C4C0 F4F260F2   *....L 42-2*   2F1360
001360   F26DF140 40404DF0 4C0F8F1F0 4C0F8F1F0   4040F0F0 F0F0F0F0 0D39C4C0 0DCDCDCD   *2-I 0CC000810 0CCC00.*   2F1380
001370   40404040 4C4C4C40 0CC0C000 43D404040   40404040 40404040 40404040 40404040   *   *   2F13A0
001380   40404040 40404040 0CD00000 43D404040   40404040 40404040 40404040 40404040   *   *   2F13C0
001390   40404040 40404040 4040D000 43040000   40404040 40404040 40404040 40404040   *   *   2F13E0
0013A0   40404040 40404040 4040D000 03040000   40404040 40404040 40404040 40404040   *   *   2F1400
0013B0   40404040 45040000 04040000 03000000   40404040 40404040 40404040 40404040   *   *   2F1420
0013C0   40404040 45040040 0404D040 0D000000   40404040 40404040 40404040 40404040   *   *   2F1440
0013D0   40404040 45040040 0404D000 0D000000   40404040 40404040 40404040 40404040   *   *   2F1460
0013E0   40404040 45040040 0000D000 00000000   40404040 40404040 40404040 40404040   *   *   2F1480
0013F0   LINES TO 001980 SAME AS ABOVE   2F14A0
001940   00000000 00CC0000 00000000 00000000   00000000 00000000 00000000 0000001C   *...................*   2F19C0
001950   00000000 00CCC002 00000000 00000000   00000000 00000000 00000000 00000000   *...................*   2F19E0
001960   00000000 00000000 00000000 00000000   00000000 00000000 00000000 00000000   *...................*   2F1A00
0019A0   LINES TO 001AC0 SAME AS ABOVE

0019C0   LINES TO 001AC0 SAME AS ABOVE   2F1A20
001AB0   6E6F7887 6C6C84C9 4DC5D01L 0D9C5C5D   6C6DF0F1 F8F97C7D C6C7C8C9 4A4B4C4D   *.... HAI(...JQR#I-/YZ.0189.*   2F1AE0
001B20   F1C2D009 07020C03 07030406 04000306   4D404040 40404040 04040406 04040406   *WX..123456789-.ABCDEFGHI.*   2F1B00
001B30   01C00300 00000163 00000C00 04C30C36   0406D030 00000000 04040C00 0000C206   *.....BWDS0LINE.*   2F1B20
001B90   5049C4EB 00000000 00000000 00000000   0D000000 00000000 00000000 00000000   *ISMPI BWCEI5M BWS0LINE.*   2F1B40
001BA0   5049C4EB 00000000 00000000 00000000   00000000 00000000 00000000 00000000   *................Y....H.*   2F1B80
001BC0   00000C00 00000000 00000000 00000000   00000000 00000000 00000000 00000000   *................M-.*   2F1BA0
001BD0   LINES TO 001D20 SAME AS ABOVE

001D30   E2E8E2D6 E4E34040 40000000 E3000000   E3000000 00480500 *.M...... OSYSOUT T....N.*   2F1C40
001D40   00000000 00000000 002F004C 00F104C0   00F104C0 004BF3A0   *................2.........3.*   2F1C60
001D50   0049FB0E 00494765 00496589 40000000   002F004C 004BF3A0   *.M......2.......3.*   2F1C80
001D60   00000000 00000000 0053F0F0 00000000   0053F0F0 00000300   *.............00....H......H.*   2F1CA0
001D70   00000000 00000000 0053F0F0 0000000F   005340FF 00000300   *..........00....*   2F1CC0
001E10   80CFD09C 0000000F 00000000 00000300   A049FD2A 00000000   *...........M......*   2F1CE0
001E40   00000000 0000000F 004CAF9C9 E340C9CD   E340C9CD 0FCF0DFF   *..........M...CAPEX CPT III.*   2F1D00
001E50   00000000 0000000F 00000000 00000000   00000000 00000000   *.2.D.574.-CBI VS2.3.MAY 6.19.* 2F1D20
001E60   F8F340FF 4BF4F940 00000000 00000000   00000000 002E9D00   *.83 08.54.49....Q.11.*   2F1D40

TERMINAL CONTROL TBL USER AREA   ADDRESS 53354C TC 53354F   LENGTH 0C0064

000000   00000000 00000000 00000000 00000000   00000000 00000000   *...................*   53354C
000020   00000000 00000000 00000000 00000000   00000000 00000000   *...................*   53356C
0000E0   00000000 00000000 00000000 00000000   *....*   5335AC

268

11.8.   CSMT And CEMT Transactions

CSMT and CEMT are master Terminal Transactions that are used by the master terminal operator to monitor and control all resources in a CICS system. For example, you can use CSMT or CEMT transaction to disable a CICS transaction when that transaction causes abend in the production CICS system. When a CICS transaction is disabled, you will get a message saying the transaction has been disabled if you try to initiate that transaction. After you have fixed the problems for that transaction, you can use CSMT or CEMT to enable the transaction. After the transaction has been enabled, it can be initiated by CICS users. Basically, CEMT performs same functions as CSMT. However CEMT has a better syntax, and performs more operations than CSMT. CSMT is still available along with CEMT. You can use CSMT or CEMT transaction to monitor or control the following:

```
. Time and interval
. Wait count and storage cushion
. CICS tasks
. CICS transactions
. CICS programs, mapsets, and dynamic tables
. VSAM files and DL/I data bases
. Terminals and printers
. Remote control units and lines
. Trace and auxiliary trace
. VTAM
. CICS shutdown
. CICS formatted dump
```

As an application programmer, you should know how to use CSMT and CEMT transaction to handle these resources in the CICS test system. For example, after you have recompiled a CICS program, you should use CSMT or CEMT transaction to make a new copy of this program into CICS. No all functions specified above should be performed by application programmers. You should only concentrate on how to control the following five CICS resources using CEMT or CSMT transaction:

```
. CICS tasks
. CICS transactions
. CICS programs, mapsets, and dynamic tables
. VSAM files and DL/I data bases
. Terminals and printers
. CICS shutdown
```

11.8.1.   CSMT Transaction

We'll discuss how to use CSMT to handle CICS tasks, CICS programs, CICS transactions, VSAM files, and terminals.

11.8.1.1.   CICS Tasks

To display a list of active CICS tasks:

Enter:

```
CSMT TAS
```

Receive:

```
TASKNO TRANID ACT/SUSP FAC.NAME TYPE
00009  CU07   SUSP              TASK
00012  CU00   ACT      L01A     TERM
```

You can use this task list to get the task number that hangs your terminal. Then you can use CORE transaction of INTERTEST and this task number to cancel that task to free your terminal.

To Terminate A Task Using Task Number:

```
CSMT TRMNAT,{YES|NO},n
```

Notes:

1. n, the task number that you want to cancel. It can be obtained using CSMT TAS.

2. YES specifies immediately termination. NO specifies the task is to be scheduled for deferred termination.

The following example shows we want to terminate the task number 12345 immediately:

```
CSMT TRMNAT,YES,12345
```

Terminate A Task Using Terminal ID:

```
CSMT TRMNAT,TERMID=xxxx
```

Notes:

xxxx in the TERMID=xxxx specifies the terminal ID associated with the task. You can get the terminal ID using CSMT TAS command. The following example shows how to terminate a task running on the terminal L01A:

```
CSMT TRMNAT,TERMID=L01A
```

Inquire Or Change Trigger Level Of A Destination

In an Automatic Task Initiation (ATI) application, you need to specify the trigger level for the transaction to be initiated in the DCT. You can inquire or dynamically change this trigger level in the DCT using CSMT transaction:

```
CSMT TRI,{INQ|n},DESTID=xxxx
```

Notes:

1. INQ specifies inquiry only, n specifies the new trigger level to be changed to.

2. xxxx in DESTID=xxxx specifies the destination (TD queue name) on the DCT.

Examples:

```
Enter:    CSMT TRI,INQ,DESTID=L880
Receive:  TRIGGER LEVEL IS 20

Enter:    CSMT TRI,10,DESTID=L880
Receive:  TRIGGER LEVEL IS CHANGED TO 10 FROM 20
```

11.8.1.2.   CICS Transactions

Enable/Disable Transactions

```
CSMT {ENA|DISAB},TRNACT,{SIN|LIS|CLA|
     ALL , {TRANID=xxxx|TRANID=xxxx
     [,...]|CLASID=xx}
```

You need to disable a CICS transaction when it abends in the CICS production system. When a CICS transaction is disabled, a message saying the transaction is disabled will be displayed on the terminal when the terminal users try to use it. After you have fixed the problems in the CICS programs that caused the transaction abend, you can then copy the new version of the CICS programs into the production CICS system and then enable that transaction. After the transaction is enabled, it can then be used by the users. The following example shows how to disable a CICS transaction ORDR:

```
CSMT DISAB,SIN,TRNACT,TRANID=ORDR
```

The following example shows how to enable the transaction ORDR after you have fixed the problems:

```
CSMT ENA,SIN,TRNACT,TRANID=ORDR
```

11.8.1.3.   CICS Programs

Each CICS program, CICS mapset, or CICS dynamic table (i.e. store table) must have one entry in the PPT. After you have compiled a CICS program, CICS mapset, or CICS dynamic table, you can get its new version into CICS by issuing the following:

```
CSMT NEW,PGRMID=xxxxxxxx
```

Where xxxxxxxx is the name of the CICS program, CICS mapset or dynamic table on the PPT. If this is the first time you have successfully compiled this CICS program, CICS mapset or CICS dynamic table, then you need to enable it first before you can issue the preceeding CSMT NEW command. When CICS is brought up every time, it will try to get the load address for each entry in the PPT. If a PPT entry does not have a load address (has never been compiled), then the entry will be disabled. If this entry is a CICS program, then its associated transaction code in the PCT will also be disabled. Therefore, you need to enable a CICS program, make a new version (CSMT NEW) and then enable its associated CICS transaction. If you do not want to use this CICS program now, you can wait until the next time CICS is brought up. In this case, you do not need to do a CSMT NEW and CSMT ENA since CICS will get the latest load address and enable this program and its transaction when it is brought up.

If your CICS program is not specified in the PPT after you have successfully compiled the program, there is no way you can enable the program or make a new copy of it. In this case, your system programmer needs to add its entry to the PPT, assemble the PPT table, shut down CICS and then bring it back up to pick up the new PPT entry. When CICS is brought up, your program will be enabled and its PPT entry will contain the load address of the latest version of the program.

If this CICS program is currently being used, and you try do a CSMT NEW, a message saying the program is in use will be displayed. The command will be ignored and the program will be disabled after it is finished with the current task. Therefore, you need to enable it before you can do a CSMT NEW.

You can enable or disable a CICS program, mapset, or dynamic table. It has the following format:

```
CSMT {ENA|DISAB},{PRO|PGRM},{SIN|LIS|
     CLA|ALL}, {PGRMID=xxxxxxxx[,...]
     CLASID=xx}
```

The following example shows how to enable a CICS program, CICS mapset or CICS dynamic table:

```
CSMT ENA,PRO,SIN,PGRMID=XCU00
```

You can also disable a PPT entry as follows:

```
CSMT DISAB,PRO,SIN,PGRMID=XCU00
```

Why do you need to disable a CICS program? If that program caused abend and you do not want the user to use it, then you can disable it. When a CICS program, CICS mapset, or CICS dynamic table is disabled and you try to use it, APCT abend occurs. APCT means the program is either disabled or not in the PPT. It is better to disable the transaction than the program.

You can also inquire about the status of a CICS program, CICS mapset, or dynamic table using the following:

```
CSMT INQ,SIN,PRO,PGRMID=xxxxxxxx
```

Where xxxxxxxx in the PGRMID=xxxxxxxx is the name specified in the PPT. You need to do this when you want to check to see if the system programmer has put your entries in the PPT. If not, you will get a message saying the program name is invalid. In this case, you can enter CANCEL and hit ENTER key to get out. CANCEL is the only way you can get out of CSMT transaction if you are prompted to enter more information. The following example shows how to inquire about a CICS program named XCU00:

```
Enter:     CSMT INQ,SIN,PRO,PGRMID=XCU00

Receive:   PROGRAM XCU00 IS IN COBOL,
           IT IS 25367 BYTES LONG,
           NOT PERMANENTLY RESIDENT,
           IT HAS BEEN USED 3 TIMES,
           ITS CURRENT USE COUNT IS 1
           PROGRAM IS ENABLED
```

From the above response, we know XCU00 is written in COBOL and it is 25K big. It is not a resident program. It has been used 3 times since CICS is brought up. There is an active task using this program. The program is enabled. A CICS program must be enabled before you can use it. Otherwise, APCT abend occurs.

11.8.1.4.   CICS Datasets

CICS supports VSAM, ISAM, or BDAM files and DL/I data bases. At least 90% of CICS shops use VSAM files. CSMT allows you to inquire about, open, close, enable or disable a VSAM file or DL/I data base, and open, close or switch a dump dataset.

Inquire About Status of Data Sets

```
CSMT DAT,INQ,{FIELID=xxxxxxxx[,...]|ALL}
```

After the above CSMT command is issued, CICS will tell you if this dataset is opened or closed, is enabled or disabled, and its service requests available (read, update, add, browse). The service requests (SERVREQ) are specified in its FCT entry. You can only issue File Control commands to request the service that has been specified in its FCT entry. Otherwise, INVREQ condition occurs. For example, you do not specify DELETE in the SERVREQ= parameter of its FCT entry and you try to issue a DELETE command within a CICS program, INVREQ (Invalid Request) exceptional condition occurs. The service request of a dataset can be dynamically changed through the use of CSMT command (see Change Status of Data Sets below).

Example:
```
Enter:     CSMT DAT,INQ,FILEID=CUSTMAST
Receive:   STATUS OF SPECIFIED FILE IS:

           FILEID -------STATUS----
           VSAM OPEN,READ,ADD,UPDATE,BROWSE,ENABLED
           **END**
```

In the above example, we inquire about the status of a VSAM file named CUSTMAST. CICS tells us that this file is opened and enabled and the service requests available are READ, ADD, UPDATE, and BROWSE. Therefore, you cannot delete the records in that file since no DELETE was specified.

Normally, a good VSAM file will be opened and enabled when CICS is brought up in the morning. It will be disabled and opened when this VSAM file is empty (no record in it). A VSAM file will be opened only when FILSTAT=OPENED (the default) is specified in its FCT entry.

Change Status of Datasets

```
CSMT DAT,{ON|OFF},{REA|UPD|ADD|EXC|
     BRO|DEL}, {FILEID=xxxxxxx[,...]
     |ALL}
```

Example:

```
Enter:     CSMT DAT,ON,REA,ADD,FILEID=CUSTMAST
Receive:   NEW STATUS OF SPECIFIED FILE IS:

           FILEID ----STATUS ----
           CUSTMAST OPEN,READ,ADD,BROWSE,
           ENABLED
           **END**
```

This will make READ and ADD request available again for this file.

Enable/Disable Data Sets

```
CSMT {ENA|DISAB},DAT,{FILEID=xxxxxxxx[,...]|ALL}
```

Notes:

1. ENA will enable the datset, DISAB will disable the dataset.

2. xxxxxxxx in the FILEID=xxxxxxxx specifies the dataset name you want to enable or disable.

Example:

```
Enter:     CSMT ENA,DAT,FILEID=CUSTMAST
Receive:   VALID FILE(S) ENABLED
```

Why do you need to enable a dataset? If this dataset is empty when CICS is brought up, it will be opened and disabled. After you have closed it to CICS and go to the batch region to load records into it, you can sign on to CICS and enable it for process.

You can disable a dataset as follows:

```
CSMT DISAB,DAT,FILEID=CUSTMAST
```

Open/Close A Dataset

```
CSMT {OPE|CLO},DAT,{FILEID=xxxxxxxx[,...]|ALL}
```

Notes:

1. OPE specifies that you want to open this dataset and CLO specifies that you want to close this datset.

2. xxxxxxxx in the FILEID=xxxxxxxx specifies the dataset name that you want to open or close. It must be specified on the FCT.

3. ALL specifies all data sets in the CICS system are to be opened or closed.

The following example shows how to open a VSAM file CUSTMAST:

```
CSMT OPE,DAT,FILEID=CUSTMAST
```

The following example shows how to close a VSAM file CUSTMAST:

```
CSMT CLO,DAT,FILEID=CUSTMAST
```

A dataset must be enabled and opened before you can issue File Control commands on it. If the dataset is not opened, then NOTOPEN condition occurs. When CICS is brought up in the morning, it will try to enable and open each file specified in the FCT with FILSTAT=(OPENED,ENABLED). Most of the files to be used in CICS are specified this way so they will be opened and enabled by CICS when it is up. A file will be disabled and closed when this file encountered some problems and cannot be opened. For example, if this file is empty, then it will be opened and disabled. If this file has never been defined, then it will be closed and disabled.

When you need to run batch update jobs using a VSAM file, you need to close it to CICS using CSMT CLO command before you can run these batch update jobs. If this file is opened to CICS and you submit these batch update jobs to the reader queue. Then these jobs will not be run since the resource (the VSAM file) is in use by CICS and is not available. After CICS is shut down, these batch jobs will be able to execute since the VSAM file is not in use by CICS. You also need to close a VSAM file to CICS when you need to rebuild it. After you have closed the VSAM file to CICS, you can use DELETE, DEFINE CLUSTER, and REPRO commands to rebuild this file. After the VSAM file has been rebuilt, you can then open it to CICS for online processing.

Most of VSAM files to be used in CICS are defined as sharable resources (SERVREQ=SHARE), so you can run read-only batch programs against these VSAM files without closing them to CICS.

In a CICS production system, VSAM files are normally opened to CICS during the day time and then closed at 5 PM to run batch jobs. It is rare that you can close production

CICS VSAM files during the day time. If you close one or more important production files (like customer master file) to CICS, not many CICS application systems can function.

Open/Close Dump Dataset

Normally, there are two dump data sets in each CICS system. But only one is active at any time. A dump dataset is used to store the storage dumps produced by CICS transaction abends and the CICS tasks that issue Dump Control commands. When a dump dataset is full, it could hang the entire CICS.

When you want to print the storage dump in the current active dump dataset, you need to close it and then make the other one active. This can be accomplished by entering:

```
CSMT SWI
```

It will close the current dump dataset and make the other one active. Now you can log off from CICS and go to the batch region to print the closed dump dataset. The dump datasets will also be printed when CICS is shut down.

Close DL/I Data Base to Updates

```
CSMT DBD,DAT,FILEID=xxxxxxxx
```

Where xxxxxxxx is the data base name. After the above command is issued, you can then back up the data base from the batch region. After the backup copy has been made, you can open the data base to CICS for updates through the use of CSMT OPE command.

Close DL/I Data Base to Reads and Updates

```
CSMT DBR,DAT,FILEID=xxxxxxxx
```

This will cause an end of volume on the system log and closes the DL/I data base to reads and updates. The system programmer can now run the recovery utility. After recovery is done, you can use CSMT OPE to open this DL/I data base to reads and updates.

11.8.1.5.   CICS Terminals

As an application programmer, you need to know how to handle terminals and printers using CSMT or CEMT transaction. You can inquire about or update the status of a terminal or printer. You can also acquire or release a VTAM-supported terminal or printer.

Inquire About Status of a Terminal

```
CSMT TERMNL,SIN,INQ,TERMID=xxxx
```

Where xxxx in the TERMID=xxxx can be a terminal or printer. It must be specified in the TCT. When a printer or a display terminal is not working, you can issue the above command to inquire about its status.

```
Enter:      CSMT TERMNL,SIN,INQ,TERMID=L01A

Receive:    STATUS IS IN SERVICE
            TRANSACTION AUTOPAGE CONNECTED
            VTAM
```

A terminal or printer must be in service and connected to VTAM before it can be used in CICS. If this terminal is out of service, then you need to put it back in service (CSMT TERMNL,INSRV). If this terminal is in service but is not connected to VTAM, then you need to acquire it (CSMT TERMNL,ACQ). A printer must be in AUTOPAGE status. A display terminal must be in TRANSCEIVE PAGE or RECEIVE status. If a terminal is not in the right status, you need to change its processing status.

```
CSMT TERMNL,{SIN|LIS},{TRNACT|REC|
     TRNCV|INP|AUTO|PAG}
     , TERMID=xxxx[,...]
```

Notes:

1. SIN specifies you want to process only one terminal and LIS specifies that more than one terminal are to be processed.

2. xxxx in the TERMID=xxxx specifies the terminal ID to be processed. It must be specified in the TCT.

Examples:

```
Enter:      CSMT TERMNL,SIN,AUTO,TERMID=L01P
Receive:    STATUS IS IN SERVICE TRANSCEIVE
            AUTOPAGE CONNECTED VTAM
```

Change Service Status of A Terminal

```
CSMT TERMNL,SIN,{INSRV|OUT},TRMNAT,TERMID=xxxx
```

Notes:

1. INSRV specifies that you want to put the terminal in service status and OUT specifies that you want to put the terminal out of service. A terminal must be in service status before it can be used.

2. xxxx in the TERMID=xxxx specifies the terminal ID to be processed. It must be specified in the TCT.

```
CSMT TERMNL,SIN,INSRV,TERMID=L01A
```

This will put the terminal L01A out of service and kill the task that is running on this terminal (if any).

```
CSMT TERMNL,SIN,OUT,TRMNAT,TERMID=L01A
```

This will put the terminal L01A in service. After you have killed the task running on this terminal through the use of CSMT OUT, you can then put it back in service.

Acquire a VTAM-Supported Terminal

```
CSMT TERMNL,SIN,ACQ[,COL],TERMID=xxxx
```

COL specifies that no message resynchronization is to be performed.

```
CSMT TERMNL,SIN,ACQ,COL,TERMID=L01A
```

This will connect printer L01A to VTAM. A VTAM-supported terminal or printer must be connected to VTAM before it can be used in CICS. If the terminal or printer is not connected to VTAM for some reason, you should connect it to VTAM using the above command. You can tell whether a terminal is connected to VTAM or not by issuing the following command:

```
CSMT TERMNL,SIN,INQ,TERMID=K01A
```


Release a VTAM-Supported Terminal

```
CSMT TERMNL,SIN,REL,TERMID=xxxx
```

Where xxxx in the TERMID=xxxx specifies the terminal ID that you want to disconnect from VTAM. The following example shows how to disconnect a terminal from VTAM:

```
CSMT TERMNL,SIN,REL,TERMID=L01A
```

If your printer is not working and its status is IN SERVICE and connected to VTAM. Then you should try to disconnect it from VTAM and then connect it with VTAM (CSMT ACQ). This may fix your printer problem.

11.8.1.6.   CICS Shutdown

You can shut down CICS immediately using the following:

```
CSMT SHU,YES[,DUMP]
```

DUMP specifies a dynamic storage dump is to be printed upon completion of the shutdown.

You can shut down CICS after all tasks have been completed and all active VTAM sessions are closed using the following:

```
CSMT SHU,NO[,DUMP],xx,yy
```

Notes:

1. XX specifies the suffix of the transaction list table to be used for this shutdown.

2. yy specifies the suffix of the program list table (PLT) to be used for this shutdown.

3. DUMP specifies that a dynamic storage dump is to be printed upon completion of the shutdown. The default is NODUMP.

11.8.2.   CEMT Transaction

CEMT (Enhanced Master Terminal Transaction) was introduced in CICS Version 1.5 to replace CSMT. To use CSMT, you need to remember the command syntax. But you can enter CEMT on a clear screen to invoke the CEMT transaction and then it will prompt you what to do next. For example, after you enter CEMT then hit ENTER key, five options (ADD, INQ, PERFORM, REMOVE, and SET) will be displayed. INQ (Inquire) and SET (change) are the two most-used options. INQ let you inquire about the CICS resource information. SET allows you to change the information of the CICS resources. For example, you can use INQ to inquire about the VSAM file status and use SET to open a VSAM file. PERFORM allows you to shut down a CICS system, produce a snap dump or reset the date and time-of-day of CICS to that of OS/VS. ADD is used to add disk volume(s) to CICS for writing the journal. REMOVE is used to inform CICS that the disk volume is no longer needed and can be removed. ADD and REMOVE options will not be used by application programmers. PERFORM is only used when you want to shut down the CICS system.

After you have entered CEMT on a clear screen, you can enter INQ and then hit ENTER key, CICS will display a list of options as follows:

```
TASK
TCLASS
TRANSACTION
PROGRAM
DATASET
QUEUE
TERMINAL
NETNAME
LINE
CONTROL
SYSTEM
MODENAME
DUMP
TRACE
AUXTRACE
PITRACE
VTAM
VOLUME
JOURNAL
BATCH
IRC
IRBATCH
```

You can then enter the desired option and hit ENTER. CICS will display next level of options for you to choose from until all options have been entered. Therefore, you do not need to remember the command syntax in order to use CEMT. But if you remember all parameters in a CEMT command, then you can enter them all at once to perform the desired function (just like using CSMT). However, you can inquire about or set more than one objects in one command. For example, when you inquire about data set information, unless you specify a particular data set, CEMT will display a page of data sets.

The operands can be entered in any sequence following CEMT and they must be separated with one another by commas or blanks. When you are ready to get out of CEMT, you must hit PF3. Any other key will not get you out of CEMT.

The following example shows we want to inquire about the VSAM file named CUSTMAST:

```
CEMT INQ,DAT,FILEID(CUSTMAST)
```

This command is very similar to the CSMT command:

```
CSMT INQ,DAT,FILEID=CUSTMAST
```

In the following sections, we'll show you how to use CEMT on tasks, transactions, programs, data sets, terminals, and dump, and how to use PERFORM to shut down CICS, produce a dump, or reset the date and time-of-day of CICS.

11.8.2.1. CICS Tasks

The command syntax for CICS tasks is:

```
{INQ|SET}
TASK[(number)]
[TCLASS(clasid)|ALL]
[TRANID(tranid)]              (INQ only)
[FACILITY(faid)]              (INQ only)
[ACTIVE|SUSPENDED]            (INQ only)
[SHORT|LONG]                  (INQ only)
[TASK|TERM|DEST]              (INQ only)
[PURGE|FORCEPURGE]            (SET only)
```

To inquire all tasks in the system, you can enter:

```
CEMT INQ TASK
```

To force to cancel the task 12345, you can enter:

```
CEMT SET TASK(12345) FORCEPURGE
```

11.8.2.2. CICS Transactions

The command syntax for CICS transactions is:

```
{INQ|SET}
TRANSACTION[(tranid)]
[CLASS(clasid)|ALL]
[PRIORITY(value)]
[ENABLED|DISABLED]
```

To inquire about the transaction CUST, you enter:

    CEMT INQ TRAN(CUST)

To enable the transaction CUST, you enter:

    CEMT SET TRAN(CUST) ENABLED

11.8.2.3. CICS Programs

The command syntax for programs is:

```
{INQ|SET}
PROGRAM[(pgrmid)]
[CLASS(clasid)|ALL]
[LENGTH(value)]                  (INQ only)
[RESCOUNT(value)]                (INQ only)
[USECOUNT(value)]                (INQ only)
[PLI|COBOL|ASSEMBLER|RPG]        (INQ only)
[ENABLED|DISABLED]
[NEWCOPY]                        (SET only)
```

You can get a new copy of program by entering:

    CEMT SET PROGRAM(XCU00) NEWCOPY

You can enable a program by entering:

    CEMT SET PROGRAM(XCU00) ENABLED

You can inquire about the status of a program by entering:

    CEMT INQ PROGRAM(XCU00)

11.8.2.4.   CICS Data Sets

The command syntax for CICS data sets is:

```
{INQ|SET}
DATASET[(fileid)]
[ALL]
[VSAM|ISAM|BDAM|DLI|REMOTE|ICIP]
    (INQ only)
[OPEN|CLOSED]
[ENABLED|DISABLED]
[READ|NOREAD]
[UPDATE|NOUPDATE]
[ADD|NOADD]
[BROWSE|NOBROWSE]
[DELETE|NODELETE]
[EXCLUSIVE|NOEXCLUSIVE]
[DUMPDB|RECOVERDB]           (SET only)
```

To inquire about the VSAM file named CUSTMAST, you enter:

```
CEMT INQ DATASET(CUSTMAST)
```

To open the VSAM file CUSTMAST, you enter:

```
CEMT SET DATASET(CUSTMAST) OPEN
```

To close the VSAM file CUSTMAST, you enter:

```
CEMT SET DATASET(CUSTMAST) CLOSED
```

11.8.2.5.   CICS Terminals

The command syntax for terminals is:

```
{INQ|SET}
TERMINAL[(termid)]
[CLASS(clasid)|SYSTEM(sysid)|ALL]
[TRANID(tranid)]              (INQ only)
[PRIORITY(value)]
[NETNAME(netname)]           (INQ only)
[PAGE|AUTOPAGE]
[INSERVICE|OUTSERVICE]
[ATI|NOATI]
[TTI|NOTTI]
[PURGE|FORCEPURGE]            (SET only)
[ACQUIRED|RELEASED]
[INTLOG|NOINTLOG]
```

To inquire about the status of the printer L01A, you enter:

```
CEMT INQ TERMINAL(L01A)
```

To put the printer in service status, you enter:

```
CEMT SET TERMINAL(L01A)
```

then enter INS on the status field.

To put a terminal out of service, you enter:

```
CEMT SET TERMINAL(K01A)
```

then you enter OUT on the status field.

11.8.2.6.   CICS Dump Data Sets

The command syntax for a dump is:

```
INQ DUMP

SET DUMP
[OPEN|CLOSED]
[SWITCH]
[AUTOSWITCH|NOAUTOSWITCH]
```

To switch the dump dataset in order to print it in the batch region:

```
CEMT SET DUMP SWITCH
```

This will close the current dump dataset and switch to the other one.

11.8.2.7.   PERFORM

The command syntax for shutting down CICS is:

```
PERFORM SHUTDOWN
[XLT(suffix)]
[PLT(suffix)]
[IMMEDIATE]
[DUMP]
```

To shut down CICS immediately without a dump, you enter:

```
CEMT PERFORM SHUTDOWN IMMEDIATE
```

The command syntax for producing a dump:

```
PERFORM SNAP
[PARTITION]
[FORMAT]
[TITLE(xxx)]
```

The command syntax for resetting the date and time-of-day of CICS/VS is:

```
CEMT PERFORM RESET
```

PART 3.   100 CICS/VS APPLICATION PROBLEMS AND
           THEIR SOLUTIONS

Chapter 12.   100 CICS/VS Application Problems And Their
              Solutions

CHAPTER 12.   100 CICS/VS APPLICATION PROBLEMS AND THEIR SOLUTIONS

This chapter will list 100 most common CICS application problems each application programmer must face on a daily basis and their solutions. This list is the result of author's 10 years of experience in CICS/VS with a total of over 280 CICS transaction installtions. It will explain why each CICS problem happens and give you the possible solutions.

001.   How to print a CICS abend storage dump?

When a CICS transaction abends, a dump will be created in the current dump dataset. The storage dump can be identified by the task number, the abend code you specified in the ABEND command or the transaction code. A dump dataset may consist of many transaction storage dumps. When CICS is shut down, the dump data sets will be printed. If you do not want to wait until CICS is shut down to get your task abend storage dump, then you need to issue the following CSMT transaction to close the current active dump and make the other dump dataset as the active one:

```
CSMT SWI
```

After the above command has been issued, CICS will let you know which one is the new active dump data set. Then you know which one (A or B) is the one we have just closed. You can then log off from CICS and go to ISPF/TSO (OS/VS) or ICCF (DOS/VSE) to print the closed dump dataset. The dump data set print utility program should be used and the dump data set (A or B) should be specified in the JCL. Normally, your system programmer will set up the dump printing JCL, all you need to change is to specify which dump you want to print. After the entire dump dataset has been printed, you can then search your storage dump using the task number, transaction code and the abend code. The trace table within the storage dump provides an excellent tool for you to determine the cause of abend and which CICS command was the last one executed. You can also use PSW, Program Storage Address, and your program compile listing to determine which statement caused the abend. For how to read a dump, please refer to Chapter 11.7.

The CICS dump datasets are normally defined as reusable. That means everytime a dump dataset is opened to CICS, it will be an empty dataset and whatever on the dataset will be erased. Therefore, when you do a CSMT SWI, the new dump dataset will be an empty one to accept the new transaction dumps.

002.   PA and CLEAR keys will not transmit data.

When the terminal user enters input data on the current CICS map and then presses PA or CLEAR key, the input data will not be transmitted into the program after the program is invoked and the RECEIVE MAP command is issued. Only ENTER key and PF keys will transmit data into the program. This is the reason why PF keys are used most often in CICS programs than PA keys. However, It is not a good design to ask the user to enter input data and then hit one of the PF keys. You should ask the user to hit ENTER key when the input data is to be entered.

003.   LOG=YES on the FCT entry for a VSAM file.

When you specify LOG=YES on FCT for a VSAM file, the transaction backout program will be invoked to restore the file back to the status where the task is started when a CICS task abends. Therefore, you can re-enter the same transaction like nothing ever happened before after you have fixed the problem. LOG=YES also provides the ENQ capability on the record when a READ command with UPDATE option, WRITE command, or DELETE command is issued. If LOG=YES is specified, you cannot request a generic delete on the VSAM file. A generic delete will delete all VSAM records with the same generic key specified.

004.   How do you specify the TS queue name in an Automatic Task Initiation application?

You should specify the terminal ID as the Destination on the DCT.

005.   VSAM file dynamic allocation.

If you have just set up a VSAM file for CICS and that file is not specified in the CICS startup JCL when CICS was brought up, you can dynamically allocated and deallocated this VSAM file to CICS by using ALLO and FREE transactions:

```
ALLO dataset-name file-id

FREE dataset-name
```

Where dataset-name is the dataset name used in the File Control commands and file-id is the VSAM file cluster name specified in the DEFINE CLUSTER command. This will dynamically allocate (ALLO) and open this VSAM file to CICS. Following that, you can issue File Control commands against this file. There is no need to open it after it has been allocated (ALLO). You can also close a VSAM file using FREE transaction. This will close and de-allocate the VSAM file.

006.   How to set up VSAM file standard label.

Each VSAM file must have a standard label in CICS startup JCL. This will relate the dataset name specified in the File Control commands to the VSAM cluster in the VSAM catalog. The VSAM cluster entry in the VSAM catalog contains all information about this VSAM file. The DD or DLBL statement provides this relationship between the dataset name and the VSAM cluster name.

```
//CICS      PROC
//CUSTMAST DD DSN=CUSTOMER.MASTER,DISP=SHR
```

If a VSAM file contains one or more alternate indexes, each alternate index path (not index itself) should have one DD or DLBL statement in the CICS startup JCL.

007.   How to compress CICS program load library

If the creation of a CICS program load module fails due to insufficient space in the CICS program load library when you try to compile a CICS program, a CICS mapset, or a CICS dynamic table, you need to compress the load library. In order to do that, you need to shut down CICS and then go to ISPF/TSO (OS/VS) or ICCF (DOS/VSE) to compress the load library. You cannot compress the CICS load library when CICS is up and running since CICS uses the load library to load the program load modules when they are invoked. If you try to compress the load library while the CICS is up, your compress job will be terminated since the load library is in use by CICS.

008.   How to bring up test or production CICS system

To bring up the CICS system, you need to submit a set of CICS startup JCL to the reader queue for execution. After this set of JCL has been executed, CICS can then be used. After CICS is up and running, you can then use CSSN transaction to sign on to CICS. The CICS startup JCL is set up by your system programmer and it is normally stored in the one of the partitioned dataset (PDS) like any other batch program JCL. You only need to submit it to the reader queue for execution to bring up CICS. However, you should not try to bring up the production CICS system. It is the responsibility of the computer operator. However, an application programmer normally can bring up the CICS test system himself.

009.   How to shut down test or production CICS system.

To shut down the test CICS system, you only need to notify all other CICS programmers who are currently using the test CICS system and then issue the following CSMT command while you are on CICS:

```
CSMT  SHU,NO
```

You are not allowed to shut down the production CICS system. This is the responsibility of your computer operator. He can also issue the above CSMT command from the console to shut down the production CICS system.

010.   Why LENGERR condition occurs when you issue a File Control command?

The LENGERR condition occurs when you try to process a variable-length VSAM file without specifying the LENGTH option or the length specified is incorrect. Most of VSAM files are fixed-length files. You do not need to specify LENGTH option in the File Control commands when you try to process a fixed-length VSAM file. However, if your system programmer does not specified RECFORM=FIXED in the FCT for that file, then CICS will assume it is a variable-length file. In this case, LENGTH option is a required parameter in the File Control command.

If indeed, this file is a variable-length VSAM file, then you should specify the maximum length in the LENGTH parameter for the input operation (READ, or READNEXT) and the actual length for the output operation (WRITE or REWRITE). After the record has been retrieved, CICS will load the LENGTH field with the actual length of the retrieved record.

011. How to re-build a VSAM file when CICS is up?

You should enter the following command while you are on CICS:

```
FREE dataset-name
```

Where dataset-name is the dataset name specified in FCT for this VSAM file. FREE transaction will dynamically close and de-allocate this VSAM file. After the VSAM file has been closed and de-allocated, no File Control commands can process it. After the file has been de-allocated, you should log off from CICS and go to the batch region and issue AMS commands (REPRO, DELETE, DEFINE CLUSTER, and REPRO) to rebuild the file. After the VSAM file has been rebuilt, you can then sign on to CICS and issue the following command:

```
ALLO dataset-name file-id
```

For example:

```
Enter:    ALLO CUSTMAST CUSTMAST.MASTER

Receive:  DYNALLOC RETURN CODE 0, ERROR CODE X'0000', REASON CODE
          X'0000' TRANSACTION END
```

This will open and dynamically allocate the VSAM file. After the VSAM file has been opened and allocated, it is ready to be processed by File Control commands.

If you do not de-allocate the VSAM file (FREE) from CICS, you will get VSAM I/O error 108 when you try to back up the VSAM file using the REPRO command in the batch region.

If you shut down the CICS system and then bring it back up after the VSAM file has been rebuilt, then there is no need to allocate this VSAM file using ALLO since it will be opened and allocated when the CICS system is brought up.

012. How to handle runaway task (AICA) abend?

Each installation can set up its own runaway task interval. A CICS task should voluntarily give up control to the task control dispatcher within the defined runaway task interval. Otherwise, AICA abend occurs. A typical runaway task time interval might be 5,000 milliseconds. It can be changed dynamically using CSMT transaction. Most of the AICA abends are the results of incorrect looping within the program logic. However, if your CICS program has to use that much of CPU time, then you need to consider using the SUSPEND command. When the SUSPEND command is issued, the execution of this task will be suspended and control goes to CICS tasks with higher priority. When there are no more CICS tasks with higher priority, the control will return to this task and the execution will be resumed.

013. Why data in the communication area is lost when it is passed to the next CICS program?

You should specify the length of the communication area of the next program in the LENGTH parameter of the XCTL or LINK command of the current program in order to pass the data. If the length you specify in the XCTL or LINK command is not equal to the length of DFHCOMMAREA of the next CICS program to be invoked, sometimes, the data you try to pass may be unpredicable.

014. Is there any CICS command that you can use to edit the input field?

Yes, the field edit build-in function (BIF DEEDIT) command can be used for this purpose. It specifies that the alphabetic and special characters are to be removed from an EBCDIC data field, the remaining digits being right justified and pedded with zeros as necessary. The following example shows how to issue a BIF DEEDIT command:

```
EXEC CICS BIF DEEDIT FIELD(AMTI) LENGTH(11) END-EXEC.
```

However, this command is very dangerous. For example, if the user enter 'A234' instead of '1234', this command will make it '0234' rather than '1234'.

015. How to handle SD37 abends when you try to assemble a CICS map?

SD37 means the library is full and there are no storages to store the symbolic description map (map copy book to be copied into CICS program) or physical map (mapset load module). Therefore, you need to look at the execution results to determine which library is full. If the map copy book library is full, then you only need to compress that library. If the mapset load library is full, then you need to sign on to CICS system and then issue the following command to shut down CICS before you can compress the load library:

```
CSMT SHU,NO
```

After the CICS has been shut down, the mapset load library is no longer in use by CICS. You can then compress the load library. After the load library has been compressed, you can then submit the CICS JCL to bring up the CICS once again and re-assemble the CICS mapset.

016. How to fix the production printer when it is not printing?

If a CICS production print program suddenly won't print on-line reports on a printer, the first thing you want to check is if the printer is powered on. The printer must be powered on before it can print the report. The second thing you want to check is if the printer is working. This can be verified by using CMSG transaction. You can send a small message to the printer from any production CICS terminal using the CMSG transaction as follows:

```
CMSG SEND,MSG='TEST PRINTER',ROUTE=L01P
```

This will print the message 'TEST PRINTER' on the printer L01P. If the printer does print the message, that means the printer is working and the CICS print program has problems.

If the printer is still not printing, that means the printer is no good and your CICS print program may be OK. You can then concentrate your efforts on this printer. In order for a printer to print, the printer must be:

1. In service
2. Acquired by VTAM (connectted to VTAM)
3. In Autopage status

You can check all these three statuses by using the CSMT INQ,TERMINAL:

```
CSMT INQ,SIN,TERMNL,TERMID=L01P
```

If the printer is out of service, you can put it back in service as follows:

```
CSMT TERMNL,SIN,INSRV,TRMNAT,TERMID=L01P
```

If the printer is in service but not acquired by VTAM, you can connect it to VTAM as follows:

```
CSMT TERMNL,SIN,ACQ,COL,TERMID=L01P
```

The printer must be in AUTOPAGE status in order to print the report, you can set the printer at this status (AUTOPAGE) as follows:

```
CSMT TERMNL,SIN,AUTO,TERMID=L01P
```

Sometimes, you need to release the printer and then acquire it before the printer can print a report. A printer could be connectted to VTAM but cannot print anything if CICS is shut down during the printing section of this printer. To release the printer from VTAM, you need to do:

```
CSMT TERMNL,SIN,REL,TERMID=L01P
```

After the printer has been released, you can then acquire it using the ACQ and COL options as we have memtioned above.

These are the most common problems for a printer. If you still cannot fix the printer, then you should call for services.

017. Why the printer would not print on-line reports for a transaction that is started through the START command?

If you use Interval Control to start a transaction to print an online report, and the report is not printed, you should look for another cause from transaction and operator security codes. In order for a printer to print, it must have an operator security code equal to the transaction security code of the print transaction. When a CICS user signs on to this terminal, its operator security codes will be loaded into TCTTE for this terminal. However, when you start the print transaction using the START command without TERMID option, a new CICS task will be initiated without an associated terminal. Thus the default security code for this printer in the TCTTE is 1. If the transaction security code for this print transaction is greater than 1, then no reports will be printed on this printer. Therefore, you need to assign 1 as the transaction security code to all print transactions in the PCT.

The operator security code is assigned in the Sign-On Table (SNT). When the operator signs on to CICS on one of the terminals, the operator security code will be stored in the TCT entry of this terminal and this terminal can only enter transactions that have been assigned with the same transaction security code. An operator may have more than one security code. An operator with security codes of 5, 6, 10, and 12 would be able to enter CICS transactions whose transaction code is defined as 5, 6, 10, or 12.

018. Why input is prohibiten on 3290 terminal following a map output operation?

If you try to send a CICS map to a 3290 terminal without specifying the cursor position, the terminal will display the map with a program check of 728 and an 'X' to indicate input prohibit. In order to fix this problem, you should do:

```
MOVE -1 TO ORDERL.
EXEC CICS SEND MAP('AXCU03')/MAPSET('XXCU03')
     ERASE CURSOR END-EXEC.
```

Just move -1 to the length field of a map field where you want to position the cursor before you issue a SEND MAP command. 3290 terminals are big terminals with four split screens. On each screen, you can use it as a 3278 terminal. For 3278 terminals, the cursor will be at (01,02) if no cursor position is specified.

019. Why a data field is not printed on an online report?

When an output field contains at least one non-printable character, then the entire field will not be printed. Therefore, when a data field contains spaces on the report, you need to see if this field contains LOW-VALUES or any other non-displayable characters.

020. Can you enter alphabetic data on a numeric field?

Yes, even you specify ATTRB=NUM for a map field, you can still enter alphabetic data by pressing the NUM lock key and entering the alphabetic data. ATTRB=NUM only means you do not need to press NUM lock key to enter numeric data.

021. **Why is your terminal still hung after the CICS has been shut down and then brought back up?**

When the CICS is hung due to some CICS tasks, you may call the computer operator to purge CICS. Before CICS is purged, the computer operator must close VTAM ACB (Access Method Control Block). The CSMT command can be used to close VTAM ACB:

```
CSMT CLOSE,VTAM
```

If the computer operator did not close ACB before CICS is purged and you are working on your terminal when CICS is purged, your terminal will be hung after CICS is shut down and brought back up again.

When your terminal is hung, the easiest way to fix it is to enter CORE transaction of INTERTEST on another CICS terminal:

```
CORE(task#)=TCA@00+18@00+18,VERX'88',CHGX'21'
```

This will change the Device Control Area (DCA) of Task Control Area (TCA) from X'88' to X'21' to cancel the task and release your hung terminal. This could be the most important INTERTEST command you need to remember since there is no other way to fix the hung terminal in most cases except to call the computer operator. However, you may be asked to enter the password in order to perform above change if your system programmer has set up a password for the CHG command of CORE. You can use the CSMT transaction to get the task number that are running on your terminal in order to fix the terminal:

```
CSMT TASK
```

After all active CICS tasks are displayed, you can get the task number that is associated with your terminal. Then you can use this task number in the above CORE transaction to cancel that task.

022. **Can you use DFHCOMMAREA as parameter value in the COMMAREA option of the LINK or XCTL command?**

Yes, you can use DFHCOMMAREA specified in LINKAGE SECTION directly in the COMMAREA option of the XCTL or LINK command since CICS will allocate DFHCOMMAREA as soon as that CICS program is invoked. Therefore, it is a dynamic storage area that has been acquired by CICS for the program and can be used in the XCTL or LINK command.

023. **Do you need to issue a RECEIVE MAP or RECEIVE INTO command in order update EIBAID field to contain the key pressed during the last input operation?**

No. When the terminal user presses one of the keys on the terminal, the transaction that post on this terminal will be invoked. After the program specified in the PCT for that transaction has been invoked, EIBAID will contain the key that was pressed by the terminal user. Thus you do not need to issue a RECEIVE INTO or RECEIVE MAP command in order to update EIBAID field with the key pressed. As soon as the CICS program is invoked, you can check this EIBAID field to see which key was pressed:

```
WORKING-STORAGE SECTION.
01  DFHAID COPY DFHAID.
LINKAGE SECTION.
01  DFHCOMMAREA    PIC X(100).
PROCEDURE DIVISION.
    IF EIBAID = DFHCLEAR
        GO TO A900-XCTL-TO-MENU.
```

024. Can you pass data from the linked subroutine program to the main CICS program that issues the LINK command?

Yes. After the linked program has been terminated by the RETURN command, the control will be returned to the very next statement following the LINK command and the communication area specified in the LINK command can be updated by the linked program and then accessed by the linking main program. Thus data can be passed from the linking program to the linked subroutine and then back from the linked program to the main program that issued the LINK command through the use of communication area specified in the COMMAREA option of the LINK command.

025. How do you get the translator listing generated by the CICS translator during the CICS program compilation?

You can add the following JCL card in the translation step to list the tranlation listing:

```
//SYSPRINT DD SYSOUT=*
```

Since the error message generated by the CICS translator is very important for a CICS programmer to determine if that CICS program has CICS commands in error. If the syntax of a CICS command is wrong, the default action specified by your system programmer is normally to drop this CICS command from the translated COBOL codes that are the input for the following compile step. This way, the compile step can continue to execute even the translation step generates some error messages. Even you can get a clean compile on that CICS program in the compile step, that does not mean the CICS program is clean. That is why you need to examine the translation lising for each compilation of your CICS program to see if any CICS command is in bad syntax. You can add the above DD card in the translation step to get the translation listing and check for the translation messages.

026. How do you get a new version of a CICS program into CICS while CICS is up and running after that CICS program has been successfully compiled?

If this program has a load module currently being used in CICS, then you can just issue the following command in CICS to get a new version into CICS:

```
CSMT NEW,PGRMID=ORDR001
```

This will get the address of the new CICS program load module to the PPT. The next CICS task that invokes that program will use the new version of the program. If this CICS program is currently being used by a CICS task while you issue the above CSMT NEW command, you will receive a message saying that the program is in used. In this case, CICS will disable the program after that CICS task has terminated. In this case, you need to enable the program first and then issue the above CSMT NEW command. You can enable a CICS program as follows:

```
CSMT ENA,SIN,PRO,PGRMID=ORDR001
```

The CICS program must be enabled before you can make a new version.

If this is the first time you have successfully compiled this CICS program, then you need to enable the CICS program before you can issue the CSMT NEW command. CICS will disable that program when CICS is brought up this morning since there is no load module for that CICS program. That is the reason why you need to enable it before you can do a CSMT NEW command.

If the PPT and PCT entries for this CICS program are not set up when CICS was brought up this morning, then you need to ask your system programmer to put its entries into the PPT and the PCT. After your system programmer has successfully compiled both PPT and PCT tables, he must shut down CICS and then bring it back up to pick up the new PCT and PPT. After CICS has brought back up, your CICS program will be enabled and ready to be used.

027. How do you get out of CSMT transaction when you do not want to continue the CSMT transaction?

For example, you try to issue a CSMT NEW command and the program you specify is invalid (not on PPT), CICS will then give you an invalid program message on the terminal. In this case, you can enter the correct program and then hit ENTER key or you can enter CANCEL and hit ENTER key to get out of the CSMT transaction. If you do not know the correct program name, then the only way out is to CANCEL it.

028. Why the program ID is invalid when you issue a CSMT transaction?

That means your system programmer has not put your CICS program, CICS mapset or CICS dynamic table into the PPT or you do not spell it right.

029.   Why the transaction ID is invalid when you issue a CSMT transaction?

That means your system programmer has not put the transaction ID and its associated program name into the PCT or you do not spell the correct transaction code.

030.   Why the dataset name is invalid when you issue a CSMT transaction?

That means your system programmer has not put the VSAM file into the FCT (File Control Table) or you do not spell it right.

031.   Why DSIDERR condition occurs during a File Control operation?

That means the dataset name you specify in the File Control command is not specified in the FCT.

032.   Why INVREQ condition occurs during File Control operation (i.e. DELETE)?

That means the function you want to perform is not specified for this VSAM file in its FCT entry. The SERVREQ= parameter in the FCT entry specifies the requests you can request upon this VSAM file. If the function (i.e. DELETE) is not specified and you try to request it in the File Control command, INVREQ condition occurs. In this case, you should ask your system programmer to change the SERVREQ parameter in the FCT entry to allow this request. Normally, all requests are specified for a VSAM file. For the FCT entry of an alternate index path, you should specify only read-only function as follows:

```
SERVREQ=(GET,BROWSE)
```

This will allow read-only (READ), and browse (STARTBR, READNEXT, ENDBR, RESETBR, and READPREV) functions.

033.   Why PGMIDERR condition occurs when you try to XCTL to another program?

The program ID error (PGMIDERR) condition occurs when the program you specify in the XCTL command is not specified in the PPT. You should ask your system programmer to put it into the PPT or check to see if you have spelled it right.

034.   Why ASRA (abend code) and protection error occur when you try to transfer the control to another CICS program through the use of the XCTL command?

The abend code ASRA means data exception and protection error means the storage area you try to process is out of the program boundry. These conditions occur when the program you try to XCTL to does not have a load module or the address of its load module in the PPT contains garbage. You should recompile this program to create a load module and then issue a CSMT NEW command to get the address of this new load module into the PPT. If this program has been compiled successfully before, then all you need to do is to issue a CSMT NEW command to reload the address of its load module into its PPT entry.

035.   Why some or all CICS transactions abend after CICS has been brought up?

This could happen once a while because the PPT table is overlayed by some garbage. You should shut down CICS, and then bring it back up to reload the addesses of load modules specified in the PPT. You can also issue CSMT NEW command to get the address of those load modules that cause the abend into PPT.

036.   Why the terminal is hung when you try to access a VSAM file?

This means the string number of this VSAM file has exceeded what is specified in the FCT. The string number in the FCT entry specifies the number of concurrent requests that can be processed against the data set. When you issue a READ with UPDATE option, the string number will be increased by 1. When you issue a REWRITE, DELETE or UNLOCK, the string number will be decreased by 1. If you forget to issue a REWRITE, DELETE or UNLOCK following a READ with UPDATE option within a CICS program, the string number will not be decreased. When the number of requests exceeds this limit, the additional tasks will be queued and never be released. This is the reason why your terminal is hung. If that VSAM file is an important file (like customer master or product master), eventually the entire CICS system will be hung. To trace this problem, you should look for any CICS program that tries to update this file. You do not need to check CICS programs that perform only read-only operations on this file. When CICS is shut down, the statistic report will show the string count for each file. If the string count exceeds the string number (STRNO) specified, that means some CICS programs that use this VSAM file do not release the file following a READ command with UPDATE option. You can use CORE transaction of INTERTEST to cancel the tasks that cause the terminals to hang and decrease the string count on its FCT entry.

There is another possibility for DOS/VSE users. If this VSAM file is a variable-length file and you try to access this file without specifying LENGTH option, your terminal may also be hung over the execution of the File Control command that tries to access this file. You should secify the maximum length for this file when you try to read the file or the actual length of the record when you try to add a record into the file. If this VSAM file is a fixed-length file, then you should ask your system programmer to put the RECFORM=FIXED into the FCT entry for this file. If there is no RECFORM= parameter specified, the default is variable-length file.

037.   Why ILLOGIC occurs when you try to access a VSAM file through its alternate index path?

That means the VSAM file and its alternate index file are out of sync or the alternate index file has not been defined or built properly. You should rebuild the alternate index file from its primary VSAM file using DELETE, DEFINE AIX, DEFINE PATH, and BLDINDEX commands. After the alternate index file has been rebuilt, the ILLOGIC condition will go away.

What makes these two files out of sync? For example, you try to add a record into the VSAM file and there is no space in the alternate index file, the record will be added to the VSAM file successfully and no index record will be created into the alternate index file. In this case, you will get a NORMAL status upon completion of this WRITE command. CICS will not warn you about the space problem in the alternate index file. However, when you try to process this VSAM file through its alternate index, ILLOGIC occurs.

038.   How can you test the CICS mapset after it is compiled successfully?

You can use CECI transaction to display this map even the CICS program that uses this CICS map is not ready to be used. However, the CICS mapset must has been specified in the PPT. You can issue the CECI command as follows:

```
CECI SEND MAP('AXCU01') MAPSET(''XXCU01')
```

After the above command is issued, CICS will display the map AXCU01 within the mapset XXCU01 on the terminal. You can then examine the map format and test these unprotected fields by entering the input data. After you have finished with this map, you can hit CLEAR key to erase the map and you are ready to enter another CICS transaction.

039.   How can you communicate with other CICS terminal users?

You can use CMSG transaction to send message to another CICS display terminal or printer. You only need to specify the terminal ID and the message in this CMSG command. You can also use CMSG command to test if a CICS printer is working. The CSMG transaction can be issued as follows:

```
CMSG MSG='HOW IS YOUR MONKEY DOING? DAVE',ROUTE=L01A,SEND
```

This will send the message to the terminal L01A. If L01A is a printer, then the message will be printed.

040. How do you monitor a CICS task that is started by a CICS transaction entered from your terminal?

For example, you enter function 6 and a customer number on the menu screen to print the customer. The menu program will start a transaction named CU07 which will print the customer. Since CU07 is started on a printer (START command with TERMID option), you cannot monitor CU07 using CEDF on the current terminal since CU07 is associated with the printer instead of the current terminal. However, you can monitor the execution of CU07 under the printer using CEDF. Before you enter the function 6 and the customer number on the menu screen, you should enter CEDF L01P on the second terminal. L01P is the printer ID that you specify in the TERMID option of the START command. You can then enter the function number 6 and the customer number on the menu screen and then hit ENTER key. When CU07 is started by the menu program, CEDF will monitor the execution of CU07 which is associated with the printer on the second terminal. You can use ENTER key on the second terminal to check out your print program one CICS command at a time.

041. Why the terminal is hung when you try to issue a SEND MAP command?

The terminal is hung because the map I/O area contains COMP-3 data which is normally non-displayable. When a map field is defined as:

```
AMT        DFHMDF POS=(03,02),LENGTH=5,ATTRB=NUM

           02   AMTL        PIC S9(4) COMP.
           02   AMTA        PIC X(1).
           02   AMTI        PIC X(5).
           02   AMTO        PIC X(5).
```

CICS will generate PIC X(5) for both its input (AMTI) and output (AMTO) fields. If you try to move a COMP-3 data into an X(5) field and then send the map to the terminal, your terminal will be hung. The following example shows how this can happen:

```
01   WS-AMT        PIC S9(5) COMP-3.
01   AMT-E         PIC 9(5).

MOVE WS-AMT TO AMTO.
EXEC CICS SEND MAP('AXCU03') MAPSET('XXCU03')
          ERASE CURSOR END-EXEC.
```

In the above example, we try to move a packed-decimal field (WS-AMT) into an alphameric field (AMTO). The move will be an alphameric move. If you send that map out, it will hang your terminal. In order to avoid that, you should move COMP-3 data to a numeric field (9(5)) and then move this 9(5) field to the X(5) field:

```
MOVE WS-AMT TO AMT-E.
MOVE AMT-E  TO AMTO.
```

or you can define the output field of AMT as follows:

```
AMT DFHMDF  POS=(3,2),LENGTH=5,ATTRB=NUM,PICOUT='99999'
```

Then AMTO will be generated in 9(5) format. Now you can move WS-AMT to AMTO directly without any problem.

```
MOVE WS-AMT TO AMTO.
```

042.   Why a CICS task is terminated with abend code AICA?

AICA means CICS has determined that CICS task is a runaway task. A runaway task is the result of incorrect logical looping within the CICS program. You should use CEDF to check which section of the CICS program is looping and correct the problem. The runaway task time interval is defined by your system programmer at the CICS system initiation time and can be changed by CSMT TIM transaction. A typical runaway task time interval is 5000 milliseconds. When a CICS task executes longer than the defined runaway task time interval, AICA abend occurs.

043.   Why a CICS task is terminated with abend code ASRA?

ARSA means data exception. That could occur when you try to process a numeric field that contains non-numeric data or you try to process a data field defined in LINKAGE SECTION that has never been acquired by this CICS task. You should use INTERTEST to locate the COBOL statement within the CICS program that caused ASRA. If INTERTEST is not installed in your shop, you should use CEDF to locate the last CICS command executed and find the numeric fields following that command which could cause ASRA abend. If INTERTEST and CEDF are not installed in your shop, you can get the storage dump and use the storage dump to determine which statement caused the ASRA abend and the contents of data fields within that statement.

044.   Can you use SEARCH verb of COBOL in a CICS program?

Yes, even the SORT verb of COBOL is not allowed in a CICS program, SEARCH is still available for CICS programs.

045.   Is CEDF or INTERTEST always available in the production system?

No. Since CEDF and INTERTEST can modify the contents of main storages and CICS system areas and change the execution flow of a CICS task without a trace, many CICS shops find that it is too dangerous to install CEDF or INTERTEST in the production CICS system. Therefore, CEDF and INTERTEST are not always available in the production CICS system. If they are installed in the production CICS system, update of main storage (i.e. CHG in CORE transaction) is not allowed. However, you do not need to update the contents of main storages in order to debug a production CICS task abend.

046.   Why MAPFAIL condition occurs during the execution of a RECEIVE MAP command when the terminal user presses PA or CLEAR key?

Since PA keys or CLEAR key will not transmit input data entered on the terminal, MAPFAIL (no data is transmitted) will occur even data was entered. If you enter input data and then hit one of PF keys or ENTER key, MAPFAIL will not occur. Both PF keys and ENTER key will transmit the input data. MAPFAIL condition occurs when no input data is to be transmitted. Even PF keys can transmit input data, it is not recommended to enter input data then hit one of the PF keys. You should ask the user to hit ENTER key if input data has been entered.

047.   Why ABM0 occurs when you try to issue a SEND MAP command?

That means the address of the mapset in the PPT has been destroyed or there is no physical map (load module) for this mapset. In order to fix this problem, you should recompile that CICS mapset to create a load module in the CICS program load library and then issue the following CSMT NEW command:

```
CSMT NEW,PGRMID=mapset-name
```

048.   Why data fields defined in WORKING-STORAGE SECTION do not contain LOW-VALUES when the CICS program is loaded?

Data fields defined in WORKING-STORAGE SECTION will be allocated when the CICS program is loaded. If you do not define a data field with initial values (VALUE), CICS will not initialize the storage acquired for that data field. Therefore, you need to move LOW-VALUES to a symbolic description map before you move output data into it. You should not count on CICS to initialize the data field with LOW-VALUES for you.

049.   Do you need to close the VSAM primary file during the rebuild of its alternate index file?

Yes. Even the rebuild of the alternate index file is a read-only operation, you still need to close its primary file to prevent CICS tasks from updating the primary VSAM file. In results, the alternate index file must be updated. In this case, you will encounter problems. Therefore, you need to close both the primary file and its alternate index path to CICS in order to rebuild its alternate index file.

050.   Why the screen data is compressed when you try to do a
        local hardcopy print using the hard-copy key on the 3270
        key board?

When you try to print the screen image to your local printer using the hard-copy key
on the key board, all blank lines on the screen which contain LOW-VALUES (X'00') in
the terminal I/O buffer will not be printed. To avoid this, you should define an one-byte
field for each blank line in the mapset definition with initial value (INITIAL=) equal
to space. Then when you try to do a local print, all blank lines will contain space instead
of LOW-VALUES and they will be printed as one blank line on the printer. This will
make the hard copy looks exactly like its screen image. The following example shows how
to define the blank line in the mapset definition to achieve this result:

```
DFHMDF   POS=(03,01),LENGTH=01,INITIAL=' '
```

Then line 3 will be printed as one space line on the printer.

051.   How do you cancel an INTERTEST task?

When you try to get out of INTERTEST and you did not hit the correct key, the task
may still active even you have got out of the INTERTEST. You can cancel this active
task by issuing the following CORE command:

```
CORE(task#)=TCA@0+18@0+18=VERX'88'=CHGX'21'
```

This will cancel the task whose number can be obtained by issuing the CSMT TASK
command.

052.   Why two tasks are running when you use CEDF to test
        your CICS program?

The first task is the CICS transaction itself and the second task is the CEDF transaction.
Thus if you need to terminate your CICS transaction under CEDF, you need to terminate
both tasks.

053.   How can you tell a run-away task?

You can tell if a task has a very old task number comparing to the other active tasks.
If the task number of this task is relatively old comparing to the task numbers that are
currently running, then you know this is a run-away task. You may need to terminate
it. CICS assigns a task number to each task when the task is started. The task number
is in ascending sequence.

054. Why a print program can hang the entire CICS system?

If you try to print an on-line report using the Message Routing technique and your CICS print program hangs the entire CICS system, the problem could come from insufficient temporary storage to store this big report. Since CICS Message Routing uses the temporary storage to store the logical message you build. If the logical message is too big, your CICS print program needs to wait for the resource (temporary storage) in order to store the logical page you have just send, then this print program will hang the entire CICS system. Thus you should put a limit on the total number of pages that can be printed on an on-line report. Normally you should not try to design an application that will print more than 20 pages (24x80) of report on-line. If you have to do that, you should use re-insert tecnique as we have memtioned earier to prevent the print program from hanging CICS system.

055. Why a print report is displayed on your terminal rather than printed on the printer?

When you try to route an on-line report to a printer during Message Routing and the printer is not available, then the report will be displayed on the terminal that originates this report.

056. Why a CICS task is terminated with APCT abend code?

That means the CICS program, dynamic table (i.e. store table) or CICS mapset to be invoked is not specified in the PPT.

057. How can you use CEDF to monitor the execution of a CICS task that is entered on a remote terminal?

You can enter CEDF L01A then hit ENTER key to set up CEDF to monitor the CICS transaction that is to be entered on the remote terminal L01A. Following that, you can call the user at the remote terminal L01A to enter the CICS transaction. After the CICS transaction has been entered, the CEDF displays will come back on your terminal just like you enter it yourself. Therefore, you can debug the CICS programs that are causing the problems at the remote terminals. This will come in handy when a user reports a problem that may only occur for that particular transaction and you want the user to enter that transaction for you at the remote terminal.

058. What would you do when a production printer is broken?

Since the on-line report programs that route the message to this printer must set up this printer in their ROUTE LIST command. Therefore when this printer is broken, you must route the message to another printer. However, it is recommanded not to hard code the printer ID in the ROUTE LIST. Instead, you should use a terminal file (VSAM KSDS file with terminal ID as the key) to assign the on-line printer to each CICS terminal. When a production printer is broken, you can use a CICS on-line transaction to change the assigned printer to the other one. When the print program is executed, it will get the new printer instead of the broken one from the terminal file. This way, you do not need to recompile this CICS print program in order to route the report to a new printer.

059. **Should you impose the security upon an Online system using the physical locations of the terminals?**

NO. Using the physical location of a terminal as a means to impose the security is not recommanded. For example, you hard code the CICS A/P menu program so that only only four terminals located in the Accounts Payable Department can use On-line A/P system. When one of the terminals is broken, you would not be able to find a temporary replacement for that terminal since no other CICS terminals are set up to use this A/P system. If there are some problems in this On-line A/P system, the CICS programmer may not be able to conduct any testing using his own terminal in the CICS test system. Therefore, it is not a good practice to use the physical location of the terminal as a means to impose the security. You should use the operator ID (OPID) that is assigned to the user in the SNT to perform the security checking. This way, the authorized user can sign on to any terminal to get into A/P system.

060. **Is it a good practice to use dynamic table (i.e. store table) in the CICS program rather than using a CICS file to store those tables?**

It depends on how many CICS programs are going to use this table and how fast you want to get to the entries of that table. A dynamic table uses main storage that ensures fast access time. If almost every CICS program must use this table and this table is a small table, then you should set it up as a dynamic table. Otherwise, you should set up all those tables in one VSAM KSDS file using the table type ('STOR') and key (store number) as the key. For example, we can put both the terminal table and the store table into a VSAM KSDS file as follows:

```
01   TABLE-RECORD.
     02   TABLE-KEY.
          03   TABLE-TYPE     PIC X(4).
          03   TABLE-SUB-KEY PIC X(26).
     02   TABLE-DATA          PIC X(49).
     02   TERM-DATA REDEFINES TABLE-DATA.
          03   TERM-PRINTER  PIC X(4).
          03   FILLER        PIC X(45).
     02   STORE-DATA REDEFINES TABLE-DATA.
          03   STORE-NAME    PIC X(20).
          03   FILLER        PIC X(29).
```

You can then move 'TERM' and terminal ID into TABLE-KEY to retrieve the associated printer for any given terminal. You can also move 'STOR' and the store number into TABLE-KEY to retrieve the store name for any given store number. Therefore, one VSAM KSDS file contains all the small tables, each contains a very small number of records. Each record in the table contains very few fields. You can then develop an on-line transaction to maintain all these tables. So everytime the table is changed, you do not need to recompile the CICS programs that use these tables. Instead, you only need to update the tables on-line.

061.   Why CECI transaction is not that popular as the FILE transaction of the INTERTEST?

Since CECI is neither a menu-driven nor a full-screen-support transaction, CICS programmers prefer FILE transaction which is a full-screen transaction. You only need to enter the file name, function to be performed and the key on the FILE screen in order to process a VSAM file. Actually, the FILE transaction is one of the major faactors that contribute to the success of INTERTEST. You can use the FILE transaction to set up the test data the way you want it.

062.   How do you get out of CICS session when your CICS transaction is looping?

No matter what key you press, the same screen keeps on coming back. In this case, you should disable the transaction of this task using another CICS terminal and then hit any key on your terminal. In results, CICS will inform you that the transaction has been disabled and your task is terminated. Now you can then hit CLEAR key to erase the message and you are ready to enter the next CICS transaction. Before you enter the CICS transaction that caused the looping, you need to enable that transaction you have just disabled. After the CICS map has been sent, you issue a RETURN command with TRANSID option. After that, you hit any key to invoke this program. This time, you should go to issue a RECEIVE MAP command. Instead, the program goes to issue the SEND MAP command. That is the reason why the transaction is looping. The following CSMT command can be used to disable the transaction:

```
CSMT DISAB,SIN,TRNACT,TRANID=CU01
```

After the transaction has been disabled and you have got out of that transaction, you should fix the problem and then enable the transaction as follows:

```
CSMT ENA,SIN,TRNACT,TRANID=CU01
```

063.   What do you do when a production CICS transaction abends?

If more than one terminal user have reported the abends on the same transaction, you should disable this CICS transaction so nobody can use it. If only one terminal user encounters the abend for that transaction, you should use CEDF, INTERTEST or CICS storage dump to determine if you need to disable that transaction. After a CICS transaction is disabled, a message saying the transaction has been disabled will be displayed on the terminal when users try to initiate that transaction.

064. Why a VSAM file is disabled when CICS is up?

When CICS is brought up in the morning, it will try to open and enable all VSAM files that are specified with FILSTAT=(OPENED,ENABLED) on the FCT. If this VSAM file does not have at least one record (empty) in the file, or the VSAM file is never being defined or VSAM file is not in normal status, CICS will not open and enable it. When a VSAM file is disabled and closed, no File Control commands can process it. You can check the file status of a VSAM file using the CSMT command:

```
CSMT INQ,SIN,DAT,FILEID=CUSTMAST
```

065. How can you test a CICS program in a menu-driven system?

You do not have to wait for the menu program to complete in order to test your CICS program. You only need to modify your program so it can be invoked by entering the transaction ID of this CICS program and the input data on the terminal. For example, your Customer Update CICS program will get the customer number from the menu program and then display the customer information on the terminal for the user to update. You can change this update program so it will be invoked by entering its transaction ID and the customer number on the terminal. After the update program has been invoked, it should issue a RECEIVE INTO command to receive the transaction ID and the customer number entered into the CICS program. Now you can use the customer number to read the customer file and display it on the terminal for the user to update:

```
01  RECE-AREA.
    02  RECE-TRAN-ID    PIC X(4).
    02  FILLER          PIC X(1).
    02  RECE-CUST-NO    PIC X(5).
01  WS-RECE-LEN         PIC S9(4) COMP VALUE +10.
LINKAGE SECTION.
01  DFHCOMMAREA         PIC X(100).
PROCEDURE DIVISION.
    IF EIBTRNID = 'CU02' AND EIBCALEN = 100
       GO TO A200-RECEIVE-MAP.
    EXEC CICS RECEIVE INTO(RECE-AREA) LENGTH(WS-RECE-LEN)
        END-EXEC.
    EXEC CICS READ DATASET('CUSTMAST')
                INTO(CUST-REC)
                RIDFLD(RECE-CUST-NO)
                END-EXEC.
.... MOVE IT TO MAP I/O AREA ....
.... SEND MAP ....
.... RETURN WITH TRANSID ....
```

In the above example, the only thing we change is to include the RECEIVE INTO command in order to get the customer number from the terminal rather than from DFHCOMMAREA. The rest of the program needs not be changed. The program will be invoked by entering the transaction ID and the customer number on the terminal. (CU01,12345).

066. How can you skip the displays during CEDF session?

You can hit PF4 at any time to skip the displays. The CEDF will stop only at the CICS commands that cause exception condition. If no exceptional condition occurs, CEDF will skip all displays and ask you whether you want to continue CEDF. After you answer YES or NO, the output screen will be displayed for you to enter input data or control key.

067. Can you ask CEDF to stop at certain CICS command?

Yes. You can hit PF9 to request CEDF to stop at certain CICS command. After PF9 has been pressed, you should enter the CICS command that you want CEDF to stop at and then hit ENTER key. After ENTER key has been pressed, you should hit PF9 again to go to that CICS command.

068. How can you look at the contents of a data field defined in LINKAGE SECTION?

When the data area is acquired or addressed, you need to write down the location displayed on the CICS command during CEDF session. For example, we define the customer record layout in LINKAGE SECTION, then we issue a READ command with SET option to read a particular customer. After the READ command has been executed successfully, the addess set for the pointer reference will be displayed. You should write down this address and then hit PF5 to examine the main storage. After the first page of the WORKING-STORAGE SECTION has been displayed, you can enter that address in the location field and then press ENTER key to display the contents of work areas starting with that address.

069. How can you examine the contents of parameters of a CICS command in hexadecimal format during CEDF sessions?

You can hit PF2 to display the current CICS command display in hexadecimal format. After you have reviewed the screen, you can go back to the character format by pressing PF2 key again.

070. How many displays do CEDF remember for you to review?

Ten displays. Since most CICS commands have two CEDF displays. That means CEDF only remembers at most five CICS commands for you to review.

071. Can you modify the parameter values of a CICS command during CEDF session?

Yes. But you need to do it before the CICS command is executed. When a CICS command is displayed by CEDF before its execution, you can change the parameter values by overriding them on the screen and then hit the ENTER key. This ENTER key will override the parameter values to what you have just entered. You need to hit the ENTER key one more time in order to execute this CICS command using the new values.

072. Can you change the execution status of a CICS command after it has been executed during CEDF?

Yes. But you must do it after the CICS command has been executed. After the execution has been completed, CEDF will display the execution status (i.e. NORMAL or NOTFND) on RESPONSE field. You can change this field to any valid exception condition or NORMAL for that CICS command. This is the best way to test those exceptional-condition-handling routines you set up within the CICS program. For example, NORMAL status is displayed after a READ command has been executed. You can change NORMAL status to NOTFND exceptional condition and then hit ENTER key to make the change. After ENTER key is hit, you need to hit ENTER key one more time in order to continue the execution. In this case, the control will go to the label set up for the NOTFND condition in HANDLE CONDITION command.

073. When do you need to enter input data or press any control key defined for a CICS program during CEDF?

The input data and control key must be entered or pressed after you have answered whether (YES) or not (NO) you want to continue CEDF session. A CICS map will be displayed twice during CEDF session, once when the SEND MAP command is executed and the second time after the task has been terminated. If you press any control key when the CICS map is first displayed, this action will be ignored by CEDF. If you enter the input data when the CICS map is first displayed, the input data will be carried over to the second display and honored by CICS. So the best time to enter input data or press control key is after you have answered whether or not you want to continue CEDF session.

074. How does CICS link the dataset name specified in the File Control command with the actual file on the disk?

The standard labels specified in the CICS startup JCL provide this linkage between the dataset and its physical location. Each dataset used in CICS must have a DD (OS/VS) or DLBL (DOS/VS) card specified in the CICS startup JCL. When you specify the dataset name in the File Control command, CICS File Control Module will get the VSAM cluster name (DSN=) from the standard label in the DD or DLBL card. Then it will use this name to search VSAM catalog to get VSAM file information.

075. Why VERRIFY command is specified in the CICS startup JCL for each VSAM file to be used in CICS?

The system programmers are told to include one VERIFY card for each VSAM file when CICS is brought up. The VERIFY command will make sure the end of file information in the VSAM catalog and VSAM file itself are consistant. The VSAM files were closed last night for batch jobs. If a batch job fails, the VSAM file may not be closed properly. This may leave the VSAM catalog with incorrect end of file information for this file. The VERIFY command is to update the VSAM catalog if necessary with the correct end of file information.

076. Is there any other way to create a VSAM file except using VSAM AMS commands?

Yes. You can issue AMS commands through TSO.

077. Do you need to issue a READ with UPDATE option in order to issue a DELETE command to delete a VSAM record?

No. You can delete the record directly using the DELETE command with RIDFLD option. The key of the record to be deleted must be in the RIDFLD field.

078. Do you need to issue the READPREV command twice in order to read the previous record during a forward-browse (READNEXT) operation?

Yes. After you issue the last READNEXT command, if you want to get the previous record of the current retrieved record, you need to issue the READPREV command twice. The first one will still get the current record, and the second READPREV will retrieve the previous record. After the previous record is retrieved, one READPREV command will retrieve one previous record.

079. Can you update the primary record during the browse of its alternate index?

Yes. You can retrieve a record through the alternate index path and then issue a READ command with UPDATE option on the primary file for this record. After the READ with UPDATE is issued, you can move the updates to record I/O area and then issue a REWRITE command to update the record. Following that, you can go to issue the READNEXT command for the next record through the alternate index path. In this case, You browse the records through the alternate index path while updating the primary file.

080. Can you update the primary record while browsing the primary file?

No. You cannot issue any File Control commands on the primary file except these browse commands (READNEXT, READPREV, RESETBR, and ENDBR) during a browse operation. If you try to update the record during a browse, INVREQ will occur. In order to update a primary file sequentially, you need to use READ with GTEQ option to retrieve the next record and then issue a READ command with UPDATE option and a REWRITE command to update this retrieved record. After the retrieved record has been updated, you need to increase the key and go back to issue another READ command with GTEQ option to retrieve the next record and repeat the above update operation.

081. How do you update all the sales order details for any given sales order? Assume that the key to the sales order detail file is the sales order number plus the detail sequence number.

As we have mentioned earier that you cannot update records during a browse operation. Instead, you should use READ command with GTEQ option to get the next record. After a qualified record (same order number) has been read, you can then issue a READ command with UPDATE option and then issue a REWRITE command to update this retrieved detail. After the current detail has been updated, you should increase the sequence number by 1 to issue a READ command with GTEQ option to get next detail. This time, the second detail will be retrieved, you can then update the second detail as you did for the first one and so on.

082. Can you specify a CICS program written in different language in the PROGRAM option in the XCTL or LINK command?

Yes you can. In fact, many of the linked CICS programs are written in Assembler language. You can even issue a LINK or XCTL command within a Command level CICS program to transfer the control to a Macro level CICS program. In this case, CEDF will not monitor the execution of that Macro level program if you are testing that Command level program using CEDF.

083. How should you name the temporary storage queue?

Since CICS is running under multiple-tasking environment, you should attach the terminal ID (EIBTRMID) as part of the TS queue name. This way, the TS queue created by your terminal can only be used by transactions entered from this terminal. Before you create the first entry in a main storage TS queue, you should always try to delete this TS queue to prevent the left-over TS queue from being used by this CICS program. A TS queue uses main storage (MAIN) will not be backed out by CICS transaction backout program. Therefore, if a CICS task has created a TS queue in main storage and then abends, the TS queue will be there next time you invoke this transaction.

084. **Why NOTFND condition occurs when you try to access a VSAM record that you have just created through its alternate index path?**

VSAM seems to have a problem that no alternate index record will be created immediately after you have created its record in the primary file. In order to force VSAM to flush its buffer to create the alternate index record after its primary record is created, you should issue STARTBR, READNEXT, and ENDBR commands to browse the VSAM alternate index file using the alternate index key as the starting key following the WRITE command.

085. **When do you need to recompile your CICS program after you have recompiled its CICS map?**

Since the CICS program must copy the symbolic description map into its WORKING-STORAGE SECTION or LINKAGE SECTION, you must recompile the CICS programs that use this map if the symbolic description map has changed. A symbolic description map consists of only CICS map fields with label. If you only change those map fields without label, the symbolic description map will not be changed. In this case, you do not need to recompile the CICS programs. Under the following situations, the CICS symbolic description map will be changed:

1. New fields with label have been added into the map.
2. Map fields with label have been re-arranged in sequence.
3. Map fields with label have been deleted from the map.
4. Lengths of map fields with label have been changed.

If you just change the attribute (ATTRB) of a map field, then its symbolic description map will not be changed.

086. **Why a shorter record is returned when you read a VSAM record through its alternate index path?**

That means your system programmer specifed the alternate index name (AIX NAME) instead of alternate index path name (PATH NAME) as the DSN= name in the DD card in the CICS startup JCL for this alternate index path. CICS assumes that you want to process the alternate index file as an independent file if its name instead of path is used in the DSN=. Therefore, the alternate index record in the alternate index file is returned instead of the record in the primary file.

087. **Why do you need to hit EOF key (Erase End of Field) after you have entered the input data on an unprotected field?**

This will insert an EOF indicator following the input data you enter on this field. If no EOF key is pressed, CICS will assume the remaining data displayed on this unprotected field as part of the input data. For example, if '12345' was displayed on the quantity field and you want to change it to '468'. You should enter '468' and then hit EOF key to erase 45 and then hit ENTER key. CICS will right justify '468' and fill the first two bytes of the input field with zeros. Therefore, '00468' will be transmitted into the map I/O area after a RECEIVE MAP command is issued. If you enter '468' and two spaces, '468 ' will be received into the map I/O area. If spaces instead of low-values are displayed on this field and you enter '468' then hit ENTER, '468 ' will be received into the program. If LOW-VALUES were displayed on this field and you enter '468', '00468' will be received into the program if this field is defined as ATTRB=NUM.

088.   How do you debug a production CICS task abend if no CEDF and INTERTEST are installed?

You should print the CICS storage dump and debug the abend using the CICS storage dump.

089.   Does half-word alignment always apply to a CICS symbolic description map?

No. The half-word alignment is the results of specification in the CICS mapset assembly JCL. The easiest way to check if the half-word alignment is specified for your symbolic description map generation is to examine it in the CICS program compile listing. If a Filler of one-byte is used following the map input field with even number of length, then half-word alignment is specified. You need to know how CICS generates its symbolic description map when you try to redefine it in the Browse/Update applications. The following example shows how to determine if half-word alignment is used by BMS:

```
01    MAPI.
      02  F1L     PIC S9(4) COMP.
      02  F1A     PIC X.
      02  FILLER REDEFINES F1A.
       03  F1F    PIC X.
      02  F1I     PIC X(30).
      02  FILLER PIC X.
      .... NEXT MAP FIELDS ....
```

In the above example, there is a one-byte filler following F1I. Therefore we know half-word alignment is used by BMS to generate the symbolic description map.

090.   Why output data displayed on the CICS map is offseted by one or more bytes?

That means your CICS program does not use the most current version of the CICS mapset. After you have made changes to a CICS mapset, you should recompile the CICS program to pick up the latest version of the CICS map copy book. Otherwise, the CICS program will still use the old symbolic description map to interpret the input or output data while the new version of CICS mapset is used to receive the map into the program or send the map to the terminal.

091. What will happen if there is no end of message (DFHBMPEM) specified as the last character in the output stream when you use the SEND FROM or SEND TEXT command to print an online report?

The end of message signals the end of output data stream to be printed. If no end of message character is inserted as the last byte of output stream, CICS will print all the remaining characters until the entire buffer is printed (1920 bytes). For example, you only want to print 1880 bytes of output data and there is no DFHBMPEM character inserted as the 1881st character in the output data stream specified in the FROM option of the SEND TEXT ACCUM or SEND command, CICS will print additional 40 bytes of data (1920 - 1880 = 40). In this case, your report will be offset by 40 bytes.

092. How do you specify an alternate index path in the FCT?

You need to specify BASE=dataset-name (only for OS/VS) in its FCT entry to relate this alternate index path to its base cluster (primary file). You also need to specify SERVREQ=(READ,BROWSE) to allow only read and browse operations. You should not specify SHARE or any update request for an alternate index path. DOS/VS users do not need to specify BASE= parameter.

093. Why INVREQ condition occurs when you try to issue a RETURN command with a TRANSID option in a subroutine program linked by a CICS main program?

You should not try to perform any terminal I/O operations in a subroutine CICS program linked by a main program. If you issue a RETURN command with a TRANSID option in a CICS program that is not at the highest level, INVREQ condition occurs. Since you expect the control to return to the main program when the subroutine CICS program has been executed. If RETURN command with TRANSID option is issued in the subroutine program, INVREQ condition occurs.

094. Why there are four bytes generated following the attribute byte of a map field in a CICS symbolic description map?

If you specify EXTATT=YES in the DFHMSD macro, BMS will generate four more bytes for each map field to support extended attributes. The extended attributes include COLOR, HIGHT, PS and validation. Most of 3270 terminals used for CICS applications do not support extended attributes. In this case, you should not specify EXTATT=YES in DFHMSD macro.

095. Can you just build the alternate index when the primary file has been defined and loaded successfully and the step that defines the alternate index fails?

Yes. You should not try to run the steps that define and load the VSAM primary file.

You should only run those job steps that define the alternate index (DEFINE AIX), define the path (DEFINE PATH) and build the alternate index file (BLDINDEX).

096. How do you retrieve a VSAM record through the alternate index path?

You should specify the data set name specified in the FCT for that alternate index path in the DATASET option, the primary record I/O area in the INTO option, and the alternate index key in the RIDFLD option:

```
EXEC CICS READ DATASET('ALTNATE')
               INTO(PRIMARY-REC)
               RIDFLD(ALT-KEY)
               END-EXEC.
```

After the READ command is issued, you will get the entire record just like you have retrieved it using the primary key.

097. How do you set up the average and maximum record lengths for an unique alternate index file?

The length should be the total of alternate index key length, primary key length and 5-byte control area.

098. How do you retrieve VSAM records through its alternate index path that is defined as non-unique?

When the first record with duplicate alternate index key is retrieved, DUPREC condition occurs. To retrieve all records with that alternate index key, a browse should be started. Each READNEXT command will retrieve a record and the DUPKEY condition will occur for each record except the last one. Therefore, when you get NORMAL status during the browse, you know all records having the same alternate index key have been retrieved. If a VSAM record has an unique alternate index key, no DUPKEY condition will occur and that record will be retrieved.

099. How do you test a CICS print program that is started by the START command without TERMID option?

Since this CICS task is initiated without an associated CICS terminal or printer, you cannot test it under CEDF. However, you can change the START command to an XCTL command and pass the data to the print program through the communication area for testing purposes. Then you can monitor this print program under CEDF. After the print program has been tested successfully this way, you can then change it back so it can be initiated by the START command.

100. How can you allow only one user to update a VSAM record at any time?

You cannot use ENQ to enqueue the customer number in order to prevent the other user from updating it concurrently in a pseudo conversational program since ENQ only lasts for that task. When you issue a RETRUEN command with TRANSID option after the SEND MAP, the resource will be dequeued. You should save the customer record in the communication area after it has been retrieved for display. After all updates to this cstomer have been edited and you are ready to update the customer, you should then issue a READ command with UPDATE option to retrieve this customer and then compare its record with the one we have saved. If they are identical, then we know we can update this customer without any problem. Otherwise, that customer was being updated by another user when you tried to retrieve it for display. In this case, you should reject the update and inform the user to start the update one more time.

PART 4. 15 MAJOR APPLICATIONS AND SAMPLE PROGRAMS

Chapter 13.   15 Major Applications And Sample Programs

CHAPTER 13.   15 MAJOR CICS APPLICATIONS AND SAMPLE PROGRAMS

In this chapter, we'll cover 15 most important CICS applications, each one is demonstrated by a complete CICS program. This will cover at least 90% of your CICS applications. Each CICS sample program is carefully designed and chosen and reprsents a typical CICS application.

13.1.   Customer Order Service System Overview

A majority of CICS/VS online systems are menu-driven systems. The user enters the transaction code of the menu program to display the menu screen. After the menu screen has been displayed, the user can then select the desired function and enter its required/optional fields to invoke the desired CICS program. The only transaction code that the user must remember is that of the menu program. The rest of the CICS programs in that CICS online system are invoked by the menu program. The required or optional fields for each function is prompted on the menu screen. So the user does not need to remember the input data for each function to be performed. The security can also be imposed in the menu program to check the authorization of using that system and the functions listed on the menu. We'll use this Customer Order Service System to demonstrate those 15 major CICS applications.

This Customer Order Service System is invoked by entering 'CUST' on a clear screen. After the menu screen is displayed, the user can perform one of the following functions listed on the menu:

```
Function Program  Description
         XCU00     Menu
   01    XCU01     Add a new customer
   02    XCU02     Inquire/Update/Delete a customer
   03    XCU03     Browse/Update customers by name
   04    XCU04     Print a sales order on 24x80 paper
   05    XCU05     Print a sales order on 24x80 paper using OVERFLOW
   06    XCU06     Print a sales order on 66x132 paper
   07    XCU07     Print a sales order on 66x85 paper
   08    XCU08     Create sales order details in TS queue
   09    XCU09     Review/Update/Create sales order details
   10    XCU10     Print sales order master list tonight
         XCU11     Print utility program
         XCU12     Automatic Task Initiation Program
         XCU13     Common Abend-Handling Program
         XCU14     Dynamic Table Loading Program
         XCU15     Screen Refreshing Program
```

After CUST is entered on a clear terminal, the menu program XCU00 will be invoked. It will then send the menu screen to the terminal for the user to select the desired function and enter required/optional fields to invoke the desired CICS program.

If function 01 is entered, XCU01 will be invoked by the menu program through the use of XCTL command. No data needs to be passed to the XCU01 program. After XCU01 is invoked, it will display a blank screen for the user to enter a new customer. After a new customer has been created, the user can hit CLEAR key to go back to the menu screen or hit PF1 to reset the screen in order to add the next customer.

If function 02 and a valid customer number is entered, the menu program (XCU00) will transfer the control to the inquire/update/delete customer program (XCU02) through the use of the XCTL command. The customer number will be passed in the communication area to the customer update program. After XCU02 program is invoked, it will use the customer number passed to read the customer file and display the customer on the terminal. After the customer has been displayed, the user can hit CLEAR key to go back to the menu screen, hit PF1 to delete the customer, or enter updates and then hit ENTER key to update the customer, or enter the next customer number to be processed. After the customer has been updated or deleted, the user can hit CLEAR key to go back to the menu screen or enter the next customer to be processed.

If function 03 and the customer name have been entered on the menu screen, the menu program will issue an XCTL command to transfer the control to the customer browse/update program XCU03. The customer name will be passed to this browse/update program through the communication area. After the browse/update customer program has been invoked, it will use the customer name passed as the starting key to browse the customer records through its alternate index path (the customer name) and display up to sixteen customers per screen on the terminal. This program is used to demonstrate how to browse a VSAM file through its alternate index. The user can hit CLEAR key to go back to the menu screen, hit PF1 to go to display the next page of customers, or hit PF2 to display the previous page of customers. If the user enters an 'X' on the desired customer, the control will go to Inquire/Update/Delete Customer (XCU02) screen to process that customer. If the user enters updates on the desired customers, the program will update those customers. At any time, the user can enter the next customer name (partial or full name) on the next customer name field to initiate the browse starting with that name.

If function 04 and a valid sales order number have been entered on the menu screen, the menu program will issue a START command without TERMID option to print that sales order. The transaction specified in the TRANSID option of that START command must be CU04 whose associated CICS program is XCU04. When XCU04 is invoked, it will use Message Routing technique to print this sales order. However, the entire page of the sales order will be defined as one header map. There are no detail map and trailer map set up in its CICS mapset. No OVERFLOW condtion needs to be handled. The SEND MAP ACCUM command will be used. The page size for this report is 24x80. The TCT page size of the printer can be defined as PGESIZE=(24,80).

If function 05 and a valid sales order number have been entered on the menu screen, the menu program will issue a START command without TERMID option to print that sales order. The transaction specified in the TRANSID option of that START command must be CU05 whose associated CICS program is XCU05. When XCU05 is invoked, it will use Message Routing technique to print that sales order. However, one header map, one detail map and one trailer map will be defined in its CICS mapset and OVERFLOW condition must be handled. The report format for this program is identical to that of XCU04. The SEND MAP ACCUM command will be used. The page size for this report is 24x80. The TCT page size of the printer can be defined as PGESIZE=(24,80).

If function 06 and a valid sales order number have been entered on the menu screen, the menu program will issue a START command without TERMID option to initiate CU06 transaction whose associated CICS program is XCU06. After XCU06 is invoked, it will use Message Routing technique to print that sales order on 66x132 paper. The SEND TEXT ACCUM command instead of the SEND MAP ACCUM command will be used to build the report. No CICS mapset needs to be defined. The TCT page size of the printer must be defined as PGESIZE=(11,132).

If function 07 and a valid sales order number have been entered on the menu screen, the menu program will issue a LINK command to link to the print program XCU07. After XCU07 is invoked, it will start the print utility transaction CU11 one or more times to print that sales order. Each START command will print up to 1920 bytes of data. If the report is greater than 1920 bytes, more than one START command must be issued. The report will be 66x85 size. The TCT page size for the printer can be PGESIZE=(24,80). After the report has been printed, XCU07 will issue a RETURN command to return to the menu program at the very statement following the LINK command. The menu program then needs to send a message saying 'SALES ORDER HAS BEEN PRINTED' on the terminal. This print utility transaction can be started by any CICS program to print any-size report. Each CICS installation normally has one such print transaction to meet the application needs.

If function 08 and a valid sales order number have been entered on the menu screen, the menu program will issue an XCTL command to transfer the control to the Create Sales Order Detail program XCU08. After XCU08 is invoked, it will display a blank screen for the user to enter sales order details. After the sales order details are entered, they will be created in a TS queue for the user to review/update/create in the next CICS program (XCU09). After the user has reviewed or updated those sales order details in the next screen, he can hit PF3 to create those details in the sales order detail file. The reason we want to create them in the TS queue is that we want the user to perform the final review or update before we create them for real in the VSAM file. XCU08 and XCU09 are used to demonstrate how to use TS queues.

If function 09 and a valid sales order number have been entered on the menu screen, the menu program will issue an XCTL command to transfer the control to the Review/Update/Create Sales Order Detail program XCU09. After XCU09 is invoked, it will read the TS queue records and display them on the terminal for the user to review or update. After the user has finished the review or update, he can hit PF3 to create those sales order details in the sales order detail file. After the records have been created in the file, we'll delete the TS queue.

If function 10 has been entered on the menu screen, the menu program will issue a LINK command to transfer the control to the CICS program XCU10. After XCU10 is invoked, it will issue the WRITEQ TD command many times to create the JCL for the sales order master list print program in the reader queue. After the JCL has been submitted to the reader queue, this program will issue a RETURN command to go back to the menu program. Following the LINK command, the menu program will display a message saying 'PRINT REQUEST IS COMPLETED' on the terminal. This program demonstrates how to design an online CICS application to submit the JCL for batch jobs to be executed at night.

XCU11 is the CICS program for the print utility transaction which can be started by any CICS program that needs to print an online report. The issuing CICS program only needs to pass the data to be printed and then issue the START command to initiate CU11. Transaction CU11 is started by XCU07 to print a sales order on 66x85 paper. Each CICS shops should develop one such print transaction so any CICS programmer can print online report without knowing how to use Terminal Control or Message Routing.

XCU12 is the CICS program for the transaction CU12 which is started when the trigger level for an intrapartition transient data queue has reached 30. After it is invoked, it will read the TD queue record which contains a sales order number to print the sales order. This program is used to demonstrate how to develop an Automatic Task Initiation (ATI) application.

XCU13 is the Common-Abend-Handling program that is to be invoked by all CICS programs when an unrecoverable error has been encountered. After it is invoked, it will collect as much information as possible and print it on the printer. After the message is printed, it will then issue an ABEND command to abend the task.

XCU14 is a CICS program that will load a dynamic table using LOAD command into the program for use. It will be used to demonstrate how to define, set up, load, process and delete a dynamic table.

XCU15 is a screen refreshing program which only needs to be started once in the morning. After it has been started, it will go get the latest information from the VSAM file, display it on the terminal, start itself within 30 seconds and then terminate itself. Therefore, the latest information will be displayed on the terminal every 30 seconds until the user terminates the task.

VSAM Files

There are three VSAM KSDS files in this Customer Order Service System. The first one is the customer file whose key is the customer number. However, we also set up an alternate index key (customer name plus customer number) upon this customer file so we can browse/update the customer file by name (XCU03). The second VSAM file is the sales order header file whose key is the sales order number. Each sales order has one header record in the Sales Order Header file and one or more sales order detail records in the Sales Order Detail file. Each detail reprsents one product customer ordered. The third VSAM file is the sales order detail file whose key is the sales order number plus the sequence number which is assigned sequentially by the system.

CICS Internal Tables

```
PPT:

*     CICS PROGRAMS
DFHPPT    TYPE=ENTRY,PROGRAM=XCU00,PGMLANG=COBOL,RES=YES
DFHPPT    TYPE=ENTRY,PROGRAM=XCU01,PGMLANG=COBOL,RES=YES
DFHPPT    TYPE=ENTRY,PROGRAM=XCU02,PGMLANG=COBOL,RES=YES
DFHPPT    TYPE=ENTRY,PROGRAM=XCU03,PGMLANG=COBOL,RES=YES
DFHPPT    TYPE=ENTRY,PROGRAM=XCU04,PGMLANG=COBOL,RES=YES
DFHPPT    TYPE=ENTRY,PROGRAM=XCU05,PGMLANG=COBOL
DFHPPT    TYPE=ENTRY,PROGRAM=XCU06,PGMLANG=COBOL
DFHPPT    TYPE=ENTRY,PROGRAM=XCU07,PGMLANG=COBOL
DFHPPT    TYPE=ENTRY,PROGRAM=XCU08,PGMLANG=COBOL
DFHPPT    TYPE=ENTRY,PROGRAM=XCU09,PGMLANG=COBOL
DFHPPT    TYPE=ENTRY,PROGRAM=XCU10,PGMLANG=COBOL
DFHPPT    TYPE=ENTRY,PROGRAM=XCU11,PGMLANG=ASSEMBLER
DFHPPT    TYPE=ENTRY,PROGRAM=XCU12,PGMLANG=COBOL
DFHPPT    TYPE=ENTRY,PROGRAM=XCU13,PGMLANG=COBOL,RES=YES
DFHPPT    TYPE=ENTRY,PROGRAM=XCU14,PGMLANG=COBOL
DFHPPT    TYPE=ENTRY,PROGRAM=XCU15,PGMLANG=COBOL
DFHPPT    TYPE=ENTRY,PROGRAM=STORTBL,PGMLANG=COBOL
*     CICS MAPSETS
DFHPPT    TYPE=ENTRY,PROGRAM=XXCU00,USAGE=MAP,RES=YES
DFHPPT    TYPE=ENTRY,PROGRAM=XXCU01,USAGE=MAP,RES=YES
DFHPPT    TYPE=ENTRY,PROGRAM=XXCU02,USAGE=MAP,RES=YES
DFHPPT    TYPE=ENTRY,PROGRAM=XXCU03,USAGE=MAP,RES=YES
DFHPPT    TYPE=ENTRY,PROGRAM=XXCU04,USAGE=MAP,RES=YES
DFHPPT    TYPE=ENTRY,PROGRAM=XXCU05,USAGE=MAP
DFHPPT    TYPE=ENTRY,PROGRAM=XXCU08,USAGE=MAP
DFHPPT    TYPE=ENTRY,PROGRAM=XXCU09,USAGE=MAP
```

```
PCT:

DFHPCT    TYPE=ENTRY,TRANSID=CUST,PROGRAM=XCU00,TRANSEC=01,     X
          TRANPRTY=150
DFHPCT    TYPE=ENTRY,TRANSID=CU01,PROGRAM=XCU01,TRANSEC=01,     X
          TRANPRTY=150
DFHPCT    TYPE=ENTRY,TRANSID=CU02,PROGRAM=XCU02,TRANSEC=01,     X
          TRANPRTY=150
DFHPCT    TYPE=ENTRY,TRANSID=CU03,PROGRAM=XCU03,TRANSEC=01,     X
          TRANPRTY=150
DFHPCT    TYPE=ENTRY,TRANSID=CU04,PROGRAM=XCU04,TRANSEC=01,     X
          TRANPRTY=150
DFHPCT    TYPE=ENTRY,TRANSID=CU05,PROGRAM=XCU05,TRANSEC=01,     X
          TRANPRTY=150
DFHPCT    TYPE=ENTRY,TRANSID=CU06,PROGRAM=XCU06,TRANSEC=01,     X
          TRANPRTY=150
DFHPCT    TYPE=ENTRY,TRANSID=CU08,PROGRAM=XCU08,TRANSEC=01,     X
          TRANPRTY=150
DFHPCT    TYPE=ENTRY,TRANSID=CU09,PROGRAM=XCU09,TRANSEC=01,     X
        TRANPRTY=150
DFHPCT    TYPE=ENTRY,TRANSID=CU11,PROGRAM=XCU11,TRANSEC=01,     X
          TRANPRTY=150
DFHPCT    TYPE=ENTRY,TRANSID=CU12,PROGRAM=XCU12,TRANSEC=01,     X
          TRANPRTY=150
DFHPCT    TYPE=ENTRY,TRANSID=CU15,PROGRAM=XCU15,TRANSEC=01,     X
          TRANPRTY=150


FCT:


DFHFCT    TYPE=DATASET,DATASET=CUSTMST,ACCMETH=(VSAM,KSDS),     X
          SERVREQ=(PUT,UPDATE,DELETE,NEWREC,BROWSE),            X
          STRNO=1,BUFND=2,BUFSP=09216,BUFNI=1,                 X
          RECFORM=FIXED,FILSTAT=(OPENED,ENABLED),LOG=YES
DFHFCT    TYPE=DATASET,DATASET=CUSTNAM,ACCMETH=(VSAM,KSDS),     X
          SERVREQ=(READ,BROWSE),BASE=CUSTMST,                   X
          STRNO=1,BUFND=2,BUFSP=09216,BUFNI=1,                 X
          RECFORM=FIXED,FILSTAT=(OPENED,ENABLED),LOG=YES
DFHFCT    TYPE=DATASET,DATASET=ORDRHDR,ACCMETH=(VSAM,KSDS),     X
          SERVREQ=(PUT,UPDATE,DELETE,NEWREC,BROWSE,SHARE),      X
          STRNO=1,BUFND=2,BUFSP=09216,BUFNI=1,                 X
          RECFORM=FIXED,FILSTAT=(OPENED,ENABLED),LOG=YES
DFHFCT    TYPE=DATASET,DATASET=ORDRDET,ACCMETH=(VSAM,KSDS),     X
          SERVREQ=(PUT,PDATE,DELETE,NEWREC,BROWSE,SHARE),       X
          STRNO=1,BUFND=2,BUFSP=09216,BUFNI=1,                 X
          RECFORM=FIXED,FILSTAT=(OPENED,ENABLED),LOG=YES


TCT:

DFHTCT    TYPE=TERMINAL,TRMTYPE=3277,TRMIDNT=K01A,              X
          TRMPRTY=25,TRMMODL=2,TRMADDR=TRMBP01,                 X
          TRMSTAT=TRANSCEIVE,POLLPOS=1,TIOAL=512,               X
          BMSFEAT=(NOROUTEALL),                                 X
          FEATURE=(AUDALARM,UCTRAN),PGESIZE=(24,80)
DFHTCT    TYPE=TERMINAL,TRMTYPE=3286,TRMIDNT=K01P,              X
          TRMPRTY=25,TRMMODL=2,TRMADDR=TRMK01P,                 X
          TRMSTAT=RECEIVE,POLLPOS=1,PGESTAT=AUTOPAGE,           X
          FEATURE=PRINT,CLASS=(VIDEO,BISYNC),TIOAL=512,         X
          PGESIZE=(24,80)
DFHTCT    TYPE=TERMINAL,TRMTYPE=3286,TRMIDNT=K02P,              X
          TRMPRTY=25,TRMTMODL=2,TRMADDR=TRMK02P,                X
          TRMSTAT=RECEIVE,POLLPOS=1,PGESTAT=AUTOPAGE,           X
          FEATURE=PRINT,CLASS=(VIDEO,BISYNC),TIOAL=512,         X
          PGESIZE=(11,132)
```

There are three entries in this TCT table. The first one is to set up a display terminal so you can enter CICS transactions from this terminal. The second one (K01P) is used in XCU04 and XCU05 and is defined with PGESIZE=(24,80). The third one (K02P) is used in XCU06 to print a report on 66x132 paper. Its page size is defined as PGESIZE=(11,132).

```
DCT:

DFHDCT      TYPE=SDSCI,BLKSIZE=136,BUFNO=1,DSCNAME=SECURI,        X
            RECSIZE=132,RECFORM=VARUNB,TYPEFLE=OUTPUT
DFHDCT      TYPE=SDSCI,BLKSIZE=80,DSCNAME=RJERDR,BLKSIZE=80,      X
            RECSIZE=80,RECFORM=FIXUNB,TYPEFLE=OUTPUT,BUFNO=1
DFHDCT      TYPE=EXTRA,DESTID=DRDR,DSCNAME=RJERDR
DFHDCT      TYPE=EXTRA,DESTID=SECR,DSCNAME=SECURI
DFHDCT      TYPE=INTRA,DESTFAC=TERMINAL,DESTID=K01P,DESTRCV=NO,   X
            REUSE=YES,TRANSID=CU12,TRIGLEV=30
```

There are three DCT entries. The first one (CRDR) is set up for the reader queue so we can submit the JCL of batch jobs from CICS in XCU10. The second one (SECR) is used to log user activities in the menu program XCU00. After CICS has been shut down, you can then sort this TD queue by user ID and then print the activity report. The third one (CU12) is used in XCU12 for Automaic Task Initiation. This is an intrapartition TD queue with destionation ID equal to the printer K01P. When the trigger level (30) has been reached, transaction CU12 will be initiated to print all 30 sales orders in that TD queue in the printer K01A.

CICS Startup JCL:

```
//CUSTMST    DD DSN=CUSTOMER.MASTER,DISP=SHR
//CUSTNAM    DD DSN=CUSTOMER.MASTER.PATH,DISP=SHR
//ORDRHDR    DD DSN=ORDER.HEADER.MASTER,DISP=SHR
//ORDRDET    DD DSN=ORDER.DETAIL.MASTER,DISP=SHR
//PRODUCT    DD DSN=PRODUCT.MASTER,DISP=SHR
//RJERDR     DD SYSOUT=(N,INTRDR),
              DCB=(LRECL=80,BLKSIZE=80,RECFM=F,BUFNO=1)

  VERIFY(CUSTMST)
  VERIFY(CUSTNAM)
  VERIFY(ORDRHDR)
  VERIFY(ORDRDET)
  VERIFY(PRODUCT)
```

Design Techniques

We'll use the following techniques to design and program this Customer Order Service System:

1. Menu-Driven
   You can only request the desired function from the menu screen.

2. Modular Program
   You can transfer the control from one program to another easily if modular programming is used. Minimum input data is needed for each CICS program.

3. One CICS program per function
   Each CICS program will perform both the input and output operations.

4. Pseudo Conversational Programming
   Following each SEND MAP command, we will issue a RETURN command with

TRANSID option to terminate the program and post the transaction code of this program on that terminal. When any response to that terminal is made, that transaction code will be initiated to receive and process the input data.

5. Transmit and edit input data only once
Each input data will be transmitted and edited only once. We'll use the communication area to store the good-edited input data. There is no need to transmit and edit input data twice.

13.2. Customer Order Service System Menu

Program ID: XCU00   Transaction code: CUST   Mapset: XXCU00

When transaction code CUST is entered on a clear screen, the menu program (XCU00) will be invoked. After XCU00 is invoked, it will send the menu screen to the terminal and then issue a RETURN command with the TRANSID option to terminate the program and post CUST on that terminal. Any response to that terminal will initiate the transaction code CUST which in turn will invoke this menu program.

After the menu screen has been displayed, the user can then enter the desired function number and the required or optional fields and then hit ENTER key. After the ENTER key is hit, this menu program will be invoked again since we have post CUST on this terminal following the last SEND MAP command. After the menu program is invoked again, you should code the program so the control will go issue a RECEIVE MAP when it is not the first time the program is invoked. After a RECEIVE MAP command is issued, the input data entered will be received into the symbloic description map (map I/O area). You can then edit each unprotected field individually, edit the required fields for the function selected, and then edit the combination of these input fields.

If any input field is invalid, you should perform dynamic attribute modification and then issue a SEND MAP command with the DATAONLY option to send the error map to the terminal. If all input fields are valid, you should issue an XCTL, a LINK or a START command to invoke the desired CICS program. The data to be passed to the desired program can be stored in the communication area (COMMAREA) if the XCTL or LINK command is to be used or in the data area specified in the FROM option if the START command is used. When the desired CICS program is invoked, the data passed to it is in DFHCOMMAREA of LINKAGE SECTION if the XCTL or LINK command is used. If the START command is used, then you need to issue a RETRIEVE command to get the data passed.

We'll also check the security in the menu program at two levels. The first level of security will check to see if the user is authorized to use this Customer Order Service System. We'll use the operator ID to perform this first level of security when the menu program is invoked the very first time. We'll then check the second level of security after the user has selected the desired function. In this case, we will check to see if this user is authorized to perform the selected function.

When the user has selected the desired function, we want to log the user activity in an extrapartition transient data queue. This TD queue will be used as output data set to collect activity information from all users that use this system. This will demonstrate how to use an extrapartition Transient Data queue to collect output data from CICS terminals for off-line batch processing. After CICS is shut down at 5 PM, we can then sort this data set by the user ID and print it.

Screen Layout:

```
CUST  XX/XX/XX HH:MM     CUSTOMER ORDER SERVICE SYSTEM           XXXX
                                MENU

FUNCTION: 99 CUSTOMER NO: 99999 CUSTOMER NAME: XXXXXXXXXXXXXXXXXXXX
             ORDER NO   : 99999

        01 CREATE A NEW CUSTOMER.
        02 INQUIRE/UPDATE/DELETE A CUSTOMER (CUSTOMER NO).
        03 BROWSE/UPDATE CUSTOMERS BY NAME (CUSTOMER NAME).
        04 PRINT A SALES ORDER ON 24X80 PAPER (ORDER NO).
        05 PRINT A SALES ORDER ON 24X80 PAPER (ORDER NO).
        06 PRINT A SALES ORDER ON 66X132 PAPER (ORDER NO).
        07 PRINT A SALES ORDER ON 66X85 PAPER (ORDER NO).
        08 CREATE ORDER DETAILS ON TS QUEUE (ORDER NO).
        09 REVIEW/UPDATE/CREATE ORDER DETAILS (ORDER NO).
        10 PRINT SALES ORDER MASTER LIST TONIGHT.

CLEAR=END, PF1=RESET
XXXXXXXXXXXXXXXXXXXXXXXXXXXXXXXXXXXXXXXXXXXXXXXXXXXXXXXXXXXXXXXXXXXXXXXXXX
```

CICS Mapset XCU00:

```
XXCU00    DFHMSD TYPE=&SYSPARM,LANG=COBOL,TIOAPFX=YES,MODE=INOUT,        X
                 STORAGE=AUTO,CTRL=(FREEKB,FRSET),TERM=3270,DATA=FIELD
AXCU00    DFHMDI SIZE=(24,80)
          DFHMDF POS=(01,01),LENGTH=04,INITIAL='CUST'
DATE      DFHMDF POS=(01,07),LENGTH=08
TIME      DFHMDF POS=(01,16),LENGTH=05
          DFHMDF POS=(01,24),LENGTH=29,INITIAL='CUSTOMER ORDER SERVICE SX
                 YSTEM'
TERMID    DFHMDF POS=(01,66),LENGTH=04
          DFHMDF POS=(02,38),LENGTH=04,INITIAL='MENU'
          DFHMDF POS=(04,01),LENGTH=09,INITIAL='FUNCTION:'
FUNNO     DFHMDF POS=(04,11),LENGTH=02,ATTRB=NUM
          DFHMDF POS=(04,14),LENGTH=12,INITIAL='CUSTOMER NO:'
CUSTNO    DFHMDF POS=(04,27),LENGTH=05,ATTRB=NUM
          DFHMDF POS=(04,33),LENGTH=14,INITIAL='CUSTOMER NAME:'
CUSTNAM   DFHMDF POS=(04,48),LENGTH=20,ATTRB=UNPROT
          DFHMDF POS=(04,69),LENGTH=01
          DFHMDF POS=(05,14),LENGTH=12,INITIAL='ORDER NO   :'
ORDRNO    DFHMDF POS=(05,27),LENGTH=05,ATTRB=NUM
          DFHMDF POS=(05,33),LENGTH=01
          DFHMDF POS=(07,11),LENGTH=25,INITIAL='01 CREATE A NEW CUSTOMERX
                 .'
          DFHMDF POS=(08,11),LENGTH=50,INITIAL='02 INQUIRE/UPDATE/DELETEX
                 A CUSTOMER (CUSTOMER NO).'
          DFHMDF POS=(09,11),LENGTH=51,INITIAL='03 BROWSE/UPDATE CUSTOMEX
                 RS BY NAME (CUSTOMER NAME).'
          DFHMDF POS=(10,11),LENGTH=49,INITIAL='04 PRINT A SALES ORDER OX
                 N 24X80 PAPER (ORDER NO).'
          DFHMDF POS=(11,11),LENGTH=49,INITIAL='05 PRINT A SALES ORDER OX
                 N 24X80 PAPER (ORDER NO).'
          DFHMDF POS=(12,11),LENGTH=50,INITIAL='06 PRINT A SALES ORDER OX
                 N 66X132 PAPER (ORDER NO).'
          DFHMDF POS=(13,11),LENGTH=49,INITIAL='07 PRINT A SALES ORDER OX
                 N 66X85 PAPER (ORDER NO).'
          DFHMDF POS=(14,11),LENGTH=47,INITIAL='08 CREATE ORDER DETAILS X
                 ON TS QUEUE (ORDER NO).'
```

```
                    DFHMDF POS=(15,11),LENGTH=49,INITIAL='09 REVIEW/UPDATE/CREATE X
                        ORDER DETAILS (ORDER NO).'
                    DFHMDF POS=(16,11),LENGTH=41,INITIAL='10 PRINT SALES ORDER MASX
                        TER LIST TONIGHT.'
                    DFHMDF POS=(18,01),LENGTH=20,INITIAL='CLEAR=END, PF1=RESET',  X
                        ATTRB=(ASKIP,BRT)
        MSG         DFHMDF POS=(19,01),LENGTH=78,ATTRB=(ASKIP,BRT)
                    DFHMSD TYPE=FINAL
                    END
```

CICS Program XCU00:

```
        ID DIVISION.
        PROGRAM-ID. XCU00.
        REMARKS. CUSTOMER ORDER SERVICE SYSTEM MENU.
        ENVIRONMENT DIVISION.
        DATA DIVISION.
        WORKING-STORAGE SECTION.
        01   COMM-AREA.
             02   CA-FUNNO         PIC 9(2).
             02   CA-CUSTNO        PIC 9(5).
             02   CA-CUSTNAM       PIC X(20).
             02   CA-ORDRNO        PIC 9(5).
             02   CA-EDIT-TAB.
                  03   EDIT        PIC X(1) OCCURS 4.
             02   CA-POS           PIC X(4).
             02   FILLER           PIC X(60).
        01   XCTL-COMM-AREA.
             02   XCA-CUSTNO       PIC 9(5).
             02   XCA-CUSTNAM      PIC X(20).
             02   XCA-ORDRNO       PIC 9(5).
             02   FILLER           PIC X(70).
        01   WS-MSG               PIC X(60).
        01   WS-MSG-LENG          PIC S9(4) COMP VALUE +60.
        01   CUST-REC.
             02   CUST-ALT-KEY.
                  03   CUST-NAME   PIC X(20).
                  03   CUST-PRIMARY-KEY.
                       04   CUST-NO PIC 9(5).
             02   CUST-CRDLMT      PIC 9(7).
             02   CUST-INVAMT      PIC S9(5)V99 COMP-3.
        01   ORDRHDR-REC.
             02   ORDRHDR-KEY.
                  03   ORDRHDR-ORDRNO PIC 9(5).
             02   ORDRHDR-CUSTNO   PIC 9(5).
             02   ORDR-CUSTNAM     PIC X(5).
        01   AXCU00I              COPY XXCU00.
        01   WS-TIME-N            PIC 9(6).
        01   FILLER REDEFINES WS-TIME-N.
             02   WS-TIME-N-HH     PIC 9(2).
             02   WS-TIME-N-MM     PIC 9(2).
             02   FILLER           PIC X(2).
        01   WS-TIME-E.
             02   WS-TIME-E-HH     PIC 9(2).
             02   FILLER           PIC X(1) VALUE ':'.
             02   WS-TIME-E-MM     PIC 9(2).
        01   XCTL-XCU03           PIC X(1100).
        01   XCTL-XCU08           PIC X(400).
        01   CA-ORDRNO-LENG       PIC S9(4) COMP VALUE +5.
        01   WS-OPID              PIC X(3).
        01   TDQ-REC.
             02   TDQ-OPID         PIC X(3).
             02   TDQ-TERMID       PIC X(4).
             02   TDQ-DATE         PIC X(8).
             02   TDQ-TIME         PIC S9(7) COMP-3.
             02   TDQ-FUNNO        PIC 9(2).
        01   TDQ-LENG             PIC S9(4) COMP VALUE +21.
        LINKAGE SECTION.
        01   DFHCOMMAREA          PIC X(100).
```

```
            PROCEDURE DIVISION.
                 EXEC CICS HANDLE CONDITION
                           NOTFND(A900-NOTFND)
                           MAPFAIL(A910-MAPFAIL)
                           ERROR(A920-ERROR)
                           END-EXEC.
                 EXEC CICS HANDLE AID
                           CLEAR(A899-EOJ)
                           PF1(A850-RESET)
                           ANYKEY(A910-MAPFAIL)
                           END-EXEC.
            *    CHECK IF 2ND TIME PGM IS INVOKED
                 IF EIBCALEN = 100 AND EIBTRNID = 'CUST'
                      MOVE DFHCOMMAREA TO COMM-AREA
                      GO TO A200-RECEIVE-MAP.
            *    CHECK IF USER IS ALLOWED TO USE CUST
                 PERFORM B400-CK-SYSTEM-SECURITY THRU
                           B409-CK-SYSTEM-SECURITY-EXIT.
            *    SECURITY IS OK, NOW DISPLAY INITIAL MENU
            A100-SEND-INIT-SCREEN.
                 MOVE LOW-VALUES     TO AXCU00O.
                 MOVE CURRENT-DATE    TO DATEO.
                 MOVE TIME-OF-DAY     TO WS-TIME-N.
                 MOVE WS-TIME-N-HH    TO WS-TIME-E-HH.
                 MOVE WS-TIME-N-MM    TO WS-TIME-E-MM.
                 MOVE WS-TIME-E       TO TIMEO.
                 MOVE EIBTRMID        TO TERMIDO.
                 MOVE -1              TO FUNNOL.
                 MOVE SPACES          TO CA-EDIT-TAB.
                 MOVE 'ENTER DESIRED FUNCTION AND REQ/OPT FIELDS' TO MSGO.
                 MOVE 'A100'          TO CA-POS.
                 EXEC CICS SEND MAP('AXCU00') MAPSET('XXCU00')
                           ERASE CURSOR END-EXEC.
                 EXEC CICS RETURN TRANSID('CUST')
                                 COMMAREA(COMM-AREA)
                                 LENGTH(100)
                                 END-EXEC.
            A200-RECEIVE-MAP.
                 EXEC CICS RECEIVE MAP('AXCU00') MAPSET('XXCU00')
                           END-EXEC.
            *    EDIT ALL FOUR FIELDS
                 PERFORM B100-EDIT-INPUT-FIELDS THRU
                           B109-EDIT-INPUT-FIELDS-EXIT.
            *    CHECK IF ANY ERROR MSG DUE TO INVALID INPUT
            *    IF ALL INPUT OK, GO TO DESIRED PGM, OTHERWISE
            *    SEND ERROR SCREEN
                 IF MSGO NOT = LOW-VALUES
                      PERFORM B300-SEND-MAP-DATAONLY THRU
                           B309-SEND-MAP-DATAONLY-EXIT.
            *    CHECK TO SEE IF FUNCTION IS ALLOWED FOR THIS USER
                 PERFORM B500-CHECK-FUNC-SECURITY THRU
                           B509-CHECK-FUNC-SECURITY-EXIT.
            *    YES, SECURITY IS OK, LOG USER ACTIVITY IN TD QUEUE
                 PERFORM B600-WRITE-TD-Q THRU
                           B609-WRITE-TD-Q-EXIT.
                 PERFORM B200-XCTL-TO-PGM THRU
                           B209-XCTL-TO-PGM-EXIT.

            A850-RESET.
                 MOVE SPACES TO COMM-AREA.
                 GO TO A100-SEND-INIT-SCREEN.
            A899-EOJ.
                 MOVE 'TRANSACTION CUST COMPLETE, HIT CLEAR' TO WS-MSG.
                 EXEC CICS SEND FROM(WS-MSG) LENGTH(WS-MSG-LENG)
                           ERASE END-EXEC.
                 EXEC CICS RETURN END-EXEC.
            A900-NOTFND.
                 IF CA-POS = 'B140'
                      MOVE 'CUSTOMER NO NOT FOUND' TO MSGO
                      GO TO B144-BAD-CUSTNO.
```

```
                IF CA-POS = 'B180'
                    MOVE 'ORDER NO NOT FOUND' TO MSGO
                    GO TO B184-BAD-ORDRNO.
                GO TO A930-ERROR.
        A910-MAPFAIL.
                MOVE -1  TO FUNNOL.
                PERFORM B300-SEND-MAP-DATAONLY THRU
                    B309-SEND-MAP-DATAONLY-EXIT.
        *   WE'LL USE A COMMON ABEND-HANDLING PGM XCU13 TO
        *   PRINT ERROR MSG AND ABEND THE TASK, XCU13 IS SHOWN IN
        *   CHAPTER 13.15.
        A920-ERROR.
                EXEC CICS XCTL PROGRAM('XCU13')
                            COMMAREA(CA-POS)
                            LENGTH(4)
                            END-EXEC.


        B100-EDIT-INPUT-FIELDS.
                PERFORM B120-EDIT-FUNNO THRU
                    B129-EDIT-FUNNO-EXIT.
                PERFORM B140-EDIT-CUSTNO THRU
                    B149-EDIT-CUSTNO-EXIT.
                PERFORM B160-EDIT-CUSTNAM THRU
                    B169-EDIT-CUSTNAM-EXIT.
                PERFORM B180-EDIT-ORDRNO THRU
                    B189-EDIT-ORDRNO-EXIT.
        B109-EDIT-INPUT-FIELDS-EXIT. EXIT.


        B120-EDIT-FUNNO.
                IF FUNNOL NOT > 0
                    IF EDIT(1) = 'G'
                        GO TO B129-EDIT-FUNNO-EXIT
                    ELSE
                        MOVE 'FUNCTION NO IS REQUIRED' TO MSGO
                        MOVE ALL '?' TO FUNNOO
                        GO TO B124-BAD-FUNNO.
                IF FUNNOI NOT NUMERIC
                    MOVE 'FUNTION NO NOT NUMERIC' TO MSGO
                    GO TO B124-BAD-FUNNO.
                IF FUNNOI > '00' AND FUNNOI < '11'
                    MOVE 'G'     TO EDIT(1)
                    MOVE '&'     TO FUNNOA
                    MOVE FUNNOI TO CA-FUNNO
                    GO TO B129-EDIT-FUNNO-EXIT.
                MOVE 'INVALID FUNCTION NO' TO MSGO.
        B124-BAD-FUNNO.
                MOVE 'B' TO EDIT(1).
                MOVE 'R' TO FUNNOA.
                MOVE -1 TO FUNNOL.
        B129-EDIT-FUNNO-EXIT. EXIT.


        B140-EDIT-CUSTNO.
                IF CUSTNOL = 0
                    IF EDIT(2) = 'G'
                        GO TO B149-EDIT-CUSTNO-EXIT
                    ELSE
                        IF EDIT(1) = 'G' AND CA-FUNNO = 2
                            MOVE 'CUSTOMER NO IS REQUIRED' TO MSGO
                            MOVE ALL '?' TO CUSTNOO
                            GO TO B144-BAD-CUSTNO
                        ELSE
                            GO TO B149-EDIT-CUSTNO-EXIT.
                IF CUSTNOI NOT NUMERIC
                    MOVE 'CUSTOMER NO NOT NUMERIC' TO MSGO
                    GO TO B144-BAD-CUSTNO.
                MOVE 'B140' TO CA-POS.
                EXEC CICS READ DATASET('CUSTMST')
                            RIDFLD(CUSTNOI)
                            INTO(CUST-REC)
                            END-EXEC.
```

330

```
            MOVE 'G'      TO EDIT(2).
            MOVE '&'      TO CUSTNOA.
            MOVE CUSTNOI TO CA-CUSTNO.
            GO TO B149-EDIT-CUSTNO-EXIT.
        B144-BAD-CUSTNO.
            MOVE 'B'      TO EDIT(2).
            MOVE -1       TO CUSTNOL.
            MOVE 'R'      TO CUSTNOA.
        B149-EDIT-CUSTNO-EXIT. EXIT.

        B160-EDIT-CUSTNAM.
            IF CUSTNAML = 0
                IF EDIT(1) = 'G' AND CA-FUNNO = 3
                    MOVE 'CUSTOMER NAME IS REQUIRED FOR BROWSE' TO MSGO
                    GO TO B164-BAD-CUSTNAM
                ELSE
                    GO TO B169-EDIT-CUSTNAM-EXIT.
            MOVE 'G'      TO EDIT(3).
            MOVE ' '      TO CUSTNAMA.
            MOVE CUSTNAMI TO CA-CUSTNAM.
            GO TO B169-EDIT-CUSTNAM-EXIT.
        B164-BAD-CUSTNAM.
            MOVE 'I'      TO CUSTNAMA.
            MOVE -1       TO CUSTNAML.
            MOVE 'B'      TO EDIT(3).
            MOVE ALL '?'  TO CUSTNAMO.
        B169-EDIT-CUSTNAM-EXIT. EXIT.

        B180-EDIT-ORDRNO.
            IF ORDRNOL = 0
                IF EDIT(4) = 'G'
                    GO TO B189-EDIT-ORDRNO-EXIT
                ELSE
                    IF EDIT(1) = 'G' AND (CA-FUNNO = 4 OR 5 OR 6 OR 7
                        OR 8 OR 9)
                        MOVE 'ORDER NO IS REQUIRED' TO MSGO
                        MOVE ALL '?' TO ORDRNOO
                        GO TO B184-BAD-ORDRNO
                    ELSE
                        GO TO B189-EDIT-ORDRNO-EXIT.
            IF ORDRNOI NOT NUMERIC
                MOVE 'ORDER NO NOT NUMERIC' TO MSGO
                GO TO B184-BAD-ORDRNO.
            MOVE 'B180' TO CA-POS.
            EXEC CICS READ DATASET('ORDRHDR')
                            RIDFLD(ORDRNOI)
                            INTO(ORDRHDR-REC)
                            END-EXEC.
            MOVE 'G'      TO EDIT(4).
            MOVE '&'      TO ORDRNOA.
            MOVE ORDRNOI TO CA-ORDRNO.
            GO TO B189-EDIT-ORDRNO-EXIT.
        B184-BAD-ORDRNO.
            MOVE 'B'      TO EDIT(4).
            MOVE 'R'      TO ORDRNOA.
            MOVE -1       TO ORDRNOL.
        B189-EDIT-ORDRNO-EXIT. EXIT.

        B200-XCTL-TO-PGM.
            MOVE SPACES   TO XCTL-COMM-AREA.
            IF CA-FUNNO = 2
                MOVE CA-CUSTNO TO XCA-CUSTNO.
            IF CA-FUNNO = 3
                MOVE CA-CUSTNAM TO XCA-CUSTNAM.
            IF CA-FUNNO = 4 OR 5 OR 6 OR 7 OR 8 OR 9
                MOVE CA-ORDRNO TO XCA-ORDRNO.
        *   FUNNO = 1, ADD NEW CUSTOMER XCU01
            IF CA-FUNNO = 1
                EXEC CICS XCTL PROGRAM('XCU01')
                            COMMAREA(XCTL-COMM-AREA)
```

```
                             LENGTH(100)
                             END-EXEC.
     *    FUNNO = 2, INQUIRE/UPDATE/DELETE A CUSTOMER
          IF CA-FUNNO = 2
              EXEC CICS XCTL PROGRAM('XCU02')
                             COMMAREA(XCTL-COMM-AREA)
                             LENGTH(100)
                             END-EXEC.
     *    FUNNO = 3, BROWSE CUSTOMERS BY NAME
          IF CA-FUNNO = 3
              MOVE XCTL-COMM-AREA TO XCTL-XCU03
              EXEC CICS XCTL PROGRAM('XCU03')
                             COMMAREA(XCTL-XCU03)
                             LENGTH(1100)
                             END-EXEC.
     *    FUNNO = 8, CREATE SALES ORDER DETAILS
          IF CA-FUNNO = 8
              MOVE XCTL-COMM-AREA TO XCTL-XCU08
              EXEC CICS XCTL PROGRAM('XCU08')
                             COMMAREA(XCTL-XCU08)
                             LENGTH(400)
                             END-EXEC.
     *    FUNNO = 9, REVIEW/UPDATE/CREATE SALES ORDER DETAILS
          IF CA-FUNNO = 9
              MOVE XCTL-COMM-AREA   TO XCTL-XCU08
              EXEC CICS XCTL PROGRAM('XCU09')
                             COMMAREA(XCTL-XCU08)
                             LENGTH(400)
                             END-EXEC.
          IF CA-FUNNO = 10
              EXEC CICS LINK PROGRAM('XCU10') END-EXEC
              MOVE 'JOB SUBMITTED' TO MSGO
              GO TO B204-SEND-MSG.

     *    FUNNO = 4, PRINT SALES ORDER 24x80
          IF CA-FUNNO = 4
              EXEC CICS START TRANSID('CU04')
                              FROM(CA-ORDRNO)
                              LENGTH(CA-ORDRNO-LENG)
                              END-EXEC
              GO TO B202-SEND-MSG.
     *    FUNNO = 5, PRINT SALES ORDER 24x80 USING OVERFLOW
          IF CA-FUNNO = 5
              EXEC CICS START TRANSID('CU05')
                              FROM(CA-ORDRNO)
                              LENGTH(CA-ORDRNO-LENG)
                              END-EXEC
              GO TO B202-SEND-MSG.
     *    FUNNO=6, PRINT SALES ORDER 66x132
          IF CA-FUNNO = 6
              EXEC CICS START TRANSID('CU06')
                              FROM(CA-ORDRNO)
                              LENGTH(CA-ORDRNO-LENG)
                              END-EXEC
              GO TO B202-SEND-MSG.
     *    MUST BE FUNNO = 7, PRINT 66x85 REPORT
          EXEC CICS LINK PROGRAM('XCU07')
                         FROM(XCTL-COMM-AREA)
                         LENGTH(100)
                         END-EXEC.
 B202-SEND-MSG.
      MOVE 'SALES ORDER PRINT COMPELETED' TO MSGO.
 B204-SEND-MSG.
      MOVE -1                              TO FUNNOL.
      PERFORM B300-SEND-MAP-DATAONLY THRU
              B309-SEND-MAP-DATAONLY-EXIT.
 B209-XCTL-TO-PGM-EXIT. EXIT.

 B300-SEND-MAP-DATAONLY.
      MOVE 'B300' TO CA-POS.
```

```
          EXEC CICS SEND MAP('AXCU00') MAPSET('XXCU00')
                          DATAONLY CURSOR END-EXEC.
          EXEC CICS RETURN TRANSID('CUST')
                          COMMAREA(COMM-AREA)
                          LENGTH(100)
                          END-EXEC.
     B309-SEND-MAP-DATAONLY-EXIT. EXIT.

     B400-CK-SYSTEM-SECURITY.
          EXEC CICS ASSIGN OPID(WS-OPID) END-EXEC.
          IF WS-OPID = 'LEE' OR 'DFG' OR 'HFG' OR 'XCL'
             NEXT SENTENCE
          ELSE
             MOVE 'SECURITY VIOLATION' TO WS-MSG
             EXEC CICS SEND FROM(WS-MSG) LENGTH(WS-MSG-LENG)
                          ERASE END-EXEC
             EXEC CICS RETUTN END-EXEC.
     B409-CK-SYSTEM-SECURITY-EXIT. EXIT.

     B500-CHECK-FUNC-SECURITY.
          EXEC CICS ASSIGN OPID(WS-OPID) END-EXEC.
          IF CA-FUNNO = 3 AND WS-OPID NOT = 'LEE'
             MOVE 'YOU ARE NOT ALLOWED TO BROWSE/UPDATE CUSTOMERS'
                     TO MSGO
             MOVE -1 TO FUNNOL
             PERFORM B300-SEND-MAP-DATAONLY THRU
                     B309-SEND-MAP-DATAONLY-EXIT.
     B500-CHECK-FUNC-SECURITY-EXIT. EXIT.

     B600-WRITE-TD-Q.
          MOVE SPACES       TO TDQ-REC.
          MOVE WS-OPID       TO TDQ-OPID.
          MOVE EIBTRMID      TO TDQ-TERMID.
          MOVE CURRENT-DATE TO TDQ-DATE.
          MOVE TIME-OF-DAY   TO TDQ-TIME.
          MOVE CA-FUNNO      TO TDQ-FUNNO.
          EXEC CICS WRITEQ TD QUEUE('SECR')
                          FROM(TDQ-REC)
                          LENGTH(TDQ-LENG)
                          END-EXEC.
     B609-WRITE-TD-Q-EXIT. EXIT.
```

13.3.   Create A New Customer

Program ID: XCU01   Transaction ID: CU01   Mapset: XXCU01

This CICS program is invoked when function number 1 was entered on the menu screen. The menu program will issue an XCTL command to invoke this Customer Add program. When this Add program is invoked, it will issue a SEND MAP command with the ERASE option to send a blank customer screen. After the blank customer screen has been sent, it will then issue a RETURN command with the TRANSID option. This will terminate this Add program and post its transaction code (CU01) on this terminal. Any response to this terminal will initiate this transaction code which in turn will invoke this Add program again.

After the initial screen has been displayed, the user can then enters the key (customer number) and all data fields and then hit ENTER key. This will invoke the Add program again since we have post its transaction code on this terminal. After the Add program is invoked again, it should go to issue a RECEIVE MAP command to receive the input data into the symbolic description map (map I/O area). You should always go to issue a RECEIVE MAP command when this program is not invoked by the menu program.

After you have edited the input data received, you should issue a SEND MAP command with the DATAONLY option if any input data is invalid. Every time you issue a SEND MAP command, you should always issue a RETURN command with TRANSID option. This technique is called pseudo conversational programming. After the error map has been displayed, the user can then correct the invalid fields and then hit ENTER key to invoke this program again.

If all input fields are valid, you should issue a WRITE command to create the new customer record in the customer file. After the record is created, you should send a message saying that the customer has been created sucessfully to the terminal and then issue a RETURN command with the TRANSID option.

After the user has seen the create completion message, he can either hit CLEAR key to go back to the menu screen or hit PF1 to reset the current screen. If PF1 is hit, you should go to display a blank customer entry screen for the user to enter the next new customer. Therefore, the user does not have to go back to the menu screen in order to add the next customer. This kind of design is very common in data entry online applications.

Screen Layout:

```
CU01  XX/XX/XX HH:MM    ADD A NEW CUSTOMER                          XXXX

CUSTOMER NO  : 99999

CUSTOMER NAME: XXXXXXXXXXXXXXXXXXXX

CREDIT LIMIT : 9999999

INVOICE AMT  : 9999999


CLEAR=MENU, PF1=RESET
XXXXXXXXXXXXXXXXXXXXXXXXXXXXXXXXXXXXXXXXXXXXXXXXXXXXXXXXXXXXXXXXXXXXXXXXXXXXXXXXX
```

CICS Mapset XXCU01:

```
XXCU01   DFHMSD TYPE=&SYSPARM,LANG=COBOL,TIOAPFX=YES,MODE=INOUT,        X
                STORAGE=AUTO,CTRL=(FREEKB,FRSET),TERM=3270,DATA=FIELD
AXCU01   DFHMDI SIZE=(24,80)
         DFHMDF POS=(01,01),LENGTH=04,INITIAL='CU01'
DATE     DFHMDF POS=(01,07),LENGTH=08
TIME     DFHMDF POS=(01,16),LENGTH=05
         DFHMDF POS=(01,25),LENGTH=18,INITIAL='ADD A NEW CUSTOMER'
TERMID   DFHMDF POS=(01,66),LENGTH=04
         DFHMDF POS=(03,01),LENGTH=14,INITIAL='CUSTOMER NO  :'
CUSTNO   DFHMDF POS=(03,16),LENGTH=05,ATTRB=NUM
         DFHMDF POS=(03,22),LENGTH=01
         DFHMDF POS=(05,01),LENGTH=14,INITIAL='CUSTOMER NAME:'
CUSTNAM  DFHMDF POS=(05,16),LENGTH=20,ATTRB=UNPROT
         DFHMDF POS=(05,37),LENGTH=01
         DFHMDF POS=(07,01),LENGTH=14,INITIAL='CREDIT LIMIT :'
CRDLMT   DFHMDF POS=(07,16),LENGTH=07,ATTRB=NUM
         DFHMDF POS=(07,24),LENGTH=01
         DFHMDF POS=(09,01),LENGTH=14,INITIAL='INVOICE AMT  :'
INVAMT   DFHMDF POS=(09,16),LENGTH=07,ATTRB=NUM,PICIN='99999V99'
         DFHMDF POS=(09,24),LENGTH=01
         DFHMDF POS=(12,01),LENGTH=21,INITIAL='CLEAR=MENU, PF1=RESET', X
                ATTRB=(ASKIP,BRT)
MSG      DFHMDF POS=(13,01),LENGTH=78,ATTRB=(ASKIP,BRT)
         DFHMSD TYPE=FINAL
         END
```

CICS Program XCU01:

```
ID DIVISION.
PROGRAM-ID. XCU01.
REMARKS. ADD A NEW CUSTOMER.
ENVIRONMENT DIVISION.
DATA DIVISION.
WORKING-STORAGE SECTION.
01   COMM-AREA.
     02   CA-CUSTNO      PIC 9(5).
     02   CA-CUSTNAM     PIC X(20).
     02   CA-CRDLMT      PIC 9(7).
     02   CA-INVAMT      PIC S9(5)V99 COMP-3.
     02   CA-EDIT-TAB.
          03   EDIT      PIC X(1) OCCURS 4.
     02   CA-POS         PIC X(4).
     02   FILLER         PIC X(56).
01   XCTL-COMM-AREA      PIC X(100).
01   WS-MSG              PIC X(60).
01   WS-MSG-LENG         PIC S9(4) COMP VALUE +60.
01   CUST-REC.
     02   CUST-ALT-KEY.
          03   CUST-NAME      PIC X(20).
          03   CUST-PRIMARY-KEY.
               04   CUST-NO   PIC 9(5).
     02   CUST-CRDLMT         PIC 9(7).
     02   CUST-INVAMT         PIC S9(5)V99 COMP-3.
01   AXCU01I             COPY XXCU01.
01   WS-TIME-N           PIC 9(6).
01   FILLER REDEFINES WS-TIME-N.
     02   WS-TIME-N-HH   PIC 9(2).
     02   WS-TIME-N-MM   PIC 9(2).
     02   FILLER         PIC 9(2).
01   WS-TIME-E.
     02   WS-TIME-E-HH   PIC 9(2).
     02   FILLER         PIC X(1) VALUE ':'.
     02   WS-TIME-E-MM   PIC 9(2).
LINKAGE SECTION.
01   DFHCOMMAREA         PIC X(100).
PROCEDURE DIVISION.
     EXEC CICS HANDLE CONDITION
               NOTFND(A900-NOTFND)
               MAPFAIL(A910-MAPFAIL)
               ERROR(A920-ERROR)
               END-EXEC.
     EXEC CICS HANDLE AID
               CLEAR(A899-XCTL-MENU)
               PF1(A850-RESET)
               ANYKEY(A910-MAPFAIL)
               END-EXEC.
     IF EIBTRNID = 'CU01' AND EIBCALEN = 100
        MOVE DFHCOMMAREA TO COMM-AREA
        GO TO A200-RECEIVE-MAP.
*    TO PREVENT USER FROM ENTERING CU01 TO INVOKE THIS PGM
     IF EIBTRNID = 'CU01'
        MOVE 'SECURITY VIOLATION' TO WS-MSG
        EXEC CICS SEND FROM(WS-MSG) LENGTH(WS-MSG-LENG)
             ERASE END-EXEC
        EXEC CICS RETURN END-EXEC.
A100-SEND-INIT-SCREEN.
     MOVE LOW-VALUES    TO AXCU01O.
     MOVE EIBTRMID      TO TERMIDO.
     MOVE CURRENT-DATE  TO DATEO.
     MOVE TIME-OF-DAY   TO WS-TIME-N.
     MOVE WS-TIME-N-HH  TO WS-TIME-E-HH.
     MOVE WS-TIME-N-MM  TO WS-TIME-E-MM.
     MOVE WS-TIME-E     TO TIMEO.
     MOVE 'ENTER NEW CUSTOMER, THEN HIT ENTER' TO MSGO.
     MOVE -1            TO CUSTNOL.
```

```
                MOVE SPACES        TO COMM-AREA.
                EXEC CICS SEND MAP('AXCU01') MAPSET('XXCU01')
                          ERASE CURSOR END-EXEC.
                EXEC CICS RETURN TRANSID('CU01')
                               COMMAREA(COMM-AREA)
                               LENGTH(100)
                               END-EXEC.
        A200-RECEIVE-MAP.
                EXEC CICS RECEIVE MAP('AXCU01') MAPSET('XXCU01')
                          END-EXEC.
                PERFORM B100-EDIT-INPUT-FIELDS THRU
                        B109-EDIT-INPUT-FIELDS-EXIT.
        *    IF ANY INVALID INPUT FIELD, SEND ERROR MAP
                IF MSGO NOT = LOW-VALUES
                    PERFORM B300-SEND-MAP-DATAONLY THRU
                            B309-SEND-MAP-DATAONLY-EXIT.
                PERFORM B200-WRITE-CUSTOMER THRU
                        B209-WRITE-CUSTOMER-EXIT.
                MOVE -1 TO CUSTNOL.
                MOVE 'CUSTOMER ADDED SUCCESSFULLY' TO MSGO.
                PERFORM B300-SEND-MAP-DATAONLY THRU
                        B309-SEND-MAP-DATAONLY-EXIT.
        A850-RESET.
                GO TO A100-SEND-INIT-SCREEN.
        A899-XCTL-MENU.
                MOVE SPACES TO XCTL-COMM-AREA.
                EXEC CICS XCTL PROGRAM('XCU00')
                               COMMAREA(XCTL-COMM-AREA)
                               LENGTH(100)
                               END-EXEC.
        A900-NOTFND.
                IF CA-POS = 'B120'
                    GO TO B122-GOOD-CUSTNO.
                GO TO A920-ERROR.
        A910-MAPFAIL.
                MOVE -1 TO CUSTNOL.
                PERFORM B300-SEND-MAP-DATAONLY THRU
                        B309-SEND-MAP-DATAONLY-EXIT.
        A920-ERROR.
        *    XCTL TO ABEND-HANDLING PGM OR YOU CAN JUST ISSUE AN ABEND
        *    EXEC CICS ABEND ABCODE('CU01') END-EXEC.
                EXEC CICS XCTL PROGRAM('XCU13')
                               COMMAREA(CA-POS)
                               LENGTH(4)
                               END-EXEC.

        B100-EDIT-INPUT-FIELDS.
                PERFORM B120-EDIT-CUSTNO THRU
                        B129-EDIT-CUSTNO-EXIT.
                PERFORM B140-EDIT-CUSTNAM THRU
                        B149-EDIT-CUSTNAM-EXIT.
                PERFORM B160-EDIT-CRDLMT THRU
                        B169-EDIT-CRDLMT-EXIT.
                PERFORM B180-EDIT-INVAMT THRU
                        B189-EDIT-INVAMT-EXIT.
        B109-EDIT-INPUT-EXIT. EXIT.

        B120-EDIT-CUSTNO.
                IF CUSTNOL = 0
                    IF EDIT(1) = 'G'
                        GO TO B129-EDIT-CUSTNO-EXIT
                    ELSE
                        MOVE 'CUSTOMER NO MUST BE ENTERED' TO MSGO
                        MOVE ALL '?' TO CUSTNOO
                        GO TO B124-BAD-CUSTNO.
                IF CUSTNOI NOT NUMERIC
                    MOVE 'CUSTOMER NO NOT NUMERIC' TO MSGO
                    GO TO B124-BAD-CUSTNO.
                MOVE 'B120' TO CA-POS.
                EXEC CICS READ DATASET('CUSTMST')
```

```
                    RIDFLD(CUSTNOI)
                    INTO(CUST-REC)
                    END-EXEC.
        MOVE 'CUSTOMER NO ALREADY EXISTS' TO MSGO.
        GO TO B124-BAD-CUSTNO.
    B122-GOOD-CUSTNO.
        MOVE 'G'       TO EDIT(1).
        MOVE '&'       TO CUSTNOA.
        MOVE CUSTNOI TO CA-CUSTNO.
        GO TO B129-EDIT-CUSTNO-EXIT.
    B124-BAD-CUSTNO.
        MOVE 'R'       TO CUSTNOA.
        MOVE -1        TO CUSTNOL.
        MOVE 'B'       TO EDIT(1).
    B129-EDIT-CUSTNO-EXIT. EXIT.

    B140-EDIT-CUSTNAM.
        IF CUSTNAML = 0
           IF EDIT(2) = 'G'
              GO TO B149-EDIT-CUSTNAM-EXIT
           ELSE
              MOVE 'CUSTOMER NAME IS REQUIRED' TO MSGO
              MOVE ALL '?' TO CUSTNAMO
              GO TO B144-BAD-CUSTNAM.
        MOVE 'G'       TO EDIT(2).
        MOVE ' '       TO CUSTNAMA.
        MOVE CUSTNAMI TO CA-CUSTNAM.
        GO TO B149-EDIT-CUSTNAM-EXIT.
    B144-BAD-CUSTNAM.
        MOVE 'B' TO EDIT(2).
        MOVE 'I' TO CUSTNAMA.
        MOVE -1  TO CUSTNAML.
    B149-EDIT-CUSTNAM-EXIT. EXIT.

    B160-EDIT-CRDLMT.
        IF CRDLMTL = 0
           IF EDIT(3) = 'G'
              GO TO B169-EDIT-CRDLMT-EXIT
           ELSE
              MOVE 'CREDIT LIMIT IS REQUIRED' TO MSGO
              MOVE ALL '?' TO CRDLMTO
              GO TO B164-BAD-CRDLMT.
        IF CRDLMTI NOT NUMERIC
           MOVE 'CREDIT LIMIT IS NOT NUMERIC' TO MSGO
           GO TO B164-BAD-CRDLMT.
        MOVE 'G'       TO EDIT(3).
        MOVE '&'       TO CRDLMTA.
        MOVE CRDLMTI   TO CA-CRDLMT.
        GO TO B169-EDIT-CRDLMT-EXIT.
    B164-BAD-CRDLMT.
        MOVE 'B' TO EDIT(3).
        MOVE 'R' TO CRDLMTA.
        MOVE -1  TO CRDLMTL.
    B169-EDIT-CRDLMT-EXIT. EXIT.

    B180-EDIT-INVAMT.
        IF INVAMTL = 0
           IF EDIT(4) = 'G'
              GO TO B189-EDIT-INVAMT-EXIT
           ELSE
              MOVE 'INVOICE AMT IS REQUIRED' TO MSGO
              MOVE ALL '?' TO INVAMTO
              GO TO B184-BAD-INVAMT.
        IF INVAMTI NOT NUMERIC
           MOVE 'INVOICE AMT NOT NUMERIC' TO MSGO
           GO TO B184-BAD-INVAMT.
        MOVE 'G'       TO EDIT(4).
        MOVE '&'       TO INVAMTA.
        MOVE INVAMTI   TO CA-INVAMT.
        GO TO B189-EDIT-INVAMT-EXIT.
```

```
B184-BAD-INVAMT.
    MOVE 'B' TO EDIT(4).
    MOVE 'R' TO INVAMTA.
    MOVE -1  TO INVAMTL.
B189-EDIT-INVAMT-EXIT. EXIT.

B200-WRITE-CUSTOMER.
    MOVE SPACES         TO CUST-REC.
    MOVE CA-CUSTNO      TO CUST-NO.
    MOVE CA-CUSTNAM     TO CUST-NAME.
    MOVE CA-CRDLMT      TO CUST-CRDLMT.
    MOVE CA-INVAMT      TO CUST-INVAMT.
    MOVE 'B200'         TO CA-POS.
    EXEC CICS WRITE DATASET('CUSTMST')
                    FROM(CUST-REC)
                    RIDFLD(CUST-NO)
                    END-EXEC.
B209-WRITE-CUSTOMER-EXIT. EXIT.

B300-SEND-MAP-DATAONLY.
    MOVE 'B300'         TO CA-POS.
    EXEC CICS SEND MAP('AXCU01') MAPSET('XXCU01')
                    DATAONLY CURSOR END-EXEC.
    EXEC CICS RETURN TRANSID('CU01')
                    COMMAREA(COMM-AREA)
                    LENGTH(100)
                    END-EXEC.
B309-SEND-MAP-DATAONLY-EXIT. EXIT.
```

13.4   Inquire/Update/Delete A Customer

Program: XCU02   Mapset: XXCU02   Transaction: CU02
CU02 and XCU02 are specified in the PCT.

This program is used to demonstrate how to code an Inquire/Update/Delete CICS program. After function number 2 and a valid customer number have been entered on the menu screen, the menu program (XCU00) will issue an XCTL command to transfer the control to this Inquire/Update/Delete program (XCU02). After this program is invoked, it will use the customer number passed from the menu program in DFHCOMMAREA of LINKAGE SECTION to read the customer in the customer file. After the customer has been retrieved, it will move this customer to the map I/O area and then issue a SEND MAP command with ERASE option to display the customer on the terminal. After the customer has been displayed, this program will then issue a RETURN command with TRANSID option to terminate itself and post its transaction code (CU02) on this terminal. Any response to this terminal will initiate this transaction which in turn will invoke this Inquire/Update/Delete program again.

After the customer has been displayed, the user can then take one of the following actions:

1. Go back to the menu screen by pressing the CLEAR key.

2. Update the customer and the hit ENTER key.

3. Delete the customer by pressing PF1 key.

4. Enter the next customer to be processed on the next customer number field and

then hit ENTER key. This program will then display the next customer for inquiry, update or delete.

If updates have been made and all updates are valid, this program will issue a READ command with the UPDATE option to retrieve the record to be updated, move updates to the record I/O area, and then issue a REWRITE command to update the record.

If PF1 has been pressed, this program should issue a DELETE command with the RIDFLD option to delete the customer.

If the next customer number has been entered, you should use this new customer number to display that customer just like you get the customer number from the menu program.

Screen Layout:

```
CU02  XX/XX/XX HH:MM    INQUIRE/UPDATE/DELETE A CUSTOMER      XXXX

CUSTOMER NO  :'99999

CUSTOMER NAME: XXXXXXXXXXXXXXXXXXXX

CREDIT LIMIT : 9999999

INVOICE AMT  : 9999999


                            NEXT CUSTOMER NO: 99999

CLEAR=MENU, PF1=DELETE
XXXXXXXXXXXXXXXXXXXXXXXXXXXXXXXXXXXXXXXXXXXXXXXXXXXXXXXXXXXXXXXXXXXXXXXXXXXXXXXX
```

CICS Mapset: XXCU02

```
XXCU02   DFHMSD TYPE=&SYSPARM,LANG=COBOL,TIOAPFX=YES,MODE=INOUT,       X
             STORAGE=AUTO,CTRL=(FREEKB,FRSET),TERM=3270,DATA=FIELD
AXCU02   DFHMDI SIZE=(24,80)
         DFHMDF POS=(01,01),LENGTH=04,INITIAL='CU02'
DATE     DFHMDF POS=(01,07),LENGTH=08
TIME     DFHMDF POS=(01,16),LENGTH=05
         DFHMDF POS=(01,25),LENGTH=32,INITIAL='INQUIRE/UPDATE/DELETE A X
             CUSTOMER'
TERMID   DFHMDF POS=(01,66),LENGTH=4
         DFHMDF POS=(03,01),LENGTH=14,INITIAL='CUSTOMER NO  :'
CUSTNO   DFHMDF POS=(03,16),LENGTH=05
         DFHMDF POS=(05,01),LENGTH=14,INITIAL='CUSTOMER NAME:'
CUSTNAM  DFHMDF POS=(05,16),LENGTH=20,ATTRB=UNPROT
         DFHMDF POS=(05,37),LENGTH=01
         DFHMDF POS=(07,01),LENGTH=14,INITIAL='CREDIT LIMIT :'
CRDLMT   DFHMDF POS=(07,16),LENGTH=07,ATTRB=NUM
         DFHMDF POS=(07,24),LENGTH=01
         DFHMDF POS=(09,01),LENGTH=14,INITIAL='INVOICE AMT  :'
INVAMT   DFHMDF POS=(09,16),LENGTH=07,ATTRB=NUM,PICIN='99999V99'
         DFHMDF POS=(12,40),LENGTH=17,INITIAL='NEXT CUSTOMER NO:'
NXTCUST  DFHMDF POS=(12,58),LENGTH=05,ATTRB=NUM
         DFHMDF POS=(12,64),LENGTH=01
         DFHMDF POS=(14,01),LENGTH=22,INITIAL='CLEAR=MENU, PF1=DELETE',X
             ATTRB=(ASKIP,BRT)
MSG      DFHMDF POS=(15,01),LENGTH=78,ATTRB=(ASKIP,BRT)
         DFHMSD TYPE=FINAL
         END
```

```
       ID DIVISION.
       PROGRAM-ID. XCU02.
       REMARKS. INQUIRE/UPDATE/DELETE A CUSTOMER.
       ENVIRONMENT DIVISION.
       DATA DIVISION.
       WORKING-STORAGE SECTION.
       01  COMM-AREA.
           02  CA-CUSTNO          PIC 9(5).
           02  CA-CUSTNAM         PIC X(20).
           02  CA-CRDLMT          PIC 9(7).
           02  CA-INVAMT          PIC S9(5)V99 COMP-3.
           02  CA-NXTCUST         PIC 9(5).
           02  CA-EDIT-TAB.
               03  EDIT           PIC X(1) OCCURS 4.
           02  CA-POS             PIC X(4).
           02  FILLER             PIC X(51).
       01  XCTL-COMM-AREA         PIC X(100).
       01  WS-MSG                 PIC X(60).
       01  WS-MSG-LENG            PIC S9(4) COMP VALUE +60.
       01  CUST-REC.
           02  CUST-ALT-KEY.
               03  CUST-NAME      PIC X(20).
               03  CUST-PRIMARY-KEY.
                   03  CUST-NO PIC 9(5).
           02  CUST-CRDLMT        PIC 9(7).
           02  CUST-INVAMT        PIC S9(5)V99 COMP-3.
       01  AXCU02I                COPY XXCU02.
       01  WS-TIME-N              PIC 9(6).
       01  FILLER REDEFINES WS-TIME-N.
           02  WS-TIME-N-HH       PIC 9(2).
           02  WS-TIME-N-MM       PIC 9(2).
           02  FILLER             PIC 9(2).
       01  WS-TIME-E.
           02  WS-TIME-E-HH       PIC 9(2).
           02  FILLER             PIC X(1) VALUE ':'.
           02  WS-TIME-E-MM       PIC 9(2).
       01  WS-INVAMT-E            PIC 9(5).99.
       LINKAGE SECTION.
       01  DFHCOMMAREA            PIC X(100).
       PROCEDURE DIVISION.
           EXEC CICS HANDLE CONDITION
                   NOTFND(A900-NOTFND)
                   MAPFAIL(A910-MAPFAIL)
                   ERROR(A920-ERROR)
                   END-EXEC.
           EXEC CICS HANDLE AID
                   CLEAR(A899-XCTL-MENU)
                   PF1(A850-DELETE-CUSTOMER)
                   ANYKEY(A910-MAPFAIL)
                   END-EXEC.
           MOVE DFHCOMMAREA    TO COMM-AREA.
           IF EIBTRNID = 'CU02' AND EIBCALEN = 100
              GO TO A200-RECEIVE-MAP.
           IF EIBTRNID = 'CU02'
              MOVE 'SECURITY VIOLATION' TO WS-MSG
              EXEC CICS SEND FROM(WS-MSG) LENGTH(WS-MSG-LENG)
                   ERASE END-EXEC.
           EXEC CICS RETURN END-EXEC.
       A100-SEND-INIT-SCREEN.
           MOVE LOW-VALUES      TO AXCU02O.
           MOVE EIBTRMID        TO TERMIDO.
           MOVE CURRENT-DATE    TO DATEO.
           MOVE TIME-OF-DAY     TO WS-TIME-N.
           MOVE WS-TIME-N-HH    TO WS-TIME-E-HH.
           MOVE WS-TIME-N-MM    TO WS-TIME-E-MM.
           MOVE WS-TIME-E       TO TIMEO.
       *   READ CUSTOMER
```

```
            MOVE 'A100'          TO CA-POS.
            EXEC CICS READ DATASET('CUSTMST')
                          RIDFLD(CA-CUSTNO)
                          INTO(CUST-REC)
                          END-EXEC.
            MOVE CA-CUSTNO       TO CUSTNOO.
            MOVE CUST-NAME       TO CUSTNAMO.
            MOVE CUST-CRDLMT      TO CRDLMTO.
            MOVE CUST-INVAMT      TO WS-INVAMT-E.
            MOVE WS-INVAMT-E      TO INVAMTO.
            MOVE -1              TO CUSTNAML.
            MOVE 'UPDATE DESIRED FIELDS, THEN HIT ENTER' TO MSGO.
            MOVE SPACES          TO CA-EDIT-TAB.
            EXEC CICS SEND MAP('AXCU02') MAPSET('XXCU02')
                    ERASE CURSOR END-EXEC.
            EXEC CICS RETURN TRANSID('CU02')
                          COMMAREA(COMM-AREA)
                          LENGTH(100)
                          END-EXEC.
        A200-RECEIVE-MAP.
            EXEC CICS RECEIVE MAP('AXCU02') MAPSET('XXCU02')
                    END-EXEC.
            PERFORM B100-EDIT-INPUT-FIELDS THRU
                    B109-EDIT-INPUT-FIELDS-EXIT.
      *     CHECK ANY INVALID INPUT FIELD
            IF MSGO NOT = LOW-VALUES
                PERFORM B300-SEND-MAP-DATAONLY THRU
                        B309-SEND-MAP-DATAONLY-EXIT.
      *     CHECK ANY UPDATE MADE
            IF EDIT(1) = 'G' OR EDIT(2) = 'G' OR EDIT(3) = 'G'
                PERFORM B200-UPDATE-CUSTOMER THRU
                        B209-UPDATE-CUSTOMER-EXIT.
      *     NEXT CUSTOMER NUMBER ENTERED ?
            IF EDIT(4) = ' '
                MOVE 'UPDATE COMPLETE SUCCESSFULLY' TO MSGO
                MOVE -1 TO NXTCUSTL
                PERFORM B300-SEND-MAP-DATAONLY THRU
                        B309-SEND-MAP-DATAONLY-EXIT.
      *     DISPLAY NEXT CUSTOMER
            MOVE CA-NXTCUST      TO CA-CUSTNO.
            GO TO A100-SEND-INIT-SCREEN.
        A850-DELETE-CUSTOMER.
            MOVE 'A850' TO CA-POS.
            EXEC CICS DELETE DATASET('CUSTMST')
                          RIDFLD(CA-CUSTNO)
                          END-EXEC.
            MOVE 'CUSTOMER DELETED' TO MSGO.
            MOVE -1  TO NXTCUSTL.
            PERFORM B300-SEND-MAP-DATAONLY THRU
                    B309-SEND-MAP-DATAONLY-EXIT.
        A899-XCTL-MENU.
            MOVE SPACES TO XCTL-COMM-AREA.
            EXEC CICS XCTL PROGRAM('XCU00')
                          COMMAREA(XCTL-COMM-AREA)
                          LENGTH(100)
                          END-EXEC.
        A900-NOTFND.
            IF CA-POS = 'B180'
                MOVE 'NEXT CUSTOMER# NOT EXISTS' TO MSGO
                GO TO B184-BAD-NXTCUST.
            GO TO A920-ERROR.
        A910-MAPFAIL.
            MOVE -1  TO CUSTNAML.
            PERFORM B300-SEND-MAP-DATAONLY THRU
                    B309-SEND-MAP-DATAONLY-EXIT.
        A920-ERROR.
            EXEC CICS XCTL PROGRAM('XCU13')
                          COMMAREA(CA-POS)
                          LENGTH(4)
                          END-EXEC.
```

```
B100-EDIT-INPUT-FIELDS.
    PERFORM B120-EDIT-CUSTNAM THRU
            B129-EDIT-CUSTNAM-EXIT.
    PERFORM B140-EDIT-CRDLMT THRU
            B149-EDIT-CRDLMT-EXIT.
    PERFORM B160-EDIT-INVAMT THRU
            B169-EDIT-INVAMT-EXIT.
    PERFORM B180-EDIT-NXTCUST THRU
            B189-EDIT-NXTCUST-EXIT.
B109-EDIT-INPUT-FIELDS-EXIT. EXIT.

B120-EDIT-CUSTNAM.
    IF CUSTNAML = 0
        GO TO B129-EDIT-CUSTNAM-EXIT.
    MOVE 'G'        TO EDIT(1).
    MOVE ' '        TO CUSTNAMA.
    MOVE CUSTNAMI TO CA-CUSTNAM.
B129-EDIT-CUSTNAM-EXIT. EXIT.

B140-EDIT-CRDLMT.
    IF CRDLMTL = 0
        GO TO B149-EDIT-CRDLMT-EXIT.
    IF CRDLMTI NOT NUMERIC
        MOVE 'CREDIT LIMIT NOT NUMERIC' TO MSGO
        GO TO B144-BAD-CRDLMT.
    MOVE CRDLMTI TO CA-CRDLMT.
    MOVE 'G'        TO EDIT(2).
    MOVE '&'        TO CRDLMTA.
    GO TO B149-EDIT-CRDLMT-EXIT.
B144-BAD-CRDLMT.
    MOVE 'B' TO EDIT(2).
    MOVE 'R' TO CRDLMTA.
    MOVE -1  TO CRDLMTL.
B149-EDIT-CRDLMT-EXIT. EXIT.

B160-EDIT-INVAMT.
    IF INVAMTL = 0
        GO TO B169-EDIT-INVAMT-EXIT.
    IF INVAMTI NOT NUMERIC
        MOVE 'INVOICE AMT NOT NUMERIC' TO MSGO
        MOVE 'B'    TO EDIT(3)
        MOVE 'R'    TO INVAMTA
        MOVE -1     TO INVAMTL
        GO TO B169-EDIT-INVAMT-EXIT.
    MOVE 'G'        TO EDIT(3).
    MOVE '&'        TO INVAMTA.
    MOVE INVAMTI TO CA-INVAMT.
B169-EDIT-INVAMT-EXIT. EXIT.

B180-EDIT-NXTCUST.
    IF NXTCUSTL = 0
        GO TO B189-EDIT-NXTCUST-EXIT.
    IF NXTCUSTI NOT NUMERIC
        MOVE 'NEXT CUSTOMER NO NOT NUMERIC' TO MSGO
        GO TO B184-BAD-NXTCUST.
    MOVE 'B180' TO CA-POS.
    EXEC CICS READ DATASET('CUSTMST')
                   RIDFLD(NXTCUSTI)
                   INTO(CUST-REC)
                   END-EXEC.
    MOVE 'G'        TO EDIT(4).
    MOVE '&'        TO NXTCUSTA.
    MOVE NXTCUSTI   TO CA-NXTCUST.
    GO TO B189-EDIT-NXTCUST-EXIT.
B184-BAD-NXTCUST.
    MOVE 'B' TO EDIT(4).
    MOVE 'R' TO NXTCUSTA.
    MOVE -1  TO NXTCUSTL.
B189-EDIT-NXTCUST-EXIT. EXIT.
```

```
        B200-UPDATE-CUSTOMER.
            MOVE 'B200' TO CA-POS.
            EXEC CICS READ DATASET('CUSTMST')
                           RIDFLD(CA-CUSTNO)
                           INTO(CUST-REC)
                           UPDATE
                           END-EXEC.
            IF EDIT(1) = 'G'
                MOVE CA-CUSTNAM TO CUST-NAME.
            IF EDIT(2) = 'G'
                MOVE CA-CRDLMT  TO CUST-CRDLMT.
            IF EDIT(3) = 'G'
                MOVE CA-INVAMT  TO CUST-INVAMT.
            MOVE 'B201' TO CA-POS.
            EXEC CICS REWRITE DATASET('CUSTMST')
                           FROM(CUST-REC)
                           END-EXEC.
        B209-UPDATE-CUSTOMER-EXIT. EXIT.

        B300-SEND-MAP-DATAONLY.
            MOVE 'B300' TO CA-POS.
            EXEC CICS SEND MAP('AXCU02') MAPSET('XXCU02')
                           DATAONLY CURSOR END-EXEC.
            EXEC CICS RETURN TRANSID('CU02')
                           COMMAREA(COMM-AREA)
                           LENGTH(100)
                           END-EXEC.
        B309-SEND-MAP-DATAONLY-EXIT. EXIT.
```

13.5.   Browse/Update Customers By Name

Program: XCU03   Mapset: XXCU03   Transaction: CU03
CU03 and XCU03 are specified in the PCT.

When the user enters function 3 and the customer name on the menu screen, the menu program will issue an XCTL command to transfer the control to this Browse/Update Customers program (XCU03). The starting customer name is the only data needs to be passed to this program. After this Browse/Update Customers program is invoked, it will use the customer name passed in DFHCOMMAREA of LINKAGE SECTION to browse the customer file through its alternate index path. We have set up an unique alternate index key (customer name plus customer number) upon this customer file. Up to 16 customers can be displayed on the screen. After a page of customers have been displayed, the user can take one of the following actions:

1. Hit CLEAR key to go back to the menu screen.

2. Hit PF1 to display the next page of customers.

3. Hit PF2 to display the previous page of customers.

4. Put an 'X' on the desired customer to go to inquire, update or delete that customer (XCU02).

5. Update name, credit limit, or invoice amount (but not customer number) of desired customers.

6. Enter the next customer name to start browse from that name.

In order to support the next page function (PF1), we need to save the alternate index key of the last customer on the current page. We can use this key to calculate (add 1 to the customer number) the starting key for the next page. We also need to save the alternate index key of the first customer on each page in order to support the previous page function (PF2). If the user hits PF2 key on the page other than the first page, we can go get the starting key of the previous page we saved in the communication area and start the browse with that key.

Screen Layout:

```
CU03  XX/XX/XX HH:MM    BROWSE/UPDATE CUSTOMERS BY NAME   XXXX PAGE: 99

NEXT CUSTOMER NAME: XXXXXXXXXXXXXXXXXXXX

SEL CUSTOMER NAME          CUST#    CRD LMT    INV AMT
X   XXXXXXXXXXXXXXXXXXXX    99999   9999999    9999999
X   XXXXXXXXXXXXXXXXXXXX    99999   9999999    9999999
X   XXXXXXXXXXXXXXXXXXXX    99999   9999999    9999999
X   XXXXXXXXXXXXXXXXXXXX    99999   9999999    9999999
X   XXXXXXXXXXXXXXXXXXXX    99999   9999999    9999999
X   XXXXXXXXXXXXXXXXXXXX    99999   9999999    9999999
X   XXXXXXXXXXXXXXXXXXXX    99999   9999999    9999999
X   XXXXXXXXXXXXXXXXXXXX    99999   9999999    9999999
X   XXXXXXXXXXXXXXXXXXXX    99999   9999999    9999999
X   XXXXXXXXXXXXXXXXXXXX    99999   9999999    9999999
X   XXXXXXXXXXXXXXXXXXXX    99999   9999999    9999999
X   XXXXXXXXXXXXXXXXXXXX    99999   9999999    9999999
X   XXXXXXXXXXXXXXXXXXXX    99999   9999999    9999999
X   XXXXXXXXXXXXXXXXXXXX    99999   9999999    9999999
X   XXXXXXXXXXXXXXXXXXXX    99999   9999999    9999999

CLEAR=MENU, PF1=NEXT PAGE, PF2=PREV PAGE
XXXXXXXXXXXXXXXXXXXXXXXXXXXXXXXXXXXXXXXXXXXXXXXXXXXXXXXXXXXXXXXXXXXXXXXXXXXXXX
```

CICS Mapset: XXCU03

```
XXCU03    DFHMSD TYPE=&SYSPARM,LANG=COBOL,TIOAPFX=YES,MODE=INOUT,          X
                 STORAGE=AUTO,CTRL=(FREEKB,FRSET),TERM=3270,DATA=FIELD
AXCU03    DFHMDI SIZE=(24,80)
          DFHMDF POS=(01,01),LENGTH=04,INITIAL='CU03'
DATE      DFHMDF POS=(01,07),LENGTH=08
TIME      DFHMDF POS=(01,16),LENGTH=05
          DFHMDF POS=(01,25),LENGTH=31,INITIAL='BROWSE/UPDATE CUSTOMERS X
                 BY NAME'
TERMID    DFHMDF POS=(01,58),LENGTH=04
          DFHMDF POS=(01,63),LENGTH=05,INITIAL='PAGE:'
PAGENO    DFHMDF POS=(01,69),LENGTH=02
          DFHMDF POS=(03,01),LENGTH=19,INITIAL='NEXT CUSTOMER NAME:'
NXTNAME   DFHMDF POS=(03,21),LENGTH=20,ATTRB=UNPROT
          DFHMDF POS=(03,42),LENGTH=01
          DFHMDF POS=(05,01),LENGTH=17,INITIAL='SEL CUSTOMER NAME'
          DFHMDF POS=(05,28),LENGTH=25,INITIAL='CUST#   CRD LMT    INV AMX
                 T'
SEL01     DFHMDF POS=(06,01),LENGTH=01,ATTRB=UNPROT
          DFHMDF POS=(06,03),LENGTH=01
NAME01    DFHMDF POS=(06,05),LENGTH=20,ATTRB=UNPROT
          DFHMDF POS=(06,26),LENGTH=01
CUST01    DFHMDF POS=(06,28),LENGTH=05
CRDLT01   DFHMDF POS=(06,36),LENGTH=07,ATTRB=NUM
          DFHMDF POS=(06,44),LENGTH=01
IVAMT01   DFHMDF POS=(06,46),LENGTH=07,ATTRB=NUM
          DFHMDF POS=(06,54),LENGTH=01
SEL02     DFHMDF POS=(07,01),LENGTH=01,ATTRB=UNPROT
          DFHMDF POS=(07,03),LENGTH=01
```

```
NAME02     DFHMDF POS=(07,05),LENGTH=20,ATTRB=UNPROT
           DFHMDF POS=(07,26),LENGTH=01
CUST02     DFHMDF POS=(07,28),LENGTH=05
CRDLT02    DFHMDF POS=(07,36),LENGTH=07,ATTRB=NUM
           DFHMDF POS=(07,44),LENGTH=01
IVAMT02    DFHMDF POS=(07,46),LENGTH=07,ATTRB=NUM
           DFHMDF POS=(07,54),LENGTH=01
           .... OCCURS 16 TIMES ....
SEL16      DFHMDF POS=(21,01),LENGTH=01,ATTRB=UNPROT
           DFHMDF POS=(21,03),LENGTH=01
NAME16     DFHMDF POS=(21,05),LENGTH=20,ATTRB=UNPROT
           DFHMDF POS=(21,26),LENGTH=01
CUST16     DFHMDF POS=(21,28),LENGTH=05
CRDLT16    DFHMDF POS=(21,36),LENGTH=07,ATTRB=NUM
           DFHMDF POS=(21,44),LENGTH=01
IVAMT16    DFHMDF POS=(21,46),LENGTH=07,ATTRB=NUM
           DFHMDF POS=(21,54),LENGTH=01
           DFHMDF POS=(23,01),LENGTH=40,INITIAL='CLEAR=MENU, PF1=NEXT PAGX
               E, PF2=PREV PAGE',ATTRB=(ASKIP,BRT)
MSG        DFHMDF POS=(24,01),LENGTH=78,ATTRB=(ASKIP,BRT)
           DFHMSD TYPE=FINAL
           END
```

CICS Program: XCU03

```
ID DIVISION.
PROGRAM-ID. XCU03.
REMARKS. BROWSE/UPDATE CUSTOMERS BY NAME.
ENVIRONMENT DIVISION.
DATA DIVISION.
WORKING-STORAGE SECTION.
01   COMM-AREA.
     02   CA-CUSTNO          PIC X(5).
     02   CA-CUSTNAM         PIC X(20).
     02   CA-CURPAG          PIC 9(2).
     02   CA-CURKEY.
          03   CA-CUR-CUSTNAM PIC X(20).
          03   CA-CUR-CUSTNO  PIC 9(5).
     02   CA-PAGE-KEY        PIC X(25) OCCURS 10.
     02   CA-LAST-KEY        PIC X(25).
     02   CA-DET-LINE        OCCURS 16.
          03   CA-DET-CUSTNO  PIC 9(5).
          03   CA-DET-SELECT  PIC X(1).
          03   CA-DET-CUSTNAM PIC X(20).
          03   CA-DET-CRDLMT  PIC 9(7).
          03   CA-DET-INVAMT  PIC S9(5)V99 COMP-3.
     02   CA-NXTNAME         PIC X(20).
     02   CA-EDIT-TAB.
          03   EDIT-NXTNAME   PIC X(1).
          03   EDIT-SEL-TAB.
               04   EDIT-SEL  OCCURS 16 PIC X(1).
          03   EDIT-T         OCCURS 16.
               04   EDIT      PIC X(1) OCCURS 3.
     02   I                  PIC 9(2).
     02   J                  PIC 9(2).
     02   CA-POS             PIC X(4).
     02   FILLER             PIC X(88).
01   WS-MSG                  PIC X(60).
01   WS-MSG-LENG             PIC S9(4) COMP VALUE +60.
01   CUST-REC.
     02   CUST-ALT-KEY.
          03   CUST-NAME      PIC X(20).
          03   CUST-PRIMARY-KEY.
               04   CUST-NO   PIC 9(5).
     02   CUST-CRDLMT        PIC 9(7).
     02   ORDR-INVAMT        PIC S9(5)V99 COMP-3.
01   XCTL-COMM-AREA.
     02   XCA-CUSTNO         PIC 9(5).
     02   FILLER             PIC X(95).
01   AXCU03I                 COPY XXCU03.
```

```
01  FILLER                    REDEFINES AXCU030.
*   66 = 12 CONTROL AREA + 11 (DATE) + 8 (TIME) + 7 (TERMID) + 5
*   (PAGENO) + 23 (CUSTNAM).
    02  FILLER                PIC X(66).
    02  DET-LINE              OCCURS 16.
        03  SELL              PIC S9(4) COMP.
        03  SELA              PIC X(1).
        03  SELI              PIC X(1).
        03  CUSTNAML          PIC S9(4) COMP.
        03  CUSTNAMA          PIC X(1).
        03  CUSTNAMI          PIC X(20).
        03  CUSTNOL           PIC S9(4) COMP.
        03  CUSTNOA           PIC X(1).
        03  CUSTNOI           PIC 9(5).
        03  CRDLMTL           PIC S9(4) COMP.
        03  CRDLMTA           PIC X(1).
        03  CRDLMTI           PIC X(7).
        03  INVAMTL           PIC S9(4) COMP.
        03  INVAMTA           PIC X(1).
        03  INVAMTI           PIC 9(5)V99.
        03  INVAMTO REDEFINES INVAMTI PIC X(7).
01  WS-TIME-N                 PIC 9(6).
01  FILLER                    REDEFINES WS-TIME-N.
    02  WS-TIME-N-HH          PIC 9(2).
    02  WS-TIME-N-MM          PIC 9(2).
    02  FILLER                PIC X(2).
01  WS-TIME-E.
    02  WS-TIME-E-HH          PIC 9(2).
    02  FILLER                PIC X(1) VALUE ':'.
    02  WS-TIME-E-MM          PIC 9(2).
01  WS-INVAMT-E               PIC 9(4).99.
LINKAGE SECTION.
01  DFHCOMMAREA               PIC X(1100).
PROCEDURE DIVISION.
    EXEC CICS HANDLE CONDITION
              NOTFND(A900-NOTFND)
              ENDFILE(A910-ENDFILE)
              MAPFAIL(A920-MAPFAIL)
              ERROR(A930-ERROR)
              END-EXEC.
    EXEC CICS HANDLE AID
              PF1(A800-NEXT-PAGE)
              PF2(A820-PREV-PAGE)
              CLEAR(A899-XCTL-MENU)
              ANYKEY(A920-MAPFAIL)
              END-EXEC,
    MOVE DFHCOMMAREA TO COMM-AREA.
    IF EIBTRNID = 'CU03' AND EIBCALEN = 1100
       GO TO A200-RECEIVE-MAP.
    IF EIBTRNID = 'CU03'
       MOVE 'SECURITY VIOLATION' TO WS-MSG
       EXEC CICS SEND FROM(WS-MSG) LENGTH(WS-MSG-LENG)
                 ERASE END-EXEC
       EXEC CICS RETURN END-EXEC.
A000-START-PGM.
*   SET UP STARTING BROWSE KEY AND PAGE NO
    MOVE 1                    TO CA-CURPAG.
    MOVE CA-CUSTNAM           TO CA-CUR-CUSTNAM.
    MOVE 0                    TO CA-CUR-CUSTNO.
A100-DISPLAY-ONE-PAGE.
    MOVE LOW-VALUES           TO AXCU030.
    MOVE EIBTRMID             TO TERMIDO.
    MOVE CURRENT-DATE         TO DATEO.
    MOVE TIME-OF-DAY          TO WS-TIME-N.
    MOVE WS-TIME-N-HH         TO WS-TIME-E-HH.
    MOVE WS-TIME-N-MM         TO WS-TIME-E-MM.
    MOVE WS-TIME-E            TO TIMEO.
    MOVE CA-CURPAG            TO PAGEO.
    MOVE 0                    TO I.
    MOVE CA-CURKEY            TO CUST-ALT-KEY.
```

```
        MOVE 'A100'              TO CA-POS.
        EXEC CICS STARTBR DATASET('CUSTNAM')
                          RIDFLD(CUST-ALT-KEY)
                          END-EXEC.
    A120-READNEXT-CUSTNAM.
        MOVE 'A120'              TO CA-POS.
        EXEC CICS READNEXT DATASET('CUSTNAM')
                           RIDFLD(CUST-ALT-KEY)
                           INTO(CUST-REC)
                           END-EXEC.
        ADD 1                    TO I.
        IF I = 1
            MOVE CUST-ALT-KEY TO CA-PAGE-KEY(CA-CURPAG).
        MOVE CUST-NAME           TO CUSTNAMI(I).
        MOVE CUST-NO             TO CUSTNOI(I).
        MOVE CUST-CRDLMT         TO CRDLMTI(I).
        MOVE CUST-INVAMT         TO WS-INVAMT-E.
        MOVE WS-INVAMT-E         TO INVAMTO(I).
        MOVE CUST-NO             TO CA-DET-CUSTNO(I).
        IF I < 16
            GO TO A120-READNEXT-CUSTNAM.
        MOVE CUST-ALT-KEY   TO CA-LAST-KEY.
    A140-ENDBR-CUSTNAM.
        EXEC CICS ENDBR DATASET('CUSTNAM') END-EXEC.
    A160-SEND-MAP.
        MOVE -1 TO SELL(1).
        MOVE 'UPDATE DESIRED FIELDS OR SELECT CUST' TO MSGO.
        MOVE SPACES TO CA-EDIT-TAB.
        EXEC CICS SEND MAP('AXCU03') MAPSET('XXCU03')
                  ERASE CURSOR END-EXEC.
        EXEC CICS RETURN TRANSID('CU03')
                         COMMAREA(COMM-AREA)
                         LENGTH(1100)
                         END-EXEC.
    A200-RECEIVE-MAP.
        EXEC CICS RECEIVE MAP('AXCU03') MAPSET('XXCU03')
                  END-EXEC.
        PERFORM B100-EDIT-INPUT-FIELDS THRU
                B109-EDIT-INPUT-FIELDS-EXIT.
    *   CHECK ANY INVALID INPUT FIELD
        IF MSGO NOT = LOW-VALUES
            PERFORM B300-SEND-MAP-DATAONLY THRU
                    B309-SEND-MAP-DATAONLY-EXIT.
    *   CHECK IF NEXT CUSTOMER NAME WAS ENTERED
        IF EDIT-NXTNAME = 'G'
            MOVE CA-NXTNAME TO CA-CUSTNAM
            MOVE SPACES      TO CA-EDIT-TAB
            GO TO A000-START-PGM.
    *   CHECK IF AN 'X' ENTERED ON SELECT FIELD
        IF EDIT-SEL-TAB NOT = SPACES
            PERFORM B200-XCTL-XCU02 THRU
                    B209-XCTL-XCU02-EXIT
            VARYING J FROM 1 BY 1 UNTIL J > I.
    *   NOW UPDATE CUSTOMERS
        PERFORM B240-UPDATE-CUSTOMER THRU
                B249-UPDATE-CUSTOMER-EXIT
                VARYING J FROM 1 BY 1 UNTIL J > I.
        MOVE 'UPDATE COMPLETED' TO MSGO.
        MOVE -1 TO NXTNAMEL.
        PERFORM B300-SEND-MAP-DATAONLY THRU
                B309-SEND-MAP-DATAONLY-EXIT.
    A800-NEXT-PAGE.
        IF I < 16
            MOVE -1  TO SELL(1)
            MOVE 'NO MORE CUSTOMERS' TO MSGO
            PERFORM B300-SEND-MAP-DATAONLY THRU
                    B309-SEND-MAP-DATAONLY-EXIT.
        IF CA-CURPAG = 10
            MOVE 0 TO CA-CURPAG.
        ADD 1                    TO CA-CURPAG.
```

```
                MOVE CA-LAST-KEY  TO CA-CURKEY.
                ADD 1                TO CA-CUR-CUSTNO.
                GO TO A100-DISPLAY-ONE-PAGE.
        A820-PREV-PAGE.
                IF CA-CURPAG = 1
                    MOVE -1   TO SELL(1)
                    MOVE 'YOU ARE ON PAGE 1' TO MSGO
                    PERFORM B300-SEND-MAP-DATAONLY THRU
                        B309-SEND-MAP-DATAONLY-EXIT.
                COMPUTE CA-CURPAG = CA-CURPAG - 1.
                MOVE CA-PAGE-KEY(CA-CURPAG) TO CA-CURKEY.
                GO TO A100-DISPLAY-ONE-PAGE.
        A899-XCTL-MENU.
                MOVE SPACES TO XCTL-COMM-AREA.
                EXEC CICS XCTL PROGRAM('XCU00')
                            COMMAREA(XCTL-COMM-AREA)
                            LENGTH(100)
                            END-EXEC.
        A900-NOTFND.
                IF CA-POS = 'A100'
                    GO TO A140-ENDBR-CUSTNAM.
                GO TO A930-ERROR.
        A910-ENDFILE.
                IF CA-POS = 'A120'
                    GO TO A140-ENDBR-CUSTNAM.
                GO TO A930-ERROR.
        A920-MAPFAIL.
                MOVE -1 TO SELL(1).
                PERFORM B300-SEND-MAP-DATAONLY THRU
                        B309-SEND-MAP-DATAONLY-EXIT.
        A930-ERROR.
                EXEC CICS XCTL PROGRAM('XCU13')
                            COMMAREA(CA-POS)
                            LENGTH(4)
                            END-EXEC.
        B100-EDIT-INPUT-FIELDS.
                PERFORM B120-EDIT-NXTNAME THRU
                        B129-EDIT-NXTNAME-EXIT.
                PERFORM B140-EDIT-CUST-LINE THRU
                        B149-EDIT-CUST-LINE-EXIT
                        VARYING J FROM 1 BY 1 UNTIL J > I.
        B109-EDIT-INPUT-FIELDS-EXIT. EXIT.

        B120-EDIT-NXTNAME.
                IF NXTNAMEL > 0
                    MOVE 'G'      TO EDIT-NXTNAME
                    MOVE ' '      TO NXTNAMEA
                    MOVE NXTNAMEI TO CA-NXTNAME.
        B129-EDIT-NXTNAME-EXIT. EXIT.

        B140-EDIT-CUST-LINE.
                PERFORM B150-EDIT-SEL THRU
                        B159-EDIT-SEL-EXIT.
                PERFORM B160-EDIT-CUSTNAM THRU
                        B169-EDIT-CUSTNAM-EXIT.
                PERFORM B170-EDIT-CRDLMT THRU
                        B179-EDIT-CRDLMT-EXIT.
                PERFORM B180-EDIT-INVAMT THRU
                        B189-EDIT-INVAMT-EXIT.
        B149-EDIT-CUST-LINE-EXIT. EXIT.

        B150-EDIT-SEL.
                IF SELL(J)  > 0
                    IF SELI(J) = 'X'
                        MOVE 'G' TO EDIT-SEL(J)
                        MOVE ' ' TO SELA(J)
                    ELSE
                        IF SELI(J) = ' '
                            MOVE ' ' TO EDIT-SEL(J)
                            MOVE ' ' TO SELA(J)
```

```
                ELSE
                    MOVE 'BAD SELECTION, MUST BE X' TO MSGO
                    MOVE 'B' TO EDIT-SEL(J)
                    MOVE 'I' TO SELA(J)
                    MOVE -1  TO SELL(J).
    B159-EDIT-SEL-EXIT. EXIT.

    B160-EDIT-CUSTNAM.
        IF CUSTNAML(J) > 0
            MOVE 'G'         TO EDIT(J, 1)
            MOVE ' '         TO CUSTNAMA(J)
            MOVE CUSTNAMI(J) TO CA-CUSTNAM(J).
    B169-EDIT-CUSTNAM-EXIT. EXIT.

    B170-EDIT-CRDLMT.
        IF CRDLMTL(J) > 0
            IF CRDLMTI(J) NUMERIC
                MOVE 'G' TO EDIT(J, 2)
                MOVE '&' TO CRDLMTA(J)
                MOVE CRDLMTI(J) TO CA-DET-CRDLMT(J)
            ELSE
                MOVE 'B' TO EDIT(J, 2)
                MOVE 'R' TO CRDLMTA(J)
                MOVE -1  TO CRDLMTL(J)
                MOVE 'CREDIT LIMIT NOT NUMERIC' TO MSGO.
    B179-EDIT-CRDLMT-EXIT. EXIT.

    B180-EDIT-INVAMT.
        IF INVAMTL(J) > 0
            IF INVAMTI(J) NUMERIC
                MOVE 'G' TO EDIT(J, 3)
                MOVE '&' TO INVAMTA(J)
                MOVE INVAMTI(J) TO CA-DET-INVAMT(J)
            ELSE
                MOVE 'B' TO EDIT(J, 3)
                MOVE 'R' TO INVAMTA(J)
                MOVE -1  TO INVAMTL(J)
                MOVE 'INVOICE AMT NOT NUMERIC' TO MSGO.
    B189-EDIT-INVAMT-EXIT. EXIT.

    B200-XCTL-XCU02.
        IF EDIT-SEL(J) = 'G'
            MOVE SPACES      TO XCTL-COMM-AREA
            MOVE CA-DET-CUSTNO(J) TO XCA-CUSTNO
            EXEC CICS XCTL PROGRAM('XCU02')
                           COMMAREA(XCTL-COMM-AREA)
                           LENGTH(100)
                           END-EXEC.
    B209-XCTL-XCU02-EXIT. EXIT.

    B240-UPDATE-CUSTOMER.
*       CHECK IF UPDATES MADE ON THIS DETAIL LINE
        IF EDIT-T(J) = SPACES
            GO TO B249-UPDATE-CUSTOMER-EXIT.
        MOVE 'B240'    TO CA-POS.
        EXEC CICS READ DATASET('CUSTMST')
                       RIDFLD(CA-DET-CUSTNO(J))
                       INTO(CUST-REC)
                       UPDATE
                       END-EXEC.
        IF EDIT(J, 1) = 'G'
            MOVE CA-DET-CUSTNAM(J)    TO CUST-NAME.
        IF EDIT(J, 2) = 'G'
            MOVE CA-DET-CRDLMT(J)     TO CUST-CRDLMT.
        IF EDIT(J, 3) = 'G'
            MOVE CA-DET-INVAMT(J)     TO CUST-INVAMT.
        EXEC CICS REWRITE DATASET('CUSTMST')
                          FROM(CUST-REC)
                          END-EXEC.
    B249-UPDATE-CUSTOMER-EXIT. EXIT.
```

```
B300-SEND-MAP-DATAONLY.
    MOVE 'B300'         TO CA-POS.
    EXEC CICS SEND MAP('AXCU03') MAPSET('XXCU03')
              DATAONLY CURSOR END-EXEC.
    EXEC CICS RETURN TRANSID('CU03')
              COMMAREA(COMM-AREA)
              LENGTH(1100)
              END-EXEC.
B309-SEND-MAP-DATAONLY-EXIT. EXIT.

A800-NEXT-PAGE.
    IF I < 16
       MOVE -1 TO SELL(1)
       MOVE 'NO MORE CUSTOMERS' TO MSGO
       PERFORM B300-SEND-MAP-DATAONLY THRU
               B309-SEND-MAP-DATAONLY-EXIT. .
    IF CA-CURPAG = 10
       MOVE 0 TO CA-CURPAG.
    ADD 1 TO CA-CURPAG.
    MOVE CA-LAST-KEY      TO CA-CURKEY.
    ADD 1                 TO CA-CUR-CUSTNO.
    GO TO A100-DISPLAY-ONE-PAGE.
A820-PREV-PAGE.
    IF CA-CURPAG = 1
       MOVE -1 TO SELL(1)
       MOVE 'YOU ARE ON PAGE 1' TO MSGO
       PERFORM B300-SEND-MAP-DATAONLY THRU
               B309-SEND-MAP-DATAONLY-EXIT.
    COMPUTE CA-CURPAG = CA-CURPAG - 1.
    MOVE CA-PAGE-KEY (CA-CURPAG) TO CA-CURKEY.
    GO TO A100-DISPLAY-ONE-PAGE.
A899-XCTL-MENU.
    MOVE SPACES TO XCTL-COMM-AREA.
    EXEC CICS XCTL PROGRAM('XCU00')
              COMMAREA(XCTL-COMM-AREA)
              LENGTH(100)
              END-EXEC.
A900-NOTFND.
    IF CA-POS = 'A100'
       GO TO A140-ENDBR-CUSTNAM.
    GO TO A930-ERROR.
A910-ENDFILE.
    IF CA-POS = 'A120'
       GO TO A140-ENDBR-CUSTNAM.
    GO TO A930-ERROR.
A920-MAPFAIL.
    MOVE -1 TO SELL(1).
    PERFORM B300-SEND-MAP-DATAONLY THRU
            B309-SEND-MAP-DATAONLY-EXIT.
A930-ERROR.
    EXEC CICS XCTL PROGRAM('XCU13')
              COMMAREA(CA-POS)
              LENGTH(4)
              END-EXEC.
```

13.6.   Print A Sales Order On 24x80 Paper

Program: XCU04   Mapset: XXCU04   Transaction: CU04

This CICS program is started by the menu program to print a sales order on 24x80 paper. Each sales order contains a sales order header in the Sales Order Header file and one or more sales order details in the Sales Order Detail file. Each sales order detail will be printed on one line. More than one page may be printed. Each page has 5 lines for the header information and 17 sales order detail lines, and 2 lines of footing. Each page has a total of 24 lines. Each line has 80 columns.

When the user enters function number 4 and a valid sales order number, the menu program will issue a START command withoutTERMID option to initiate CU04 transaction. After this XCU04 program is invoked, it will issue a RETRIEVE command to retrieve the sales order number and use it to print the sales order. We'll use the order number to read the Sales Order Header file to get the order header information for the top portion of each page. We'll then use the sales order number to browse the Sales Order Detail file to retrieve all details for that order number. The key to this Sales Order Detail file is the sales order number plus a 3-byte sequence number.

We'll use Message Routing technique to print this sales order. We'll issue a ROUTE command to set up the printer list. Then we can issue a SEND MAP ACCUM command to build each page in the message. We'll define the entire page as one header map. No detail map and trailer map are to be defined in the CICS mapset because only one printer type (3287 model 2) is to be used to print the sales order. Therefore, we only need to move sales order header information and 17 sales order details to the map I/O area and then issue a SEND MAP ACCUM command to create this page in the message. When there are no more details in the Sales Order Detail file for this sales order number, we'll then end the browse and issue a SEND PAGE command to print the sales order. After the sales order has been printed, we should issue a RETURN command to terminate this task. Following the START command in the menu program, you should send a message saying the sales order has been printed to the terminal.

In the menu program (XCU00):

```
IF CA-FUNNO = 4
    EXEC CICS START TRANSID('CU04')
                    FROM(CA-ORDRNO)
                    LENGTH(CA-ORDRNO-LENG)
                    END-EXEC
    GO TO B202-SEND-MSG.
    ....
B202-SEND-MSG.
    MOVE 'SALES ORDER PRINT COMPLETED' TO MSGO
    MOVE -1   TO FUNNOL.
    PERFORM B300-SEND-MAP-DATAONLY THRU
            B309-SEND-MAP-DATAONLY-EXIT.
```

Report Format:

```
CU04   XX/XX/XX HH:MM     SALES ORDER (24X80)              PAGE: 99

ORDER NO: 99999   CUSTOMER NO: 99999   CUSTOMER NAME: XXXXXXXXXXXXXXXXXXXX

SEQ#   PRODUCT            DESC                ORDQTY      PRICE
999    XXXXXXXXXXXXXX     XXXXXXXXXXXXXXXXXXXX  99999    99999.99
999    XXXXXXXXXXXXXX     XXXXXXXXXXXXXXXXXXXX  99999    99999.99
999    XXXXXXXXXXXXXX     XXXXXXXXXXXXXXXXXXXX  99999    99999.99
999    XXXXXXXXXXXXXX     XXXXXXXXXXXXXXXXXXXX  99999    99999.99
999    XXXXXXXXXXXXXX     XXXXXXXXXXXXXXXXXXXX  99999    99999.99
999    XXXXXXXXXXXXXX     XXXXXXXXXXXXXXXXXXXX  99999    99999.99
999    XXXXXXXXXXXXXX     XXXXXXXXXXXXXXXXXXXX  99999    99999.99
999    XXXXXXXXXXXXXX     XXXXXXXXXXXXXXXXXXXX  99999    99999.99
999    XXXXXXXXXXXXXX     XXXXXXXXXXXXXXXXXXXX  99999    99999.99
999    XXXXXXXXXXXXXX     XXXXXXXXXXXXXXXXXXXX  99999    99999.99
999    XXXXXXXXXXXXXX     XXXXXXXXXXXXXXXXXXXX  99999    99999.99
999    XXXXXXXXXXXXXX     XXXXXXXXXXXXXXXXXXXX  99999    99999.99
999    XXXXXXXXXXXXXX     XXXXXXXXXXXXXXXXXXXX  99999    99999.99
999    XXXXXXXXXXXXXX     XXXXXXXXXXXXXXXXXXXX  99999    99999.99
999    XXXXXXXXXXXXXX     XXXXXXXXXXXXXXXXXXXX  99999    99999.99
999    XXXXXXXXXXXXXX     XXXXXXXXXXXXXXXXXXXX  99999    99999.99
999    XXXXXXXXXXXXXX     XXXXXXXXXXXXXXXXXXXX  99999    99999.99

(CONTINUED ON NEXT PAGE)
```

CICS Mapset XXCU04:

```
XXCU04     DFHMSD TYPE=&SYSPARM,TIOAPFX=YES,MODE=OUT,LANG=COBOL,TERM=ALL,X
                  STORAGE=AUTO,CTRL=(PRINT,L80,FREEKB),DATA=BLOCK
AXCU04     DFHMDI SIZE=(24,80),JUSTIFY=FIRST,HEADER=YES
           DFHMDF POS=(01,01),LENGTH=04,INITIAL='CU04'
DATE       DFHMDF POS=(01,07),LENGTH=08
TIME       DFHMDF POS=(01,16),LENGTH=05
           DFHMDF POS=(01,25),LENGTH=19,INITIAL='SALES ORDER (24X80)'
           DFHMDF POS=(01,64),LENGTH=05,INITIAL='PAGE:'
PAGENO     DFHMDF POS=(01,70),LENGTH=02
           DFHMDF POS=(03,01),LENGTH=09,INITIAL='ORDER NO:'
ORDRNO     DFHMDF POS=(03,11),LENGTH=05
           DFHMDF POS=(03,18),LENGTH=12,INITIAL='CUSTOMER NO:'
CUSTNO     DFHMDF POS=(03,31),LENGTH=05
           DFHMDF POS=(03,38),LENGTH=14,INITIAL='CUSTOMER NAME:'
CUSTNAM    DFHMDF POS=(03,53),LENGTH=20
           DFHMDF POS=(05,01),LENGTH=14,INITIAL='SEQ#    PRODUCT'
           DFHMDF POS=(05,26),LENGTH=04,INITIAL='DESC'
           DFHMDF POS=(05,48),LENGTH=17,INITIAL='ORDQTY       PRICE'
DETLIN     DFHMDF POS=(06,01),LENGTH=79,OCCURS=17
LASTLIN    DFHMDF POS=(24,01),LENGTH=24,INITIAL='(CONTINUED ON NEXT PAGE)X
                  '
           DFHMSD TYPE=FINAL
           END
```

CICS Program XCU04:

```
ID DIVISION.
PROGRAM-ID. XCU04.
REMARKS. PRINT A SALES ORDER ON 24X80 PAPER.
ENVIRONMENT DIVISION.
DATA DIVISION.
WORKING-STORAGE SECTION.
01   CA-ORDRNO                PIC 9(5).
01   CA-ORDRNO-LENG           PIC S9(4) COMP VALUE +5.
01   WS-MSG                   PIC X(60).
01   WS-MSG-LENG              PIC S9(4) COMP VALUE +60.
01   ROUTE-LIST.
     02   ROUTE-TAB.
          03   ROUTE-ENTRY    OCCURS 2.
               04   RL-TRMID  PIC X(4).
               04   FILLER    PIC X(5).
               04   RL-STATUS PIC X(1).
               04   FILLER    PIC X(6).
     02   ROUTE-END           PIC S9(4) COMP VALUE -1.
01   CA-POS                   PIC X(4).
01   ORDRHDR-REC.
     02   ORDRHDR-KEY.
          03   ORDRHDR-ORDRNO PIC 9(5).
     02   ORDRHDR-CUSTNO      PIC 9(5).
     02   ORDRHDR-CUSTNAM     PIC X(20).
01   ORDRDET-REC.
     02   ORDRDET-KEY.
          03   ORDRDET-ORDRNO PIC 9(5).
          03   ORDRDET-SEQNO  PIC 9(3).
     02   ORDRDET-PRODUCT     PIC X(15).
     02   ORDRDET-DESC        PIC X(20).
     02   ORDRDET-ORDRQTY     PIC S9(5) COMP-3.
     02   ORDRDET-PRICE       PIC S9(5)V99 COMP-3.
*    USE OUTPUT MAP SINCE NO INPUT MAP (MODE=OUT IN DFHMSD)
01   AXCU04O                  COPY XXCU04.
01   WS-PAGENO                PIC 9(2).
01   WS-TIME-N                PIC 9(6).
01   FILLER                   REDEFINES WS-TIME-N.
     02   WS-TIME-N-HH        PIC 9(2).
     02   WS-TIME-N-MM        PIC 9(2).
     02   FILLER              PIC X(2).
```

```
01  WS-TIME-E.
    02  WS-TIME-E-HH        PIC 9(2).
    02  FILLER              PIC X(1) VALUE ':'.
    02  WS-TIME-E-MM        PIC 9(2).
01  WS-LINE-CTR             PIC 9(2) VALUE 0.
01  WS-TOT-DETAILS          PIC 9(3) VALUE 0.
01  DET-LINE.
    02  DL-SEQNO            PIC Z(3).
    02  FILLER              PIC X(4).
    02  DL-PRODUCT          PIC X(15).
    02  FILLER              PIC X(3).
    02  DL-DESC             PIC X(20).
    02  FILLER              PIC X(3).
    02  DL-ORDRQTY          PIC Z(4)9.
    02  FILLER              PIC X(3).
    02  DL-PRICE            PIC Z(5).99.
PROCEDURE DIVISION.
    EXEC CICS HANDLE CONDITION
            NOTFND(A900-NOTFND)
            ENDFILE(A910-ENDFILE)
            ENDDATA(A920-ENDDATA)
            ERROR(A930-ERROR)
            END-EXEC.
A000-RETRIEVE-DATA.
*   RETRIEVE ORDER NO PASSED FROM MENU PROGRAM
    MOVE 'A000' TO CA-POS.
*   IF ENDDATA OCCURS, ISSUE RETURN
    EXEC CICS RETRIEVE INTO(CA-ORDRNO) LENGTH(CA-ORDRNO-LENG)
            END-EXEC.
*   SET UP ROUTE LIST
    MOVE SPACES         TO ROUTE-TAB.
    MOVE 'L01P'         TO RL-TRMID(1).
    MOVE 'L02P'         TO RL-TRMID(2).
    MOVE LOW-VALUES TO RL-STATUS(1) RL-STATUS(2).
    EXEC CICS ROUTE LIST(ROUTE-LIST) END-EXEC.
*   READ ORDER HEADER FOR HEADER INFO
    MOVE 'A002'         TO CA-POS.
    EXEC CICS READ DATASET('ORDRHDR')
                RIDFLD(CA-ORDRNO)
                INTO(ORDRHDR-REC)
                END-EXEC.
*   MOVE HEADER TO PAGE TOP PORTION
    MOVE LOW-VALUES     TO AXCU040.
    MOVE CURRENT-DATE TO DATEO.
    MOVE TIME-OF-DAY  TO WS-TIME-N.
    MOVE WS-TIME-N-HH TO WS-TIME-E-HH.
    MOVE WS-TIME-N-MM TO WS-TIME-E-MM.
    MOVE WS-TIME-E    TO TIMEO.
    MOVE 1            TO WS-PAGENO.
    MOVE WS-PAGENO    TO PAGENOO.
    MOVE CA-ORDRNO    TO ORDRNOO.
    MOVE ORDRHDR-CUSTNO  TO CUSTNOO.
    MOVE ORDRHDR-CUSTNAM TO CUSTNAMO.
*   START BROWSE DETAIL FILE TO GET DETAIL RECORDS
    MOVE 0              TO WS-LINE-CTR WS-TOT-DETAILS.
    MOVE CA-ORDRNO      TO ORDRDET-ORDRNO.
    MOVE 1              TO ORDRDET-SEQNO.
    MOVE 'A010'         TO CA-POS.
    EXEC CICS STARTBR DATASET('ORDRDET')
                RIDFLD(ORDRDET-KEY)
                END-EXEC.
A120-READNEXT-ORDRDET.
    MOVE 'A120'         TO CA-POS.
    EXEC CICS READNEXT DATASET('ORDRDET')
                RIDFLD(ORDRDET-KEY)
                INTO(ORDRDET-REC)
                END-EXEC.
*   CHECK TO SEE IF SAME ORDER
    IF ORDRDET-ORDRNO NOT = CA-ORDRNO
        GO TO A140-ENDBR-ORDRDET.
```

```
        ADD 1                   TO WS-LINE-CTR WS-TOT-DETAILS.
        MOVE SPACES             TO DET-LINE.
        MOVE ORDRDET-SEQNO      TO DL-SEQNO.
        MOVE ORDRDET-PRODUCT TO DL-PRODUCT.
        MOVE ORDRDET-DESC       TO DL-DESC.
        MOVE ORDRDET-ORDRQTY TO DL-ORDRQTY.
        MOVE ORDRDET-PRICE      TO DL-PRICE.
        MOVE DET-LINE           TO DETLINO(WS-LINE-CTR).
*       CHECK IF PAGE IS FULL (17 DETAILS)
        IF WS-LINE-CTR < 17
            GO TO A120-READNEXT-ORDRDET.
*       NOW THE PAGE IS FULL, WE SHOULD SEND MAP ACCUM
        EXEC CICS SEND MAP('AXCU04') MAPSET('XXCU04')
                  ERASE ACCUM PAGING END-EXEC.
*       UP TO 255 DETAILS (15 PAGES) CAN BE PRINTED
        IF WS-TOT-DETAILS NOT < 255
            GO TO A140-ENDBR-ORDRDET
        ADD 1                   TO WS-PAGENO.
        MOVE WS-PAGENO TO PAGENOO.
        MOVE 0                  TO WS-LINE-CTR.
        MOVE LOW-VALUES TO DETLINO(1) DETLINO(2) DETLINO(3)
             DETLINO(4) DETLINO(5) DETLINO(6) DETLINO(7) DETLINO(8)
             DETLINO(9) DETLINO(10) DETLINO(11) DETLINO(12)
             DETLINO(13) DETLINO(14) DETLINO(15) DETLINO(16)
             DETLINO(17).
        GO TO A120-READNEXT-ORDRDET.
    A140-ENDBR-ORDRDET.
        EXEC CICS ENDBR DATASET('ORDRDET') END-EXEC.
        EXEC CICS SEND PAGE END-EXEC.
*       ALWAYS GO BACK TO SEE IF THIS PGM CAN ALSO PROCESS OTHER
*       TASKS
        GO TO A000-RETRIEVE-DATA.
    A800-EOJ.
        EXEC CICS RETURN END-EXEC.
    A900-NOTFND.
        IF CA-POS = 'A010'
            EXEC CICS PURGE MESSAGE END-EXEC
            GO TO A000-RETRIEVE-DATA.
        GO TO A930-ERROR.
    A910-ENDFILE.
        IF CA-POS = 'A120'
            GO TO A140-ENDBR-ORDRDET.
        GO TO A930-ERROR.
    A920-ENDDATA.
        IF CA-POS = 'A000'
            GO TO A800-EOJ.
    A930-ERROR.
        EXEC CICS XCTL PROGRAM('XCU13')
                       COMMAREA(CA-POS)
                       LENGTH(4)
                       END-EXEC.
```

13.7.   Print A Sales Order On 24x80 Paper Using OVERFLOW

Program: XCU05   Mapset: XXCU05   Transaction: CU05

This print program will be started by the menu program to print a sales order. The report
format is the same as that used in XCU04. We'll still use the Message Routing technique
to print the sales order. However, we'll define three maps within the mapset: header
map, detail map and trailer map. The header map contains the sales order header
information. The detail map occupies only one line and contains one sales order detail.
Therefore, you'll need to send 17 detail maps in order to make up one page. When we
try to send the detail map the 18th time, OVERFLOW condition occurs. In this case,
you should send the trailer map to complete the current page, send the header map for

the top portion of the next page and then go back to send the detail map that caused the OVERFLOW as the first detail on the next page. The OVERFLOW condition will be set off when you send the header map for the next page. So when you try to send the detail map that caused the OVERFLOW again, there will be no OVERFLOW condition.

When the user enters function 5 and a valid order number on the menu screen, the menu program will issue a START command without the TERMID option to initiate CU05 transaction. When this XCU05 program is invoked, it will print the sales order. After this sales order has been printed, this program will try to retrieve the next sales order to print for other CICS tasks. When ENDDATA condition occurs, it will then issue a RETURN command to terminate itself.

The report format for this XCU05 program is identical to that shown in the preceeding section.

Report Format:

```
CU05  XX/XX/XX HH:MM    SALES ORDER (24X80)                   PAGE: 99

ORDER NO: 99999  CUSTOMER NO: 99999  CUSTOMER NAME: XXXXXXXXXXXXXXXXXXXX

SEQ#   PRODUCT            DESC                  ORDQTY      PRICE
999    XXXXXXXXXXXXXXX    XXXXXXXXXXXXXXXXXXXX  99999     99999.99
999    XXXXXXXXXXXXXXX    XXXXXXXXXXXXXXXXXXXX  99999     99999.99
999    XXXXXXXXXXXXXXX    XXXXXXXXXXXXXXXXXXXX  99999     99999.99
999    XXXXXXXXXXXXXXX    XXXXXXXXXXXXXXXXXXXX  99999     99999.99
999    XXXXXXXXXXXXXXX    XXXXXXXXXXXXXXXXXXXX  99999     99999.99
999    XXXXXXXXXXXXXXX    XXXXXXXXXXXXXXXXXXXX  99999     99999.99
999    XXXXXXXXXXXXXXX    XXXXXXXXXXXXXXXXXXXX  99999     99999.99
999    XXXXXXXXXXXXXXX    XXXXXXXXXXXXXXXXXXXX  99999     99999.99
999    XXXXXXXXXXXXXXX    XXXXXXXXXXXXXXXXXXXX  99999     99999.99
999    XXXXXXXXXXXXXXX    XXXXXXXXXXXXXXXXXXXX  99999     99999.99
999    XXXXXXXXXXXXXXX    XXXXXXXXXXXXXXXXXXXX  99999     99999.99
999    XXXXXXXXXXXXXXX    XXXXXXXXXXXXXXXXXXXX  99999     99999.99
999    XXXXXXXXXXXXXXX    XXXXXXXXXXXXXXXXXXXX  99999     99999.99
999    XXXXXXXXXXXXXXX    XXXXXXXXXXXXXXXXXXXX  99999     99999.99
999    XXXXXXXXXXXXXXX    XXXXXXXXXXXXXXXXXXXX  99999     99999.99
999    XXXXXXXXXXXXXXX    XXXXXXXXXXXXXXXXXXXX  99999     99999.99

(CONTINUED ON NEXT PAGE)
```

CICS Mapset XXCU05:

```
XXCU05    DFHMSD TYPE=&SYSPARM,TIOAPFX=YES,MODE=OUT,LANG=COBOL,TERM=ALL,X
                 STORAGE=AUTO,CTRL=(PRINT,L80,FREEKB),DATA=BLOCK
AXCU05H   DFHMDI SIZE=(05,80),JUSTIFY=FIRST,HEADER=YES
          DFHMDF POS=(01,01),LENGTH=04,INITIAL='CU05'
DATE      DFHMDF POS=(01,07),LENGTH=08
TIME      DFHMDF POS=(01,16),LENGTH=05
          DFHMDF POS=(01,25),LENGTH=19,INITIAL='SALES ORDER (24X80)'
          DFHMDF POS=(01,64),LENGTH=05,INITIAL='PAGE:'
PAGENO    DFHMDF POS=(01,70),LENGTH=02
          DFHMDF POS=(03,01),LENGTH=09,INITIAL='ORDER NO:'
ORDRNO    DFHMDF POS=(03,11),LENGTH=05
          DFHMDF POS=(03,18),LENGTH=12,INITIAL='CUSTOMER NO:'
CUSTNO    DFHMDF POS=(03,31),LENGTH=05
          DFHMDF POS=(03,38),LENGTH=14,INITIAL='CUSTOMER NAME:'
CUSTNAM   DFHMDF POS=(03,53),LENGTH=20
          DFHMDF POS=(05,01),LENGTH=14,INITIAL='SEQ#    PRODUCT'
          DFHMDF POS=(05,26),LENGTH=04,INITIAL='DESC'
```

```
                DFHMDF POS=(05,48),LENGTH=17,INITIAL='ORDQTY        PRICE'
AXCU05D  DFHMDI SIZE=(01,80),LINE=NEXT
DETLIN   DFHMDF POS=(01,01),LENGTH=79
AXCU05T  DFHMDI SIZE=(02,80),LINE=23,TRAILER=YES
                DFHMDF POS=(01,01),LENGTH=01,INITIAL=' '
LASTLIN  DFHMDF POS=(02,01),LENGTH=24,INITIAL='(CONTINUED ON NEXT PAGE)X
        '
                DFHMSD TYPE=FINAL
                END
```

CICS Program XCU05:

```
ID DIVISION.
PROGRAM-ID. XCU05.
REMARKS. PRINT A SALES ORDER ON 24X80 PAPER USING OVERFLOW.
ENVIRONMENT DIVISION.
DATA DIVISION.
WORKING-STORAGE SECTION.
01  CA-ORDRNO          PIC 9(5).
01  CA-ORDRNO-LENG     PIC S9(4) COMP VALUE +5.
01  WS-LINE-CTR        PIC 9(2) VALUE 0.
01  WS-TOT-DETAILS     PIC 9(3) VALUE 0.
01  DET-LINE.
    02  DL-SEQNO       PIC Z(3).
    02  FILLER         PIC X(4).
    02  DL-PRODUCT     PIC X(15).
    02  FILLER         PIC X(3).
    02  DL-DESC        PIC X(20).
    02  FILLER         PIC X(3).
    02  DL-ORDRQTY     PIC Z(4)9.
    02  FILLER         PIC X(3).
    02  DL-PRICE       PIC Z(5).99.
01  WS-PAGENO          PIC 9(2).
01  ROUTE-LIST.
    02  ROUTE-TAB.
        03  ROUTE-ENTRY    OCCURS 2.
            04  RL-TRMID PIC X(4).
            04  FILLER   PIC X(5).
            04  RL-STATUS PIC X(1).
            04  FILLER   PIC X(6).
    02  ROUTE-END          PIC S9(4) COMP VALUE -1.
01  ORDRDET-REC.
    02  ORDRDET-KEY.
        03  ORDRDET-ORDRNO  PIC 9(5).
        03  ORDRDET-SEQNO   PIC 9(3).
    02  ORDRDET-PRODUCT     PIC X(15).
    02  ORDRDET-DESC        PIC X(20).
    02  ORDRDET-ORDRQTY     PIC S9(5) COMP-3.
    02  ORDRDET-PRICE       PIC S9(5)V99 COMP-3.
01  ORDRHDR-REC.
    02  ORDRHDR-KEY.
        03  ORDRHDR-ORDRNO  PIC 9(5).
    02  ORDRHDR-CUSTNO      PIC 9(5).
    02  ORDRHDR-CUSTNAM     PIC X(20).
01  CA-POS             PIC X(4).
01  AXCU05O            COPY XXCU05.
01  WS-TIME-N          PIC 9(6).
01  FILLER REDEFINES WS-TIME-N.
    02  WS-TIME-N-HH   PIC 9(2).
    02  WS-TIME-N-MM   PIC 9(2).
    02  FILLER         PIC X(2).
01  WS-TIME-E.
    02  WS-TIME-E-HH   PIC 9(2).
    02  FILLER         PIC X(1) VALUE ':'.
    02  WS-TIME-E-MM   PIC 9(2).
PROCEDURE DIVISION.
    EXEC CICS HANDLE CONDITION
            NOTFND(A900-NOTFND)
            ENDFILE(A910-ENDFILE)
```

```
                        ENDDATA(A920-ENDDATA)
                        OVERFLOW(A930-OVERFLOW)
                        ERROR(A940-ERROR)
                        END-EXEC.
A000-RETRIEVE-DATA.
        MOVE 'A000' TO CA-POS.
        EXEC CICS RETRIEVE INTO(CA-ORDRNO) LENGTH(CA-ORDRNO-LENG)
                        END-EXEC.
*     READ ORDER HEADER
        EXEC CICS READ DATASET('ORDRHDR')
                        RIDFLD(CA-ORDRNO)
                        INTO(ORDRHDR-REC)
                        END-EXEC.
        MOVE LOW-VALUES         TO AXCU05HO.
        MOVE CURRENT-DATE       TO DATEO.
        MOVE TIME-OF-DAY        TO WS-TIME-N.
        MOVE WS-TIME-N-HH       TO WS-TIME-E-HH.
        MOVE WS-TIME-N-MM       TO WS-TIME-E-MM.
        MOVE WS-TIME-E          TO TIMEO.
        MOVE 1                  TO WS-PAGENO.
        MOVE WS-PAGENO          TO PAGENOO.
        MOVE CA-ORDRNO          TO ORDRNOO.
        MOVE ORDRHDR-CUSTNO     TO CUSTNO.
        MOVE ORDRHDR-CUSTNAM    TO CUSTNAMO.
        MOVE 'A010'             TO CA-POS.
*     SET UP ROUTE LIST
        MOVE SPACES            TO ROUTE-TAB.
        MOVE 'L01P'            TO RL-TRMID(1).
        MOVE 'L02P'            TO RL-TRMID(2).
        MOVE LOW-VALUES        TO RL-STATUS(1) RL-STATUS(2).
        MOVE 'A020'            TO CA-POS.
        EXEC CICS ROUTE LIST(ROUTE-LIST) END-EXEC.
*     SEND HEADER MAP
        EXEC CICS SEND MAP('AXCU05H') MAPSET('XXCU05')
                ACCUM PAGING ERASE END-EXEC.
*     BROWSE SALES ORDER DETAILS
        MOVE 0                  TO WS-LINE-CTR.
        MOVE CA-ORDRNO          TO ORDRDET-ORDRNO.
        MOVE 1                  TO ORDRDET-SEQNO.
        MOVE 'A030'             TO CA-POS.
        EXEC CICS STARTBR DATASET('ORDRDET')
                        RIDFLD(ORDRDET-KEY)
                        END-EXEC.
A120-READNEXT-ORDRDET.
        MOVE 'A120'             TO CA-POS.
        EXEC CICS READNEXT DATASET('ORDRDET')
                        RIDFLD(ORDRDET-KEY)
                        INTO(ORDRDET-REC)
                        END-EXEC.
*     CHECK IF SAME ORDER NO
        IF ORDRDET-ORDRNO NOT = CA-ORDRNO
            GO TO A140-ENDBR-ORDRDET.
        ADD 1                  TO WS-LINE-CTR WS-TOT-DETAILS.
        MOVE SPACES            TO DET-LINE.
        MOVE ORDRDET-SEQNO     TO DL-SEQNO.
        MOVE ORDRDET-PRODUCT   TO DL-PRODUCT.
        MOVE ORDRDET-DESC      TO DL-DESC.
        MOVE ORDRDET-ORDRQTY   TO DL-ORDRQTY.
        MOVE ORDRDET-PRICE     TO DL-PRICE.
        MOVE DET-LINE          TO DETLINO.
A130-SEND-DETAIL-MAP.
        MOVE 'B130'            TO CA-POS.
*     OVERFLOW CONDITION MAY OCCUR WHEN SEND MAP COMMAND
*     IF SO, YOU NEED TO SEND TRAILER MAP FOR CURRENT PAGE, HDR MAP
*     FOR NEXT PAGE AND THEN SEND THIS DETAIL MAP AGAIN
        EXEC CICS SEND MAP('AXCU05D') MAPSET('XXCU05')
                ACCUM PAGING END-EXEC.
*     MAXIMUM 15 PAGES (255 = 17 X 15)
        IF WS-TOT-DETAILS < 255
```

357

```
            GO TO A120-READNEXT-ORDRDET.
A140-ENDBR-ORDRDET.
    EXEC CICS ENDBR DATASET('ORDRDET') END-EXEC.
    EXEC CICS SEND PAGE END-EXEC.
*   ALWAYS GO BACK TO SEE IF ANY DATA TO BE PROCESSED FOR OTHER
*   CICS TASKS, ENDDATA OCCURS WHEN NO DATA
    GO TO A000-RETRIEVE-DATA.
A800-EOJ.
    EXEC CICS RETURN END-EXEC.
A900-NOTFND.
    IF CA-POS = 'A030'
        EXEC CICS PURGE MESSAGE END-EXEC
        GO TO A000-RETRIEVE-DATA.
    GO TO A940-ERROR.
A910-ENDFILE.
    IF CA-POS = 'A120'
        GO TO A140-ENDBR-ORDRDET.
    GO TO A940-ERROR.
A920-ENDDATA.
    IF CA-POS = 'A000'
        GO TO A800-EOJ.
    GO TO A940-ERROR.
A930-OVERFLOW.
*   SEND TRAILER MAP FOR CURRENT PAGE
    MOVE LOW-VALUES TO AXCU05TO.
    EXEC CICS SEND MAP('AXCU05T') MAPSET('XXCU05')
              PAGING ACCUM END-EXEC.
*   SEND HEADER MAP FOR NEXT PAGE
    ADD 1           TO WS-PAGENO.
    MOVE WS-PAGENO  TO PAGENOO.
    EXEC CICS SEND MAP('AXCU05H') MAPSET('XXCU05')
              ERASE ACCUM PAGING END-EXEC.
*   GO TO SEND DETAIL MAP THAT CAUSED OVERFLOW
    GO TO A130-SEND-DETAIL-MAP.
A940-ERROR.
    EXEC CICS XCTL PROGRAM('XCU13')
                   COMMAREA(CA-POS)
                   LENGTH(4)
                   END-EXEC.
```

13.8.   Print A Sales Order On 66X132 Paper

Program: XCU06   CICS Mapset: None   Transaction: CU06

When the user enters function 6 and a valid sales order number, the menu program will issue a START command without TERMID option to initiate CU06 transaction to print that sales order. When XCU06 program is invoked, it will issue a RETRIEVE command to retrieve the sales order number. It'll then use this sales order number to retrieve and print the sales order. Instead of using the SEND MAP ACCUM command, XCU06 will use the SEND TEXT ACCUM command to build the message. This is still a Message Routing technique. Since the SEND TEXT ACCUM command is to be used, there is no need to code the CICS mapset. The report format will be defined in WORKING-STORAGE SECTION. In order to print the sales order on 66 (lines) X 132 (columns), we need to set up the page size of the printer in the TCT as PGESIZE=(11,132). The reason we choose 11 is because a regular computer paper has 66 lines in a page which is a multiple of 11.

We still issue a ROUTE command to set up the printer list. Then we'll issue one SEND TEXT ACCUM command to build each print line in the report. When there are no more sales order details, we'll end the browse and issue a SEND PAGE command to print

the report. After the report has been printed, we can then go back to retrieve data for
the next CICS task. If ENDDATA condition occurs, you should then issue a RETURN
command to terminate the task.

Report Format:

```
CU06  XX/XX/XX HH:MM     SALES ORDER (66X132)                    PAGE: 99

ORDER NO: 99999  CUSTOMER NO: 99999  CUSTOMER NAME: XXXXXXXXXXXXXXXXXXXX

SEQ#   PRODUCT            DESC                   ORDQTY      PRICE   EXT PRICE
999    XXXXXXXXXXXXXXX    XXXXXXXXXXXXXXXXXXXX    99999   99999.99   99999.99
999    XXXXXXXXXXXXXXX    XXXXXXXXXXXXXXXXXXXX    99999   99999.99   99999.99
(TOTAL OF 58 DETAILS)
999    XXXXXXXXXXXXXXX    XXXXXXXXXXXXXXXXXXXX    99999   99999.99   99999.99
999    XXXXXXXXXXXXXXX    XXXXXXXXXXXXXXXXXXXX    99999   99999.99   99999.99
```

CICS Mapset: None

CICS Program XCU06:

```
      ID DIVISION.
      PROGRAM-ID. XCU06.
      REMARKS. PRINT A SALES ORDER ON 66X132 PAPER.
      ENVIRONMENT DIVISION.
      DATA DIVISION.
      WORKING-STORAGE SECTION.
      01   CA-ORDRNO              PIC 9(5).
      01   CA-ORDRNO-LENG         PIC S9(4) COMP VALUE +5.
      01   WS-LINE-CTR            PIC 9(2) VALUE 0.
      01   WS-TOT-DETAILS         PIC 9(3) VALUE 0.
      01   HDG-1.
           02   FILLER            PIC X(7) VALUE ' CU06  '.
           02   HDG-DATE          PIC X(8).
           02   FILLER            PIC X(1) VALUE ' '.
           02   HDG-TIME.
                03   HDG-TIME-HH  PIC 9(2).
                03   FILLER       PIC X(1) VALUE ':'.
                03   HDG-TIME-MM  PIC 9(2).
           02   FILLER            PIC X(4) VALUE SPACES.
           02   FILLER            PIC X(20) VALUE 'SALES ORDER (66X132)'.
           02   FILLER            PIC X(18) VALUE SPACES.
           02   FILLER            PIC X(6) VALUE 'PAGE: '.
           02   HDG-PAGENO        PIC 9(2).
      01   HDG-2.
           02   FILLER            PIC X(11) VALUE ' ORDER NO: '.
           02   HDG-ORDRNO        PIC 9(5).
           02   FILLER            PIC X(15) VALUE '  CUSTOMER NO: '.
           02   HDG-CUSTNO        PIC 9(5).
           02   FILLER            PIC X(17) VALUE '  CUSTOMER NAME: '.
           02   HDG-CUSTNAM       PIC X(20).
      01   HDG-3.
           02   FILLER            PIC X(26)
                VALUE      ' SEQ#   PRODUCT               '.
           02   FILLER            PIC X(22) VALUE 'DESC'.
           02   FILLER            PIC X(28) VALUE
                'ORDRQTY      PRICE   EXT PRICE'.
      01   DET-LINE.
           02   FILLER            PIC X(1).
           02   DL-SEQNO          PIC Z(3).
           02   FILLER            PIC X(4).
           02   DL-PRODUCT        PIC X(15).
           02   FILLER            PIC X(3).
           02   DL-DESC           PIC X(20).
           02   FILLER            PIC X(3).
```

359

```
        02  DL-ORDRQTY          PIC Z(4)9.
        02  FILLER              PIC X(3).
        02  DL-PRICE            PIC Z(5).99.
        02  FILLER              PIC X(3).
        02  DL-EXTPRC           PIC Z(5).99.
    01  PRT-LINE                PIC X(132).
    01  PRT-LINE-LENG           PIC S9(4) COMP VALUE +132.
    01  WS-PAGENO               PIC 9(2).
    01  WS-EXTPRC               PIC S9(5)V99 COMP-3.
    01  ROUTE-LIST.
        02  ROUTE-TAB.
            03  ROUTE-ENTRY     OCCURS 2.
                04  RL-TRMID    PIC X(4).
                04  FILLER      PIC X(5).
                04  RL-STATUS   PIC X(1).
                04  FILLER      PIC X(6).
            03  ROUTE-END       PIC S9(4) COMP VALUE -1.
    01  ORDRHDR-REC.
        02  ORDRHDR-KEY.
            03  ORDRHDR-ORDRNO  PIC 9(5).
        02  ORDRHDR-CUSTNO      PIC 9(5).
        02  ORDRHDR-CUSTNAM     PIC X(20).
    01  ORDRDET-REC.
        02  ORDRDET-KEY.
            03  ORDRDET-ORDRNO  PIC 9(5).
            03  ORDRDET-SEQNO   PIC 9(3).
        02  ORDRDET-PRODUCT     PIC X(15).
        02  ORDRDET-DESC        PIC X(20).
        02  ORDRDET-ORDRQTY     PIC S9(5) COMP-3.
        02  ORDRDET-PRICE       PIC S9(5)V99 COMP-3.
    01  CA-POS                  PIC X(4).
    01  WS-TIME-N               PIC 9(6).
    01  FILLER REDEFINES WS-TIME-N.
        02  WS-TIME-N-HH        PIC 9(2).
        02  WS-TIME-N-MM        PIC 9(2).
        02  FILLER              PIC 9(2).
    01  WS-BLANK-LINES          PIC 9(2).
    PROCEDURE DIVISION.
        EXEC CICS HANDLE CONDITION
                    NOTDFND(A900-NOTFND)
                    ENDFILE(A910-ENDFILE)
                    ENDDATA(A920-ENDDATA)
                    ERROR(A930-ERROR)
                    END-EXEC.
    A000-RETRIEVE-DATA.
        MOVE 'A000'         TO CA-POS.
        EXEC CICS RETRIEVE INTO(CA-ORDRNO) LENGTH(CA-ORDRNO-LENG)
                    END-EXEC.
    *   SET UP ROUTE LIST
        MOVE SPACES         TO ROUTE-TAB.
        MOVE 'L01P'         TO RL-TRMID(1).
        MOVE 'L02P'         TO RL-TRMID(2).
        MOVE LOW-VALUES     TO RL-STATUS(1) RL-STATUS(2).
        EXEC CICS ROUTE LIST(ROUTE-LIST) NLEOM END-EXEC.
    *   READ ORDER HEADER
        EXEC CICS READ DATASET('ORDRHDR')
                        RIDFLD(CA-ORDRNO)
                        INTO(ORDRHDR-REC)
                        END-EXEC.
        MOVE 0              TO WS-PAGENO.
        PERFORM B100-PRINT-HDGS THRU
                B109-PRINT-HDGS-EXIT.
    A100-STARTBR-ORDRDET.
        MOVE CA-ORDRNO          TO ORDRDET-ORDRNO.
        MOVE 1                  TO ORDRDET-SEQNO.
        MOVE 0                  TO WS-LINE-CTR WS-TOT-DETAILS.
        MOVE 'A100'             TO CA-POS.
        EXEC CICS STARTBR DATASET('ORDRDET')
                        RIDFLD(ORDRDET-KEY)
                        END-EXEC.
```

```
      A120-READNEXT-ORDRDET.
            MOVE 'A120'               TO CA-POS.
            EXEC CICS READNEXT DATASET('ORDRDET')
                             RIDFLD(ORDRDET-KEY)
                             INTO(ORDRDET-REC)
                             END-EXEC.
      *     CHECK IF SAME ORDER NO
            IF ORDRDET-ORDRNO NOT = CA-ORDRNO
               GO TO A140-ENDBR-ORDRDET.
            ADD 1                     TO WS-TOT-DETAILS.
            MOVE SPACES               TO DET-LINE.
            MOVE ORDRDET-SEQNO        TO DL-SEQNO.
            MOVE ORDRDET-PRODUCT      TO DL-PRODUCT.
            MOVE ORDRDET-DESC         TO DL-DESC.
            MOVE ORDRDET-ORDRQTY      TO DL-ORDRQTY.
            MOVE ORDRDET-PRICE        TO DL-PRICE.
            COMPUTE WS-EXTPRC ROUNDED = ORDRDET-PRICE * ORDRDET-ORDRQTY.
            MOVE WS-EXTPRC            TO DL-EXTPRC.
            MOVE DET-LINE             TO PRT-LINE.
            PERFORM B300-PRINT-DET-LINE THRU
                  B309-PRINT-DET-LINE-EXIT.
      *     LIMIT TO 255 DETAILS
            IF WS-TOT-DETAILS < 255
               GO TO A120-READNEXT-ORDRDET.
      A140-ENDBR-ORDRDET.
            EXEC CICS ENDBR DATASET('ORDRDET') END-EXEC.
      *     CALCULATE NUMBER OF SPACES LINES TO MAKE UP 66 LINE PAGE
            COMPUTE WS-BLANK-LINES = 58 - WS-LINE-CTR + 3.
            MOVE SPACES      TO PRT-LINE.
            PERFORM B200-PRINT-ONE-LINE THRU
                  B209-PRINT-ONE-LINE-EXIT WS-BLANK-LINES TIMES.
            EXEC CICS SEND PAGE END-EXEC.
      *     ALWAYS GO BACK TO GET DATA FOR NEXT TASK
            GO TO A000-RETRIEVE-DATA.
      A850-EOJ.
            EXEC CICS RETURN END-EXEC.
      A900-NOTFND.
            IF CA-POS = 'A100'
               GO TO A140-ENDBR-ORDRDET.
            GO TO A930-ERROR.
      A910-ENDFILE.
            IF CA-POS = 'A120'
               GO TO A140-ENDBR-ORDRDET.
            GO TO A930-ERROR.
      A920-ENDDATA.
            IF CA-POS = 'A000'
               GO TO A850-EOJ.
      A930-ERROR.
      *     XCTL TO ABEND-HANDLING PGM
            EXEC CICS XCTL PROGRAM('XCU13')
                        COMMAREA(CA-POS)
                        LENGTH(4)
                        END-EXEC.
      B100-PRINT-HDGS.
            ADD 1                     TO WS-PAGENO.
            MOVE CURRENT-DATE         TO HDG-DATE.
            MOVE TIME-OF-DAY          TO WS-TIME-N.
            MOVE WS-TIME-N-HH         TO HDG-TIME-HH.
            MOVE WS-TIME-N-MM         TO HDG-TIME-MM.
            MOVE WS-PAGENO            TO HDG-PAGENO.
            MOVE CA-ORDRNO            TO HDG-ORDRNO.
            MOVE ORDRHDR-CUSTNO       TO HDG-CUSTNO.
            MOVE ORDRHDR-CUSTNAM      TO HDG-CUSTNAM.
            MOVE HDG-1                TO PRT-LINE.
            PERFORM B200-PRINT-ONE-LINE THRU
                  B209-PRINT-ONE-LINE-EXIT.
            MOVE SPACES               TO PRT-LINE.
            PERFORM B200-PRINT-ONE-LINE THRU
                  B209-PRINT-ONE-LINE-EXIT.
            MOVE HDG-2                TO PRT-LINE.
```

```
      PERFORM B200-PRINT-ONE-LINE THRU
              B209-PRINT-ONE-LINE-EXIT.
      MOVE SPACES              TO PRT-LINE.
      PERFORM B200-PRINT-ONE-LINE THRU
              B209-PRINT-ONE-LINE-EXIT.
      MOVE HDG-3               TO PRT-LINE.
      PERFORM B200-PRINT-ONE-LINE THRU
              B209-PRINT-ONE-LINE-EXIT.
      MOVE 0                   TO WS-LINE-CTR.
  B100-PRINT-HDGS-EXIT. EXIT.
  *     PRINT ONE LINE
  B200-PRINT-ONE-LINE.
      EXEC CICS SEND TEXT FROM(PRT-LINE) LENGTH(PRT-LINE-LENG)
              ACCUM PAGING FREEKB NLEOM END-EXEC.
  B209-PRINT-ONE-LINE-EXIT. EXIT.
  *     PRINT DETAIL LINE AND HANDLE PAGE OVERFLOW
  B300-PRINT-DET-LINE.
  *     IF PAGE IS FULL (58 DETAILS), PRINT 3 SPACE LINES AT BOTTOM
  *     PRINT HDR FOR NEXT PAGE, THEN PRINT THIS DETAIL LINE
      IF WS-LINE-CTR = 58
          PERFORM B400-PRINT-TRAILER THRU
                  B409-PRINT-TRAILER-EXIT
          PERFORM B100-PRINT-HDGS THRU
                  B109-PRINT-HDGS-EXIT.
      ADD 1               TO WS-LINE-CTR.
      PERFORM B200-PRINT-ONE-LINE THRU
              B209-PRINT-ONE-LINE-EXIT.
  B309-PRINT-DET-LINE-EXIT. EXIT.
  *     PRINT 3 SPACES LINES AT THE BOTTOM OF EACH PAGE
  B400-PRINT-TRAILER.
      MOVE SPACES TO PRT-LINE.
      PERFORM B200-PRINT-ONE-LINE THRU
              B209-PRINT-ONE-LINE-EXIT 3 TIMES.
  B409-PRINT-TRAILER-EXIT. EXIT.
```

13.9.   Print A Sales Order On 66X85 Paper

CICS Program: XCU07   CICS Mapset: None   Transaction: None

When the user enters function 7 and a valid sales order number on the menu screen, the menu program will issue a LINK command to invoke this XCU07 program. We use LINK command to invoke this program because this program will issue one or more START commands to initiate a print utility transaction (CU11). Each START command that initiates CU11 can print up to 1920 bytes of data. Therefore, XCU07 may need to issue more than one START command to print the entire sales order. This is the reason why we use the LINK command rather than the START command in the menu program to invoke XCU07. Following the LINK command in the menu program, you should send a message saying the sales order has been printed to the terminal.

This print utility transaction CU11 will be listed in 13.13. It can be initiated by any CICS program that needs to print any-size report. The issuing CICS program only needs to supply the data to be printed in line format along with its line length, and form feed information in the FROM option of the START command. This transaction will then issue a SEND FROM command to print the output data. It can print up to 1920 bytes of data. XCU07 will demonstrate how to initiate this transaction to print 66X85 report. You can use it to print any-size report without knowing how to issue CICS commands to print an online report. The page size for the printer specified in the TCT does not matter if you use this print utility transaction.

362

Before you issue the first START command, you need to issue an ENQ command to enqueue the printer. After you have printed the report, you should issue a DEQ command to release the printer. This will prevent other CICS tasks from printing reports in the same printer between two START commands. If ENQBUSY condition occurs when you issue an ENQ command, you should reject the print request and inform the user to request it again later.

It is recommended that each CICS shop have this type of print utility transaction so any one who needs to print something does not need to know how to print it.

Report Format:

```
CU07  XX/XX/XX HH:MM    SALES ORDER (66X85)                      PAGE: 99

ORDER NO: 99999  CUSTOMER NO: 99999  CUSTOMER NAME: XXXXXXXXXXXXXXXXXXXX

SEQ#    PRODUCT            DESC                  ORDQTY       PRICE
999     XXXXXXXXXXXXXX     XXXXXXXXXXXXXXXXXXXX   99999     99999.99
999     XXXXXXXXXXXXXX     XXXXXXXXXXXXXXXXXXXX   99999     99999.99
(TOTAL OF 58 DETAILS)
999     XXXXXXXXXXXXXX     XXXXXXXXXXXXXXXXXXXX   99999     99999.99
999     XXXXXXXXXXXXXX     XXXXXXXXXXXXXXXXXXXX   99999     99999.99
```

CICS Mapset: None

Menu Program XCU00:

```
            EXEC CICS LINK PROGRAM('XCU07')
                           FROM(XCTL-COMM-AREA)
                           LENGTH(100)
                           END-EXEC.
        B202-SEND-MSG.
            MOVE 'SALES ORDER PRINT COMPLETED' TO MSGO.
            MOVE -1  TO FUNNOL.
            PERFORM B300-SEND-MAP-DATAONLY THRU
                    B309-SEND-MAP-DATAONLY-EXIT.
```

CICS Program XCU07:

```
        ID DIVISION.
        PROGRAM-ID. XCU07.
        REMARKS. PRINT A SALES ORDER ON 66X85 PAPER.
        ENVIRONMENT DIVISION.
        DATA DIVISION.
        WORKING-STORAGE SECTION.
        01  COMM-AREA.
            02  CA-ORDRNO    PIC 9(5).
            02  FILLER       PIC X(95).
        01  HDG-1.
            02  FILLER       PIC X(7) VALUE ' CU07  '.
            02  HDG-DATE     PIC X(8).
            02  FILLER       PIC X(1) VALUE ' '.
            02  HDG-TIME.
                03  HDG-TIME-HH PIC 9(2).
                03  FILLER      PIC X(1) VALUE ':'.
                03  HDG-TIME-MM PIC 9(2).
            02  FILLER       PIC X(4) VALUE SPACES.
            02  FILLER       PIC X(19) VALUE 'SALES ORDER (66X85)'.
            02  FILLER       PIC X(19) VALUE SPACES.
            02  FILLER       PIC X(6) VALUE 'PAGE: '.
            02  HDG-PAGENO   PIC 9(2).
        01  HDG-2.
```

```
                02   FILLER          PIC X(11) VALUE ' ORDER NO: '.
                02   HDG-ORDRNO      PIC 9(5).
                02   FILLER          PIC X(15) VALUE '  CUSTOMER NO: '.
                02   HDG-CUSTNO      PIC 9(5).
                02   FILLER          PIC X(17) VALUE '  CUSTOMER NAME: '.
                02   HDG-CUSTNAM     PIC X(20).
        01   HDG-3.
                02   FILLER          PIC X(26) VALUE
                '  SEQ#    PRODUCT             '.
                02   FILLER          PIC X(22) VALUE 'DESC'.
                02   FILLER          PIC X(17) VALUE
                'ORDQTY         PRICE'.
        01   DET-LINE.
                02   FILLER          PIC X(1).
                02   DL-SEQNO        PIC Z(3).
                02   FILLER          PIC X(4).
                02   DL-PRODUCT      PIC X(15).
                02   FILLER          PIC X(3).
                02   DL-DESC         PIC X(20).
                02   FILLER          PIC X(3).
                02   DL-ORDRQTY      PIC Z(4)9.
                02   FILLER          PIC X(3).
                02   DL-PRICE        PIC Z(5).99.
        01   PRINT-DATA-LENG PIC S9(4) COMP.
        *    PRINT-DATA CANNOT BIGGER THAN 1920 BYTES
        01   PRINT-DATA.
                02   PD-LINE-LENG PIC S9(4) COMP VALUE +85.
                02   PD-FORM-FEED PIC X(1).
                02   PD-LINES.
                     03   PD-LINE   OCCURS 22 PIC X(85).
        01   PRINT-LINE-CTR   PIC 9(2) VALUE 0.
        01   WS-DETAIL-CTR    PIC 9(2) VALUE 0.
        01   WS-TOT-DETAILS   PIC 9(3) VALUE 0.
        01   PRT-LINE         PIC X(85).
        01   WS-PAGENO        PIC 9(2).
        01   WS-PRINTER       PIC X(4) VALUE 'L01P'.
        01   WS-TIME-N        PIC 9(6).
        01   FILLER REDEFINES WS-TIME-N.
                02   WS-TIME-N-HH PIC 9(2).
                02   WS-TIME-N-MM PIC 9(2).
                02   FILLER       PIC X(2).
        01   WS-MSG           PIC X(60).
        01   WS-MSG-LENG      PIC S9(4) COMP VALUE +60.
        LINKAGE SECTION.
        01   DFHCOMMAREA      PIC X(100).
        PROCEDURE DIVISION.
            EXEC CICS HANDLE CONDITION
                      NOTFND(A900-NOTFND)
                      ENDFILE(A910-ENDFILE)
                      ERROR(A920-ERROR)
                      ENQBUSY(A930-ENQBUSY)
                      END-EXEC.
            MOVE DFHCOMMAREA TO COMM-AREA.
        *   READ ORDER HEADER
            MOVE 'A000'      TO CA-POS.
            EXEC CICS READ DATASET('ORDRHDR')
                      RIDFLD(CA-ORDRNO)
                      INTO(ORDRHDR-REC)
                      END-EXEC.
            MOVE 0           TO WS-PAGENO.
            MOVE 0           TO WS-DETAIL-CTR WS-TOT-DETAILS
                                PRINT-LINE-CTR.
            MOVE SPACES      TO PD-LINES.
        *   ENQ THE PRINTER
            EXEC CICS ENQ RESOURCE(WS-PRINTER) LENGTH(4) END-EXEC.
            PERFORM B100-PRINT-HDGS THRU
                    B109-PRINT-HDGS-EXIT.
        A100-STARTBR-ORDRDET.
            MOVE CA-ORDRNO TO ORDRDET-ORDRNO.
            MOVE 1           TO ORDRDET-SEQNO.
```

```
                MOVE 'A100'       TO CA-POS.
                EXEC CICS STARTBR DATASET('ORDRDET')
                            RIDFLD(ORDRDET-KEY)
                            END-EXEC.
         A120-READNEXT-ORDRDET.
                MOVE 'A120'          TO CA-POS.
                EXEC CICS READNEXT DATASET('ORDRDET')
                            RIDFLD(ORDRDET-KEY)
                            INTO(ORDRDET-REC)
                            END-EXEC.
         *    CHECK IF SAME ORDER NO
                IF ORDRDET-ORDRNO NOT = CA-ORDRNO
                    GO TO A140-ENDBR-ORDRDET.
                ADD 1                TO WS-TOT-DETAILS.
                MOVE SPACES          TO DET-LINE.
                MOVE ORDRDET-SEQNO   TO DL-SEQNO.
                MOVE ORDRDET-PRODUCT TO DL-PRODUCT.
                MOVE ORDRDET-DESC    TO DL-DESC.
                MOVE ORDRDET-ORDRQTY TO DL-ORDRQTY.
                MOVE ORDRDET-PRICE   TO DL-PRICE.
         *    IF PAGE IS FULL, PRINTER 3 SPACES LINES AT BOTTOM, PRINT
         *    HEADER FOR NEXT PAGE
                IF WS-DETAIL-CTR = 58
                    PERFORM B300-PRINT-TRAILER THRU
                            B309-PRINT-TRAILER-EXIT
                    PERFORM B100-PRINT-HDGS THRU
                            B109-PRINT-HDGS-EXIT.
                ADD 1                TO WS-DETAIL-CTR.
                MOVE DET-LINE        TO PRT-LINE.
                PERFORM B400-PRINT-ONE-LINE THRU
                        B409-PRINT-ONE-LINE-EXIT.
         *    LIMIT TO 195 DETAILS
                IF WS-TOT-DETAILS < 195
                    GO TO A120-READNEXT-ORDRDET.
         A140-ENDBR-ORDRDET.
                EXEC CICS ENDBR DATASET('ORDRDET') END-EXEC.
         *    CHECK IF ANY LINE TO BE PRINTED
                IF PRINT-LINE-CTR > 0
                    PERFORM B200-START-CU11 THRU
                            B209-START-CU11-EXIT.
                EXEC CICS DEQ RESOURCE(WS-PRINTER) LENGTH(4) END-EXEC.
         *    RETURN TO MENU PROGRAM
                EXEC CICS RETURN END-EXEC.

         A900-NOTFND.
                IF CA-POS = 'A100'
                    GO TO A140-ENDBR-ORDRDET.
                GO TO A920-ERROR.
         A910-ENDFILE.
                IF CA-POS = 'A120'
                    GO TO A140-ENDBR-ORDRDET.
                GO TO A920-ERROR.
         A920-ERROR.
                EXEC CICS XCTL PROGRAM('XCU13')
                            COMMAREA(CA-POS)
                            LENGTH(4)
                            END-EXEC.
         A930-ENQBUSY.
                MOVE 'PRINTER K01P IS IN USE, PRINT ORDER LATER' TO WS-MSG.
                EXEC CICS SEND FROM(WS-MSG) LENGTH(WS-MSG-LENG)
                            ERASE END-EXEC.
                EXEC CICS RETURN END-EXEC.
         B100-PRINT-HDGS.
                MOVE CURRENT-DATE    TO HDG-DATE.
                MOVE TIME-OF-DAY     TO WS-TIME-N.
                MOVE WS-TIME-N-HH    TO HDG-TIME-HH.
                MOVE WS-TIME-N-MM    TO HDG-TIME-MM.
                ADD 1                TO WS-PAGENO.
                MOVE WS-PAGENO       TO HDG-PAGENO.
                MOVE CA-ORDRNO       TO HDG-ORDRNO.
```

```
            MOVE ORDRHDR-CUSTNO  TO HDG-CUSTNO.
            MOVE ORDRHDR-CUSTNAM TO HDG-CUSTNAM.
            MOVE HDG-1           TO PRT-LINE.
            PERFORM B400-PRINT-ONE-LINE THRU
                    B409-PRINT-ONE-LINE-EXIT.
            MOVE SPACES          TO PRT-LINE.
            PERFORM B400-PRINT-ONE-LINE THRU
                    B409-PRINT-ONE-LINE-EXIT.
            MOVE HDG-2           TO PRT-LINE.
            PERFORM B400-PRINT-ONE-LINE THRU
                    B409-PRINT-ONE-LINE-EXIT.
            MOVE SPACES          TO PRT-LINE.
            PERFORM B400-PRINT-ONE-LINE THRU
                    B409-PRINT-ONE-LINE-EXIT.
            MOVE HDG-3           TO PRT-LINE.
            PERFORM B400-PRINT-ONE-LINE THRU
                    B409-PRINT-ONE-LINE-EXIT.
            MOVE 0               TO WS-DETAIL-CTR.
        B109-PRINT-HDGS-EXIT. EXIT.
        *    WHEN THE PRINT TABLE IS FULL, INITIATE CU13 TO PRINT IT
        B200-START-CU11.
            COMPUTE PRINT-DATA-LENG = PRINT-LINE-CTR * 85 + 3.
        *    FORM FEED IF FIRST PAGE
            IF WS-TOT-DETAILS = 0
                MOVE 'Y' TO PD-FORM-FEED
            ELSE
                MOVE 'N' TO PD-FORM-FEED.
        *    START CU11 TO PRINT 22 LINES ON PRINTER K01P
            EXEC CICS START TRANSID('CU11')
                            FROM(PRINT-DATA)
                            LENGTH(PRINT-DATA-LENG)
                            TERMID('K01P')
                            END-EXEC.
            MOVE 0               TO PRINT-LINE-CTR.
            MOVE SPACES          TO PD-LINES.
        B209-START-CU11-EXIT. EXIT.

        B300-PRINT-TRAILER.
            MOVE SPACES          TO PRT-LINE.
            PERFORM B400-PRINT-ONE-LINE THRU
                    B409-PRINT-ONE-LINE-EXIT 3 TIMES.
            MOVE 0               TO WS-DETAIL-CTR.
        B309-PRINT-TRAILER-EXIT. EXIT.

        B400-PRINT-ONE-LINE.
            ADD 1                TO PRINT-LINE-CTR.
            MOVE PRT-LINE TO PD-LINE(PRINT-LINE-CTR).
        *    IF PRINT-DATA IS FULL, START CU11 TO PRINT 22 LINES
            IF PRINT-LINE-CTR = 22
                PERFORM B200-START-CU11 THRU
                        B209-START-CU11-EXIT.
        B409-PRINT-ONE-LINE-EXIT. EXIT.
```

13.10.   Create Sales Order Details In TS Queue

CICS Program: XCU08   CICS Mapset: XXCU08   Transaction: CU08

When the user enters function 8 and a valid sales order number on the menu screen, the menu program will issue an XCTL command to transfer the control to this program (XCU08). After XCU08 is invoked, it will display a blank data entry screen for the user to enter sales order details. Up to 16 details can be entered. If all details entered are valid, it will create one TS queue record for each detail entered. If the user wants to enter more sales order details, he needs to hit PF1 to display a blank data entry screen. When the user has entered all the sales order details, he can hit PF2 to go to Review/Update/Create Details screen to perform the final review or update. After final review or update has been completed, he can then hit PF3 on Review/Update/Create Sales Order Details screen to create those sales order details from the TS queue into the Sales Order Detail file. At any time, the user can hit CLEAR key from this Create Sales Order Details screen to go back to the menu screen.

In order to use a TS queue, you must include the terminal ID (EIBTRMID) as part of the TS queue name so the user will be able to create and access his own TS queue. This program XCU08 and the next one XCU09 will be used to demonstrate how to use TS queues to store data in one CICS program and then pass it to another CICS program for processing.

Screen Layout:

```
CU08  XX/XX/XX HH:MM    CREATE SALES ORDER DETAILS       XXXX

ORDER NO: 99999 CUSTOMER NO: 99999 CUSTOMER NAME: XXXXXXXXXXXXXXXXXXXX

PRODUCT          ORDQTY
XXXXXXXXXXXXXX   99999
XXXXXXXXXXXXXX   99999
XXXXXXXXXXXXXX   99999
XXXXXXXXXXXXXX   99999
XXXXXXXXXXXXXX   99999
XXXXXXXXXXXXXX   99999
XXXXXXXXXXXXXX   99999
XXXXXXXXXXXXXX   99999
XXXXXXXXXXXXXX   99999
XXXXXXXXXXXXXX   99999
XXXXXXXXXXXXXX   99999
XXXXXXXXXXXXXX   99999
XXXXXXXXXXXXXX   99999
XXXXXXXXXXXXXX   99999
XXXXXXXXXXXXXX   99999

CLEAR=MENU,PF1=NEW PAGE,PF2=REVIEW/UPDATE/CREATE DETAILS
XXXXXXXXXXXXXXXXXXXXXXXXXXXXXXXXXXXXXXXXXXXXXXXXXXXXXXXXXXXXXXXXXXXXXXXXXXXXX
```

CICS Mapset XXCU08:

```
XXCU08    DFHMSD TYPE=&SYSPARM,LANG=COBOL,TIOAPFX=YES,MODE=INOUT,           X
                 STORAGE=AUTO,CTRL=(FREEKB,FRSET),TERM=3270,DATA=FIELD
AXCU08    DFHMDI SIZE=(24,80)
          DFHMDF POS=(01,01),LENGTH=04,INITIAL='CU08'
DATE      DFHMDF POS=(01,07),LENGTH=08
TIME      DFHMDF POS=(01,16),LENGTH=05
          DFHMDF POS=(01,25),LENGTH=26,INITIAL='CREATE SALES ORDER DETAIX
              LS'
TERMID    DFHMDF POS=(01,59),LENGTH=04
          DFHMDF POS=(03,01),LENGTH=09,INITIAL='ORDER NO:'
ORDRNO    DFHMDF POS=(03,11),LENGTH=05
          DFHMDF POS=(03,17),LENGTH=12,INITIAL='CUSTOMER NO:'
CUSTNO    DFHMDF POS=(03,30),LENGTH=05
          DFHMDF POS=(03,36),LENGTH=14,INITIAL='CUSTOMER NAME:'
CUSTNAM   DFHMDF POS=(03,51),LENGTH=20
          DFHMDF POS=(05,01),LENGTH=7,INITIAL='PRODUCT'
          DFHMDF POS=(05,18),LENGTH=6,INITIAL='ORDQTY'
PROD01    DFHMDF POS=(06,01),LENGTH=15,ATTRB=UNPROT
          DFHMDF POS=(06,17),LENGTH=01
QTY01     DFHMDF POS=(06,19),LENGTH=05,ATTRB=NUM
          DFHMDF POS=(06,25),LENGTH=01
PROD02    DFHMDF POS=(07,01),LENGTH=15,ATTRB=UNPROT
          DFHMDF POS=(07,17),LENGTH=01
QTY02     DFHMDF POS=(07,19),LENGTH=05,ATTRB=NUM
```

```
               DFHMDF POS=(07,25),LENGTH=01
               .... OCCURS 16 TIMES ....
PROD16         DFHMDF POS=(21,01),LENGTH=15,ATTRB=UNPROT
               DFHMDF POS=(21,17),LENGTH=01
QTY16          DFHMDF POS=(21,19),LENGTH=05,ATTRB=NUM
               DFHMDF POS=(21,25),LENGTH=01
               DFHMDF POS=(23,01),LENGTH=56,ATTRB=(ASKIP,BRT),INITIAL='CLEAR=X
                   MENU,PF1=NEW PAGE,PF2=REVIEW/UPDATE/CREATE DETAILS'
MSG            DFHMDF POS=(24,01),LENGTH=78,ATTRB=(ASKIP,BRT)
               DFHMSD TYPE=FINAL
               END
```

CICS Program XCU08:

```
ID DIVISION.
PROGRAM-ID. XCU08.
REMARKS. CREATE SALES ORDER DETAILS IN TS QUEUE.
ENVIRONMENT DIVISION.
DATA DIVISION.
WORKING-STORAGE SECTION.
01   COMM-AREA.
     02   CA-ORDRNO          PIC 9(5).
     02   EDIT-TAB.
          03   EDIT-T        OCCURS 16.
               04   EDIT     PIC X(1) OCCURS 2.
     02   CA-DET-LINE        OCCURS 16.
          03   CA-PROD       PIC X(15).
          03   CA-QTY        PIC S9(5) COMP-3.
     02   J                  PIC 9(2).
     02   CA-POS             PIC X(4).
     02   CA-TS-Q-CREATED PIC X(1).
     02   FILLER             PIC X(68).
01   TS-Q-REC.
     02   TS-PROD            PIC X(15).
     02   TS-QTY             PIC S9(5) COMP-3.
01   TS-Q-LENG              PIC S9(4) COMP VALUE +18.
01   TS-Q-NAME.
     02   TS-Q-TRMID         PIC X(4).
     02   FILLER             PIC X(4) VALUE 'CU08'.
01   WS-TIME-N              PIC 9(6).
01   FILLER                 REDEFINES WS-TIME-N.
     02   WS-TIME-N-HH       PIC 9(2).
     02   WS-TIME-N-MM       PIC 9(2).
     02   FILLER             PIC X(2).
01   WS-TIME-E.
     02   WS-TIME-E-HH       PIC 9(2).
     02   FILLER             PIC X(1) VALUE ':'.
     02   WS-TIME-E-MM       PIC 9(2).
01   ORDRHDR-REC.
     02   ORDRHDR-KEY.
          03   ORDRHDR-ORDRNO PIC 9(5).
     02   ORDRHDR-CUSTNO     PIC 9(5).
     02   ORDRHDR-CUSTNAM    PIC X(20).
01   PRODUCT-REC.
     02   PROD-KEY.
          03   PROD-PRODUCT PIC X(15).
     02   PROD-DESC          PIC X(20).
     02   PROD-PRICE         PIC S9(5)V99 COMP-3.
01   XCTL-XCU09.
     02   XX-ORDRNO          PIC 9(5).
     02   FILLER             PIC X(395).
01   XCTL-XCU00             PIC X(100).
01   WS-MSG                 PIC X(60).
01   WS-MSG-LENG            PIC S9(4) COMP VALUE +60.
01   AXCU08I                COPY XXCU08.
01   FILLER                 REDEFINES AXCU08O.
*    77 = 12 (TIOA PRFX) + 11 (DATE) + 8 (TIME) + 7 (TERMID) +
*    8 (ORDRNO) + 8 (CUSTNO) + 23 (CUSTNAM)
     02   FILLER            PIC X(77).
```

```
        02  DET-LINE          OCCURS 16.
            03  PRODL         PIC S9(4) COMP.
            03  PRODA         PIC X(1).
            03  PRODI         PIC X(15).
            03  QTYL          PIC S9(4) COMP.
            03  QTYA          PIC X(1).
            03  QTYI          PIC 9(5).
            03  QTYO          REDEFINES QTYI PIC X(5).
 LINKAGE SECTION.
 01  DFHCOMMAREA           PIC X(400).
 PRODUCRE DIVISION.
        EXEC CICS HANDLE CONDITION
                   NOTFND(A900-NOTFND)
                   MAPFAIL(A910-MAPFAIL)
                   ERROR(A920-ERROR)
                   END-EXEC.
        EXEC CICS HANDLE AID
                   CLEAR(A899-XCTL-MENU)
                   PF1(A800-NEXT-PAGE)
                   PF2(A840-XCTL-XCU09)
                   ANYKEY(A910-MAPFAIL)
                   END-EXEC.
        MOVE DFHCOMMAREA     TO COMM-AREA.
        IF EIBTRNID = 'CU08' AND EIBCALEN = 400
             GO TO A200-RECEIVE-MAP.
 *      TO PREVENT USER FROM ENTERING CU08 ON TERMINAL
        IF EIBTRNID = 'CU08'
           MOVE 'SECURITY VIOLATION' TO WS-MSG
           EXEC CICS SEND FROM(WS-MSG) LENGTH(WS-MSG-LENG)
                   ERASE END-EXEC
           EXEC CICS RETURN END-EXEC.
        MOVE 'N'   TO CA-TS-Q-CREATED.
 *      SEND BLANK DATA ENTRY SCREEN
 A000-SEND-INIT-SCREEN.
        MOVE LOW-VALUES    TO AXCU080.
        MOVE CURRENT-DATE  TO DATEO.
        MOVE TIME-OF-DAY   TO WS-TIME-N.
        MOVE WS-TIME-N-HH  TO WS-TIME-E-HH.
        MOVE WS-TIME-N-MM  TO WS-TIME-E-MM.
        MOVE WS-TIME-E     TO TIMEO.
        MOVE EIBTRMID      TO TERMIDO.
 *      READ ORDER HEADER
        MOVE 'A000'        TO CA-POS.
        EXEC CICS READ DATASET('ORDRHDR')
                   RIDFLD(CA-ORDRNO)
                   INTO(ORDRHDR-REC)
                   END-EXEC.
        MOVE CA-ORDRNO         TO ORDRNOO.
        MOVE ORDRHDR-CUSTNO    TO CUSTNOO.
        MOVE ORDRHDR-CUSTNAM   TO CUSTNAMO.
        MOVE 'ENTER DETAILS THEN HIT ENTER KEY' TO MSGO.
        MOVE -1               TO PRODL(1).
        MOVE SPACES           TO EDIT-TAB.
        EXEC CICS SEND MAP('AXCU08') MAPSET('XXCU08')
                   ERASE CURSOR END-EXEC.
        EXEC CICS RETURN TRANSID('CU08')
                   COMMAREA(COMM-AREA)
                   LENGTH(400)
                   END-EXEC.
 A200-RECEIVE-MAP.
        EXEC CICS RECEIVE MAP('AXCU08') MAPSET('XXCU08')
                   END-EXEC.
 *    EDIT DETAILS
        PERFORM B100-EDIT-DET-LINE THRU
                B109-EDIT-DET-LINE-EXIT
                VARYING J FROM 1 BY 1 UNTIL J > 16.
 *    CHECK ANY INVALID INPUT FIELD?
        IF MSGO NOT = LOW-VALUES
           PERFORM B300-SEND-MAP-DATAONLY THRU
                   B309-SEND-MAP-DATAONLY-EXIT.
```

```
*    NOW CREATE ORDER DETAILS IN TS Q
     MOVE EIBTRMID  TO TS-Q-TRMID.
     PERFORM B200-CREATE-TS-Q THRU
             B209-CREATE-TS-Q-EXIT
             VARYING J FROM 1 BY 1 UNTIL J > 16.
     MOVE 'DETAILS CREATED SUCCESSFULLY' TO MSGO.
     MOVE -1    TO PRODL(1).
     PERFORM B300-SEND-MAP-DATAONLY THRU
             B309-SEND-MAP-DATAONLY-EXIT.
 A800-NEXT-PAGE.
     GO TO A000-SEND-INIT-SCREEN.
 A840-XCTL-XCU09.
*    CHECK TO SEE IF ANY DETAIL CREATED IN TS Q
     IF CA-TS-Q-CREATED NOT = 'Y'
         MOVE 'NO DETAILS WERE CREATED' TO MSGO
         MOVE -1        TO PRODL(1)
         PERFORM B300-SEND-MAP-DATAONLY THRU
                 B309-SEND-MAP-DATAONLY-EXIT.
     MOVE SPACES        TO XCTL-XCU09.
     MOVE CA-ORDRNO     TO XX-ORDRNO.
     EXEC CICS XCTL PROGRAM('XCU09')
                    COMMAREA(XCTL-XCU09)
                    LENGTH(400)
                    END-EXEC.
 A899-XCTL-MENU.
     MOVE SPACES        TO XCTL-XCU00.
     EXEC CICS XCTL PROGRAM('XCU00')
                    COMMAREA(XCTL-XCU00)
                    LENGTH(100)
                    END-EXEC.
 A900-NOTFND.
     IF CA-POS = 'B120'
         MOVE 'PRODUCT CODE NOT FOUND' TO MSGO
         GO TO B124-BAD-PROD.
     GO TO A920-ERROR.
 A910-MAPFAIL.
     MOVE -1         TO PRODL(1).
     PERFORM B300-SEND-MAP-DATAONLY THRU
             B309-SEND-MAP-DATAONLY-EXIT.
 A920-ERROR.
     EXEC CICS XCTL PROGRAM('XCU13')
                    COMMAREA(CA-POS)
                    LENGTH(4)
                    END-EXEC.
 B100-EDIT-DET-LINE.
     PERFORM B120-EDIT-PROD THRU
             B129-EDIT-PROD-EXIT.
     PERFORM B140-EDIT-QTY THRU
             B149-EDIT-QTY-EXIT.
 B109-EDIT-DET-LINE-EXIT. EXIT.


 B120-EDIT-PROD.
     IF PRODL(J) = 0
         IF EDIT(J, 2) = 'G' OR QTYL(J) > 0
             MOVE 'PRODUCT CODE MUST BE ENTERED' TO MSGO
             MOVE ALL '?' TO PRODI(J)
             GO TO B124-BAD-PROD
         ELSE
             GO TO B129-EDIT-PROD-EXIT.
*    CHECK TO SEE IF PRODUCT CODE EXISTS
     MOVE 'B120' TO CA-POS.
     EXEC CICS READ DATASET('PRODUCT')
                    RIDFLD(PRODI(J))
                    INTO(PRODUCT-REC)
                    END-EXEC.
     MOVE 'G'       TO EDIT(J, 1).
     MOVE ' '       TO PRODA(J).
     MOVE PRODI(J)  TO CA-PROD(J).
     GO TO B129-EDIT-PROD-EXIT.
 B124-BAD-PROD.
```

```
        MOVE 'B'      TO EDIT(J, 1).
        MOVE -1       TO PRODL(J).
        MOVE 'I'      TO PRODA(J).
 B129-EDIT-PROD-EXIT. EXIT.

 B140-EDIT-QTY.
     IF QTYL(J) = 0
         IF EDIT(J, 1) = 'G' OR PRODL(J) > 0
             MOVE 'QTY MUST BE ENTERED' TO MSGO
             MOVE ALL '?' TO QTYO(J)
             GO TO B144-BAD-QTY
         ELSE
             GO TO B149-EDIT-QTY-EXIT.
     IF QTYI(J) NOT NUMERIC
         MOVE 'QTY NOT NUMERIC' TO MSGO
         GO TO B144-BAD-QTY.
     MOVE QTYI(J)   TO CA-QTY(J).
     MOVE '&'       TO QTYA(J).
     MOVE 'G'       TO EDIT(J, 2).
     GO TO B149-EDIT-QTY-EXIT.
 B144-BAD-QTY.
     MOVE 'B'       TO EDIT(J, 2).
     MOVE 'R'       TO QTYA(J).
     MOVE -1        TO QTYL(J).
 B149-EDIT-QTY-EXIT. EXIT.

 B200-CREATE-TS-Q.
 *   CHECK ANY DATA ENTERED ON THIS DETAIL LINE
     IF EDIT-T(J) = SPACES
         GO TO B209-CREATE-TS-Q-EXIT.
     MOVE CA-PROD(J)     TO TS-PROD.
     MOVE CA-QTY(J)      TO TS-QTY.
     MOVE 'B200'         TO CA-POS.
     EXEC CICS WRITEQ TS QUEUE(TS-Q-NAME)
                         FROM(TS-Q-REC)
                         LENGTH(TS-Q-LENG)
                         END-EXEC.
     MOVE 'Y'            TO CA-TS-Q-CREATED.
 B209-CREATE-TS-Q-EXIT. EXIT.

 B300-SEND-MAP-DATAONLY.
     MOVE 'B300'    TO CA-POS.
     EXEC CICS SEND MAP('AXCU08') MAPSET('XXCU08')
             CURSOR DATAONLY END-EXEC.
     EXEC CICS RETURN TRANSID('CU08')
                     COMMAREA(COMM-AREA)
                     LENGTH(400)
                     END-EXEC.
 B309-SEND-MAP-DATAONLY-EXIT. EXIT.
```

13.11.   Review/Update/Create Sales Order Details

CICS Program: XCU09   CICS Mapset: XXCU09   Transaction: CU09

When the user enters function 9 and a valid sales order number on the menu screen, the menu program will issue an XCTL command to transfer the control to this XCU09 program. The user can also hit PF2 key on Create Sales Order Details screen to invoke this XCU09 program after the order details have been created. After XCU09 is invoked, it will read the TS queue and display up to 16 sales order details on the screen. After one page of the sales order details has been displayed, the user can take one of the following actions:

1. Hit CLEAR key to go back to the menu screen.

2. Hit PF1 key to display the next page of details.

3. Hit PF2 key to display the previous page of details.

4. Update details and hit ENTER key.

5. Hit PF3 key to create the sales order details on file.

The TS queue to be reviewed or updated is created in XCU08. Each sales order detail has one record in ths TS queue. XCU09 will read the TS queue records and display them for review or update. After the user has reviewed or updated sales order details in the TS queue, he can then hit PF3 to create those sales order details into the sales order detail file. After the records have been created in the file, XCU09 will delete the TS queue.

Screen Layout:

```
CU09  XX/XX/XX HH:MM    REVIEW/UPDATE/CREATE SALES ORDER DETAILS XXXX PAGE: 99

ORDER NO: 99999   CUSTOMER NO: 99999 CUSTOMER NAME: XXXXXXXXXXXXXXXXXXXX

PRODUCT          ORDQTY
XXXXXXXXXXXXXX    99999
XXXXXXXXXXXXXX    99999
XXXXXXXXXXXXXX    99999
XXXXXXXXXXXXXX    99999
XXXXXXXXXXXXXX    99999
XXXXXXXXXXXXXX    99999
XXXXXXXXXXXXXX    99999
XXXXXXXXXXXXXX    99999
XXXXXXXXXXXXXX    99999
XXXXXXXXXXXXXX    99999
XXXXXXXXXXXXXX    99999
XXXXXXXXXXXXXX    99999
XXXXXXXXXXXXXX    99999
XXXXXXXXXXXXXX    99999
XXXXXXXXXXXXXX    99999

CLEAR=MENU,PF1=NEXT PAGE,PF2=PREV PAGE,PF3=CREATE DETAILS
XXXXXXXXXXXXXXXXXXXXXXXXXXXXXXXXXXXXXXXXXXXXXXXXXXXXXXXXXXXXXXXXXXXXXXXXXXXX
```

CICS Mapset XXCU09:

```
XXCU09    DFHMSD TYPE=&SYSPARM,LANG=COBOL,TIOAPFX=YES,MODE=INOUT,          X
                 STORAGE=AUTO,CTRL=(FREEKB,FRSET),TERM=3270,DATA=FIELD
AXCU09    DFHMDI SIZE=(24,80)
          DFHMDF POS=(01,01),LENGTH=04,INITIAL='CU09'
DATE      DFHMDF POS=(01,07),LENGTH=08
TIME      DFHMDF POS=(01,16),LENGTH=05
          DFHMDF POS=(01,25),LENGTH=40,INITIAL='REVIEW/UPDATE/CREATE SALX
             ES ORDER DETAILS'
TERMID    DFHMDF POS=(01,66),LENGTH=04
          DFHMDF POS=(01,71),LENGTH=05,INITIAL='PAGE:'
PAGENO    DFHMDF POS=(01,77),LENGTH=02
          DFHMDF POS=(03,01),LENGTH=09,INITIAL='ORDER NO:'
ORDRNO    DFHMDF POS=(03,11),LENGTH=05
          DFHMDF POS=(03,18),LENGTH=12,INITIAL='CUSTOMER NO:'
CUSTNO    DFHMDF POS=(03,31),LENGTH=05
          DFHMDF POS=(03,37),LENGTH=14,INITIAL='CUSTOMER NAME:'
CUSTNAM   DFHMDF POS=(03,52),LENGTH=20
          DFHMDF POS=(05,01),LENGTH=07,INITIAL='PRODUCT'
```

```
                 DFHMDF POS=(05,18),LENGTH=06,INITIAL='ORDQTY'
PROD01           DFHMDF POS=(06,01),LENGTH=15,ATTRB=UNPROT
                 DFHMDF POS=(06,17),LENGTH=01
QTY01            DFHMDF POS=(06,19),LENGTH=05,ATTRB=NUM
                 DFHMDF POS=(06,25),LENGTH=01
PROD02           DFHMDF POS=(07,01),LENGTH=15,ATTRB=UNPROT
                 DFHMDF POS=(07,17),LENGTH=01
QTY02            DFHMDF POS=(07,19),LENGTH=05,ATTRB=NUM
                 DFHMDF POS=(07,25),LENGTH=01
                 .... OCCURS 16 TIMES ....
PROD16           DFHMDF POS=(21,01),LENGTH=15,ATTRB=UNPROT
                 DFHMDF POS=(21,17),LENGTH=01
QTY16            DFHMDF POS=(21,19),LENGTH=05,ATTRB=NUM
                 DFHMDF POS=(21,25),LENGTH=01
                 DFHMDF POS=(23,01),LENGTH=57,ATTRB=(ASKIP,BRT),INITIAL='CLEAR=X
                      MENU,PF1=NEXT PAGE,PF2=PREV PAGE,PF3=CREATE DETAILS'
MSG              DFHMDF POS=(24,01),LENGTH=78,ATTRB=(ASKIP,BRT)
                 DFHMSD TYPE=FINAL
                 END
```

CICS Program XCU09:

```
ID DIVISION.
PROGRAM-ID. XCU09.
REMARKS. REVIEW/UPDATE/CREATE ORDER DETAILS.
ENVIRONMENT DIVISION.
DATA DIVISION.
WORKING-STORAGE SECTION.
01   COMM-AREA.
     02  CA-ORDRNO       PIC 9(5).
     02  CA-CURPAG       PIC 9(2).
     02  CA-CURITEM      PIC S9(4) COMP.
     02  EDIT-TAB.
         03  EDIT-T      OCCURS 16.
             04  EDIT    PIC X(1) OCCURS 2.
     02  CA-DET-LINE     OCCURS 16.
         03  CA-ITEM     PIC S9(4) COMP.
         03  CA-PROD     PIC X(15).
         03  CA-QTY      PIC S9(5) COMP-3.
     02  CA-PAGITEM      PIC S9(4) COMP OCCURS 10.
     02  I               PIC 9(2).
     02  J               PIC 9(2).
     02  CA-POS          PIC X(4).
     02  FILLER          PIC X(11).
01   ORDRHDR-REC.
     02  ORDRHDR-KEY.
         03  ORDRHDR-ORDRNO PIC 9(5).
     02  ORDRHDR-CUSTNO  PIC 9(5).
     02  ORDRHDR-CUSTNAM PIC X(20).
01   ORDRDET-REC.
     02  ORDRDET-KEY.
         03  ORDRDET-ORDRNO PIC 9(5).
         03  ORDRDET-SEQNO  PIC 9(3).
     02  ORDRDET-PRODUCT PIC X(15).
     02  ORDRDET-DESC    PIC X(20).
     02  ORDRDET-ORDRQTY PIC S9(5) COMP-3.
     02  ORDRDET-PRICE   PIC S9(5)V99 COMP-3.
01   PRODUCT-REC.
     02  PROD-KEY.
         03  PROD-PROD   PIC X(15).
     02  PROD-DESC       PIC X(20).
     02  PROD-PRICE      PIC S9(5)V99 COMP-3.
01   TS-Q-REC.
     02  TS-PROD         PIC X(15).
     02  TS-QTY          PIC S9(5) COMP-3.
01   TS-Q-LENG           PIC S9(4) COMP VALUE +18.
01   TS-Q-NAME.
     02  TS-Q-TRMID      PIC X(4).
```

```
        02  FILLER          PIC X(4) VALUE 'CU08'.
01  XCTL-XCU00              PIC X(100).
01  WS-MSG                  PIC X(60).
01  WS-MSG-LENG             PIC S9(4) COMP VALUE +60.
01  WS-TIME-N               PIC 9(6).
01  FILLER                  REDEFINES WS-TIME-N.
        02  WS-TIME-N-HH    PIC 9(2).
        02  WS-TIME-N-MM    PIC 9(2).
        02  FILLER          PIC X(2).
01  WS-TIME-E.
        02  WS-TIME-E-HH    PIC 9(2).
        02  FILLER          PIC X(1) VALUE ':'.
        02  WS-TIME-E-MM    PIC 9(2).
01  AXCU09I                 COPY XXCU09.
01  FILLER                  REDEFINES AXCU09O.
*   82 = 12 (TIOAPFX) + 11 (DATE) + 8 (TIME) + 7 (TERMID) +
*   5 (PAGENO) + 8 (ORDRNO) + 8 (CUSTNO) + 23 (CUSTNAM)
        02  FILLER          PIC X(82).
        02  DET-LINE        OCCURS 16.
            03  PRODL       PIC S9(4) COMP.
            03  PRODA       PIC X(1).
            03  PRODI       PIC X(15).
            03  QTYL        PIC S9(4) COMP.
            03  QTYA        PIC X(1).
            03  QTYI        PIC 9(5).
            03  QTYO        REDEFINES QTYI PIC X(5).
LINKAGE SECTION.
01  DFHCOMMAREA             PIC X(400).
PROCEDURE DIVISION.
    EXEC CICS HANDLE CONDITION
            NOTFND(A900-NOTFND)
            QIDERR(A910-QIDERR)
            MAPFAIL(A920-MAPFAIL)
            ITEMERR(A930-ITEMERR)
            ERROR(A940-ERROR)
            END-EXEC.
    EXEC CICS HANDLE AID
            CLEAR(A899-XCTL-MENU)
            PF1(A800-NEXT-PAGE)
            PF2(A820-PREV-PAGE)
            PF3(A840-CREATE-DETAILS)
            ANYKEY(A920-MAPFAIL)
            END-EXEC.
    MOVE DFHCOMMAREA TO COMM-AREA.
    IF EIBTRNID = 'CU09' AND EIBCALEN = 400
        GO TO A200-RECEIVE-MAP.
    IF EIBTRNID = 'CU09'
        MOVE 'SECURITY VIOLATION' TO WS-MSG
        EXEC CICS SEND FROM(WS-MSG) LENGTH(WS-MSG-LENG)
                  ERASE END-EXEC
        EXEC CICS RETURN END-EXEC.
    MOVE EIBTRMID       TO TS-Q-TRMID.
    MOVE 1              TO CA-CURITEM.
    MOVE 1              TO CA-CURPAG.
A000-SEND-INIT-SCREEN.
    MOVE LOW-VALUES     TO AXCU09O.
    MOVE CURRENT-DATE   TO DATEO.
    MOVE TIME-OF-DAY    TO WS-TIME-N.
    MOVE WS-TIME-N-HH   TO WS-TIME-E-HH.
    MOVE WS-TIME-N-MM   TO WS-TIME-E-MM.
    MOVE WS-TIME-E      TO TIMEO.
    MOVE EIBTRMID       TO TERMIDO.
    MOVE CA-CURPAG      TO PAGENOO.
*   READ ORDER HEADER
    MOVE 'A000'         TO CA-POS.
    EXEC CICS READ DATASET('ORDRHDR')
                   RIDFLD(CA-ORDRNO)
                   INTO(ORDRHDR-REC)
                   END-EXEC.
```

```
            MOVE CA-ORDRNO        TO ORDRNOO.
            MOVE ORDRHDR-CUSTNO   TO CUSTNOO.
            MOVE ORDRHDR-CUSTNAM  TO CUSTNAMO.
            MOVE 0                TO I.
        A100-READ-NEXT-DETAIL.
            MOVE 'A100'           TO CA-POS.
            EXEC CICS READQ TS QUEUE(TS-Q-NAME)
                               INTO(TS-Q-REC)
                               LENGTH(TS-Q-LENG)
                               ITEM(CA-CURITEM)
                               END-EXEC.
            ADD 1                 TO I.
            IF I = 1
                MOVE CA-CURITEM   TO CA-PAGITEM(CA-CURPAG).
            MOVE CA-CURITEM       TO CA-ITEM(I).
            MOVE TS-PROD          TO PRODI(I).
            MOVE TS-QTY           TO QTYI(I).
            IF I < 16
                ADD 1             TO CA-CURITEM
            GO TO A100-READ-NEXT-DETAIL.
        A160-SEND-MAP.
            MOVE -1               TO PRODL(1).
            MOVE SPACES           TO EDIT-TAB.
            MOVE 'UPDATE DETAILS THEN HIT ENTER KEY' TO MSGO.
            EXEC CICS SEND MAP('AXCU09') MAPSET('XXCU09')
                    ERASE CURSOR END-EXEC.
            EXEC CICS RETURN TRANSID('CU09')
                               COMMAREA(COMM-AREA)
                               LENGTH(400)
                               END-EXEC.
        A200-RECEIVE-MAP.
            EXEC CICS RECEIVE MAP('AXCU09') MAPSET('XXCU09')
                    END-EXEC.
            PERFORM B100-EDIT-DET-LINE THRU
                    B109-EDIT-DET-LINE-EXIT
                    VARYING J FROM 1 BY 1 UNTIL J > I.
        *   CHECK ANY INVALID INPUT FIELD?
            IF MSGO NOT = LOW-VALUES
                PERFORM B300-SEND-MAP-DATAONLY THRU
                    B309-SEND-MAP-DATAONLY-EXIT.
        *   UPDATE ORDER DETAILS IN TS Q
            PERFORM B200-UPDATE-DETAIL THRU
                    B209-UPDATE-DETAIL-EXIT
                    VARYING J FROM 1 BY 1 UNTIL J > I.
            MOVE 'UPDATE COMPLETED' TO MSGO.
            MOVE -1               TO PRODL(1).
            PERFORM B300-SEND-MAP-DATAONLY THRU
                    B309-SEND-MAP-DATAONLY-EXIT.
        A800-NEXT-PAGE.
        *   IF CURRENT PAGE IS NOT FULL, REJECT THE REQUEST
            IF I < 16
                MOVE 'NO MORE DETAILS' TO MSGO
                MOVE -1           TO PRODL(1)
                PERFORM B300-SEND-MAP-DATAONLY THRU
                        B309-SEND-MAP-DATAONLY-EXIT.
        *   ONLY KEY OF THE LAST 10 PAGES WILL BE SAVED
            IF CA-CURPAG = 10
                MOVE 0 TO CA-CURPAG.
            ADD 1       TO CA-CURPAG.
            COMPUTE CA-CURITEM = CA-ITEM(16) + 1.
            GO TO A000-SEND-INIT-SCREEN.
        A820-PREV-PAGE.
            IF CA-CURPAG = 1
                MOVE 'YOU ARE ON PAGE 1' TO MSGO
                MOVE -1     TO PRODL(1)
                PERFORM B300-SEND-MAP-DATAONLY THRU
                        B309-SEND-MAP-DATAONLY-EXIT.
            COMPUTE CA-CURPAG = CA-CURPAGE - 1.
            MOVE CA-PAGITEM(CA-CURPAG) TO CA-CURITEM.
```

```
            GO TO A000-SEND-INIT-SCREEN.
    A840-CREATE-DETAILS.
            MOVE 0         TO CA-CURITEM.
            MOVE EIBTRMID TO TS-Q-TRMID.
    A842-READ-NEXT-DETAIL.
            MOVE 'A842'   TO CA-POS.
            ADD 1 TO CA-CURITEM.
            EXEC CICS READQ TS QUEUE(TS-Q-NAME)
                             INTO(TS-Q-REC)
                             LENGTH(TS-Q-LENG)
                             ITEM(CA-CURITEM)
                             END-EXEC.
    *    READ PRODUCT FILE TO GET DESC AND PRICE
            MOVE 'A843'   TO CA-POS.
            EXEC CICS READ DATASET('PRODUCT')
                             RIDFLD(TS-PROD)
                             INTO(PRODUCT-REC)
                             END-EXEC.
    *    CREATE SALES ORDER DETAIL ON FILE
            MOVE SPACES        TO ORDRDET-REC.
            MOVE CA-ORDRNO   TO ORDRDET-ORDRNO.
            MOVE CA-CURITEM TO ORDRDET-SEQNO.
            MOVE TS-PROD      TO ORDRDET-PRODUCT.
            MOVE PROD-DESC    TO ORDRDET-DESC.
            MOVE PROD-PRICE TO ORDRDET-PRICE.
            MOVE TS-QTY       TO ORDRDET-ORDRQTY.
            MOVE 'A844'       TO CA-POS.
            EXEC CICS WRITE DATASET('ORDRDET')
                             FROM(ORDRDET-REC)
                             RIDFLD(ORDRDET-KEY)
                             END-EXEC.
            GO TO A842-READ-NEXT-DETAIL.
    A844-DELETE-TS-Q.
            MOVE 'A845'      TO CA-POS.
            EXEC CICS DELETEQ TS QUEUE(TS-Q-NAME)
                     END-EXEC.
            MOVE 'DETAILS CREATED ON FILE' TO MSGO.
            MOVE -1    TO PRODL(1).
            PERFORM B300-SEND-MAP-DATAONLY THRU
                    B309-SEND-MAP-DATAONLY-EXIT.
    A899-XCTL-MENU.
            MOVE SPACES        TO XCTL-XCU00.
            EXEC CICS XCTL PROGRAM('XCU00')
                             COMMAREA(XCTL-XCU00)
                             LENGTH(100)
                             END-EXEC.
    A900-NOTFND.
            IF CA-POS = 'B120'
                MOVE 'BAD PRODUCT CODE' TO MSGO
                GO TO B124-BAD-PROD.
            GO TO A940-ERROR.
    A910-QIDERR.
            IF CA-POS = 'A100'
                MOVE 'NO SALES ORDER DETAILS TO BE PROCESSED' TO WS-MSG
                EXEC CICS SEND FROM(WS-MSG) LENGTH(WS-MSG-LENG)
                             ERASE END-EXEC
                EXEC CICS RETURN END-EXEC.
            GO TO A940-ERROR.
    A920-MAPFAIL.
            MOVE -1    TO PRODL(1).
            PERFORM B300-SEND-MAP-DATAONLY THRU
                    B309-SEND-MAP-DATAONLY-EXIT.
    A930-ITEMERR.
            IF CA-POS = 'A100'
                GO TO A160-SEND-MAP.
            IF CA-POS = 'A842'
                GO TO A844-DELETE-TS-Q.
            GO TO A940-ERROR.
    A940-ERROR.
            EXEC CICS XCTL PROGRAM('XCU13')
```

```
                        COMMAREA(CA-POS)
                        LENGTH(4)
                        END-EXEC.
    B100-EDIT-DET-LINE.
        PERFORM B120-EDIT-PROD THRU
                B129-EDIT-PROD-EXIT.
        PERFORM B140-EDIT-QTY THRU
                B149-EDIT-QTY-EXIT.
    B109-EDIT-DET-LINE-EXIT. EXIT.


    B120-EDIT-PROD.
        IF PRODL(J) = 0
            GO TO B129-EDIT-PROD-EXIT.
        MOVE 'B120'   TO CA-POS.
        EXEC CICS READ DATASET('PRODUCT')
                        RIDFLD(PRODI(J))
                        INTO(PRODUCT-REC)
                        END-EXEC.
        MOVE 'G'    TO EDIT(J, 1).
        MOVE ' '    TO PRODA(J).
        MOVE PRODI(J) TO CA-PROD(J).
        GO TO B129-EDIT-PROD-EXIT.
    B124-BAD-PROD.
        MOVE 'B'    TO EDIT(J, 1).
        MOVE 'I'    TO PRODA(J).
        MOVE -1     TO PRODL(J).
    B129-EDIT-PROD-EXIT. EXIT.


    B140-EDIT-QTY.
        IF QTYL(J) > 0
            IF QTYI(J) NUMERIC
                MOVE 'G'     TO EDIT(J, 2)
                MOVE '&'     TO QTYA(J)
                MOVE QTYI(J) TO CA-QTY(J)
            ELSE
                MOVE 'QTY NOT NUMERIC' TO MSGO
                MOVE 'B'    TO EDIT(J, 2)
                MOVE 'R'    TO QTYA(J)
                MOVE -1     TO QTYL(J).
    B149-EDIT-QTY-EXIT. EXIT.


    B200-UPDATE-DETAIL.
    *   CHECK TO SEE IF UPDATE MADE ON THIS DETAIL LINE
        IF EDIT-T(J) = SPACES
            GO TO B209-UPDATE-DETAIL-EXIT.
        MOVE CA-ITEM(J) TO CA-CURITEM.
        MOVE 'B200'     TO CA-POS.
        MOVE EIBTRMID    TO TS-Q-TRMID.
        EXEC CICS READQ TS QUEUE(TS-Q-NAME)
                        INTO(TS-Q-REC)
                        LENGTH(TS-Q-LENG)
                        ITEM(CA-CURITEM)
                        END-EXEC.
        IF EDIT(J, 1) = 'G'
            MOVE CA-PROD(J) TO TS-PROD.
        IF EDIT(J, 2) = 'G'
            MOVE CA-QTY(J)  TO TS-QTY.
        MOVE 'B202'       TO CA-POS.
        EXEC CICS WRITEQ TS QUEUE(TS-Q-NAME)
                        FROM(TS-Q-REC)
                        LENGTH(TS-Q-LENG)
                        ITEM(CA-CURITEM)
                        REWRITE
                        END-EXEC.
    B209-UPDATE-DETAIL-EXIT. EXIT.


    B300-SEND-MAP-DATAONLY.
        MOVE 'B300' TO CA-POS.
        EXEC CICS SEND MAP('AXCU09') MAPSET('XXCU09')
                DATAONLY CURSOR END-EXEC.
```

```
          EXEC CICS RETURN TRANSID('CU09')
                     COMMAREA(COMM-AREA)
                     LENGTH(400)
                     END-EXEC.
          B309-SEND-MAP-DATAONLY-EXIT. EXIT.
```

13.12.   Print Sales Order Master List Tonight (XCU10)

CICS Program: XCU10   CICS Mapset: none   CICS Transaction code: none

This CICS program is used to demonstrate how to submit batch job JCL to the reader queue from CICS/VS region. A CICS/VS online system cannot be complete without batch jobs. In order for the CICS users to request these batch jobs, you can develop a CICS program that creates TD queue records (JCL cards) into the reader queue which must be defined in the DCT as an extrapartitition transient data queue. Each JCL card must be created as one TD queue record with 80-byte length. You can also ask the user to enter the control card data (i.e. date) on the menu screen and then pass it through the communication area to this CICS program. After that, this CICS program will include this control card as input data to the desired batch program. After the JCL has been submitted to the reader queue by this CICS program, it will be executed after the CICS/VS system has been shut down at 5 P.M.. The computer operator will release this set of JCL only after the CICS has been shut down. You cannot execute a batch update job while CICS is up and running since the VSAM files are in use by CICS and your batch update job must wait until they becomes available.

This program is invoked when the user enters function number 10 on the menu screen. The menu program will issue a LINK command to link to this CICS program. The reason we use LINK instead of XCTL command is because this CICS program does not have a mapset. Therefore, we can let the menu program sends the completion message after the control is returned from this CICS program (XCU10).

CICS Program XCU10:

```
          ID DIVISION.
          PROGRAM-ID. XCU10.
          REMARKS. SUBMIT BATCH JOB JCL TO READER QUEUE.
          ENVIRONMENT DIVISION.
          DATA DIVISION.
          WORKING-STORAGE SECTION.
          01  JCL-CARD-LENG      PIC S9(4) COMP VALUE +80.
          01  I                  PIC 9(2).
          01  JCL-CARDS.
              02  JCL-CARD-1     PIC X(80) VALUE
                  '//ORDR100 JOB (1500,ORDR),PRODUCTION,'.
              02  JCL-CARD-2     PIC X(80) VALUE
                  '//         CLASS=2,MSGCLASS=X,NOTIFY=LEE'.
              02  JCL-CARD-3     PIC X(80) VALUE
                  '/*ROUTE      PRINT RMT4'.
              02  JCL-CARD-4     PIC X(80) VALUE
                  '//JOBLIB   DD DSN=CCD.PROD.LINKLIB,DISP=SHR'.
              02  JCL-CARD-5     PIC X(80) VALUE
                  '//ORDR100  EXEC ORDR100'.
              02  JCL-CARD-6     PIC X(80) VALUE
                  '//STEP1    DD *'.
              02  JCL-CARD-7     PIC X(80).
              02  JCL-CARD-8     PIC X(80) VALUE
                  '/*EOF'.
          01  JCL-CARDS-AREA.
```

```
        02  JCL-CARD        PIC X(80) OCCURS 8 TIMES.
    01  CA-POS              PIC X(4).
    LINKAGE SECTION.
    PROCEDURE DIVISION.
        EXEC CICS HANDLE CONDITION
                  ERROR(A900-ERROR)
                  END-EXEC.
        MOVE 'A000'         TO CA-POS.
 *      MOVE CURRENT-DATE INTO CONTROL CARD
 *      IT WLL BE USED AS CONTROL DATA TO THIS BATCH PROGRAM
        MOVE CURRENT-DATE TO JCL-CARD-7.
        MOVE JCL-CARDS      TO JCL-CARDS-AREA.
        PERFORM A100-SUBMIT-JCL-CARD THRU
                A109-SUBMIT-JCL-CARD-EXIT
                VARYING I FROM 1 BY 1 UNTIL I > 8.
 *      RETURN TO MENU PGM FOLLOWING LINK COMMAND
        MOVE 'A020'         TO CA-POS.
        EXEC CICS RETURN END-EXEC.

    A100-SUBMIT-JCL-CARD.
        MOVE 'A100'            TO CA-POS.
        EXEC CICS WRITEQ TD QUEUE('DRDR')
                            FROM(JCL-CARD(I))
                            LENGTH(JCL-CARD-LENG)
                            END-EXEC.
    A109-SUBMIT-JCL-CARD-EXIT. EXIT.

    A900-ERROR.
        EXEC CICS XCTL PROGRAM('XCU13')
                       COMMAREA(CA-POS)
                       LENGTH(4)
                       END-EXEC.
```

13.13. Print Utility Program (XCU11)

CICS Program: XCU11   CICS Mapset: None   Transaction: CU11

This program is used to demonstrate how to develop a print utility transaction that is to be started by any CICS program that needs to print an online report. Each CICS shop should have such a print utility transaction so CICS programmers do not need to know how to issue CICS commands to print an online report. They only need to supply data to be printed in line format and initiate this transaction (CU11).

When we try to print the sales order on 66x85 paper in CICS program XCU07, we build an output area that contains 22 lines of 85-byte data and then issue a START command with FROM option to initiate CU11 to print the report. More than one START command may be issued in order to print the entire report. We specify the output data to be printed in the FROM option of the START command. You can also start this print utility transaction to print any-size report. You only need to pass the line length, form feed information and output data to be printed in line format. However, the length of output area you specify in the FROM option of the START command must not exceed 1920 bytes since we'll issue a SEND FROM command to print up to 1920 bytes of data. 3286 and 3287 model 2 printers are the most popular CICS printers and their buffer size is 1920 bytes.

In XCU07 (Sales Order Print Program):

```
01  PRINT-DATA-LENG      PIC S9(4) COMP.
01  PRINT-DATA.
    02  PD-LINE-LENG      PIC S9(4) COMP VALUE +85.
    02  PD-FORM-FEED      PIC X(1).
    02  PD-LINES.
        03  PD-LINE       OCCURS 22 LINES PIC X(85).

EXEC CICS START  TRANSID('CU11')
                 FROM(PRINT-DATA)
                 LENGTH(PRINT-DATA-LENG)
                 TERMID('K01P')
                 END-EXEC.
```

In the above example, you need to specify the line length in which the data is to be printed in the first two bytes of PRINT-DATA. The second field in PRINT-DATA is the form feed information. If you need to jump to a new page before you print the PRINT-DATA, then you should move 'Y' (Yes) to this field. Otherwise, you should move 'N' (No) to this field. PD-LINES in PRINT-DATA contains 22 lines of output lines to be printed, each line is 85 bytes long. Since you can only define up to 1920 bytes for PRINT-DATA, you can have a maximum of 22 lines (85 * 22 = 1870). You should specify the printer where you want to print this report in the TERMID option of the START command. In the CICS program XCU11, we'll use SEND FROM command instead of MESSAGE ROUTING commands. Therefore, you need to specify TERMID in the START command so the output will be delivered (printed) to the asociated terminal (printer) of that task.

After XCU11 is invoked, you should issue a RETRIEVE command to retrieve the data (PRINT-DATA) passed by the issuing CICS program (XCU07). After the data has been retrieved, you need to build an output area that is to be used in the FROM option of the SEND command from the retrieved data. This output area will contain the data to be printed along with printer control characters. The data to be printed will be in compressed form. That means we'll truncate the trailing spaces for each line passed from XCU07. Following each compressed line, we'll insert a new line character (DFHBMPNL). When the printer encounters this new line character, it will advance one line and return the carriage to the column one before it prints the next compressed line. At the end of the last line to be printed, we'll insert an end of message printer control character (DFHBMPEM). When the printer encounters this end of message printer control character, it will terminate the print operation. If there is no DFHBMPEM inserted as the last character in the output area, the printer will continue to print the filler in the printer buffer until 1920 bytes of data have been printed. Therfore, if your output area contains 1870 bytes of data and no DFHBMPEM has been inserted as the last character, 50 (1920 - 1870 = 50) more bytes of data in the buffer will be printed.

If form feed has been requested ('Y' in PD-FORM-FEED), then you need to insert X'0C' and X'0D' as the first two bytes in the output area. X'0C' will perform the form feed and X'0D' will return the carriage to the first column of the line before the printer prints the first compressed line.

We'll write this CICS Program XCU11 in Assembler language since it will be started by any CICS program that needs to print an online report.

CICS Program XCU11:

```
SAMPLE    DSECT
INPDATA   DS    0CL1920
LINELEN   DS    H
FORMFED   DS    C
PDLINES   DS    CL1917
OUTLENG   DS    H
LENGL1    DS    H
INLENG    DS    H
OUTAREA   DS    CL1920
R0        EQU   0
R1        EQU   1
R2        EQU   2
R3        EQU   3
R4        EQU   4
R5        EQU   5
R6        EQU   6
R7        EQU   7
R8        EQU   8
XCU11     CSECT
          BALR  11,0
          USING *,11
          MVC   INLENG,=H'+1920'
          EXEC CICS HANDLE CONDITION ERROR(ERROR) ENDDATA(ENDDT)
RETDATA   EQU   *
          EXEC CICS RETRIEVE INTO(INPDATA) LENGTH(INLENG)
          LA    R1,PDLINES    R1=FIRST BYTE OF INPUT DATA
          LH    R2,INLENG
          SH    R2,=H'3'      R2=LENG OF INPUT DATA
          STH   R2,INLENG
          LR    R3,R1
          AR    R3,R2
          LH    R7,LINELEN
          SH    R7,=H'1'
          STH   R7,LENGL1     LINE LENG - 1
          LA    R4,OUTAREA    R4=ADR FOR OUTAREA
          LR    R5,R4         R4 CONTAINS ADR FOR OUTDATA
          CLI   FORMFED,C'Y'  CK IF FORMFEED REQUESTED ?
          BNE   NXTLINE       TO MOVE NEXT LINE TO OUTDATA
          MVC   0(2,R4),=X'0C0D'
          AH    R4,=H'2'
          SH    R1,LINELEN
NXTLINE   EQU   *
          AH    R1,LINELEN
          CR    R1,R3 CK ANY MORE INPUT LINE FOR PROCESS
          BNL   SENDFRM NO MORE INPUT DATA, GO PRINT
          LR    R7,R1
          AH    R7,LENGL1 R7 POINTS TO LAST BYTE OF LINE
CKBLK     EQU   *
          CLI   0(R7),X'40'
          BNE   MOVEINP MOVE INPUT LINE TO OUTPUT
          SH    R7,=H'1'
          CR    R7,R1     CK IF FIRST BYTE OF LINE REACHED?
          BNL   CKBLK   GO TO CK NEXT CHAR
          B     MOVENL WHOLE LINE IS SPACE, INSERT NL ONLY
MOVEINP   SR    R7,R1 CAL ACTUAL LENG OF DATA TO BE MOVED
          AH    R7,=H'1'
          EX    R7,OUTLINE
          AR    R4,R7
MOVENL    EQU   *
          MVI   0(R4),X'15' INSERT NL CHAR
          AH    R4,=H'1' CALC NXT OUTPUT BYTE ADDR
          B     NXTLINE GO BACK TO PROCESS NEXT INPUT LINE
OUTLINE   EQU   *
          MVC   0(0,R4),0(R1)
SENDFRM   EQU   *
          MVI   0(R4),X'19' INSERT EOM CHAR
          AH    R4,=H'1'
          SR    R4,R5   CALCU OUTDATA LENGTH
          STH   R4,OUTLENG
```

```
          EXEC CICS SEND FROM(OUTAREA) LENGTH(OUTLENG) WAIT    *
                ERASE CTLCHAR('H')
*  GO GET NEXT DATA FOR NEXT TASK, IF ENDDATA OCCURS, NO NEXT
*  DATA FOR PROCESS
          B     RETDATA
ERROR     EQU   *
          EXEC CICS ABEND ABCODE('CU11')
ENDDT     EQU   *
          EXEC CICS RETURN
          END   XCU11
```

13.14.   Automatic Task Initiation (ATI) Program (XCU12)

CICS Program: XCU12   CICS Mapset: XXCU12   Transaction: CU12

This program is used to demonstrate how to design an Automatic Task Initiation application. We want to print a sales order after the sales order has been created in XCU09. However, we do not want to invoke the sales order print program every time the sales order is created. Instead, we want to print sales orders only after 30 sales orders have been created. Therefore, the sale order print transaction only needs to be invoked once for every 30 sales orders. This way, you can save some loading time of this sales order print program.

In order to accomplish the above application, we can define an intrapartition transient data queue in the DCT and specify the printer ID as its destination in its DCT entry. We also specify 30 as the trigger level (TRIGLEV=30) for this TD queue. In CICS program XCU09, we need to create a TD queue record into this TD queue after the sales order has been created. When there are 30 records in the queue, CICS will initiate transacxtion CU12. After XCU12 is invoked, it will issue the READQ TD command to retrieve the queue record and use the sales order number in the record to print the sales order. When there are no more records in the TD queue, QZERO condition occurs. In this case, we should issue a RETURN command to terminate CU12. The storage occupied by this TD queue will be released after the record has been retrieved.

The DCT entry for the TD queue used in this ATI application is as follows:

```
DFHDCT    TYPE=INTRA,DESTFAC=TERMINAL,DESTID=K01P,DESTRCV=NO, X
          REUSE=YES,RSL=1,TRANSID=CU12,TRIGLEV=30
```

The CICS program (XCU09) that creates the sales order must create a TD queue record in K01P TD queue:

In XCU09:

```
01  TD-Q-REC.
    02  TD-Q-ORDRNO    PIC 9(5).
01  TD-Q-LENG          PIC S9(4) COMP VALUE +5.

EXEC CICS WRITEQ TD QUEUE('K01P')
                FROM(TD-Q-REC)
                LENGTH(TD-Q-LENG)
                END-EXEC.
```

CICS Mapset XXCU12:

```
XXCU12   DFHMSD TYPE=&SYSPARM,LANG=COBOL,TIOAPFX=YES,MODE=OUT
AXCU12   DFHMDI SIZE=(01,80)
         DFHMDF POS=(01,01),LENGTH=09,INITIAL='ORDER NO:'
ORDRNO   DFHMDF POS=(01,11),LENGTH=05
         DFHMDF POS=(01,17),LENGTH=12,PICOUT='CUSTOMER NO:'
CUSTNO   DFHMDF POS=(01,30),LENGTH=05
         DFHMDF POS=(01,36),LENGTH=05,INITIAL='NAME:'
CUSTNAM  DFHMDF POS=(01,42),LENGTH=20
         DFHMSD TYPE=FINAL
         END
```

CICS Program XXCU12:

```
ID DIVISION.
PROGRAM-ID. XCU12.
REMARKS. ATI TO PRINT SALES ORDERS.
ENVIRONMENT DIVISION.
DATA DIVISION.
WORKING-STORAGE SECTION.
01  TD-Q-REC.
    02  TD-Q-ORDRNO     PIC 9(5).
01  TD-Q-LENG           PIC S9(4) COMP VALUE +5.
01  WS-MSG              PIC X(60).
01  WS-MSG-LENG         PIC S9(4) COMP.
01  AXCU12O             COPY XXCU12.
PROCEDURE DIVISION.
    EXEC CICS HANDLE CONDITION
              QZERO(A800-EOJ)
              ERROR(A900-ERROR)
              END-EXEC.
*   READ NEXT TD QUEUE RECORD UNTIL QZERO OCCURS
A100-READ-NEXT-Q-REC.
    EXEC CICS READQ TD QUEUE('K01P')
                    INTO(TD-Q-REC)
                    LENGTH(TD-Q-LENG)
                    END-EXEC.
*   USE TD-Q-ORDRNO IN THE RETRIEVED TD RECORD TO READ ORDR HDR
    EXEC CICS READ DATASET('ORDRHDR')
                   INTO(ORDRHDR-REC)
                   RIDFLD(TD-Q-ORDRNO)
                   END-EXEC.
*   MOVE ORDER HDR TO MAP I/O AREA
    MOVE LOW-VALUES       TO AXCU12O.
    MOVE ORDRHDR-ORDRNO  TO ORDRNOO.
    MOVE ORDRHDR-CUSTNO   TO CUSTNOO.
    MOVE ORDRHDR-CUSTNAM TO CUSTNAMO.
*   PRINT ORDR HDR ON K01P
    EXEC CICS SEND MAP('AXCU12') ERASE PRINT L80 END-EXEC.
*   GO GET NEXT TD Q RECORD FOR PROCESS
    GO TO A100-READ-NEXT-Q-REC.
*   WHEN QZERO CONDITION OCCURS, THAT MEANS NO MORE RECORDS
*   YOU SHOULD TERMINATE CU12
A800-EOJ.
    EXEC CICS RETURN END-EXEC.
*   ANY ERROR OCCURS, YOU NEED TO ABEND THE TASK AND PRODUCE
*   A STORAGE DUMP
A900-ERROR.
    EXEC CICS ABEND ABCODE('CU12') END-EXEC.
```

13.15.   Common-Abend-Handling Program (XCU13)

CICS Program: XCU13   CICS Mapset: None   Transaction: None

When an unrecoverable error has been encountered, you can either issue an ABEND command to abend the task or issue an XCTL command to transfer the control to a common-abend-handling program. If an ABEND command is issued, the task is terminated abnormally and all you get is a storage dump. If you XCTL to a common-abend-handling program, you can print error message on a printer and then issue the ABEND command to abend the task. Therefore, you get the error message in the printer in addition to the storage dump. In many situations, the error message is all you need to debug a CICS abend and there is no need to read the storage dump. The error message can be designed to contain the following information:

1. Abend location (passed from issuing program).
2. Transaction code (EIBTRNID).
3. CICS Program (passed from issuing program).
4. Terminal ID (EIBTRMID) if any.
5. The last resource used (EIBRSRCE).
6. The last record key (passed from issuing program).
7. The last CICS command issued (EIBFN).
8. The return code of last CICS command execution (EIBRCODE).
9. The operator ID (OPID).
10. CICS task number (EIBTASKN).

We will transfer the control to this program in the routine specified for ERROR exceptional condition in every CICS program within this Customer Order Service system. After XCU13 is invoked, we'll collect the above information and then print it by starting CU11 (print utility transaction). After the error message has been printed, you must abend the task by issuing an ABEND command. This will abend the task to produce a storage dump and cause dynamic transaction backout to be performed on that task. If you issue a RETURN command instead of an ABEND command, the task will be terminated normally by CICS. In this case, no storage dump will be produced and no dynamic transaction backout will be performed. CICS considers this task is terminated normally.

In the menu program XCU00:

```
        EXEC CICS HANDLE CONDITION
                  NOTFND(A900-NOTFND)
                  MAPFAIL(A910-MAPFAIL)
                  ERROR(A920-ERROR)
                  END-EXEC.
        ....
    A920-ERROR.
        EXEC CICS XCTL PROGRAM('XCU13')
                       COMMAREA(CA-POS)
                       LENGTH(4)
                       END-EXEC.
```

CICS Program XCU13:

```
        ID DIVISION.
        PROGRAM-ID. XCU13.
        REMARKS. COMMON ABEND HANDLING PROGRAM.
        ENVIRONMENT DIVISION.
        DATA DIVISION.
        WORKING-STORAGE SECTION.
        01  LINE-1          PIC X(22) VALUE 'CICS TASK ABEND ******'.
```

```
01  LINE-2.
    02  DATE        PIC X(8).
    02  FILLER      PIC X(1) VALUE ' '.
    02  TIME.
        03  TIME-HH PIC 9(2).
        03  FILLER  PIC X(1) VALUE ':'.
        03  TIME-MM PIC 9(2).
        03  FILLER  PIC X(1) VALUE ':'.
        03  TIME-SS PIC 9(2).
    02  FILLER      PIC X(9) VALUE ' TRANSID='.
    02  TRANSID     PIC X(4).
    02  FILLER      PIC X(9) VALUE ' PROGRAM='.
    02  PROGRAM     PIC X(8).
    02  FILLER      PIC X(7) VALUE ' TASK#:'.
    02  TASKNO      PIC 9(7).
    02  FILLER      PIC X(8) VALUE ' TERMID='.
    02  TERMID      PIC X(4).
01  LINE-3.
    02  FILLER      PIC X(18) VALUE SPACES.
    02  FILLER      PIC X(9) VALUE 'RESOURCE='.
    02  RESOURCE    PIC X(8).
    02  FILLER      PIC X(10) VALUE ' FUNCTION='.
    02  FUNCTION    PIC 9(4).
    02  FILLER      PIC X(9) VALUE ' DATASET='.
    02  DATASET     PIC X(8).
01  LINE-4.
    02  FILLER      PIC X(18) VALUE SPACES.
    02  FILLER      PIC X(12) VALUE ' RETURN CODE='.
    02  RCODE1      PIC 9(4).
    02  FILLER      PIC X(1) VALUE SPACE.
    02  RCODE2      PIC 9(4).
    02  FILLER      PIC X(8) VALUE ' REQ ID='.
    02  REQID       PIC X(8).
01  LINE-5.
    02  FILLER      PIC X(18) VALUE SPACES.
    02  FILLER      PIC X(9) VALUE 'LOCATION='.
    02  CA-POS      PIC X(4).
    02  FILLER      PIC X(8) VALUE ' OPERID='.
    02  OPERID      PIC X(3).
01  LINE-6          PIC X(80) VALUE SPACES.
01  PRINT-DATA-LENG PIC S9(4) VALUE +483.
01  PRINT-DATA.
    02  PD-LINE-LENG PIC S9(4) COMP VALUE +80.
    02  PD-FORM-FEED PIC X(1) VALUE 'N'.
    02  PD-LINES.
        03  PD-LINE     OCCURS 6 PIC X(80).
01  WS-PRINTER      PIC X(4) VALUE 'K01P'.
01  WS-TIME-N       PIC 9(6).
01  FILLER REDEFINES WS-TIME-N.
    02  WS-TIME-N-HH PIC 9(2).
    02  WS-TIME-N-MM PIC 9(2).
    02  WS-TIME-N-SS PIC 9(2).
01  WS-FUNCTION     PIC X(2) SYNC.
01  WS-FUNCTION-N REDEFINES WS-FUNCTION PIC S9(4) COMP.
01  WS-RCODE        PIC X(4) SYNC.
01  WS-RCODE-N REDEFINES WS-RECORD.
    02  WS-RCODE1   PIC S9(4) COMP.
    02  WS-RCODE2   PIC S9(4) COMP.
01  WS-ABEND-CODE   PIC X(4).
LINKAGE SECTION.
01  DFHCOMMAREA     PIC X(4).
PROCEDURE DIVISION.
*   MOVE ERROR MESSAGE TO LINE 1 - 6
    MOVE CURRENT-DATE   TO DATE.
    MOVE TIME-OF-DAY    TO WS-TIME-N.
    MOVE WS-TIME-N-HH   TO TIME-HH.
    MOVE WS-TIME-N-MM   TO TIME-MM.
    MOVE WS-TIME-N-SS   TO TIME-SS.
    MOVE EIBTRNID       TO TRANSID.
*   PROGRAM NAME CAN BE PASSED FROM ISSUING PROGRAM
```

```
        MOVE SPACES         TO PROGRAM.
        MOVE EIBTASKN       TO TASKNO.
        MOVE EIBTRMID       TO TERMID.
        MOVE EIBRSRCE       TO RESOURCE.
        MOVE EIBFN          TO WS-FUNCTION.
        MOVE WS-FUNCTION-N  TO FUNCTION.
        MOVE EIBDS          TO DATASET.
*       NOW CONVERT EIBRCODE TO NUMERIC NUMBER
        MOVE EIBRCODE       TO WS-RCODE.
        MOVE WS-RCODE1      TO RCODE1.
        MOVE WS-RCODE2      TO RCODE2.
        MOVE EIBREQID       TO REQID.
        MOVE DFHCOMMAREA    TO CA-POS.
        EXEC CICS ASSIGN OPID(OPERID) END-EXEC.
        MOVE LINE-1         TO PD-LINE(1).
        MOVE LINE-2         TO PD-LINE(2).
        MOVE LINE-3         TO PD-LINE(3).
        MOVE LINE-4         TO PD-LINE(4).
        MOVE LINE-5         TO PD-LINE(5).
        MOVE LINE-6         TO PD-LINE(6).
*       START PRINT UTILITY TRANSACTION CU11 TO PRINT ERROR MESSAGE
        EXEC CICS START TRANSID('CU11')
                        FROM(PRINT-DATA)
                        LENGTH(PRINT-DATA-LENG)
                        TERMID('K01P')
                        END-EXEC.
*       NOW ABEND THIS TASK TO PRODUCE DUMP AND CAUSE DYNAMIC
*       TRANSACTION BACKOUT
        MOVE EIBTRNID   TO WS-ABEND-CODE.
        EXEC CICS ABEND ABCODE(WS-ABEND-CODE) END-EXEC.
```

The function (EIBFN) is a very important field that contains the last CICS command executed. However, it is stored in hexadecimal format. Therefore, you need to convert it to a number before you can print it. After the function has been converted into a numeric number and printed, you need to check it with the EIBFN table in the manual to see which is the last function executed. We also do the same thing to EIBRCODE to produce two numeric numbers. Only the first four bytes of EIBRCODE will be used for VSAM files.

The error message has the following format:

```
CICS TASK ABEND ******
MM/DD/YY HH:MM:SS TRANSID=XXXX PROGRAM=XXXXXXXX TASK#=9999999 TERMID=XXXX
                  RESOURCE=XXXXXXXX FUNCTION=9999 DATASET=XXXXXXXX
                  RETURN CODE=9999 9999 REQ ID=XXXXXXXX
                  LOCATION=XXXX OPERID=XXX
```

13.16.   Load Dynamic Table Program (XCU14)

CICS Program: XCU14   CICS Mapset: None   Transaction: None   Store table: STORTBL (in PPT)

In this section, we'll discuss how to define a dynamic store table and how to process it in a CICS program (XCU14). A dynamic table is loaded into a CICS program through the use of the LOAD command. After the table is no longer needed, it can then be deleted by issuing a RELEASE command. If a table is to be used by many CICS programs and it is to be changed constantly, you need to consider to set it up as a dynamic table. When a dynamic table is changed, you only need to recatalog the table and there is no need to recompile all CICS programs that use this table since the table is loaded dynamically into the CICS program.

When a dynamic table is loaded, it is loaded into the main storage. The speed of accessing the dynamic table in main storage is many times faster than retrieving a record from a VSAM KSDS file. This is the advantage of using dynamic table over using VSAM KSDS file to store the table. You can also load the dynamic table only once and let it stay in main storage whole day until CICS/VS is shut down. This can be accomplished by specifying HOLD option in the first LOAD command that loads the table.

In order to set up a dynamic table, you need to catalog it in the CICS program load library. After it is cataloged, you need to set it up in the PPT. When CICS is brought up, the dynamic table will be enabled and ready to be loaded. In the CICS program that uses this table, you need to set up the table in LINKAGE SECTION and then issue a LOAD command to load it into the program. After the table has been loaded, you can then search the table to find the desired table entry. After the table is no longer needed, you should then issue a RELEASE command to delete the table. After the table is deleted, the contents in the table are no longer available to the CICS program. If you have changed the contents of a dynamic table, you need to recatalog it in the program load library and then do a CSMT NEW to get its new version into CICS/VS. There is no need to recompile the CICS programs that use this table. After the new version of the table is copied into the PPT through the use of CSMT NEW command, it will be loaded into the main storage when the next CICS program issues the LOAD command.

13.16.1. Catalog The Dynamic Table

This is the first step to set up a dynamic table. You should use Assembler language to catalog this table:

```
DOS/VS:

* $$ JOB JNM=STORTBL
* $$ LST CLASS=X,DISP=H
// JOB STORTBL CATALOG A STORE TABLE
// OPTION CATAL
  PHASE STORTBL,+0
// EXEC PROC=ASMLNK
STORTBL   START 0
STOR1     DC      CL25'00001DALLAS               '
STOR2     DC      CL25'00002FORT WORTH           '
STOR3     DC      CL25'00003AUSTIN               '
STOR4     DC      CL25'00004HOUSTON              '
STOR5     DC      CL25'00005ADDISON              '
          END
/*
/&
* $$ EOJ


OS/VS:

//STORTBL   JOB (1500,ORDR),'LEE',
//          NOTIFY=LEE,MSGCLASS=H,USER=LEE,PASSWORD=WS,CLASS=A
//STEP1     EXEC PGM=ASMBLR,REGION=768K,
//  PARM='LIST,NODECK,LOAD'
```

```
//SYSPRINT   DD SYSOUT=A
//SYSUT1     DD UNIT=DISK,SPACE=(CYL,(5,5)),DISP=(NEW,DELETE)
//SYSUT2     DD UNIT=DISK,SPACE=(CYL,(5,5)),DISP=(NEW,DELETE)
//SYSUT3     DD UNIT=DISK,SPACE=(CYL,(5,5)),DISP=(NEW,DELETE)
//SYSGO      DD UNIT=DISK,SPACE=(CYL,(5,5)),DISP=(NEW,PASS)
//SYSIN      DD *
          PRINT ON,GEN,DATA
          TITLE 'STORE TABLE'
STORTBL   START 0
STOR1     DC    CL25'00001DALLAS              '
STOR2     DC    CL25'00002FORT WORTH          '
STOR3     DC    CL25'00003AUSTIN              '
STOR4     DC    CL25'00004HOUSTON             '
STOR5     DC    CL25'00005ADDISON             '
          END
/*
//STEP2      EXEC PGM=IEWL,PARM='LIST,XREF,SIZE=(106K,16K)'
//SYSPRINT   DD SYSOUT=*
//SYSUT1     DD UNIT=DISK,SPACE=(CYL,(1,1)),DISP=(,DELETE)
//SYSLMOD    DD DSN=CICS.LOAD.LIB,DISP=SHR
//MODIN      DD DSN=*.STEP1.SYSGO,DISP=(OLD,DELETE)
//SYSLIN     DD *
 INCLUDE MODIN
 NAME STORTBL(R)
/*
```

After you have executed the above job, the dynamic table (STORTBL) will be cataloged into the program load library.

13.16.2.   Set Up The Dynamic Table In The PPT

A dynamic table is considered a CICS program. Therefore, you need to set it up in the PPT as follows:

```
DFHPPT TYPE=ENTRY,PROGRAM=STORTBL,PGMLANG=ASSEMBLER
```

13.16.3.   Process It in The CICS Program

You should define the dynamic table in LINKAGE SECTION of the CICS program and then issue a LOAD command to load it into the program. After the dynamic table is loaded, you can use it to search the desired entry. After the table is no longer needed, you should issue a RELEASE command to delete it. After the table has been deleted, its contents are not available to the CICS program. If you do not issue a RELEASE command to delete the table and HOLD option is not specified in the LOAD command that loads this table, then the table will be deleted when the task is terminated.

```
LINKAGE SECTION.
01   DFHCOMMAREA          PIC X(100).
01   BLLCELLS.
*    FIRST POINTER RESERVED FOR CICS
     02   FILLER          PIC S9(8) COMP.
*    2ND POINTER POINTS TO 1ST 01-LEVEL DATA AREA
     02   TBL-PTR         PIC S9(8) COMP.
01   STOR-TBL.
     02   STOR-ENTRY          OCCURS 5 TIMES.
          03   STOR-NO        PIC 9(5).
          03   STOR-LOCATION PIC X(20).
PROCEDURE DIVISION.
```

```
        EXEC CICS LOAD PROGRAM('STORTBL') SET(TBL-PTR) END-EXEC.
*       NOW YOU CAN USE THE TABLE
        MOVE STOR-NO(1)         TO STORNOO.
        MOVE STOR-LOCATION(1) TO LOCATO.
*       DELETE THE TABLE WHEN IT IS NO LONGER NEEDED
        EXEC CICS RELEASE PROGRAM('STORTBL') END-EXEC.
        ... STOR-TBL IS NO LONGER AVAILABLE ...
```

13.17. Screen Refeshing Program (XCU15)

CICS Program: XCU15   CICS Mapset: XXCU15   Transaction: CU15

This program is used to demonstrate how to design a screen refreshing application. A screen refreshing transaction only needs to be initiated once after CICS is brought up and it will initiate itself at each specified time interval until it is cancelled by the user or until CICS is shut down. The user can enter the transaction code (CU15) on a clear terminal to initiate the screen refreshing transaction the very first time. It will then start itself within a specified time interval.

For example, an airline company may use this technique to display the arrival and departure time of the flight schedule every 60 seconds. The arrival and departure time are constantly updated in the VSAM file. After the screen refreshing program is invoked, it will go get the latest information (READ command) on the VSAM file and display it on the terminal (SEND MAP command), initiate its own transaction within 60 seconds (START command) and then terminate itself (RETURN command). Now the users can review the latest information on the terminal. After 60 seconds elapse, this screen refreshing transaction will be initiated once again. It will go get the latest information, display it on the terminal, initiated its own transaction and then terminate itself. This cycle goes on and on until the user has decided to cancel the session by pressing any key on the terminal or until CICS is shut down.

You can also use this technique to display today's current total sales amount on the terminal for the sales manager and the president of the company. You need to update the sales total when a sales order is created online in order to support this application. The bank uses this technique to display its position in the federal reserve bank. At any time, the bank must maintain a certain percentage of its asset as the reserved fund. In order to support this application, the federal reserve position must be posted when a debit or credit transaction is executed.

You must design the screen refreshing program to be able to handle the cancellation of the session requested by the user. This can be accomplished by cancelling the un-expired future transaction, delete the TS queue and then check to see if the TS queue exists in the beginning of the task to see if this task is to be cancelled.

CICS Mapset XXCU15:

```
XXCU15    DFHMSD TYPE=&SYSPARM,LANG=COBOL,TIOAPFX=YES,MODE=INOUT,           X
                 STORAGE=AUTO,CTRL=(FREEKB,FRSET),TERM=3270,DATA=FIELD
AXCU15    DFHMDI SIZE=(05,80)
          DFHMDF POS=(01,25),LENGTH=11,INITIAL='SALES TOTAL'
          DFHMDF POS=(03,01),LENGTH=16,INITIAL='SALES TOTAL AMT:'
AMT       DFHMDF POS=(03,18),LENGTH=10,PICOUT='Z(7).99'
```

```
                 DFHMDF POS=(05,01),LENGTH=16,INITIAL='TOTAL ORDERS    :'
       ORDR      DFHMDF POS=(05,18),LENGTH=05,PICOUT='ZZZZ9'.
                 DFHMSD TYPE=FINAL
                 END
```

CICS Program XCU15:

```
       ID DIVISION.
       PROGRAM-ID. XCU15.
       REMARKS. DISPLAY CURRENT SALES TOTAL.
       ENVIRONMENT DIVISION.
       DATA DIVISION.
       WORKING-STORAGE SECTION.
       01  TS-Q-REC           PIC X(10).
       01  TS-Q-NAME.
           02  TS-Q-TERMID    PIC X(4).
           02  FILLER         PIC X(4) VALUE 'CU15'.
       01  TS-Q-LENG          PIC S9(4) COMP VALUE +10.
       01  TS-Q-ITEM          PIC S9(4) COMP VALUE +1.
       01  SALES-REC.
           02  SALES-KEY      PIC X(5).
           02  SALES-TOT-AMT  PIC S9(7)V99 COMP.
           02  SALES-TOT-ORDR PIC 9(5).
       01  DFHAID             COPY DFHAID.
       01  CA-POS             PIC X(4).
       LINKAGE SECTION.
       01  DFHCOMMAREA        PIC X(10).
       PROCEDURE DIVISION.
           EXEC CICS HANDLE CONDITION
                QIDERR(A900-QIDERR)
                NOTFND(A910-NOTFND)
                ERROR(A920-ERROR)
                END-EXEC.
      *    IF ANY KEY IS ENTERED, EIBCALEN WILL BE = 10
      *    THAT MEANS THE USER WANTS TO CANCEL SESSION
           IF EIBTRNID = 'CU15' AND EIBCALEN = 10
              GO TO A200-CANCEL.
      *    IF USER ENTERS CU15 ON A CLEAR TERMINAL OR THIS IS INITIATED
      *    BY THE LAST START COMMAND, DISPLAY INFO
       A100-DISPLAY-SALES.
           MOVE EIBTRMID    TO TS-Q-TERMID.
      *    IF CU15 IS NOT INITIATED BY ENTERING CU15 ON TERMINAL
      *    THEN WE NEED TO CHECK IF ANY CANCEL HAS BEEN REQUESTED BY
      *    CHECKING IF TS QUEUE EXISTS. WHEN TS QUEUE DOES NOT EXIST,
      *    WE KNOW THE USER HAS TRIED TO CANCEL THE SESSION
      *    IF USER ENTERS CU15, THEN EIBAID = DFHENTER
           IF EIBAID NOT = DFHENTER
              MOVE 'A100' TO CA-POS
              EXEC CICS READQ TS QUEUE(TS-Q-NAME)
                               INTO(TS-Q-REC)
                               LENGTH(TS-Q-LENG)
                               ITEM(TS-Q-ITEM)
                               END-EXEC.
      *    ASSUME THE KEY TO SALES INFO IS LOW-VALUES
           MOVE LOW-VALUES TO SALES-KEY.
           EXEC CICS READ DATASET('SALES')
                          INTO(SALES-REC)
                          RIDFLD(SALES-KEY)
                          END-EXEC.
      *    MOVE SALES INFO TO MAP I/O AREA
           MOVE LOW-VALUES     TO AXCU15O.
           MOVE SALES-TOT-AMT  TO AMTO.
           MOVE SALES-TOT-ORDR TO ORDRO.
           MOVE -1             TO AMTL.
           EXEC CICS SEND MAP('AXCU15') MAPSET('XXCU15')
                     ERASE CURSOR END-EXEC.
      *    CREATE TS Q TO SUPPORT CANCELLATION OF SESSION
      *    YOU ONLY NEED TO CREATE TS Q WHEN CU15 IS INITIATED 1ST TIME
```

```
            IF EIBAID NOT = DFHENTER
                GO TO A120-START-CU15.
            MOVE LOW-VALUES        TO TS-Q-REC.
            MOVE EIBTRMID          TO TS-Q-TERMID.
            EXEC CICS WRITEQ TS QUEUE(TS-Q-NAME)
                                FROM(TS-Q-REC)
                                LENGTH(TS-Q-LENG)
                                MAIN
                                END-EXEC.
        A120-START-CU15.
        *   START ITSELF ON THIS TERMINAL WITHIN 60 SECONDS, WE
        *   SPECIFY TERMID AS REQID IN CASE WE NEED TO CANCEL THIS TASK
            EXEC CICS START TRANSID('CU15')
                            TERMID(EIBTRMID)
                            REQID(EIBTRMID)
                            INTERVAL(60)
                            END-EXEC.
        *   TERMINATE ITSELF AND POST CU15 ON THIS TERMINAL, SO
        *   IF USER HITS ANY KEY, CU15 WILL BE INITIATED & EIBCALEN=10
        *   IN THIS CASE, WE WILL CANCEL THE CU15 SESSION
            EXEC CICS RETURN TRANSID('CU15')
                             COMMAREA(COMM-AREA)
                             LENGTH(10)
                             END-EXEC.
        A200-CANCEL.
            MOVE EIBTRMID        TO TS-Q-TERMID.
        *   CANCEL THE FUTURE TASK WE INITIATED IN THE LAST DISPLAY
        *   IF THIS FUTURE TASK HAS EXPIRED THIS CANCEL WILL FAIL
            MOVE 'A200' TO CA-POS.
            EXEC CICS CANCEL TRANSID('CU15') REQID(EIBTRMID) END-EXEC.
        *   WE DELETE THE TS QUEUE SO FUTURE TASK WILL GET QIDERR WHEN
        *   IT TRIES TO READ IT. IF QIDERR, WE'LL TERMINATE THE TASK
        *   WITHOUT DISPLAY ANY INFORMATION. THE SESSION IS ENDED
        A202-DELETE-TS-Q.
            MOVE 'A202'   TO CA-POS.
            EXEC CICS DELETEQ TS QUEUE(TS-Q-NAME) END-EXEC.
            EXEC CICS RETURN END-EXEC.
        A900-QIDERR.
            IF CA-POS = 'A100' OR 'A202'
                EXEC CICS RETURN END-EXEC.
            GO TO A920-ERROR.
        A910-NOTFND.
            IF CA-POS = 'A200'
                GO TO A202-DELETE-TS-Q.
            GO TO A920-ERROR.
        A920-ERROR.
            EXEC CICS ABEND ABCODE('CU15') END-EXEC.
```

When the user hits any key on the terminal to cancel the session, it may be too late to cancel the future task started by the last task. If the task has been started when you issue the CANCEL command, you need to delete the TS queue so the next task started by this expired future task will not display any information and will terminate itself after it gets QIDERR condition when it tries to read the TS queue. This double cancellation will ensure the tasks will be terminated and the session will be cancelled.

N

O

P

Q

R

ORDER FORM

Send the ORDER FORM to:

CCD Online Systems, Inc.
P.O. Box 795759
Dallas, Texas 75379

To Order By Credit Card (VISA or M/C):

Call TOLL FREE 1-800-851-5072 (Outside Texas)
1-214-248-7642 (In Texas)
(9 AM to 5 PM Central time)

Please send me the book(s) I've indicated below. I must be completely satisfied, or I'll send them back at any time for a full refund.

QTY	Title	Price
____	CICS/VS Command Level Programming With COBOL Examples	$29.95
____	IMS/VS DB/DC Online Programming Using MFS And DL/I	$29.95
____	IMS/VS DL/I Programming With COBOL Examples	$29.95
____	VSAM Coding In COBOL And VSAM AMS	$19.95
____	CICS/VS Online System Design And Implementation Techniques	$29.95
____	Contract Programming For DP Professionals (12/86)	$29.95

Sub Total .... $ _____

6.125% Tax (Texas Resident Only) .... $ _____

Total Amount .... $ _____

Discount Schedule

15% discount if Sub Total is greater than $100.00
18% discount if Sub Total is greater than $200.00
20% discount if Sub Total is greater than $300.00
(Apply the discount to the above Sub Total)

____ I want to save shipping & handling charges.
   Here is my check for Total Amount .... $ _____

____ Bill me for Total Amount plus shipping & handling charges.

____ Please charge to my ____ VISA ____ M/C

   Card no. _____ Exp Date: _____

   Signature: _____
                   (Required)

Name (Print) _____

Address _____

City/State/Zip _____

Office Telephone _____
                   (Required if payment is not enclosed)

Allow 1 to 2 weeks for delivery.